American Caesars

Lives of the Presidents from
Franklin D. Roosevelt to George W. Bush

American Caesars

*Lives of the Presidents
from Franklin D. Roosevelt to
George W. Bush*

NIGEL HAMILTON

THE BODLEY HEAD
LONDON

Published by The Bodley Head 2010

2 4 6 8 10 9 7 5 3 1

First published in Great Britain in 2010 by
The Bodley Head
Random House, 20 Vauxhall Bridge Road,
London SW1V 2SA

www.bodleyhead.co.uk
www.rbooks.co.uk

Addresses for companies within The Random House Group Limited can be found at:
www.randomhouse.co.uk/offices.htm

The Random House Group Limited Reg. No. 954009

A CIP catalogue record for this book
is available from the British Library

ISBN 9781847920027 (HBK)
ISBN 9781847921253 (TPK)

The Random House Group Limited supports The Forest Stewardship
Council (FSC), the leading international forest certification organisation. All our titles
that are printed on Greenpeace approved FSC certified paper carry the FSC logo. Our
paper procurement policy can be found at www.rbooks.co.uk/environment

Mixed Sources
Product group from well-managed
forests and other controlled sources
www.fsc.org Cert no. TT-COC-2139
© 1996 Forest Stewardship Council
FSC

Typeset in DanteMT by Palimpsest Book Production Limited,
Grangemouth, Stirlingshire

Printed and bound in Great Britain by
Clays Ltd, St Ives plc

Contents

Preface

Gaius Suetonius Tranquillus – known as Suetonius – had written a whole series of biographies of Roman poets, orators and historians (*The Lives of Illustrious Men*) when the idea came to him, early in the second century AD, to address the first twelve Caesars of Rome. Beginning with the dictator Julius Caesar, he recounted the lives of emperors Augustus, Tiberius, Caligula, Claudius, Nero, Galba, Otho, Vitellius, Vespasian, Titus and Domitian.

The result was *The Twelve Caesars*, which became a classic of classical times: a virtuoso imperial portrait gallery by a distinguished author, remarkable not only for its frank, often salacious accounts (in contrast to contemporary commemorations) of Rome's emperors, but also because the twelve men whose lives he chronicled were the embodiment – both good and awful – of Rome's greatest century and a half, between 49 BC and AD 96.

As Roman hegemony became more contested in the second century AD, and ultimately fractured into the decline and fall that Gibbon later chronicled, Suetonius' extraordinary work only increased in interest. Some of his chosen Caesars had been deified, but Suetonius showed little reverence for the divine, preferring to chronicle their lives as human beings, each with his own story from birth to supreme power. His emperors were thus portrayed not as sanctified icons, but as distinctive individuals, often effective but also perverse – ruthless characters whom Suetonius treated fairly, without needing to curtsey. Here was the prototype of Lytton Strachey's later masterpiece, *Eminent Victorians*, published in 1918, but without the need for irony, and unforgettable not only as portraits, but because the selected group personified the 'beautiful and the base' that Dr Johnson later saw as essential facets of 'useful' biography rather than hagiography. Bucking the contemporary approach taken by Greek and Roman biographers, moreover, Suetonius divided each portrait into three parts: first an account of how the Caesar rose to power; then his public life as emperor; and finally, an account of the emperor's private life.

Fast-forward to today. Though few US citizens care for the word 'empire' to describe their own country, American historians have reluctantly begun to accept the designation, since by most indices – military, economic and cultural – the United States has incontrovertibly been the world's dominant hegemony since its entry into World War II in 1941. With its massive rearmament programme, its struggle to defeat Hitler's Third Reich and fascism, and its use of the atom bomb to defeat the Japanese Empire, it stepped up to the plate in defence of democracy. Then, after the war's end, it did not turn away from international leadership as it had done after World War I, but undertook a role as ongoing guardian of its allies and those countries which espoused democratic values – and also some that didn't, as long as it was in America's interest to do so. Isolationism thus died, and the United States attempted, as best it could, to maintain a Pax Americana, or liberal peace, across much of the post-war world, using its economic, military, diplomatic and even subversive power. At times the Pax turned distinctly belligerent, as it did under presidents Truman, Johnson, Nixon, Bush Sr and Bush Jr – indeed, by the beginning of the twenty-first century, a presidential adviser at the imperial court could shamelessly tell reporters: 'We're an empire now, and when we act, we create our own reality.'[1] Overseas US military bases increased from fourteen in 1938 to more than a thousand in the new millennium.[2]

In writing this account of the last twelve American presidents and using, somewhat loosely, the words 'Caesars', 'imperial' and 'empire', my object is not to scorn the difficulties which the United States has faced and still faces today. Rather, my purpose is to look back over the past six decades since the United States became the world's foremost military and economic power, and to shine a spotlight on the men who have led their often unruly nation on its post-World War II 'imperial' journey. Although there have been empires and emperors aplenty in the world since Roman times, I doubt there has been a succession of such remarkable individuals who have launched and led a hegemony as potent as that of the United States, paralleling the might of the Roman Empire.

Who were they, then, these American 'Caesars'? How did they get to be president? How did they confront the challenges of empire once they got there? How effectively did they assert their growing power in the Oval Office, in the role that came to be called the 'imperial presidency'? How authoritatively did they assert Pax Americana through the long years of Cold War, and thereafter? And what, for good or ill, was the course of their private lives? These are the questions I have sought to answer, as a biographer, within the context of recent American and global history. Of the twelve men who held the office of US president from the onset of World War II, four showed undoubted (to me) greatness. As in ancient Rome some American Caesars started wars; others ended them. Some authorized assassination attempts on foreign leaders threatening American hegemony; almost all became victims of assassination attempts; one was actually murdered in office. But from the time of America's entry into World War II, each president was required, on a world stage, to show leadership – and it is the quality of each one's imperial leadership that I have tried to judge in *American Caesars*.

Each chapter tells the story of a human journey, as its protagonist makes his way to the heart of American power, and there confronts the salient challenges of his time. The book begins with the greatest of American emperors, the Caesar Augustus of his time: President Franklin D. Roosevelt. It continues with the lives of his great successors, Harry S. Truman, Dwight D. Eisenhower and John F. Kennedy; then examines the lives of Lyndon Johnson, Richard Nixon, Gerald Ford, Jimmy Carter, Ronald Reagan, George H. W. Bush and Bill Clinton; and ends with arguably the worst of all the American Caesars, George W. Bush, and his deputy Dick Cheney, who wilfully and recklessly destroyed so much of the moral basis of American leadership in the modern world.

Where the American Empire will go from here – how long it will last, as it competes with other, rising empires, and how it will manage its epic struggle to embrace the values enshrined in its great Constitution – is not for me to predict. In the meantime there are too many lessons to be learned from the lives of these twelve men to neglect or forget them. The reader will not necessarily agree with my judgements, embedded in these life stories. The reader will also have his or her own views on which of the twelve American Caesars (and deputy Caesars) most resemble Suetonius' heroes – or his tyrants such as Tiberius, Caligula and Nero. Whether we like it or not, however, these were the men chosen, one after another, to lead the United States in what will be regarded as its greatest days in the role of dominant world superpower. They surely deserve to be seen, as Suetonius saw their Roman forebears, unflinchingly and yet with charity, together with their private lives that remind us, in their affections, how intensely human and individual they were, despite the great burdens they undertook on behalf of the empire.

That said, let us begin with the greatest Caesar of all.

CHAPTER ONE

FRANKLIN D. ROOSEVELT

Later Deified

Democrat
32nd President
(March 4, 1933–April 12, 1945)

Part One: The Road to the White House

Franklin Delano Roosevelt was born on January 30, 1882, at Springwood, Hyde Park, a grand estate overlooking the Hudson River, seventy-five miles above New York City. The birth of the ten-pound baby, which lasted twenty-six hours, almost killed his mother, Sara Delano Roosevelt. Because of the difficult parturition she was advised not to have more children.

FDR was suckled at his mother's breast – unusual at the time – and was kept in dresses and long curls until the age of five, schooled at home, wore kilts, and then pants for the first time at age seven. He had his first bath alone at age nine. In Washington DC, President Cleveland patted FDR's curly head and, reflecting on the burdens of the Oval Office, pronounced 'a strange wish for you. It is that you may never be president of the United States.'[1]

The wish would not be granted.

Mr and Mrs James Roosevelt doted on FDR – so much so, they made do with private tutors and took him with them to Europe, visiting it no less than eight times in FDR's first fourteen years. It was only then, reluctantly, they let him go to his first full-time school, Groton, three years later than his contemporaries. They had forbidden him to try for entry to naval college at Annapolis, saying they would miss him too much if he went to sea.

The sea, nevertheless, became part of FDR's lifeblood. Mr James, as his father was known to all, had built a summer home in 1883 off the coast of Maine on the island of Campobello, and there FDR learned to sail, being given his first yacht, the *New Moon*, at age sixteen, as well as Alfred Thayer Mahan's works on the influence of sea power in history. He began a collection of stamps, stuffed birds, naval prints and books, all of which he catalogued meticulously.

At Harvard FDR finished his four-year degree course in three, and became a much admired editor-in-chief of the university newspaper, the *Crimson*. He had a fine singing voice, learned nothing by rote, but instead developed from an early age a surprisingly independent mind, confident in his own opinions, and positive in his outlook on life. Standing 6' 2" tall, he towered over most of his contemporaries; handsome, energetic, blessed with a genial sense of humour, yet as happy alone as with companions.

The secret of FDR's early success was his mother, Sara. On Mr James' death in 1900 FDR inherited half his father's financial estate, from which he drew an annuity of $12,000, but Sara retained ownership of the Springwood mansion; moreover she controlled the principal of FDR's inheritance. The following year, on the death of her own father she inherited a fortune of $1.2 million ($28 million in today's money). A very rich widow, she avoided fortune hunters and rented an apartment in Boston, Massachusetts, to be close to her son across the Charles River, at Harvard. After graduating, he married in 1905 and Sara built him a house (which she continued to own) close to hers in Manhattan.

'Nothing like keeping the name in the family' remarked Republican President Theodore Roosevelt when he insisted on being allowed to give away his orphaned but wealthy niece, Eleanor Roosevelt, to her fifth cousin, FDR.[2] It was Sara Delano, however, not Eleanor, who continued to be the linchpin of FDR's rising career, socially, professionally and emotionally. Sara encouraged FDR not to overestimate his talents, but to use his abundant skills – his intelligence, charm, humour, education and connections – to make his way in the world beyond the inbred Roosevelts, just as her father had done when facing bankruptcy after the 1857 financial meltdown. She was, and remained all her life, FDR's litmus test in considering his options. When he began to support the local Democratic Party, she supported his decision, recalling later that 'I was one of the few sympathizers Franklin had among his own people. Many of our friends said it was a shame for so fine a young man to associate with "dirty" politicians.'[3]

So close was FDR to his mother, in fact, that he was almost rejected by the local Democratic Party as a mama's boy. Asked by a state committeeman if he would like to run for the New York State legislature as an assemblyman in 1910, he responded he would first have to ask his mother. 'Frank,' the committeeman responded, as he looked up at the building where they'd parked, 'the men that are looking out that window are waiting for an answer. They won't like to hear that you had to ask your *mother*.'[4]

FDR never concealed his political ambition. A fellow law clerk at Carter, Ledyard and Milburn, who had also been at Harvard with FDR, recalled how, in 1907, FDR confided to his young colleagues he was determined to become president of the United States, like his uncle-in-law, and outlined the exact steps by which he would do so: a seat in the New York State Assembly, Assistant Secretary of the Navy, governor of New York, the White House. None mocked him; it seemed, as his colleague recalled, 'entirely reasonable'.[5]

In fact Roosevelt stood for the New York State Senate rather than the Assembly – and won. His resounding victory made him, at age twenty-eight, a force to be reckoned with in the New York Democratic Party in 1911. However, in the same way that the Republican Party split between progressives and conservatives, so did the Democrats. FDR found himself a progressive, fighting the forces of corruption in his own party, known in New York as Tammany Hall.

Beaten in every fight for legislation and party appointments, it was only when FDR threw his support to the Democratic outsider, Governor Woodrow Wilson of New Jersey, in the 1912 presidential election that he was given his chance to leapfrog the closed ranks of Tammany Hall Democrats into the corridors of Washington power. Wilson won. As a reward for his help FDR was offered the posts of Assistant Secretary of the Treasury or the Navy. He chose the Navy.

FDR was the youngest man (at thirty) ever to hold the office. Like Winston Churchill – First Lord of the Admiralty in Britain at the time – FDR was energetic, impetuous, arrogant. His boss, Josephus Daniels, was a short, rumpled newspaper owner from Raleigh, North Carolina, who knew nothing of the sea or the navy, in fact was a pacifist and teetotaller who ordered naval officers' messes to stop serving alcohol. Daniels did, though, know a lot about America and its people. While the European nations allowed power to devolve on to the military once war began, leaving their politicians powerless either to overrule the generals or to make peace, Daniels taught FDR the greatest lesson of the twentieth century: 'the politicians' must retain control of the generals, and must use that power wisely.

Under Daniels' tutelage, FDR learned the exercise of political command. In peacetime the US Navy absorbed 20 per cent of America's annual federal budget, employed 63,000 servicemen in all ranks, and provided employment for hundreds of thousands more in shipyards across the nation, with 197 ships on active service.[6] When President Wilson reluctantly asked Congress to authorize national rearmament involving the building of 176 new ships – the biggest peacetime construction project in the nation's history (ten battleships, a hundred submarines, six battle cruisers, fifty destroyers and ten light cruisers) – FDR applied his formidable energies to the task. Not only did he propose a Council of National Defense to oversee war production, but while Daniels was out of Washington he created, in September 1916, a 50,000-strong Naval Reserve. Thus, by the time President Wilson declared war on April 4, 1917, in response to the kaiser's authorization of unrestricted submarine warfare against neutral countries, FDR was considered indispensable, and the president – narrowly re-elected in November 1916 – refused to hear of FDR's request to join up as a naval officer. 'Tell the young man to stay where he is' Wilson instructed Daniels.[7]

In the 1880s the US economy had become the biggest in the world. With the surrender of the German armed forces at Compiègne on November 11, 1918, the United States finally established its claim to be a world empire in all but name, boasting an army of five million men and a navy of half a million, second only to that of the British Empire, once the German fleet was scuttled at Scapa Flow. America's moral power, however, was founded in a revered Constitution, idealistic principles of justice and, in Wilson's view, the ideal of self-determination by all nations. On his way to the Versailles Peace Conference, Wilson – welcomed by his Assistant Secretary of the Navy – was celebrated at Brest with banners reading 'Hail the Champion of the Rights of Man', and in Paris by two million people as 'Wilson the Just'.

War-weariness in America, however, quickly set in, leading to renewed isolationism. On his return, President Wilson barnstormed across America to sell his League of Nations accord – the core of the Versailles Treaty – in the fall of 1919, but suffered first a minor and then a massive stroke. 'He looked as if he were dead' a White House usher recalled candidly, and although, over time, the president regained some speech and movement in his right arm, his new wife, Edith, kept him out of sight even of his secretaries.[8]

It was in these circumstances that, with the president clearly unable to run for a third term in the summer of 1920, the Assistant Secretary of the Navy put himself forward as a candidate for the number two place on the Democratic Party's presidential ticket, next to the Ohio governor James M. Cox, and was nominated. He was only thirty-eight.

To launch their campaign, Cox and FDR went to the White House to meet President Wilson and get his blessing, Cox having agreed that the League of Nations would be, as FDR recalled, 'the paramount issue' of their platform, in deference to Wilson. 'It was one of the most impressive scenes', the Democratic vice-presidential nominee afterwards described, 'I have ever witnessed.'[9]

The truth was rather different. Roosevelt had greeted the president in full health in France only a year before. Now, 'as we came in sight of the portico, we saw the president in a wheelchair', FDR later confided.[10] A shawl covered President Wilson's left arm, his head hung down, the left side of his face was paralyzed, and his words were barely audible. Without realizing it, FDR was staring at his own destiny.

Amazingly, the press declined to publish the truth of the president's condition. Wilson was awarded that year's Nobel Peace Prize (which he was too ill to collect). But the further west that FDR travelled as vice-presidential candidate, the more he recognized that the United States, a nation of immigrants, was not yet ready to assume the mantle and responsibilities of world leadership.

President Wilson's aide, Joseph M. Tumulty, recalled the White House as the 'loneliest place on election night' in 1920. Not only were Cox and Roosevelt soundly defeated by the Republican senator, Warren G. Harding of Ohio – 404 to 127 in the Electoral College, and by almost two to one in the popular vote – but the vote was seen as a total 'defeat of the solemn referendum on the League of Nations'. It was also the Democratic Party's worst showing since the Civil War.

Roosevelt soon had his own medical disaster to face. Travelling to Campobello for his summer vacation in July 1921, he made good a promise he'd made to attend, as chairman of the New York Boy Scouts, a youth camp by the Hudson River. His enthusiasm and energy were infectious, but so was something else. In Maine, sailing and playing with his children, his legs gave way beneath him. The local doctor diagnosed a summer cold, while a nearby specialist, when summoned, a spinal clot. But with the lower half of FDR's body paralyzed, his trusted aide, Louis Howe, wrote urgently to FDR's uncle Fred in New York, telling him the symptoms. A diagnosis of polio was confirmed by the national authority on the disease the moment he reached the island of Campobello.

Polio changed FDR's life. He had already begun planning a run for the US Senate in 1922. Unkind people now called him a cripple. Even his mother Sara thought he should retire to Springwood, Hyde Park, and become a country squire, though this seemed premature when he was only thirty-nine. There was no way, however, in which the illness could be kept from the public. On its front page the *New York Times* announced 'F. D. ROOSEVELT ILL OF POLIOMYELITIS.'[11]

Since the majority of polio patients recovered at least partial use of their limbs, FDR's team stressed to the media that the former vice-presidential candidate was heading towards recovery, not disability. This was untrue, but not wholly dishonest. Roosevelt's willpower in learning to walk with two fourteen-pound steel braces holding him upright from his heels to his hips, mesmerized those who met him. When he swung himself forward on crutches to the podium at Madison Square Garden in New York to give the nominating speech for Governor Al Smith as candidate for the Democratic presidential nomination on June 26, 1924, no one dared breathe, as Frances Perkins – later Secretary of Labor – recalled. 'Eight thousand delegates, alternates, and spectators watched spellbound while FDR fought his way across the stage, the personification of courage' one biographer recounted.[12] 'When he finally reached the podium, unable to wave for fear of falling but flashing that famous smile, head thrown back, shoulders high, the Garden erupted with a thunderous ovation.'[13]

Four years later, in Houston, FDR again gave the nominating speech for Governor Smith – without crutches this time, and with 15,000 people in the audience, as well as radio microphones transmitting his speech. By using the arm of his son for support on one side, and a cane in his other hand, FDR gave the impression of mild, residual stiffness, but otherwise rude good health. A president, he declared in his lilting tenor voice, needed a 'quality of soul' that 'makes him a strong help to those in sorrow or trouble, that quality which makes him not merely admired but loved by all of the people – the quality of sympathetic understanding of the human heart, or real interest in one's fellow man.'[14] He was extolling Smith, but the words applied much more to himself.

Asked to stand for the governorship of New York, FDR decided to take his chances, despite the fact that Wall Street was experiencing an unregulated, feverish speculation bonanza and he had no real hope of winning. 'Mess is no name for it' Louis Howe wired him.[15] Speaking as many as fourteen times a day, Roosevelt criss-crossed the state, and finally went home to bed in Manhattan on election night, assuming he had lost the battle. He awoke to hear his mother shouting from the front door (she still lived in the next house) that he was governor-elect.

Inaugurated on January 1, 1929, Governor Roosevelt predicted neither the Great Crash that year, nor the Great Depression that followed. However, thanks to his farm and rehabilitation centre in Warm Springs, Georgia, FDR's finger was on the pulse of American life in an unusual way. In the state capitol in Albany, the new governor responded to the economic collapse that took place as he had in his Navy Department days, using government purchasing power to modernize not a fleet but a state. He set up the first state commission in the nation to stabilize employment, and became the first governor in America to endorse un-employment insurance. He pushed for a massive electrification programme, stressed farm relief and employment projects. In 1930, running for re-election as governor, more than 90 per cent of registered voters went to the polls in New York City, giving FDR the largest win in New York history, as well as returning Democratic majorities in both houses of the state legislature. The way was clear to presidential nomin-ation in 1932.

As national unemployment doubled to eight million, the bread and soup lines grew longer. FDR called the New York Assembly into special session, asking for an immediate $20 million to provide work, and where work was not feasible, 'food against starvation'. President Hoover had claimed that 'mutual self-help' was the answer – prin-ciples which, if departed from, would strike at the very 'roots of self-government'. By contrast, FDR claimed it was the duty of 'modern society, acting through its government' to prevent starva-tion as 'a matter of social duty'. In August 1931, he set up a Temporary Emergency Relief Administration (TERA) to distribute state funding, and raised state income taxes. TERA would, over the following five years, assist 40 per cent of New York State residents, five million people – with 70 per cent returning to employment.[16]

FDR's activist success was not appreciated by his rival, former New York Governor Al Smith. But with Democratic leaders across the country despairing of their losing streak in presidential elections since 1920, they wanted a winner, and early polls showed FDR as the only front-runner who could beat President Hoover in 1932. A scurrilous campaign to damn FDR's chances on the grounds that he was physic-ally unfit for the rigours of the presidency was scotched by a panel of distinguished doctors, given free access to Governor Roosevelt during his workday. They reported him 'able to take more punishment than many men ten years younger'. When asked her own opinion, FDR's wife, Eleanor, remarked sourly: 'If the infantile paralysis didn't kill him, the presidency won't.'[17]

At Oglethorpe University in Georgia on May 22, 1932, FDR gave one of his most famous speeches. 'Must the country remain hungry and jobless while raw materials stand unused and factories idle?' he asked, and gave his famous answer: 'The country needs, the country demands, bold, persistent experimentation. Take a method and try it. If it fails admit it frankly and try another. But above all, try something.'[18]

Imaginative, pragmatic, non-partisan and activist in his response to a growing national emergency: this was Roosevelt's contribution to the history of democracy, at a time when more draconian solutions were being aired in Europe and the Far East.

For President Herbert Hoover, the 1932 election campaign proved a fiasco. The self-made millionaire and former mining engineer lost to FDR by almost seven million votes out of a record forty million cast. Huge new Democratic majorities in both houses of Congress, moreover, meant that no Republican filibuster would suffice to stop the president-elect's New Deal programme, once his official inaugur-ation took place in March 1933. A bullet, however, could – and nearly did, when an unemployed Italian bricklayer in Miami, having bought a handgun at a local pawnshop, took aim at the president-elect, sitting in his open, parked car as he talked to the Chicago mayor, Anton Cermak. A spectator swung her purse and deflected his shot. Cermak was mortally wounded: FDR was unscathed.

Part Two: The Presidency

'This great Nation will endure as it has endured,' declared the 32nd president in his historic inaugural speech on March 4, 1933, 'will revive and will prosper. So first of all, let me assert my firm belief that the only thing we have to fear is fear itself – nameless, unreasoning, unjustified terror which paralyzes needed efforts to convert retreat into advance.'

Those who scorned FDR's words as empty rhetoric received a rude awakening. Summoning Congress back into emergency session, the new president made good on his promise: using the federal government to put capitalism back on its feet. Issuing a proclamation closing the nation's banks, he sought the means to keep them solvent. Within days he had it; the government would issue the money, backed not by gold but by its own security. The ruse worked. A week later – after federal scrutiny – banks reopened, with federal insurance backing them, and they stayed open. The dollar soared. 'Capitalism', as Raymond Moley, one of FDR's 'brain trust', remarked, 'was saved in eight days.'[19]

In a series of initiatives he pushed through with the cooperation of Republicans and Democrats, as well as the support of the nation's state governors and the press, FDR then kept Congress in session – repealing Prohibition, increasing farm incomes by tackling surpluses (paying for the reduction by special taxes), refinancing farm mortgages threatened by foreclosure, and creating a Civilian Conservation Corps that would offer employment to three million young people. 'It smacks of fascism, of Hitlerism, of a form of sovietism' the president of the American Federation of Labor complained, afraid the measure would depress ordinary workers' wages. But the Boy Scout in Franklin Roosevelt would not back down. Some 2,500 camps across the nation were set up, FDR taking the president of the AFL to see the first of them, that summer, in Shenandoah National Park.

The creation of the CCC presaged the creation of the Federal Emergency Relief Agency, assisting seventeen million people that year, with a staff of only 121. A public works bill was also put before Congress, with $3.3 billion of federal stimulus funding approved by June 16, 1933, less than a hundred days since FDR entered the White House.

Regulation of Wall Street, the revival of the Tennessee Valley hydroelectric programme stalled since its opening in World War I, in deference

to the objection that it offered unfair federal competition with private
energy companies – and the creation of a Homeowners' Loan
Corporation to rescue the collapsing housing market; these and other
measures added to the president's remarkable domestic achievement.
A week after the inauguration, the president had also begun broadcasting 'fireside chats' in which, via radio, he explained to listeners
across America in articulate yet homey language what he was seeking
to do, and why. Instantly, a new bond was established between the
president and the public. What surprised listeners most was Roosevelt's
sheer energy, confidence, humour and faith, a testament both to his
indomitable courage as a paraplegic, and his positive temperament.
As his mother Sara put it, his 'disposition is such that he can accept
responsibilities and not let them wear him out'.[20]

In contrast to Adolf Hitler – who was granted full emergency powers
by the German Reichstag on March 23, 1933, and who in *his* first days
as dictator announced he would rule Germany with an iron, anti-
Semitic fist ('Treason towards the nation and the people shall in future
be stamped out with ruthless barbarity' Hitler declared, as he ordered
the rounding up of his political opponents, to be held in concentration camps) – FDR's first Hundred Days showed America and the
world that democracy could be saved, without barbarism.

Try as the Republican right did, it was difficult to portray as a mad
fascist, or as a Nazi or Soviet dictator, a patrician president working so
closely with the nation's Congress and governors. Four of Roosevelt's
senior cabinet members were Republicans, and the president went out
of his way to show he was not *parti pris*, but party-free. He took the
United States off the gold standard, insisted on balancing the national
budget, cut the pay of government officials – including himself – and
radiated courage, optimism and confidence. Marxist historians who
interpreted history as the implacable movement of economic and social
forces would never be able to explain the impact made by a single such
individual, drawn from the 'landed gentry', who marshalled the
positive energies of his nation, rather than the punitive.

The November 1934 midterm elections returned even larger
Democratic majorities in both House and Senate. With that fair wind
FDR announced the Securities and Exchange Commission, the new
regulatory agency for Wall Street, and a revolutionary federal
programme to provide unemployment pay, sick pay and old-age

pensions. 'Keep it simple', FDR ordered his Secretary of Labor. 'So simple that everybody will understand it.'[21] To fend off opposition and make sure the programme could never be derailed by later congressional budget manoeuvres, he made it self-financing through contributions by employers and employees rather than the government. Signed by the president on August 14, 1935, the Social Security Act became FDR's signature domestic achievement as president of the United States, and a demonstration to both fascists and Communists across the world that there was a middle way.[22]

Social-security legislation was followed by the Works Progress Administration, whereby Congress gave FDR power to disburse $4.8 billion to employ 'the maximum number of persons in the shortest time possible'. Using the Army Corps of Engineers, his chief overseer, Harry Hopkins, set to work, employing 8.5 million people over the following eight years and injecting $11 billion into the working economy. Without being aware of it, FDR was in fact rehearsing the nation for the moment when the US government would have to administer an even bigger programme: the manning of a military empire.

Unemployment was cut by two thirds, national income rose 50 per cent, industrial production doubled, stock prices went up, as did corporate profits and farm income. The Rural Electrification Administration Act of 1935 appealed to those outside the cities, while the Wagner Act, recognizing (in the wake of growing violence in San Francisco, Minneapolis and Toledo) workers' rights to unionize, appealed to urban industrial voters. Criticized by economists for his employment initiatives, rather than the provision of a dole, FDR was unrepentant. 'That is true' he allowed, with regard to his rejection of a weekly handout rather than federally funded employment. 'But the men who tell me that', he pointed out, 'have, unfortunately, too little contact with the true America to realize most Americans want to give something for what they get. That something, which in this case is honest work, is the saving barrier between them and moral degradation.'[23]

FDR's empathy with the lot of ordinary Americans was the quality that raised him head and shoulders above his contemporaries. At the Democratic National Convention in Philadelphia in June 1936, a crowd of 100,000, as well as half the population of America who owned radios, listened as the president – who fell on the way to the podium when one of his leg braces failed to lock tight – was lifted back on to his feet and gave thanks to those who had helped defeat the Depression. Candidly and with humility he acknowledged the mistakes made along the way. 'Governments can err. Presidents do make mistakes' he acknowledged. But there was, he said, echoing Dante, a difference between 'the sins of the cold-blooded and the sins of the warm-hearted'. As he put it – thinking of former president Herbert Hoover, who was currently stomping across the country in an attempt to recast his own bruised legend – 'Better the occasional faults of a government that lives in a spirit of charity than the consistent omissions of a government frozen in the ice of its own indifference.' Then, lowering his voice a register, FDR came to the words that would define his presidency: 'To some generations much is given. Of other generations much is asked. This generation of Americans has a rendezvous with destiny.'

For ten long minutes the cheering overwhelmed the rhetoric in the formal start to an election that again made history when, on November 3, 1936, FDR won by the largest margin in electoral annals to that date: carrying 523 electoral votes to Governor Alf Landon's eight, and trouncing his opponent by a margin of more than eleven million votes in the popular vote.

Father Coughlin, who had helped launch a new party to split Roosevelt's support, had boasted he would 'teach' the public 'how to hate'. 'Religion and patriotism,' Coughlin urged Congressman Lemke and the new Union Party, 'keep going on that. It's the only way you can get them really "het up"' – a view that so alarmed Pope Pius XI that he dispatched Cardinal Pacelli to America to calm concerns over Coughlin's increasingly anti-Semitic invective.[24] Fortunately for Roosevelt, however, the Union Party's showing proved even worse on election night than that of the Republican Party.

Roosevelt's second term, ironically, proved as disappointing as his first had been inspiring. Not only did his Supreme Court-packing agenda fail miserably (as well as proving unnecessary, once vacancies on the court allowed FDR to nominate his own replacements), but he backed off his great economic stimulus package at the point of its maximum success, fearing inflation and loss of control over the national deficit. The result was a balanced budget, but a new recession. Unionization in big industrial plants such as the Republic steelworks in South Chicago led to brutality and mass murder by the police, with FDR caught in the metaphorical middle. Similarly, an antilynching bill split the Democratic Party in the South, and the president, for all his sympathy for the black cause, was loath to intervene lest he lose his traditional Dixiecrat base, should southern Democrats turn to the Republicans. The stock market crashed, unemployment rose by two million in two months, and the president suddenly seemed mortal again – unsure whether to restimulate the economy or sit tight.

By the spring of 1938, as the 'Roosevelt recession' worsened, FDR was finally persuaded to abandon his balanced budget demands, and instead revive the Public Works Administration, as well as the Works Progress Administration, with billions of dollars in new federal spending. This duly did the Keynesian trick – though not swiftly enough to avoid a midterm election reverse for Democrats in Congress, the party losing eighty-one seats in the House, eight in the Senate, and thirteen governorships across the country. The outlook for FDR, if he wished to run again for the presidency in 1940, looked unpromising.

It was at this juncture, however, that foreign affairs began to play a major part in the role of the American president, for the first time since Republicans refused to ratify the League of Nations and the United States opted out of a global role in the post-World War I universe.

Roosevelt had recognized the USSR in 1933, and withdrawn American troops from Haiti as part of his 'Good Neighbor' policy, but American appeasement seemed only to encourage war elsewhere, not halt it. When Japanese troops invaded China and their warplanes deliberately attacked and sank the USS *Panay* at anchor in the Yangtse River in December 1937, neither Congress nor the American navy seemed anxious to retaliate. Instead, the State Department sent the Japanese government a bill! This the Japanese happily paid.

In Europe, the same was the case. Neutrality Acts forbade the trading of American war materials with belligerents, let alone American military intervention, unless with congressional approval. Annual immigration quotas had been set by Congress in 1924, with no caveats for refugees, and remained unaltered despite the worsening situation in Europe. No effort was made by the US to make an issue of General Franco's insurgency, backed militarily by Italian and German forces, against the elected Spanish Republican government. American impotence to intervene abroad was illustrated yet again when Hitler annexed Austria with impunity on March 11, 1938, then went on to challenge the major European powers by threatening war if western Czechoslovakia (which included the Sudetenland) was not also ceded to the Nazi Third Reich.

The fact was, with only 185,000 men in its army, the United States of America now ranked a lowly eighteenth on the scale of military forces in the world. It could do nothing to help Britain, France and Russia in protesting Hitler's opportunism, even had Congress wished. 'We in the United States do not seek to impose on any other people either our way of life or our internal government' FDR assured the international community. 'But we are determined', he warned, 'to maintain and protect that way of life and form of government for ourselves.' Beyond offering help to Canada if it was attacked, however, the truth was that the president of the United States was, thanks to public sentiment and congressional pusillanimity, powerless: an extraordinary reversal of its situation at the end of World War I.

'It's a terrible thing to look over your shoulder when you are trying to lead', FDR told one of his speechwriters, who was Jewish, '– and to find no one there.'[25] News of Kristallnacht in November 1938 shocked Americans. 'I myself could scarcely believe such things could occur in a twentieth-century civilization' FDR commented, but outrage led neither to higher immigration quotas for Jewish refugees, nor to a change in American isolationist sentiment.[26] Protected by the Atlantic, the New World seemed to be severing its links with the Old.

With Hitler's march into the rest of Czechoslovakia and seizure of Prague in March 1939, the situation resembled, as Winston Churchill memorably commented, 'feeding the crocodiles'. German troops duly drove into Poland on September 1, 1939, from the west, followed two weeks later by Russian troops advancing from the east as part of a Nazi–Soviet Pact. To Hitler's surprise, however, Britain declared war in order to honour its agreement to aid Poland, followed by France. World war was now unleashed – with the United States, as in 1914, on the sidelines.

FDR's experience in the Navy Department under Josephus Daniels in World War I now became invaluable. By remaining neutral in Europe's struggle, rather than rushing in, the United States had been able to intercede in 1917 with decisive effect. FDR's approach therefore mirrored that of President Wilson twenty-five years before: declaring a steadfast faith in democracy, but avoiding any commitment abroad, while quietly increasing American preparedness, should war be forced upon the United States.

For FDR, this 'phony war' period became perhaps the greatest trial of his political life. France, Britain and Russia had all held firm in the face of German military attack in 1914, but would they do so now, in the face of modern air warfare and German troops, sent into battle by a ruthless Nazi dictator? American aviator Charles Lindbergh thought not, as did Roosevelt's ambassador to London, Joseph P. Kennedy. Their defeatist views were amply confirmed when Hitler overran Denmark and Norway in April 1940, then invaded Holland, Belgium and France on May 10. No Battle of the Marne came to save the Allies. Instead, surrounded on three sides, the British Army was authorized by the new prime minister, Winston Churchill, to evacuate at Dunkirk, and several weeks later Marshal Pétain surrendered on behalf of a provisional French government in Vichy. This left Hitler master of western and central Europe by sheer force of arms, only six years since becoming chancellor of a bankrupt Weimar Republic, facing massive unemployment.

'I suppose Churchill was the best man in England' FDR said, reluctantly acknowledging King George VI's wisdom in choosing Winston Churchill rather than Lord Halifax to be prime minister, 'even if he was drunk half of his time.'[27] The president found it difficult to forget Churchill's snooty attitude when FDR had tried to visit British Admiralty units on behalf of the US Navy Department in 1916, and then in person in London at a banquet in 1918. Now, however, their roles were reversed: Churchill (who had conveniently forgotten his faux pas) begged for material US assistance in pleading telegrams each day.

President Hoover would have scoffed, but Roosevelt was torn. It was an election year, and although the public remained predominantly isolationist, the president found it hard to take pride in one form of democratic life in North America, yet turn his back on it in Europe. Churchill might be an alcoholic, but Hitler was far worse: a 'madman', as FDR had called him already in 1933, drunk with power.[28] The president made up his mind to assist Churchill, as far as he could, overruling his ambassador in London, and treating Britain as an outpost of the US.

This was the turning point in the history of American Empire and the modern world, as the president chose to align the United States with the one major surviving, embattled democracy left in combat in Europe in the summer of 1940. The president had made General George C. Marshall, who had served on the staff of General Pershing in World War I, head of the US Army. Within weeks of the fall of France, under a 'cash and carry' bill he had pushed Congress to pass the previous autumn, FDR and Marshall more than made up for the weapons British troops had left at Dunkirk. From London, Ambassador Kennedy continued to predict defeat for England, but the aerial Battle of Britain – equivalent to the Battle of the Marne in 1914 – ended Hitler's hopes of a swift German invasion that summer. With the Luftwaffe's failure in the air, the course of the war became a matter not of blitzkrieg but of attrition; a war Hitler knew from his economic and military advisors he could not win, yet would not as Führer relinquish.

Whether FDR could win re-election for a third term in November 1940, meanwhile, was far from a foregone conclusion. The president was still only fifty-eight, but his long struggle with polio and his eight taxing years in the presidency, leading his country out of the Depression, had worn him out. In February he had suffered what his doctor called 'a very slight heart attack', falling unconscious across the table. He'd already signed a contract to be contributing editor of *Collier's* magazine after he left the White House (at $75,000 per year), and had confided to the Teamsters union president 'I am tired. I really am. I can't be president again.' He wanted to 'have a rest' and to 'write history', not have to make it. 'No, I just can't do it.'[29] But with the war in Europe heating up, and calls from Chicago that there were 'nine hundred leaderless delegates milling about like worried sheep waiting for the inspiration of leadership that only you can give them', he had to accede.[30] FDR thus became the first elected president in American history to be nominated as his party's candidate for a third consecutive term in office.

The autumn of 1940, FDR knew, would determine America's survival, as he struggled to stop isolationist sentiment across America from preventing his re-election. In August he announced he favoured a selective military service bill or draft, to increase the nation's defence forces – the first ever in peacetime. If Wendell Willkie, chairman of the largest utility holding company and the Republican presidential nominee, had chosen to denounce the president's proposal at that point, he might well have carried the election, such was the nervousness in the country about being dragged into a war that seemed unwinnable for the democracies in Europe. 'I would rather not win the election than do that' Willkie nobly declared, however.[31] Congress passed the Selective Service Bill in September, and by October, 1940, some sixteen million Americans between the ages of twenty-one and thirty-five were registered for a year's military training.

From a mere 189,000 men America's tiny army would grow by the following summer to 1.4 million. Willkie, seeing his polls slide, was urged by his Republican advisers to try a dirty tricks strategy accusing the president of 'secret agreements' to take America into war if he were re-elected. This time Willkie cooperated, and immediately the polls swung in his favour as the 'peace candidate'. Stung, the president travelled to Philadelphia. There, in the cradle of American constitutional democracy, he gave a ringing, categorical denial of the charges. 'There is no secret treaty, no secret obligation, no secret commitment, no secret understanding in any shape or form, direct or indirect, with any other government, to involve this nation in any war or for any other purpose' the president declared.[32] And to nail down the lid on Willkie's coffin, he proclaimed in Boston, where the American Revolution had begun: 'I have said before, but I shall say it again and again and again. Your boys are not going to be sent into any foreign wars.'[33]

'That hypocritical son of a bitch. This is going to beat me' Willkie sighed as he listened to his opponent on the radio.[34] It did. On November 5, 1940, FDR won his third presidential election with fifty million people voting, the largest number in American history. The president received 449 electoral votes to Willkie's meagre eighty-two, and in the popular vote FDR won five million more ballots than Willike. It was not quite the landslide of 1936, but given the isolationist temper of the times in America, it was a magnificent achievement. With selective military service launched and Congress authorizing massive supplementary funding for military production, the US would be in a position not only to defend itself if it was attacked, but to intervene where and when the president and Congress decided.

In 1936, in addressing domestic policy, Roosevelt had spoken of America's 'rendezvous with destiny'. Now, abjuring as an 'obvious delusion' the isolationist notion of America as 'a lone island in a world dominated by the philosophy of force', as he put it in the summer of 1940, he saw a second destiny: that America should rise not only to the challenge of modern social equality and dignity in a free capitalist society, but gird itself to become the world's leading power in international affairs, once its defence forces were rebuilt.[35] For that to happen, he needed Britain to hold out against the Nazi offensive. At Churchill's request he therefore not only pushed through a naval-destroyers-for-bases deal, by which fifty mothballed American World War I destroyers could be traded with Britain for strategically import-ant military garrison rights in the western hemisphere, but pressed Congress to ignore Britain's impending bankruptcy and continue to supply it on unspecified credit, or 'Lend-Lease'.

Roosevelt's Lend-Lease proposal was bitterly opposed by many Republicans, even by Democrats like Joseph P. Kennedy, the US ambas-sador to Britain. But by flattering Kennedy – who left his post in London to exert pressure on FDR and sink Lend-Lease as wasted money ('Democracy is finished in England') – the president was able to pressure Congress into passing the bill, while keeping America out of the war.

Speaking to the nation, the president's fireside chat of December 29, 1940, provided a vivid example of the difference between the everyday democratic values expressed by the elected leader of America in the White House and the venomous, mesmerizing rhetoric of Adolf Hitler. 'The experience of the past two years has proven beyond doubt that no nation can appease the Nazis' FDR explained – and poured cold water on the notion of an American 'negotiated peace' with Hitler, such as Ambassador Kennedy was proposing.[36] 'Nonsense! Is it a nego-tiated peace if a gang of outlaws surrounds your community and on threat of extermination makes you pay tribute to save your skins?' he asked listeners. Hitler was not only clinically insane, but implacable. 'No man can tame a tiger into a kitten by stroking it. There can be no appeasement with ruthlessness' the president declared. 'If Britain goes down, the Axis powers will control the continents of Europe, Asia, Africa, Australasia, and the high seas – and they will be in a position to bring enormous military and naval resources against this hemisphere.' In that case, 'Crawling into bed and pulling the cover over our heads' was no answer. 'The people of Europe who are defending themselves do not ask us to do their fighting. They ask us for the implements of war,' he spelled out, 'the planes, the tanks, the guns that will enable them to fight for their liberty and for our security.' And with that the president used the phrase that would redefine the status of the United States in 1941: 'the arsenal of democracy'.[37]

Several days later, in his State of the Union address, the president raised the stakes still further, urging Americans to lift their sights from mercantilism to a restatement of fundamental democratic principles, setting out what became known as 'the essential Four Freedoms' of modern democratic life: the freedoms of speech and of worship, from want and from fear.[38]

Lend-Lease, endorsed by Wendell Willkie, was signed by Roosevelt into law on March 11, 1941 – not only the largest congressional appropriation in American history but, as FDR put it, 'the end of any attempts at appeasement'.[39]

Appeasement might be over as a policy for the United States, but entering the war was a different issue. Eighty-one per cent of Americans still opposed American involvement. As German troops went on to invade Greece, the cradle of western civilization, after overrunning Bulgaria and Yugoslavia, Churchill again appealed to Roosevelt to join Britain as an ally and declare war on Nazi Germany, to no avail. Using paratroopers, Hitler's Wehrmacht even seized Crete, birthplace of Zeus and considered an impregnable island, dominating the Mediterranean. With General Rommel racing his Panzerarmee across North Africa towards Tobruk, and the Mediterranean controlled by Axis air power, the future for democracy looked bleak, even if the US were to declare war.

In view of Hitler's blitzkrieg success, then, the question arose: were isolationists such as Ambassador Kennedy, Colonel Lindbergh, Senator Burton K. Wheeler and Herbert Hoover right? Was Britain doomed? Between them, Hitler's Third Reich, Mussolini's Italian Empire, and Stalin's Soviet Union would in that case become the ultimate masters of a modern industrial, militarized, totalitarian Europe.

As if to prove the wisdom of Roosevelt's warning about stroking tigers, however, Hitler now shocked the world – though not intelligence services – by attacking his own ally, Russia. Beginning before dawn on the same day of the same month in which Napoleon had once attacked Russia, June 22, almost four million German troops, marshalled in 180 infantry and Panzer divisions, crossed the German–Soviet border in 1941, and made for Leningrad, Moscow, Minsk and the Crimea, executing Russian political commissars and Jews as they went, and herding hundreds of thousands of bewildered Soviet soldiers into captivity.

For FDR, Hitler's apparent success, though welcomed by many in America as a blow against Bolshevism, only increased the threat of

Nazism – the more so if, as Hitler was requesting, Japan were also to declare and wage war on Russia in the Far East, forcing the Soviets to fight on two fronts. The Japanese would thereby increase their growing hegemony in the Far East, following their invasions of China and Indochina, while Hitler would become the undisputed master of all Europe and Russia. The United States of America would then be forced into yet further isolation, indeed be pressed to start appeasement negotiations with the Third Reich and the Empire of Japan, in a new Munich.

The fate of the democratic world now rested, to an extraordinary extent, in one man's hands. Mulling over the situation, President Roosevelt sent word via his emissary Harry Hopkins to Prime Minister Churchill that he'd like to meet him – in secret. Their 'summit' aboard the battleships *Augusta* and *Prince of Wales* in Placentia Bay, off the coast of Newfoundland, early in August 1941, infuriated Hitler, who felt upstaged; but it disappointed Churchill too.

Churchill had assumed Roosevelt would not have suggested such a meeting – fraught with danger for the prime minister in avoiding German U-boats as he sailed across the Atlantic with his senior staff – unless the president 'contemplated some further forward step': namely an announcement of America's entry into the war, on the British Empire's side, and that of the Soviet Union, too, in resisting fascism.[40] However, though the two leaders clasped hands and began their summit by calling each other 'Winston' and 'Franklin', and though they lunched, dined and sang rousing English hymns together, and though they reviewed the global scenario in considerable detail, and though FDR made sympathetic noises, no formal commitment was given by the president beyond further Lend-Lease aid and a decision, in the light of the recent dispatch of US Marines to help defend Iceland, that the Atlantic Ocean between the United States and Iceland would be declared an American maritime security zone, patrolled by US warships. Beyond that, FDR would not go. Instead, the president proposed, they should jointly issue a declaration of principles.

Principles? Churchill was driven almost apoplectic with rage. Buoyed by a report from an emissary to Moscow whom he trusted, however, the president was certain that both Russian and British forces would hold out. He was therefore determined to step into the shoes of President Wilson, whose 'Fourteen Points' had been the only explicit statement of war aims presented by any side in World War I. Where

Wilson had produced his document in January 1918, ten months *after* America's declaration of war, however, FDR wanted his charter to *precede* America's entry into the world conflict, and thus inspire not only those peoples still holding out against the tide of Nazi aggression, but the American public. To Churchill's chagrin, therefore, Roosevelt insisted in the joint declaration that there be no post-war territorial gains coveted by, or given to, the US or Britain; that any alteration in national boundaries should only take place by consent of the peoples concerned; and that all peoples – including those in the colonies – had the right to self-determination. This sent ice running through Churchill's veins.

Churchill's dream of the continuation of the British Empire, with the ongoing subjection of India, Burma, Singapore, Malaya and other colonies in Africa, the Middle East and the Far East, was thus shaken. FDR himself stood behind the American version of the declaration, however, and Churchill, desperate for America to become a participating ally (Field Marshal Smuts, his strategic adviser, had reported that the war against Germany could never be won without American intervention), was forced to present the document to his cabinet in London as a fait accompli.[41] The joint declaration henceforth became known as the Atlantic Charter, without even a commitment that the US would fight. It was on Roosevelt's part a masterstroke, though a bitter pill for the beleaguered British prime minister to swallow, as he read newspaper reports of what the president had told reporters on his return to Washington: the US was no closer to 'entering the war' as a result of the summit.[42]

The Atlantic Charter, though never formally signed, spelled the end of British colonial imperialism – indeed the imminent end of Britain as a world power. As Roosevelt congratulated himself when telling his wife about his trip, Churchill had been 'the orator', but he had been the realist.[43]

Because Roosevelt did not survive World War II, he was unable to write his memoirs; whereas Churchill, purloining most of Downing Street's secret documents, was able later to portray himself, in his multi-volume history of the war, as the master strategist of ultimate Allied victory. Despite Churchill's undoubted moral and physical courage, this was to say the least debatable.

In truth, FDR exhibited a far better feel for the likely course the war would follow than Churchill, indeed than any senior politician in the world. With his now legendary powers of persuasion he had gone before Congress to get the Selective Service Act renewed and extended to eighteen months. Congress responded by passing the measure by only a single vote on August 12, against growing resistance from isolationists. Meanwhile the president accelerated war production of planes, tanks, guns, ships and munitions to the point where, unhampered by bombs or invading armies, US output of material in 1942, as a still neutral country, promised to dwarf that of all belligerents combined. If Russia and Britain could survive until the winter, the US would thus be in a position, FDR calculated, to intervene decisively, and thereby emerge as the master of the post-war universe; an economic and military mastery that would, thanks to the Atlantic Charter, be predicated on *moral* principles.

Roosevelt's political, strategic, industrial and diplomatic skill in guiding the US not only on the sidelines of a world war, but with a clearly articulated moral framework for the world that would come thereafter, was – and remains – perhaps the greatest example of presidential leadership in American history. To the relief of those like Frances Perkins who feared the clash of prima donnas in Placentia Bay, the president had afterwards remarked that he'd liked Churchill, indeed had found him much improved since 1918. 'I'm sure that he's got a greater mind than he had twenty years ago', he remarked of the prime minister. 'He's got a more developed mind.'⁴⁴ If this was true of Churchill, it was doubly so of Roosevelt. By extending his American security zone as far as Iceland in the summer of 1941, and by then placing an embargo on oil exports to Japan, the president now turned the screw on the Axis alliance, challenging both the Third Reich and the Empire of the Rising Sun to respond in the only way they knew how: by force of arms, thus giving the United States a *casus belli* that would turn the isolationist tide at home.

Bogged down in his titanic struggle to crush the Soviet Union's armies before winter, Hitler was forced to cede control of the western Atlantic to the US Navy, and he gave U-boat captains direct orders to avoid any incident that might provoke an American declaration of war. Japan was equally loath to incite war with the US. Without essential raw materials such as oil from America, however, it was stymied in its plans to expand its Greater East Asia Co-prosperity Sphere. Aware from decrypts of Japanese secret signals how hysterical the Japanese leaders were becoming, FDR ratcheted up his diplomatic pressure, not only refusing to lift his embargo on the export of oil and other materials to Japan, but demanding that the Japanese withdraw from conquered territories in China.

Convinced that the United States would declare war on Japan if they invaded the Dutch East Indies and Malaya, the new hard-line Japanese government headed by Hideki Tojo therefore proposed in November 1941 a pre-emptive attack on American forces in the Pacific before US units could be reinforced. The war was becoming a game of cat and mouse; but America, thanks to Roosevelt's massive re-armament programme and military draft, was the cat.

Aware of Japanese intentions from intercepts, Roosevelt ordered all American commanders in the Pacific to be on the highest alert, and sent a squadron of new B-17s to Hawaii. Not even FDR, however, could credit the utter ineptitude of the peacetime US garrison at Pearl Harbor, when now attacked in broad daylight on December 7, 1941: the 'day of infamy', as the president called it in his speech to Congress. In two hours Admiral Yamamoto's attack on Pearl Harbor managed to sink eighteen American warships, including no less than eight battle-ships, smash or cripple 283 aircraft, and kill 2,403 servicemen, with almost total impunity.

Hitler, with his armies beleaguered in snow outside Moscow and lacking winter clothing, was ecstatic when he heard the news (he had not been informed by the Japanese in advance), but completely misread the fact that the US had, in the aftermath, declared war only on Japan. Four days after Pearl Harbor the Führer made a long, impassioned speech to deputies in the Reichstag in Berlin. In it he announced some-thing that would cost him the war – and his life.

President Roosevelt, Hitler explained to Reichstag deputies, 'comes from a family rolling in money', with social advantages that 'pave the way and secure success in life in the democracies'. By contrast, Hitler himself had returned from World War I 'just as poor as I had left for it in the autumn of 1914'. While Roosevelt the millionaire had then pursued the 'career of a normal politician, who is experienced in busi-ness, has economic backing, and is protected by his birth, I fought as a nameless and unknown man for the resurrection of my *Volk*, a people which had just suffered the greatest injustice in its history. The course

of the two lives!' the Führer reflected, amazed to think how different
they were, as men and leaders. 'When Franklin Roosevelt became the
head of the United States, he was the candidate of a thoroughly capitalist party, which used him. When I became the chancellor of the
German Reich, I was the Führer of a popular movement which I
myself had created.' Where Roosevelt was guided by a 'brain trust'
of Jews – people 'we once fought in Germany as a parasitic phenomenon of mankind, and which we had begun to remove from public
life' – he, Adolf Hitler, had fought against such people on behalf of
'the fate of my *Volk* and my sacred inner beliefs'.[45] Roosevelt's and
Churchill's Atlantic Charter was 'tantamount to a bald hairdresser
recommending his unfailing hair restorer. These gentlemen, who live
in socially retarded states, should have taken care of their unemployed
instead of agitating for war' the Führer commented. Germany, whose
Volk had 'a history of nearly two thousand years', had 'never been as
united and unified as it is today and as it will be in the future', nor
'so aware of its honour'. As Führer, he announced, he had therefore
given the American chargé d'affaires his passport and had told him to
leave Berlin. He was declaring war on the United States.

The challenge that now faced the Third Reich would not only be
one of arms, but of will and ruthlessness. 'Just as we were mercilessly
harsh in our struggle for power,' the Führer warned, 'we will be merciless and harsh in our struggle for the preservation of our *Volk*.' Any
German who questioned, criticized, mocked or sabotaged 'the efforts
of the homeland' would be executed.[46] Six days later, on December
17, 1941, having arrived back at his Rastenburg headquarters in East
Prussia, Hitler then relieved Field Marshal von Brauchitsch of his post
as commander-in-chief of the army, and made himself supreme
commander or generalissimo of the Wehrmacht and Waffen SS.
'Anyone can do that little bit of operational planning' he sneered.

For his part, FDR also took on the role of generalissimo, yet took
care while exercising his constitutional authority as commander-in-
chief to direct the strategy of the war but not to interfere with its
implementation, as Hitler now did, to the cost of his armies' chances
of battlefield success. In casting Roosevelt as a mere functionary and
'profiteer' in the 'shadow' of President Wilson in World War I, Hitler
– who had never visited America – had made a big mistake. FDR's
eight years in the US Navy Department, from 1913 to 1920, had given

him the very training Hitler lacked – indeed it is impossible for an historian to imagine how otherwise a huge but militarily impotent democracy, which had refused to militarize in the inter-war years, could have transformed itself into the Rome of the twentieth century as, under Roosevelt's presidency, the United States now did.

From that earlier administrative experience in Washington, working with Josephus Daniels, FDR had learned the fundamental lesson of war, as set out by Clausewitz and other military thinkers: the organization of a nation's resources is crucial to achieving success – the means that enable the end. The fact that Yamamoto's daring sneak attack had proven so damaging to America's naval and military standing in the Far East was shameful (FDR could not understand why, despite his warnings sent to Hawaii, the battleships were 'tied up in rows', and the airplanes parked by their runways as at a polo meet), but the president was not downcast.[47] His 500-word speech to Congress on December 8, 1941 on the infamy of Pearl Harbor would go down in history alongside Lincoln's Gettysburg Address, but it was his State of the Union address four weeks later that actually *made* history.

On January 6, 1942, outlining American production targets for the coming year, President Roosevelt announced numbers that took Congress' and the world's breath away: six million tons of new ships; 45,000 tanks; 60,000 airplanes – in 1942 alone! On this basis, there could be no doubt who would win the war, only how long it would take.

Churchill, hearing these figures from Roosevelt himself while staying in the White House for three weeks, was reborn. In a fireside chat two days after Pearl Harbor FDR had told listeners that there would be 'bad news and good news', 'defeats and victories', but that these were the 'fortunes of war' – and would be shared by the nation. The fundamental fact was that 'we are all in it – all the way. Every single man, woman and child is a partner in the most tremendous undertaking in American history.'[48]

The first eight months of 1942 bore out the president's warning about bad news. Hong Kong, Guam, Wake Island, New Britain, the Gilbert Islands and most of the Solomon Islands had fallen to the Japanese. On January 2, the capital of the Philippines, Manila, fell too, forcing the Americans to fall back into the Bataan Peninsula, while another Japanese army captured Kuala Lumpur in Malaya, advanced through Borneo and invaded New Guinea, to the north of Australia.

General Rommel raced to Benghazi, routing the British Commonwealth army in North Africa, while Hitler, authorizing the annihilation of all German and captured Jews, told his propaganda minister Dr Goebbels not to 'get sentimental' about the Hebrews, but to 'speed up the process with cold brutality', whatever the 'resistance in some circles'. (As Goebbels coyly noted in his diary several weeks later, in relation to the mass deportation of Jews to extermination camps in the east: 'Here will be used a fairly barbarous method which one can't come close to describing; not much will remain of the Jews themselves. On the whole, it can be determined that 60 per cent of them will have to be liquidated, only 40 per cent being usable for the purposes of labour.')[49]

German barbarity was matched by Japanese atrocities committed against captured enemy troops in Asia, South East Asia and the Pacific. In February, the Japanese invaded Burma, and after landing in Malaya, took Singapore, together with 85,000 troops defending it. In the Battle of the Java Sea, all five Allied cruisers were sunk, and five of the nine accompanying destroyers. The Dutch East Indies also fell to Japanese invaders, and Japanese warplanes began bombing Darwin on the northern Australian peninsula. And worse was to come.

As the spring of 1942 turned to summer, German forces launched another spectacular armoured offensive in the Crimea. The Japanese took the surrender of General King's 76,000-strong army in the Bataan Peninsula of the Philippines – the largest surrender in American history, and precursor to the infamous Bataan Death March. With the Russian armies defeated in the Crimea, opening the gateway to the rich oilfields of the Caucasus, Stalin sent his foreign minister Vyacheslav Molotov to Washington to plead for more American munitions and an urgent invasion of France to create a second front and relieve the pressure on Russia.

Roosevelt's and Churchill's responses to the pleas of the Soviet Union differed markedly. To Molotov's appeal for a second front, Roosevelt replied yes: the Allies would launch an invasion of France in 1942, to draw off German air squadrons and divisions, and drive straight for Berlin. Churchill, when he heard what Roosevelt had verbally promised Molotov, was appalled. The Allies would never be able to launch such an amphibious attack across the often stormy seas of the English Channel; no one had done so successfully since 1066. As the Spanish Armada had come to grief in 1588, so too had Hitler's mighty Luftwaffe in the Battle of Britain; it was an impossible task. In June 1942, therefore, Churchill made haste to Washington to attempt to dissuade FDR against mounting a second front – at least, across the Channel. It was in the White House, in fact, that Churchill's defeatism in terms of head-to-head battle with the German armies was seemingly justified, when Roosevelt relayed to him the bad news. Tobruk in North Africa, with its entire British garrison of 33,000 soldiers, had surrendered to Rommel's German-Italian Panzerarmee without serious fighting. 'Defeat is one thing,' Churchill commented, in shame at British cowardice, 'disgrace is another.'[50]

Roosevelt was remarkably unfazed. For him, it was another indication of Britain's need for more and better equipment – which America could provide. He thus magnanimously offered a convoy of the latest American Sherman tanks and 105 mm self-propelled artillery guns to be re-routed to Suez, to ensure that Egypt, too, was not lost.[51]

By the summer of 1942, then, it was clear that Washington DC – not London or Moscow – was the epicentre of the Allies' war on Germany and Japan. To prosecute the war, Roosevelt had established a Joint Chiefs of Staff Committee, with its offices forming the Anglo-American High Command headquarters, and the new Pentagon – the world's largest office building – to house it. Meanwhile FDR also set up a series of War Boards to maximize US industrial output, and gave the green light to the development of a highly secret weapon of mass destruction: the Manhattan Project.

With Congress' backing, FDR was, in short, not only the US president but now the generalissimo of the Allied cause, weighing carefully the political, economic and military priorities in winning the war. Aged sixty that year, and despite the military reverses overseas, he radiated confidence and vitality, sure that he could manage the leaders of the various supplicant nations and emissaries seeking his aid. He was, in this sense, the pharaoh not only of peacetime, but of war. America, he was certain, would win in the end, with its subordinate partners. He had only to communicate positive energy and compassion, and exercise good judgement, and the United States would emerge as leader of a democratic New World it could oversee economically and, if necessary, by superior force.

Roosevelt's patience was the quality that perhaps raised him above all his peers. To the apoplexy of his generals he not only accepted Churchill's argument that Germany should be defeated first, then Japan (since the fall of Germany would inevitably lead to the fall of Japan, whereas the reverse was not true), but deferred to Churchill's qualms about a cross-Channel attack on France in 1942. He therefore delayed the undertaking for two years, until American forces were seasoned enough by battles in North Africa and Italy, to launch what would be the decisive battle of World War II: D-Day, on June 6, 1944. 'If anything happens to that man, I couldn't stand it' Churchill said with tears in his eyes as Roosevelt's plane took off from Casablanca, where they concerted plans in January 1943. 'He is the truest friend; he has the furthest vision; he is the greatest man I have ever known.'[52]

Meeting President Roosevelt in Casablanca on behalf of the Free French, quartered in London, General de Gaulle did not agree. De Gaulle was incensed by the president's presumptuousness regarding the future. 'Roosevelt meant the peace to be an American peace, convinced that he must be the one to dictate its structure,' de Gaulle later chronicled, 'and that France in particular should recognize him as its saviour and its arbiter.' Given the tens of thousands of Americans, Britons and Canadians who would still have to give their lives to liberate France, this seemed a fair presumption to most combatants, but not to de Gaulle. The Frenchman was furious that 'beneath his mask of courtesy, Roosevelt regarded me without benevolence'.[53]

Malevolence might have been more accurate. Roosevelt remarked to Supreme Court Justice Felix Frankfurter that de Gaulle was 'a bit touched' in the head, and later 'a nut'.[54] At any event, with allies such as these, the president would have been forgiven for wishing, like his military staff, to return his forces to the US and concentrate on the defeat of Japan – where, in crucial naval battles in the Coral Sea and Midway, US naval superiority had been reasserted in the summer of 1942, and the campaign to retake the Solomon Islands had begun in earnest at Guadalcanal. Yet to his lasting credit Roosevelt resisted, aware that this time, unlike 1918, the United States must take a more effective leadership role in the post-war world, not back away.

Upon his success in first setting the United States back on the path to economic prosperity in the 1930s, then commanding America's war effort, and finally in positioning the United States to guide the post-war world, Franklin Delano Roosevelt must ultimately be judged. None were easy tasks – in fact it is hard to imagine any other American figure who could have managed what FDR achieved. Compromise in keeping the Grand Alliance unified was in this respect Roosevelt's greatest contribution to grand strategy, and though mocked by those who counselled a more rational, clear-cut American military approach, time would prove him right. Roosevelt, as generalissimo-in-chief, was vindicated, able to take heed of Churchill's warnings, overrule his military advisers, use his understanding of the Vichy French, and prosecute a patient strategy that allowed the Allies to employ their combination of forces – naval, air and ground troops, as well as military intelligence – that promised to defeat even the most fanatical German armies. Moreover he ensured that Stalin would refuse possible German offers of an armistice, knowing that the Americans were, eventually, coming, and would not accept anything but the 'unconditional surrender' of the Nazis, as FDR announced at Casablanca.

By the fall of 1943, with the Soviets pushing back Hitler's armies towards Prussia, Anglo-American forces in control of the Mediterranean, and General MacArthur making headway in the Solomon Islands, the war certainly seemed to have reversed itself since the dark days of 1941. Even the U-boat menace in the Atlantic – where, in the spring of 1943, more than 200 German submarines had caused havoc in intercepting Allied convoys – was lifted when Roosevelt ordered back sixty long-range Liberator airplanes from the Pacific, which led to the sinking of eighty German submarines, and Hitler's order to withdraw the remainder.

American war production hit new records that year, with the US producing a new B-24 bomber every sixty-three minutes, tens of thousands of tanks, thousands of ships, and hundreds of thousands of vehicles of all kinds; more than the output of all other combatants combined. It was small wonder that, at a summit in Tehran in November 1943, Stalin raised his glass to acknowledge what 'the president and the United States have done to win this war. The most important thing in this war are machines. The United States has proven it can turn out 10,000 planes a month. Russia can turn out, at most, 3,000 airplanes a month. The United States is a country with machines' the Russian dictator remarked with awe. 'Without the use of those machines, through Lend-Lease, we would lose this war.'

This was, in the end, Roosevelt's greatest single achievement. Fearing an English Channel running with English blood, Churchill had frankly never believed in an Allied invasion of France. The Germans themselves had baulked at a cross-channel assault in 1940. The one-day assault on Dieppe in 1942 (in which more than 1,000 Canadian soldiers had been mown down in a few hours, and 2,000 captured) had proven an unmitigated catastrophe, completely defeating its strategic aim of proving to the Russians that the Allies were serious in preparing for a cross-Channel invasion of France. Moreover Churchill's pet project, his personally promoted amphibious landing near Rome at Anzio, in January 1944, was an even greater disaster, incurring a horrific 29,000 American and British casualties to little, if any, purpose. In overruling Churchill, therefore, and insisting the Allies must and *would* carry out Operation Overlord, Roosevelt showed supreme patience and, at the appropriate moment, decisive judgement. Moreover, in deciding that General Eisenhower, not General Marshall, should command the Allied D-Day invasion, Roosevelt once again demonstrated his talent for choosing effective subordinates.

D-Day, June 6, 1944, was thus the triumph of President Roosevelt's role as generalissimo-in-chief. It would become the greatest successful military operation of the twentieth century, mounted under the supreme command of an American general, and combining the arms not only of all the services, but all the western Allies. When Churchill telegraphed Stalin to say the D-Day landings would commence the next day, the marshal – who had waited two long years for the moment – sneered: 'if there is no fog. Until now there was always something that interfered. I suspect tomorrow it will be something else. Maybe they'll meet up with some Germans! What if they meet up with some Germans! Maybe there won't be a landing then, but just promises as usual.'[55]

The Russian dictator, however, was stunned and surprised by the ferocity of the Allied onslaught. Landing almost 200,000 troops in Normandy in a single day, in overwhelming force, across a storm-blown sea, and reinforcing them with two million troops in the weeks thereafter, the western Allies finally proved they could not only supply the means to fight the Nazis, but the will, determination and professionalism to do so – and to win. It was a lesson that not only the Germans, but also the Soviets, took to heart.

Summoning James Byrnes back from the Supreme Court to act as his domestic affairs deputy, Roosevelt increasingly concentrated his unique political skills on the business of working with America's allies, and plans for a post-war world. Inevitably, the latter impinged on the former; Churchill recalled how, at the Tehran summit, 'I sat with the Russian bear on the one side of me, with paws outstretched, and on the other side the great American buffalo, and between the two sat the poor little English donkey who was the only one', he claimed, 'who knew the right way home.'[56]

But did he? Churchill had proven an historic figure when England stood alone against the Nazis after the fall of France, Russia complacent in its Nazi–Soviet Pact, the United States still in isolation mode. But as World War II wound to its climax, Churchill's vision of a Britain restored to colonial greatness, at the heart of a global empire, rang hollow to Roosevelt's ears, for all Churchill's eloquence. When Stalin jokingly suggested, at Tehran, shooting 50,000 German officers at the conclusion of the war, and Roosevelt demurred, suggesting 49,000 as a better number, Churchill walked out of the room, chased by Stalin and Molotov, who insisted it was a jest.[57] 'I would rather be taken out into the garden here and now and be shot myself than sully my own country's honour by such infamy' Churchill had protested: the voice of a great humanitarian, but one who looked to revive an imperial past, not embrace a post-colonial future.

President Roosevelt, though later criticized for his naivety in dealing with his Russian counterpart, was far more prescient than Churchill about the future of the democratic rather than the Communist world. Churchill evinced little interest in the concept of a United Nations organization, or UN trusteeships that would, against strict timetables, immediately prepare former colonized countries for swift independence. The colonial system, Roosevelt had told his son Elliott at Casablanca, was not merely unjust, but inevitably it led to protest, terrorism and war. 'Exploit the resources of an India, a Burma, a Java; take all the wealth out of those countries but never put anything back into them, things like education, decent standards of living, minimum health requirements – all you're doing is storing up the kind of trouble that leads to war.'[58] Churchill was still so opposed to Indian self-rule that Roosevelt had told Stalin, at Tehran, 'it would be better not to discuss the question of that country's independence with Churchill', given the prime minister's Tory views.[59] Roosevelt felt similarly about

French colonialism – indeed with regard to Indochina, FDR had also agreed '100%' with Stalin in wishing to stop France from taking it back as a colony, stating bluntly that 'after 100 years of French rule in Indochina, the inhabitants were worse off than they had been'.[60]

One British historian of the Tehran conference wondered, forty years later, if it had 'crossed Stalin's mind that Roosevelt was, wittingly or unwittingly, pointing towards a world of Soviet/American dictatorship' – later to be called 'hegemonism'.[61] Whether or not it did, the prospect certainly crossed many a British (and French) mind, with concerns as to whether such a dual dictatorship of the world could possibly work without eventual war between the two, given their contrary systems of government.

Roosevelt had no illusions either about Soviet Communism or Stalin. To his lasting credit, however, FDR felt impelled at least to try to co-opt Russian involvement in shaping a free and democratic post-war world. Certainly no other American figure could have attempted to reach an accommodation with Stalin, nor with such legendary charm, humour and goodwill. If Soviet–American relations were destined to go down the drain after the war, given a Bolshevist system based upon fear, intimidation and indifference to human life, Roosevelt was determined that, on his watch, he would first do everything in his power to make the dual hegemony work. And this, by standing for election for an unprecedented fourth term as president of the United States, despite failing health, he was determined to achieve.

His hand shook when he poured tea, he had long since stopped using the White House swimming pool, and he rarely stood, finding his leg braces too heavy and the effort too tiring. Deep circles below his eyes began to make his huge, once handsome face, with his trademark small pince-nez, seem haggard – yet still the president insisted, in the summer of 1944, he was fit to run. Eventually, at the insistence of his daughter Anna, he went for a check-up at the Bethesda Naval Hospital, where he was found to be suffering congestive heart failure, causing his face, lips and nail beds to discolour. If not treated, he was given a year to live.

Aged sixty-two, the president suddenly looked seventy-two, and should never have placed his name in contention, given his prognosis. Instead, the press was told he was in fine health and, after being nominated on the first ballot at the Democratic Party Convention in July

1944, he set off for Hawaii to mediate between General MacArthur and Admiral Nimitz over strategy in the Pacific – having dropped the unpopular vice president, Henry Wallace, from the ticket, and having taken Senator Harry S. Truman of Missouri as his running mate.

Few who met the president in person were confident he would stand up to the rigours of an election campaign. After conferring with FDR aboard the USS *Baltimore*, MacArthur told his wife on July 26, 1944, 'In six months he will be in his grave.' The president was, MacArthur felt, 'just a shell of the man I knew'.[62] Roosevelt had lost nineteen pounds, and when he spoke to dock workers in Washington State, after donning his leg braces for the first time in a year, he rambled and was almost incoherent. 'It's going to look mighty sad when he begins to trade punches with young Dewey' the *Washington Post* predicted, referring to the Republican candidate, Governor Thomas E. Dewey of New York.[63]

In fact the campaign that autumn turned out to be the reverse, as Roosevelt twitted the young governor for 'attacking my little dog, Fala'. Addressing an audience in Washington, FDR added: 'Well, of course, I don't resent attacks, and my family doesn't resent attacks, but Fala does resent them.'[64] Campaigning in New York the president appeared before three million people in October 1944, riding in an open White House car, even in pouring rain, and speaking before 125,000 people in Chicago's Soldier Field (with 150,000 outside), ending with an appearance in Boston, where Frank Sinatra warmed up the crowd. There, in the city's Fenway Park, the president reminded his audience that America was a nation of immigrants, and it was 'our duty to make sure that, big as our country is, there is no room in it for racial or religious intolerance' – nor for 'snobbery'.[65]

Six months later, Roosevelt's partner in the Grand Alliance, Winston Churchill, would be ejected from the prime ministership by British voters, but for his part FDR seemed in November 1944 just as popular as when first elected, winning the presidential election by three million more votes than in 1932, and receiving 432 electoral votes to Dewey's ninety-nine.

The president was over the moon; but under the weather. He had lost more weight, had no appetite, and his blood pressure was higher than ever. 'He looked like an invalid who had been allowed to see guests for the first time and the guests had stayed too long' Frances

Perkins recalled, after congratulating him on his win.[66] The president gave his fourth inaugural speech under the South Portico of the White House on January 20, 1945, before 7,000 people gathered in the snow – his last ever while standing. Peace was now close, 'a just and honorable peace, a durable peace' that America would work for, 'as today we work and fight for total victory in war'. In working for peace, moreover, 'We shall strive for perfection' he declared; a goal that would not be achieved 'immediately – but we shall still strive. We may make mistakes – but they must never be mistakes which result from faintness of heart or abandonment of moral principle.' He reminded his audience that the US Constitution was not a perfect instrument, but a 'firm base upon which all manner of men, of all races and colors and creeds, could build our solid structure of democracy', a democracy he had sought, as president, to protect. 'We have learned', he stated, 'that we cannot live alone, at peace; that our well-being is dependent on the well-being of other nations far away . . . We have learned to be citizens of the world.' Isolationism, in other words, was dead.

Two days later the ailing president sailed to Malta, then flew to Yalta on the Black Sea, where the sequel to the Tehran summit was to be held, beginning on February 4, 1945.

No conference in World War II would later give rise to more partisan argument than Yalta. Reversing their role as the party of isolationism up to World War II, Republicans would assert the summit was a sell-out by a sick president to Stalin. Yalta was, they claimed, a veritable invitation to diehard Soviet Communists to do what Hitler had failed to do: control Europe and infect the globe with their ideological doctrines.[67]

The president was certainly unwell – indeed was dying, whether of heart disease or cancer, or both. Edith Wilson, the widow of President Wilson, had commented at the inauguration that Roosevelt looked 'exactly as my husband did when he went into his decline'.[68] But with the war not yet over in either Europe or the Far East – and anywhere between half a million and a million American casualties estimated as necessary to force the Japanese to accept unconditional surrender – the president was determined to get Stalin's formal agreement to join the US in defeating Japan, once Berlin fell. Moreover, he wanted the mechanism of the United Nations – successor to the League of Nations – locked down, while Stalin still supported the notion. The rest, he recognized, would be a matter of barter.

Barter there certainly was at Yalta. The Soviets were already occupying much of Poland, having refused to support the Warsaw uprising, clearly determined to use the country as a permanent buffer against any future Barbarossa-like attack from the West. Poland would thus be part of a Soviet cordon sanitaire against Germany and any other western power seeking to invade Russia – a form of paranoid Soviet isolationism that would, behind a veil of mischief-making in foreign parts, characterize Russian relations with the West for the next half-century.

Roosevelt, fully aware of this, did his best at Yalta to charm and encourage Stalin in a less negative approach to the future world. It was, sadly, a losing battle. Moreover, the president was still adamant that the British should honour the Atlantic Charter and abandon their dreams of post-war colonial paradise, putting him on a confrontational course with Winston Churchill.

Roosevelt did his dying best at the eight-day Yalta conference. He fudged a compromise over Poland, knowing he was clothing rape; he agreed to Far Eastern bases for the Soviet military, in order not only to get Russian entry into the war against Japan, but to build a co-bulwark against renascent Japanese military adventurism in post-war years. He settled for a four-power occupation of Germany in distinct zones, including Berlin. He engineered a joint declaration on Liberated Europe, pledging free elections that would be 'broadly representative of all democratic elements', knowing that Russia, in those countries it overran on its own, would stretch the word 'democratic' to breaking point. Above all, he got agreement on the set-up for the United Nations, with a preparatory conference to assemble in San Francisco that April.

Sailing back to America aboard the USS Quincy, the president was depressed. Meeting King Ibn Saud of Saudi Arabia on Great Bitter Lake in the Suez Canal on February 12, 1945, Roosevelt attempted to get the king's agreement to 10,000 more Jewish refugees being allowed to settle in Palestine. Ibn Saud refused, saying the refugees should be sent back to the countries from which they came, compelling the president to promise that whatever Congress or the American media might say, he himself 'would do nothing to assist the Jews against the Arabs and would make no move hostile to the Arab people', while confiding to his new Secretary of State, Edward Stettinius, that Jews and Arabs, sadly, were on a collision course, but that he would do his best to find a way of avoiding war between them.[69] 'I didn't say the result was good,' FDR said to an aide on his return to Washington, 'I said it was the best I could do.'[70]

On March 1, 1945, the president made his last speech to a joint session of Congress, asking the senators and congressmen to forgive him if he remained seated, given the weight of his steel leg braces – the first time he had ever mentioned his disability. As one historian noted, 'His voice faltered, he was hoarse, he hesitated or lost his place fourteen times' and kept departing from the text.[71] He joked that he wanted to do in one hour 'what Winston did in two', and made reference to the Roosevelts' reputation for travel.[72] 'No plan is perfect' he said of his efforts at Yalta to assure the democratic freedom of Poland and other countries in Europe, but he hoped that overall the summit marked 'the end of the system of unilateral action', or heedless war by militarist states, and even – if the United Nations worked as was hoped – the end of imperial 'balances of power, and all other expedients that have been tried for centuries – and have always failed'. He denied he was unwell – unfounded 'rumors' that had circulated in his absence, but which could be seen, he claimed, to be untrue.

It was a bravura performance. Six weeks later, having travelled to Warm Springs to recover his failing energy, he was signing papers when he felt a terrible headache, slumped forward, and died.

Part Three: Private Life

Pampered by a rich, devoted, somewhat imperious mother, FDR grew up in very privileged circumstances, as Hitler noted, but as an only, often lonely child. Wanting to please his mother, yet also wanting to escape her control over his financial and social life, were the twin leitmotifs of his early manhood as he courted a number of eligible girls while at Harvard. He seemed, in fact, almost feminine in his desperation to get married before he graduated, proposing to at least three teenagers.

The most beautiful and serious of these student infatuations was tiny Alice Sohier, daughter of a wealthy businessman, who bewitched him.[73] Her doctor claimed her womb was too small to bear children, so Franklin's declaration that he wanted to have six fell on unfavourable Sohier ears ('I did not wish to be a cow' she told a friend afterwards).[74]

Whether from pique or *noblesse oblige*, FDR then courted another teenager, a girl he had known all his life: the orphaned daughter of his godfather, Elliott Roosevelt. She was the legendary ugly duckling of the family, unnaturally tall for those days (5' 10"), with big feet, big protruding teeth, and a receding chin. Plain was a euphemism. Moreover, she had no sense of humour and was – after several years in a finishing school in Paris, run by a left-wing lesbian martinet, Mlle Souvestre – dedicated to helping the poor and disadvantaged, which would free her from the trite and unattainable expectations of her class.

However, thanks to her deceased parents Eleanor Roosevelt was set to inherit a lot of money. To cap this, her uncle (the brother of her deceased father) was none other than the president of the United States. Franklin – who never kissed her before they were engaged, and certainly never went further than kissing before they were married – called her an 'angel' in his diary, and 'Babs' in conversation. Looks aside, he was proud of his 'catch'. He had grown tall and hugely handsome by the time he left Harvard, and was politically ambitious. Eleanor, who was well read, compassionate and obedient to the point of subservience in her adoration of him, would do fine. He wanted to be admired and loved, but by someone other than just his mother. And by Eleanor he was, once they married in 1905. They would have six children (one died), and houses full of servants. What more could he want?

Yachting, hiking, golf. Parties too, at which he was not only the tallest at 6' 2" but also the most handsome, intelligent, witty and charming. Eleanor herself predicted she would 'never be able to hold him', telling her cousin Ethel 'He's too attractive.'[75] Exhausted after child number six, Eleanor did not refuse to have further sex, but she did ask for, and get, her own bedroom and a good night's sleep in 1916.[76] In terms of marital stitching, however, it was a mistake, as she eventually discovered.

In 1918 Roosevelt sailed to England and France in order to inspect the US Navy's installations there, and to see the US Marine Corps in combat in the final year of World War I. On the way home he caught flu, in the global pandemic, and arrived aboard the *Leviathan* having barely survived a high fever and difficulty in breathing. Eleanor, alerted by telegram, met the ship at New York and arranged his conveyance by ambulance to his mother Sara's house on East 65th Street. As she unpacked his things, she came to his leather valise, and opened it.

Inside were beribboned love letters addressed to him from Eleanor's former secretary, Lucy Mercer.

Eleanor had already fired the twenty-six-year-old Ms Mercer in 1917 for being too intimate with Franklin, only for Lucy to join the navy as a yeoman, and Franklin to hire her in the Assistant Secretary of the Navy's office. There too Lucy had been fired, by Franklin's boss, Josephus Daniels, who knew that in Washington tongues wagged harder than in any other city. FDR still saw the stunningly beautiful Miss Lucy, however, and supported her financially when she lost her job. The discovery of the cache of her love letters – which she had continued to send while Franklin was in Europe – was an affront Eleanor could not endure.

'The bottom dropped out of my world' Eleanor later wrote. To her daughter Anna she later confided that she 'questioned' her husband about his intentions, if he was so in love with the woman, and 'offered him a divorce and asked that he think things over before giving her a definite answer'.[77]

No one in the Roosevelt family had ever been divorced, however, and though Eleanor herself had told a friend in a similar predicament 'not to accept ½ loaf of love', this was what, in the event, she was forced to take. For when FDR's mother, Sara, heard of Franklin's plans to divorce, she put her foot down, telling FDR he would not get another penny from her, nor would he inherit Springwood. FDR's amanuensis, Louis Howe, said the same thing, only more bluntly. FDR would be dismissed as Assistant Secretary of the Navy by Josephus, and his career would be ruined.

Thanks to Sara and to Howe, the crisis was averted. FDR lied to Lucy, telling her Eleanor would not agree to a divorce. But knowing FDR so well – they had conducted the affair for two years – Lucy also knew FDR was slated for greatness. Divorce, even if Eleanor did agree to one, would end all talk of his reaching the presidency one day. Lucy thus released him from any obligation, he 'returned' to his wife, and by the summer of 1920 FDR was campaigning as the Democratic candidate for the vice presidency of the United States, posing as a happily married man with five children.

To her credit, Lucy Mercer faded completely into the background – indeed emulated Franklin's mother, by marrying a fabulously wealthy widower twice her age, Winty Rutherford, by whom she also had a child. She continued to correspond with FDR, as a 'friend', but allowed no hint of their relationship to surface in her lifetime.

Eleanor, by contrast, was neither convinced that, as a result of his treachery, FDR still had the makings of greatness in him, nor could she exonerate him for loving Lucy, whose beauty made her feel exactly as she'd felt (and suffered) throughout her childhood: ugly and unwanted. 'I have the memory of an elephant. I can forgive, but never forget' she later confessed.[78] She took to visiting Rock Creek Cemetery and sitting before Saint-Gaudens' memorial statue to Clover Adams, who had killed herself in grief over her husband's love affair.[79] She lost weight and threw up so much the acid caused her teeth to separate and appear even more prominent.[80] She had once declared her belief in his future; now she appeared indifferent. When New York governor Al Smith ran for the presidency in 1928, and Franklin ran for the governor's mansion that Smith would vacate, she worked for Smith, not for FDR. 'Governor Smith's election means something,' she told a friend, 'but whether Franklin spends two years in Albany or not matters comparatively very little.' And when Smith lost, and FDR won, she was sour. 'I don't care' she snorted to a journalist. 'What difference does it make to me?'[81]

Eleanor's humourless, punitive response to FDR's betrayal changed their marriage into one of lingering convenience. She nursed him almost single-handedly when he was struck by polio, out of charity and duty, but at a deeper level considered it his just reward. When he began going down to Warm Springs to build his polio centre, to which polio sufferers of all backgrounds could come for treatment, she did not accompany him. She even ignored rumours that he had 'girlfriends' there, among them, Marguerite (Missy) LeHand, a former campaign worker who became his secretary and girl Friday. Young, lively, but neither beautiful nor from a classy background, Missy was accepted by Eleanor as a substitute wife for her husband. Sex, Eleanor told her daughter, 'is an ordeal to be borne'; she was perfectly happy for Franklin to have it, *à la française*, in his post-polio state (his potency not being affected by the paralysis in his lower limbs), if that was what he wanted, since she did not.[82] What she insisted upon was discretion ('I haven't told Mama that Missy is back' Eleanor wrote FDR in the spring of 1924, because Sara would have 'more peace of mind when she doesn't know such things'), while she carved a career for herself as an activist for social causes.[83]

Though he had promised Eleanor he would never see Lucy again, it was a promise Franklin and Lucy found difficult to keep. Lucy Mercer's husband proved more jealous of FDR than Eleanor of Lucy. Franklin and Lucy therefore maintained a clandestine correspondence throughout the 1920s and 1930s, and it was only when her husband's health failed in his mid-seventies, and he required full-time nursing that, in 1937, the relationship was revived in person. In 1935 FDR had suggested to author Fulton Oursler a magazine series by different detective novelists, devoted to the theme of how a rich man, 'married for twenty years' but with a wife who 'bores him' and tired of the 'hollowness of all the superficial friendship surrounding him', could engineer a getaway in order 'to begin a secret life in some small town where he can escape his past' – the series to be called 'The President's Mystery Story'. Oursler complied, earning $9,000 for the president (who gave it to his polio foundation).

The president had found his own secret solution: being driven to Q Street in Georgetown, picking Lucy up ('Go look out the window,' Lucy's niece would shout, 'President Roosevelt is coming to pick up Aunt Lucy!') and taking a ride with her in his car through Rock Creek Park.[84] In 1940, Lucy attended FDR's third inauguration as his guest, and when her husband suffered a stroke in 1941, the president took to meeting her in small lanes in the Virginia countryside. ('There seems to be a lady waiting on the road. Let us ask her if she needs a ride' he'd tell his driver.)[85]

On June 5, 1941, under the alias Mrs Paul Johnson in the White House log, Lucy visited the president in the Oval Office for the first time, while Eleanor was away at Hyde Park where she had her own house, Stone Cottage, or Val-Kill.[86]

FDR had always enjoyed the thrill of subterfuge, which appealed to his adventurous nature. Some have speculated that the knowledge of Lucy's impending visit to the White House caused Missy LeHand to have the first stroke that disabled her, on June 4, 1941, so possessive had she become as FDR's 'office wife' and gatekeeper. If so, FDR showed no guilt. Not only did he see Lucy for an hour and a half on June 6, but kept seeing her thereafter, either at the White House, Hyde Park, her estate at Allamuchy, or at Warm Springs. At the White House, one biographer noted, Eleanor's departure and Lucy's arrival 'suggested the banging doors in a French bedroom farce'.[87]

Lucy – whose husband died in 1944 – had worried lest she be

burdening the president by such clandestine trysts. 'This kind of letter is best unwritten and unmailed, and poor darling, to give you one more thing to read or think about is practically criminal'[88] she acknowledged in one missive – yet she still mailed it, knowing how lonely he was in the 'white sepulcher' of the White House, and how their romance allowed him, however nostalgically, to fantasize about a 'small house' that would be 'a joy', where 'one could grow vegetables as well as flowers'. 'I know one should be proud, very proud of your greatness,' she mused, 'instead of wishing for the soft life, of joy – and the world shut out.'[89]

By initiating his daughter Anna in the subterfuge, FDR was able to see Lucy time and time again – even at Bernard Baruch's estate at Hobcaw, in South Carolina, in April 1944, before D-Day – and taking her to Shangri-La, a Maryland summer camp in the Catoctin Mountains, seventy-five miles from Washington (later called Camp David) in July. In November 1944, he had her to stay at Warm Springs again, in the Little White House, like husband and wife. On a drive to Dowdell's Knob nearby, he told her in confidence of 'the real problems facing the world now', and his plan to meet Stalin and Churchill in the hope of committing Russia to the war against Japan – matters he simply couldn't share with Eleanor who, instead of hearing him out, would have pressed her own views, as FDR's daughter said. 'Mother was not capable of giving him this – just listening' Anna reflected.[90]

Another house guest, Daisy Suckley, a neighbour from Hyde Park, noted in her diary how concerned Lucy was about the president's health. 'She has worried & does worry terribly, about him, & has felt for years that he has been terribly lonely . . . We got to the point of literally weeping on each other's shoulders & we kissed each other, I think because we each feel thankful that the other understood & wants to help Franklin.'[91]

This was, sadly, no longer the case with Eleanor, who spent only a few days with FDR in his last two years. The affection he inspired in those around him, from world leaders to his black maid at Warm Springs, was remarkable. Born an American aristocrat, he had become a man of the people. Lizzie McDuffie 'told funny stories, laughed unrestrainedly, & gestured most amusingly & even poked him on the shoulder on one occasion to press home her point. She then resumed her position as maid', Daisy noted.[92]

As his health failed, FDR almost gave up the subterfuge, having Lucy travel with him on his special train back to Washington in December, and taking her with him to Hyde Park in January before his fourth inauguration. After Yalta, they were almost never apart. Recognizing how close to the end her father might be, Anna saw nothing morally wrong in the relationship; 'they were occasions', she later confided, 'which I welcomed for my father because they were light-hearted and gay, affording a few hours of much needed relaxation for a loved father and world leader in a time of crisis'.[93]

In Warm Springs, the president became so excited by Lucy's imminent arrival, on April 9, 1945, that he told his chauffeur to drive him eighty miles to Macon, Georgia, to intercept her as she came from her estate at Ridgely Hall in Aiken, South Carolina. Finally, at Manchester, they met up, and shooing away Ms Shoumatoff – who was to paint his portrait at Lucy's suggestion – to finish the journey on her own, FDR had Lucy sit beside him in the back of his automobile, enchanted. The following evening he insisted on driving Lucy himself in his hand-controlled car, with Fala, up to Dowdell's Knob to see the sun go down. Again, the next day, he drove Lucy, with Daisy Suckley and the dog in the back, for a two-hour drive. 'Lucy is so sweet with F—' Daisy noted in her diary that night. 'No wonder he loves having her around – Toward the end of the drive, it began to be chilly and she put her sweater over his knees.'[94]

It was the president's last drive. The next morning he worked on his government papers, then telephoned Washington to ensure he would get the first stamp commemorating the United Nations Conference he was to address on April 25, and began sitting for Ms Shoumatoff at midday. Lucy, next to him, was talking to Daisy about the barbecue planned for the evening when he collapsed.[95] He'd been haggard, but happy, a last idyll that came to an end several hours later at 3.35 p.m., when the enlightened pharaoh of the twentieth century was pronounced dead. By then Lucy, ever discreet, had slipped away into an obscurity that would last for decades thereafter.

CHAPTER TWO

HARRY S. TRUMAN

Later deified

Democrat
33rd President
(April 12, 1945–January 20, 1953)

Part One: The Road to the White House

Harry S. Truman was born on May 8, 1884, in Lamar, Missouri, the eldest son of a Baptist farmer and cattle futures trader. (The S in his name was left unpunctuated on Truman's birth certificate. It is said to have referred to his grandfather, Sol Young, a Confederate sympathizer in the Civil War.)

Truman suffered from deformed eyeballs. Without thick glasses he was, he admitted later, 'blind as a mole'.[1] Adored by his mother, he was only sent to school at age eight; at age ten his right side was paralyzed by diphtheria, and for a time he was unable to walk. His mother, who came from a well-off landowning family, was convinced he was a prodigy he read so much (history, biography and poetry). She insisted the family move from Lamar to Independence, where there were better schools. She paid for piano lessons through high school, encouraging Truman to believe he could make a career in music. Once his father lost everything in 1902 and went effectively bankrupt, there was insufficient money, and Truman never attended college. (He later took night-school courses in law, but never graduated.) 'My choice early in life was either to be a piano player in a whorehouse, or a politician' he later joked – adding there was little difference.

In actuality Truman's early reading of the Roman historians, from Julius Caesar to Plutarch and Tacitus, caused him to set his sights on a career in the military. His application to West Point in 1902 was rejected, however, owing to his optical 'deformity'.

To help support his family, Truman studied basic bookkeeping and worked for the local railroad, where he learned 'all the cuss words in the English language, not by ear, but by note'.[2] Switching to clerking in a bank, he finally joined his father and brother in 1906, working on his uncle's farm close to Grandview, Jackson County, without plumbing or electricity. His brother left to start a family of his own; Truman stayed on for a decade with his taciturn, implacable father, who would shout from the bottom of the stairs at 5 a.m. every day to rouse him to the fields.

For those early adult years Truman ploughed, fed pigs and cattle, cut wheat, shucked corn and kept the farm's books. 'We always owed the bank something – sometimes more, sometimes less – but we always owed the bank.'[3]

Meanwhile, to fulfil his childhood dream, and despite his eyesight, Truman applied to join the Missouri National Guard in 1905 as a junior lieutenant in the field artillery. His grandmother, whose property had been razed by Union troops for siding with the Confederacy in Kentucky, was appalled. Eyeing him standing proudly in his blue dress uniform, she thundered: 'Harry, this is the first time since 1863 that a blue uniform has been in this house. Don't bring it here again!'[4] (He didn't.)

Farming taught Truman how to get along with a demanding father, in an occupation to which he was entirely unsuited. He was at least spared the temptations of the big city in his twenties, learned the value of relentlessly hard work, and appreciated the joviality, tensions and loyalty of a close family. Most of all, he trained himself to get along with rural people of lesser intelligence and ambition, but no less wisdom. His vision of democracy – American democracy – was thus forged on farmland, a very different outlook from that of his patrician predecessor as president, FDR. Truman regretted that the US had not stopped immigration to America in the 1880s; then 'we'd have been an agricultural country forever', he said. 'When it is made up of factories and large cities it soon becomes depressed and makes classes among people.'[5] Yet it would be these growing American cities, ironically, that would later ensure his election when all opinion polls showed him going down to defeat.

A four-year lawsuit over his grandmother's will (which brought the still almost bankrupt Trumans 518 acres of her high-value land, but also heartbreaking family strife) altered Truman's nostalgia – especially the sight of a white-haired aunt 'tearing up truth just for a few dollars'. The suit only ended after the death of the aunt, when a settlement, or family peace treaty, was concluded. This, and a lawsuit over a few hundred barren acres in another state that went before the Supreme Court, caused Truman to temper his idealization of the land. 'No man that's any good would be a farmhand', he reflected in 1914, and by 1917, although well past draft age, he was ready to re-enlist in the National Guard and, if possible, serve overseas.[6]

Cheating on the eye test Truman joined the 2nd Missouri Field Artillery Regiment, where troopers elected their officers. The unit was soon federalized as the 129th. During training he befriended a fellow volunteer, James Pendergast, whose uncle, Tom Pendergast, was the political 'boss' of Kansas City. Truman also ran a successful unit canteen to make extra money with the help of a Jewish subordinate, Eddie Jacobson, who would have a profound influence on Truman's future.

Truman was soon promoted to artillery captain. His battery, shipped to Europe, took part in a series of actions in support of infantry in north-east France against German forces in the autumn of 1918. Truman's steadfastness under fire earned him a high reputation and official commendation that would help him greatly when later seeking political office. His moral fury over French extortionism – 'These people love francs better than their country and they are extracting just as many of them from us as they possibly can' – also gave him an increasing scepticism about human greed.[104]

Following the November 1918 Armistice Truman was recommended for a major's appointment in the regular US Army, which would have enabled him to serve with all the significant generals whom he would later direct as commander-in-chief of the US armed services, from Eisenhower to MacArthur, Bradley, Patton, Marshall and Ridgway. Instead, he turned down the opportunity and set up a haberdashery with Eddie Jacobson in Kansas City, Missouri.

'Truman & Jacobson' failed. The experience taught Truman many lessons, however, from tact with difficult customers to stoicism in the face of insolvency. Saddled with debts that would take a decade to pay off (he declined to declare bankruptcy), Truman was forced to face up to reality: he was too small a figure to be playing alone in the big leagues. If he was ever to win elected office – as, increasingly, the ex-artillery captain wished to do – he would need not only support from fellow veterans (he became a reserve officer, rising to colonel commanding the 381st Field Artillery Regiment in 1932), but financial and political 'sponsors'.

It was young Jim Pendergast's father, Mike Pendergast, who first suggested Truman run for eastern county judge, Jackson County, Missouri, in 1922. ('Judge' was the name given for what was, effectively, a county governor, responsible for appointing most public officials and overseeing the financial running of the community through its tax revenues.) With the 'help' of Tom Pendergast, the 'boss' of Kansas City, Truman – though an execrable speaker – duly 'won' the Democratic Party nomination and the post.

'Machine' politics and the 'boss' system were a political equivalent of the mafia in major US cities. Providing a guarantee of victory for their candidates through intimidation, multiple voting and ballot theft, the system was a Faustian bargain for someone with higher than local aspirations. By accepting such help, Truman the would-be politician was tainted from the start, though there was no other way in which, lacking money, charisma or rhetorical ability, the thick-bespectacled former haberdasher from Independence could make his way up the electoral ladder. Without Pendergast's support Truman lost re-election for eastern country judge in 1924, took up Masonry in a big way, became membership secretary of the Auto Club of Kansas City in 1925, lost yet more money when taking over a Citizens Community Bank in 1926 (it failed), and was fortunate to be sponsored again by Tom Pendergast (who had become the 'boss of bosses' in Kansas City politics) for presiding judge for the entire region in the autumn of 1926.

Truman seems to have been personally incorruptible, pocketing none of the rake-offs that Pendergast notoriously took from major public contracts. 'Am I a fool or an ethical giant?' he asked himself in his diary, hurt by press excoriation of his fealty to a corrupt political puppeteer.[8] Concerned lest newspaper readers send his family poisoned gifts he forbade them to eat anything delivered to the door. Without Pendergast, however, he was, in terms of election, a Missouri nobody; indeed, he only visited the nation's capital for the first time at age forty-four. He had joined a slew of associations in a bid to gain wider recognition, but without financial and organizational backing in the nuts and bolts of running an election campaign he remained, in the end, beholden to Pendergast.

Missouri had straddled both sides in the American Civil War, but had formally sided with the Union. Its population of Scots, Irish, Germans, Jews and blacks was tough, socially conservative, segregated, and in the 1920s equally divided between rural and urban Americans. The Ku Klux Klan was active, as were gangsters and loan sharks in Kansas City and St Louis. Truman stood out among political leaders in the state because, as Judge Truman, he held greedy contractors to a strict budget, while his literary and cultural interests caused him to want his community to boast better services, from roads and schools to libraries and concert halls. When the Great Depression hit Missouri, therefore, he did not hesitate in promoting a massive public works program: major public investments that were brought in on time, under budget, with full employment. He was twice re-elected presiding judge, despite worsening gangsterism and political corruption in Kansas City itself.

In 1934 Truman's Faustian bargain reached a crossroads. He had been made director of the Federal Re-employment Service in Missouri, answering to Harry Hopkins in Washington DC, and had found work for some 100,000 Missourians. He had thought about running either for tax collector, with Pendergast's backing – which would have given him a safe salary of $10,000 per annum – or for Congress. He was fifty years old, unknown outside his home state and unable to make up his mind. Pendergast made it up for him. He was told to run for the US Senate.

Despite Mussolini's dictatorship in Italy, the clampdown by Stalin in the Soviet Union, and the rise of Hitler in Germany, as well as worsening problems in Asia, there was zero interest among new or old immigrant Missourians in foreign affairs. Interest in how their next senator would work in tandem with the Roosevelt administration in handling jobs, welfare and mortgage relief was, however, high, and though some saw Truman as a mere pawn in Tom Pendergast's corrupt political machine, others were impressed by the honesty, candour, simplicity, courage and dependability of the candidate. 'You folks won't get a chance very often to vote for a farmer for United States senator' one Democrat introduced Truman at a picnic gathering. 'He's our kind of people. Why, his hands fit cultivator handles just like owls' claws fit a limb.'[9]

Not even a car crash which broke two of his ribs stopped Truman from barnstorming for the Democratic nomination under the Rooseveltian banner of 'A New Deal for Missouri'. To a large extent, however, this remained show. In truth, Truman relied heavily on Pendergast, who controlled the Kansas City vote, in a fight against the boss of St Louis, who controlled the Democratic primary vote there. Election records reflected the corruption: Kansas City recorded a staggering 137,529 votes for Truman, but only 1,525 for his opponent, John Cochran; in St Louis, by contrast, Cochran polled 121,048 votes, against Truman's meagre 4,614. At any event, Truman won the Democratic senatorial nomination in November 1934 almost entirely thanks to Pendergast.

Once installed in Washington DC, Senator Truman found himself the poorest member of the legislature. His wife and family stayed in Independence, where there was insufficient money to pay off the loans on the family farm, which was repossessed by the banks. In itself this was the ultimate demonstration that Truman himself was incorrupt-ible, however much he relied on Pendergast for electoral support in the jungle of urban interwar politics. 'My connection with Pendergast was, of course, purely political' the senator explained to a journalist when Pendergast was eventually indicted and imprisoned for election fraud, at the prompting of Roosevelt's Justice Department. 'He has been a friend to me when I needed it. I am not one to desert a ship when it starts to go down.'[10] But down it went.

In the Senate Truman focused on interstate commerce and trans-portation – rail and air – as the most practical means to combat the Depression and revive America's economic prosperity. With Pendergast imprisoned, his mother's farm foreclosed and no capital, Truman faced an uphill re-election battle for the Senate in 1940, when his six-year term ended. 'He is a dead cock in the pit' as the St Louis *Post-Dispatch* commented.[11] Unsure whether or not to resign, Truman filed for re-nomination and had the fight of his life with a rival, popular Democratic governor, Lloyd Stark. Tall, handsome and a charismatic speaker, Governor Stark looked unbeatable: a distinguished World War I veteran who had inherited the world's largest apple-growing farm, had supported all Roosevelt's New Deal programmes, and had done his best to clean up election fraud in Missouri – especially Pendergast's. Stark was even bruited as a possible vice president if Roosevelt ran a third time.

Roosevelt ran, but didn't choose Stark. Down 11,000 votes, Truman went to bed on primary polling day, August 6, 1940, thinking he'd lost; 'I guess this is one time I'm beaten' he sighed, but was woken early the next morning to hear he was re-elected, thanks to the state's two great urban populations: Kansas City, where Truman's loyalty to the convicted Pendergast was admired, and St Louis, where the machine boss now also plumped for him.[12] It was a victory he then repeated against his Republican opponent in the November 1940 contest.

Roosevelt had been re-elected on the promise that he would keep America's sons out of foreign wars. There was no guarantee, though, that foreign wars would keep out America's sons. Appointed to the Senate Military Affairs Committee, Truman asked to head a special subcommittee to investigate the national defence programme, known thereafter as the Truman Committee.

Truman's job thus became central to America's reluctant preparation for its new 'manifest destiny'. By getting to know and assess every major (and many a minor) military installation and supplier in the United States, and as the boss finally of his own organization (albeit tiny in staff and funding), the senator grew twelve inches – until the Japanese attack on Pearl Harbor on December 7, 1941. Assuming his investigatory subcommittee would be unnecessary in actual war – indeed might embarrass the president (and the country's enemies) by exposing gaps and failures in the country's war machinery – Truman volunteered for the military again. He was turned down in person by General Marshall with the immortal words: 'We don't need old stiffs like you – this will be a young man's war.'[13]

Returning to his Senate subcommittee work, Truman realized that, as the president reassured him, it would probably be more important than ever. 'The chairman is a fine fellow, presiding like some trim, efficient, keen-minded businessman,' a journalist described, 'which is just what he looks like, with his neat appearance, heavy-lensed glasses and quick, good-natured smile.'[14] Truman boasted he saved the country billions of dollars, ensured the manufacture of vital synthetic rubber, facilitated the employment of an army of factory women, and stopped Standard Oil from choking 'the country to death' – for his suspicion of the greed of American big business corporations, as well as union labour racketeers, was sincere, if tinged with envy.[15] 'I'm glad I can sleep well' he solaced himself, despite his relative impecuniousness – still unable to buy back the family farm, and without real hope of advancement.[16]

Then, on Thursday July 20, 1944, Roosevelt finally made up his mind whom he wanted as his new vice-presidential nominee, having dropped Henry Wallace. A colleague from St Louis took the call from the president at the Blackstone Hotel.

'Bob, have you got that fellow lined up?' the president demanded.

'No, he is the contrariest Missouri mule I've ever dealt with.'[17]

'Well, tell the senator that if he wants to break up the Democratic party by staying out', Roosevelt shouted, it 'is his responsibility.'

The colleague looked at Truman.

'Jesus Christ!' Truman exploded, after saying yes (despite his wife's objections; she feared his assassination if he succeeded to the presidency). 'But why the hell didn't he tell me [he wanted me] in the first place?'[18]

Truman criss-crossed America on behalf of the Roosevelt-Truman ticket in the 1944 autumn election campaign, aware that, though the president's mind still seemed alert, 'physically he's just going to pieces'.[19] The result, nevertheless, on November 8, 1944, was FDR's triumphant re-election to a fourth term. Thereafter, Truman did not travel to Yalta, saw the president only twice following the inauguration, and was totally unprepared for the moment when, out of the blue on April 12, 1945, came the shattering news from Warm Springs, Georgia, that President Roosevelt was dead.

Part Two: The Presidency

Even in the Soviet Union black-bordered flags flew on government buildings, while in Washington DC the Stars and Stripes above the White House were lowered to half-mast for the first time since the death of President Harding in office in 1923. In the Cabinet Room at the White House, President Truman was sworn in by Chief Justice Harlan Fiske at 6 p.m.

The cabinet was then summoned. 'He looked to me like a very little man as he sat waiting in a huge leather chair' FDR's press secretary later recalled.[20] It seemed an impossible seat to fill, in a nation inheriting the mantle of empire – but a nation which, since throwing off the yoke of England's monarchical empire in 1777, professed an aversion to thinking of itself in imperial terms. After all, in 1919 the Senate had forced the country to reject its own president's founding role in setting up and joining the League of Nations. Twenty-five years later, with a new president who had only once been to Europe and lacked even a college degree, how would the nation rise to the looming challenges? Would there be a retreat into isolationism, as in the 1920s – after ensuring German industry was first razed, as Treasury Secretary Morgenthau recommended, so that there could never be a Fourth Reich (or commercial competitor)?

Truman claimed his predecessor's death struck him like a 'bolt of lightning'.[21] If so, it seemed to others not to paralyze so much as galvanize him. Lunching with the main congressional leaders, the former senator assured them that Congress would be an equal partner in fashioning post-war America and America's place in the post-war world. Congressmen and senators were pleased, unaware how quickly the two competing secular ideologies of the 1920s and 1930s, Communism and capitalism, would rise up in revived mutual confrontation, once the war against Hitler and Hirohito was won.

World events moved swiftly after FDR's sad demise. Only two weeks later, Italian dictator Benito Mussolini and his mistress were executed by his fellow countrymen; then, on April 30, news came that Adolf Hitler had shot himself and his mistress, lest execution be his fate too. By May 7, Hitler's successor, Grand Admiral Dönitz, agreed unconditional German surrender to the Allied supreme commander, General Dwight D. Eisenhower.

The American divisions (sixty in Europe by May 1945), backed by a vast air force of bomber and fighter aircraft, had ended the German threat to western civilization. On May 8, 1945 the war in Europe ended, though the war against Japan had still to be won. Roosevelt's widow, Eleanor, finally moved out of the White House (requiring two months and twenty army trucks), so that the Trumans (requiring one) could move in.

The global balance of power was now set to shift completely. The Dutch and French empires were bankrupt after their defeat in 1940 and appeared doomed, even as Allied troops reasserted control of German- and Japanese-occupied territories across the world. The British Empire, which had prevailed in its long struggle against Hitler's

Third Reich, was – at least in terms of its mother country – effectively penniless. Whatever the fantasies of its redoubtable prime minister, Winston Churchill, the United Kingdom seemed ill-placed to police a global network of colonies, at a time when its indigenous population was exhausted by six years of war. This left only China, the Soviet Union and the United States of America to take up the batons of supranational rule. Since China no longer had an emperor and was embroiled in a civil war between Communists, led by Mao Zedong, and Nationalists, led by Chiang Kai-shek, it would be several years before its destiny would become manifest. Thus the rest of the world looked to Stalin and to America's new generalissimo, President Truman, to see not only how the world war would end, but how the post-war world would be shaped. They did not have long to wait.

Thanks to his four years inspecting American war production (and from 1943 helping prepare for reconversion to a post-war economy) Truman was initially, if naively, confident in his ability to take over the reins of the Roosevelt administration. For the most part, he re-employed Roosevelt's cabinet and senior appointees. 'It won't be long until I can sit back and study the picture and tell 'em what is to be done in each department' he wrote in a letter to his wife. 'When things come to that stage there'll be no more to running this job than there was to running Jackson County and not any more worry.'[22]

These were famous last words, reflecting the innocence of a rising empire. The notion that the United States, let alone large parts of the economically dependent world, could be run by a board of American directors and a happy-go-lucky chairman was quickly challenged when Prime Minister Churchill warned on May 12, 1945, that, with regard to Soviet behaviour and intentions in central and eastern Europe, 'an iron curtain' had been 'drawn down'.[23]

Ignoring Churchill, Truman instructed Harry Hopkins, on a mission to Moscow in May 1945, not only to try and get a fig leaf to cover Soviet tyranny in Soviet-occupied Poland but also to tell Stalin – who outraged the diplomatic community by arresting the members of Poland's government-in-exile when they flew to Moscow – that Romania, Bulgaria, Czechoslovakia, Austria, Yugoslavia and the Baltic states were not important to US 'interests'. 'The smart boys in the State Department, as usual, are against the best interests of the US' he noted naively in his diary, 'if they can circumvent a straightforward hard hitting trader for the home front.' That trader, of course, was Truman himself. 'I shall expect our interests to come first' he emphasized as he made his way to the Big Three summit in Potsdam, close to Sanssouci, the mini Versailles on the outskirts of Berlin established by Frederick the Great of Prussia. 'I'm not working for any interest but the Republic of the United States. I [am] giving nothing away except to save starving people and even then I hope we can only help them to help themselves.'[24]

Potsdam, however, would change Truman's life, and the course of American history, as the president awoke not only to global reality, but to America's destiny.

Truman was driven from his villa – aptly called Number 2 Kaiserstrasse, or Caesar Street – on July 16, 1945, in an open car, along an avenue lined with US soldiers and tanks, into the ruined capital of the Third Reich. Coming from Washington, he found the utter devastation surreal. The ruined Reich Chancellery, in the basement of which Hitler had recently committed suicide, Truman dubbed 'Hitler's Folly'. As he noted in his diary, Hitler 'overreached himself by trying to take in too much territory. He had no morals and the people backed him up. Never did I see a more sorrowful sight.'[25]

The bookworm child was taken back to his early reading. As he recorded that night: 'I thought of Carthage, Baalbeck, Jerusalem, Rome, Atlantis, Peking, Babylon, Nineveh; Scipio, Rameses II, Titus, Herman, Sherman, Jenghis Khan, Alexander, Darius the Great.'[26] Though he shrank from adding his name or Washington DC to that imperial pantheon, and reflected humbly how humans were but 'termites on a planet', he was acutely aware from latest communications with the White House that the United States was about to become more powerful than any nation in history, having successfully developed an atomic bomb. The question now arose whether to use it to destroy the empire of Japan. And how to handle America's partner on the world-historical stage, the USSR.

Truman's first meeting with Churchill did not impress him. Churchill's golden-tongued unctuousness contrasted poorly with the no-nonsense demeanour of Joseph Stalin, who raised a host of questions about the post-imperial world – from getting rid of the fascist dictator Franco in Spain to the future of territories once mandated by the League of Nations in the Middle East, even in Africa.

Compared to Churchill, Stalin was of a different, more bracing (and less alcoholic) calibre. Stalin's list was 'dynamite – but I have some dynamite too which I'm not exploding now' Truman noted cryptically in his diary.[27] The two emperors of the world now measured each other over the fate of Poland, in an effort to see how powerful the other truly was.

For Truman the realist, Poland's doom was a fait accompli, already occupied by hundreds of thousands of Soviet troops. Meanwhile Truman needed the USSR to participate actively in the newly created United Nations, whose founding he had just attended, if it was ever to succeed as an international body. He also needed Russia to follow through and enter, as promised, the fight against Japan, if conventional war was to be pursued to the bitter end. Truman therefore accepted the saddest, yet unavoidable compromise: recognizing a Polish puppet government that did not look like espousing democracy – and wouldn't be permitted to for the next fifty years. This was deplorable, but inexorable. As Churchill feared, Communists throughout Europe would feel emboldened by the Polish example to seize power in their own countries, and win protection from the USSR and fellow Communist regimes, if they could – indeed it was already happening in Bulgaria, Albania and Greece. There, following the exit of Nazi occupiers, Communist insurgents, supported by arms furnished by the Yugoslav Communist dictator Tito, were causing British liberation forces grave concern. If most of the nations of Europe merely exchanged the swastika for the hammer and sickle, Truman began to wonder, what purpose would the removal of Adolf Hitler have served, in terms of American interests?

Despite his reservations about the 'striped pants' diplomats of the US State Department, therefore, Truman was forced at Potsdam to recognize that the looming confrontation between the USSR and the USA was less about Marxist ideologies and democratic ideals – Communism and capitalism – than between two systems of *power*: dictatorship and electoral-based democracy.

Having learned how to handle 'Boss' Pendergast in Missouri, Truman remained amazingly, if innocently, confident he could, within limits, handle both Stalin and Soviet opportunism. Don't contest what you cannot control; be firm as a rock over those things you can; give financial help to rebuild industry and commerce among your allies;

trust in God. 'I can deal with Stalin. He is honest – but smart as hell' Truman recorded in his diary after their first meeting. The next day he invited him to visit the US.

Like FDR, Truman laboured under no illusions about the Russian quest for 'security'. Soviet troops occupied all of central Europe to the Elbe and the Danube. What Truman could and did do was hold Stalin to the Yalta agreement on the four occupation zones of Germany. 'If Russia chooses to allow Poland to occupy a part of her [German occupation] zone I am agreeable but title to territory cannot and will not be settled here' Truman made clear as chairman of the super-power summit, and began to listen more attentively to America's 'striped pants' brigade, especially those who were stationed in Communist countries, or where Communists were seeking power.[28] The 'Russian variety' of Communism 'isn't Communism at all but just police government pure and simple' the president noted. 'A few top hands just take clubs, pistols and concentration camps and rule the people on lower levels. The Communist Party in Moscow is no different in its methods and actions toward the common man than were the czar and the Russian Nobleman (so-called: they were anything but noble). Nazis and Fascists were worse.'[29]

With the news on July 26 that Churchill had been defeated in the British general election, and Stalin's 'indisposition' on July 30, however, Truman began to reflect on the prospects for post-war peace if Stalin were to die. 'If some demagogue on horseback gained control of the efficient Russian military machine he could play havoc with European peace for a while. I also wonder if there is a man with the necessary strength and following to step into Stalin's place and maintain peace and solidarity at home . . . Our only hope for good from the European War is restored prosperity to Europe and future trade with them. It is', he reflected, 'a sick situation.'[30]

Years later, Truman considered he had been 'an innocent idealist' at Potsdam. Stalin showed no interest in Truman's proposals to inter-nationalize the main arterial waterways of Europe or to restore European prosperity, and broke most of the Potsdam agreements as soon as he returned to the Soviet Union.[31] 'And I like the little son of a bitch' Truman afterwards lamented. 'He was a good six inches shorter than I am and even Churchill was only three inches taller than Joe! Yet I was the little man in stature and intellect! So the Press said.'[32]

Was the press right? Had Truman been too compliant? Russian-occupied eastern Europe was certainly confirmed as lost to democracy at Potsdam; but without the US declaring war on the Soviet Union (which Congress would not have supported), it is difficult to see how Truman could have saved the defenceless, 'Soviet-liberated' nations. He proved correct in seeing Stalin as the linchpin of Russian Communism – a barbaric dictator, but one who was at least forthright and consistent, especially in comparison with his successor, Nikita Khrushchev.

However naive Truman was, then, it was he who stepped up to the plate at Potsdam, and on behalf of the western world. It was in Potsdam that he recognized the bankruptcy and impotence of the once awe-inspiring British Empire as it attempted to hang on to 'control [of] the Eastern Mediterranean', and to 'keep India, oil in Persia, the Suez Canal and whatever else was floating loose' – imperial interests that would all too soon be shorn away.[33] This left the United States a simple choice: either return to its pre-war isolationism, keeping its distance, or take up the fallen baton and lead the free world by imposing a new Pax Americana on the territories that Stalin's troops had not already overrun.

On July 24 in Potsdam, Truman had given his approval for the new weapon to be used on Japan as soon as possible, after due warning – 'asking the Japs to surrender and save lives'. 'I'm sure they will not do that,' he noted laconically in his diary, 'but we will have given them the chance.'[34] Since Roosevelt's death, 50,000 American servicemen had died in the Pacific and another quarter of a million would be killed, he was told by the chief of staff of the army, General Marshall, if Japan refused to surrender and the US had to invade with conventional forces.[35] In his diary the president had written that the weapon was 'to be used against Japan between now and August 10th. I have told the Sec of War, Mr Stimson, to use it so that military objectives and soldiers and sailors are the target and not women and children. Even if the Japs are savages, ruthless, merciless and fanatic, we as the leader of the world for the common welfare cannot drop this terrible bomb on the old capital or the new. He & I are in accord . . . It is certainly a good thing for the world that Hitler's crowd or Stalin's did not discover the bomb.'[133]

Reviewing the situation with the US ambassador to Moscow, Averell

Harriman, and the other 'Wise Men' of the State Department on his return from Potsdam, Truman expressed satisfaction that, although it took two atomic bombs, dropped on Hiroshima on August 6 and Nagasaki on August 9, to achieve, the Japanese government finally surrendered unconditionally to the Allies on August 10, saving countless American (and Japanese) lives and ending World War II without the need for Russian intervention. But Potsdam, he also made clear to Harriman, had clarified his own new view: that the United States must embrace a global post-war leadership role and, in effect, become a counter-empire to the Communist USSR.

Thus, before either the famous Kennan policy of containment or the Marshall Plan were mooted, Truman not only made a momentous decision regarding the use of the world's first atomic weapon, but also grasped at Potsdam in essence how and why he would direct American quasi-imperial power in the post-war world. It was a guns-and-butter vision that lacked Roosevelt's noble rhetoric, and it would expose him to attacks from both right and left in America. It would also lead the United States, under the leadership of subsequent imperial presidents, into countless strategic difficulties and questionable actions, including major wars. It is difficult to imagine, however, that Roosevelt would not have done the same had he lived.

In due course Truman would have to contend with schisms in his own Democratic Party, caused in part by liberals, and also by union greed. He would suffer nefarious attacks from rabid anti-Communist Republicans such as the young Richard Nixon (who would call him a traitor – an insult Truman never forgave). Nevertheless Truman's epiphany at Potsdam gave rise to the essential architecture of American empire, for good and bad, for the next half-century and more.

Leftist historians would argue that a more Russia-friendly policy by the United States might have encouraged a less repressive, less paranoid Soviet system over time. It is more likely, however, that the opposite would have been the case. The USSR's boasts of higher agricultural, industrial and commercial output in the ensuing decades were almost all fabrications which, behind its 'iron curtain', could only escape exposure by denying access to independent reporters, and by absolute control of the media. Only by ruling its constituent and satellite peoples with 'clubs, pistols and concentration camps' (exemplified in Soviet military clampdowns in Hungary and later Czechoslovakia) and cheap

bread, was the Soviet Union able to stave off the collapse of an inher-
ently unworkable system for so many decades. In short, the USSR *had*
to continue to tyrannize its Communist empire merely in order to
survive, forcing the United States to find a counterweight if its democratic vision was to prevail in the West.

Given the weak state of Europe's liberated western countries,
Truman's historic role, he recognized, was to reverse the conduct of
post-World War I America in foreign affairs. This he decided to do by
maintaining a major American military presence in Europe (later establishing, equipping and leading the forces of NATO), while pumping
money into the rebuilding of European nations with whom the United
States could trade – and profit. It was enlightened capitalistic imperialism such as had characterized relations between the United Kingdom
and its dominions; but like the British Empire (which had traded slaves
for cotton, opium for tea, and upheld many a corrupt ruler in order
to maintain its overall hegemony) its record would be less than
honourable in the more contested reaches of its influence.

As Britain divested itself of its imperial obligations under its new
prime minister, Clement Attlee, the US was faced with grave decisions. If Britain had 'stumbled into empire' as one historian put it, it
was now stumbling out of it, leaving its former American colony,
under President Truman, to pick up the pieces – and the tab.[37] On
February 21, 1947, Attlee announced the end of British rule in India –
the 'jewel' in the British crown that had made Queen Victoria an
empress – no later than June the following year. The next day Attlee
told Truman's new Secretary of State, General Marshall, that Britain
was effectively bankrupt, and could no longer afford the cost and
troops (which would be withdrawn before April 1) to guarantee either
security in Greece – where Communist insurgents were inciting civil
war – or aid to Turkey, which was being subjected to Soviet pressure
over the Dardanelles Straits.

Truman's advisers begged him to be less diffident in public and to
galvanize post-war America as he had the nation when ending World
War II: to be an American warrior, with a vision for the country.
Addressing Congress on Wednesday March 12, 1947, Truman finally
did so. 'It had to be clear and free of hesitation or double talk' Truman
later recalled instructing his speech writers, and wisely invited the
leading lawmakers of Congress to the White House to hear him

explain his policy two days before he gave the speech, and to ask questions.[38]

Whether or not the president was exaggerating the threat posed by the USSR or was wise to exhort America to challenge Communism 'on every front', his speech made history. As he recorded in his memoirs, 'I could never quite forget the strong hold which isolationism had gained over our country after World War I. Throughout my years in the Senate I listened each year as one of the senators would read Washington's farewell address. It served little purpose to point out to the isolationists that Washington had advised a method suitable under conditions of *his* day to achieve the great end of preserving the nation . . . For the isolationists this address was like a biblical text.'[39] His own speech to Congress became, by contrast, as he put it, 'the turning point in America's foreign policy, which now declared that wherever aggression, direct or indirect, threatened the peace, the security of the United States was involved' – the Truman Doctrine, as it became known.[40] American Empire, under the rubric of Pax Americana, was thus born, and the bill sanctioning aid to Greece and Turkey was passed by 287 to 107 on May 9, 1947 by the new Republican-dominated House of Representatives.

Backing Truman's bill with finance and implied military assistance, Congress thus ensured that Greece avoided a Communist coup and Turkey maintained its army and complete independence, in spite of Soviet threats and pressure. Both nations would join NATO in 1952, with their forces serving under an American supreme commander.

American isolationism, or non-imperialism, was dead; the burdens of empire were lifted from the shoulders of the floundering British, and assumed now by the United States. 'At the present moment in world history nearly every nation must choose between alternative ways of life' Truman explained. 'The choice is too often not a free one. One way of life is based upon the will of the majority, and is distinguished by free institutions, representative government, free elections, guarantees of individual liberty, freedom of speech and religion and freedom from political oppression. The second way of life is based upon the will of a minority forcibly imposed upon the majority. It relies upon terror and oppression, a controlled press and radio, fixed elections, and the suppression of personal freedoms.'[41]

In the years that followed, as in ancient Rome, many aspects of

democracy, both within the United States and in the actions of its official and unofficial personnel abroad, would be compromised. Yet
almost no historian has doubted Truman's integrity or honesty in
switching America's course from isolationism to world dominance.
'The world looks to us for leadership' Truman stated at the Jefferson
Day dinner on April 5, 1947. 'The force of events makes it necessary
that we assume that role.'[42]

The president was not exaggerating. Marshal Voroshilov, the Soviet
commander in Hungary, had ignored the results of the 1945 election in
which the Independent Smallholders' Party won 57 per cent of the votes.
Voroshilov insisted that the Hungarian Communist Party be invited to
participate in a coalition government, followed by executions, purges,
show trials, political imprisonment, exile to Siberia and savage repression of criticism or uprising. Czechoslovakia suffered a similar fate, as
did Romania and Albania; only Tito in Yugoslavia dared claim a certain
murderous independence (all Yugoslav monarchists were executed).

Truman's espousal of the Marshall Plan, which he persuaded
Congress to take up in 1947 following his 'Doctrine' speech, demonstrated the man from Independence at his best. Truman wanted to
aid *all* the shattered economies of post-war Europe, not simply Greece
and the strategically critical Turkey. On the urging of his Secretary of
State, George Marshall, he therefore offered massive American financial aid to free as well as to Communist countries, including the USSR.

Stalin, who had gratefully accepted grain and convoys of materiel
from the US during World War II, had already made a speech
denouncing capitalism and the US in February 1946. Now, a year later,
he forbade all Soviet satellite countries in eastern and central Europe,
as well as the USSR, to accept American aid. His Foreign Secretary
denounced the US plan as 'dollar imperialism'. Czechoslovakia and
Poland had agreed to send representatives to the Paris conference on
the Marshall Plan, but they were summoned to Moscow and warned
not to think of attending. Even the nominally independent Finland
declined Marshall Plan aid in order not to antagonize Stalin. Isolationist
Republicans in Congress also protested against the plan, as did Henry
Wallace, the former Democratic vice president. Once news came in
of the elected government of Czechoslovakia being overthrown by
Stalinists, however, Congress relented, and after six months' wran-
gling, passed a $12.4 billion aid package.

Economic historians later claimed that the Marshall Plan was a wolf in sheep's clothing that helped US trade and industry more than the western European beneficiaries (for example, half of all purchases had to be transported in US vessels). Nevertheless, the plan proved to be the touchstone of renewed European economic confidence among the democracies; indeed in many ways it became the building block for the creation of the European Economic Community (today the EU). Moreover Truman, selflessly, was quite content to have the plan named after the man he called 'the greatest living American' – the 'organizer of victory' in World War II, General George C. Marshall – rather than himself. (Marshall won the Nobel Peace Prize in 1953 for the plan). 'The assistance we gave, which averted stark tragedy and started progress towards recovery in many areas of the world, was in keeping both with the American character and with America's new historic responsibility' Truman later wrote.[43] (He also confided how he had to order Marshall to accept authorship of the plan: 'He blushed . . . He was just about the most modest man I ever did know, and he said, "I can't allow a thing like that to happen, Mr President."'[44]) It also helped guarantee America's security, for by 'rebuilding Europe and Asia, we would help to establish that healthy economic balance which is essential to the peace of the world' – even if Third World economists later questioned how healthy such a balance really was, for them.[45]

As the effects of the Marshall Plan began to be felt, the British, French and American governments authorized not only a commercial merging of the three western occupation sectors of Germany, but also a common West German currency (the Deutschmark, replacing the Reichsmark or Imperial Mark) to hasten economic recovery. This signalled the first major, inexorable step towards a West German constitution and republic, rather than the gutted, compliant and, above all, demilitarized or neutered state that the Soviets (and Allies, originally) had in mind.

Germany – at least that part occupied by American, British and French forces – would thus be rebuilt. Given that Germany had twice invaded Russia in the past thirty-three years, Stalin was furious, and decided to twist off the growing serpent's head. Relying on a legal loophole, since there was no formal, signed document permitting road and rail access from West German occupation zones to the capital,

Berlin, Stalin ordered a blockade. The Allied occupation zones of the city, merged as West Berlin, would starve.

If Stalin thought blockading West Berlin would force the western Allies to back down over German economic revival in the summer of 1947, he was misguided. It had the opposite effect. The western Allies could do nothing to rescue Poland, Hungary or Czechoslovakia (which was taken over completely by Quisling-style Communists the following year). American troops, however, were still stationed, fully armed, in Berlin. On June 28, 1947, Truman made the decision that 'we would stay, period', and reaffirmed it in the days afterwards. The Secretary of State, Jim Byrnes, 'wants to hedge', Truman snorted in his diary on July 19; 'he always does'. The president had made his decision and stuck with it. 'I don't pass the buck, nor do I alibi out of any decision I make.'[46]

Overriding his US Air Force chief of staff, General Vandenberg, Truman authorized a massive airlift until a diplomatic solution was found. The airlift was expected to take three weeks; brilliantly marshalled by General William Turner – who had organized from Burma the famous 'Hump' air supply of General Stilwell's forces fighting the Japanese in China in World War II – it lasted, in the event, almost a year. French engineers built the new Tegel airfield, while pilots from Britain, Australia, Canada and South Africa flew 50,000 of the staggering 277,000 unarmed American and RAF flights required, bringing more than 2.3 million tons of food and supplies into the beleaguered city, at the cost of sixty-five Allied lives. At one point, an Allied supply aircraft was landing every minute in West Berlin.

Stalin – who did not dare permit an unarmed Allied transport plane to be shot down, lest he thereby provoke a third world war – eventually brought the Russian fiasco to an end in the spring of 1948. He had played poker, even risking atomic war, and had lost.

The net result of the Berlin airlift was that, as Truman later wrote, 'we demonstrated to the people of Europe that with their cooperation we would act, and act resolutely, when their freedom was threatened. Politically it brought the peoples of western Europe more closely to us.'[47] This was not an exaggeration. Five of the west European nations formed a new military alliance, Western Union, in March 1948, which was the basis for the twelve-nation North Atlantic Treaty Organization, or NATO, set up in April 1949 under American supreme command. The Federal Republic of West Germany was then established on May 23, 1949.

Instead of offering the downtrodden nations of central Europe an example of socialism at its best, Russia had thus shown itself at its worst. Though they would maintain a vice-like military grip upon its 'liberated' nations for another four decades, Soviets became as hated as the Nazis had been – with, sadly, no single political, cultural, economic or social benefit to show their puppet states, in retrospect, for all the years of occupation, save for ballet, good (if heavily censored) public education, and vodka. By contrast, Harry Truman, the haberdasher from Kansas City, emerged from the Berlin airlift as one of the greatest of modern emperors in the eyes of most people in the free world: a simple man, but, for all that, a well-intentioned, brave internationalist, generous with American aid, firm in conflict, and cautious in taking advice from wilder-minded military advisers and subordinates.

Not all Truman's decisions as American emperor worked as successfully as the Marshall Plan, the Berlin airlift and NATO. Two, in particular, would adversely affect the peace and stability of the world, though each was pursued with the best of intentions: Palestine and Korea.

If Truman's performance over the Berlin airlift was exemplary, his performance over the crisis in Palestine in 1948 was the opposite. War upon war, hatred piled upon hatred was the result of what writer Robert Fisk would call 'an epic tragedy whose effects have spread around the world and continue to poison the lives not only of the participants but of our entire western political and military policies towards the Middle East and the Muslim lands'.[48]

What Truman faced in 1945 was, however, a veritable debacle not of his own or American making: namely an ongoing contractual obligation by Britain, signed and sealed under international law more than twenty years before in 1923, to 'reconstitute' a homeland for Jews in Palestine, 2,000 years after their expulsion by the Romans. That obligation, incurred in 1917 (the Balfour Declaration) in an effort to secure Jewish support for the Allies in World War I, directly contradicted promises made to the Arab tribes and kingdoms of the Middle East when securing their help in overthrowing the Ottoman Turkish Empire.

Protests – and ultimately revolts by Palestinian Arabs in the 1930s – had caused the British (who had been awarded a League of Nations Mandate to govern the country while establishing the Jewish home- land) to limit annual Jewish immigration lest it create, overnight, civil war in an Arab territory considered strategically vital to Britain's commercial and military empire. By the end of World War II, however, the situation was reaching crisis levels once again. Some five to six million European Jews, it was realized, had been murdered in the coldest blood by the Nazis. Their survivors were in refugee camps for 'displaced persons'. A safe homeland in Palestine seemed the obvious, least expensive and most compassionate solution for them. Truman, who had never visited the Middle East, felt so, at any rate; indeed he pressured the British government to grant 100,000 immigration visas into Palestine immediately, and offered to pay all transport and feeding costs. Such people would, the legendary president of the Jewish World Zionist Organization, Chaim Weizmann, assured Truman, 'make the desert bloom'.

Truman, brought up on the stories of the Bible, was entranced by Chaim Weizmann, and moved by the tears of his haberdashery partner Eddie Jacobson, who had persuaded Truman to meet the Zionist leader. He was also deluged by letters and telephone calls from Jewish voters across America who wanted the US to ease the plight of the refugees. Between 1945 and 1948 he attempted vainly to steer a neutral course. 'I am not a New Yorker' Truman told one pleader of the Jewish cause. 'All these people are pleading for a special cause. I am an American.'[49] He received delegations from neighbouring Arab states who warned of the consequences of 'giving away' Arab land to European Jews; he was warned by his own State Department officials not to destabilize Britian's unenviable task in keeping order in Palestine – where Jewish terrorists of the Haganah, Irgun and Stern Gang groups were taking British soldiers hostage, executing them, and exploding bombs in British buildings, such as the King David Hotel. ('They seem to have the same attitude toward the "underdog" [i.e. Arabs] when they are on top as they have [suffered] as "underdogs" themselves' Truman fumed.)[50] 'Jesus Christ couldn't please them when he was here on earth,' Truman said in exasperation over Zionist lobbyists, 'so how could anyone expect that I would have any luck?'[51] Their number reflected, however, a political reality in America. 'I am sorry, gentlemen,' he told a group of US diplomats working on the Middle East, 'but I have to answer to hundreds of thousands who are anxious for the success of Zionism; I do not have hundreds of thousands of Arabs among my constituents.'[52]

Truman's heart, in the end, was with the European refugees – and, by extension, the minority of Jews in Palestine (625,000 out of a population of almost two million) who would look after them. His advisers (the 'Wise Men' George Marshall, Dean Acheson, Averell Harriman, Charles Bohlen, James Forrestal) explained the long-term consequences of instability in the Middle East, especially in regard to the supply of oil to the West, and the possibility that Arab nations might turn towards the USSR, thus giving the Soviets new influence in the region, even a base in the Mediterranean. However, other political and electoral advisers warned the president that if he did not support the Jewish refugee exodus to Palestine, then Republicans would, with politically fatal consequences for Democrats, first in the 1946 midterm elections, then in the 1948 presidential election.

Truman was thus caught between two stools. Had he employed the same robust, far-sighted determination that he'd evinced in promulgating the Truman Doctrine, the Marshall Plan and the Berlin airlift, he could have accepted American responsibility to ensure a just, internationally negotiated settlement in Palestine. Instead, with the US refusing to grant extra immigrant visas to Jewish refugees and Holocaust survivors, he meddled from afar, to the point where the British Foreign Secretary, Ernest Bevin, washed his hands of Palestine's fate in September 1947, announcing that Britain, in one of the worst examples of spinelessness in its history, would withdraw all forces in May the following year, and surrender its Mandate back to the UN – which had *no* forces to keep order.

Fairly or unfairly, the UN eventually recommended partition of Palestine, by a two-thirds majority, in November 1947. When neither the Palestinian leaders nor the surrounding Arab neighbours accepted the terms of the UN partition (which awarded 53 per cent of the country, including the Negev Desert, the home of Bedouin Arabs for 4,000 years, to the Jews), Truman then recognized the new State of Israel only eleven minutes after the official departure of the last British troops, on May 14, 1948. This did nothing to assuage Arab despair or acceptance of the UN partition plan, or to advance UN calls for a temporary trusteeship while further negotiations took place, or to head off plans for military attack by neighbouring Arab countries.

Throughout the sad saga Truman, urged on by his former naval aide and subsequently White House adviser, Captain Clark Clifford, had acted against the warnings of his own State Department. As Under Secretary Acheson put it to Truman, by surrendering the Mandate in the face of mounting American calls for more Jewish immigration, the British prime minister had by 1947 'deftly exchanged the United States for Britain as the most disliked power in the Middle East'.[53] It is a title the US still holds.

Secretary of State General Marshall was driven to the point of unique insubordination (for a trained soldier), telling the commander-in-chief and chief executive of the United States to his face that if the US election was taking place that day, he would 'vote against the president'.[54] It was a savage indictment of Truman's conflicted conduct. Thinking to do right by his former partner Eddie Jacobson, Dr Weizmann and Clark Clifford (who warned Truman even before the British departure he would lose the 1948 election unless he recognized the establishment of Israel), and the many Jewish Americans agitating for a Jewish homeland rather than for issuing more visas into the US, Truman had ensured an accelerated homeland for Holocaust survivors and Jews – but at a terrible cost. 'There'd never been anything like it before,' Truman later recalled the pressure he was under, 'and there wasn't after. Not even when I fired MacArthur.'[55] In the second half of 1947 alone, 135,000 letters, telegrams and petitions bombarded him.

Though recognized by Truman's fiat in a matter of minutes, Israel would never survive, isolated in the heartland of Islam, without American financial and military aid, or achieve peace in the long run without negotiated treaties with the former Palestinian majority and its Arab neighbours, thus dragging the United States into a responsibility it had never sought, or wanted, and which continues to this day.

Truman's opponent in the 1948 presidential election turned out to be the silk-spoken Republican governor of New York State, Thomas Dewey, whose polls suggested such an inevitable victory that on an election platform in Idlewild, Truman was reported to have muttered, 'Tom, when you get to the White House, for God's sake do something about the plumbing.'[153] (Not only the plumbing but the entire interior of the White House was due to be gutted and rebuilt.)

Aware he was behind both in public opinion in media support, Truman became as energized as he'd been in 1940 when running against another governor, Lloyd Stark, telling an aide that he knew 'he was catching up and he was confident that on election day he would be out front'.[57] He even predicted the states he would win to the last handful. While Dewey stayed home, Truman grounded his presidential airplane, the *Independence*, and took out the 'Presidential Special' train with its bombproof Pullman car: the 'Ferdinand Magellan', equipped with microphone and loudspeakers. In cities like Detroit he spoke to crowds of industrial workers as many as 100,000 strong. He gave up reading speeches in his hopeless monotone and spoke extempore, as he had in his earlier days, lambasting Dewey, the Republican 'do nothing' Congress, and Republican 'red-baiters' and 'red-herring' chasers, earning the sobriquet 'Give 'em hell Harry'. With former vice president Henry Wallace running as an independent, as well as the southern Democrat Strom Thurmond standing in opposition to Truman's civil rights bill, which Dixiecrats had killed, Truman felt licensed to let rip – and did, coming across as the people's underdog president, while Dewey (like Stark before him) looked aristocratic and out of touch with ordinary Americans.

It was a masterly self-reinvention on Truman's part, combative and firm in standing up to Communism abroad, without risking accidental or thoughtless war. He secretly took a room in a hotel in Missouri on election night. NBC television called the race for Dewey, and Truman went to bed. He was woken at 4 a.m. by aides telling him that Illinois, the tell-tale state, had plumped for Truman. 'That's it!' Truman responded. 'Now let's go back to sleep, and we'll go down tomorrow and wait for the telegram from the other fellow.' It was hard for aides not to feel admiration for such a boss – especially when the president eyed the bottle of bourbon on his dresser and added: 'Well, boys, we'll have one and then we'll all go to sleep. I'll pour the first one.'[58]

Reversing Gallup poll predictions, Truman won the election on November 2, 1948, by 49.5 per cent to Dewey's 45.1 per cent, which translated into 303 electoral delegates to Dewey's 189, and segregationist Thurmond's thirty-nine. (Wallace won nil.)

Truman's unexpected second (though first elected) presidential term turned out to be far less fulfilling than his first three years in the White House – or 'Great White Jail' as he and his wife called it. With the

Truman Doctrine helping to stabilize a Cold War (a term invented in 1947) in Europe, but unable to stop an Arab–Israeli war in the Middle East from breaking out in 1948, Truman was unwilling to commit troops or ask Congress for vast monies to prop up the Nationalist regime of Chiang Kai-shek in China – where General Marshall had attempted fruitlessly to sponsor a coalition between Chiang and the Communist leader, Mao Zedong. As Marshall predicted, the Nationalists were too corrupt and badly led to be worth supporting militarily. By late 1949 Mao's forces seized Beijing, and together with two million refugees, the Nationalist forces finally retreated to Taiwan. Mao proclaimed a Communist People's Republic of China on the mainland, comprising 550 million people. Britain and other countries immediately recognized Mao's regime de facto, just as the US had instantly recognized Israel. Truman, in deference to Congress, declined to do so, however – putting US–Chinese relations into deep sleep for a generation – with right-wing American imperialists berating Truman for having 'lost' China to Mao.

The US had never had China to 'lose', but this did not stop Republicans turning from isolationists into warmongers. Though lucky to avoid a war in Asia that would have dwarfed in casualties even the magnitude of the war against Japan, Truman would not be so fortunate in Korea.

Under Japanese imperial rule since 1910, Korea had been divided at the end of World War II into two territories, North and South, under Russian and American UN trusteeship. On June 24, 1950, a North Korean Communist army under Kim Il-sung ('Our Great Leader') swept south across the 38th Parallel into the American zone. This put Truman in a fix he could not easily escape.

Attacking at dawn on a Sunday when most South Korean soldiers were off duty, Kim Il-sung's invasion, employing 135,000 troops, 242 Soviet-made tanks, and 180 Soviet-made aircraft, was a military master-stroke, but a political disaster. Stalin had stopped him the year before, and more recently had warned him not to invade the southern zone unless he was satisfied he could swiftly win. Everything thus depended on speed.

Receiving reports of the North Korean attack, President Truman flew straight back to Washington from Independence, Missouri, where he was staying the weekend. In order to save time he immediately placed the matter before the UN's Security Council, without waiting for a formal resolution in Congress. Since the USSR had temporarily walked out of the Council – reflecting Stalin's ambivalence over the issue – Truman was able to avoid a Soviet veto; he asked for, and got, a clear resolution (later three), condemning the attack and calling upon the North Koreans to withdraw or face economic and military sanctions.

Thus far, Truman had taken the lead international role, and elicited the applause of the entire free world. Events thereafter spiralled out of political control, thanks to General Douglas MacArthur.

MacArthur was now seventy years old. Tall, egocentric to the point of paranoia, he had remained the commander-in-chief of US forces in East Asia and Allied supreme commander, stationed in Japan. When South Korean troops abandoned the capital, Seoul, and continued to fall back south, MacArthur, appointed generalissimo of UN forces, dispatched American troops from Japan. These men could only slow the North Korean advance, not stop it. But by landing a fresh contingent behind the North Korean lines, on the midwest coast of the peninsula at Inchon on September 15, 1950, MacArthur then brilliantly routed Kim Il-sung's invading army, and was soon back in possession of the 38th Parallel, gung-ho to pursue the enemy northwards and unify Korea not as a Communist but as as a democratic nation, under American protection.

On September 28, 1950, the Cold War became red hot. The history of the American Empire may be said to have hinged on two men: MacArthur and Truman. Certainly, in the flush of a great victory at Inchon (an operation he had ordered despite a thousand voices counselling him against such a precarious landing), MacArthur was certain he had routed the enemy, and could destroy the remnants of the fleeing North Korean army in a matter of weeks, if not days – if permitted to cross the 38th Parallel. From there he would strike north to the frontiers of China and the Soviet Union. MacArthur thus cabled Washington, demanding consent.

The UN resolution, however, had not authorized a crossing of the 38th Parallel. The Pentagon was also concerned lest Soviet and Chinese forces become involved by an American-led advance, Chinese foreign minister Chou En-lai having warned of military action if the Parallel was crossed. All too easily the war might escalate into a third world war.

In a miscalculation that proved to be one of the colossal errors in military history, MacArthur dismissed such fears, assuring Washington that there were negligible Sino-Soviet forces in North Korea, and no signs of outside forces being readied to enter the country.

Had Truman overruled MacArthur and stopped all US–UN forces on the 38th Parallel, and then threatened atomic warfare if the North Koreans dared repeat their incursion, historians could not have faulted him – indeed he might have gone down as one of the greatest of American presidents, in the same league as Franklin Roosevelt. He might even have been asked to stand again for a second elected term in the White House as the quiet but firm guardian of international peace and security. Neither the Soviets nor the Chinese Communists had yet committed troops to the front line – and would have been unlikely to do so, merely to aid a second, doomed North Korean attack on the forces of the UN. Historians, however, only write history – they do not make it.

Later, Truman cursed himself for not having dismissed MacArthur. 'I've given it a lot of thought, and I have finally concluded', he told an interviewer, 'that there were times when he [MacArthur] . . . well, I'm afraid, when he wasn't right in the head . . . He just wouldn't let anybody near him who wouldn't kiss his ass . . . I should have fired him.'[59] Firing such a legendary figure – who had masterminded World War II in the Pacific and taken the Japanese surrender – was, however, something no one in the Truman administration was anxious to do, lest it stir further accusations of being 'soft' on Communism. At a meeting of the inner cabinet and Joint Chiefs of Staff, Truman 'told them I wanted to fire him, and I wanted to send over General Bradley to take his place. But they talked me out of it. They said it would cause too much uproar, so I didn't do it, and I was wrong.'[60]

Truman's advisers were right about Republican uproar; when Truman fired his Secretary of Defense, Louis Johnson, a few days later and appointed General Marshall in his stead, Marshall was denounced by Republicans at his confirmation hearing in the Senate as 'a frontman for traitors'.[61]

With MacArthur promising total victory (and thus the reunification of Korea by force as a democratic state), Truman and his advisers, including Marshall, gambled on MacArthur's battlefield prowess.

As Kim Il-sung had hoped to present the UN with a fait accompli, so did MacArthur. General Marshall radioed MacArthur on September 29, 1950 to keep quiet about crossing the 38th Parallel, while he wrapped up his campaign.

Betting on a headstrong, seventy-year-old general worried President Truman, however. He ordered the CIA (an organization he had set up after World War II to take over the role of the fabled OSS) to check out MacArthur's assertion that no Chinese armies would, or could, intervene. The CIA confirmed MacArthur's view; nevertheless, Truman remained sceptical.

In the midst of patriotic jubilation over MacArthur's victory at Inchon, Truman dared not face accusations of halting his country's star general on the cusp of sudden, 'definitive' American victory. However, every fibre of his humble Missouri background cautioned him against hubris. Truman flew 14,000 miles to meet MacArthur in person, for the first and only time in his life, on the island of Wake in the mid-Pacific, on 15 September, 1950. There, like Julius Caesar first attempting collegial relations with Pompey, the president tried to be civil and get to know, face to face, the notoriously vain, self-seeking general – who once again, both privately and in front of witnesses (including the Joint Chiefs of Staff and the Secretary of the Army) assured Truman that 'organized resistance throughout Korea will be ended by Thanksgiving' (November 23, 1950); that he would have the troops of the US Eighth Army back in Japan 'by Christmas'; and that neither the Soviets nor the Chinese would 'throw good money after bad' by entering the conflict.[62]

The result was disaster. The Chinese *did* commit troops to battle, and in vast numbers (260,000), since they could not sit idly by and watch their Communist next-door neighbour be destroyed, even though Kim Il-sung had brought the business on himself. 'The Chinese have come in with both feet' Truman memorably remarked, but resisted calls from colleagues that he should fire MacArthur, feeling that national unity was more important than scapegoating.[63]

Truman's magnanimity towards MacArthur was not reciprocated. The campaign in Korea became a bloodbath – with Seoul changing hands four times, and atrocities committed on both sides. What had been a brilliant demonstration of UN-supported firmness in the face of Communist military invasion turned into a moral as well as physical quagmire. By the beginning of December 1950, most US military and diplomatic officials favoured evacuation of Korea entirely. The head of the US Army, General 'Lightnin' Joe' Collins, felt Korea was 'not worth a nickel',[64] while the head of the CIA felt it important to 'get out of Korea'.[65] MacArthur, by contrast, condemned such 'Munich defeatism'; he favoured, instead, taking the war into China, blockading its seaports, attacking its cities from the air, using atomic weapons, bringing Nationalist Chinese forces from Taiwan to fight in Korea, launching an attack on the mainland of China from Taiwan . . .

Truman's gamble had needlessly turned a potential silk purse into a sow's ear in two fatal months. The leadership of the United States, so brilliantly asserted in a 'UN policing' role in September 1950 (as Stalin had warned Kim Il-sung in 1949), had led to a major war: the wrong war, as the chairman of the Joint Chiefs of Staff, General Bradley, had warned, at the wrong time, in the wrong place. Moreover, it was now a war to salvage America's military pride and honour (General Walker had been forced to make the longest retreat of an American army since the Civil War, chased by the Chinese), supporting a right-wing Korean nationalist, Syngman Rhee, about whom no American knew anything. UN cohesion, fused in facing the North Korean invasion, had also been exploded – McArthur's atomic-bomb sabre-rattling giving understandable rise to grave strains among European allies of the United States, whose NATO solidarity, in 1950, was of far greater import to the future of democratic freedoms in the world than the fortunes of a former Japanese colony.

In every respect, MacArthur's misjudgement, and Truman's acquiescence in it, had altered America's destiny – for the worse. When in the spring of 1951 MacArthur proceeded to publicly blame Truman and his administration (in an open letter to the Republican Minority Leader in Congress), rather than himself, Truman finally relieved him of his post. On Monday April 9, 1951, Truman told General Bradley: 'The son of a bitch isn't going to resign on me' and go into politics. 'I want him fired.'[66]

It was too late. MacArthur's 'martyrdom' (he was feted with ticker-tape parades attended by millions on his return to the US) only inflamed the rhetorical fantasies of 'the China lobby' in America, as well as those who advocated atomic measures to assert American hegemony abroad. Meanwhile at home, the monster of McCarthyism – Senator Joe McCarthy's crusade to root out secret Communists he saw in every area of government, industry and entertainment in America – was treated to a luscious bone.

Declaring a national emergency on December 15, 1950, Truman was forced to pay for MacArthur's mistake by the ruin of his own legacy, and terrible slaughter. The two years that followed were marked by stoic heroism on the battlefront – to little purpose, other than to restore what the US had achieved by September 1950: restitution of the 38th Parallel as the border between North and South Korea. The US armed services suffered almost 137,000 casualties: 33,686 dead in combat and 103,284 wounded. Other UN forces sustained 16,000 dead, while the South Koreans suffered a staggering 415,000 mortalities, military and civilian. North Korean dead were estimated at an even more staggering 520,000 – with an estimated 900,000 Chinese military casualties.

On November 1, 1950, two assassins from New York, having travelled by train and taken rooms in Washington DC's Harris Hotel, walked to Blair House, the temporary residence of the president, and opened fire on the security detail outside the building, intending to rush in and kill Truman.

It being a hot day, Truman was resting on his bed in his underwear, after a worrying morning meeting across the road, in the West Wing of the White House, at which the CIA director had announced the CIA had made a mistake, and that some 15,000–20,000 Chinese troops were in combat in northern Korea.

Had the Puerto Rican nationalists carried more powerful weapons than two pistols (a Luger and a P-38, with sixty-nine rounds of ammunition) they might well have been successful. Within two minutes twenty-seven shots were fired; one assassin was dead, and one White House policeman; the other assassin and two White House policemen were badly wounded. When the president ran and looked out of the open window to see for himself the source of the commotion, a voice from the sidewalk barked 'Get back! Get back!'[67] Undaunted, Truman dressed, went downstairs and attended an unveiling ceremony for a statue of Churchill's military representative during World War II, Field Marshal Sir John Dill, in Arlington Cemetery.

Convicted and sentenced to death, the surviving assassin was surprised, afterwards, to have his sentence commuted to life imprisonment – by the president. 'My opinion has always been that if you're in an office like that and someone wants to shoot you, they'll probably do it, and there's nothing much can help you out. It just goes with the job, and I don't think there's any way to prevent it' Truman mused later.[68] The secret service disagreed. He was provided with an armoured limousine with a landmine-proof floor and grenade-secure roof simply to cross Pennsylvania Avenue, and forbidden to walk. He had, he reflected, become a prisoner of the presidency.[69]

Assassination attempts by Puerto Ricans were one thing, but why, historians later asked, when the United States emerged as the most powerful economic and military nation on earth after World War II, did it become so infected by the bug that was eventually called McCarthyism? Moreover, why did Truman not do more to nip the disease in the bud before it became a pandemic, reducing the US for years to the status, in some respects, of a near police state with the FBI acting as a sort of western STASI rather than a criminal investigation bureau, with 'political' files on almost every actual and potential political leadership figure in the country, and many thousands of ordinary citizens?

The answer is that Truman did attempt to head off the looming scourge. By executive order on March 21, 1947, he set up a Loyalty Review Board in the Civil Service Commission tasked with investigating any and every government employee against whom a rumour or allegation of 'disloyalty' to the United States was made. The board, using FBI investigators, examined tens of thousands of people. Between 400 and 1,200 were fired during Truman's presidency. Between 1,000 and 6,000 resigned, many in disgust and protest.[70] This seemed a small, indeed pathetic, number in such a huge empire, with more than 2.5 million government employees, but rather than demonstrating the patriotism and reliability of the vast majority of Americans, the results only seemed to feed fear and loathing among anxious citizens seeking scapegoats in a difficult post-war reconstruction environment, as prices rose and news broke that atomic secrets had been stolen and given to the Russians. Inevitably, a politician stepped forward to ride the wave of apprehension, even panic: Senator Joe McCarthy.

At Wheeling, West Virginia, on February 9, 1950, Senator McCarthy, an alcoholic loudmouth who had switched from the Democratic to the Republican Party, achieved grotesque notoriety by holding up a phony piece of paper, claiming it contained the names of more than 200 Communist 'spies' currently working in the American government.[71] The list was fictitious, the assertion a lie, and the senator a corrupt charlatan; almost everything in his curriculum vitae was, in fact, a fabrication, from heroism as 'Tail-Gunner Joe' to war wounds. Nevertheless, with the help of Senator Robert Taft, who hated Truman and was eyeing the next presidential election, and J. Edgar Hoover, the director of the FBI who also despised the president, McCarthy's position as chair of the Senate Subcommittee on Investigations gave him carte blanche to paint the inner workings of American government as red.

Perhaps all empires are prone to internal pogroms in the pursuit or maintenance of power. Joseph McCarthy's hate-ridden sallies against the great and the good in America's government smacked of the social misfit, poisoned by envy rather than any observable ideology. In the context of bitter war against Communists in Korea, and concerns over the leaking of America's atom bomb secrets, however, his talk of spies and accusations of treachery in the highest places began to gain political and social traction.

Alarmed lest the unity of the nation, in a grave national emergency, be subverted by the Wisconsin demagogue, President Truman summoned a meeting of advisers on February 28, 1951. Congressional privilege had allowed McCarthy to speak without fear of slander, encouraging 'hectoring and innuendo', 'dirty tricks' and a 'bully's delight in the ruin of innocent'.[72] Where would it end, the president asked, and what would they suggest he do?

The Attorney General had come prepared for just such a question, and to the assembled group he confided he had a 'thick and devastating dossier'[73] on McCarthy and his corrupt financial and private life, including details of his bedmates over recent years – 'enough to blow Senator McCarthy's show sky high'.[74]

The president banged the table with the flat of his hand but, fatefully, it was not to announce they now had the means to expose the Wisconsin phony. The writer John Hersey, who was present, later recalled Truman's reasons for not leaking the dossier. 'You must not ask the president of the United States to get down in the gutter with a guttersnipe. Nobody, not even the president, can approach too close to a skunk, in skunk territory, and expect to get anything out of it except a bad smell. If you think someone is telling a lie about you, the only way to answer is with the whole truth.'[75]

This was Trumanian naivety of a tragic kind. The result was worse than anyone imagined. As one cultural chronicler of the period, Joseph Goulden, noted, fear, apathy and ignorance meant that 'for a full decade, that of the 1950s, America went into a holding period – intellectually, morally, politically'.[76] Dean Acheson, Truman's valiant Secretary of State, wrote of the '1950s' shameful and nihilistic orgy' of 'irresponsible character assassination'[77] which had a dire effect on the US government, as well as universities, and the Civil Services (whose members had to submit to loyalty oaths and FBI investigation) – requiring 'a decade to recover from this sadistic pogrom'.[78] Clark Clifford, who was also present at the McCarthy-dossier meeting, later wrote: 'It is easy to make light of McCarthy today, when even conservatives use the word "McCarthyism" to mean unfair political smear tactics – but the harsh fact, which must never be forgotten, is that until he destroyed himself . . . Joe McCarthy literally terrorized Washington and much of the nation', giving free ammunition to Communists abroad who could legitimately describe America as a quasi-police state, not a genuine democracy.[79] Too honourable to sink to McCarthy's level, Truman thereby permitted him to pursue his 'tricks' for a further three years, and his influence lasted for even longer.

Truman was in his fifth year as Caesar when he decided, in the spring of 1950, before the Korean War even began, that he would not stand again. 'Cincinnatus and Washington pointed the way. When Rome forgot Cincinnatus its downfall began' he noted tersely in his diary on April 16, 1950, reflecting on the way that, after their public duties were over, President Washington and Cincinnatus had both returned to their farms, the latter after his time as temporary dictator of Rome ended in 439 BC. By the end of his elected term Truman had served as president for seven years and nine months. 'I am not a candidate,' he wrote (but did not announce publicly, lest it cause him to be seen as a lame-duck president), 'and will not accept the nomination for another term.'[80]

As it happened, Truman would not be offered the nomination. The continuing stalemate in the Korean War, and the defection of more and more southern Democratic segregationists to the Republican Party, meant there was little or no support left for the beleaguered president among congressmen and senators anxious about their own re-election chances. Wherever his name was entered by others on primary presidential nomination ballot lists, Truman was roundly beaten. Moreover, when General Eisenhower, as the hugely popular supreme commander of NATO in Europe, indicated that he would resign his command and stand for the presidency as a Republican if drafted by the Republican Party at its summer 1952 political convention, Truman – who had hoped the general might stand as a Democrat – was mortified.

Eisenhower's victory in the presidential election in November 1952, as well as the clean sweep by the Republicans in the Senate and House of Representatives, reflected a nation tired of war. General Eisenhower had promised that the first thing he would do would be to 'go to Korea', and end the stalemate: either fighting the war to a definitive conclusion, or bringing the troops home. Biting his tongue, Truman offered the president-elect his plane, transition briefings with his staff, and a personal meeting in the newly refurbished White House.

There, in the Oval Office, Harry Truman gave back the globe which Eisenhower had given him some years before, in recognition of Truman's imperial responsibilities. In private, Truman was disconsolate. 'He'll sit right here,' Truman's daughter Margaret recalled her father's prediction, 'and he'll say do this, do that!! And nothing will happen. Poor Ike – it won't be a bit like the army. He'll find it very frustrating.'[81]

And with that, the Cincinnatus of modern America – former farmer and haberdasher – left the White House, without even a bodyguard, let alone a pension.

Part Three: Private Life

Harry S. Truman differed both in background and character from his predecessor, FDR. Where Franklin Roosevelt was expansive – overwhelming people with his presence and the toss of his great lion-like head when he laughed or dismissed his opponents – Truman was compact in build with alert, penetrating eyes behind his thick glasses.

He was the only president in the twentieth century, in fact, to wear spectacles permanently – which he kept on, even when swimming in the White House pool.

Truman stood 5' 10", and weighed a steady 185 lb as president. He liked to wear a double-breasted, light-coloured suit, with immaculately laundered shirts, a five-pointed handkerchief in the breast pocket, and a World War I veteran's pin in his lapel. He had no disarming warmth, only an air of no-nonsense honesty and firmness. It was said that on charisma alone, Dwight Eisenhower, had he run for president in 1948 rather than 1952, would have beaten Truman easily.

Recognizing his lack of photogenic or charismatic appeal, Truman adopted early on in life a self-deprecating, humorous way of talking in company, while constantly clarifying his own thoughts and feelings in his diary and in letters, many hundreds of them not sent.

Truman adored his wife, Bess. When she greeted him coldly in Independence, after he had flown from Washington in a snowstorm to be with her for Christmas, he was hurt almost beyond words. 'You can never appreciate', he wrote in a letter, 'what it means to me to come home as I did the other evening after doing at least 100 things I didn't want to do [as president in 1945] and have the only person in the world whose approval and good opinion I value look at me like I'm something the cat dragged in and tell me I've come in at last because I couldn't find any reason to stay away . . .'[82] He did not send it.

The truth was that for all his high sense of responsibility and goodwill, Truman was by temperament short in patience and irascible. Very rarely, however, did he ever allow himself to lose his cool in public, although there were occasions when his mask would slip: when the *Washington Post*'s music correspondent dared criticize his daughter Margaret's first singing concert, for example, the president's rage knew no bounds. The vitriolic letter he penned he actually stamped and posted himself. 'Some day I hope to meet you' he wrote the hapless journalist. 'When that happens you'll need a new nose, a lot of beefsteak for black eyes, and perhaps a supporter below!'[83]

Truman's lack of observable ego caused others with greater egos to imagine they could best him, from Lloyd Stark to James Byrnes and Douglas MacArthur. None did. Truman's mother-in-law, wealthy Madge Wallace, was a great trial, however. For years she would not give her blessing to her daughter Bess' marriage to Truman, whom she considered a mere 'dirt farmer'. It took many years of courtship before Truman could persuade Bess, the object of his childhood adoration (he first met her in Bible class at age six) to finally persuade her mother to accept him as her son-in-law. True to form, at the wedding she criticized him for wearing a light woollen suit with waistcoat, instead of linen.

Madge Wallace's own husband had been a no-good, loudmouth alcoholic who shot himself in his bath, causing Mrs Wallace to cling to her daughter and pursue respectability at all costs. The price she exacted for her eventual agreement to the wedding was that she should be permitted to live with her daughter and her daughter's husband in every one of their residences – which she did. She died in the White House the month before Truman left office.

One of the president's English biographers called Truman 'about the most devoted husband in American presidential history'.[84] He was certainly one of the most faithful letter-writers to his spouse, which pleased historians, about whom Bess was sceptical. Dubbed 'dull, dumpy and distant' as First Lady, she espoused no grand (or minor) causes; her hands perspired if she had to speak in public (which she attempted always to avoid); she did not believe in advancing women's rights; she was attacked by the black congressman Adam Clayton Powell for once attending a reception of the segregated Daughters of the American Revolution; was excoriated for crossing a picket line to see Ingrid Bergman act in a still racially segregated theatre. Nevertheless Bess was and remained throughout Truman's life his one and only love, along with their daughter, Margaret ('Margie').

Bess Wallace never went out to work after completing finishing school. Content with being a homemaker, she helped Truman keep his books as a haberdasher, and with his paperwork when a senator. He rarely wrote a speech or letter that she did not vet before he gave or sent it, knowing that her intensely private, cautious, principled character was the necessary counterpoise to his feistier, fiery-tempered, often impetuous nature. 'How does it feel being engaged to a clodhopper who has ambitions to be governor of Missouri and chief executive of the US?' Truman asked his new fiancée in a letter in 1913. 'He'll do well if he gets to be a retired farmer' he added; 'I intend to keep peggin' away and I suppose I'll arrive at something. You'll never be sorry if you take me for better or for worse because I'll always try to make it better.'[85]

Truman's loyalty to his wife knew no bounds. If anyone spoke or wrote ill of her, he or she was forever banished. As Bess aged, Truman's devotion only grew more pronounced. Seeing an advertisement for Marilyn Monroe in *Gentlemen Prefer Blondes*, he memorably commented: 'real gentlemen prefer gray'. His letters to Bess numbered in the thousands, written every day they were apart. When later he found Bess burning some of their correspondence, he asked what on earth she was doing. 'I'm burning your letters to me.' 'Bess!' he objected, 'You oughtn't to do that.' 'Why not? I've read them several times.' 'But think of history!' 'I *have*' Bess remarked.[86]

How many of Truman's letters Bess destroyed, we do not know. More than 1,000 survive, however, providing a fascinatingly intimate insight into Truman's witty, observant, ambitious, entertaining, loyal and sharing heart.

Once, at Potsdam, Truman gave a ride back to his villa to a young American officer who offered to do anything for the president, even 'you know, like women'. Truman cut him short. 'Listen, son, I married my sweetheart' he said. 'She doesn't run around on me, and I don't run around on her. I want that understood. Don't ever mention that kind of stuff to me again.'[87]

If Truman was a marital paragon in comparison to his predecessor FDR (and his successors Eisenhower, Kennedy and Johnson), he was by no means a prude, or averse to boisterous company, especially if it involved music. At a stage show for servicemen shortly after his 1945 inauguration as vice president, he astonished the world by playing an upright piano in front of 800 people with Lauren Bacall perched, long-legged, on the piano. (The photo elicited sacks of mail from 'old ladies' who felt it unbecoming for a vice president.) He even astonished Prime Minister Churchill, according to Lord Moran, Churchill's doctor. 'When he was on his way out, passing a piano in one of the rooms,' Moran noted in his diary at Potsdam, 'he stopped and, pulling up a chair, played for a while.'[88] At Number 2 Kaiserstrasse in Potsdam, the president gave a party for both Stalin and Churchill at which the he played Paderewski's Minuet in G, which Paderewski himself had helped Truman master as a child after a concert in Kansas City, when Truman was twelve. Then, when Clement Attlee, a former infantry major, replaced Churchill as British prime minister, the two World War I veterans sang bawdy soldiers' songs they'd learned at the front. During the live televised reopening of the White House in May 1952 Truman suddenly sat down at the Steinway grand – 'the most wonderful tones of any piano I have ever heard' – and played part of Mozart's Ninth Sonata. His favourite was Chopin's A flat Waltz, Opus 42.[89] When he left the White House he claimed his record collection took up more space on the moving truck than his files. Music, clearly, was in Truman's bones.

Best of all, however, Truman loved to drink bourbon on the rocks and play poker with colleagues and cronies, who were obliged to tell tales along with him, tall as well as true. He insisted on a loss-limit for individuals, with a common bank, made up from a portion of winner's chips for losers to draw on. He played poker, it was said, recklessly and with gusto. 'He drank bourbon continuously but never got tight' an aide recalled. 'He just got exhilarated and told terrible stories.'[90]

Truman was a modest man who lived modestly. In contrast to Churchill, who rose late and stayed up late, Truman rose early and retired early, save when partying, when he rose early and retired late. Even as vice president of the United States he continued to live in a rented five-room apartment on Connecticut Avenue. Once he, his wife, their daughter and Mrs Madge Wallace, moved into the White House, they treated the White House staff as equals, to the astonishment – and delight – of the personnel. 'He could talk to anyone! He could talk to the lowly peasant. He could talk to the king of England' one of his secret service agents recalled. 'He never got swellheaded – never got, you know, swagly.'[91] 'They treated the staff with respect' the assistant to the chief usher reflected. 'When a butler or doorman or usher would enter the room, the Trumans would introduce him to whoever happened to be sitting in the room, even if it were a king or a prime minister. They introduced all the staff to their visitors – something I've never seen the Roosevelts do.'[92]

Truman's personal honesty was, in the context of American politics, power and temptation, remarkable. From 1935 Truman had no income other than his salary as senator, vice president and finally president, which reached $100,000 by 1952, but was insufficient to cover the costs of his thirteen staff, let alone formal White House hospitality expenses. (He had to be voted a further $50,000 by Congress to help run the White House.[93]) When he left the Oval Office at age sixty-nine, he had nothing bar his savings and his military pension, amounting to $112.56 per month. He moved back to his wife's family home at 219 North Delaware Street in Independence, Missouri. Five years later in 1958, Congress voted him (and subsequent ex-presidents) a pension and office expenses – and, after the Kennedy assassination, a bodyguard.

In the corrupt world of American politics, Harry S. Truman had been personally incorruptible. On December 26, 1972, he died in a Kansas City hospital, aged eighty-eight. He was buried in the court-yard of the Presidential Library bearing his name – 'the captain with the mighty heart', as Dean Acheson once called him.[94]

CHAPTER THREE

DWIGHT D. EISENHOWER

Later Deified

Republican
34th President
(January 20, 1953–January 20, 1961)

Part One: The Road to the White House

Dwight David Eisenhower (named Dwight after a popular evangelist preacher of the time) was born on October 14, 1890 in the small town of Denison, Texas. His father, David Eisenhower, had moved there to find work as a railway-engine wiper, earning $10 per week (his general store in Abilene, Kansas, had failed and he had consumed his promised inheritance).

Engine-wiping offered little future, however, and after several years in Texas David Eisenhower and his Jehovah's Witness wife, Ida, returned to Abilene with $24, three small children, and a fourth on the way. The third of David's and Ida's six boys (one of whom died), Dwight Eisenhower grew up from age two in the once lawless Wild West town and railroad cattle centre, pacified and made famous by Wild Bill Hickok. All his life Eisenhower would be addicted to Westerns.

The Eisenhowers' small house in Abilene had no indoor plumbing, and the boys had to help their mother keep chickens, two cows, poultry and rabbits to supplement their father's meagre income as a maintenance man at the local dairy. (He never earned more than $150 per month in his life.) Like his brothers – 'those little roughnecks from the wrong side of the tracks' people said of them – Eisenhower (nicknamed 'The Swede', and later 'Ike') wished to get out of Abilene as fast as possible.[1] At school he was good at maths, and athletic. Tall for the time (5' 10"), with unusually large hands, bright blue eyes and a smooth, handsome head, 'The Swede' made an agreement with his brother: one would work for several years to pay for the other to go to college, then reverse the arrangement. His older brother Edgar duly went to the University of Michigan – but never returned the favour.

It did not matter. After working eighty-six hours per week for two years at the local creamery following high-school graduation, Eisenhower won through competitive exams and high recommendations a place at West Point, which he entered as a cadet in 1911. He was a born leader, had a good memory, and inherited from his father an explosive temper which he spent his life controlling. 'He who conquers his temper is greater than he who taketh the city' his mother instilled in him.[2] It helped Eisenhower, too, to conceal his real views. As he later confided, 'I got where I did by knowing how to hide my ego and my intelligence.'[3]

Commissioned a second lieutenant in 1915, the West Point graduate was impecunious but popular, capable but unpretentious, and a magnet to both men and women, despite his shyness with the latter. In 1916 at Fort Sam Houston he married the daughter of a millionaire meatpacking businessman, who forbade the lieutenant go into the army's nascent aviation wing lest his daughter become a young widow. Instead, after US entry into World War I, Eisenhower was asked to organize the training of some 10,000 tank personnel for combat in France. To his chagrin he proved so effective as an administrator that he was retained in America, as the army mushroomed from a mere 106,000 men in 1916 to 2.4 million three years later. He was awarded the Distinguished Service Medal for his work.

Reduced from temporary lieutenant colonel to captain, then rising again to major and lieutenant colonel over the next twenty years in the military, Eisenhower never did hold combat field command. He was, however, highly regarded for his skills as a football coach, as a superlative staff officer – and chain-smoking poker player.

Interested in modernization and mechanization, despite the contraction of the post-war army to 300,000 men, in 1919 Eisenhower participated as an observer in the army's first transcontinental road crossing by a motorized army formation – the genesis of his US highway system, commissioned during his presidency. He served in Panama, then in Europe (on General Pershing's American Battlefields Commission), and Washington DC. There, as a staff officer serving as assistant to the then chief of staff of the US Army, General Douglas MacArthur, he witnessed MacArthur refuse to take direct orders from the Secretary of the Army. In an act of deliberate defiance of political authority, MacArthur instructed US Army units (led by tanker

George S. Patton) to cross the Anacostia Bridge and destroy the shanty town ('Hooverville') of World War I army veterans pleading for early payment of their promised bonuses, on July 28, 1932, at the height of the Depression. It was 'one of the most disgraceful incidents in American history' Eisenhower's military biographer later considered.[4]

'I just can't understand how such a damn fool could ever have gotten to be a general' Eisenhower said later of MacArthur.[5] But at the time, as a mere major, he was unwilling to confront his aristocratic boss, who considered the Bonus Marchers to be Communists and malingerers. Though he considered himself to have been 'a slave in the War Department' under MacArthur, Eisenhower's five years in the capital nevertheless enabled him to meet, break bread with, and work with cabinet ministers, senators and congressmen – a political experience invaluable as preparation for later elective office, and a merciful counter to his years in 'exile' in the Pacific.[6]

Posted to the Philippines (a US colony slated for independence in 1945) by FDR in 1934 as head of the US Military Mission, General MacArthur took the absurd rank of field marshal of the skeletal Philippine Army – and insisted Eisenhower accompany him, in the rank of a Philippine general. Eisenhower agreed to go but refused the rank, earning MacArthur's enduring spite. 'He was the best clerk who ever served under me' MacArthur later derided the tireless staff officer.[7]

Had he remained in the Philippines, Eisenhower might well have ended the war in Japanese captivity – if he had survived the Bataan Death March and horrific POW conditions. Instead, the lieutenant colonel – who had spent much of his time at the presidential palace in Manila playing bridge with the Philippine president, Manuel Quezon, and had been deprived of further contact with his army contemporaries – was posted back to Washington DC late in 1939. He commanded briefly a battalion on manoeuvres, then served as chief of staff of a corps, first as a full colonel, then brigadier general. His clear mind and capacity for hard work eventually paid off when, following Pearl Harbor in December 1941, he became part of General George Marshall's War Department operations planning team. In that capacity he was sent to England by Marshall the following spring to assess the feasibility of an Allied cross-Channel invasion in 1942.

Well liked by the British, Eisenhower was soon appointed US

commander for the European theatre. As he wrote home to his wife, he had to be 'a bit of a diplomat – lawyer – promoter – salesman – social hound – *liar* (at least to get out of social affairs) – mountebank – actor – Simon Legree – humanitarian – orator and incidentally (sometimes I think most damnably incidentally) a soldier!'[8]

Eisenhower fulfilled most of these conditions brilliantly. His strategic and tactical ideas were questionable, as were his assessments of effective commanders. (He was impressed by a young British admiral, Lord Louis Mountbatten, for example, and argued strongly for D-Day to be launched in 1942 with a single division; when Mountbatten did mount such a one-division attack across the English Channel at Dieppe that August, more than 3,500 Canadian and Allied troops were killed, wounded or captured in a single day, discouraging any further notions of cross-Channel invasion for two years.) Yet Eisenhower's absolute sincerity and his supranational dedication made up for his failings in a war the Allies could not lose – so long as the Russians kept fighting in the east, and the American war machine kept making planes, ships, tanks and artillery.

In deference to the US decision to follow a 'Germany First' strategy, Eisenhower – having been made Allied commander-in-chief of the air, naval and ground forces for Operation Torch, the Allied invasion of north-west Africa in November 1942 – made his name and reputation as a supreme commander who could weld a truly international team, despite his unease in such a rear-headquarters role. 'I used to read about commanders of armies and envied them what I supposed to be great freedom in action and decision' he wrote his wife from Algiers, many hundreds of miles from the battlefield. 'What a notion! My life is a mixture of politics and war. The latter is bad enough – but I've been trained for it!' Politics, by contrast, was 'straight and unadulterated venom' – demanding not only his valuable time, but 'my good disposition' in order to marshal the Allied cause.[9]

The surrender of all German and Axis troops in North Africa on May 12, 1942 at Tunis made the politics and the venom worthwhile, however, and the subsequent Allied invasions of Sicily in July 1943, and finally the mainland of Italy in September 1943, added lustre to Eisenhower's growing reputation. On December 7, the second anniversary of Pearl Harbor, the president visited Eisenhower in Tunis on his way back from his summit with Churchill and Stalin in Tehran.

'Well, Ike,' FDR announced, 'you are going to command Overlord' – the D-Day invasion, set for the spring of 1944.[10]

Asked afterwards by his son James why he had chosen Eisenhower rather than General Marshall, FDR explained: 'Eisenhower is the best politician among the military men. He is a natural leader who can convince other men to follow him, and this is what we need in his position more than any other quality.'[11] Projecting transparent openness of mind and firm purpose, Eisenhower transcended the internecine squabbling that bedevils coalition warfare. Even Stalin was impressed by his character, remarking 'General Ike is a very great man, not only because of his military accomplishments but because of his human, friendly, kind and frank nature. He is not a "grubyi" [coarse] man like most military.'[12]

Eisenhower's ability to lead the senior combat team of the western Allies paid off. As supreme commander he backed General Montgomery's plans for the D-Day landings, then General Bradley's plans for the breakout in Normandy (using heavy bombers to blast a way out of the Normandy *bocage*), then Patton's race to the Loire – and Germany. He would be criticized by military historians for taking personal field command in September 1944, leading to the dispersion of his forces ('broad front'), failure at Arnhem (the 'Bridge Too Far') and worst of all, the German counteroffensive in the Ardennes (the 'Battle of the Bulge'), in which the US armies suffered 80,000 casualties. Montgomery and Patton closed down this German counter-attack, and two months later had forces across the Rhine racing for Berlin and Vienna.

Eisenhower was criticized for not ordering the seizure of Berlin from the west after American troops had already crossed the Elbe, and for failing to secure written terms from the Russians for Allied access to the city. However, his absolute sincerity of Allied purpose outshone his naivety and tactical shortcomings. After German unconditional surrender on May 7, 1945, he became the hero of liberated Europe, and the most honoured American on the continent – indeed he emerged from the Allied 'Crusade In Europe' (as he titled his subsequent account) so popular in the United States that there were growing calls for him to stand, like victorious General Ulysses S. Grant after the Civil War, for the presidency.

So great was Eisenhower's popularity back home that the new president, Harry Truman – only three months in office and on his way to the summit at Potsdam – generously assured Eisenhower that if he stood for election as a Democrat, Truman would be happy to stand down and serve again as vice president.[13] The general assured the president, however, that he had no political ambitions, having never voted in a presidential election in his life.

On General Marshall's retirement following the Japanese surrender, Eisenhower took Marshall's place as chief of staff of the army, having been made a five-star general – a heady achievement for an engine-wiper's son. (His father died in 1942, before Eisenhower's meteoric rise, but his mother lived to see him return triumphantly from Europe.) On a tour of American forces serving abroad (including China, where he was briefed by the president's emissary, General Marshall, on the inevitability of Chiang Kai-shek's defeat), Eisenhower visited Japan. It was there that he met with his former commanding officer, and fellow five-star general: the commander of US forces in the Far East, Douglas MacArthur.

In the library of the general's residence next to the US embassy in Tokyo, the two American supreme commanders of World War II faced each other after dinner on May 10, 1946, Eisenhower now technically MacArthur's boss. The unspoken matter of the 1948 presidential election, still two years away, hung over them. Both men were considered prime candidates to be nominated by acclamation. When Eisenhower finally raised the subject, MacArthur claimed that, at age sixty-six and by ten years the older man, he was too old to stand a chance, but was certain Ike would be asked. Eisenhower resisted. 'That's right,' MacArthur said, with a twisted smile. 'You go on like that and you'll get it for sure!'[14]

As Eisenhower's official biographer noted, 'Neither man convinced the other.'[15] Upon his retirement as head of the US Army Eisenhower did become president, but of New York's Columbia University, not the United States. In the fall of 1950, with deepening strategic anxiety over Russian intentions in the wake of the bitter war in Korea, President Truman asked Eisenhower to return to military duty as the first supreme commander of NATO in Europe. Dutifully accepting the appointment, General Eisenhower took up his post in Paris in January 1951. As he sought to weld the nations of western Europe into a cohesive military defence force, American politics were never far away, especially when the prospective Republican contender for the 1952 election, Senator Robert Taft (son of President Taft), protested against American involvement in NATO, and said he wished to bring home all American forces still in Europe.[16]

Concerned lest the United States slide back into isolationism under a Taft-led Republican administration, as it had after World War I, Eisenhower tore up a note he'd penned, to the effect that he would remain at NATO as a soldier and would 'repudiate' any efforts to draft him for the Republican nomination the following year.[17] Instead, he indicated, he was open to the notion of running for president – and stamping out Taft's isolationist movement in America.

After being shown, in Paris, a hand-delivered film of a tumultuous two-hour Madison Square Garden rally in New York in February 1952, with huge crowds sporting 'I Like Ike' buttons and chanting 'We want Ike!' (the film had been flown over by the aviator Jacqueline Cochran, who tellingly addressed him as 'Mr President'), Eisenhower then made his historic decision to resign from the army, if nominated, and stand.[18] As a Republican.

At the White House, Truman – who had hoped Eisenhower would run in order to 'keep the isolationists out of the White House' – was gutted, noting sardonically that Republicans were showing the general 'gates of gold and silver', which the president was quite certain 'will turn out but copper and tin'.[19]

There were, Eisenhower quickly recognized, Faustian-like bargains he would have to make in joining the ranks of politicians, a breed for which he had professed contempt all his life.[20]

Fortunately Eisenhower had become a master at swallowing his pride and seeking compromise, as well as taming his temper, throughout his career. Years later, when an interviewer implied that he was not cut out to be a politician, he retorted: 'What the hell are you talking about? I have been in politics, the most active sort of politics, most of my adult life. There's no more active political organization in the world than the armed services of the US.'[21]

In the event, thanks to the hard work of Senator Lodge and his team, General Dwight D. Eisenhower pipped Senator Taft to the post on the first ballot at the Chicago Republican Convention on July 11, 1952 and became the first US general in the twentieth century to be nominated by a political party as its presidential candidate. Eisenhower's triumph, however, raised the question of running mate.

To unify Republicans, Eisenhower was advised, a candidate was required who would be acceptable to those who had supported his isolationist opponent – the 'reactionaries', as Eisenhower called them, or 'Old Guard'. There was such a man, who nursed – as his biographer wrote – a 'Cassius-like appetite for power': Senator Richard M. Nixon of California.[22]

Eisenhower had met with Nixon for an hour in Paris while still supreme commander of NATO in 1951, and had found the Californian unctuous but clever. Nixon had gained a national reputation for Communist-bashing, but he promised to bring geographical balance to the ticket by representing the West Coast. Thus, immediately after Eisenhower's nomination, the general summoned Nixon to his suite in the Blackstone Hotel and asked if Nixon would join his 'crusade of ideals'.[23] Nixon said yes. It was an offer Ike would deeply regret.

Part Two: The Presidency

On November 4, 1952, having covered 21,000 miles by whistle-stop campaign train and 30,000 miles by air, and having reluctantly kept Nixon on as his vice-presidential running mate despite allegations of a 'Secret Nixon Fund', Eisenhower won the presidency easily – 55 per cent to 45 per cent in the popular vote, and 442 to eighty-nine in the Electoral College.

Chagrined – especially over Eisenhower's failure to rein in Republican denunciations of General Marshall for having 'lost' China – Truman magnanimously invited the president-elect, who seemed uncommonly grumpy, to the White House. There, the president offered the first genuine transition assistance in history by instructing his staff to brief the president-elect's team; Eisenhower was even offered Truman's plane, the *Independence*, to take him to Korea on the fact-finding mission he had promised the public.

From afar, Eisenhower had considered MacArthur's 1950 landings at Inchon and his bold campaign across the 38th Parallel to be militarily 'perfect' – even favouring McArthur's controversial willingness to use atomic weapons. But his visit to Korea as president-elect (though in an ordinary military plane) brought him up against reality. General Mark Clark, the UN commander, favoured another MacArthur-style attack against the North Korean and Chinese forces. Seeing for himself the 300-mile-wide front and rugged terrain, the veteran commander-in-chief of campaigns in Morocco, Tunisia, Sicily, Italy, France and Germany estimated it would require at least 300,000 American troops. 'I know how you feel, militarily,' he told Clark, 'but I feel I have a mandate from the people to stop this fighting. That's my decision.'[24] There would be no UN attack.

MacArthur, meanwhile, announced he had his own 'secret plan' to end the Korean War – one that he would only reveal in person to the president-elect. In New York on December 14, 1952, the would-be Caesar explained to the about-to-be Caesar his solution – threatening Mao Zedong, the ruler of Communist China, he would mercilessly bomb China's main cities with atomic weapons and destroy the Chinese industrial base. If this failed, MacArthur proposed dropping a radioactive belt across the Chinese–North Korean border, to stop Chinese troops crossing into North Korea, while the US–UN forces were to cross the 38th Parallel and mount new amphibious and land offensives.

Eisenhower, knowing that the sixteen UN participant nations would not, as America's allies in Korea, consent to such World War III measures, realized he was talking to a madman. His own historic responsibility, he recognized, was not to pursue fantasies, but to keep the world safe and if possible at peace.

The president-elect's response to MacArthur's plan was admirably cool. However, his behaviour towards President Truman, still his commander-in-chief, was less worthy. Asked to step into the White House for traditional coffee before the inauguration of 20 January, 1953, Eisenhower declined. The car ride to the reviewing stand at the Capitol was equally frosty. When Eisenhower found his son John on the stand, brought back from military duty in Korea for the occasion, he was furious and demanded to know who had ordered him home. Truman stared in disbelief at Ike. 'The president of the United States ordered your son to attend your inauguration' Truman responded.[25]

Three days later, Eisenhower thanked Truman for his thoughtfulness, in a letter, but the damage was done; for the next eight years the two greatest living American emperors did not speak or communicate with each other.

The strain of the election campaign, and the problem of how to end the war in Korea, were clearly weighing on the new president, as his contempt for the command set-up in the White House showed, once he took office. 'If I'd had a staff like this during the war, we'd have lost it' Eisenhower fumed.[26] He soon instituted a more imperial staff structure at the White House, appointing for the first time in presidential history a no-nonsense chief of staff, Sherman Adams, a first-class secretariat, weekly National Security Council meetings, regular press conferences, and weekly cabinet meetings – which did not vote, but advised the president. This was the start of modern White House headquarters-style administration: the imperial presidency, as it would later be termed. 'Organization cannot make a genius out of a dunce' he would say. 'But it can provide its head with the facts he needs, and help him avoid misinformed mistakes.'[27] The president started early, disliked the telephone, encouraged one-page summaries of documents from his staff, listened patiently, asked penetrating questions and took time to mull over his decisions, even at the risk of appearing indecisive.

By the spring of 1953, with the death of Stalin and the failure of another massive Chinese ground attack in Korea, prospects for a ceasefire in Korea grew. The seventy-nine-year-old South Korean president, Syngman Rhee, refused to accept a divided nation, but Eisenhower bluntly told him he must accept such a compromise or the United States would pull out its forces altogether. Meanwhile Eisenhower prepared nuclear-tipped artillery and fighter-borne weapons for potential combat, and sent a message via the Indian prime minister that they would be used if China launched another invasion of the South (a threat Truman should have used, had he resolutely forbidden MacArthur to cross the 38th Parallel two years earlier). On July 26, 1953, an armistice was signed. As Eisenhower went to the White House Broadcast Room to announce the end of hostilities, he told a photographer: 'The war is over – I hope my son is coming home soon.'[28]

Eisenhower's judgement, whether about people or issues, was certainly not infallible, but he had the crucial blessing Napoleon had looked for in a general: luck. Moreover he was not an ideologue, or self-serving. Given Senator Taft's death from cancer in 1954 and the resultant elevation of MacArthur to the presidency that would have occurred had the two men been the successful Republican candidates in the 1952 election, historians could only marvel in retrospect at America's good fortune in having had Eisenhower at the imperial

helm. With his high intelligence, noble ideals and ability to weld people
– from prima donnas to effective public servants – into a team,
Eisenhower proved more successful in his first year in office than his
detractors ever thought possible. His popularity regularly reached 70
per cent, and 80 per cent of his legislation was passed by the Republican-
controlled Congress (Eisenhower had wisely taken to golfing with the
Senate Majority Leader). He had promised a reduction of taxes, but
refused to fulfil that promise until the budget was balanced. He issued
a new National Security Council directive outlining American strategy
in supporting and protecting western Europe and Japan, with defence
of Taiwan, South Korea and Israel as the perhaps unfortunate 'extra'
legacies of the Truman era, yet an inheritance America could not,
morally, abandon. It was an overall strategy that would make certain
America stayed out of foreign wars for the rest of Eisenhower's presidency, indeed a strategy that would last for fifty years, ensuring the
United States' continuing wealth as the world's largest economy. Yet
at every step he was crossed, not by the Democrats, but the right-
wing extremists in his own party – beginning with Senator McCarthy.

Later, after McCarthy self-destructed, people found it difficult to
understand the fear and trembling he had aroused by his Senate investigations, so similar to the dreaded Inquisition during the Spanish
Empire, or the Soviet Union's worst show trials; but this was to treat
McCarthy as an aberration in an otherwise civilized American society
– which was unfair to aberrants. The truth was, McCarthy represented
not only himself but the dark side of political extremism in America,
expressed in both the Republican Party and the Democratic Party. Like
many a turncoat, the former Democrat became more aggressive and
fanatical once a Republican than most Republicans – and when a
Republican president and Congress assumed power in 1953, McCarthy's
power to create headlines and headaches increased exponentially. At
the start of the 81st Congress, with a Republican majority in both
houses (albeit by only one vote in the Senate), McCarthy was appointed
chairman of the Senate Committee on Government Operations – and
made himself chair of its Permanent Subcommittee on Investigations,
normally a backwater, without objection.

No sooner was Eisenhower's 1953 inauguration over than, to his
amazement, McCarthy dared contest the nomination of General
Walter Bedell Smith, Eisenhower's famous wartime chief of staff and

subsequent US ambassador to Russia and first director of the CIA, to be Under Secretary of State. When Eisenhower, furious, managed to warn off McCarthy via the Senate Majority Leader, McCarthy switched to the nomination of Dr James B. Conant, the president of Harvard, as US high commissioner to Germany. Though Eisenhower again got McCarthy to withdraw his opposition – this time via McCarthy's former Senate colleague, the vice president – he then found McCarthy contesting the nomination as US ambassador to Russia of Charles E. Bohlen, a career officer who had been present at Yalta and whom McCarthy targeted for not repudiating the Yalta agreement.

Bohlen's Senate hearing lasted four entire days, by which time Eisenhower had a clearer picture of the Republican Party in action. McCarthy's subcommittee then began hearings on supposed subversives in the new administration. No lie became too gross, no accusation too outrageous, no libel too exaggerated, no demonization too grotesque for McCarthy, aided by his legal counsel Roy Cohn, to pass up in his self-appointed pogrom to expose the Communist enemy within America – an ideology supposedly responsible for all the ills without. A paranoid culture of fear and suspicion was deliberately inculcated in the manner – ironically – of Stalin's and Hitler's purges. He coerced John Foster Dulles, Eisenhower's new Secretary of State, to demand 'loyalty state-ments' from all 16,500 State Department employees and to purge the State Department of 'Communists, left-wingers, New Dealers, radicals and pinkos' – reducing the Voice of America to rank propaganda, and eliminating all liberal or leftist literature from American embassy libraries worldwide.

A poor and rambling speaker, McCarthy was a strangely repellent demagogue, the last of a breed of politicians who for centuries had grabbed headlines in print, and by their congressional immunity were able to lie and slander with impunity. Like his predecessor in the Oval Office, Eisenhower refused to speak to or deal directly with McCarthy, declaring privately, 'I will not get into a pissing contest with that skunk.'[29] The president tellingly blamed 'the people who have built him up, namely writers, editors, publishers. I really believe', Eisenhower noted in his diary, 'that nothing will be so effective in combating his particular kind of troublemaking as to ignore him. This he cannot stand.'[30]

Eisenhower was right about McCarthy's reaction, but wrong about the senator's troublemaking, never dreaming that he might go for the very organization the president most revered: the US Army.

The army had dared draft G. David Schine, who was the favourite aide of McCarthy's chief counsel, Roy Cohn. Furious, McCarthy turned his spotlight on the Pentagon, and the army's top personnel soon found themselves subpoenaed by McCarthy's Senate committee. The army responded by claiming that McCarthy and Cohn (a homosexual who later died of AIDS) had improperly used their power to get special treatment for Schine. The hearings, chaired by Senator Karl Mundt once McCarthy was forced to step down, became a national spectacle and were the first congressional inquiry to be fully televised, gavel to gavel, with an audience of twenty million.

Live coverage of McCarthy berating one of the army's senior officers, Brigadier General Ralph Zwicker (who had landed on D-Day, was wounded and decorated), as 'not fit to wear' his uniform, and lacking even the 'brains of a five-year-old child', proved scandalous. The TV hearings became a uniquely American disgrace. With McCarthy demanding access to Pentagon documents and subpoenaing White House officials on Eisenhower's staff, however, it was not only the Senate that was open to world ridicule. McCarthy and McCarthyism had got out of hand, the president belatedly recognized, causing him to feel shame for the Republican Party as well as the Senate.[31] While watching McCarthy's antics on his television set at the White House, he was heard to remark 'It saddens me that I must feel ashamed for the United States Senate.'[32]

Eisenhower, whose friends were all millionaires and who was an anti-Communist to his fingertips, could no longer stand by and watch McCarthy transform America into a version of the USSR through accusation, intimidation, fear and show trials aired on national TV. There was even talk of McCarthy running for the presidency in 1956, a prospect that prompted Eisenhower, who had only intended to serve a single term, to say the 'only reason I would consider running again would be to run against him'.[33] 'He's ambitious', Eisenhower judged McCarthy's supposed presidential aspirations, but 'he's the last guy in the whole world who'll ever get there, if I have anything to say.'[34]

Having hitherto downplayed the McCarthy threat, the president became so deeply concerned that he confided to aides he might leave the Republican Party, with its clique of right-wing desperadoes

including Senator Barry Goldwater, and 'set quietly about the formation of a new party'. He considered making a personal appeal to every
member of Congress and every governor 'whose general political
philosophy [is] the middle way'. In the meantime, however, he became
determined to beat McCarthy over the army hearings.

Instead of denouncing McCarthy directly, as president, the former
supreme commander decided on a different strategy. Summoning his
Attorney General, Herbert Brownell, Eisenhower invented a new judicial rule: 'executive privilege', a rule that would bar Congress from
subpoenaing any serving employee on the president's team, or his or
her documents, lest they thereby inhibit the president of the United
States in the execution of his constitutional duties as chief executive
of the country. Not one member of his staff would therefore go before
McCarthy's kangaroo court.

'Executive privilege' undoubtedly changed the nature of the presidential power in America, cementing for good or ill what had already
become, thanks to American military and economic power across the
globe, an increasingly imperial presidency. It certainly stymied
McCarthy's witch-hunt. Denied victims or their documents, McCarthy
was helpless. The president had then only to wait for McCarthy himself
to be investigated over his alleged improprieties in the Schine case.
On the afternoon of June 9, 1954, the subcommittee hearings finally
reached their climax. In a pre-hearing contractual arrangement,
McCarthy had agreed not to make personal accusations of
Communism against any member of the army counsel's legal team.
Now, under cross-examination himself, McCarthy gave way to a malevolence he could no longer control. On camera, he suddenly announced
a new charge: accusing the army chief counsel's law office of
harbouring a lawyer with Communist sympathies.

Before twenty million viewers the army's chief lawyer, Joseph
Welch, paused, and after a deep breath addressed the Republican
senator. 'Until this moment, Senator, I think I never really gauged
your cruelty or your recklessness . . . Have you no sense of decency,
sir, at long last? Have you left no sense of decency?' As McCarthy
attempted to respond, Welch cut him off, asking the chairman, Senator
Mundt, to 'call the next witness'.[35] Spectators in the gallery erupted
with applause. McCarthy, slain on live TV, turned to Cohn and in a
stunned voice, croaked: 'What happened?' The president, watching

in the White House, was ecstatic, and invited Welch to the Oval Office in order to congratulate him in person. 'You handled a tough job like a champion' Eisenhower beamed.[36]

Eisenhower's close encounter with McCarthy's evil altered his view of his own role as US president or Caesar. Senator McCarthy was declared *persona non grata* at the White House, indeed all government receptions, on the express orders of the president. In retaliation McCarthy announced he was 'breaking' with the Republican leader and accused the president publicly of 'weakness and supineness' in ferreting out Communists, indeed claimed he himself had made a terrible mistake – namely to have voted for Eisenhower in 1952 as a staunch anti-Communist.[37]

The president was undaunted. He seemed, in fact, energized by the fight with McCarthy, telling his press secretary, Jim Hagerty, he was 'glad the break has come'. 'I have just one purpose, outside of keeping this world at peace,' Eisenhower explained, 'and that is to build up a strong progressive Republican Party in this country. If the right wing wants a fight, they're going to get it. If they want to leave the Republican Party and form a third party, that's their business, but before I end up, either this Republican Party will reflect progressivism or I won't be with them anymore.'[38] And if the fanatics thought they could nominate a right-wing ideologue like McCarthy for the presidency, he declared, 'they've got another thought coming. I'll go up and down this country, campaigning against them. I'll fight them right down the line.'[39]

The American Empire was, in effect, at the crossroads. 'There is so much resentment,' Eisenhower reflected upon the very Republicans who had helped make him president, 'and those people will never give up.' The dieharders wanted to ban all trade with Communist countries, refusing to accept Eisenhower's view that once those countries were lifted out of poverty, the appeal of Communism would wither. 'Trade is the strongest weapon of the diplomat and it should be used more', not less, the president declared. 'Anyone who says that to trade with a Red country is in effect advocating a traitorous act just doesn't know what he is talking about' he snorted.[40] When the vice president began using the same hard-line language as McCarthy, Eisenhower called him to the White House and told him to 'back off'. When Nixon gave the excuse that he had meant to attack only Acheson and

Truman, not the entire Democratic Party, Eisenhower cut him short. Use of the word treason was 'indefensible', he told Nixon, and ordered him to stop it, immediately.[41]

Scapegoating and an almost fascistic patriotism had produced a potent right-wing Republican brew – moreover a uniquely dangerous one, given the power of America's growing atomic arsenal. The US was producing a new atomic bomb *every day*, in addition to the 1,600 bombs it had when Eisenhower became president. By contrast the Soviet Union had no nuclear weapons deployed operationally. As a result McCarthy called for General MacArthur to replace John Foster Dulles, in order to exert a more muscular American foreign policy. Again, Eisenhower ignored him, knowing that had 'the Old Guard', as Eisenhower termed them, been privy to the USSR's weakness in operational nuclear weapons, McCarthy's bellicosity would have been even harder to control.

Vietnam became a test case. The newly fortified French position at Dien Bien Phu supposedly guarded the Laotian border, across which Vietnam's nationalist-Communist insurgent leader Ho Chi Minh got the supplies he needed to evict the French colonists. The French had claimed their garrison was impregnable, but once in danger of being surrounded and overrun by Ho Chi Minh's troops, they asked for American help.

Eisenhower had already sent Under Secretary of State General Bedell Smith to study the French situation. Worried about the expansion of Communism in South East Asia, Bedell Smith recommended using Chiang Kai-shek's Nationalist Chinese Army, while Admiral Radford, the chairman of the Joint Chiefs of Staff, recommended the use of atomic weapons. 'You boys must be crazy' Eisenhower said. 'We can't use those awful things against Asians for the second time in less than ten years. My God!'[42] A Franco-American war in the jungles of Vietnam made no military sense to Eisenhower, nor did there seem any chance that members of Congress would condone a US-led war in Vietnam, when no American to date had been attacked and no American commercial trade route, major market or mineral source was affected.

Having rehearsed all the options (and changed his mind a dozen times), Eisenhower wisely overruled his advisers. He let the French be defeated at Dien Bien Phu. In June 1954, an armistice was signed in Geneva, similar to the one Eisenhower had obtained in Korea. This ended hostilities in Indochina, partitioning Vietnam temporarily on the 17th Parallel, its sovereign independence formally granted by the evacuating French, and national reunification elections slated for 1956.

In September 1955 Eisenhower suffered a heart attack, the severity of which was hushed up. Recovering, the president attempted to dump Nixon, suggesting on December 26 that, since Nixon's popularity was still low, he would benefit from more experience, in a cabinet position to which Eisenhower could appoint him, and then easily dismiss him. Eisenhower even spoke of running for re-election as a Democrat, perhaps with the Democratic governor of Ohio, Frank Lausche, or the progressive chief justice, Earl Warren, or the navy secretary, Robert Anderson, even his brother Milton, as his vice president. Anyone rather than with Nixon. 'He never liked me . . . he's always been against me' Nixon complained.[43] Backed by his wife, Pat, Nixon declined to quit, however, lining up as many pledges of support for the summer Republican National Convention as possible by having his name specially written in on tens of thousands of New Hampshire presidential primary ballots as vice-presidential nominee, and getting former colleagues in Congress to give written support for his continued place as a good anti-Communist and anti-tax Republican on the ticket.

It was clear that Richard Milhous Nixon, unlike FDR's vice president Henry Wallace in 1944, would not surrender his claim to the vice-throne. Belatedly, Eisenhower realized the time to dump Nixon had been in 1952, at the time of Nixon's financial scandal. Now, however, it was too late. Eisenhower had to grit his teeth and renew his offer of the vice-presidential ticket, hoping that his frail health (he suffered an attack of ileitis, requiring an emergency bypass operation on his small intestine, performed on June 8, 1956) would see him through the inevitable crises of a second term, if re-elected – for the nation's sake.

The next major crisis came, in fact, before the election could even take place. On June 29, 1956, the president had finally been able to sign the Federal Aid Highway Act he'd been urging on Congress for over a year, to create a national system of intercity highways comparable to the great Roman roads of classical times.[44] On August 22 the president was re-nominated by acclamation at the Republican National Convention in San Francisco. Soon after, a major international crisis arose in the Middle East over ownership of the Suez Canal.

At first Eisenhower, recovering from his surgery, could not believe Britain and France would take unilateral military action without UN support, or act secretly in concert with Israel, a country which above all other states in the Middle East needed the goodwill of its Arab neighbours. Eisenhower at first assumed such reported plans to be the brainchild of Winston Churchill, whose notions and misadventures from Gallipoli in World War I to the Dodecan Islands in World War II had taxed the patience of all who had to work with, and under, him. In fact, however, the Suez invasion was the idea of Churchill's successor, Sir Anthony Eden, who insisted that Abdel Gamal Nasser, the president of Egypt, was a second Hitler in the making.

Eisenhower did not share Eden's view. Nasser's decision in July 1956 to nationalize the Suez Canal had certainly reignited the dying embers of British and French imperialism ('The fat was now really in the fire' Eisenhower wrote in his memoirs[45]) but the president felt Nasser was 'in his rights' to take over the canal, under eminent domain, and ridiculed the British assertion that Egyptian pilots would be unable to guide vessels through it without British supervision.[46] (Within the first week Egyptian pilots had shepherded 254 ships without help, a canal record.) Moreover, while 'initial military successes might be easy', Eisenhower warned Prime Minister Eden, 'the eventual price might become too heavy'.[47]

Once again Eisenhower's savvy was pitted against members of his own party. The Senate Majority Leader, Democrat Lyndon B. Johnson, counselled Eisenhower to 'tell them [the British and the French] they have our moral support and go on in'.[48] John Foster Dulles, as Secretary of State, also favoured American strong-arm tactics. Again, Eisenhower demurred. He would only risk embroilment in war if the nation was threatened or attacked. To his great credit, he urged Eden 'not [to] make Nasser an Arab hero', given that Nasser loved drama; as in Truman's magnificent Berlin airlift approach to such a challenge, Eden should, he advised, quietly work on supertankers, new oil pipelines and oil supply from the US, while the United States built upon its special relationship with Saudi Arabia.[49]

Neither Eden nor the Israelis complied. Flying over the Middle East, Ike's new spy plane, the U-2, discovered that Israel had obtained sixty French Mystère fighter planes, not the twenty-four it had owned up to under the 1950 Tripartite Declaration, which maintained the military status quo in the region. Reports indicated, moreover, that the British and French were preparing an invasion force on the island of Cyprus, while the Israelis were doing likewise – ready, it was believed, to invade Jordan. Urged by the CIA to approve the assassination of Nasser, Eisenhower refused permission, point blank. It would inflame 'the Arab world' even if it succeeded, and besides, Nasser might be followed by a far worse leader. Eisenhower instructed Dulles to tell the Israelis to drop any idea of attacking Jordan, since that would only force other Arabs to turn to the Soviet Union for weapons with which to defend themselves, and 'the ultimate effect would be to sovietize the whole region'.[50]

To Eisenhower's chagrin, the British, French and Israelis persisted. The Israeli prime minister, David Ben-Gurion, seemed determined to take the West Bank, gambling on American distraction over the presidential election, the support of Jews in America, and Egyptian preoccupation with defending its newly nationalized canal against the French and British. Such an Israeli offensive, Eisenhower warned bluntly, 'cannot fail to bring catastrophe'.[51] In fact Eisenhower began to wonder whether he would 'have to use force' to stop the Israelis, even if this lost him the election. 'There would go New York, New Jersey, and Connecticut at least' he mused. But, as he told Dulles, he was not going to allow that fear 'to influence my judgement'.[52] 'I just can't figure out what the Israelis think they're up to. Maybe they're thinking they just *can't* survive without more land' Eisenhower confided to an aide. But how would expansionist Israeli tactics make more sense than Hitler's had, in the long run? 'I don't see how they can survive without coming to some honorable and peaceful terms with the whole Arab world that surrounds them.'[53]

On October 28, 1956, the Israelis attacked – not Jordan, as the CIA had predicted, but across the Egyptian-held Sinai Desert towards the Suez Canal, which they hoped the Egyptians would then close, giving the British and French a *casus belli* to invade also. The 'catastrophe' Eisenhower predicted had begun.

The London Tripartite Declaration, which Britain, France and the US had signed on May 25, 1950, had warned that, in the interests of peace and stability in the Middle East, the signatories would take military action if Israel or any of the Arab states violated 'frontiers or armistice lines'. With absolute indifference to their own Declaration,

France and Britain now worked not to stop the Israelis from violating borders, but to assist them, threatening to invade Egypt unless it withdrew its canal staff and military forces ten miles from the canal. Appalled, President Eisenhower issued a White House statement deploring such perfidy; 'he did not care in the slightest whether he is re-elected or not' his staff secretary noted; if the voting public threw him out the following week, at the November election, 'so be it'.[54] The president felt he had been double-crossed, and sided with Egypt. 'I've never seen great powers make such a complete mess and botch of things' Eisenhower lamented.[55] It was 'the biggest error of our time' he declared, and he called not only for a ceasefire, but also a military and trade embargo against Israel until it withdrew its forces.[56]

The smaller nations at the UN were overwhelmed with admiration for Eisenhower, as were American voters. Yet Eden simply ignored the president, went ahead with the Anglo-French part of the plot and on October 31, 1954 authorized the bombing of Cairo. Nasser retaliated by ordering the sinking of block-ships in the canal. In the last speech of his re-election campaign, Eisenhower said of the Middle East imbroglio and arrant colonialism on the part of his allies, 'We cannot subscribe to one law for the weak, another for the strong; one law for those opposing us, another for those allied with us. There can be only one law – or there shall be no peace.'[57]

Saddest of all to Eisenhower was that Britain's and France's myopia gave Russia a perfect opportunity to bring a popular anti-Soviet uprising in Hungary, which had begun on October 23, to heel with impunity. The USSR had promised to withdraw its troops; instead, it dispatched some 200,000 soldiers and 4,000 tanks to Budapest, where they murdered 40,000 Hungarian protesters. The CIA recommended airdropping supplies to the dissidents, while others urged Eisenhower to invade Hungary with US troops from bases in Germany, but he shook his weary head. Hungary, behind the Iron Curtain, was as 'inaccessible to us as Tibet'.[58] Ignoring world outrage over the crackdown (the Hungarian prime minister was forced to seek diplomatic asylum, but was intercepted by the Russians and executed), the Soviet prime minister, Nikolai Bulganin, suggested in a letter to Eisenhower that Russia and the US should join forces and together send troops into Egypt. 'If this war is not stopped', the Russian emperor warned his American counterpart, it could 'grow into a Third World War'.[59]

Eisenhower ignored Bulganin's suggestion, instead insisting that the UN police a ceasefire, with no troops permitted in the area from the Big Five powers: a ceasefire that, on November 6, 1956 – American election day – Prime Minister Eden reluctantly accepted, though Ben-Gurion did not.

In a major international crisis, the president had acted calmly, and had refused to go along with recidivist Anglo-French colonial imperialism, or Israeli adventurism. Although Democrats made further gains in the Senate and House of Representatives in the election, Eisenhower's personal popularity swept him back into the Oval Office, trouncing his presidential election opponent, Adlai Stevenson, for a second time. It was a landslide victory, Eisenhower defeating the Democrat by 457 to seventy-three in the Electoral College, and by almost ten million votes in ballots cast.

With Eisenhower commanding such manifest popular support, Republican and Democratic warmongers in Congress were silenced. The president was allowed to impose sanctions on Ben-Gurion – cutting off $40 million in private American tax gifts made to Israel and $60 million raised in bonds – in order to force him to submit to the UN resolution and withdraw Israeli forces from Gaza.

Ben-Gurion resisted, demanding the right to administer and police the 'strip' and to get international guarantees so that Israel could use the Gulf of Aqaba. But if Ben-Gurion hoped the Jewish lobby in America would compel Congress to force Eisenhower to follow such an agenda, as had been the case in Truman's presidency, he had mistaken Eisenhower's firmness. Congressional leaders left the matter up to the president, and on March 1, 1957, a chastened Golda Meir, on behalf of Ben-Gurion, announced Israel's 'full and complete withdrawal' from the territory it had overrun in the Suez war. Nasser thereupon ordered the Suez Canal – which would now be an Egyptian waterway – to be cleared. The war was over.

In retrospect Eisenhower's calmness throughout the Suez crisis bespoke his long military training and experience of war. By staying out of hostilities in the Middle East, and compelling the participants to withdraw – while ensuring the Soviets were denied a new presence in the region, or a reward for their mass butchery in Hungary – Eisenhower had shown great leadership.

Crises abroad were not the only ones Eisenhower sought to defuse.

In his handling of America's foreign policy the president enjoyed the
support of the vast majority of Americans, as well as most members
of Congress, and he was loath to endanger that buttress by espousing
domestic causes that were divisive, such as civil rights. Events, however,
now forced his hand.

The Supreme Court's *Brown* vs *Board of Education* ruling in 1954
'gave some time' to begin integrating segregated public schools in
America, from kindergarten to twelfth grade, he had reminded his
cabinet before the 1956 election. 'Our complaint is, that time is not
being used' he warned. 'Instead states have merely sat down to say
"We Defy."'[60] Even the right to vote was not being accorded to blacks.
Out of almost a million African Americans living in Mississippi, for
instance, only 7,000 were permitted to vote![61] Despite defeat in a monumental Civil War over slavery and states rights, southern Democrats
had successfully resisted civil rights legislation since Reconstruction,
and were clearly not going to give up on segregation without a fight.
The FBI reported that membership of the Ku Klux Klan was soaring,
as were sales of handguns in the South. As racial tensions escalated,
and more blacks were murdered without law enforcement or judicial
response (since white juries refused to find white defendants guilty),
the danger of civil insurrection arose.

Eisenhower's natural instinct was to wait out the venom, but since
it showed no sign of abating, he reluctantly – and to the fury of
southern political leaders – submitted to Congress a modest civil rights
bill in 1957, involving federal rather than state judicial process. The
House of Representatives passed the bill on June 18, but southern
senators baulked, and with a filibuster, which lasted a record twenty-
four hours, mounted by Strom Thurmond (despite the senator having
secretly fathered a child by a black woman) and other bigots, Lyndon
Johnson as Majority Leader was forced to limit the legislation to an
emasculated voting and housing rights bill which Eisenhower felt
would require a decade to revisit. One northern senator called the bill
'a soup made from the shadow of a crow which had starved to death'.[62]
Eisenhower signed the bill into law on September 9, 1957. Far from
calming tempers in the South, however, it seemed only to inflame
them, on both sides.

Even more threatening to whites in the South than voting rights
was the impending desegregation of public schools, on which southern

racists were prepared to take matters into their own hands. When schools reopened after the summer and education boards attempted to introduce black children into hitherto white-only schools, mob violence ensued – but with state governors backing the white mobs, not the black children. Governor Orval Faubus of Arkansas became an international celebrity by ordering the state's National Guard to stop nine black children from attending Little Rock's Central High School. It was not a message the president wanted to be broadcast to the world, and fearing further insurrection, Eisenhower – who was vacationing in Newport – summoned Governor Faubus to Rhode Island to explain himself.

On September 14, 1957, Faubus faced the president. The governor had been an infantry major in Europe in World War II, serving under General Eisenhower, who as president now had the power to federalize the National Guard unless Faubus followed the law. A trial of strength between the president and a state governor could have only one outcome, Eisenhower warned: 'the state will lose'.[63] He recommended the governor return to Arkansas and ensure the black children be permitted to enter the school in safety. Faubus promised Eisenhower he would do so but, once back in Arkansas, reneged on his word, resulting in mayhem as hordes of white racists, summoned by telephone and radio, poured into Little Rock with guns and steel bars to bar the black children from entering.

By September 23, 1957, the situation had become both a national and an international disaster. Shortly after midday Eisenhower called the head of the US Army, General Maxwell Taylor – a paratroop commander who had dropped on D-Day, under Eisenhower's supreme command – and by nightfall some 500 paratroopers of the 101st Airborne Division had assumed positions in the centre of the city, with bayonets fixed. Governor Faubus went on national television to decry the 'warm red blood of patriotic citizens staining the cold, naked, unsheathed knives' of the airborne division's soldiers holding back the white mob, while Senator Richard Russell charged the president with using Hitler-like storm-trooper tactics on ordinary Americans.[64]

For Eisenhower, these charges took a great deal of swallowing. The fact that the US Army had to be called out to protect less than a dozen students seeking to go to school was a terrible indictment of white bigotry. The Soviets, Eisenhower said, were 'gloating over this incident and using it everywhere to misrepresent our whole nation'.[65] Did Faubus and his ilk have no shame? 'Failure to act', he replied in a letter to Senator Russell, 'would be tantamount to acquiescence in anarchy and the dissolution of the union.'[66]

A Gallup poll three weeks later showed 58 per cent of respondents supported Eisenhower's 'handling of the situation at Little Rock'. Over 30 per cent disapproved, however, and in Arkansas Faubus became a folk hero, especially when, as Eisenhower feared, Faubus closed the school altogether once the National Guard was defederalized at the end of the school year. No high-school education, in the governor's view, was better than integration.

Eisenhower's decision to send the 101st Airborne Division into Little Rock marked the pinnacle of his presidency, as an upholder of the Constitution: a signal to the world that, in the struggle of free peoples against the tyranny of Communism, he would not accept the tyranny of white bigots and lynch mobs in his own country. As he clarified in his letter to Senator Russell, 'I completely fail to comprehend your comparison of our troops to Hitler's storm troopers. In one case military power was used to further the ambitions and purposes of a ruthless dictator; in the other to preserve the institutions of free government.'[67]

Eisenhower was ill-rewarded for his reluctant firmness, however. Though liberals congratulated him, he knew from his dealings with Faubus – a Democratic governor – that anti-black racism could not be cauterized permanently by force, any more than it had been by Union troops in and after the Civil War. It was a peculiarly American disease that had infected successive waves of white European immigrants to the South for 300 years, and in the months following the Central High School crisis, Eisenhower's popularity, once so unassailable, began to dip – especially after news was broadcast on October 4, 1957 that Russia had successfully fired into orbit a satellite they called the 'travelling companion': *Sputnik 1*.

Americans were stunned by First Secretary Khrushchev's statement in Moscow that the USSR had 'won' the space race – and, by extension, the arms race. With no bombers able to strike the United States, the USSR seemed to have performed an end run: capable now, by implication, of launching not only a satellite but nuclear-armed intercontinental ballistic missiles, reminiscent of V-2 bombs in World War II.

Such missiles would be capable of striking every American city with impunity, since interception would be impossible. Even subsequent retaliation was questionable, given that three quarters of the American B-52 fleet would be destroyed on the ground in the initial Russian onslaught. Some US advisers even counselled Eisenhower to launch an immediate pre-emptive atomic holocaust on the Soviet Union, before its missile launchers were operational.

The president demurred, though he did give the go-ahead for more hydrogen-bomb testing, more B-52s to be churned out, and accelerated competition between the navy and army in developing America's own sputnik.

Making haste, unfortunately, only produced less speed. On December 6, 1957, America's first attempted satellite launch ended ignominiously – the rocket exploded only a few seconds after blast-off. The sequel, on February 5, 1958, fared no better, exploding within the first minute. Moreover it carried only a 4 lb payload, as compared with *Sputnik 3*'s successful 3,000 lb payload, launched into orbit in May 1958.

By then Eisenhower's once magisterial presidency was reeling, the president having suffered a stroke on November 25, 1957, aged sixty-seven.

Though in due course he recovered all his faculties, Eisenhower fell into depression. In January 1958, he told his Secretary of State, John Foster Dulles, that given his heart attack, his ileitis and then the stroke, he should, if he was unable to attend a planned meeting of NATO, perhaps 'abdicate'.[68]

Fearful of Richard Nixon, the vice president, commanding the US nuclear arsenal, Dulles dissuaded the president. Nevertheless the writing appeared to be on the wall. Eisenhower had never liked or trusted Nixon, nor did he feel confident about Nixon holding the reins of America's imperial power. More important, Eisenhower was losing confidence in himself. A number of the president's most senior cabinet officials had already abandoned ship, America was in the grip of an economic recession, unemployment was approaching 8 per cent, and there was pressure to offer federal funding for people to build their own nuclear shelters. Though Eisenhower tried to pour oil on troubled waters in his press conferences, speeches and addresses to the nation, he had never been an articulate speaker (as opposed to writer), and his paternalistic phrasing made him appear increasingly out of touch and unreasonably complacent, thus providing ammunition to ambitious Democrats like Lyndon Johnson to begin eyeing the throne.

At the nadir of his depression in February 1958, Eisenhower drew up a secret personal agreement with the vice president, allowing Nixon to decide whether to assume presidential power if Eisenhower was too incapacitated to hand over authority. Dulles was himself terminally ill; the mood was bleak. Then on March 27, 1958, Bulganin resigned. Nikita Sergeyevich Khrushchev became both Soviet premier and party leader, and thus the effective leader of the USSR. It was possible, Eisenhower reckoned, that by personal diplomacy the relationship between the two world superpowers could be transformed – for the better.

Given the attention paid to the later legendary nuclear confrontation between Kennedy and Khrushchev, which brought the world to the very brink of World War III, its prequel should not be forgotten.

As president, Dwight Eisenhower saw his role as that of a conservative brake on younger imperialistic hotheads, far preferring to use what historians called 'hidden hand' strategy: using the CIA to police compliant regimes across the world, such as Iran (where the CIA overthrew the prime minister and put the Shah back on his Peacock Throne) and South America (where the president of Guatemala was overthrown). Dealing with Khrushchev, however, was of a different order, and Eisenhower's failure would, sadly, tarnish his legacy after six extraordinary years of world leadership.

It was not for want of trying. Deploring the arms race, and saddened by the death on May 24, 1958 of his Secretary of State, John Foster Dulles, Eisenhower decided to try personal peacemaking with the USSR. On July 10, 1958, the president therefore issued an invitation to Khrushchev to visit the US and twelve days later Khrushchev accepted, the visit scheduled for the summer of 1959. It would be the first time a leader of the Soviet Union had ever visited the United States, its former ally – but since World War II's aftermath, its sworn 'imperialist enemy'.

Khrushchev's tape-recorded memoirs later revealed the profound suspicion he had to overcome before leaving the USSR in September 1959. 'I'll admit I was worried' he recalled. He'd already travelled to India and to England, 'But this was different – this was America.' He didn't think the US was necessarily superior to Britain in culture, 'but American power was of decisive significance'.[69] Power *mattered*.

Khrushchev had in fact met General Eisenhower twice before, in Moscow in 1945 and Geneva in 1955. He'd sparred with Vice President Nixon at the opening of the American National Exhibition in Moscow in late July 1959, in the show kitchen of a labour-saving modern American home (the so-called 'Kitchen Debate'). That, however, had been on Russian soil, where Khrushchev could mercilessly mock idle American consumerism before compliant Soviet reporters. Now, however, he would be on American soil, with only his foreign minister, Andrei Gromyko, and their wives. Even the planned visit to the president's hideaway home in Maryland, renamed Camp David for Eisenhower's grandson, aroused paranoid fears (calmed when informed it was simply a dacha, and thus a special honour). 'You shouldn't forget that all during Stalin's life, right up to the day he died', Khrushchev noted in his memoirs, the Russian dictator 'kept telling us we'd never be able to stand up to the forces of imperialism, that the first time we came into contact with the outside world our enemies would smash us to pieces; we would get confused and be unable to defend our land. In his words, we would become "agents" of some kind.'[70]

Khrushchev admitted to having butterflies, his nerves 'strained with excitement' that he 'was about to meet with the leader of the country which represented the biggest military threat in the world and to discuss with him the major issues of the times: peaceful coexistence, an agreement on the ban of nuclear weapons, the reduction of armed forces, the withdrawal of troops, and the liquidation of bases on foreign territories. I was also looking forward to establishing contacts with the American business world.'[71]

Eisenhower was also nervous with anticipation. He and Khrushchev shared many common experiences. Khrushchev, three years younger than Eisenhower and even balder, had been born the son of an illiterate peasant and raised in rural poverty. 'Our countries have different social systems' Khrushchev acknowledged at the state dinner held in his honour at the White House. 'We believe our system to be better – and you believe yours to be better. But surely we should not bring quarrels out on to the arena of open struggle. Let history judge which of us is right. If we agree this principle, then we can build our relations on the basis of peace and friendship.'[72]

If only! Eisenhower took the Russian premier in his presidential helicopter to Camp David, where Khrushchev regaled the president with stories of Comrade Stalin and the war in Russia. Known as 'The Butcher of the Ukraine', Khrushchev had, as political commissar, been responsible for ensuring Stalin's orders were carried out on the battle-fields of Kiev, Kharkov, Stalingrad and Kursk – with monumental, often criminal casualties (such as Stalin's refusal to evacuate the city of Stalingrad and to fight on the more defensible high ground to the east), as Khrushchev told Eisenhower.

The president admitted to finding Khrushchev's war stories 'fascin-ating'. But in the context of the post-war world, the question was how could the two empires coexist more peacefully in the present, and future. Eisenhower even took Khrushchev to see his farm at Gettysburg and promised to send one of his prime Angus cattle to Russia. The two men confided in each other that they were constantly being badgered and cajoled by their military advisers to spend more money on weapons and defence, thus constantly ratcheting up the arms race, as before World War I. ('How many times can you kill the same man?' Eisenhower had asked one of his Republican gadflies from Congress, in exasper-ation.[73]) But when the two imperial leaders discussed practical measures to further 'peace and friendship', it became clear there was little either emperor could do without impeachment, removal or assassination. Congress, dominated since the 1958 midterm elections by right-leaning Democrats on defence, would never agree to arms control that would inhibit American nuclear superiority; the Soviets would never allow weapons inspections in their closed society. Beyond the military stand-off, moreover, there was the political system divide. Khrushchev was used to banging the table in order to get things done, indeed prided himself on his power as a virtual dictator, imagining that, though 'you [Americans] are richer than we are at present . . . tomorrow', by the ability of the Politburo to direct the Soviet economy, 'we will be as rich as you are, and the day after tomorrow we will be even richer'.[74]

Eisenhower could only shake his head. He had sent Khrushchev across America to visit American people and factories for ten days, and to see at first hand state and city – as opposed to federal – govern-ment. He had arranged for him to visit Hollywood and privately owned farms, hoping the premier might see the cumulative, peaceful energy of individualism, once unleashed and encouraged in an educated, democratic society observing a written constitution and federal, state and local laws.

The effort, however, seemed to have the opposite effect to the one Eisenhower had intended. Though impressing Khrushchev with capitalism's undeniable virtues, the trip seemed actually to raise Khrushchev's anxiety level rather than diminish it, increasing his sense of Soviet inferiority in everything save repressive militarism and secret police. Moreover Eisenhower was polite but implacable over West Berlin, and the need for access routes from the West to remain under western Allied military aegis; was unwilling to countenance the disbandment of NATO merely on the promise of Russian military withdrawal from the occupied countries of eastern Europe; was unable to promise an end to Congress' trade embargo, or forgiveness of debt, since he did not have that power.

The talks between the two emperors – both born into the 'working class' – thus 'failed', as Khrushchev put it. The arms race – or rather, the Russian race to try and catch up with America's technological advances – would go on. The 'Americans had us surrounded on all sides with their military bases' Khrushchev noted. Russia 'lagged significantly behind the US in both warheads and missiles, and the US was out of range of our bombers. We could blast into dust America's allies in Europe and Asia, but America itself – with its huge economic and military potential – was beyond our reach . . . I was convinced that as long as the US held a big advantage over us, we couldn't submit to international disarmament'[75] or to having 'inspectors criss-crossing around the Soviet Union' who 'would have discovered that we were in a relatively weak position', leading them 'to attack us'.[76]

'I could tell Eisenhower was deflated' Khrushchev recalled. 'He looked like a man who had fallen through a hole in the ice and been dragged from the river with freezing water still dripping off of him. Lunchtime came. It was more like a funeral than a wedding feast. Well, maybe that's going too far: it wasn't so much like a funeral as it was like a meal served at the bedside of a critically ill patient.' The two men then travelled from Camp David to Washington by car. 'I could see how depressed and worried Eisenhower was; and I knew how he felt, but there wasn't anything I could do to help him.'[77]

Khrushchev's visit convinced him the United States was outstripping the USSR in every area of production, both civilian and military. Like a chess player who knows he will lose if a game is continued methodically, on his return to Moscow Khrushchev sought every opportunity to turn the tables by provoking dramas that would put the United States (and its allies) on the defensive. The first was sabre-rattling over Berlin. When Eisenhower refused to be disconcerted by Khrushchev's threatened deadline for the western Allies to vacate West Berlin (a deadline Khrushchev had to keep postponing), thus leading the Russian premier to lose face at home, Khrushchev grew even more denunci-atory of American 'imperialism' in his speeches. Nothing seemed to go his way, however, until, to his surprise and delight, he was presented on May 1, 1960 with the perfect opportunity to trick the man who, by virtue of his patience, goodwill and firmness, had become his nemesis.

A disarmament and détente summit meeting had been planned to take place in Paris in mid-May, and in order to have a better idea of current Russian operational missile capability, President Eisenhower had authorized the use of the high-flying American spy planes, the U-2s. Aware that, if shot down by a new Russian SAM missile, this might jeopardize the Paris summit, as well as his own visit to the USSR planned thereafter (in return for Khrushchev's to the US the previous September), Eisenhower only permitted a single final flight which confirmed that there was no missile 'gap', as both Democrat and Republican loudmouths were proclaiming. The US still had over-whelming nuclear superiority.

Had Eisenhower accepted the CIA report, and had he refused to sanction another, he might well have saved his presidency from the abyss into which it now fell – much as Truman's opportunity to stop General MacArthur's forces from crossing the 38th Parallel in 1950 might have saved his. But the deputy director of the CIA begged for one more U-2 flight to confirm the lack of Russian ICBMs, and Eisenhower reluctantly gave his authorization.

The U-2, unreachable by Soviet fighter planes, was, however, hit by lucky Russian anti-aircraft fire, and brought down on May 1, 1960, hundreds of miles inside Russian territory, exactly as Eisenhower had feared. CIA officials hoped against hope that its pilot, Captain Gary Powers, had been killed, and could tell no tales.

Unfortunately for them, Powers parachuted to safety, thereby giving Khrushchev a wholly unexpected way to trap Eisenhower and admin-ister a humiliating snub to the Americans. It was childlike, yet would have dire consequences.

For days Khrushchev deliberately kept the survival of the American pilot quiet, as well as the tell-tale remnants of his plane. As news of a missing plane got out, Eisenhower and the US government were compelled to issue a series of ever more embarrassing lies, beginning with outright denial of any mishap, followed by an assertion that the flight had only been a weather-reporting plane over Turkey that had strayed. Finally, like a magician, Khrushchev brought the drama to a climax by exhibiting on Soviet state television the captive pilot, Gary Powers, his incriminating spy film and bits of the U-2.

Premier Khrushchev's performance, as public theatre, was masterly, even claiming the flight had been a deliberate affront to the Soviet Union's May Day festival. In a country relying on patriotism rather than home appliances, it earned the delight of the Politburo and the outrage of the Russian people: a propaganda victory of the first magnitude in an otherwise losing imperial game. However, in then demanding that President Eisenhower – whom Khrushchev portrayed as having been probably unaware of what his intelligence services were doing – issue a humiliating rebuke to his subordinate military advisers in America, and fire someone senior in order to complete the Russian global propaganda coup, 'The Butcher of the Ukraine' made an unfortunate miscalculation.

Eisenhower was a man of his word, and of great natural dignity. He was also a soldier by training as well as having a long, distinguished career in the military. His high sense of honour – rather than his political common sense – refused to let him either scapegoat anyone else, or deny his own decision as commander-in-chief. He thus took personal and public responsibility for the mission, explaining in a statement that intelligence-gathering was often regrettable, but part of national security in the real world. Yet for the very reason of national security – i.e. secrecy – he could not explain publicly the most vital aspect of the affair: that the previous spy flight had proved there was no disadvantageous missile 'gap' between the United States and the USSR, as Democratic hopefuls such as senators John F. Kennedy and Lyndon B. Johnson were claiming in the presidential primaries.

Keeping silent over the U-2's revelation, Eisenhower was thus forced to fall on his sword, not only causing him to look ineffective at home, but giving Khrushchev another huge propaganda opportunity. A veritable battle between the two empires began to rage in their countries' press, radio and television, with neither side backing down. The issue grew bigger by the day, and threatened to overwhelm what should have been a constructive Paris summit conference, in the interests of détente, only two weeks after the downed flight.

Instead of Gary Powers' flight thus providing Eisenhower with the quiet confidence to be magnanimous at the Paris conference table, safe in the knowledge that America enjoyed nuclear operational superiority, his May Day mission had turned into a Mayday call.

Eisenhower flew to Paris intending to confess to Khrushchev that as he had indeed authorized the U-2 mission, but had now ordered that no more spy flights would ever be flown over Russia – in part because orbiting American satellite rockets would soon be able to do the job. He left it too late, however. According to his diplomatic aide Oleg Troyanovsky, Khrushchev decided on a whim to sabotage the summit, and use American embarrassment as the launch pad for a new propaganda campaign that would mask Russian military inferiority – indeed give the Soviet Union time to catch up militarily with the United States. He would therefore stage a new opera, demanding at the conference that Eisenhower openly apologize for the violation of Russian airspace 'and punish those responsible. He went on to say that it seemed next to impossible that Eisenhower could accept those terms. Consequently the summit would almost certainly collapse before really starting.' Those Russians who were present felt sick: 'most, if not all, were upset at the realization that we were sliding back to the worst times of the Cold War and would have to start from Square One again.' The deputy Russian foreign minister went around the embassy in Paris repeating 'What a situation! What a situation!'[78]

The charade duly took place on May 16, 1960, when Khrushchev asked his host, President de Gaulle, for the right to speak first. Then, to the consternation of the assembled world leaders and their staffs, the Soviet premier began his promised tirade against President Eisenhower and the American government, and their perfidy over the U-2 incident. De Gaulle asked Khrushchev to lower his voice as 'the acoustics in this room are excellent. We can all hear the chairman.'[79] Even the Russian delegation became concerned how to 'keep him from overplaying the part of a person outraged at the insult suffered'.[80] When Khrushchev raised his arm, pointing at the ceiling, and complained he had been 'overflown', de Gaulle pointed out that France, too, had already been overflown eighteen times by *Sputnik 4*, launched the previous day, 'without my permission. How do I know you do not have cameras aboard which are taking pictures of my country?'

At this, Khrushchev became even angrier, denying the possibility in strangely religious terms for a Communist atheist: 'As God is my witness, my hands are clean. You don't think I would do a thing like that?'[81] Eisenhower then attempted to cool the temperature. He said he was sad, but not upset that Khrushchev had seen fit to withdraw his invitation to visit the USSR, but he hoped they could move on to the more substantive matters of disarmament.

It was no good, however; attitudes had been struck, pride ruffled, dignity compromised.[82] Khrushchev recalled how, when he was done ranting, he 'sat down. Frankly, I was all worked up, feeling combative and exhilarated. As my kind of simple folk would say, I was spoiling for a fight. I had caused quite a commotion.' He claimed that when Eisenhower and his delegation stood up, the summit came to an end. 'Then we all left. We had set off an explosion that scattered the four delegations into their separate chambers. The conference table, which was to have united us, had crumbled into dust.'[83] Metaphorically this was true; the chance for meaningful détente between the competing empires was set back by decades.

With his failure to force the West to surrender West Berlin or its access routes to the city, then his amateur dramatics in Paris, Khrushchev had turned himself into a world heavyweight shadow-boxer instead of wise peacemaker. 'We had shown that anyone who slapped us on our cheek would get his head kicked off' said the former commissar, recalling his pride over the Paris summit. 'The Americans had been taught a lesson. They had learned the limit of our toler-ance. They now knew that American imperialism would not go unpunished if it overstepped this limit. We showed the whole world that while all other western powers might crawl on their bellies in front of America's mighty financial and industrial capital, we wouldn't bow down – not for one second.' Under no circumstances would he or his fellow Soviets 'let ourselves be abused and degraded'.[84] Instead, he would – as at Stalingrad and Kursk – switch to counter-attack. In America.

Travelling to New York and denouncing the 'mighty' American 'imperialists' at the United Nations General Assembly in the autumn of 1960, castigating the old colonial nations for their slowness in granting independence to their colonies, and publicly befriending the new Cuban dictator Fidel Castro at his downtrodden hotel in Harlem, Khrushchev now posed and strutted as a Communist hero to the Third World. Wherever there were cameras, he felt obliged to make a scene. In the Big Apple on September 29, 1960, for example, he famously banged the United Nations podium with his fists, then, on October 11, his desk with his shoe. As Oleg Troyanovsky (who accompanied Khrushchev) euphemistically recalled, there had always been something 'puckish' in Khrushchev's nature, but now it was exhibited in 'an irresistible urge to humiliate the prince of Darkness, as he had begun to regard Eisenhower'.

For Eisenhower, the sight of Premier Khrushchev, emperor of the Soviet Union, turning into a dangerous and unpredictable clown, was disheartening. Eisenhower had had to deal with other bombastic leaders in his lifetime – MacArthur, Montgomery and Patton in particular – and he did not allow Khrushchev's antics to spoil his day. Nevertheless the picture of Khrushchev acting out in the final weeks before the 1960 election (which would mark the end of Eisenhower's distinguished eight-year presidency) was depressing. The two nominated American presidential candidates of the major parties – Vice President Nixon and Senator John F. Kennedy – seemed now to be competing not to pursue peace, but to be seen as toughest on defence and military spending, with ridiculous allegations of a missile 'gap' between the US and Russia, and nonsensical rhetoric over Cuba. The chance to make quiet progress with Russia over nuclear disarmament (especially in the knowledge that Communist China was building an atomic bomb) had gone up in U-2's smoke, ruining Eisenhower's imperial legacy.

In a televised farewell address from the Oval Office, Eisenhower memorably warned against the country's own 'military industrial complex' becoming too potent. An 'immense military establishment' and a 'large arms industry', acting in concert, were seeking 'unwarranted influence' in 'every city, every statehouse, every office of the federal government,' thus posing the risk of a 'disastrous rise of misplaced power'.[85] Then, on January 20, 1961, Eisenhower handed over the burdens of office to his successor, the young Democratic senator and president-elect John F. Kennedy, who had beaten Nixon by the narrowest of margins in the November 1960 election. 'I had longed to give the world a lasting peace' Eisenhower would write in retirement. 'I was only able to contribute', he lamented, 'a stalemate.'[86]

Part Three: Private Life

From the time he was a child the people around Dwight Eisenhower wanted to win his affection, and his approval. This was the secret of his leadership in war, but also in peace, as a politician. Highly intelligent, with a great gift of empathy, Eisenhower was astute enough to recognize the power of benevolent charisma in modern communications, as FDR had shown. And with the era of television, after World War II, he found himself in a position to apply his famous smile to the living-room screen. Eisenhower became the first president to give televised press conferences. Taking instruction and advice from American television's star anchor, Edward R. Murrow, and from Hollywood actor Robert Montgomery, he learned how to put himself across not as an actor but as himself: a man with natural dignity, modesty and genuineness – a man you would be proud to have living next door. Thenceforth 'likeability' would become a crucial ingredient in the public's expectations of a presidential candidate – to the detriment of Eisenhower's heir apparent, 'Tricky Dick' Nixon, who sounded wise on radio, but looked like a crook on television.

The ability to inspire affection raised, of course, the question of fidelity. Few charismatic male leaders exude magnetism without being tempted by the rewards. Like Franklin D. Roosevelt, Eisenhower was no exception. His strict upbringing by his Jehovah's Witness mother was a lifelong moral compass, but not enough to fight all temptation. From schooldays onwards Eisenhower chain-smoked as many as four packs a day. He adored football, and was gutted when a knee injury at West Point precluded further play. He also hunted and loved to fish. Once rain and darkness fell, however, poker and bridge, with bourbon, were Eisenhower's favourite pastime, as they were for Truman. Eisenhower's prowess at the poker table helped fund his cadetship at West Point, to the point where he was sometimes barred from groups.

Eisenhower's love life followed an equally conventional course. Like Truman, he had first set his marital sights on a fellow high-school student: a blue-eyed blonde beauty named Gladys Harding. On August

5, 1915, on his graduation from West Point, Eisenhower asked Gladys
to marry him. As in Truman's case the romance was sabotaged by the
young lady's parent – in Gladys Harding's case her father, who predicted
that 'That Eisenhower kid will never amount to anything.'[87]

Fearful of her father's reaction, Gladys – who was set on making
a career as a pianist – temporized, leading Eisenhower to pour his
heart out in a series of lovelorn letters that demonstrated how romantic
he was, behind his disciplined, ambitious facade. 'More than ever, now,
I want to hear you say the three words [I love you] with "Better than
I ever have anyone in the world"' he implored Gladys. 'If you can say
that to me . . . then I'll know that I've won. From that time – if it
ever comes – I'll know you're mine – no matter where you go – or
what you do . . . For girl I do love you and want you to KNOW it –
to be as certain of it as I am – and to believe in me and trust me as
you would your dad.'[88]

Gladys Harding wouldn't, however, citing her own musical ambition. Thus, when the handsome young second lieutenant on the
rebound was posted to Fort Sam Houston in San Antonio, Texas, he
turned his attention to a new campaign: this time to win the heart of
a flighty eighteen-year-old, Mamie Doud: the short, pretty, spoiled
daughter of a rich dad who would deny his daughter nothing, and
who condoned the romance. The pair made an unlikely couple – 'a
classic romantic mismatch' in the words of one biographer, between
a twenty-five-year-old penniless infantry officer (known as a 'woman-
hater' after the collapse of his relationship with Gladys Harding) and
an 'outrageous flirt', a vivacious teenage air-head, fresh out of
'finishing' school.[89]

'The girl I'm running around with now is named Miss Doud, from
Denver' Eisenhower wrote to another high-school friend. '[She] winters
here. Pretty nice – but awful strong for society – which often bores
me. But we get along well together – and I'm at her house whenever
I'm off duty.'[90] Perhaps hoping his letter would be passed on to Gladys
Harding, the unrequited love of his life, he repeated he would write
more fully 'about the girl I run around with *since* I learned that
G[ladys]. H[arding]. cared so terribly for her *work*'.[91]

The wedding of Dwight D. Eisenhower and Miss Mamie Doud
took place on July 1, 1916, in the Doud family home in Denver. For a
man of such high intelligence and ambition, however, marriage to

Mamie – an inveterate socialite – became a trial, as did the profession of soldiering after World War I. Their first son, Little Ike or 'Ikky', died of scarlet fever and meningitis in 1921, and something of the light went out of Eisenhower's genial personality, causing people to find him difficult to fathom. 'Ike has the most engaging grin of anybody I ever met' his wife would later say of him. 'Though when he turns it off,' she added, 'his face is as bleak as the plains of Kansas.'[92]

The death of their first son steeled both Ike and Mamie for the difficult years that followed in different postings, from Panama to the Philippines. It was neither a passionate nor a spiritual union, neither calming nor mentally stimulating. Instead it became yet another test of Eisenhower's loyalty and patience – as was his career, serving under men like Douglas MacArthur – and in curbing his own explosive temper.

For Mamie Doud it was also a long trial. Eisenhower preferred to stay at home and read, or spend time with close friends, rather than party or 'socialize'. 'Ike is the kind', she would say ruefully, 'who would rather give you a fried egg in his own home than take you to the finest nightclub in the world.'[93] He was obstinate, too. 'No woman can run him' she confided to a girlfriend. And later to her grand-daughter-in-law: 'There can be only one star in the heaven, Sugar, and there is only one way to live with an Eisenhower. Let him have his own way.'[94] Divorce was mooted in 1922 and again in 1936, in view of Mamie's flirtations, but neither she nor Eisenhower wanted the stigma or the adverse effect it might have on their surviving second son, David. They loyally soldiered on, so to speak, until in 1942 Eisenhower's female driver, resurrecting shades of Gladys Harding, turned the general's head.

A former model for Worth, Kay Summersby was a stunningly attractive, tall, slender, Irish redhead, daughter of a British cavalry officer, married to a British officer in India and being sued for divorce for carrying on an affair with an American officer in England when Eisenhower became her boss. Thereafter she devoted herself to Eisenhower's welfare and comfort. Inevitably tongues wagged – including Kay's. She later wrote two books, *Eisenhower Was My Boss* and *Past Forgetting*, the latter claiming that she'd had a wartime love affair with Eisenhower, with much fun, tenderness and kissing but no sexual consummation, after a trial-and-error performance had ended in impotence on the general's return to London, prior to D-Day. This may indeed have been the simple truth; Eisenhower's deep loyalty to Mamie, after almost thirty years of marriage and the death of their first child, may well have made the sexual act of infidelity, or gratification, simply too frightening, given also the enormous responsibilities he carried as supreme commander in Europe and the hopes and fears of so many millions of soldiers and citizens of the free world vested in him.

If Eisenhower could not consummate his love affair with Kay, however, did he propose marriage to Mrs Summersby, which might allow him to become potent again? No less a person than President Truman later believed so, recalling a letter which Eisenhower purportedly sent General Marshall at the end of World War II, 'saying that he wanted to come back to the United States and divorce Mrs Eisenhower so that he could marry this Englishwoman'. It was, Truman remembered, 'a very, very shocking thing to have done, for a man who was a general in the army of the United States' – a five-star general, no less. 'Well,' Truman went on, 'Marshall wrote him back a letter the like of which I never did see. He said that if . . . Eisenhower even came close to doing such a thing, he'd not only bust him out of the army, he'd see to it that never for the rest of his life would he be able to draw a peaceful breath . . . a living hell. General Marshall didn't often lose his temper, but when he did, it was a corker.' And, Truman claimed, 'one of the last things I did as president, I got those letters from his file in the Pentagon, and I destroyed them'.[95]

Published in 1973 by a journalist and interviewer, Truman's allegation could never be verified – indeed the journalist's recording of the conversation was never found.[96] Most historians discounted it as the rambling of an old man, the summer before his own death, and four years after Eisenhower's. Could such a story have been invented out of thin air? Even Mamie suspected (and accused) Eisenhower of having an affair with Kay, and Eisenhower did admit to Mamie that he had briefly been infatuated. Enough to countenance retirement from the army and a post-war life with Kay, though? If so, he would not have been the first American to dread return to a sterile marriage at home, after the extraordinary experience of struggle and military conquest in Europe; moreover the days he'd spent with Mamie at her apartment in New York, before flying to England to undertake command of the D-Day invasion, had been miserable and had held out little prospect of post-war happiness.

Whatever the truth, reality set in once he was home. 'Kay, it's impossible. There's nothing I can do' Eisenhower had said when accidentally meeting Kay in New York in 1948 (he had arranged for her to become an American citizen).[97] The great general, vanquisher of the German armies in the West, thus opted for the nobler, more loyal outcome – and became, as a result, the hugely popular president of the United States, with Mamie an all-American, beloved and devoted First Lady, who said she liked to reach over in the double bed she'd ordered for Ike's return from the war 'and pat Ike on his old bald head anytime I want to'.[98] The bed, in a refurbished pink and green room, became Mamie's command post, from which she rarely rose before midday, relishing the White House personal staff and the social distinction that came with the title after so many years of isolation, while 'the general' was away fighting.

Something of his long-suffering stoicism, along with his genial nature, was thus the mark of Eisenhower's character, and gave confidence to Americans that the empire was in safe hands. Even his passion for golf, though mocked by comedians, symbolized a president who knew the importance of relaxation as a counterpart to his high sense of duty (and his constantly controlled temper). He read Westerns in the same way – as escapism from the problems he faced by day. In 1950 he had purchased a farmhouse at Gettysburg as a country retreat (the first house he ever owned). There, inspired by Winston Churchill, he began to paint, avidly and therapeutically. He accepted gifts, just as he took for granted the valet who dressed him each day, the drivers and pilots who transported him, the staff who worked for him, as well as the millionaire companions who vacationed and visited with him. Yet woe betide any who expected special favours as a result! He prided himself on his absolute impartiality, which made him the greatest internationalist American since FDR, perhaps even greater. 'Without allies or associates the leader is just an adventurer like Genghis Khan' he liked to say.[99]

Legions of subordinates, from MacArthur to Patton and Bradley, decried this impartiality, accusing Eisenhower of being insufficiently nationalistic; yet it was this very quality that made him stand head and shoulders above any other American of his time. He was slow to advance the cause of racial integration at home (and wholly ignorant of the merits of feminism), but in accepting the Supreme Court decision on public education, and in ordering the 101st Airborne Division to Little Rock, he had shown he would not shirk his ultimate duty. Though disparaged by racists, moreover, he never questioned the rightness of his action. He had become, he recognized, the embodiment of the noble American in an age of empire, with a duty to represent all Americans, not simply a party.

As President Theodore Roosevelt had famously recommended, Eisenhower talked softly abroad, but wielded a big, indeed atomic, stick – which, unlike his predecessor, he never had occasion to use. Under his presidency America flourished economically, without bankrupting itself through military expenditure and overreach. 'Rarely in American history has the craving for tranquility and moderation commanded more general support' wrote the pioneer political pollster Samuel Lubell, who did door-to-door research.[100] Though mocked by historians after his departure from the White House for his lack of flamboyance in the new 1960s decade – he was ranked twenty-second of thirty-one presidents, just above Andrew Johnson, who was impeached – Eisenhower had fulfilled his generation's trust.[292] He died on March 28, 1969, at Walter Reed Army Hospital in Washington DC, and was buried in the grounds of the Presidential Library established in his name. He was, after Theodore Roosevelt, Woodrow Wilson and FDR, probably the greatest American president of the twentieth century – and, in the years after his departure from the White House, his calm, worldly experience and safe hands would be sorely missed.

CHAPTER FOUR

JOHN F. KENNEDY

Later deified

Democrat
35th President
(January 20, 1961–November 22, 1963)

Part One: The Road to the White House

John Fitzgerald Kennedy was born in Brookline, a suburb of Boston, Massachusetts on May 29, 1917. He was named after his maternal grandfather, John 'HoneyFitz' Fitzgerald, who made history as a congressman and then as the first Irish-American Catholic mayor of Boston, a New England port-city in which WASP (White Anglo-Saxon Protestant) elitism had secured virtually all senior political posts since the Pilgrims landed in 1620. 'No Irish Need Apply' had still been a common sign on hiring boards when HoneyFitz grew up. Hugely popular, funny and hardworking, Fitzgerald *had* applied, however – and had won. Thereafter he humorously referred to the difference between himself and the Cabots and the Lodges, whose families had arrived early in the seventeenth century, as the difference of 'only a few ships'.

John F. Kennedy's father, by contrast, was a man of little humour, save that of cynicism. Son of an East Boston bar owner, Joseph P. Kennedy was clever, ruthlessly ambitious, and made history in America in a different way: first as its youngest bank president, then wartime shipyard manager, stock-market swindler, millionaire movie production company owner, and first chairman of the Securities Exchange Commission (SEC) in New York (appointed by FDR as 'a thief to catch a thief'). As reward for his support for FDR, Kennedy asked to be made US ambassador to London in 1938. A passionate isolationist (he had avoided military service in World War I), Kennedy opposed involvement in Europe's troubles, and by 1940, as Britain faced Hitler's Third Reich alone, Ambassador Kennedy became Churchill's bitterest foe in London.

Joseph P. Kennedy Jr, Joseph P. Kennedy's eldest son, was a chip off the block – a devoted but shallow-minded mouthpiece for his father's sympathies with the Nazis and American isolationism in 1940 and 1941. Ambassador Kennedy's second son, John F. Kennedy, however, was made of different stuff. Suffering recurrent illnesses, he spent much of his childhood in either a hospital, sick room or sanatorium. He disliked the Catholic boarding school to which his devout but distant mother sent him, so was switched at age fourteen to his brother's Episcopalian boarding school, Choate, in Connecticut. There he scored at the top of intelligence tests, read voraciously, yet did little class work and was finally threatened with expulsion for irreverence and subversion. When asked by a school-affiliated psychologist why he so misbehaved, the seventeen-year-old replied: 'If my brother were not so efficient, it would be easier for me to be efficient. He does it so much better than I do.'[1]

While no other member of the Kennedy family had ever willingly picked up a book, 'Jack' Kennedy was never without one. Endowed with a near-photographic memory and self-deprecating humour he was, like Dwight Eisenhower, blessed with a magnetic charm. Even his Choate school headmaster, who was tormented for four years by Kennedy's anti-Establishment, schoolboy subversion, later recalled how winning Jack could be, with his tousled hair, wide cheeks, perfect teeth and mischievous blue eyes. 'His smile was, as a young boy, when he first came to school – well, in any school he would have got away with some things just on his smile.'[2]

To the smile was added a quick, sharp mind, and a fascination with world politics. As a Harvard University student he interned at the US embassies in London and Paris, then travelled through Russia and Germany in the weeks before the Nazi invasion of Poland in September 1939. He took charge of American survivors of the first passenger vessel to be sunk by a German submarine in World War II (the SS *Athenia*) on behalf of his father, and chose as the subject of his senior thesis at Harvard Britain's failure to rearm in time to meet Hitler's aggression, a subject so topical it was issued as a book, *Why England Slept*, in the summer of 1940, as France fell and the people of Britain prepared for Nazi invasion. Thereafter, in California, deeply involved in a peace conference, the young author took issue with his father, who had disobeyed Roosevelt and blackmailed the president to be able to return to America from the London embassy prior to the November 1940 presidential election.

'If England is defeated America is going to be alone in a strained and hostile world' the twenty-three-year-old warned his father in a letter – indeed, Britain might be 'on the verge of defeat or defeated – by a combination of totalitarian powers. Then there will be a general turning of the people's opinions. They will say "Why were we so stupid not to have given Britain all possible aid."'[3]

The letter was brilliantly effective. Ambassador Kennedy withdrew his planned opposition to the Lend-Lease Bill. Britain did survive, and was able to join the United States in declaring war on the Japanese Empire after Pearl Harbor.

By then JFK had wangled a doctor's pass to serve in the US Navy, first in naval intelligence in Washington before transferring to high-speed wooden torpedo boats. Posted to the Solomon Islands in 1943 he took command of the ill-fated PT-109, which was rammed and sunk by a steel-hulled Japanese destroyer at night, when the lead US boat, equipped with radar, quit the patrol and returned to base. Two crew members were killed, but Kennedy brought the remaining nine back to safety after four days and five nights behind Japanese lines.

Written up by novelist John Hersey in the *New Yorker* in 1944, the PT-109 story made Kennedy a minor national hero, but the episode was disastrous for Kennedy's physical health, eventually causing him to be medically discharged. The death of his healthy older brother, who had joined the navy as a pilot, upset him so deeply that he wrote a collection of essay tributes to Joe Jr, who had been expected to go into politics after the war.

The privately published volume was a mark of fierce family loyalty, and perfectly sincere, yet avoided the bitter truth – that Joe Jr lacked an independent mind and good political judgement (he was an early admirer of Hitler, and had opposed FDR's re-nomination at the Democratic National Convention in 1940). By contrast JFK seemed not only to have inherited his grandfather's legendary charm and compassion, but also evinced precociously mature political judgement. Encouraged by his college and navy friends, with his father's backing and at the urging of his adoring grandfather, JFK thus ran for a vacant congressional seat in Massachusetts in 1946. To Ambassador Kennedy's amazement – in view of his son's appalling health – JFK proved a born campaigner, exuding a kind of natural grace both on the platform and in person, and concealing his exceptional intelligence behind his quick humour. He was well informed, well travelled, inquisitive, competitive, ruggedly handsome, tough, and happy-go-lucky. Women adored him; men were less easily seduced, but his mix of insouciance and thoughtfulness, for a decorated young veteran, eventually won their votes too. He was elected three times as a congressman for Massachusetts between 1946 and 1950, then ran for the Senate in 1952 against the distinguished incumbent, Republican Henry Cabot Lodge, who had moved mountains to draft Eisenhower for the presidency.

In a memorable campaign, despite a national landslide for Republicans, JFK triumphed and took Lodge's Senate seat. The difference of a few ships had worked in JFK's favour, putting him ahead of his WASP rival as the young representative of an old state in which veterans, immigrants, community groups and college faculty now warmed to his liberal, Truman-style notion of government: firm on defence and international alliances, and compassionate on domestic issues from veteran's housing to education, the minimum wage and social security.

Marrying Jacqueline Bouvier, a New England WAFC (White Anglo-French Catholic), added to the allure of the freshman senator, who defied his father's wishes, and ran for vice president at the 1956 Democratic Convention – the same summer that Vice President Richard Nixon stood for re-nomination as the Republican vice-presidential candidate.

Nixon was successful in his bid; Kennedy was not. The Democratic vice-presidential nomination went to Senator Estes Kefauver by a handful of votes. The convention was televised, however, and Kennedy's performance (which included his narration of the official thirty-minute documentary film on the history of the Democratic Party, as well as his beguiling concession remarks) garnered Kennedy national face-and-voice recognition as a young candidate, barely thirty-nine, to be reckoned with.

Determined to show he was on a rising tide, JFK stood again for election to the US Senate in 1958, and won by the largest majority in Massachusetts history, as well the largest in that year's elections to the Senate. With Adlai Stevenson withdrawing from the presidential fray after two defeats, unless drafted, the time seemed propitious for JFK to make his expected bid for the Democratic presidential nomination in 1960. His work in the Senate was undistinguished but, once promoted to a place on the Senate Foreign Relations Committee, he spoke widely on foreign policy. His youthfulness, his idealism, his intelligence, his photogenic (and expensively dressed) new wife, and his own good looks augured well in the television age. His third book, *Profiles in Courage*, though largely researched and first-drafted by others (like Winston Churchill's books) had won a Pulitzer Prize for biography in 1957, which gave him an unusual literary pedigree. Moreover his heroic war record mitigated his youth and executive inexperience, making Governor Stevenson look fusty even to many liberals.

The national press, like the public, thus found much to laud in Kennedy's candidature, though many remained disturbed not only by JFK's faith (no Catholic had ever been elected to the presidency), but by his sinister father, Joseph P. Kennedy, in the background, bankrolling his candidature.

To run successfully against powerful Democratic rivals such as the supremely effective Senate Majority Leader, Lyndon B. Johnson, JFK thus needed to campaign vigorously, widely and combatively, in order that his distinctive personality emerge and win over sceptics. To this end his father furnished him with his own plane, *The Caroline* (named after his daughter, born in 1957). Despite recurrent (and sedulously concealed) ill health, JFK duly won the party nomination in Los Angeles in August 1960, offering his beaten rival, Lyndon Johnson, the vice presidency as a gesture of magnanimity and respect, though never dreaming Johnson would surrender his powerful legislative position in the Senate to accept it.

To Kennedy's surprise Johnson did, and in a thrilling campaign that autumn, the race for the presidency looked too close to call.

Two confrontations helped tip the national scales towards Kennedy: a brave appearance in Houston, Texas, before a meeting of 300 Protestant ministers, where he defended his right as a Catholic to run for the nation's highest office; and the first ever televised presidential debates, to which his opponent, Republican Richard Nixon, an excellent debater with a deep baritone voice, agreed. On radio, where Nixon's voice conveyed his vice-presidential stature, he seemed to win the three debates, but on television the reverse seemed to be the case (according to Gallup polls), the vice president sweating profusely under the klieg lamps, and looking untrustworthy beside the confident, smiling, handsome Democrat.

The presidential election on November 8, 1960, proved one of the closest in American history, indeed closer than that of Truman against Dewey in 1948. The difference between winning and losing appeared to boil down to a number of disputed counties in Illinois, where Chicago Mayor Daley's machine was operating, and where large amounts of cash (organized by Joe Kennedy) changed hands and fraudulent voting was suspected. ('Mr President, with a little bit of luck and the help of a few close friends, you are going to carry Illinois' Daley had confidently promised earlier that evening.[4])

Kennedy, when asked how he would take the news if he were to lose the election, admitted: 'Badly. But I won't take it as hard as Nixon will.'[5] He was right.

Nixon was urged to contest the result. Such an investigation might, however, have encountered electoral fraud on Nixon's own behalf. At 9 a.m. Nixon's press secretary conceded. Nixon did not, and in fact only officially conceded on January 6, 1961, in Congress, after Kennedy had visited him by helicopter in Florida and offered him a senior position in the new administration (which Nixon declined).

Part Two: The Presidency

On January 20, 1961, John Fitzgerald Kennedy, aged forty-three, took the oath of office as thirty-fifth president of the United States, with Lyndon Baines Johnson sworn in as the new vice president, standing beside the outgoing thirty-fourth president, Dwight D. Eisenhower, and outgoing vice president, Richard Nixon. Together they comprised four consecutive presidents of the United States, none of whom had ever served as a state governor, the traditional means of ascent.

Kennedy's inagural speech, written by the even younger Ted Sorensen, was widely considered the best of its kind in American annals. 'Let the word go forth from this time and place,' Kennedy declared in his confident tenor voice, with its distinctive Boston intonation, 'to friend and foe alike, that the torch has been passed to a new generation of Americans – born in this century, tempered by war, disciplined by a hard and bitter peace, proud of our ancient heritage – and unwilling to witness or permit the slow undoing of those human rights to which this nation has always been committed, and to which we are committed today at home and around the world. Let every nation know, whether it wishes us well or ill, that we shall pay any price, bear any burden, meet any hardship, support any friend, oppose any foe, in order to assure the survival and the success of liberty.' Televised across the world, it signalled a new captain at America's imperial helm.

With Kennedy's younger brother Robert F. Kennedy nominated as Attorney General, and JFK's Senate seat 'kept warm' for when his youngest brother Ted would be old enough to serve, as well as Joseph Kennedy operating in the background as a grey eminence, the British prime minister Harold Macmillan likened the Kennedy clan to a medieval Italian family taking over the capital. The Kennedys were, of course, Irish-American, but there was undeniably something of a Medici feel to the takeover, following the staid, solid and respectable Eisenhowers, who suddenly looked like yesterday's pudding, despite the international crises Eisenhower had so maturely met, and the domestic wonders he had performed as president.

Living standards had risen more than 30 per cent during Eisenhower's two terms; almost every American home had television; grand highways were being constructed to connect the main cities of the continent from coast to coast and north to south; no wars had been declared; no riots had marred the rising national prosperity after Little Rock; and there was little if any inflation. President Eisenhower was understandably miffed. 'This is the biggest defeat of my life' he had remarked the morning after the election, sensing that, with a new era beginning, his legacy would quickly be forgotten, even trampled.[6] In particular he deplored 'naive' reporters who welcomed JFK as 'a new genius in our midst who is incapable of making any mistakes, and therefore deserving no criticism whatever'.[7]

Certainly, having raised public – indeed world – expectations on behalf of a new generation, Kennedy had to work hard to meet them. The first great achievement of his new administration took place some weeks later, in March 1961: the establishment of the Peace Corps, a volunteer programme to send young Americans abroad to help especially in Third World countries, and which tapped into the native idealism of a younger American generation.

The Peace Corps would exemplify the best and most inspiring element of the new broom in Washington, where the White House was swiftly transformed by the 'best and brightest' new incumbents, such as Defense Secretary Robert McNamara, former head of Ford Motor Company, and National Security Adviser McGeorge Bundy, the former (and youngest ever) Dean of the Faculty at Harvard. The First Lady had just given birth to a boy, in addition to their daughter Caroline, so the private quarters were quickly transformed into a charming nursery. The press was captivated by the picture, later memorialized as a modern Camelot.

Peace Corps volunteers fanned across the Second and Third Worlds, without weapons. Fidel Castro, by contrast, favoured the export both of Marxist ideas *and* weapons, thus posing a potent threat in the poorer countries of Latin America. President Eisenhower had already warned 'we could lose all of South America' unless the US took action, yet felt the United States must 'conduct itself in precisely the right way' lest it merely fan the flames of anti-Americanism.[8] A straightforward imperialist invasion of Cuba was off the table, in Eisenhower's view, since it would only confirm Castro's depiction of the US as a military empire out of control; he had therefore favoured the same hidden-hand tactic he'd used in Iran and Guatemala: a coup, backed by Cuban exiles, covertly sponsored by the CIA, with a $13 million budget. Eisenhower directed that no US military personnel be sanctioned for the mission, however, at least in combat status; nor was Vice President Nixon allowed to be part of the planned operation. Finally, Eisenhower insisted, there had to be a credible alternative leader to put in Castro's place.

Operation Zapata had thus hardly promised to be a great success before President Kennedy took office, and it certainly did not promise to become better in the weeks after his inauguration, for all the talk of paying any price and bearing any burden. The truth was, it was already ridiculed by diplomats: the plan 'known all over Latin America' and even 'discussed in UN circles', as Eisenhower's Under Secretary of State, Douglas Dillon (whom Kennedy had made Treasury Secretary), protested.[9] Kennedy's new Secretary of State, Dean Rusk, felt similarly unenthusiastic, as was the chairman of the Senate Foreign Relations Committee, William Fulbright. Castro could not but be aware of the impending operation, and threw out most of the American embassy personnel in Havana, calling it, correctly, 'a nest of spies'.

Swollen to 1,500 men and targeted on to another Cuban beachhead, the CIA-supported Cuban exiles, still lacking a leader, were authorized by President Kennedy to invade Cuba on April 17, 1961, at the so-called

Bay of Pigs. Within hours the landing threatened to become a catastrophe.

Certainly the Kremlin expected US forces to invade. But Kennedy did not take either course. As the entire rebel force was reported as having been killed or taken captive, the First Lady and White House staff found JFK weeping at the needless loss of life and liberty. 'A great nation must be willing to use its strength' Senator Goldwater told the president, urging him to snatch victory from the jaws of defeat. 'Power belongs to those who use it [and] I would do whatever is necessary to assure the invasion is a success.'[10] Richard Nixon said the same, while Richard Bissell, on behalf of the CIA, begged for at least two US jets to 'shoot down enemy aircraft'. 'No,' Kennedy responded, 'I've told you over and over again, our forces won't engage in combat.'[11] When the chief of the US Navy Staff, Admiral Burke (Kennedy's former naval commander in the Solomon Islands) asked permission to send a US destroyer into action to knock out Castro's advancing tanks, the president again refused: 'Burke, I don't want the United States involved in this' – and in the ensuing days, as calamity became a rout, he held by that decision.[12]

Instead, the president did the unthinkable. He accepted failure – and turned down Nixon's offer, on behalf of the Republican Party, to publicly support him if he now launched a formal US invasion of Cuba (using, if necessary, a phony threat to the naval base at Guantanamo as a pretext). At the president's live press conference on April 21, 1961, a reporter defied the injunction (in the interests of national security) against questions over Cuba; the president paused, then looked the journalist in the eye without irritation. 'There's an old saying that victory has a hundred fathers,' he stated, 'and defeat is an orphan. I am the responsible officer of this government.'[13]

Defeat, then, it was. Viewers – like the reporters present – were stunned. And impressed. Even Kennedy was amazed at the public's response to his admission of responsibility for the blunder. In a Gallup survey his popularity rating jumped *ten* points, hitting 83 per cent approval. 'Jesus, it's just like Ike' he mocked the results of the poll with typically self-deprecating wit. 'The worse you do, the better they like you.'[14]

As became clear to the president, a commander-in-chief must in the end live with his own conscience and ignore the gung-ho chiding of subordinates eager for imperial glory, usually at the cost of other men's lives. In his heart of hearts, tempered by savage war in the Solomon Islands, JFK had not really believed in Operation Zapata, either as an operation of war or as a political objective, given that no replacement for Castro was at hand. He himself had visited Cuba (and its massage parlours) numerous times in its pre-Castro, Batista era. Was Batista's corrupt political, social and economic system what the United States should be seeking to restore, along with the United Fruit Company's property? What credible leader or government were the Cuban rebels offering the poor in Cuba?

The 1960s were not the 1890s, the president recognized from the young people he was meeting in launching his Peace Corps. The idealistic rhetoric that had brought him the presidency (but only just) was based on an inspirational, *moral* quality he exuded in spades, not cynicism, or the methods the Soviets had used in Hungary. Chastened by the disaster, he assured Eisenhower that the next time he would not mess up; he would choose his battlefields more carefully.

Cuba was not the only point of maximum impact between capitalism and Communism. Alongside the drama of the Bay of Pigs, the world was treated in the spring of 1961 to a race between the two nuclear superpowers to see which of them could, following the success of the sputnik programme, be the first to put a human being into orbit around the earth. The race was won by the Soviet Union when Lieutenant Yuri Gagarin was rocketed into space on April 12, 1961, beating US astronaut Alan Shepard – who only reached a height of 115 miles, and did not orbit the earth – by three weeks. It secured another great propaganda victory for the Soviets, fostering the illusion not only of technological superiority over the capitalist world, but also of the USSR's peaceful intentions.

Eisenhower's response as president would have been to ignore the propaganda, and proceed patiently with the science. President Kennedy, however, was nothing if not sensitive to the battle of modern ideas between the US and USSR. In the wake of Lieutenant Gagarin's triumph he therefore ordered a crash programme to put the first man on the moon – though it would not happen in his lifetime.

No sooner had the waves of Cuba and Lieutenant Gagarin subsided, than Kennedy emplaned to meet his fellow emperor in Vienna.

The summit meeting, on June 3, 1961, was a second disaster for

Kennedy in as many months. Kennedy's charm and good manners had entranced America, and the majority of people had forgiven his freshman faux pas over Cuba; but his charm now acted as a disadvantage in confronting 'The Butcher of the Ukraine'.

Kennedy admitted afterwards to James Reston, a *New York Times* journalist, that the confrontation was the 'roughest thing in my life'.[15] Dean Rusk, Kennedy's Secretary of State, recalled that the president was 'very upset. He wasn't prepared for the brutality of Khrushchev's presentation' – a *nyet*-studded performance during which Khrushchev rejected any nuclear disarmament that entailed military inspection; proposed again to recognize East Germany and thereby abandon four-power control and access to Berlin; and insisted Russia would continue to back Communist movements worldwide, whatever the danger of miscalculation leading to inadvertent nuclear war.[16]

Drugged with cortisone for his Addison's disease – an invariably fatal, progressive deterioration of the adrenal glands – novocaine for his back pain, and a concoction devised by Dr Max Jacobson for celebrities to combat his low energy level, Kennedy seemed to Khrushchev 'very inexperienced, even immature. Compared to him, Eisenhower was a man of intelligence and vision.'[17]

Back in Moscow Khrushchev spoke of Kennedy as 'the boy': a president who 'doesn't have any backbone' or, worse still, 'the courage to stand up to a serious challenge'.[18] A KGB operative in America confided to Robert Kennedy that Khrushchev's bombast in Vienna seemed to have downright 'scared' the president. 'When you have your hand up a girl's dress,' the operative sneered, 'you expect her to scream, but you don't expect her to be scared.'[19] Better in fact that war 'begin now', over Berlin, the Russian premier had told Kennedy, than later, when even more destructive weaponry would be developed by the two empires. 'If that's true,' Kennedy had sighed, 'it's going to be a cold winter.'[20]

To America's allies, the president was disturbingly pessimistic in the aftermath of Vienna. Prime Minister Macmillan, whom Kennedy visited in London on his way back to America, noted in his diary that the president was still in shock and that for Kennedy the Vienna summit had been 'rather like somebody meeting Napoleon (at the height of his power) for the first time'.[21] 'Talking to *Time*'s correspondent Hugh Sidey, Kennedy said 'I talked about how a nuclear exchange would kill seventy million people in ten minutes and he just looked at me as if to say, "So what?"'[22] Vice President Johnson said 'Khrushchev scared the poor little fellow dead' and later imitated JFK falling to his knees in abject supplication to the Russian premier.[23]

Those seeking to understand the Russian premier's Napoleonic posturing did not have far too look. The fact was, Khrushchev – a man with a tough, peasant approach to negotiating – had been amazed by apparent American pusillanimity over Cuba, and had fully expected Castro to be overwhelmed by a full-scale American invasion force in a matter of days. When no American troops landed, however, he'd been puzzled. 'I don't understand Kennedy,' he had told his son Sergei one evening. 'What's wrong with him? Can he really be that indecisive? Perhaps he lacks determination.'[24]

The results of JFK's failed charm offensive in Vienna, on top of his Bay of Pigs 'weakness', thus tipped the scales in the now icy Cold War. The Russian premier had never underestimated President Eisenhower's imperial resolve, especially after seeing for himself the magnitude of America's industrial might and energy; but Eisenhower was like an older brother, four years older than Khrushchev, whereas 'the boy' Kennedy was twenty-three years younger – younger even than Khrushchev's son. In Moscow Khrushchev was soon heard discussing with aides 'what we can do in our [Soviet] interest and at the same time subject Kennedy to a test of strength'.[25]

If Khrushchev was an opportunist, JFK was a pragmatist. Growing up with a ruthless businessman for a father, JFK was no stranger to tough goliaths driven by their own manic agendas. What Kennedy misunderstood – as Eisenhower had – was the extent to which Khrushchev was out of his intellectual depth, and at war with the world, both at home and abroad; a denouncer of Stalin who was himself a tyrant; a man who thrived on hand-to-hand combat in the pursuit of power, like a Roman gladiator. Thus, to test Kennedy's mettle, Khrushchev had announced at Vienna that he was going to separate West Berlin from the West, a threat that had caused even Khrushchev's own fellow Presidium members to wince. Seeking to wield the initiative in inter-empire relations was one thing; but testing American resolve by risking nuclear war over *Berlin*? Should tens of millions of Russian lives be put in jeopardy, Presidium members asked, over western access to a fragment of a bombed-out German city, a place forever linked with Adolf Hitler and the Nazis, which they would then have to hand over to the very people Khrushchev and his generation had fought to the death to defeat in World War II? Even Khrushchev, pondering his own gambler's impetuousness, recognized why his colleagues were baulking at that. Thus when Kennedy belatedly made clear at Vienna, as Eisenhower had done at Camp David, that the US would never surrender West Berlin, but implied that the US would not go to war over East Berlin, Khrushchev had seen his chance: namely the opportunity to partition the still-open city permanently and physically, with a wall. At a stroke he could thereby halt the tide of East German nationals currently fleeing the so-called German Democratic Republic in their tens of thousands. He made a personal, secret tour of Berlin in an unmarked limousine. Then, in an inspired example of 'imperial' Soviet leadership, Khrushchev ramped up his public rhetoric about the many hundreds of millions who would die in a nuclear holocaust if the US became belligerent over Berlin, while secretly giving orders for barbed wire to be rolled out on August 13, 1961, followed by demolitions and the erection of the wall. He then waited for western reaction.

Had the western Allies or West Berliners begun immediately tearing down the wire, Khrushchev had in reality no idea what he would do, believing in Napoleon's dictum, *on s'engage, et puis on voit*: you throw yourself into the fray, then see what happens.

'Father was delighted' Sergei Khrushchev remembered, however, for the building of the Berlin Wall went entirely unopposed. Once again Khrushchev emerged the propaganda victor; Kennedy implicitly accepted the Soviet challenge by doing nothing beyond sending 1,500 Marines to guarantee military access to East Berlin, under the old four-power World War II agreement.

The fact was, the Berlin Wall, however unfortunate for East Germans, was a blessed relief to President Kennedy, since it finally removed Berlin as a potential *casus belli* after months of dire Soviet threats and warnings – a draconian yet peaceful resolution, at a moment when the US was facing up to its own barrier, between whites and blacks. Attacks on Freedom Riders in the South had become murderous, and then, in September 1962, the first major race riot of Kennedy's presidency took place as a crowd of 2,000 white students and troublemakers gathered on the campus of the University of Mississippi, in Oxford, to stop the first ever black student from registering. Wielding lead pipes and guns, and throwing rocks and Molotov cocktails, they met the federal marshals whom the Attorney General Robert Kennedy had sent in, with bullets – inviting bloodshed. 'Go to hell, JFK!' was one epithet they screamed; 'Go to Cuba, nigger lovers, go to Cuba!' another.[26]

President Kennedy held his fire, finally appearing on national television at 10 p.m. on Sunday September 30, 1962, in the Oval Office. Taking his cue from his predecessor during the Little Rock crisis, he appealed to the honour and dignity of Mississippians in accepting the ruling of the Fifth Circuit southern judges who had voted to send the black student, James Meredith, to Old Miss. The law was the law – even if the governor, Ross Barnett, was afraid to uphold it, as Governor Faubus had defied President Eisenhower in 1957. 'Our nation is founded on the principle that observance of the law is the eternal safeguard of liberty,' the president reminded viewers, 'and defiance of the law is the surest road to tyranny. The law which we obey includes the final rulings of the courts, as well as the enactments of our legislative bodies. Even among law-abiding men few laws are universally loved, but they are uniformly respected and not resisted . . . The eyes of the nation and all the world are upon you and upon all of us' the president ended. 'I am certain the great majority of the students will uphold that honor.'[27]

The majority did – but a vocal, armed minority, however, held out for drama and the sight of blood. Tear gas had to be fired to prevent hysterical rioters from becoming a lynch mob; photographs of US marshals wearing gas masks were flashed across the world. An Agence France Press journalist was killed by the rioters, as well as a bystander. Twenty-eight marshals were shot, and several hundred sustained other injuries from bricks and projectiles. 'People are dying in Oxford. This is the worst thing I've seen in forty-five years' Kennedy yelled at the Defense Secretary and chief of the US Army, telling them to transmit his orders to General Billingslea, a distinguished paratroop leader who'd fought in North Africa, Sicily, Italy and the Netherlands, but who, as designated area commander, had not gotten the military police in to protect Meredith, an American in his own country.[28] Finally, reluctantly, the president ordered regular army units to be flown from Tennessee to Oxford, just as Eisenhower had been compelled to do at Little Rock five years before.

No sooner had President Kennedy dealt with the crisis in Mississippi – the 'most interesting time' he'd had 'since the Bay of Pigs' he remarked in mocking understatement, as he sent 23,000 soldiers to protect Meredith – than he was compelled to meet an even greater challenge: nuclear weapons being secretly shipped by the Soviet Union to Cuba.[29]

Neither Kennedy nor his cabinet had believed the CIA warnings that Soviet vessels might be shipping nuclear missiles to Castro. Had not Khrushchev, in an exchange of letters (dubbed the 'pen pal letters'), personally denied that Russia had any intention of introducing offensive missiles into the hemisphere? Had not Khrushchev's unofficial emissaries vowed the same, in confidential meetings with Robert Kennedy and others? Above all, why would Khrushchev take such a premeditated risk, requiring not only absolute secrecy until the weapons were fully installed and operational – when they could be announced as a fait accompli – but a progression of lies that would poison hopes of better relations between East and West for another generation? It didn't make sense, prompting the president to ridicule the CIA director's dire predictions.

Kennedy did worry, however, about the political ramifications at home of a Russian military build-up in Cuba. Right-wing post-McCarthyites (McCarthy had died in 1957) had been calling Kennedy a pushover ever since the Bays of Pigs disaster, and had bayed for renewed invasion of Cuba, this time with overwhelming American force. To placate them and show that his administration would not bow to Soviet warmongering, Kennedy had approved Operation Mongoose, a CIA plan to destabilize Cuba by any means possible. He also called up another 150,000 reservists, while at the same time authorizing an official speech, by the Deputy Secretary of Defense, that would reveal for the first time, publicly and officially, that he had been mistaken when campaigning against Vice President Nixon over a perceived missile gap in favour of the Soviets. Not only was there no such gap, but the truth was – as President Eisenhower's U-2 flights had shown – the US had a huge superiority in nuclear weapons and delivery systems from the ground, sea and air. Even if the USSR did launch a first atomic strike, the US would be able to retaliate with such force it would eradicate the entire Soviet Union in a matter of hours.

The official speech mollified American hawks, but proved, in the event, a terrible miscalculation, egging the Soviet leader even further in his search for an opportunity to 'stick it' to the United States. 'Rodion Yakovlevich,' Khrushchev had said to Malinovsky, his defence minister, in April that year, 'what if we throw a hedgehog down Uncle Sam's pants?'[30] With the Berlin crisis effectively defused by the new wall, there were still many other opportunities to humiliate the American government, such as in Laos or the Congo, but these were far, far from the American continent. Using Cuba, only ninety miles from the Florida Keys, as the platform for weapons aimed at the mainland, offered Khrushchev the chance to make Americans understand how Russians felt, surrounded by American nuclear missiles from Norway to Turkey.

When Kennedy first learned of the successful transfer of nuclear weapons to Cuba, after breakfast at the White House on October 16, 1962, he was stunned by the sheer audacity of Khrushchev's new gamble. For months Khrushchev and his underlings must have deliberately lied, the president recognized, while Russian vessels quietly shipped the nuclear arsenal across the Atlantic. The new US photos – ironically taken by a U-2 spy plane, as well as by satellite – provided unmistakeable evidence. Castro's Cuba was to be transformed into a Russian nuclear missile base.

In the years that followed, commentators and historians would rake over the ashes, origins, context, steps and missteps that constituted the Cuban Missile Crisis. Kennedy's initial misreading of the situation certainly put the US government on the spot. Both Truman and Eisenhower would doubtlessly have sent in the air force to obliterate the missile sites, followed by naval and ground forces – as Castro predicted when being told of Khrushchev's plan. But Khrushchev, a wily veteran of World War II, had first checked with his marshals. As he reassured Castro, it would take a full week for the US to mount an amphibious invasion after an air strike. During that interval Khrushchev would announce he was standing behind Cuba, and warn that any US invasion would trigger World War III. A rock-solid, nuclear-tipped mutual-support pact between Cuba and the USSR would then be signed in public in November, Khrushchev promised, insisting that, in the meantime, secrecy was essential so that the Americans would be faced with a fait accompli. Once the Soviet intercontinental and medium-range ballistic missiles were *in situ* (with 50,000 accompanying troops) on November 6, it would be too late for the US to risk attacking them, Khrushchev was certain.[31] Kennedy, soft and indecisive, would have to climb down. 'The missiles will already be in place,' Khrushchev explained his reasoning later, 'ready to fire. Before taking the decision to eliminate them by military means, the United States would have to think twice. America could knock out some of those installations, but not all. What if a quarter, or one-tenth survived . . .'

Khrushchev's reasoning was correct. 'We are probably going to have to bomb them' were the president's first words, which he quickly withdrew, however, when he examined the timetable.[32] Nuclear missiles or bombs were probably already on the island, complicating any notion of instant reprisal such as US bombing, which could not be guaranteed to be 100 per cent effective. (Four decades later, historians confirmed the appraisal: a slew of medium-range Soviet missiles had arrived in mid-September, followed by their nuclear warheads on October 4, and by October 16, the nuclear warheads for the intercontinental ballistic missiles had also reached Cuba, although they remained in port on a Russian ship, waiting to be unloaded.[33] By the time Kennedy saw the U-2 photographs there were thus already 'eighty cruise missile warheads, six atomic bombs for Il-28 bombers and twelve Luna warheads' in Cuba, as Khrushchev's biographer summarized.[34])

Beyond the uncertainty about whether nuclear weapons had already arrived and were operational, there was the looming political fallout for Kennedy in having failed to credit his own CIA director's warnings. 'He thought', one biographer later wrote, 'he was going to go down as the commander-in-chief who looked the other way while the Soviets put nuclear missiles ninety miles from the United States.'[35] As he set down the photos, Kennedy realized he had been snookered.

Perhaps no plan since the blitzkrieg campaigns of Adolf Hitler – often against the advice of his generals – so demonstrated the role of individuals in history as Khrushchev's fantastical plot. 'It was his brainchild,' his aide Troyanovsky recalled, 'and he clung to it in spite of all the dangers and warnings.'[36]

To his great credit, the president finally recognized what the former Secretary of State, Dean Acheson, had said of Khrushchev: they were 'dealing with a madman'.[37] Even Khrushchev's own generals thought he had taken leave of his senses and, as Admiral Amelko remarked, that the Cuban venture was 'a crackpot scheme'.[38] The 'crackpot' Soviet premier, however, had made it impossible for Kennedy to take military action without risking a nuclear disaster, either by accident or chain of events. The question was, how would Kennedy react.

Over six fateful days in October, the president reviewed his options.

The Russians had kept silent about what they were doing. Very well, then, Kennedy determined, so would we. He deliberately said nothing to the Soviet foreign minister, Gromyko, who visited him at the White House on October 18. 'It was incredible to sit there and watch the lies coming out of his mouth' the president afterwards told an aide – but still said nothing.[39] Finally, having obtained further incontrovertible evidence of the Soviet missile bases, and having lined up his ducks, Kennedy said he was going to make an important announcement on national television.

At 9.30 p.m. on October 22, 1962, having sent copies of his text by special delivery to Moscow and the capitals of the globe, President Kennedy addressed the world. Composed in part by Ted Sorensen (who was summoned from hospital, where he was being treated for ulcers), the broadcast set out in harrowing detail the new threat ninety miles off the coast of Florida, with Soviet nuclear missiles being transferred to Cuban launch sites at that very moment 'under a cloack of secrecy and deception'. The president called upon Khrushchev to 'halt and eliminate this clandestine, reckless and provocative threat to world peace and to stable relations between our two nations' by withdrawing them from the western hemisphere, or face the consequences. In the meantime, the president announced, he had ordered the establishment of a naval blockade or 'quarantine' around Cuba, so that no more nuclear weapons could be shipped to the island. Addressing his countrymen, the president ended his speech with an appeal for calm and unity of American purpose:

> The path we have chosen for the present is full of hazards, as all paths are; but it is the one most consistent with our character and courage as a nation and our commitments around the world. The cost of freedom is always high, but Americans have always paid it. And one path we shall never choose, and that is the path of surrender or submission.
>
> Our goal is not the victory of might, but the vindication of right; not peace at the expense of freedom, but both peace and freedom, here in this hemisphere, and, we hope, around the world. God willing, that goal will be achieved.
>
> Thank you and good night.

Khrushchev, reading the advance text at the Kremlin, was shocked. Having brimmed with pride at sending to Cuba, without detection, a vast shipment of nuclear weapons that would alter the entire balance of power between the two empires at a stroke, he was now beside himself with anger, fear and frustration. He called for a crisis meeting of the Presidium. 'The missiles aren't operational yet. They're defence-less; they can be wiped out from the air in one swipe' he confessed in panic to his son.[40] To his colleagues in the Kremlin he now backpedalled, explaining he'd never wanted to provoke the threat of nuclear war, he 'just wanted to intimidate' the Americans in order to deter 'the anti-Cuban [i.e. exile] forces'.[41]

For hours the meeting became surreal, as different options were debated, from a 'big war' between Russia and the US, to a small one between Cuba and the US, with the Soviets washing their hands and handing over 'tactical' (i.e. battlefield) nuclear weapons to the Cubans. Eventually the meeting broke up in dissension. As Khrushchev's biog-rapher noted, the premier, not the president, had screwed up. 'Instead of preventing war, his masterstroke might trigger one' – and all for an island more inconsequential than Berlin, which no Berlin-type airlift from the Soviet Union could now save, nor Soviet ships even reach, since they could not breach the imminent US blockade without inciting war.[42]

Intense and secret negotiations went on between Washington and the Kremlin, while across the world people protested, blamed, excused, and vented their anxiety. Finally Khrushchev backed down. On October 24, six Russian vessels laden with military material approached the 500-mile exclusion perimeter – then stopped dead in the water. Dean Rusk, the Secretary of State, turned to McGeorge Bundy, the national security adviser, and made the remark for which he would become famous: 'We're eyeball to eyeball, and I think the other fellow just blinked.'[43]

Khrushchev had. He had gambled, and only two weeks away from triumph, had to admit defeat. In the following days, in return for Russian withdrawal, he obtained a non-binding promise from a magnanimous Kennedy that the United States would never invade Communist Cuba, and also that, some time later and without public admission of the arrangement, redundant American nuclear missiles would be removed from Turkey, on the Soviet Union's border. This was, in actuality, a not inconsiderable outcome, though bringing the world to the very brink of nuclear war to achieve it was not considered a victory by anybody in the Kremlin, or in Havana.

To his own surprise, President John F. Kennedy emerged a global hero. All twenty members of the Organization of American States had voted to support Kennedy's quarantine, and thereafter continued to impose it as a commercial quarantine. Instead of becoming the Lenin of Latin America, Fidel Castro became a pariah; his Communist revolution, for all its supposedly idealistic socialist aims and objectives, was stillborn. Furious, Castro bad-mouthed Khrushchev ('Son of a bitch ... bastard ... asshole ... No *cojones. Maricón*'), and excoriated the 44,000 departing Russian troops and their precious hardware, claiming later that he could never find out who had dreamed up such a crazy scheme in the first place.

In the greatest international crisis since World War II, Kennedy had shown firmness and great statesmanship, overruling the hawks in his own country and ensuring the peaceful resolution of an extraordinary adventure. Without bluff and bluster, Khrushchev 'was lost' and would soon be deposed.[44] To his chagrin, moreover, it was Mao Zedong who took over the propaganda role of godfather to the Marxist-Leninist revolutionary world, accusing Khrushchev's Cuban policy of being nothing but 'adventurism' followed by 'capitulationism'.[45]

As 1962 came to a close, with the Cuban Missile Crisis thankfully over, President Kennedy's approval rating rose to the upper seventies.

While the Soviet Union retreated into an ageing imperial shell, its agriculture still failing to feed its people and its industry incapable of furnishing the things people really wanted, from refrigerators to cars, the United States seemed to have overcome its shame over the sputnik programme, and to be exploding with young, creative energy in manufacturing, commerce, science, pop music, pop art, literature, and access to college education. In a special one-hour ABC television interview on December 16, 1962, the president was asked about his two years in office to date. Had they matched his expectations?

Kennedy shook his head. The problems he'd encountered were, he said, 'more difficult than I had imagined they were. The responsibilities placed on the United States are greater than I imagined them to be, and there are greater limitations upon our ability to bring about a favorable result than I imagined them to be. And I think that is probably true of anyone who becomes the president, because there is such a difference between those who advise or speak or legislate, and between the man who must select from the various alternatives proposed and say that this shall be the policy of the United States.' Wistfully he pointed out that 'If you take the wrong course, and on occasion I have, the president bears the burden of the responsibility quite rightly. The advisers', he added tartly, 'may move on to new advice.'[46]

This was John F. Kennedy at his most reflective – and realistic. Nevertheless he did allow himself and his American viewers a brief moment of pride in the accomplishments of the United States as a great power since World War II – 'One hundred and eighty million people' who, 'for almost twenty years, have been the great means of defending the world against the Nazi threat, and since then against the Communist threat, and if it were not for us, the Communists would be dominant in the world today . . . I think that is a pretty good record with 6 per cent of the world's population. I think we ought to be rather pleased with ourselves this Christmas.'[47]

In the glow of prosperity (the US had emerged from a minor recession in 1960–1, and was beginning to boom), as well as peaceful resolution of the Cuban Missile Crisis, the president enumerated to his secretary the twenty-seven probable troubles requiring solution in 1963.[48] Neither civil rights nor Vietnam were on the list.

Like Eisenhower at the time of the *Brown* vs *Board of Education* case, Kennedy hoped against hope he could defer the matter of civil rights to his second term, after the 1964 election, walking in the meantime on eggshells in order to placate both whites and blacks. Yet the very energy that was impelling the 1960s – with gross national product (GNP) rising by 4 per cent per capita in 1962 – made black leaders less rather than more patient. The very aspirations aroused by Kennedy's 1960 rhetoric could not now be stopped, or shelved, merely because the president feared he might then lose the 1964 election. A civil rights voting bill the president introduced to Congress in February 1963 was mocked by blacks as whitewashing. In April, the city of Birmingham, Alabama, saw protest marches, and the arrest of Dr King for leading them. By May, when, released from jail, Dr King turned to children for his marches, the temperature rose higher still. Thousands were arrested. Alarming photos were transmitted across the world of Eugene 'Bull' Connor, the Commissioner of Public Safety, turning fire hoses on 1,000 black children as they came out of a Baptist church, and German shepherd dogs being used against them. After the humiliation of the Cuban Missile Crisis, Radio Moscow now had ample opportunity to hit back, in the court of world opinion.

Kennedy was called upon to get off the fence and to use his presidential bully pulpit, whether or not it sundered his own or the Democratic Party's re-election chances. He resisted, but as a summer of increasing civil rights demonstrations in the face of southern intransigence promised to grow hotter and hotter, the day of reckoning came. George Wallace, the governor of Alabama, arrived on the campus of the state university on June 11, 1963, vowing he would personally halt court-ordered desegregation by stopping the university's first two black students from registering.

Many had mocked Kennedy's book, *Profiles in Courage*, as the work of Ted Sorensen, Kennedy's talented young speechwriter from Nebraska. Yet the notion of political courage as the willingness to challenge conventional power structures had been Kennedy's own, and he had been sincere in his admiration of those figures in political history who had shown it. Now, at last, his own turn had come. Hitherto he had, like Eisenhower, sheltered behind his legal and constitutional responsibility to carry out the laws of the land, as chief executive of the nation. Now, in an eighteen-minute television address at 8 p.m. on June 11, having federalized the Alabama National Guard under his own ultimate command, the president set out the inequities of education, society, business, finance, employment and health care as they affected black people of America. 'This is not even a legal or legislative issue alone,' he declared in the 'deeper', stronger voice Eleanor Roosevelt had recommended he adopt, shortly before she died. 'We are confronted primarily with a moral issue. It is as old as the Scriptures,' he added for the benefit of segregationists in the Bible Belt, 'and is as clear as the American Constitution.' Who 'among us' would change 'his skin' if faced by unending segregation and humiliation in public places, in restaurants, public schools, and in the denial of the right to vote; 'Who among us would then be content with the counsels of patience and delay?' he asked. 'We face, therefore, a moral crisis as a country and as a people. It cannot be met with repressive police action. It cannot be left to increased demonstrations in the streets . . . It is time to act in the Congress, in your state and local legislative body, and above all in our daily lives. A great change is at hand, and our task, our obligation, is to make that revolution, that change, peaceful and constructive for all.'

With those words, the president announced he would be introducing a new comprehensive civil rights bill into Congress. Aware that this might mean the loss of the southern Democrats, he'd told his legislative counsellor he was well aware that 'I can kiss the South goodbye.' But he had, at last, chosen sides.[49]

Led by Martin Luther King Jr, a march on Washington took place at the end of August 1963. 'The Vandals are coming to sack Rome' one Washington newspaper warned, but the march proved peaceful, and the voices of Mahalia Jackson and Dr King made history. Kennedy was moved. 'He's damned good. Damned good!' he remarked with genuine admiration as he watched and listened to King's passionate 'I have a dream' speech on television.[50] After the march was over, he invited Dr King to a private meeting in the Cabinet Room of the White House, and there congratulated the preacher – who was twelve years younger than himself – in person. Together, the two most inspirational figures of their generation began detailed discussions on how enough votes could be secured in Congress for a civil rights bill. 'It's going to be a crusade, then' said seventy-four-year-old Philip Randolph, founder of the Brotherhood of Sleeping Car Porters. 'And I think that nobody can lead this crusade but you, Mr President.'[51] Taking a deep breath, Kennedy vowed he would.

Even as civil rights marches and protests dominated the agenda at home, meanwhile, the difficulty of leading and cheerleading the democratic nations of the world proved just as challenging, especially in a prosperous empire bristling with hawks. In June, the president gave a deeply idealistic speech on world peace at the American University in Washington to reinforce his view of the impending negotiations in Moscow over a limited nuclear test-ban treaty which, to the disgust of the Chinese Communists, the Russians agreed to sign on July 25. 'What kind of peace do we speak?' Kennedy asked rhetorically. 'Not a Pax Americana, enforced on the world by American weapons of war' but one in which inevitable tensions were eased by 'mutual tolerance' and respect.

In the light of the US–Soviet brokered settlement reached in Laos, long considered the 'hot spot' of South East Asia, as well as the ultimately peaceful resolution of the Cuban Missile Crisis, this sounded noble and realistic – but as Khrushchev pointed out to Averell Harriman (the chief US negotiator of the test-ban treaty), such words, though broadcast uncut on Soviet radio and television, did not make Americans any the less 'imperialist'. There were, Khrushchev explained, 'many capitalists who only deal with matters in their own country, whereas an imperialist is a capitalist who interferes in other people's affairs, as you are in South Vietnam.'[52]

Coming from Khrushchev, after his imperialist fiasco in Cuba, this was rich – but not unmerited. Two years before, President de Gaulle had warned Kennedy that intervention in Vietnam 'will be an endless entanglement', as the French had cause to know. 'You will sink into a bottomless military and political quagmire, however much you spend in men and money.'[53] He was right, but had little idea how loud the drums of war echoed in the citadel of American democracy. Twenty years before, Republican isolationists had stopped the president from committing troops to defend democracy in Europe; now, Kennedy had spent the first two years of his presidency attempting to shoot down hawks he had himself appointed to his administration, in an effort to show bipartisanship over American security: Dean Rusk, Robert MacNamara, Walt Rostow and the brothers William and McGeorge Bundy. The president 'expressed his strong feeling' against committing US troops to Vietnam, since America's primary allies, France and Britain, were against such a move, as the minutes of the National Security Meeting on November 14, 1961 had recorded. Going to war in Vietnam without the support of allies would invoke 'sharp domestic criticism' as well as 'strong objections from other nations in the world' the president warned, pointing out that he could make 'a rather strong case against intervening in an area 10,000 miles away against 16,000 [Vietcong] guerrillas,' backed by 200,000 nationalist Communist troops in North Vietnam – a region where 'millions have been spent for years and with no success'.

Instead of simply silencing the hawks, however, the president had sought to placate them by agreeing to what turned out to be a disastrous compromise – sending, between 1961 and 1963, some 16,000 US military 'advisers', tasked with propping up the thoroughly corrupt and ineffective, undemocratic government of the self-appointed South Vietnamese ruler, Ngo Dinh Diem.

Kennedy had no illusions. After all, he had fought in bitter combat against the Japanese in the Solomon Islands in 1943, and knew the level of air, navy and infantry required to dislodge entrenched enemy troops, particularly guerrillas, in tropical conditions. He had been to Vietnam (North and South) in 1951, where he had concluded that the French were not only wrong to remain in colonial occupation of the country, but also deluded in thinking they could ever subdue Ho Chi Minh's essentially nationalist uprising. He acknowledged in a press conference in December 1962 the 'great difficulty' in 'fighting a guerrilla war', especially, he emphasized, 'in terrain as difficult as South Vietnam'.[54] He told his navy chief, Arleigh Burke, that the distinguished fighting admiral was 'wrong' when he said the United States *had* to fight in Laos, and had declined to give further CIA support to anti-Communist General Phoumi Nosavan, who failed miserably in fighting the Communist Pathet Lao. 'General Phoumi is a total shit' Kennedy told a journalist friend, and he rejected Admiral Burke's insistence that, if not in Laos, at least in South Vietnam the US must stand and fight.[55] 'And if it's not South Vietnam, is it going to be Thailand?' Burke had sneered – to the president's discomfort.[56]

Kennedy appreciated that great empires could only prosper when able to establish and protect their sources of wealth and sustenance; in doing so, they had to focus on vital spheres of influence, not be sidetracked into expensive and distracting conflict that only added to their headaches. President Eisenhower had overruled his advisers and had declined to help the French maintain Vietnam as a non-Communist colony. Having hopefully mollified the hawks of his administration and the Pentagon, JFK desperately tried to keep Vietnam off the administration's agenda, out of its press conferences, and away from the front pages of American newspapers, in the forlorn hope he could erase it as a political issue in America and in due course either negotiate a settlement, or abandon President Diem and his associates to their own national destiny. But patience was required, he felt. Divided Berlin – where on July 26, 1963 Kennedy had given the massively popular *'Ich bin ein Berliner'* speech before a million cheering West Berliners – was still the most potent symbol of the Cold War and western democratic resolve. But South Vietnam, where Buddhist monks were incinerating themselves in protest against Diem's corrupt regime? Senator Mike Mansfield, the Senate Majority Leader, advised the president not to listen to the CIA and the military, who were gung-ho to exploit the opportunity for bloodshed far away from Washington control, and stressed the 'the relatively limited importance of the area in terms of specific US interests'. In words that would ring through subsequent American history, the senator urged the president to ask himself whether 'South Viet Nam' was truly as 'important to us' as the supposed advocates for fighting there claimed.[57] Kennedy nodded, as he calculated how a withdrawal could be effected.[58] 'If I tried to pull out completely now from Vietnam,' he explained to an aide after talking with Mansfield, 'we would have another Joe McCarthy scare on our hands, but I can do it after I'm re-elected' in 1964.

Beset by other troubles and issues, from civil rights to re-election concerns, and finding his group of advisers on the subject of Vietnam equally divided between hawks and doves, Kennedy now made the same intrinsic mistake he'd made over the Bay of Pigs and Operation Mongoose. To appease the right he appointed a fiercely anti-Communist Republican, the former senator Cabot Lodge, as the new American ambassador to Saigon, and in a cable he would regret to the day he died, gave Lodge the green light to support a coup against Diem that would supposedly usher in a military junta, with whom the CIA and the military could better work in fighting the Vietcong insurgency.

How this American-sponsored junta in South Vietnam could be seen as an outpost of 'democracy', and whether it would prove any less corrupt or more effective in administering the Asian country, were questions Kennedy failed to ask in the autumn of 1963, let alone demand an answer to. He did not have Eisenhower's experience and prestige as a general in high command, dealing with the military; moreover he lacked Eisenhower's 'hidden hand' intimacy with the CIA. Most of all, he lacked Eisenhower's luck.

Belatedly, in the days after cabling Lodge, he realized he'd made a poor, indeed potentially awful decision, and tried to recall or reverse the cable. He was, he realized, trapped; if the coup failed, the US would look exactly like the nefarious, imperial, meddling Uncle Sam it had been portrayed as over the Bay of Pigs. 'If we miscalculate, we could lose our entire position in South East Asia overnight' he signalled to Lodge.[59] Were it to succeed, though, it would still look the same, with no guarantee the new junta, even with American help, would be any more successful in fighting the Communist insurgency than Diem.

The Vietnam coup thus went ahead, with secret American backing, at 1.45 p.m. on November 1, 1963. President Diem and his brother were taken prisoner on the orders of the South Vietnamese generals, and despite Kennedy's attempts to arrange for the brothers to be flown out of the country, they were swiftly assassinated in the personnel carrier in which they were travelling, along with the $1 million in cash the CIA was supplying to ease their exile. The chairman of the Joint Chiefs of Staff, General Maxwell Taylor (who did not favour the plan for a coup), recalled how, when the news was passed to Kennedy, he 'leaped to his feet and rushed from the room with a look of shock and dismay on his face'.[60] Upstairs, he burst into tears, as Jackie recalled.[61] Like Julius Caesar, he saw it not only as a mistake, but as an omen.

Kennedy blamed himself. He went into depression, knowing he had been party not only to a *coup d'état*, in a faraway, difficult country whose fortunes should not have skewed American strategy, but also to the killing in cold blood of Diem, a man he'd met and admired. Was this the act of a great democracy, that had overthrown the British yoke in 1776 and set down the world's most precious political document, the Constitution of the United States? 'I should never have given my consent to it without a round-table conference,' he said in a statement taped for the record three days later. 'I was shocked by the death of Diem and Nhu. I'd met Diem with Justice Douglas many years ago. He was an extraordinary character. While he became increasingly difficult in the last months, nevertheless over a ten-year period, he'd held his country together, maintained its independence under very adverse conditions. The way he was killed made it particularly abhorrent.'[62]

A fortnight later Kennedy was himself assassinated, seemingly by a lone gunman, Lee Harvey Oswald, who was in turn murdered while in police custody two days later.[63]

Part Three: Private Life

JFK's father suffered lifelong stomach problems, and was rendered mute and unable to walk by a massive stroke in 1961; his sister Eunice also suffered from mild Addison's disease, but JFK's ill health was of a completely different order, resulting in disabilities almost as severe as FDR's polio and heart disease, and requiring the same magnitude of courage. Scarlet fever, chicken pox, bronchitis, German measles, mumps, whooping cough, ear infections; these were easily diagnosable, if almost incessant, illnesses during JFK's childhood. During adolescence and early manhood, however, his afflictions became more serious and less easy to identify, beyond 'colitis', suspected leukaemia and gastritis. He neither smoked nor drank, and only ate bland food such as soup. Doctors had no idea what caused his frequent physical collapses.

At college, and with the help of his best friend from school (who was homosexual and adored him slavishly), JFK began a checkered romantic career as 'Don Juan' or 'Don John Kennedy', as he described himself.[64] Mozart's Don Giovanni, had, according to his servant Leporello, racked up some 2,085 conquests. It was a catalogue raisonné that JFK was resolved to match in his own lifetime. Handsome, witty, educated, well travelled and exciting to be with, against all the medical odds he seemed to be succeeding when, at twenty-four, Ensign John F. Kennedy fell in love in late 1941 with a beautiful, exotic – and married – siren.

Six years older than JFK, Inga Arvad was the only woman who came near to stealing his almost proverbially stone heart; indeed, Inga might well have become Mrs John F. Kennedy had war and J. Edgar Hoover not intervened. Radiantly attractive, sensitive and intelligent, Inga exuded more charm even than her young Massachusetts beau. A former Miss Denmark, then successful journalist, she had followed her second husband, Hungarian anthropologist and film-maker Paul Fejos, to New York. After retraining at the Columbia School of Journalism, she was writing an interview column for the *Washington Herald* when introduced to Kennedy.

For the first and only time in his life, JFK became utterly infatuated and they quickly became a Washington item, causing Inga's jealous husband to pay for a private detective to trail her, and her female colleagues to denounce her to the FBI as a possible enemy spy. (While in Denmark in the 1930s Inga had got exclusive interviews with Hitler and a number of senior Nazis in neighbouring Germany.)

The denunciations were groundless, but once the FBI began a surveillance operation on Mrs Fejos, alarm bells sounded when the man staying overnight at her apartment was identified as the son of the US ambassador to Great Britain. More worrying still, in the case of a woman being investigated as a possible German spy, the junior officer was found to be working in the office of the chief of naval intelligence, raising the possibility of a scandal neither the navy nor the ambassador to Great Britain were keen, in the wake of Pearl Harbor, to see explode. JFK was therefore swiftly removed from his intelligence post in Washington and sent to Charleston, South Carolina, where he was assigned to training and security duties.

Warned not to continue the affair, JFK simply refused to comply – indeed begged Inga to marry him. Head over heels in love, he wanted to have a baby with her. 'Dammit, Jack, she's already married!' his father protested, but Jack 'said he didn't care', Inga's newspaper editor recalled.[65]

To the end of his days, JFK kept Inga's love letters, as she kept his. But the love affair, ignited just as the US Navy suffered the worst defeat in its history, was itself doomed to defeat, Inga realized – especially when told so by none other than Ambassador Kennedy. To Inga, JFK's ambition seemed both real and achievable, despite his youth, given his personality, intelligence and talents. Transcripts of their lovemaking, taped by the FBI as part of their ongoing investigation, revealed not only repeated carnal relations but JFK's relentless dissections of world affairs, the probable future course of the war, and his ambition to become president of the United States.

'We are so well matched' Inga reflected, knowing marriage was impossible yet certain JFK would one day get to the very pinnacle of politics. 'Should I die before you reach to the top of the golden ladder, then Jack, dear – if there is a life after death, as you believe in – be I in heaven or hell, that is the moment when I shall stretch a hand out and try to keep you balancing on that – the most precarious of all steps.'[66]

Even had JFK followed his smitten heart rather than his head and married Inga, pursuing thereafter a career as a writer and political journalist (as he did briefly, after the war), could Inga have altered his Don Juan behaviour? The serious biographer must doubt it. Nevertheless Inga was, without doubt, the only woman in JFK's life who bewitched him *von Kopf bis Fuss* ('from head to toe', as Marlene Dietrich had mesmerizingly sung in *The Blue Angel*), and of whom he was sexually jealous: a true femme fatale. Blonde, quick-witted, instinctively empathetic, gifted in languages, well travelled, experienced in life, not afraid of sex, profoundly feminine and so beautiful men old and young melted before her, 'Inga Binga' (as JFK dubbed her) tormented the young ensign – indeed his decision to leave his 'safe' shore-based post in Charleston, South Carolina, and volunteer for active duty at sea, despite his chronic ill health, can be seen as a crazed reaction to the battle for Inga – a battle he could only have won by getting himself dishonourably discharged from the navy, in wartime, and ignoring his father's warnings. Given his patriotism and vaulting ambition, that was something he would not do.

In the Solomon Islands, where he played Sinatra love ballads incessantly on a portable Victrola between night sorties behind the Japanese lines, JFK dreamed of Inga. He seemed unfazed by the prospect of death, impelled by love and his old standby, his self-deprecating sense of humour. When he crashed his PT boat against the dock, racing back to base after one mission, and faced court martial for recklessly endangering government property, he was unapologetic and is reported to have said, 'Well, you can't stop that PT-109!'[67]

Certainly JFK could not be stopped after his affair with Inga; indeed there was something almost suicidal in his behaviour. Telling Inga in a letter how much he longed to see her again, he wrote 'If anything happens to me I have this knowledge that if I had lived to be a hundred, I could only have improved the quantity of my life, not the quality. This sounds gloomy as hell . . . I'll cut it . . . You are the only person I'd say it to anyway. As a matter of fact knowing you has been the brightest point in an extremely bright twenty-six years'.[68]

How had a privileged, repeatedly sick, gangly youth got himself into combat anyway, his colleagues wondered? Wherever he went, men were magnetized. His courage in saving his surviving crew after the sinking of his PT boat would become legendary, but when captaining a subsequent vessel, PT-59, he demonstrated even more determination under fire, as well as being promoted executive officer of his squadron with a perfect 4.0 rating for overall performance and leadership. Though JFK had written lovelorn letters to Inga from the tropics, he weighed only 140 lb, was yellow, barely able to walk for back pain, and 'just looked like hell' Inga later told her son.[69] It was over.

Along with broken health and the disillusioning, death-filled experience of war, the end of the affair with Inga marked the end of innocence in the life of JFK. His brother Joe Jr was killed while courageously piloting a navy bomber packed with explosives on a secret mission over England in August 1944.[70] Then in September, his sister Kathleen's young husband, Captain Lord Hartington, was killed in Belgium during the Allied breakout from Normandy.

With Inga elsewhere, his brother dead and his sister widowed, JFK alternated between depression and a sort of manic determination to make every second count in terms of his two obsessions: politics and women. On a whim, shortly after his election to Congress, he is believed to have secretly married a pretty, petite, blonde, twice-divorced Inga lookalike, Durie Malcolm, an Episcopalian socialite in Palm Beach.

If true, and if JFK thought this act of insouciant defiance of his fate would go down well in the Kennedy compound, he was much mistaken. His father 'went ballistic' recalled his friend Chuck Spalding, who was ordered by Joe Kennedy to get the marriage 'eradicated' at the County Court, which (in days of handwritten paper records) was swiftly done.[71]

The problem of an unwise first marriage was less fatal to JFK's political aspirations, however, than the revelation, in 1947, that his recurrent illnesses were due to the fact that he was slowly dying of a fatal disease – Addison's. On a trip to Ireland and England as a young congressman, JFK was given this shocking diagnosis by the king's doctor, Sir Daniel Davis. Seeing JFK's suspiciously bronzed flesh, he diagnosed advanced Addison's disease – and gave Kennedy perhaps a year to live. Aboard the Queen Elizabeth on the way home, JFK again fell ill and it seemed even that prognosis was optimistic; a Catholic priest administered the last rites. Fortunately for Kennedy, an American doctor Dr George Thorn, had pioneered the use of synthetic cortisone to treat Addisonian patients. In great secrecy the congressman began taking Thorn's medication, and the terminal disease was arrested – for how long no doctor could say. In 1951, on a visit to Japan, JFK suffered a repeat Addisonian crisis, and was again given the last rites – but survived.

Life, which had always been a game that JFK played competitively and for maximum amusement, now became a serious challenge: how, like FDR after polio, to become a real politician with a clear vision, and cheat death, to fulfil not only his own long-standing ambition, but the dreams of his family, the good wishes of his friends, the expectations of colleagues, and the hopes of his growing number of supporters who believed in his sad-looking, disabled yet magnetic leadership ability.

As in Shakespeare's portrait of young Prince Hal, JFK now threw himself into his political career in Washington while ensuring his Massachusetts base was covered. Politics – in terms of issues and personalities – proved to be a new battlefield. Political calculation marked every decision, even that of marriage. Interviewed in the late 1940s, Congressman Kennedy claimed he'd like to marry a 'homebody type of girl. One who is quiet and would make a nice, understanding wife and mother for [my] children. The color of her hair or her height wouldn't make much difference. Just as long as she's a homebody is all that counts. When I find her, even politics will take a back seat then.'[72]

This was garbage. JFK neither looked for such a consort seriously, nor would he ever allow politics to take a back seat; indeed after the affair with Inga and the putative marriage to Durie Malcolm, he showed no inclination to marry at all. So little did he date 'homebody' types, or even eligible women, in fact, that his father, as his chief funder, launderer and political rooter, grew anxious over his son's playboy reputation, as did others on JFK's staff. Marrying Inga, a divorced woman, would have spelled the end of any presidential aspirations (as would his secretly expunged nuptials with Durie) – but remaining unmarried made Kennedy an equally vulnerable candidate.

It was in this way that Senator John Fitzgerald Kennedy, the most eligible bachelor in Congress following his victory over Senator Lodge in 1952, surrendered to his father's importunings and the following year took Jackie Bouvier, daughter of divorced parents but a Roman Catholic, as his bride.

Jackie Bouvier was well mannered (she had been named Debutante of the Year in the 1947–8 Newport, Rhode Island, season) and well educated, having attended Vassar, the Sorbonne and George Washington University. Significantly, she was working as the Inquiring Photographer on the *Washington Times-Herald* – the same position that Inga Arvad had held – when JFK met her. There the similarity ended, however. Jackie was twelve years younger than the senator, and not considered conventionally beautiful, with wide shoulders, no figure, size-ten shoes, an accomplished equestrienne and a budding cultural snob par excellence. As an impecunious stepdaughter of the very wealthy Standard Oil heir, Hugh D. Auchincloss of Hammersmith Farm in Connecticut, she was also obsessed with what she termed 'real money'.[73]

There was tantalizingly little initial interest or affection on JFK's part. A sullen, desultory romance ensued with but a single postcard sent by JFK to his fiancée when out of town. When one of JFK's ushers danced with her at the big wedding on September 12, 1953, and asked when had she first fallen in love with JFK, Jackie stopped dancing and demanded: 'Who says I am in love with him?'[74] Yet when a photographer took JFK's picture as he danced with another attractive woman

– rumoured to be one of his paramours – she smashed the photo-grapher's camera.[75]

Jackie's efforts at self-protection were futile, however. Like most women who fell under his spell, she adored him, in her case as help-lessly as she'd loved her own errant father, 'Black Jack' Bouvier, who had proven too drunk to give her away on her wedding day. Thus began the tragic marriage of Mr and Mrs John F. Kennedy.

In *The Twelve Caesars*, Suetonius described the private life of the emperor Caligula with undisguised disgust. 'It would be hard to say whether the way he got married, the way he dissolved his marriages, or the way he behaved as a husband was the more disgraceful.' Certainly there were many sad similarities between Caligula's and JFK's marital and extramarital conduct. According to his friends, JFK dated more women during his *fiançailles* than ever, as if determined to prove he would not be tamed. Certainly he refused to give up the chase after-wards, as if punishing Jackie for imagining they could be a real couple.

JFK's travels in pre-war Europe had given him an understanding of the European class system, a set-up whereby the privileged upper classes could, behind a mask of 'polite behaviour', do exactly as they pleased in whatever beds they pleased, protected by a hierarchical social struc-ture and strict libel laws. This amorality was much to JFK's liking, as the privileged son of an American multimillionaire; its ethos would always define his reckless private life. However, in contrast to his wife's sincere and gushing admiration for all things European – clothes, cuisine, history – JFK was, and remained, all-American in his tastes, interests and, above all, in his aggressive approach to living. He loved compet-itive sports – football, touch-football, sailing, golf. He loved dancing, show business, Broadway and Hollywood, priding himself on bedding more stars of the silver screen in his career than almost any actor, from Gene Tierney and Grace Kelly to Jayne Mansfield and Marilyn Monroe. Uncertain how long he had to live, he demanded – and got – the maximum out of life, whether in politics or in pleasure. As a journalist friend, Gloria Emerson, later recalled, at weekend parties he walked around 'half naked, with just a towel wrapped around him – all bone, all rib, all shank. You have to have tremendous self-assurance to do that. I've never met anyone like that again. It was the audaciousness, the intensity, the impatience, the brusqueness. Here was a man who wasn't going to wait; he was going to get what he wanted. He was going to go from the House to the Senate to the White House. And it was quite thrilling.'[76]

In 1954 JFK's sister Pat married the British actor Peter Lawford, who then facilitated JFK's intimacy with Sinatra's jet-setting entertainment mafia, the so-called 'Rat Pack'. Though as president he would eventually be forced to spurn Sinatra and his naked poolside orgies for fear of stories leaking in the press, JFK's recklessness did not diminish. He despised Jackie's pretentious social and artistic snobbery (she was nicknamed 'the Deb' in the Kennedy family), and found her whims and moodiness unbearable when he was in almost constant pain. His life by 1953 had reduced to two demands: sexual distraction or serious, challenging political engagement, neither of which, given the differences of their personalities, Jackie supplied. ('Oh, Jack, I'm so sorry for you that I'm such a dud' she apologized.[77]) He had always been cruelly indifferent to women, at heart – save for Inga, who had broken his. Now he took it out on Jackie that, for purely political and dynastic reasons, he had felt obliged to take her as his wife: their wedding, their honeymoon and their marriage, in his eyes, as much a sham as his first – merely more pretentious.

For Jackie, this was far more than she had bargained for. By 1959, it was later reported, her feelings had turned from love to despair – as was all too understandable, given JFK's behaviour. She had nursed him through his back surgeries but had got little in return since, like JFK's parents, siblings, friends and colleagues she was sworn to secrecy about the severity of his ailments and the extent of his womanizing. Concerned lest his sexually transmitted diseases might have made him impotent, JFK had had himself tested for fertility, the results of which were positive. Nevertheless Jackie had miscarried once, and was understandably careful when she became pregnant again in 1956, at the time of the Chicago Democratic Convention. Once the politicking was over, JFK simply flew to Europe without her, disappearing on a privately rented yacht in the Mediterranean with his younger brother and a fellow philanderer, wealthy William Thomson, to 'relax' with young women. When Jackie haemorrhaged and the baby died in America, JFK simply sailed on, only returning home when a friend in the Senate, George Smathers, called from Washington and read him the riot act. It was small wonder Jackie eventually wanted out, demanding, it was said, a huge money-guarantee from the 'paymaster', Joseph P. Kennedy, for her to drop her divorce application and continue as the senator's spouse for the duration of the 1960 presidential election campaign. Convinced that he could ensure his son's election, but that Jackie's defection could damn it, Joseph Kennedy willingly agreed.

When JFK won the election – just – Jackie played fair to the agreement. JFK, however, had not made any agreement regarding his conduct. When asked by his deputy speechwriter, Dick Goodwin, whether being president in the White House cramped his philandering, given the intense media scrutiny, he grinned and shook his head. 'Dick,' he responded, 'it's never been easier!'[78]

Jackie had loyally borne JFK two healthy children – a girl in 1957 and a boy in 1960. In the White House, to her great credit, she made a new role for herself as First Lady. She would not be a toiling feminist and defender of the rights of the poor, like Eleanor Roosevelt, nor would she stay out of the limelight under her mother's watchful eye, like shy Beth Truman. Nor did she aspire to quiet TV dinners with her husband once he returned from the Oval Office to the family quarters, as Mamie Eisenhower had done. Instead Jackie set herself the task of becoming not only the mother of young children in the White House, complete with nursery and crèche, but also the photogenic young doyenne of modern taste, fashionable clothes and appreciation of cultural history, casting a spell on invited foreign dignitaries, artists and diplomats in the manner of a twentieth-century Cleopatra, while decorating with flair a hideaway country estate, Glen Ora, that she rented in Virginia's horse country, where she was able to indulge her love of fox-hunting.

Warming to his role of father, JFK's attitude towards Jackie softened, even if his extramarital behaviour didn't change. As Jackie became a world celebrity in her own right as First Lady, he also began to appreciate her style, famously remarking in Paris, on his way to Vienna, that he was but the 'man who accompanied Jacqueline Kennedy to Paris'.[79] His wit, self-deprecating and worldly-wise, together with Jackie's trend-setting fashion sense and dignity, made the Kennedys an entrancing couple, especially when photographed or filmed with their children (which Jackie only permitted by tasteful photographers such as Richard Avedon).

Behind the super-elegant facade, however, JFK found himself more challenged by the job of president than he'd expected, and more and more in need of medication, both pharmaceutical and extramarital. The tougher the responsibilities of presidency became, the fiercer grew his addiction, and the more his staff worried – especially once his father was out of the picture, following his stroke. It was as if Jackie's immaculately dressed, beautifully manicured posing (she adopted a husky whisper when talking to people she wished to beguile), though graceful and fashionable, only reinforced JFK's desire to 'stick it' to those who bowed to such elitism and snobbery. His mother Rose's cold, dry insistence on aping the manners of the upper classes, as well as her obsession with top dressmakers, had infuriated him as a child, and was now replicated as Jackie and Rose fought for the title of 'best-dressed woman in America'. For all his legendary compassion, JFK seemed unable to see that such pretensions were their answer to otherwise crushing marital infidelity.

The more Jackie dressed, the more, it seemed, JFK undressed, even receiving visitors in the nude, such as his paralyzed father's nurse, after his father's stroke. 'All I could really think of was what in heaven's name does one say to a naked president?' Rita Dallas later recalled – and how she had thrown a washcloth into the bath with the words 'For heaven's sake, cover up.'[80] Such playfulness masked, however, a much deeper, almost pathological subversion by which, in his private life, JFK deliberately cocked a snook at decorum. In public, he was famed for his quick, intelligent articulateness, which his speechwriter Ted Sorensen further refined, adding noble cadences; but in private, impatient with those who bored, crossed or disappointed him, JFK cussed and swore like a proverbial trooper, his speech peppered with 'prick' and 'shit' and 'fuck' and 'nuts' and 'bastard' and 'son of a bitch'.[81] A speed-reader with a photographic memory, he was famously able to absorb information and distil its essence. But working at high velocity, at once inspirational and realistic, intelligent and compassionate, his private life, he felt, was his own, to do as he pleased. And what pleased him was casting off the uniform of the presidency, almost literally, as he sought nudity and 'fun' in the White House swimming pool, or the family compound at Palm Beach.

Because he was president, the secret services were able (and obliged) to protect such privacy, even as, amazed, they witnessed the leader of the free world casting caution to the four winds and behaving, when Jackie was not present, like a teenager whose parents were on vacation. His White House staff became his pimps, escorting 'Jane Does' into the residence whenever Jackie was away, without logging their names or bothering with security at the gates. The White House pool often resembled a Roman bathhouse, the scene of orgy after orgy, which the secret services were compelled to protect both from assassins and from public view.

'Was he really that bad?' an Argentine girlfriend, who had known JFK from the age of nineteen, later asked, distressed at revelations concerning Kennedy's many hundreds of extramarital 'conquests', ranging from mafia trollops like Judith Campbell, to well brought up daughters of the upper class. 'How could he have had the *time?*'[82]

The answer was perhaps that the president spent so little time with each of his belles. Even Jackie, according to her psychotherapist (who spoke after her death), complained that JFK had no idea of foreplay. The president seemed not to be interested in loving intimacy – something which remained a distant and somewhat forbidding city. In matters of public policy such as poverty or mental retardation or racial oppression, JFK felt and could uninhibitedly show curiosity, compassion and a determination to effect change through political courage; but in matters of after-hours distraction he became, as his life went on and he continued to cheat death, simply too addicted to stop. It was, moreover, an area where not even his closest male friends, marvelling at the polarities of his character, could restrain him. Thus in his public life he could be the most disciplined and rational of men, yet in his private life could simply ignore danger or even – perhaps especially – decency. At the end of a private lunch with his friend Chuck Spalding in JFK's suite in the Carlyle in New York, JFK asked Spalding's new young girlfriend if she'd like to go into the bedroom with him for 'dessert' – which she did. Recalling the episode almost thirty years later, Spalding could not explain why he had neither stopped JFK, nor called him on his *droit de seigneur* behaviour, then or afterwards. 'I didn't . . . I just didn't' Spalding shrugged. 'That's how he was.'[83] And that was the man Spalding loved, as a friend.

This was, perhaps, the crux of the matter. While JFK seemed unable, after Inga, to show love in a reciprocal, caring relationship, this did not stop people – of both sexes – loving *him*. Jackie's response was exactly the same as that of Spalding. She called JFK 'Bunny' for his insatiable need for sex, and would at times introduce visitors to her twenty-three-year-old secretary with the words 'This is Miss Turnure – with whom my husband is sleeping.'[84] Two young campaign assistants, twenty-year-old Priscilla Wear and Jill Cowan, were put on the White House payroll as secretaries, yet were known to all as 'Fiddle' and 'Faddle' with instructions to service the president whenever summoned. They, too, would be introduced to certain visitors by Jackie as 'my husband's tarts'. 'Why? Are you starting to get ambitious?' the president asked when Priscilla announced she'd like to take a typing course.[85]

Air hostesses, women journalists, artists, mothers and wives (like Marella Agnelli, the wife of the boss of Fiat) all succumbed, often unaware, like Helen Chavchavadze, a classmate of Jackie's sister Lee, that JFK was simultaneously carrying on similar affairs with other women. 'It was a compulsion, a quirk in his personality' Helen would later reflect, having had a breakdown. 'He was out of control.'[86] 'He's like a god, fucking anybody he wants to,' remarked political aide Fred Dutton, 'anytime he feels like it.'[87] Even Jackie was reduced to finding attractive young women, such as Mary Meyer, Robyn Butler, Fifi Fell and Mary Gimbel, to amuse her husband at table – and beneath. As Helen Chavchavadze put it, 'Jackie was in charge' of the harem – indeed Jackie later commissioned and edited, at Doubleday, a book on eastern harems: 'choosing his playmates. It was very French.'[88] Less French and more Roman was the president's penchant for group sex, perhaps ensuring his partners understood the terms of trade as much as for enhanced excitement; sex as distraction, in other words, not love, which was something else, long buried in the past.

Though the JFK's private shenanigans astonished newcomer aides and secret servicemen, none 'ratted', in large part because such private misbehaviour could not be seen as adversely affecting the president's professional performance in the White House. Indeed the opposite might be said. From initial naivety in handling the presidency, JFK had grown more and more confident in his unique role as youthful leader or steward of the free world, as his handling of the Cuban Missile Crisis showed.

Was it, then, as Jackie believed, an abiding fear of boredom, of wasting precious off-duty hours in a life he was certain from the start would be short, that explained JFK's recklessness as president? Was the chase, the planning, the constant challenge of promiscuity with pretty – and young – women an escape, however temporary, from often crippling pain, age and depression? Was it, in the White House, a tried and tested means to slough off the relentless expectations and heavy burdens of head of state?

Whatever it was that impelled JFK to take such risks it went back too far, too deep, and was too insistent in its urgency for him to countenance reform. Moreover the women he bedded were the last to complain, raised in an era when 'it was assumed that women compete with each other for the best men' as one young mistress recalled.[89] 'Somehow it didn't register with me at any deep level that what I was doing was absolutely immoral, absolutely atrocious behavior' – a twenty-year-old reflected, describing 'having dinner in the White House' with sex to follow in 'the Abraham Lincoln bedroom'.[90]

How long such behaviour could have continued without becoming public knowledge is a question that vexed many writers in subsequent years. Certainly it made the president vulnerable to blackmail; indeed by the autumn of 1963 he was being warned by well-meaning friends about serious financial corruption on the part of his personal staff in the White House, corruption he chose not to investigate or rein in lest, in return, the accused accuse him of other, scandalous improprieties.[91]

In any event, JFK himself never abandoned his primary love: politics. He was determined to stand for re-election in 1964, and to win with a significant majority. With this in mind he persuaded Jackie to accompany him on November 21, 1963 to Fort Worth, Texas, to rally support for the Democratic Party. He'd once told Clare Booth Luce 'I can't go to sleep without a lay.'[92] He'd wanted Jackie to come, yet whenever Jackie was with him, one of his secret service agents recalled, his private life 'was no fun. He just had headaches. You really saw him droop because he wasn't getting laid. He was like a rooster getting hit with a water hose.'[93] Nevertheless he was grateful she'd agreed to accompany him into what he called 'nut country', knowing how she hated campaigning and having to meet 'common' people who called her 'Jackie' instead of her preferred 'Jacqueline'.[94]

The next day, 22 November, 1963, the president and First Lady flew to Love Field outside Dallas, where they got into their open limousine and made their way downtown where there was to be a $100-a-plate fundraising luncheon at the Trade Mart. Amazingly, it was the first time since the inauguration in 1961 that she had ever been west of her house at Glen Ora, Virginia – despite a number of trips abroad, including a recent month-long stay in Europe as house guest of Aristotle Onassis.

While JFK beamed his warm, grateful smile at the crowds, hoping the estimated 200,000 would all vote Democrat in the next year's election, Jackie seemed unable or unwilling to fake delight, insisting on wearing dark sunglasses, as if married to a South American dictator. JFK asked her to take them off, so that well-wishers lining the route could see her better.

Jackie took them off, but the bright sunlight hurt her eyes. 'Jackie: *take your glasses off!*' the president repeated, when she put them back on. They were his last words to her. Just as the open Lincoln Continental (he had rejected the covered limousine that had been offered as an alternative) picked up gentle speed after slowing down to walking pace around the right-angle bend on Dealey Plaza, a shot rang out. 'If someone wants to shoot me from a window with a rifle, nobody can stop it', the president had remarked earlier.[95] He was right. The bullet, aimed from above, went through his neck. Two more shots made it murder most foul, ending the life of the last of the Great Caesars.

CHAPTER FIVE

LYNDON B. JOHNSON

Later reviled

Democrat
36th President
(November 22, 1963–January 20, 1969)

Part One: The Road to the White House

Lyndon Baines Johnson was born on August 27, 1908 in a two-room shack by the Pedernales, a small, muddy tributary of the Colorado River, in the Hill Country, sixty-five miles from Austin, Texas.[1]

A speculator on cotton futures, Lyndon's father Sam Ealy Johnson Jr had lost all but the clothes on his back. Rebekah Baines Johnson, Lyndon's mother, was a devout, college-educated journalist, big on literacy, poetry and dreams. The Baines family had a rich tradition of producing Baptist preachers and politicians – her father, a lawyer, became a Secretary of State for Texas – but had then gone bankrupt.

For the first five years of his life Lyndon was brought up in rural poverty until the family finally moved to a rented house in the small town of Johnson City. Becoming a real-estate broker, Lyndon's father – who had once before been elected to the Texas state legislature in Austin – was re-elected three times following the end of World War I. However the Johnsons remained short of money, and their house remained without indoor plumbing.

When her husband was away, Rebekah, a strong-willed woman, kept Lyndon, her firstborn, in her bed. Though she gave birth to four more children, Lyndon – smart, gangly and wild – would always be her favourite.

At age fifteen Lyndon ran away from home with a group of friends to work in California for a year. Further months labouring on highway construction in rural Texas convinced him that without an education he was never going to achieve much in life. On a working scholarship he therefore attended San Marcos College in south-west Texas, studying first for a two-year teaching certificate then a full four-year BS degree in education and history. To earn his tuition money he worked as an aide to the college principal, and for a year took a job as a principal himself in a small rural Mexican American school – an experience that made him a lifelong warrior for the poor, the wronged and the racially oppressed. He became a high-school teacher in Houston in 1930.

Johnson had been called 'incorrigibly delinquent' as a teenager, but his phenomenal energy on behalf of his Mexican American students, then his Houston High students, bespoke responsibility and ambitions that would not be contained in a classroom. As a youth he had acted as a messenger for his father in the state legislature in Austin, where he had fallen in love with democracy – expressed in a marbled atmosphere of ritual, oratory, legal niceties, constantly quoted history and political barter behind closed doors. When approached for help in running a local politician's campaign for the state legislature, he offered his services to be his campaign manager. He was then asked to go to Washington DC in 1931, as legislative secretary to his local congressman, Richard Kleberg.

No man in the history of Congress embraced the everyday business of Capitol Hill as did Lyndon Baines Johnson upon his arrival in Washington. Alternately obsequious in his willingness to be of service to superiors, and tyrannically domineering towards those over whom he had power, LBJ was from the start a phenomenon. He revived a discussion group, Little Congress, and became its Speaker at age twenty-three. On March 4, 1933 he attended Roosevelt's inauguration, dreaming of one day standing there as president himself, instead of as a mere legislative secretary. In a delusion of Napoleonic grandeur the junior congressional aide, who slept only four to five hours per night, even put himself forward to be president of Texas College of Arts and Industries in Kingsville, South Texas. Turned down for presumptuousness he was, however, offered a $10,000 per year job as lobbyist for General Electric, and was on the point of accepting when Roosevelt announced on June 26, 1935 the formation by executive order of a new National Youth Administration. There would be, it was also announced, a director for each of the forty-eight states, and a $27 million budget.

Johnson pounced, and with the help of his mentor, Texas congressman Sam Rayburn, he got FDR to revoke the appointment of an experienced union boss as the Texas director, and instead assign twenty-six-year-old Lyndon Johnson to the post in Austin.

The youngest director of any New Deal programme in America, Johnson – who had married in 1934 – saw a chance, with twenty million people nationwide on relief, not only to help find employment (and, thereby, college funding) for the 125,000 young Texans who needed work and direction, but to prove his ability as a leader. He did. By the following year Eleanor Roosevelt, on a visit to Texas – which comprises a ninth of the area of the continental United States – asked to meet the young director who was 'doing such an effective job.'[2]

By then, in fact, Johnson had already begun plotting his electoral ascent. A seat in the Texas State Senate initially looked appealing, but he had reservations. He had promised his colleagues at the Capitol in Washington he would return one day as an elected congressman, and in February 1937 he made a successful bid for the House of Representatives for the Tenth District of Texas, in a special election. Johnson thereby not only became the youngest member of Congress, but got to meet the president, who was visiting Galveston on a trip aboard the presidential yacht in the Gulf of Mexico that spring, and who asked to meet the young Democratic prodigy. Greeting FDR as he came ashore, the newly elected congressman 'came on like a freight train', Roosevelt later commented. Johnson accompanied the president the next day on his way to Kingsville, and from there to Fort Worth. 'I've just met a remarkable young man. Now I like this boy, and you're going to help him with anything you can' the president told his key strategist Tommy Corcoran, once back in Washington.[3] 'That was all it took' remarked Corcoran years later, 'one train ride.'[4]

So successful was Congressman Johnson in getting Works Progress Administration (WPA) projects, housing and rural electrification to his area of Texas that Roosevelt asked him to become head of the Rural Electrification Administration (REA) itself. Johnson declined. His relationship with the president continued to prosper in the years that followed, however, to mutual benefit: Roosevelt steered huge military contracts Johnson's way in Texas, and in turn Johnson steered them to Brown & Root, Inc., which financed Texas-for-Roosevelt campaigns, as well as Brown-for-Lyndon support. So certain did Johnson become that he could vault into the US Senate, that when Texas senator Morris Sheppard died of a brain haemorrhage in April 1941, shortly after Roosevelt's third inauguration, the thirty-two-year-old congressman threw his ten-gallon hat into the ring and fought a tough race against his fellow Democrat, Texas governor 'Pappy' O'Daniel.

All his adult life Johnson had done everything possible to ensure that, when he went out to attain something, no stone was left unturned. On election night, however, having unwisely made public the tiny margin of his victory, Johnson went exhausted to his hotel room in Johnson City to sleep, his door guarded by Rebekah, his proud mother, against all intrusion. When he awoke it was to find his opponent had raided the ballot boxes kept in various judges' homes. Johnson eventually lost by 1,311 'late' votes. 'Lyndon,' the president said, tipping back his head in laughter when the distraught congressman came back to see him at the White House on July 30, 1941, 'apparently you Texans haven't learned one of the first things we learned up in New York State, and that is that when the election is over, you have to sit on the ballot boxes.'[5]

With the Japanese attack on Pearl Harbor in December 1941, Johnson's failed Senate campaign receded into the background. He had already unsuccessfully volunteered for service in the US Navy in 1940, when Roosevelt revived the draft; moreover, he had helped save the year-old Selective Service Act, or draft, from defeat by isolationists the following year, by a single vote. In recognition the navy now ignored his poor medical report and commissioned him as a lieutenant commander. The navy drew the line at active service at sea, however, since Johnson did not know one end of a vessel from the other. Granted leave of absence by the House, the young congressman commander was instead charged with gingering naval war production in Texas and the Southwest, under the auspices of the Secretary of the Navy's office.

Frustrated that he was not the boss, Lieutenant Commander Johnson pressed the president first to make him an admiral in charge of all wartime navy production, then, following a harrowing mission to Australia and the Solomon Islands on behalf of the president, Secretary of the Navy.[6]

Roosevelt, a lifelong sailor, had been Assistant Secretary of the Navy for eight years, but had never made Secretary, and was not going to appoint to that position a junior congressman aged thirty-four. With Roosevelt blocking naval promotion, and his chairmanship of a House subcommittee on problems in wartime production overshadowed by

Senator Truman's powerful, high-profile Senate subcommittee, Johnson languished. By April 1945, when Roosevelt died and Truman became president, Johnson feared the worst. Roosevelt had, at least, been impressed by the young congressman's superhuman energy and drive. Truman, aware of murky financial dealings in Texas, refused to have anything to do with him.

With no hope of attaining a full committee chairmanship for a further twenty years owing to House seniority rules, Johnson thus decided to make another bid for the Senate in 1948, at age thirty-nine.

Johnson's 1948 Senate campaign was as brutal as Congressman Nixon's simultaneous contest in California – only in Texas, Johnson was crusading against 'Coke' Stevenson, a fellow Democrat who was the state's most popular former Speaker of the House of Representatives, former lieutenant governor, and former governor, from 1941 to 1947. Twenty years older than Johnson, Stevenson opposed the Marshall Plan, axed funding for the needy, and had, as governor of the state, ignored a lynching in Texarkana with the words 'certain members of the Negro race' deserved to be lynched.[7]

The run-off campaign for the Democratic nomination proved to be the fight of Johnson's life. Stevenson – a quiet, simple man, known as 'our cowboy governor' – was backed by Texas oil interests and conservative, largely racist sentiment; Johnson by a mix of political and financial supporters. With both sides spending almost $1 million the campaign was so surreal it could have been a rehearsal for George Orwell's novel *Nineteen Eighty-Four* (published the following year): Johnson pioneered the use of a campaign helicopter, a sixty-foot-long Sikorsky S-51 with three rotor blades (quickly christened the 'Flying Windmill')[8] that hovered over Texas farms and constituents. 'Hello down there!' Johnson would blare through a loudspeaker attached to the wheel struts, 'This is your friend, Lyndon Johnson, your candidate for United States Senate. I hope you'll vote for me on Primary Day. And bring along your relatives to vote, too!'[9]

This was not *deus ex machina*, but Lyndon Johnson's version of it. Advance men paved his way in the cities and radio advertising blasted night and day, as the young congressman battled the ageing former governor. Taking Roosevelt's words to heart, Johnson not only sat on the ballot boxes, but concealed the interim tallies from his opponent, the better to amend them when, as feared, Stevenson outpolled him.

In the days following the election Johnson thus whittled Stevenson's lead down to zero, and then overtook him. At eighty-seven votes' majority for Johnson, it was the tightest result in Texas history.

The vicious 1948 Texas campaign was the making of Lyndon B. Johnson. Like his fellow freshman senator Richard M. Nixon, Johnson had supped with the devil to get there, and like Nixon he instantly used his formidable energies to aim higher. Within two years he was appointed Democratic Party whip, and within four he became the Democratic Minority Party Leader in the Senate.

Where Nixon had used his political acumen to boost Joe McCarthy, however, Johnson used it to destroy his fellow senator. In the spring of 1954 Johnson authorized and arranged for McCarthy's army hearings to be televised so that the American people could see, as Johnson put it, 'what the bastard is up to'.[10] In the autumn he then orchestrated Senate hearings that, by sixty-seven votes to twenty-two, recommended Senator McCarthy be 'condemned' for having abused Senate rules and pilloried an innocent American general.[11] By 1955, when a Republican senator changed his party affiliation, Johnson became, at age forty-six, Senate Majority Leader – the swiftest ascent in the history of an institution known for its white hair.

Inevitably, 'The Tornado' was spoken of as a future president. But in the fickle way that American populist politics ran – and would continue to run – an alternative Democratic contender came forward in 1956 who seemed at first glance too young, too charming, too spoiled, too handsome, too father-dominated, and too lightweight to win the deputy Democratic crown as vice-presidential candidate: Senator John F. Kennedy.

Kennedy failed in his bid for the vice-presidential nomination in 1956, but when he won the nomination for the number one spot at the Democratic National Convention four years later in Los Angeles and as a courtesy asked Johnson to be his running mate, Johnson surprised even his closest aides by taking the offer seriously. John Adams had called the post 'the most insignificant office that ever the invention of man contrived', but Johnson did the maths. Unknown to the general public Kennedy was suffering from Addison's disease, an often terminal illness. Kennedy's offer would give Johnson a better than one-in-four chance of reaching the Oval Office by reason of the incumbent's death – a goal he might otherwise never achieve on his own, he calculated. To Kennedy's surprise, Johnson therefore accepted. In a presidential election that also made history for its ballot stuffing and bloc-voting, the Kennedy–Johnson ticket then squeezed past the winning post in November 1960. Johnson thus became, in January 1961, vice president of the United States, taking the place of his nemesis, outgoing vice president Richard Nixon.

Nixon had made the same calculation when surrendering his Senate seat to run for the vice presidency in 1962, next to General Eisenhower, but in his case the gamble had not paid off. Once elected, Nixon had been almost wholly sidelined by the president save at campaign times – and in much the same way, from January 1961 to the fall of 1963, Vice President Lyndon B. Johnson found himself largely ignored by Kennedy, spending less than two hours in one-on-one discussion with him in the whole of 1963.[12] Worse still, without Johnson's masterly influence in the Senate as Majority Leader, President Kennedy had a tough time pushing his liberal legislative agenda through Congress. Then, on November 22, 1963 – a day that, like Pearl Harbor, would live in infamy – disaster struck.

Part Two: The Presidency

To the end of his life Johnson suspected a more nefarious plot behind the Kennedy assassination than the lone-gunman conclusion arrived at by the Warren Commission, which the new president straightaway established. No serious evidence emerged, however, of such a conspiracy, notwithstanding suspicions of mafia involvement and/or Cuban exiles, still smarting over the Bay of Pigs.

Johnson had been a human tornado in the years of his ascent. As the 36th president of the US he now became a hurricane. Within two days of the assassination he was masterminding successful passage through Congress of Kennedy's imperilled civil rights bill and $11 billion of tax cuts. As Truman had begun his surprise presidency, in a moment of national mourning, with an address to Congress, so President Johnson prepared a special speech three days after Kennedy's death, dictating for his speechwriters 'a whole page' of notes on hate: 'hate internationally – hate domestically – and just to say this hate that produces inequality, this hate that produces poverty, that's why we've got to have a tax bill

– the hate that produces injustice – that's why we've got to have a civil rights bill. It's a cancer that just eats out our national existence.'[13]

Johnson was as good as his word. Whatever Johnson wanted badly enough, he got, as when he overcame the resistance of his mentor and all-powerful southern senator, Richard Russell of Georgia, against serving on the Warren Commission, one week after the assassination. 'You've never turned your country down' Johnson barked on the telephone, working on Russell's patriotism. 'This is not me. This is your country . . . You're my man on that *commission*, and you're going to *do* it! And don't tell me what you can do and what you *can't* because I can't *arrest* you and I'm not going to put the *FBI* on you. But you're *goddammed* sure going to *serve* – I tell you *that!*'[14]

Russell served. Then, to the slain president's interrupted legislative agenda, Johnson added a third rail: a war on poverty. 'This administration,' he memorably declared in his famous State of the Union address to Congress on January 8, 1964, 'today, here and now, declares unconditional war on poverty in America . . . Our aim is not only to relieve the symptom of poverty, but to cure it and, above all, to prevent it.'[15]

Backed by liberal Democrats wanting to turn the tragedy into an opportunity for real change in America, Johnson was unstoppable. The 'smear and fear' tactics of Republicans and conservative Dixiecrats would unfortunately continue, Senator Hubert Humphrey of Minnesota stated, but 'while they are digging there, we will just be building a better America': rebuilding the republic on the basis of 'war on poverty, economic growth, world peace, security and medicare, human dignity, human rights, education, opportunity for the young.' To which Johnson responded 'Goddamn, that couldn't be better; that's as fine a statement as I ever saw of that view in a few words', and eight months later chose him as his election running mate.[16]

In due course Johnson's and Humphrey's visionary dreams would turn sour. But for the moment, at the opening stage in Johnson's crusade as a liberal, he swept aside all obstacles in the greatest demonstration of domestic presidential leadership since FDR's first term. As vice president, Johnson had been shunned by his former colleagues in the Senate, to the point where, as Senate president, he had stopped stepping down on to the Senate floor, or even going into the Democratic cloakroom where for twelve years he had held court, so unwelcome did the bullying former 'Master of the Senate' feel. Now, however, he had a mission, blazing a trail on behalf of his country, and was determined to use the assassination of his predecessor as his launch pad to greatness. 'I had to take the dead man's program and turn it into a martyr's cause' he later explained, his goal being to clarify the cause, in terms of legislation, and to turn it into reality. 'That way,' as he put it, 'Kennedy would live on forever and so would I.'[17]

Kennedy aficionados were not necessarily grateful, however. The Widow Jacqueline – a Paris-educated lover of style over substance par excellence – innocently fashioned, in her grief, a romantic legend of a lost Camelot, while former Kennedy operatives connived and calculated the chances of putting another Kennedy sibling on the imperial throne. Faint whiffs of treason thus emanated from Massachusetts and certain suburbs of the capital, reminding historians of Shakespeare's history plays, with their tart insights into the machinations of a perpetually jockeying Renaissance court.

Johnson's political courage made such murmurings of discontent in his own Democratic Party especially unworthy. 'I'm going to be the president who finishes what Lincoln began' Johnson insisted. When Senator Russell warned the president not to steamroller Kennedy's stalled civil rights bill through Congress, Johnson responded, 'Dick, you've got to get out of my way. I'm going to run over you. I don't intend to cavil or compromise.' And when Russell warned that 'it's going to cost you the South and cost the election', the president tilted his powerful head lower still. 'If that's the price I've got to pay,' he thundered, 'I'll pay it gladly.'[18]

Russell was unmoved. 'We will resist to the bitter end any measure or movement which would have a tendency to bring about social equality' the senator declared openly. At the end of March 30, 1964, however, following fifty-four days of Republican-Dixiecrat filibuster in the Senate, Johnson's civil rights bill was judged to have enough votes (two thirds of the Senate) to merit cloture, which concluded legislative opposition to racial integration in America, a century after the Civil War.

Signing the Civil Rights Act on July 2, 1964 in front of a hundred witnesses in the East Room of the White House, Johnson could take pride in an extraordinary accomplishment. It was, literally and metaphorically, his signature achievement as president of the United States, rectifying an injustice that had plagued America since colonial times. Yet although the president had used every tactic in his huge arsenal of persuasion, both public and private, to get the bill passed as a bipartisan measure, he was nervous about marking the ceremony with television cameras, knowing it would accelerate the ending of Dixiecrat support for the Democratic Party.

As Senator Russell had warned, the Civil Rights Act would have profound consequences for the Democrats. Johnson's aide, Bill Moyers, found the president far from elated in his bedroom that night. Asked why he looked so depressed, Johnson sighed: 'Because, Bill, I think we just delivered the South to the Republican Party for a long time to come.'[19]

If so, it would not happen overnight. In the meantime Johnson obtained a huge, Keynesian tax cut for the American middle class, lowering taxes an average of 19 per cent for eighty million individuals, with low-income earners paying little or none at all, and corporations also benefiting from a 2 per cent reduction in company tax rates. This was a stimulus bill that would, it was claimed, lead to increased consumer spending, higher industrial investment, reduced unemployment, and a higher gross national product. Reaction to the tax cuts was immediate. The stock market broke its 800-point ceiling for the first time, causing Democrats to anticipate a landslide in the November election, despite the contentious civil rights legislation.

Would Johnson stand, however? It was a quirk in his tornado-like character that, at certain times, he would lose faith in himself and, recalling his hardscrabble childhood, would suddenly feel too wounded, too unlovable, too sinful, too humble in terms of his background to go on. Compared with most northern liberals he was a southern progressive who had actually known poverty, yet he still felt inferior, at times, to those who talked poverty so eloquently. To them, he claimed, 'my name is shit and always has been and always will be. I got their goddamn legislation passed for them, but they gave me no credit.'[20] In particular, a spat he had with privileged Robert F. Kennedy, whom he had kept on as his Attorney General but whom he had decided not to take as his running mate if he ran, rankled. 'I don't want to have to go down in history', Johnson – a worrier to his toenails – explained, 'as the guy to have the dog wagged by the tail and have the vice president elect me.'[21]

The feeling was mutual. For his part, Robert Kennedy described the president as 'mean, bitter, vicious – an animal in many ways', a carnivore 'able to eat people up, and even people who are considered rather strong figures – I mean Mac Bundy or Bob McNamara. There's nothing left of them. *Our* president [Kennedy] was a gentleman and a human being. This man is not.'[22]

Johnson may have been an animal, but whatever was said of him, he was the leader who had brought the country together after his predecessor's shocking assassination, and who had used the tragedy to push a liberal agenda through Congress in posthumous homage to JFK. What concerned Johnson at a much deeper level were the antics at the Republican National Convention in New Jersey, especially those of Senator Barry Goldwater.

Like many Democrats, Johnson did not initially believe Senator Goldwater's *Conscience of a Conservative* political philosophy (against big government at home, yet for big American government action abroad) could win Goldwater the Republican nomination. Domestically, the Republicans 'don't stand for anything' the president mocked. 'And if they don't stand for something – hell if they just come out here and talk revival of the corn tassel or . . . Tom Watson's[23] watermelons, it would be something, but they're just, by God, *against* things – against everything,' he commented, 'and trying to smear and fear.'[24]

The smearing worked, however, not only against Democrats but against opponents in Goldwater's own party. Thus moderate Republican governor Nelson Rockefeller of New York, who had bucked Goldwater's call for 'values' by daring to get divorced in 1961 and remarrying in 1963, was trounced by Goldwater in the California Republican primary, and neither Nixon nor Senator Lodge found it possible to halt the wave of support that Goldwater's jingoism was creating. There was 'a bunch of screwballs in California', as Johnson put it, with money to burn – and a potential nominee 'as nutty as a fruitcake',[25] calling to send the Marines into Vietnam and to 'bomb' the North Vietnamese[26] – yet Goldwater was winning enough delegates to become the official presidential candidate of the Republican Party. 'He wants to drop atomic bombs on everybody' the president sighed. 'I don't believe the people will stand for that' – but even he acknowledged that, in a country as ornery as America, they 'may do it'.[27]

Republicans *did* – many of them, like Clare Boothe Luce, the wife of *Time* magazine founder Henry Luce, delighted that Goldwater had voted against the civil rights bill on June 18. At the Republican National Convention in San Francisco the next month Goldwater duly seized the Republican Party crown – ironically, the party of emancipator Abraham Lincoln – and in his nomination acceptance speech on July 16, 1964, Goldwater proceeded to excoriate America's decades-old containment policy.

Goldwater's rhetoric was chilling in its fanaticism: 'It's been during Democratic years that our strength to deter war has stood still, and even gone into a planned decline. It has been during Democratic years that we have weakly stumbled into conflict, timidly refusing to draw our own lines against aggression, deceitfully refusing to tell even our people of our full participation, and tragically, letting our finest men die on battlefields unmarked by purpose, unmarked by pride or the prospect of victory.'

To those who'd wondered what on earth he meant, Goldwater was all too clear. 'The administration which we shall replace', he sneered, 'has talked and talked and talked and talked the words of freedom' but had done no actual face-to-face fighting on its behalf. American policy since JFK's election, he claimed, had been nothing but a wilful belief in 'the illusion that a world of conflict will somehow mysteriously resolve itself into a world of harmony, if we just don't rock the boat or irritate the forces of aggression' – a continuing containment policy that he called 'hogwash'. Failures in the fight against Communism, he maintained, 'cement the wall of shame in Berlin. Failures blot the sands of shame at the Bay of Pigs. Failures mark the slow death of freedom in Laos. Failures infest the jungles of Vietnam . . . Failures proclaim lost leadership, obscure purpose, weakening wills, and the risk of inciting our sworn enemies to new aggressions and to new excesses.'

What all this was leading to, Goldwater revealed, was a new show-down in South East Asia. 'Yesterday it was Korea. Tonight it is Vietnam. Make no bones of this. Don't try to sweep this under the rug. We are at war in Vietnam. And yet the president, who is commander-in-chief of our forces, refuses to say – *refuses* to say, mind you – whether or not the objective over there is victory. And his Secretary of Defense continues to mislead and misinform the American people, and enough of it has gone by.' The would-be

Republican president wanted to 'set the tides running again in the cause of freedom'; indeed to hysterical cheering he reminded his audience 'that extremism in the defense of liberty is no vice'.[28] The former ferry-pilot from World War II gave notice he would, if elected, give up the timid policy of American 'advisers' helping the South Vietnamese junta in its attempts to deal with the Vietcong insurgency. He wanted war.

As publication of Johnson's secret White House tapes revealed three decades later, the president and the senior members of his administration and the Democratic Congress were all intimately aware of the disastrous French experience in the 1950s and were not anxious to repeat it. Time and again through the spring and early summer of 1964 Johnson had discussed the nightmare scenario of direct American intervention in a war in the jungles of the Vietnamese peninsula with his colleagues, opponents, members of the press and academics, as the primaries took place and the Democratic National Convention in Atlantic City drew closer.[29] 'It's a tragic situation. It's one of those places where you can't win', Senator Russell warned the president on May 27, 1964 as the two men talked through the worsening conditions in South Vietnam, where national elections – mandated by the Geneva Peace Accords – had been turned down by the United States government lest the Communists win. The latest 'democratic' government in Saigon was no more than a right-wing military junta, capitalizing on its *coup d'état* against President Diem nine months before. 'Anything that you do is wrong' commented Senator Russell, chairman of the Senate Armed Services Committee. As he memorably put it, the US was 'like the damn cow over a fence out there in Vietnam'.[30] 'The French report that they lost 250,000 men and spent a couple billion of their money and two billion of ours down there and just got the hell whipped out of them' he reminded the president.[31] At which point Johnson posed the $64,000 question: 'How important is it to us?' Russell shook his head. 'It isn't important a damned bit, with all these new missile systems' with which the United States could deter possible Soviet aggression.[32]

South Vietnam, however, *was* important to Goldwater, a symbol of his mission to export American 'spiritual values' and 'to bomb' those who disagreed, as Johnson noted in frustration. Behind Goldwater, moreover, stood Nixon, Ronald Reagan and the ageing

Republican conservatives who had savaged Truman over the 'loss' of China in 1948.[33]

Like Senator Russell, the president thus felt sandwiched between his predecessor's fateful decision to station 16,000 American military 'advisers' in South Vietnam, on the one hand, and Goldwater's gung-ho war rhetoric – with its shades of MacArthur's willingness to use nuclear weapons in Korea – on the other. Truman had eventually fired MacArthur; but did Johnson have the same strength of will to over-rule his own military advisers by withdrawing those in Vietnam? Would he not be called defeatist, chicken, and worse?

Johnson, in terms of foreign policy, was no Truman. At heart he felt fatally torn: doomed if he allowed the US to become directly engaged in a Vietnamese civil war it could no more win than the French had been able to in the early 1950s, but damned by Goldwater's Republican tribe – indeed fearful of 'impeachment' – if he pulled Kennedy's 16,000 American 'advisers' out of Vietnam.[34] Afraid that Goldwater would turn the American tide against Democrats in November, Johnson attempted to toe a line of cautious indecision, refusing to allow himself to be stampeded by Goldwater Republicans as the Democratic National Convention in Atlantic City approached.

On August 4, 1964, an alarming report reached the White House that the USS *Maddox*, a World War II specialist communications destroyer operating off the coast of North Vietnam in the Gulf of Tonkin, was under attack by North Vietnamese PT boats. Johnson was urged by his advisers to bomb North Vietnamese installations in reprisal.

'It looks to me like the weakness of our position is that we respond only to an action and we don't have any [strategy] of our own' the president wisely reflected.[35] By taking punitive retaliatory action, America would get lured into war without a real plan, and with the initiative held by the enemy. What if American bombing didn't scare the North Vietnamese, but on the contrary encouraged them to goad the US into outright war? President Eisenhower's emissary to South East Asia, General Matt Ridgway, had famously told Eisenhower that taking up the falling French colonial baton in Vietnam would require eight US divisions and eight years. Senator Russell had told Eisenhower it would take fifty years.[36] Was America up for such a struggle, in support of a corrupt, unpopular and completely undemocratic mili-tocracy in South Vietnam?

The president therefore demanded proof that North Vietnamese vessels had attacked US ships. He was right to question the evidence: Admiral Sharp's initial reports from his headquarters in Honolulu – 6,000 miles from the Gulf of Tonkin, where the incident was said to have taken place – turned out to be less than firm, once challenged. 'Freak weather' conditions had apparently affected the US destroyer's radar, its captain reported, and the ship's sonar operator might, he warned, have been seeing things that weren't there. No North Vietnamese vessels had actually been identified, he admitted. He therefore recommended no further action be taken until a 'complete evaluation' had been undertaken.

It was too late, however. The die was cast at the height of a presidential election-year battle, Johnson ultimately deciding that the minor incident would give him his chance to defang Goldwater warmongers without having to go to war, so long as he, as commander-in-chief, exercised a restraining hand on those in the US military and among his national security staff who were spoiling for bigger blood. On August 7 and 8, 1964, after McNamara had issued a series of outright lies to conceal US direction of, and participation in, the CIA's operations, Johnson got Congress to grant him retaliatory war powers, yet insisted in a national television broadcast that he was only authorizing an American airstrike on North Vietnam in response to 'open aggression on the high seas', and was *not* thereby escalating the US advisory mission in Vietnam into outright war.

Only two senators dared oppose the Tonkin Gulf Resolution, and no congressmen. With wisdom and guile Johnson seemed thereby to have cauterized the growing threat from Senator Goldwater by demonstrating his own firmness of purpose as president.

Just over a hundred American 'advisers' had been killed in support of South Vietnamese forces between 1961 and 1964. The Tonkin Gulf Resolution, however, would change that picture: a veritable death sentence, as Senator Russell had feared, for more than 59,000 American sons in the coming years. It would also spell wounds and disability, drug addiction and trauma for hundreds of thousands of American servicemen, who survived service in Vietnam. Instead of teaching the North Vietnamese a lesson in the Gulf of Tonkin – namely to desist from attacking American military personnel – the American 'retaliatory' bombing and naval-shelling raid on the North Vietnam PT boat base achieved the opposite; indeed evoked the great lesson of war in history: it is far easier to get into hostilities than out of them.

Since the Geneva conference of 1954, North Vietnam had thus far committed no regular forces south of the Demilitarized Zone, or 17th Parallel. Under American protection the South had then teetered in a long, festering civil strife, not only between South Vietnamese non-Communists and Communists (the Vietcong), but between Buddhists and Catholics. The Gulf of Tonkin Resolution, however, changed the dynamic, licensing the militaries of both North Vietnam and the United States to prepare for outright war, with only Lyndon B. Johnson able to halt the slide.

Johnson's genius as a politician had always been to watch for bad omens, an example of which was his refusal ever to let his wife send his 'lucky' shoes away to be resoled, lest they not be available in a crisis. Now, in the summer of 1964, Johnson hesitated. In a declaration to be read to the Democratic National Convention, he claimed he was not 'physically and mentally' equipped to carry the burden of the presidency – the 'responsibilities of the bomb and the world and the Negroes and the South'. The dangers America faced were such that he rightly doubted he could be his country's leader. There were, he told his aide Walter Jenkins, 'younger men and better-prepared men and better-trained men and Harvard-educated men. I know my limitations.'[37] He would not therefore stand for the nomination. 'My God, he's going up there tomorrow [to] resign; the convention will be thrown into chaos', said a long-time assistant, recalling the panic that gripped him and others.[38]

Johnson's withdrawal statement was serious; indeed it presaged his actual withdrawal from the presidency four years later. But in the summer of 1964, with his war on poverty proposals having been officially submitted to Congress in March and his civil rights bill just signed, the still-unelected president knew, in his heart of hearts, he couldn't simply back out of the White House and leave Senator Goldwater to take the reins of American Empire. Robert Kennedy, Johnson's only real rival in the Democratic Party, would never hold the South in a presidential election, and would never beat Goldwater in November that year. Besides, Kennedy held the same views as Johnson domestically and in foreign policy, including (at this time) Vietnam. Withdrawing from the presidential race would make Johnson a lame-duck president for his remaining five months, with waning power to hold back the forces of patriotic gore in the wake of Tonkin.

In the end, what the president had wanted was loving reassurance and, once his wife gave it (telling him he was 'as brave a man as Harry Truman – or FDR – or Lincoln' and 'to step out now would be wrong for your country', leaving his 'enemies jeering' and nothing but a 'lonely wasteland for your future'), Johnson rescinded his resignation statement.[39] He thus accepted his party's unanimous nomination on August 29, and went all out to defeat Goldwater in the fall election on November 3.

Using the 'Daisy' (nuclear mushroom cloud) television ad, Johnson's election team cast his maverick Arizona opponent as unstable and liable to cause an atomic war, leading to a landslide victory for the president (forty-three million votes to twenty-seven million, the highest popular vote percentage – 61 per cent – in US history), as well as winning the largest Democratic majorities in both chambers of Congress since FDR in 1936. Lyndon Baines Johnson had been elected president of the United States in his own right.

With the country enjoying a forty-two-month economic boom, and every prospect of the war on poverty rivalling FDR's New Deal, Democrats were delighted. Johnson's victory at the polls, however, did not mean the problem of Vietnam went away. It got worse.

On the campaign trail in New Hampshire the president had insisted he was not going to allow 'American boys to do the fighting for Asian boys'. But if Asian boys would not fight, he had little option, unless he ordered the national elections, mandated by the Geneva Accords, or got the South Vietnamese junta to fight better. Choosing the latter course, Johnson was infuriated by the farce taking place in Saigon. Following the CIA-assisted assassination of President Diem, a second coup had ousted General Minh in January 1964, and resulted in yet another general, Nguyen Khanh, taking power. In August, 1964, Khanh – who recommended that South Vietnamese forces attack North Vietnam – himself faced an attempted coup. Acting Prime Minister Oanh, a Harvard-educated economist, lasted three days; the former mayor of Saigon became titular 'president' while General Khanh held military power. Then, on September 13, 1964, Khanh faced yet another military coup attempt. President Johnson's aide, Jack Valenti, searched later for an apt metaphor for the exasperation felt by the White House:

'I guess you might call [it] . . . a *turnstile*, for God's sake. You know, coups were like fleas on a dog, and Johnson said, "I don't want to hear any more about this coup shit. I've had enough of it, and we've got to find a way to stabilize those people out there."'[40] In the absence of a competent national authority in South Vietnam, Johnson's military advisers and the chiefs of staff pressed him to let American forces take over the job, as they had in Korea.

The Under Secretary of State, George Ball, reminded his colleagues Korea had been different: that in 1950 the American government had been responding to a massive land invasion by regular North Korean forces, and moreover had acted under the aegis and banner of the United Nations. Ball, however, was speaking into the wind – the wind of war.

The sheer imperial hubris of Johnson's military planners and advisers takes the historian's breath away half a century later, ranging from their pre-emptive plans to bomb China's nuclear weapons production plants to plans for mass bombing of North Vietnam, with utter disregard for the need for allies, or even for the danger of losing respect across the world if the plans failed.

As John F. Kennedy had allowed himself to be browbeaten into greenlighting the disastrous Bay of Pigs operation in 1961 and the subsequent dispatch of 16,000 'advisers' to South Vietnam, so Johnson now, in his turn, hesitantly but inexorably allowed himself to be infected by the Goldwater-led vision of 'kicking ass' in the winter of 1964–5 following his election: the notion of teaching the world a lesson about modern American military firepower in confronting 'Communism'. It would serve, Johnson was assured, as a potent warning to both Russia and China, and to any smaller countries that accepted help from them.

In vain the State Department warned that neither Japan nor Thailand – Vietnam's neighbour, beyond Laos – wanted a US air or ground war, and that not even the countries in the region believed the 'domino' theory: that 'losing' South Vietnam would entail the 'loss' of all South East Asia to Communism. Moreover, a turn to war – especially a mass-bombing war – would, the State Department cautioned, not impress Russia and China. Nor would it impress America's NATO allies, who felt it misguided and unlikely to produce a political solution – indeed it would probably *rule out* a political solution.

The superlative judgement that had enabled Lyndon Johnson to get his domestic agenda enacted over the past year, even without having been elected president, now failed him completely. Instead of taking charge of the issue and pressing for an internationally mediated settlement, or national Vietnamese elections as mandated by the Geneva Accords, Johnson handed the matter over to 'the experts', his military advisers, allowing them to set and define his choices, whereupon he would, he promised, select what he thought was the best option. This was not only government by committee, but also unilateral imperialism, in that it was prosecuted 'regardless of opinion in other [foreign] quarters' as the US chief planner put it.

The concept of unilateral American Empire pursuing its destiny regardless of allies now swept aside the patient work of presidents Roosevelt, Truman and Kennedy. Two weeks after Johnson's inauguration, a mortar attack on an American airfield at Pleiku on February 7, 1965, killed eight Americans. Like the Tonkin incident, this was the *casus belli* the US military had been praying for.

Having summoned the Senate Majority Leader and House Speaker to the Oval Office, the president explained how he and his cabinet had 'kept our gun over the mantle and our shells in the basement for a long time now. And what was the result? They are killing our men while they sleep in the night. I can't ask our American soldiers out there to continue to fight with one hand tied behind their backs.'[41] Claiming that 'cowardice has gotten us into more wars than response has', Johnson told them he had, finally, authorized massive US bombing raids over North Vietnam.[42] The Vietnam War now formally began.

In vain George Ball warned that 'Once on the tiger's back we cannot be sure of picking the place to dismount.'[43] Instead of searching for ways to defuse the growing crisis by diplomacy, in conjunction with America's allies, the president now hunkered down with his generals and national security advisers, hoping to find, or invent, an all-American military solution. Even if it meant ultimate withdrawal from Vietnam, Johnson wanted first to make a grand show of American military might, lest anyone question imperial American power and superiority. Thus, instead of educating the public on the need for an internationally negotiated resolution to preserve the peace, Johnson greenlighted immediate – and secret – preparations for modern war that would use America's unrivalled arsenal of latest weaponry: still unsure, however, as commander-in-chief, whether the new jungle war should be conducted from the air, on the ground or at sea – and how to avoid it spilling over into war with China and the Soviet Union.

By opting for graduated bombing raids, codenamed Rolling Thunder, beginning March 2, 1965, Johnson certainly succeeded in avoiding Goldwater's preference for nuclear warfare, in direct confrontation with the Chinese or Russians. By the same token, though, he thereby invoked a bloodbath of holocaust proportions over the next several years: between 52,000[44] and 182,000[45] North Vietnamese civilians were slaughtered in American air attacks that dropped some 864,000 tons of high-explosive bombs.

The president had been warned – as had Kennedy before him – that air power alone would be ineffective in bombing the North Vietnamese to America's negotiating table, indeed would only redouble North Vietnamese determination, just as the Nazi bombing blitz over England had done in 1940 and 1941. Bombing, in other words, would only encourage the North Vietnamese to send more, not fewer troops to help the Vietcong in South Vietnam. This, in turn, would make it harder, not easier, to 'win the war' in South Vietnam, since ground combat in the forbidding jungle terrain was fraught with problems for the US military. And so it transpired; instead of forcing the North Vietnamese to back off, Operation Rolling Thunder merely incited them to commit to a war unto the death.

The story of Johnson's direction of US forces over the subsequent four years, as *de jure* generalissimo, turned out to be a nightmare of argument, disagreement, disappointment, anger, recrimination – and bloodshed on an ever increasing scale, perhaps as many as a million civilian deaths by the end. 'Bomb, bomb, bomb. That's all you know. Well, I want to know why there's nothing else' the president berated his chief airman. 'You generals have all been educated at taxpayer's expense, and you're not giving me any ideas and any solutions for this damn little piss-ant country.'[46] Yet if Johnson thought there was a solution other than negotiating peace via the South Vietnamese government, not simply the North Vietnamese, he was to be terribly mistaken.

Despairing of North Vietnamese willingness to negotiate in response to US carpet-bombing from the air (with relatively few American casualties), the president was inevitably compelled to order a ground war in South Vietnam, using US forces operating on their own, without even a semblance of South Vietnamese involvement: mercenaries by any other name. By June 1965, some 75,000 US troops were in the country; by July, another 100,000 were authorized, with a further 100,000 to be sent over in 1966.

Though well armed and well led, they offered easy targets to Vietcong guerrilla units, backed by weapons and personnel from North Vietnam via the Ho Chi Minh Trail, which the US Air Force was unable to interdict even for a single day, just as Senator Russell had warned, from bitter experience in Korea. American casualties mounted. A third of the US Army had already comprised conscripts; all too soon huge numbers of new draftees between the ages of eighteen and twenty-seven were being sent out from the United States, fuelling an anti-war movement that took fire in what was already being termed a generational cultural revolution in America and the West.

Within months, Johnson's war in Vietnam thus produced the very opposite results to those he had intended. His wife, Lady Bird, later claimed he 'had no stomach for it, no heart for it; it wasn't the war he wanted', but that whenever he went before a crowd to talk about civil rights and poverty and combating disease, the 'audience would begin to shift their feet and be restive and silent and maybe hostile. But then the moment you said something about defending liberty around the world – bear any burden – everybody would go cheering.'[47] Polls showed Mrs Johnson partially right: three quarters of Americans favoured negotiations to resolve the Vietnamese imbroglio, but even more, 83 per cent, supported the bombing of North Vietnam, and 79 per cent still credited the 'domino theory' of Communism.

Clearly, the war in Vietnam, embarked upon with patriotic fervour, was not unifying America but dividing it, threatening to ruin the very causes Johnson had made his own: racial justice and the war on poverty.

Five days after the Rolling Thunder bombing sorties over North Vietnam began, racial unrest in the US showed the world the most alarming face of an America in violent social transition. At Selma, Alabama, the Reverend Martin Luther King Jr led a peaceful 'Black Sunday' civil rights march across the Edmund Pettus Bridge in support of voting rights, only to be attacked by state and local police brandishing clubs and tear gas. Only a third of the marchers reached Montgomery, with three killed. Though Johnson was able to push through his Voting Rights Act, which he signed into law on August 6, 1965, outlawing racial discrimination at the polling station, this proved a pyrrhic victory when, five days later, one of the worst urban riots in American history broke out in a section of Los Angeles known as Watts. Most of the area was razed, thirty-five people were killed, and 4,000 arrested. The mayor blamed 'Communists', while the predominantly black population, enduring 30 per cent unemployment in an otherwise booming Californian economy, blamed the 5,000 strong white police force, whom they saw as armed 'pigs'.

A just war, such as World War II, might have unified the country, and helped Johnson's domestic agenda. But in choosing to send hundreds of thousands of young Americans to fight for a military junta halfway across the world, Johnson soon found himself attacked on all fronts. Far from galvanizing NATO and his allies, Johnson's decision to go to war in Vietnam exasperated the French president Charles de Gaulle, who in 1966 withdrew France from NATO's command structure and expelled NATO's headquarters in France. With no NATO country willing to support American combat in Vietnam, the Atlantic Alliance fell into disarray, while the North Vietnamese took heart from American protest demonstrations and refusals by draftees to serve.

Like many political leaders of empire before him, Johnson had initially calculated it would be a short war, fought by regulars. Once Hanoi saw that the US was serious in shoring up South Vietnam's coup-riddled, chaotic regime and was going to apply its vast military forces to stamp out the Vietcong insurgency and stop any talk of Communists sharing power, the North Vietnamese would negotiate a peace treaty. The terms would then be the same as in Korea: a commitment by the Vietnamese in the North to leave an American-protected, non-Communist South Vietnamese authority in power, thus allowing the US to withdraw its forces in 'six months', as Johnson declared – indeed, in a desperate televised plea, the president even offered billions of dollars in funding to Communist North Vietnam, if it would only leave South Vietnam to follow its junta-led destiny. Since this destiny was conceived only as a sort of Americanized puppet nation under the eagle-like wing of the US president as a global imperial patriarch, with no Communist participation in government permitted, the North Vietnamese refused to countenance such terms. Johnson had gambled on the use of force, in what his national security adviser called 'all-out limited war' to keep the country partitioned. It was not working.

Johnson's political skill had always been his ability to put himself in the shoes of an opponent, and calculate what was needed to get his way. In the case of South Vietnam, however, the giant Texan found that by embracing rather than rejecting war, he had committed himself to a mistake. 'If I were Ho Chi Minh, I would never negotiate' he admitted, forcing the US into a 'long war' for which the American people would have little stomach.[48]

From being a 'trouble spot' few Americans were even aware of, Vietnam now became the overarching issue dominating America's airwaves and political debate, as the war's financial costs, the military draft, and growing public opposition escalated. Congress had passed Johnson's request for a special supplemental appropriation to fund expansion of the war effort by 408 votes to seven in May 1965, but only out of patriotism and in the hope of a quick fix. Where would such an open-ended commitment end, more and more people began to ask. With the tap turned on, who could turn it off? At a White House meeting that Johnson convened, his Defense Secretary Robert McNamara urged expanding the army by another 200,000 men and an even larger call-up of 225,000 reserves, while George Ball, Under Secretary of Defense, countered 'We can't win': that the war would be a 'long protracted' campaign with a 'messy conclusion' – namely defeat and withdrawal, as the French had learned. A 'great power cannot beat guerrillas' he cautioned; this, not respect for American resolve, would be the lesson others would take from the war, if it was pursued. For Johnson it was a bitter pill, and as president of the United States, he simply refused to swallow it.

Though the war had initially provided a stimulus to the buoyant American economy, its escalation was another matter. Inexorably interest rates began to rise, and the budget deficit started to explode. To continue the war in Vietnam would, Johnson recognized, drain the treasury and signal the end of his war on poverty in America; in fact the Voting Rights Act of 1965 turned out to be the last major civil rights legislation enacted in America. A tax increase was necessary to pay for the war, but since the Tonkin Resolution gave Johnson only a congressional mandate to prosecute retaliatory military action and he lacked a popular mandate for a longer war, the tax was considered too politically dangerous to impose. By the spring of 1966 Johnson had to ask Congress for yet another $4.8 billion supplemental appropriation, and by the summer of 1966 was having to propose massive cuts in federal expenditures, at the very moment when his ambitious social legislation needed financial reinforcement if it was to succeed without more violence.

Violence came, irrespective of finance. The summer of 1966 saw urban riots in some thirty-eight American cities, from Chicago to Philadelphia, as newly empowered blacks vented their frustration over the disparity between white and black incomes, education and urban blight, symbolized in destructive young black rioters screaming 'Burn, baby, burn.'

Thus arose the ultimate contradiction of the 1960s: the American government marshalling its financial, military and political forces to impose a fantasy notion of American 'democracy' abroad, on a fractured and fractious people – Buddhists, Catholics and others – almost 10,000 miles away, while in America itself the ideal of a Great Society, unified and strong, disintegrated into urban mayhem, characterized by student protests and rising social tensions ranging from black militancy to gay rights and feminism.

Punctuating the era of violence were repeated assassinations. On February 21, 1965, Malcolm X – an African American minister who had dared join the Nation of Islam, then had left it to become a Sunni Muslim – was murdered by black Muslims in Manhattan. More and more Johnson feared for his own life when travelling outside the White House – and not without reason.

Vietnam gradually infected every part of American life, most especially since the war could not be fought without calling up reserves and untrained conscripts. Unwilling students sought to avoid the draft by deferments or exile – eventually more than 100,000 fled abroad to escape serving – which further contributed to the increasing generational divide. Paying for the war also became an ever worsening problem; by 1967, some 400,000 US troops had been committed and a two-year surcharge on individual taxpayer's income became inevitable, as well as complete cessation of new Great Society spending programmes and cutbacks in recently instituted ones.

Detroit led the urban riots and burn-downs that summer, breaking Johnson's heart after all the effort and determination he had invested in civil rights legislation and his war on poverty. Yet inasmuch as he had chosen, as president and commander-in-chief, to go to war in

Vietnam, he had only himself to blame. With American casualties mounting week by week, gradually reaching into the tens of thousands, Johnson's approval rating sank to 34 per cent. Even his loyal aide Jack Valenti resigned from the White House, begging Johnson to 'find some way out of Vietnam. All that you strive for and believe in, and are accomplishing is in danger, as long as this war goes on'.[49]

Surrounded by loyal national security advisers and generals promising eventual victory if he but stayed the course, Johnson shook his lined, tormented head. As the 'told-you-sos' berated him in the media, he burned with shame and frustration. 'Don't give me another goddamn history lesson' he roared at Senator McGovern. 'I don't need a lecture on where we went wrong. I've got to deal with where we are now.' But since he refused either to withdraw, or to offer meaningful terms of negotiation, or to force the South Vietnamese to go along with whatever he decided, he was effectively a prisoner of his own mistake. 'I can't get out' he lamented. 'So what the hell can I do?'[50]

Another casualty of Johnson's war in Vietnam, meanwhile, was peace in the Middle East. For three years Johnson had known of Israel's race to build an atomic bomb at Dimona, in the Negev desert. By 1966 evidence showed that Israel was putting nuclear warheads into missiles, but Johnson was so committed to his unilateral full-scale war in Vietnam that he found himself unable to object. Matters could only get worse. When, early in June, 1967, a special adviser asked Johnson if he was going to ask Israel to be patient in waiting for an international initiative to open the Strait of Tiran, which President Nasser of Egypt had closed to shipping the week before (thus depriving Israel of access to the Red Sea and Indian Ocean), Johnson shook his head. The Israelis wouldn't wait, he told John Roche – and America was impotent to intercede. 'They're going to hit' Johnson confided, having received secret intelligence reports of massive Israeli mobilization. 'There's nothing we can do about it.'[51] Israel was going to war.

Perhaps no other catastrophe so demonstrated the price of American imperial overreach in Vietnam as the Six Day War, launched by Israel on June 5, 1967. In less than a week Israel managed to secure all its planned military conquests without the use of its nuclear weaponry, defeating the Egyptian and Syrian armies, seizing the Egyptian Sinai desert, occupying the entire West Bank, capturing East Jerusalem, and taking the Golan Heights.

Johnson, who saw Israel's victory as a disaster for the Middle East and the security of the western world, was now, thanks to his imbroglio in Vietnam, as helpless in restraining Israeli ambitions as he had been in restraining Nasser from closing the Tiran Straits.[52] Jews in America berated the president for insisting on American neutrality during Israel's war, while Arabs across the Middle East damned him for covertly equipping, aiding and resupplying Israel's blitzkrieg. 'You Zionist dupe!' Johnson shouted at his aide Larry Levinson when Levinson begged him to address a pro-Israel rally in Washington's Lafayette Park and thus garner more Jewish support – especially from Jewish anti-Vietnam voters – by backing Israel. 'Why can't you see I'm doing all I can for Israel? That's what you should be telling people', the president cried, knowing he was as powerless to break up the brawl as he had been to stop it from starting.[53]

Several days later US impotence was stunningly illustrated when in broad daylight, Israeli bombers and three Israeli PT boats attacked the USS *Liberty*, an American naval intelligence vessel similar in purpose to the *Maddox* but operating in international waters off Port Said. After strafing the American warship with cannon and napalm, the PT boats launched five torpedoes which further crippled the smoking vessel. Thirty-four American crew were killed, and another 171 were wounded. Though Israel afterwards excused the attack as one of mistaken identity, no one was taken in. As historian Robert Dallek noted, 'The Israelis were determined to avoid a repeat of 1956, when US, Soviet, and UN pressure forced them to give up the fruits of their victory against Egypt.'[54] The US Navy would not be permitted to monitor Israeli progress, let alone pass on information about it to their enemies.

Chastened, Johnson could do nothing. Once Israel had achieved its objectives – tripling the size of Israel from 8,000 to 26,000 square miles, forcing a third of a million Arabs to flee from the West Bank, which Israel then annexed, conquering the whole city of Jerusalem, securing the 'Kashmir of the Middle East', the Golan Heights, and racing its armoured forces right up to the banks of the Suez Canal, as well as the Gulf of Suez and the Gulf of Tiran coastlines – a UN ceasefire was arranged.

Although the ceasefire mandated eventual Israeli withdrawal from the territories it had conquered, the document was worthless, save as a testament to Israeli's astonishing military success. Holding on to most of its military conquests for another forty years, it not only permitted Israelis to establish settlements in what became 'the occupied territories', but also allowed it to refuse for the next half-century to withdraw from any land seized unless an agreement was signed by its former owner accepting Israel's 'right to exist' and other terms, such as no right of return by Palestinian refugees to their former homes. Thus, while defeat in Vietnam would go down as the greatest military reverse in America's history, for Israel the Six Day War would represent the greatest triumph in its military annals.

To add to Johnson's woes, the American debacle in Vietnam meant that the US was unable to take advantage of what otherwise would have been a signal opportunity to improve East–West relations. The Soviet Union had become deeply concerned about the hostile attitude of its former ally and Communist partner, the People's Republic of China, to which it had once given technical assistance in developing an atomic bomb. Now the Chinese had developed a hydrogen bomb, and felt not only the equal of Russia, but a rival for North Vietnamese affections. Instead of being able to exploit this inter-Communist rivalry to America's advantage, Johnson's war in Vietnam achieved the very opposite.

In challenging Ho Chi Minh to armed combat, Johnson found himself grappling with an opponent increasingly able to get both Moscow and Peking to compete with each other to offer assistance. Observers and chroniclers of the region could thus only watch in bemused disbelief as France, having extricated its defeated army from Vietnam in 1954, recognized the People's Republic of China in 1964 and began trading profitably with Beijing, a move that prompted Washington to send a diplomatic note deploring President de Gaulle's decision as 'unwise and untimely'.[55] By contrast President Johnson found himself not only stuck with France's abandoned war in Vietnam, but also without access to China's trade market. Moreover, thanks to Israel's triumphant victory in the Middle East, America's access to oil was severly curtailed at the very moment when American oil production was falling, in relation to its industrial, commercial and domestic needs.

With China and Israel developing their own nuclear weapons, the Soviet premier, Aleksei Kosygin, reckoned it was time for a summit with his fellow emperor, President Johnson. Two weeks after the Israeli ceasefire he proposed that they meet in New York, on the occasion of his visit to the UN. But in a vivid illustration of the negative repercussions of the Vietnam War, Johnson was forced to turn down the Russian proposal – for fear of anti-war demonstrations by his own people.

Johnson was now at the nadir of his presidential fortunes. Eventually it was decided to hold the summit at a small state college in New Jersey, Glassboro State College (later renamed Rowan University) on June 23, 1967, out of sight and reach of protesters and assassins.

Glassboro demonstrated what no one was willing to admit: both the Soviet and the American empires had reached the limits of their imperial hegemony. The states to which Russia had sent arms – Egypt and Syria – had been trounced in combat, while the crippling of the USS *Liberty* and America's inability to influence its own client state in the Six Day War had demonstrated US impotence, despite its vast wealth and power. In the interests of stability in the region, Kosygin asked Johnson to join with Russia in pressuring Israel to withdraw from the territories it had just conquered in order to start permanent peace talks, but Johnson knew it would be political suicide in terms of the following year's presidential election, and warned Kosygin to back off. When Kosygin asked Johnson to withdraw American forces from Vietnam, the dialogue chilled even more.

What might have been a decade of détente after the Cuban Missile Crisis – thus disproving Goldwater's belligerent 1964 rhetoric – had frozen into mutual finger-wagging. No nuclear arms reduction was agreed; indeed the arms race would continue full tilt, as the Russians attempted to deploy as many ABMs as possible to counter American offensive capability, and the two most inflammable conflicts in the world went unresolved.

As if to prove the impotence of the summit leaders, Ho Chi Minh – who was now dying – directed a mass uprising against military and civilian control centres across South Vietnam to break the military deadlock. Beginning on January 31, 1968, the day of Tet Nguyen Dan (the Vietnamese festival celebrating the lunar start of the New Year), the offensive stunned American commanders as well as South Vietnamese officers by its ferocity and breadth. A 'Battle of the Bulge' attack had been expected by Johnson and the generals, targeted on the US Marine base of Khe Sanh. Instead, the Communists simultaneously besieged some thirty-six provincial capitals, five of the half-dozen largest cities, and 30 per cent of South Vietnam's district centres.

At first, President Johnson's polls went up, as Americans rallied around the flag. But as the weeks and months went by, Johnson could not prevent the casualty figures from being broadcast and public opposition to the war resumed. Though the battlefields were far away from ordinary American life, television brought the pity of war finally home, especially after reports of an American massacre at My Lai (code-named 'Pinkville') of South Vietnamese civilians, many hundreds of them women and children. The victims had been beaten, tortured, raped, and their bodies mutilated. Though the three US servicemen who tried to stop the massacre were vilified on their return home, the majority of the American public was now wearied of the war and ashamed of its excesses. The Defense Secretary, Robert McNamara, had admitted to the president and his colleagues the previous autumn that 'everything I and Dean Rusk have tried to do since 1961 has been a failure', and he warned that to continue the war 'would be dangerous, costly in lives, and unsatisfactory'.[56]

At a State Department meeting on February 27, 1968, McNamara's 'controlled exterior cracked', his successor Clark Clifford recalled later. 'Speaking between suppressed sobs', he burst out with the words: 'The goddamned air force, they're dropping more on North Vietnam than we dropped on Germany in the last year of World War II, and it's not doing anything! We simply have to end this thing . . . It is out of control.'[57]

Johnson described McNamara as mentally unbalanced, disoriented by stress, even suicidal, and accepted his resignation; but Johnson's own health, mental and physical, almost four years since Tonkin, was taking a tremendous beating. His war had split the nation, the administration, and Johnson himself. He'd flown to Vietnam on the eve of Christmas 1967, when he temporarily halted the bombing of Hanoi, and had encouraged US troops to 'nail that coonskin to the wall' in the pursuit of 'victory' on the ground, but in private he'd begun to do what he had refused to allow for four years: pressure the corrupt South Vietnamese president to open talks with the Communist National Liberation Front, even flying to Rome and begging the Pope to see if he could persuade Lieutenant Colonel Thieu, a Roman Catholic, to agree to negotiate with the NLF in South Vietnam.

Thieu refused, thus forcing Johnson back into fighting for American 'honor', in support of an odious regime. 'I'm not going to be the first American president to lose a war' Johnson said, continuing to defend his own obstinacy, and hoped against hope that in beating back the Tet Offensive, he might yet compel the North Vietnamese to negotiate.[58] But with 525,000 US troops in the field in Vietnam – the largest army fielded by the United States since World War II – and the Joint Chiefs of Staff asking for another 205,000 reserves to be called up, as well as Congress baulking at having to pass an unpopular tax to pay the ever escalating cost, General Westmoreland's gung-ho optimism was not shared by Clark Clifford, the new Secretary of Defense.

On March 4, 1968, Clifford gave the president his task force's assessment of the situation. Keeping his voice deliberately low and dispassionate, using 'the dry-as-dust language of a Dickensian lawyer', he quietly laid out the sheer impossibility of winning a misbegotten war in support of a corrupt regime in a distant country, at punitive cost to America's spiralling deficit, its young men, its gold reserves, its responsibilities in the rest of the world, its standing with its allies, and its fracturing national morale. 'We are not sure that a conventional military victory, as commonly defined, can be achieved.' The prospects were dim. 'We seem to have gotten caught in a sinkhole' he said bluntly. Reversing the view he'd expressed only a few months before, he made clear he now saw 'no end in sight'. Sending another 205,000 men to the meat grinder would only prolong the agony.[59]

At a moment when the president was being fed positive reports of US combat units in countering the Tet Offensive, Clifford's assessment forced Johnson to stop focusing on tactical operations and to see the utter vacuousness of his grand strategy. 'Clifford changed the course of US policy' Johnson's press secretary, George Reedy, considered. Westmoreland's intelligence chief later claimed that Johnson had 'fired a doubting Thomas [i.e. McNamara] only to replace him with a Judas', but similar accusations had been made against those of Hitler's advisers like Rommel who had counselled the Führer to make peace in 1944 after the Allied invasion of Normandy.[60] Even Dean Acheson, who had been the toughest of hawks over Vietnam, now described the war as 'unwinnable'.

Reluctantly Johnson recognized, even if he capped the number of

US troops in South Vietnam and stopped the bombing of North Vietnam, he would not necessarily be able to persuade the South Vietnamese junta to accept a power-sharing peace deal, let alone sit down with the North Vietnamese. As more advisers pressed for Johnson to hold firm, indeed to escalate the war still further, others now joined Clifford's camp, forcing Johnson to face up to the impasse to which he had led his beloved country.

The president's brother Sam Houston Johnson recalled a domino game they played one night in the White House: 'He just sat there, staring way off yonder.' 'It's your move Lyndon' he reminded the president. 'That's just the trouble,' LBJ finally spoke, 'it's always my move.' With 'his big tough fingers', he played with the blank domino in his hand. 'Sam Houston,' he finally said. 'I've just got to choose between my opposing experts. No way of avoiding it. But I sure as hell wish I could *really* know what's right.'[61]

In the end, and despite the defections of McNamara, Acheson and Clifford, Johnson opted to continue the war. 'He had never, in his entire life, learned to confess error,' Reedy reflected later, 'and this quality – amusing or exasperating in a private person – resulted in cosmic tragedy for a president. He had to prove he was right all along.'[62]

Clifford, as a consummate Washington insider, had never known such a crisis in American government. The war was threatening to tear the nation apart at every level: in families (President Johnson's own daughter hysterically opposed the war, as her husband was shipped out to Vietnam), in anti-war demonstrations, in the media, in Congress, in the administration. Johnson had promised to make a national broadcast at the end of the month to address the issue, but what would he decide to do, and what would he say?

Once again he summoned his advisers, the majority of whom now recommended he 'stop the bombing and negotiate' with the North Vietnamese. Johnson was stunned. 'Who poisoned the well with these guys?' he demanded afterwards, like an angry headmaster whose staff had crossed his plans. 'The Establishment bastards have bailed out' he sneered.[63] Yet he knew in his heart of hearts that the Wise Men were right and that only he, as American Caesar, could manage the next step: negotiating a peace agreement while his troops held the fort. Having swallowed that bitter pill, however, Johnson then made the biggest error since Tonkin in trying to put his decision into effect.

On March 31, 1968, he went before the cameras in the Oval Office
and made his historic statement. He would stop bombing North Vietnam
and seek a peace agreement with the North Vietnamese. But there was
a further announcement he wished to make. 'With America's sons in
the fields far away, with America's future under challenge right here at
home, with our hopes and the world's hopes for peace in the balance
every day, I do not believe that I should devote an hour or a day of my
time to any personal partisan causes or to any duties other than the
awesome duties of this – the presidency of your country. Accordingly,
I shall not seek, and I will not accept, the nomination of my party for
another term as your president.' His political career was over.

No one, including his own wife, could ever quite explain this.
Though the announcement seemed to bring him a brief moment of
comfort as the burden of the imperial crown finally lifted from his
shoulders, the notion that the leader of the free world could simply
and suddenly terminate his duties, in the midst of a war, without
diminishing his authority as president and mortally wounding his own
political party, was an illusion. Shock and disbelief greeted the news
among his cabinet, staff and citizens, especially Democrats. Whatever
his failings, Lyndon Johnson had been, by force of personality, a far
bigger, more dominating figure in the firmament of American politics than his detractors – from East Coast Kennedy-liberals to southern
Dixiecrats – had ever allowed.

Nineteen sixty-eight, the year of Tet, now turned into one of the
worst years in American history. Four days after the president's
announcement, on April 4, 1968, Dr Martin Luther King Jr was assassinated in Memphis, Tennessee. America descended into a nationwide
orgy of urban rioting. City by city, including Washington, America
went up in flames.

'By the dawn of April 6, a pall of black smoke hung over the national
monuments' one observer wrote. 'The capital of the United States
was under military occupation', some 75,000 soldiers having been
deployed lest the country disintegrate into anarchy.[64] Then on June 4,
Senator Robert F. Kennedy was assassinated in Los Angeles, having
just won the California Democratic presidential primary, leaving only
Eugene McCarthy and the vice president, Hubert Humphrey, to fight
it out for the Democratic nomination in Chicago in July.

For a moment Johnson, regretting his decision not to stand, explored whether the convention might draft him, but, given the fury of anti-war protests outside and the president's ever deepening unpopularity, it was a mirage. His ratings had remained stuck in the mid-thirties, and negotiations in Paris were deadlocked thanks to the continued American bombing that Johnson would not halt. His 'fantasy that the convention would be such a mess that he would go in on a flying carpet and be acclaimed as the nominee' was derided even by his own press secretary.[65] In any event, Mayor Daley's police brutality at Chicago in dealing with anti-war protesters put the final kibosh on the idea, making it unsafe for the embattled president even to go near the city, or face crowds chanting 'Hey, hey, LBJ, how many kids did you kill today?' On August 28, 1968, Johnson sent word to the party chairman that his name 'not be considered by the convention', and Vice President Hubert Humphrey was duly nominated.[66]

Instead of backing him, however, Johnson now did the unthinkable: he deliberately destroyed Humphrey's candidacy.

After visiting Saigon, Secretary of Defense Clark Clifford had reported to the President that he was 'absolutely certain' the South Vietnamese government did not want an end to the war while they were protected by over 500,000 American troops and a 'golden flow of money'. In other words, the South Vietnamese were the problem, not the Communists. But when Hubert Humphrey recommended forcing the South Vietnamese to compromise, in order to get peace, Johnson labelled him a turncoat and gave orders that Humphrey's telephone was to be tapped. Thus when Humphrey – still vice president of the United States – came to see Johnson at the White House after campaigning in Maryland in September 1968, Johnson refused to meet with him. 'You tell the president he can cram it up his ass!' the distraught vice president expostulated as he left the White House.[67] Johnson thereafter refused to campaign for Humphrey in Texas and key border states on the grounds that Richard Nixon, the nominated Republican candidate for the presidency in the November election, 'is following my policies more closely than Humphrey'.[68]

Johnson's misreading of Richard Nixon – who had promised never to speak ill of the president if he continued bombing North Vietnam – would now doom the American Empire to yet more years of bloodshed. On October 2, 1968, word came that the North Vietnamese, nervous lest Nixon become president, were prepared to negotiate

seriously with the representatives of the South Vietnamese government present at the table in Paris, in return for a cessation of American
bombing. Johnson immediately made preparations for the bombing
to stop. 'Nixon will be disappointed' he acknowledged, but decided
at long last that peace in Vietnam was more important than helping
Nixon defeat Humphrey.[69]

It was too late. 'He promised me he would not [end the bombing]'
Nixon screamed, unwilling at first to credit the report from his double
agent, working under Johnson at the White House; 'He has sworn
he would not.'[70] Told 'It's going to happen', however, Nixon searched
for ways to sabotage Johnson's peace negotiations, lest his fight for
the presidency be lost at the eleventh hour, with Vice President
Humphrey garnering the fruits of an October surprise: peace. When
Johnson called Nixon to confirm the breakthrough, and that he was
going to halt the bombings now that North Vietnam had agreed to
his conditions, Nixon 'reaffirmed his support for a deal on that
basis'[71] but in reality went ahead with a plan he'd secretly drawn up
to derail the peace talks: persuading the South Vietnamese *not* to
participate.[72]

Illegally tapping Nixon's phones, Johnson quickly became aware of
Nixon's skullduggery: Nixon and his chief of staff, John Mitchell, had
used Anna Chennault – the co-chair of 'Republican Women for Nixon'
– to persuade President Thieu in Saigon not to participate in the talks,
on the promise of better terms for the South Vietnamese if he held
out and Nixon were elected. 'I was constantly in touch with Mitchell
and Nixon' boasted Mrs Chennault decades later, but at the time there
was nothing the president could do, lest his wiretapping became
known.[73] Like Eisenhower before him, he had become trapped by his
own clandestine operations.

Johnson yelled at his aides that it was 'treason' on Nixon's part,
'American boys dying in the service of Nixon's political ambitions'.[74]
He even telephoned Nixon to complain, but Nixon swore 'There was
absolutely no truth in it, as far as he knew.' Nixon and his staff then
'collapsed with laughter' after he put the phone down.[75]

'We must tell them [the South Vietnamese] we won't stand for
them vetoing this' Johnson railed. 'We have attained what we worked
for. We must not let this get away from us.'[76] But with President
Thieu stonewalling, the peace negotiations failed. Nixon, not Vice

President Humphrey, won the election on November 5 to become the thirty-seventh president of the United States – by 0.7 per cent in the popular vote.

Part Three: Private Life

Explosive forces seemed to drive Lyndon Johnson's larger-than-life nature. Everything about him, from his ears to his nose to his height and his feet, was outsize – and his personality was the same. From the start of his career, colleagues, relatives and chroniclers noted that whatever Lyndon undertook, he took over, not so much because he was a control freak (though he was) as because his tremendous energy, intelligence and drive made such an outcome inevitable. Moreover, in relentless hard work he discovered a talent that would have ensured he reach the top in any profession he chose: namely the ability to read with relentless cynicism other people's motives, their characters and their weaknesses. He was not always right, but his often sneering 'fix' on others enabled him either to bend them to his will or, if they did not bend, to thwart their attempts to best him. The most sensible, the most sensitive, and the best walked away from him; but those who remained were broken, and enchained.

Where Johnson's cynicism came from is hard to know. Certainly his humble circumstances as a child in Texas, his restless adolescence, his familiarity with the soil, farms and their folk, domestic animals, wild animals, hunting, the Texas range, meant that although he'd never gone without food or needed to do manual work, he had no illusions or compunctions about human nature as animal nature: including his own. Inasmuch as he despised himself for not having a purer, more noble character, he sought to compensate by working harder, aiming higher, doing more for the less privileged or empowered – not mechanically but manically. There was no spiritual or religious component to this ceaseless drive; indeed he was never religious from childhood on, and until he reached the White House, his brother said, he never attended a church. What propelled him was nothing biblical or even political in any ideological or carefully thought-out sense. But like those men who go into the armed services and rise to the highest rank, he was by nature – that is, by temperament and inclination – a *warrior*: a political warrior. He was born to fight, not with his fists (a fellow student would recall his utter cowardice if there was any danger of physical violence) but with intensity and relentless determination to get his own way, whether by guile or by exerting himself harder than anyone else.

Succeeding, almost from the word go, he recognized what many a leader of men before him had discovered: strength of will trumped all. Human beings were like pack wolves, with himself as the alpha wolf. Fighting for 'the poor' or weak or disadvantaged actually increased his dominance. Moreover, to maintain that dominance, especially with rivals, he instinctively applied his X-ray ability, measuring their boundaries in morality and endurance, exploiting their gratitude, their fear, their greed or their innocence.

At every step in his ascent to supreme power Johnson first attached himself to mentors – older men to whom by industry and servility he could be useful – until he himself inherited their power.

Love was an early casualty in this grand quest. At eighteen, while he was at San Marcos College, Johnson met Carol Davis, an unusually tall (6'), stunningly attractive fellow student. However much he boasted ('Well, I've got to take ol' Jumbo here and give him some exercise' he would declare, sporting himself naked after a shower at his shared apartment), and however much he groomed his wavy, slicked locks and clothes for a night out, he was disliked by the majority of girls he dated, who found his braggadocio and exaggerations almost pathological.[77] Carol, however, was two years older than Johnson, clever and shy. She was also rich. 'I fell in love with her the first moment we met' Johnson claimed. She 'played the violin and wrote poetry', he recalled, but also had a big white convertible her father – owner of a major wholesale grocery business in San Marcos – had bought her. The romance lasted two years. 'Lying next to the river in a waste-high mass of weeds,' Johnson related, 'we began to talk about marriage', but the relationship, though it promised him access to money and power (her father had been mayor of San Marcos) was doomed. Not only was Carol not interested in politics ('Miss Sarah,' Johnson complained to his landlady, 'this girl loves opera. But I'd rather sit down on an old log with a farmer and talk'[78]), but her father wasn't interested in Lyndon as a suitor, having already moved his wife and four daughters from Dripping Springs to San Marcos lest they be inclined to 'marry those goatherders up there' in the Hill Country, where Johnson came from.[79] 'I won't let you, I won't have my daughter marrying into that no-account Johnson family' Carol's father told her. 'I've known that bunch all my life, one generation after another of shiftless dirt farmers and grubby politicians . . . None of them will ever amount to a damn.'[80]

If Johnson was hurt by Carol's rejection after two years' courting, he did not show it; indeed the episode merely reinforced his view that romantic love was a waste of energy. Sex could be had with whores or women of easy virtue.[81] What he wanted in a wife was a woman of means, who would devote herself to his career, night and day – but keep out of his way when not required. When he met petite Claudia Alta in 1934, he was certain he'd found the right partner. On their first date – morning coffee at a store in Austin – he could sense he was making a big impression and wasted no time. He told her about his job (secretary to Congressman Kleberg), his salary, his insurance policies, his family – then asked her to marry him.

Claudia, nicknamed Lady Bird since infancy, lived alone with her widower father, a millionaire businessman and landowner with tens of thousands of acres to his name. Still only twenty-one, she already had two degrees from the University of Texas, and though working as a journalist, was almost pathologically shy. 'I thought it was some kind of joke' she said later of Johnson's proposal.[82]

It wasn't. The next day Johnson whisked Lady Bird off to meet his parents in Johnson City. 'The house was extremely modest' she recalled. 'Lyndon knew it, and I knew it, and he was kind of watching me look at it.'[83] No beauty – indeed considered by her peers and even her friends to be plain and dowdy – Claudia thought Lyndon strikingly handsome: 'excessively thin, but very, very good-looking, with lots of black wavy hair, and the most outspoken, straightforward, determined manner I had ever encountered'.[84]

Lady Bird asked him to wait twelve months while they got to know each other better, but Lyndon refused. He pressed for an immediate engagement, and a wedding. 'I see something I know I want – I immediately exert efforts to get it' he said of his character and modus operandi in the frankest of love letters to her, sent from his congressman's office in Washington. 'You see something you might want . . . You tear it to pieces in an effort to determine if you should want it . . . Then you . . . conclude that maybe the desire isn't an "ever-lasting" one and the "sane" thing to do is to wait a year or so'.[85] Less courting than pressuring, this was a manner of business he was making his own: working on people's weaknesses, hesitations, uncertainty, while contrasting these with his own tough-love energy, focus and determination.

Ten weeks later the twenty-six-year-old congressman's secretary drove the car he'd borrowed from his boss the 1,300 miles from Washington to Texas and gave Claudia an ultimatum. 'We either get married now or we never will. And if you say goodbye to me, it just proves to me that you just don't love me enough to dare to. And I can't bear to go on and keep wondering if it will ever happen.'[86]

Lady Bird caved in. They were married forthwith without any member of either of their families present, using a $2.50 ring purchased from a Sears, Roebuck store across the street for the hastily arranged civil ceremony in St Mark's Episcopal Church, San Antonio. 'Lyndon and I committed matrimony last night' Lady Bird telephoned the stunned friend who'd first introduced her to Johnson.[87]

From insistent, adoring suitor, Lyndon Baines Johnson, alias Dr Jekyll, instantly turned into a Mr Hyde, trampling over Lady Bird as though she were a servant, not his wife. 'He'd embarrass her in public. Just yell at her across the room, tell her to do something' one person recalled. 'All the people from Texas felt very sorry for Lady Bird. I don't know how she stands for it.'[88] 'Put your lipstick on' he'd snarl when they went out. 'You don't sell for what you're worth.'[89]

Lady Bird did as ordered – as others did, too – because Lyndon was Lyndon: a human tsunami, sweeping all in his path, men as well as women. Her father was similarly tall (6' 2"), dictatorial, obsessively neat and at the same time foul-mouthed. Lyndon was no different. He seemed to enjoy defying convention or good manners: 'a very intense crudity,' George Reedy reflected, 'an obviously deliberate effort to be disgusting' in the sight of snobs or sophisticates.[90] He was rude, boorish, taunting, humiliating, thinking nothing of urinating into the sink in his office while still interviewing someone,[91] standing naked in company,[92] or later, when he had his own bathroom, leaving the door open and defecating while dictating, or speaking with an aide or visitor. 'Have you ever seen anything as big as this?' he asked a friend visiting from Texas, unzipping his pants.[93]

Behind Johnson's outrageously boorish behavior was an unspoken challenge: accept me as I am, or get out. He rendered Lady Bird unhappy by his more or less constant fornication, practised in Washington on a truly pasha-like scale using every space, from his office desk to his car and closet. Unlike JFK, who charmed ladies to surrender their virtue in the hope of love, he never allowed any of his conquests to even dream of usurping his wife's place. He believed – or made himself believe – he was unique in his drive and ambition; his attention was thus a gift a man or a woman rejected at his or her cost or peril. His Washington harem was compared by one observer to *The King and I*. 'It worked that way; you know, the scene where she sits at the table and all the babes – Lady Bird was the head wife.'[94]

Lyndon's behaviour, in Lady Bird's eyes, simply reflected the biological dynamism of an oversexed man – *her* man. 'You have to understand,' she later explained to a journalist, 'my husband loved people. All people. And half the people in the world were women. You don't think I could have kept my husband away from half the people?'[95] Lyndon's womanizing did upset her, however, when he went overboard, and sex became affection that took him away from her emotionally, rather than being the expression of mere exuberance. His seven-year affair with Alice Marsh, the mistress and later wife of his Texas patron Charles Marsh, was a case in point. Likened to a 'Viking princess', the tall, red-haired beauty fell deeply in love with Lyndon who, together with Charles Marsh, agreed to a *ménage à trois*. Lyndon needed Marsh's money for his campaigns; she (twenty-four years younger than her husband) needed Johnson's youthful ardour; while Marsh – who felt he owned Lyndon – was content to let her amuse herself. Only Lady Bird lost out, suffering miscarriage after miscarriage, and only finally giving birth to two daughters in her thirties.

Apart from Alice Marsh, however, Lady Bird was in no danger from Lyndon's myriad conquests. 'Yes, but that's just one side of him,' she excused him to a friend who seemed outraged by Lyndon's philandering.[96] Johnson made no secret of it, either. As a newly minted senator he met a beautiful twenty-three-year-old radio ad executive at a party in Dallas, and had her flown to Austin. 'I threw away all my morals for him' she sighed later, knowing she was not alone.[97] Helen Gahagan Douglas, wife of actor Melvyn Douglas, was a congresswoman whom Richard Nixon later defeated in their fight for the Senate;

she too discarded her morals when Congressman Johnson hit on her in 1944, continuing to have an 'on-call' sexual relationship with him for the following twenty years. 'Bird knows everything about me, and all my lady friends are hers, too' Lyndon assured Speaker Sam Rayburn when Rayburn warned him not to endanger his marriage.⁹⁸ And it was true, as Lady Bird's confidences, interviews and her diary attest.⁹⁹

'Sex to Johnson was one of the spoils of victory' George Reedy would later say.¹⁰⁰ It was also a means to evade the shadow of the Grim Reaper. When his mother died of cancer in September 1958, just after he had turned fifty, Lyndon began to behave more like a high-school dropout than the Senate Majority Leader. 'He intermingled, almost daily, childish tantrums; threats of resignation; wild drinking bouts; a remarkably non-paternal yen for young girls; and an almost frantic desire to be in the company of young people' said Reedy.¹⁰¹ Five years later, the corrupting influence – or mystique – of the White House only fanned the excesses to which Johnson was prone. Flirtation with 'a very pretty young woman' led to casual sex on an office desk, as one of his many willing 'victims' recalled.¹⁰² In fact there were so many that, in a moment of boastfulness and sneering, Johnson claimed he'd 'had more women by accident than Kennedy had on purpose'.¹⁰³

Working eighteen hours a day in the Oval Office Johnson came to feel he *deserved* the brief spoils of imperial victory, unworried by the parallels with Caligula and Nero. As Jackie Kennedy had become her husband's enabler, so too did Lady Bird, soothing his brow, maintaining her composure, and continuing to adore her husband as Vietnam and riots incinerated the dreams they had once shared.

Another White House aide, the Princeton historian Eric Goldman, blamed Texas – not so much for its border traditions of wild Scots-Irish behaviour as for the lack of an early education to match the sheer natural intellect of the man. 'After years of meeting first-rate minds in and out of universities, I am sure I have never met a more intelligent person than Lyndon Johnson' he wrote, correcting those who saw only the loudmouth, the exaggerator, the liar. By intelligence the professor meant 'in terms of sheer IQ, a clear swift, penetrating mind, with an abundance of its own type of imagination and subtleties'. Yet for all his gifts, Johnson was a 'great sonofabitch', a throwback to the Huey Longs of the 1930s, a man who, despite his elevation to the highest office in the land – indeed the world – 'could not command that respect, affection and rapport which alone permit an American president genuinely to lead' in a modern democratic world.[104]

'If he did not exist, we'd have to invent him' Charles de Gaulle had said, *pace* Voltaire, of the new 'Texas cowboy' president of the United States he had met at the funeral of President Kennedy in 1963. A whole era of American imperial grandeur – its conduct of power across the world tempered by presidents of global vision and wisdom – was coming to an end, de Gaulle recognized, with Johnson's accession. 'Roosevelt and Kennedy were masks over the real face' of the United States, de Gaulle felt. By contrast 'Johnson is the very portrait of America. He reveals the country to us as it really is, rough and raw' – and the world would have to live with the consequences.[105]

Convinced that her husband's health would not permit him to serve out a second elected term, Lady Bird had also been a proponent of his decision not to run again for the presidency in 1968. But retirement to the Texas ranch was, if anything, worse for Johnson's health. He had stopped chain-smoking after a heart attack in 1955, and had followed a strict diet throughout his years in the White House, exercising regularly. All this he abandoned once 'home' in Texas. On January 22, 1973, Lyndon Baines Johnson suffered another heart attack, aged sixty-four. This time it was fatal.

Lady Bird was distraught (Lyndon had died in his study alone, his biggest dread). Though African Americans felt gratitude, the majority of the nation, sickened by Johnson's mad war in Vietnam, was unforgiving, and hardly mourned his passing. After a state memorial service in Washington the great champion of civil rights and equality was buried in the Johnson family plot by the Pedernales River, whence he had come.

CHAPTER SIX

RICHARD NIXON

Later reviled

Republican
37th President
(January 20, 1969–August 9, 1974)

Part One: The Road to the White House

Richard Milhous Nixon was born in Yorba Linda, in southern California, on January 9, 1913. He was the second son of a devout Quaker, Hannah Milhous, and her uneducated but hard-working, irascible Irish-American husband, Frank Nixon.

Frank Nixon made his living as a repairman, carpenter, streetcar driver, citrus picker and finally orange and lemon grove farmer on the ten acres his wife's family gave him. The simple Sears, Roebuck house Frank built was tiny, with a diminutive, five-foot high attic room for their five boys, two of whom died of tuberculosis in childhood; but it did have an indoor bathroom and plumbing. Unable to afford fertilizer, and not making enough to survive, Frank gave up his failed lemon grove in 1919, worked for Union Oil while his wife worked as a lemon packer, and in 1922 started a gas station and grocery store in nearby Whittier.

Working in the summers as a picker in the bean fields for twelve hours a day, at age seven and eight, Richard – named after King Richard the Lionheart – grew up a somewhat morose, introspective child, walking to school barefoot, carrying his shoes and socks in a paper bag.

Though he never learned to read music, Nixon was blessed with near total recall, and learned to play the piano in the family's small sitting room; indeed for a while he seemed destined, like Harry Truman, for a musical career. At age eleven he applied, unsuccessfully, for a job at the Los Angeles Times. He did brilliantly at school and was pressed to apply to Harvard University, but for financial reasons was unable to do so. Instead, because his grandfather had left a $250 bequest for members of the family to study locally, he attended tiny Whittier College (its student body totalling only 300) nearby, where he achieved prominence as an organizer, debater, student president and amateur actor.

Just under six feet tall, with wavy hair, an extruded nose and deep baritone voice, Nixon was thought by his drama teacher to be talented enough to become a professional actor – which in certain ways is what he did become. He was not unattractive, but was too self-absorbed, emotionally brittle and self-seeking to attract women. His mother hoped he might become a clergyman. Instead he devoted himself to getting ahead in the temporal world, beginning with law, which he studied on a scholarship at Duke Law School in North Carolina. In 1940 he voted against Franklin Roosevelt in the presidential election.

When the United States was attacked at Pearl Harbor, Nixon – who had been turned down for a job in the FBI and had become a small-town lawyer and assistant city attorney in Whittier – served in Washington as a government price control official, then in the navy as a logistics officer. He saw brief service in the Pacific, in adminis-trative work behind the front lines, before returning to the States as a base administrator in California.

Posted to Washington DC in the autumn of 1945 as a navy contract lawyer, Lieutenant Commander Nixon was approached by the Committee of One Hundred, mostly arch right-wingers of the Twelfth Congressional District of California. 'Are you serious?' Nixon responded to the phone call, and promised to give the post-war battle his all. He'd married a local secondary school teacher; with her earnings and his own (including poker winnings) he had $5,000 to contribute to his campaign. The rest came from a cabal of local Republicans, including the owner of the *Los Angeles Times*.

The Committee of One Hundred judged their man correctly. 'I always felt, because he was poor,' reflected California governor Pat Brown later, 'he got in with those rich Republicans, who changed him.'[1]

Since he had not stood for office before, Nixon could not be attacked on his record; by contrast he attacked his opponent's record with every-thing he was able, as a trained lawyer, to research and misrepresent. Using identical tactics to Joe McCarthy in Wisconsin, Nixon was thus able to smear the five-term Democratic incumbent, Congressman

Jerry Voorhis, as pro-Communist. The climax came in the first of five debates to which Voorhis unwisely challenged the challenger. Held on September 13, 1946, in South Pasadena High School, the debate treated its audience to Richard Nixon's first political drama, starring himself: a performance in which, like Iago using Desdemona's stolen handkerchief, he suddenly waved a phony document, which he claimed as 'proof' that his opponent was a near-Communist.[2]

That Congressman Voorhis, son of a millionaire and a dedicated liberal, could be smeared as a pro-Communist was a testament to Richard Nixon's success as a campaigner. 'I like to win and I play hard to win' he would later admit. 'You have to fight all the way; you never get on the defensive. Nice guys and sissies don't win many elections.'[3] 'Of course, I knew that Jerry Voorhis wasn't a Communist' he confessed after the election, which he won by 64,784 votes to 49,431.[4] He was, also, a 'marked man', as a member of the Committee of One Hundred warned him in a congratulatory phone call.[5]

Licensed – and paid – to become his party's attack dog against powerful unions ('I was elected to smash the labor bosses' he confided) and to target influential 'pinkos' during the two years when Republicans held majorities in both chambers of Congress, from 1947 to 1949, Nixon was determined to seize his opportunity.[6] He had no distinguished record of combat experience like his fellow congressman John F. Kennedy, but he did have a credential that could catapult him into the headlines. 'I was the only lawyer on the committee, so that's why I played such a major role' he later explained his high profile on the House Un-American Activities Committee (HUAC).[7] Though nothing of substance was ever unearthed by the committee, in a climate where the director of the FBI was publicly claiming there were 'at least 100,000 Communists at large in the country', HUAC would set the course of virulent McCarthyism for the following seven years, specializing in guilt and personal ruin via calculated leaks and innuendo.[8] Nixon himself was responsible for the Mundt-Nixon bill, requiring registration of American Communist Party members, denial of passports, and barring of non-elective federal jobs, which even the FBI objected to, since it would only drive Communists underground. For Nixon, however, it provided the necessary kudos he needed for his next political step: the congressional investigation of a specific, high-profile government 'pinko', Alger Hiss.

Using his amateur theatrical experience as well as his training as a lawyer, Nixon deliberately portrayed Hiss – a distinguished senior State Department official who had advised President Roosevelt at Yalta and was founding secretary of the United Nations – as the quintessential, pinstriped New Dealer, while casting himself as the patriotic all-American commoner. Since Hiss was a self-made man whose father had been a bankrupt who committed suicide, the polarity was entirely manufactured, but it more than achieved the national attention the young congressman desired. Nixon deliberately leaked confidential information he'd been given, spread unsubstantiated rumours, and promised his main witness freedom from perjury for having lied about his own treason in the 1930s, while working night and day to 'get' Hiss. He did. Indicted for perjury in January 1950, Alger Hiss was found guilty and imprisoned for four years in a federal penitentiary. Nixon, meanwhile, emerged a national figure, re-elected to Congress, and his name a byword as a dedicated, no-holds-barred Republican anti-Communist prosecutor. Inevitably, he raised his sights to the Senate.

In private, Nixon was – to Democrats – a surprisingly liberal figure: a strong proponent of health care, public education and civil rights, 'a liberal', as he himself put it, 'but not a flaming liberal', representing 'Main Street rather than Wall Street', a believer in bipartisanship and 'practical liberalism' or 'progressive liberalism'. As a prosecutor and campaigner, by contrast, he was ruthless, vindictive, amoral, and wholly devoted to his own cause: namely self-advancement. The Speaker of Congress, Sam Rayburn, declared Nixon, even after a single term, to be 'the most devious face of all those who have served in the Congress in all the years I've been here', but Nixon was unbowed.[9] He began plotting his campaign for the Senate in 1949, eighteen months before the election. Tarring Democrats as the party of 'state socialism', he declared 'They can call it a planned economy, the Fair Deal, or social welfare. It's still the same old socialist baloney any way you slice it.'[10] Thanks to the Hiss case, he boasted, he had won publicity 'on a scale that most congressmen only dream of achieving'.[11]

Nixon's 1950 Senate campaign against Helen Gahagan Douglas, a fellow member of Congress, would become infamous. He proceeded to tar and feather Douglas – with whom he had hitherto been on collegial, first-name terms – as a Communist fellow traveller, 'pink down to her underwear'.[12]

Nixon vowed to 'put on a fighting, rocking, socking campaign'.[13] With anonymous phone calls, half a million libellous copies of 'The Pink Sheet' and the support of Republican financiers and oil men, he proceeded to do so. No claim or accusation was too outrageous as Nixon called for American forces to cross the 38th Parallel in Korea following the invasion of the South by North Korea, and damned Congresswoman Douglas for advocating Chiang Kai-shek's seat on the UN Security Council should be given to the Communist Chinese government – the very policy he would himself espouse two decades later, to Douglas' incredulity.

As best she could, Douglas attempted to warn voters of Nixon's willingness to lie and cheat, coining the epithet 'Tricky Dick', but to no effect. Wherever he campaigned, Nixon claimed 'personal knowledge' of HUAC files containing frightening information on Communist fifth-columnist intentions in America, including the poisoning of the nation's water and food supplies, attacking public facilities, derailing trains, seizing armouries and the like.[14] With J. Edgar Hoover declaring that there were now over half a million subversives at large in the country, and Joe McCarthy having waved before reporters a phony list of 205 active Communists in the higher echelons of the US government, this was rank demagoguery on Nixon's part. It won him the Senate seat, however, by a near-landslide (2.1 million votes to Douglas' 1.5 million), on November 7, 1950.

Nixon was only thirty-seven, the second youngest member of the upper chamber, representing the second most populous state in America. There, as Senator Nixon, he could have remained for the rest of his life, had he so chosen – a politician able and willing to back enough social causes in Washington, from civil rights to health care, to be amenable to Democrats, while posing as a diehard right-wing anti-Communist and anti-New Dealer in election campaigns. Nixon almost immediately evinced, however, higher aspirations. Travelling to Europe in the early summer of 1951, he visited the supreme commander of NATO, General Eisenhower. Thereafter he let it be known to Eisenhower's main promoter, Senator Henry Cabot Lodge of Massachusetts, that he would be able to help in getting California delegates at the 1952 Republican National Convention to back the general – and did, earning himself the offer of the vice-presidential ticket.

Matters did not then go according to Nixon's plan. On September 18, 1952, under the headline 'Secret Rich Men's Trust Fund Keeps Nixon in Style Far Beyond His Salary', an article in the *New York Post* claimed Nixon was a kept man, funded by Republican backers in California. A scandal erupted.

Eisenhower, running on a campaign slogan of absolute probity in government (following scandals dogging several outgoing Truman administration officials), was distraught at the notion of losing the presidential election because of an ambitious but corrupt young running mate, about whom he had always had qualms. For his 'crusade' to be successful, Eisenhower insisted his team be 'as clean as a hound's tooth'. In at least two cases, Nixon had interceded with the Justice Department on behalf of rich contributors, despite his demand that key Democrats resign from Congress for similar favours. Eisenhower therefore favoured dumping Nixon immediately. Nixon, however, refused.

Aboard his campaign train, Nixon declared at whistle-stops he was the victim of a 'filthy left-wing smear' – an irony, given his own past election tactics. A first-class lawyer, he recognized that his accusers had exaggerated some of their claims to include his home furnishings and his wife's fur coat – an article of clothing she did not possess. Nixon therefore pleaded with Eisenhower for the chance, at least, to clear his name in a television broadcast. Uncertain whether to give him that leeway lest it only attract more public attention to the business, Eisenhower procrastinated, prompting Nixon to exclaim: 'General, a time comes in politics when you have to shit or get off the pot!'[15]

It is impossible to overstate the critical importance of the 'Checkers speech' (as it became known) to the survival of Richard Nixon as a politician. Even Eisenhower, used to the histrionics of generals like George Patton, Bernard Montgomery and Charles de Gaulle, was awed by Nixon's performance in a national broadcast before sixty million viewers – the largest television audience ever for a political speech.

Ironically, Nixon's wife had earlier begged him not to take Eisenhower's offer of the vice-presidential ticket, and thereby have to surrender his safe Senate seat. The fur-coat scandal now threatened to ruin Nixon's career, however, even if his resignation saved Eisenhower and the Republican Party. Were he to 'crawl away', she

warned him, 'you will destroy yourself. Your life will be marred
forever and the same will be true of your family and, particularly,
your daughters.'[16] 'Just tell them that I haven't the slightest idea [what
I'll say],' Nixon snapped back at Eisenhower's emissary, Governor
Dewey, 'and if they want to find out they'd better listen to the broadcast. And tell them', he added, ominously, 'I know something about
politics too!'[17]

Nixon did. He later confided he 'staged' the entire show, from the
desk in front of which he stood, to his wife in a chair by his side in
a home-made woollen dress, and the absence of a script, using only
notes that he held. 'He oscillated between the slick southern California
salesman and Uriah Heep', one biographer described, but the performance was magnetically effective, as Nixon first refuted the allegations
made against him, then turned the tables.[18]

Listing his assets and his liabilities, the embattled senator declared:
'Well, that's about it. That's what we have and that's what we owe.
It isn't very much, but Pat and I have the satisfaction that every dime
we have is honestly ours. I should say this, that Pat doesn't have a
mink coat. But she does have a respectable Republican cloth coat and
I always tell her that she would look good in anything.' He then
corrected himself, saying they *had* accepted one gift, after the last election. 'A man in Texas heard Pat on the radio mention the fact that
our two young daughters would like to have a dog. And, believe it or
not, the day before we left on this campaign trip we got a message
from Union Station in Baltimore saying they had a package for us . . .
It was a little cocker spaniel dog in a crate that he sent all the way
from Texas. Black and white and spotted, and our little girl, Tricia,
the six-year-old, named it Checkers. And you know, the kids love the
dog and I just want to say this right now, that regardless of what they
say about it, we're going to keep it.'

Many viewers wept at this. But it was not all. The senator then
made a plea for 'the little man' in American politics, saying Eisenhower's
Democratic opponent, Governor Adlai Stevenson, was a wealthy man
who inherited a fortune from his father, which was fine, but men 'of
modest means' deserved a chance too, he said, quoting Republican
president Abraham Lincoln, who had remarked, 'God must have loved
the common people – he made so many of them.' Thereupon Nixon
called upon Governor Stevenson and other candidates to 'come

before the American people as I have and make a complete statement as to their financial history. And if they don't it will be an admission that they have something to hide.'[19]

The Checkers speech made political and television history. Though Eisenhower waited another day before making up his mind – in order to show who was boss – the vast positive public response made it impossible for him to dump Nixon. Eisenhower would have to put up with him – as would America.

Nixon had read the public mind and its need to identify with the candidate as an ordinary, not extraordinary American: a man with a spouse, children, a house, a mortgage, debts and a dog. With his own heavy-jowled, morose, underdog face he shamelessly played upon the ordinary viewer's sympathy – and got it. No subsequent American Caesar would be able to campaign successfully without making that familial, human connection, presented on television.

'You're my boy!' General Eisenhower declared when summoning Nixon to a meeting in Virginia and let him rip on the campaign trail (though even he blanched when Nixon referred to President Truman as a 'traitor').

Once he had won the 1952 election and was installed as president, however, Eisenhower barely allowed Nixon entry to the White House. He would not tolerate the vice president's participation in cabinet and senior government meetings, save as an observer, and censored Nixon's speeches. Moreover, he tried to remove him from the re-election ticket in 1956 by offering him a senior cabinet post, which Nixon understandably declined lest he thereby miss the opportunity to inherit the crown if the president died in office. Four years later, Eisenhower's tepid imprimatur ensured that Nixon did not succeed him when the vice president was beaten in the 1960 election by Senator John F. Kennedy.

Nixon was gutted by the president's ill will, especially given the fact that Eisenhower's grandson, David, had wedded Nixon's attractive daughter Julie. In any event, Nixon's years in the wilderness now began. He declined offers to join a New York law firm and returned to California as an attorney. On President Kennedy's advice he wrote a book, *Six Crises*, which became a bestseller and enabled him to buy a nice house in Bel Air next to Groucho Marx. 'Let's not run, let's stay at home. Let's be a private family' his wife begged, hoping she could persuade him to abandon his political dream.[20] Despite his promises, however, Nixon was far from being done with politics. Against his wife's advice, and that of many advisers, in autumn 1961 he threw his hat into the ring for the governorship of California, a stepping stone to the presidency.

Times had changed, however. 'That's what you have to expect from these fucking local yokels' Nixon complained when attendance at his campaign meetings was thin. 'I wouldn't give them the sweat off my balls.'[21] Nixon's concession speech made history for its mournful bitterness, following a night of drinking and, according to some sources, spousal abuse so severe his wife could not go out in public. 'One last thing,' Nixon told reporters, 'as I leave you I want you to know – just think how much you're going to be missing. You won't have Nixon to kick around any more because, gentlemen, this is my last press conference.'[22] He was, he claimed, leaving political life for good; it had been his 'last play'. 'Barring a miracle,' *Time* magazine declared, 'Richard Nixon can never hope to be elected to any political office again.'[23]

With President Kennedy's approval polls rising to record levels after the safe conclusion to the Cuban Missile Crisis that autumn, Nixon concentrated on making money ($250,000 per annum) and cultivating wealthy connections, from Walter Annenberg to Elmer Bobst, Bebe Rebozo and Don Kendall. He moved to a twelve-room apartment on Fifth Avenue, New York City, and began to travel the world as a youthful elder statesman of the Republican Party, gaining audiences with the world's leaders from General Franco to Willy Brandt, de Gaulle to Gamal Nasser. He also visited Vietnam.

With Rockefeller and Goldwater first tearing each other apart for the 1964 presidential nomination, then Goldwater being trounced by President Johnson, Nixon's gubernatorial misstep in California was gradually forgotten. Despite the new statesmanlike role he had adopted, however, even people who worked with him remained worried by his weird psyche. 'He is', Tom Wicker warned in the *New York Times*, 'as difficult as ever to know, driven still by deep inner compulsion toward power and personal vindication, painfully conscious of slights and failures, a man who has imposed upon himself a self-control so rigid as to be all but invisible' to all but his wife – and his psychiatrist.

Though sworn to secrecy, Dr Arnold Hutschnecker was especially concerned. When looking in a mirror, Nixon confided to him, 'it was as if there were nobody there'. Nixon continued to suffer from insomnia and depression, and seemed to have difficulty in living up to the exalted, saintly figure of his Quaker mother. At the same time, he seemed oddly at home with his own duplicity, in a political world largely based upon dissembling and 'dirty tricks'. 'John,' Nixon said to an aide after telling 'some pretty awful lies' to an audience, 'I can say things that when other people say them, they are lies, but when I say them people don't believe them anyway!' From then on, the aide recalled, 'I realized I was dealing with a very complicated person.'[24]

Journalists might write Nixon off as a has-been, a self-pitying failure, sour and out of sync with flower power and the 1960s, but his influence in Republican circles remained strong. As President Johnson's Great Society began to crumble in the face of mounting casualties in an unpopular war in Vietnam and race riots at home, Nixon's hour again approached. He assembled the largest Republican financial backing in history, and won the early primaries for the 1968 Republican presidential nomination against governors Romney, Rockefeller and Reagan (nicknamed the Three Rs). At the national convention in Miami in August 1968, he won an overwhelming first-ballot victory, but to general consternation then chose an unknown (and uninvestigated) governor of Maryland, Spiro T. Agnew, as his vice presidential running mate, instead of the more distinguished Senator George Romney – an ominous, if little noticed, indication of Nixon's distrust of others and inability to share the limelight, in an otherwise extraordinary act of self-reinvention.

Measured, statesmanlike rhetoric characterized Nixon's second bid for the White House, with new speechwriters Pat Buchanan and William Safire reaching for a Republican high road. 'As we look at America, we see cities enveloped in smoke and flame. We hear sirens in the night. We see Americans dying on distant battlefields abroad' Nixon had said in his acceptance speech in Miami. 'We see Americans hating each other; killing each other at home. And as we see and hear these things, millions of Americans cry out in anguish: Did we come all this way for this? Did American boys die in Normandy and Korea and Valley Forge for this?' Pausing first, he heard an 'answer to these questions': another, quieter voice 'in the tumult of the shouting. It is the voice of the great majority of Americans, the forgotten Americans, the non-shouters, the non-demonstrators. They're good people. They're decent people. They work and they save and they pay taxes and they care. They work in American factories, they run American businesses, they serve in government. They provide most of the soldiers who die to keep it free. They give drive to the spirit of America. They give life to the American dream.'[25]

This was a vastly different approach from the anti-Communist, anti-tax, anti-government 'values' Republicanism that Governor Ronald Reagan was trumpeting. Moreover it represented the better, compassionate, responsible voice of Richard Nixon himself: the 'good' son of Quaker Hannah Milhous: a dutiful, hard-working son who had helped his father buy, stock and sell, even deliver, vegetables for his small grocery store in Yorba Linda, long before Nixon turned to rich backers and gave in to the demons in his soul. Sadly, it was a side of Nixon that was completely contradicted by what he next did – namely, in an act of rank treason, sabotage President Johnson's last-minute breakthrough in peace negotiations with North Vietnam to end the Vietnam War.

By dissuading President Thieu from attending the Paris peace talks, Nixon brilliantly scotched the president's triumph, and destroyed Vice President Hubert Humphrey's challenge for the 1968 presidential crown. At midnight on November 5, 1968, Humphrey seemed to be leading by almost 1 per cent, but in the Electoral College the picture was less rosy. At 3 a.m. Nixon, calculating his Electoral College numbers on his familiar yellow legal pad, claimed success. He had won victory by a sliver – a margin of less than 1 per cent of votes cast – snatching it from the jaws of defeat and avenging his loss to John F. Kennedy in 1960.

Part Two: The Presidency

Immediately after his inauguration on January 20, 1969, Nixon shunned the Oval Office. Instead, he selected a secret suite or hideaway: Room EOB 175, in the Old Executive Office Building next door along Pennsylvania Avenue, amid a rabbit warren of offices. He had assembled a cabinet of mediocrities, including a Secretary of State, William

Rogers, who would be a cipher, so that he could himself direct and manage American foreign policy – with political scientist Dr Henry Kissinger, from Harvard University, as his national security adviser.

From Room 175, using his coterie of protective loyalists and henchmen, the new president now issued edicts and instructions without having to meet people face to face. 'I have never met such a gang of self-seeking bastards in my life' Kissinger remarked of Nixon's clique, reminiscent of a medieval monarch's courtiers – worse even than Kissinger's colleagues at Harvard.[26] William Rogers, however, saw Kissinger as the problem: 'Machiavellian, deceitful, egotistical, arrogant, and insulting.'[27]

Voters had been made to believe Nixon had a better chance of immediately ending the war than his opponent by virtue of a 'secret plan',[28] but as historian Robert Dallek noted, this had been 'nothing more than an election ploy'[29] that turned into national disaster when Nixon now found it impossible to shift President Thieu's opposition to a peace settlement with North Vietnam. Nixon and Kissinger were thus stymied; they 'had no good alternative for ending the war except the application of more force' against North Vietnam.[30]

Protected by his chief of staff Bob Haldeman, and his domestic affairs czar John Ehrlichman, Nixon ate lunch alone in Room 175, and kept late hours there, brooding, plotting, spinning, dictating, as he set out to recast American foreign policy while dismissing domestic concerns as 'building outhouses in Peoria'.[31] He thus declined to give a State of the Union address, refused to give press conferences on a regular basis, and decided to rely on occasional, very carefully controlled appearances. As far as possible he even shut down direct contact with the State Department and foreign diplomats. Instead, he began to fly from one hideaway to another with a retinue of staffers, while Dr Kissinger, Haldeman and Ehrlichman were under orders to translate his decisions into direct action, without reference to the cabinet or Congress or even the Pentagon. He also relied on loyalist John Mitchell, whom he made Attorney General, to police any leaks to the Fourth Estate. Anyone publishing details or revelations of the president's intentions or decisions was immediately subjected to wiretapping – including Kissinger himself. The first victim of this new secretive approach to the presidency was to be Cambodia.

How, historians later asked, was a democratically elected leader of

the United States able to recast the constitutional role of the presidency, and bypass the famed checks and balances, namely Congress,
the Supreme Court, and a free press?

The answer – as it would be three decades later – was the veil of
war. President Johnson had launched the war in Vietnam to satisfy
jingoists and armchair strategists preoccupied by domino theories of
Soviet expansionism. He had then acted as the chairman of successive committees of advisers. Nixon had no such interest. As Kennedy
had 'hit the Republicans from the right', in the parlance of historians,
Nixon's intention was equally radical: namely to hit Democrats from
the left, hoping to reverse his old anti-Communist agenda and seek a
new world order based on rapprochement and equivalence between
the US, the Soviet Union and Communist China as the world's three
superpowers, each with their own spheres of influence. To achieve
this, however, he needed to close down the Vietnam War as swiftly
as possible. With President Thieu resisting all blandishments, Nixon
decided he would have to escalate the war, on a scale not seen since
World War II.

Using his commander-in-chief's prerogative, Nixon thus drew up,
in his second month in office, a secret new bombing plan to interdict
the Ho Chi Minh Trail, the gateway for the North Vietnamese army's
supplies and troops to operations in the South.

The US Air Force bombed Cambodia and southern Laos (Operation
MENU) from March 18 to May 26, 1969, without the Secretary of the
Air Force or the outside world knowing – using phony coordinates,
in literal double-entry bookkeeping.

Had the secret escalation worked, Nixon and his national security
adviser might have been able to excuse such deliberate mass murder
as a necessity in achieving peace. But to Dr Kissinger's disappointment, the bombing evinced no change in Hanoi's position, indeed
produced nothing save the tipping of Cambodia into a catastrophic
spiral of civil war, the creation of 600,000 refugees in Laos (20 per
cent of its population), and the start of yet more illegal wiretapping
in America when the *New York Times* finally revealed the bomber raids
on Cambodia.

By the summer of 1969 Nixon was privately admitting that there
was no possibility of 'victory', or even an armistice, along the lines
of Korea, with the country remaining divided into two. The question

was simply one of American imperial pride: how the commander-in-chief could get the US Army out of Vietnam without America's standing as the most powerful nation in the free world suffering too severely.

President de Gaulle had recommended swallowing national pride and making a simple decision to leave the country, as the French had left Algeria. However, France had been a waning empire, with withdrawal a mark of painful adjustment to a post-colonial, European reality. Though some commentators predicted the imminent collapse of the American Empire as evidenced by its anarchic, draft-burning, drug-taking, campus-occupying and anti-war-protesting students, Nixon was sure they were wrong; in this, at least, he was right. The American economy, despite inflation and unemployment, was more productive than ever, busting to expand on a global scale, if only the troops could be brought home.

Finding an 'honourable' Vietnam exit strategy thus posed the same problem that it had for President Johnson. Still beholden to President Thieu for his role in getting him elected, Nixon kept Operation MENU secret for another four years, during which some half a million tons of bombs were dropped. In the meantime he and his national security adviser lurched from one alternative exit to the next, unwilling to accept the 'first defeat in the nation's history', as Nixon put it.[32]

Not to be able to smash up 'a fourth-rate power like North Vietnam' without resorting to nuclear weapons tormented Nixon. He refused to believe Ho Chi Minh 'doesn't have a breaking point'. He even explored the possibility of applying his 'Madman Theory', namely feigning crazy and unpredictable behaviour. Like Nikita Khrushchev before him, he would, he told Kissinger, thus be seen by North Vietnam and their 'sponsors' as a wild card, dangerous and nuclear-tipped, so that North Vietnam would *have* to negotiate a settlement in Paris, if only for safety's sake. 'We'll just slip the word to them' the President explained to his chief of staff. The enemy would be compelled to cower, saying: 'We can't restrain him when he is angry – and he has his hand on the nuclear button.' 'Ho Chi Minh himself will be in Paris in two days,' the president fantasized, 'begging for peace.'[33]

Not even Nixon, a consummate actor, believed he would get away with this on its own, however. He therefore ordered plans to be drawn up for a monster-offensive to be called Operation Duck Hook, which would apply 'maximum political, military, and psychological shock' on the enemy – indeed the president regretted he hadn't kicked off with such clout on winning the White House. 'We should have bombed the hell out of them the minute we took office' he told his speechwriter, Bill Safire. Simultaneously he also continued to pursue his 'Madman' idea. Word thus went round the White House that 'the Old Man is going to have to drop the bomb before the year is out and that will be the end of the war'.[34] To further the 'madman-as-president' notion, Nixon even ordered the dispatch of 'nuclear capable forces to their operating bases' in an effort to intimidate the Russians into pressuring the North Vietnamese to relent.

Nothing worked, however; indeed protests in America grew ever more vocal. Finally, in response to the Moratorium, a huge national anti-war protest held on October 15, 1969, Nixon finally bowed to the un-silent majority in America, just as President Johnson had before him. He wished to win the midterm congressional elections in 1970, and if possible be re-elected as president in 1972. He therefore rejected Kissinger's proposals to increase the bombing or send over more American troops. Instead he proposed the opposite: namely to force Thieu to accept 'de-Americanization' of the conflict: a policy that was quickly retitled 'Vietnamization'.

'Vietnamization' sounded a lot better than defeat, but was based on the same premise: that South Vietnam was doomed, since the South Vietnamese could no more defend themselves effectively, without American help, than the South Koreans.

In a speech on November 3, 1969, Nixon attempted to put a brave face on his failure to resolve the conflict in Vietnam, blaming the North Vietnamese for refusing to cave in. Meanwhile, pretending the war was going well, he announced he would begin withdrawing tens of thousands of troops as part of his successful 'Vietnamization' policy. He also announced the termination of the draft, once the war – for America – ended, addressing the young people of America with the words 'I want peace as much as you do.'[35]

Behind a veil of pretence – that the South Vietnamese were suddenly and miraculously able to shoulder the burden of fighting the Vietcong and North Vietnamese – the Great Retreat was beginning. By the end of the year, Nixon had ordered the repatriation of more than 115,000 American troops, with huge numbers slated to follow them home the following year.

Nixon the politician had gauged correctly, if belatedly. His public approval rating leaped to an all-time high (68 per cent). By continuing a punitive B-52 bombing policy, meantime, he hoped he could at least play to the patriotic American gallery. 'If, when the chips are down, the world's most powerful nation, the United States of America, acts like a pitiful, helpless giant,' he claimed, 'the forces of totalitarianism and anarchy will threaten free nations and free institutions throughout the world.' As a rationale for continuing mass slaughter from the air, especially in laying waste a poor and neutral country such as Cambodia by massive carpet-bombing, it proved unconvincing to protesters, and filled later historians with indignation – poor Cambodia becoming 'the most heavily bombed country in history'.[36] Transcripts of Nixon's deliberations with Henry Kissinger, released decades later, certainly make sickening reading. 'They [the USAF] have got to go in there and I mean really go in,' Nixon emphasized to Kissinger in 1970. 'I want everything that can fly to go in there and crack the hell out of them. There is no limitation on mileage and there is no limitation on budget. Is that clear?' Lest there be any doubt (since Kissinger had warned that the US Air Force was trained to attack Soviet air forces and conventional armies, not guerrillas embedded in civilian communities[37]), Nixon reiterated: 'I want a plan where every goddamn thing that can fly goes into Cambodia and hits every target that is open . . . everything. I want them to use the big planes, the small planes, everything they can.'[38]

The Cambodian 'Sideshow', as William Shawcross sarcastically called it – a campaign in which 15,000 American troops invaded the country, without congressional approval, while 2.75 million tons of bombs were dropped by the US Air Force – was a veritable holocaust from a humanitarian point of view. Upwards of 10 per cent of the bombing was indiscriminate, resulting not only in some 600,000 Cambodian deaths, it was later estimated in a Finnish government report, but also the death of a further million Cambodian civilians by starvation, and the rise of Pol Pot's Khmer Rouge.

Meanwhile huge advances in western technology and the manufacture of consumer appliances in the 1960s had proved Nixon, in his Kitchen Debate with Nikita Khrushchev in 1959, correct: consumer capitalism *was* fulfilling ordinary people's desires for a better life more effectively than ideological Marxism was doing. Thanks to President

Kennedy's decision to fund a race to the moon, moreover, even the Soviet Union's one scientific and engineering triumph, sputnik, was relegated to a footnote when, on Sunday July 20, 1969, nearly a billion people around the world – the largest television audience ever – watched as the *Eagle* (the lunar module of *Apollo 11*) landed, and two American astronauts set foot on the moon's powdery surface.

'This certainly has to be the most historic telephone call ever made from the White House' Nixon declared excitedly as he spoke to the men, Neil Armstrong and Buzz Aldrin. It was the 'beginning of a new age' he claimed. 'For one priceless moment in the whole history of man all the people on this earth are truly one.' Welcoming the men three days later aboard an American aircraft carrier in the Pacific Ocean, Nixon then congratulated them in person, saying (to the consternation of evangelical Christians) that it was 'the greatest week in the history of the world since the Creation'.[39]

As five further manned moon landings then built upon the American achievement over the following three years, the question arose: might the 1970s usher in that 'new age', an age of peaceful coexistence, leading to an end to the Cold War? If so, how far could the United States push that process, while turning it to its own economic and security advantage? Did the answer lie in what, after the first moon landing, Nixon called his new 'Doctrine'?

Speaking to journalists in Guam, Nixon had described his view of US policy across the world, in particular the face-saving 'Vietnamization'. Reading reporters' articles afterwards, he decided to give it the title 'Nixon Doctrine', in contrast to the Truman Doctrine, and Cambodia, he declared, 'is the Nixon doctrine in its purest form'.[40]

Pure was a relative term. In his new approach to foreign affairs there would be 'no more Vietnams'. Although the US would do its best to help meet Communist insurgencies when they arose, it 'would not fight the war' for other people's democracies.[41] Instead, America would pursue a radically new approach to empire: seeking an accommodation with the Soviets, a freeze on the arms race, and reversal of his own long-held attitude towards Communist China by embracing it now as a 'neighbour' in the Pacific, with the prospect of real trade between the continents – once a major facet of the United States economy. The Cold War would thus no longer be fought as a struggle to be won, but would be recast as the interplay of great powers, as in the nineteenth century, with 'spheres' of influence but no direct colonization.

Reporters who had covered Nixon since the 1940s rubbed their eyes in disbelief. Was such a volte-face real? And could Nixon put it into effect?

In seeking psychiatric help in the 1950s, Nixon had attempted to alter his political persona into one he could accept in the mirror and with which he could be more comfortable. The result had been, for the most part, a more dignified, statesmanlike Richard Nixon, willing to see the world more realistically than many of his Republican, even Democratic colleagues: the foundation for his new Nixon Doctrine. But, as his deliberate stymieing of President Johnson's peace negotiations had demonstrated, the old Richard Nixon – ambitious, resentful, tormented – had not gone away, and in the bunker-style life he then led as president, protected by amoral courtiers, it was bound eventually to resurface. 'Isolation', Kissinger said of him later, 'had become almost a spiritual necessity' – a 'tormented man who insisted on his loneliness'.[42]

Unable to share the limelight or give credit to others, the president was, Kissinger described, 'a very odd man, an unpleasant man. He didn't enjoy people.'[43] Nixon himself was aware of this. Of President Eisenhower he said in amazement, 'Everybody loved Ike. But the reverse of that was that Ike loved everybody . . . Ike didn't hate anybody. Ike was puzzled by that sort of thing. He didn't think of people who disagreed with him as being the "enemy". He just thought: "They don't agree with me."'[44] This was not how Richard Nixon felt or worked, with the consequence that the bunker mentality that pervaded his presidency poisoned even the most progressive of his initiatives.

The Strategic Arms Limitation Treaty (SALT) between the United States and the Soviet Union was an example of Nixon at his best – and worst. Halting the arms race had been a goal of presidents since Dwight Eisenhower. It had been pursued by Kennedy, who got a treaty ban against testing nuclear weapons, and again by President Johnson, who got the Soviets to agree a common approach to the spread of nuclear weapons. Yet it was President Nixon who got Congress to ratify Johnson's nuclear non-proliferation treaty and, in a tied vote in the Senate (broken by the vice president) to back a failing US anti-ballistic-missile (ABM) programme, as a bargaining tool in getting a strategic missile limitation. Instead of proceeding methodically through his SALT team and Secretary of State, however, Nixon pursued a tortuous up-and-down, back-room, ad hoc series of 'negotiations' as Byzantine as they were protracted, all conducted with, or through, his National Security Adviser, Kissinger, lest the State Department or defence experts garner any credit or acclaim.

This was the 'Madman Theory' written into the script of the increasingly imperial White House itself: an American Empire propelled by capitalist wealth, investment, trade and hard work, but led by a whim-driven president who seemed able only to operate in secret, hoping that his eccentric, maverick style would keep everybody guessing and thereby preserve the initiative in his own hands. Thus, instead of getting a considered arms treaty with the Soviets in reasonable time, Nixon attempted endless manoeuvres as part of his negotiating tactics to try and trick-or-treat them into pressuring the North Vietnamese to make peace – a linkage that failed completely, and left Nixon, facing growing unpopularity over continuation of the Vietnam War in May 1972, having to agree to a five-year arms moratorium that was largely specious.

Characteristically the president announced SALT to the world as if it were the beginning of the end of the Cold War. Moreover, having used Dr Kissinger rather than his formal team to get the agreement, he became paranoid lest Kissinger take credit for it. 'It won't mean a damn thing' he privately acknowledged of the SALT agreement, but agreed with Kissinger it might well produce a worthwhile outcome by stealing the peacenik thunder from under Democrats' noses, and thus 'break the back of this generation of Democratic leaders'.[45] More so, in fact, if he and Kissinger pursued their dual-Machiavellian approach to government. 'We've got to break – we've got to destroy the confidence of the people in the American Establishment' the president confided to Kissinger, so that 'the people' of America would turn to Richard M. Nixon as their true leader.[46]

This was no longer a matter of an imperial presidency, centred on the White House, in other words, but of a maverick president operating from a hidden office, on the sly, *away* from the White House; unpredictable, isolated, often out of control. Certainly, it was becoming clear to many observers abroad that America was being ruled by a new kind of leader, an untrustworthy chief executive playing poker on a world stage while exploiting the docility and support of a 'silent majority' at home.

For all Nixon's mistakes and self-isolation, however, such observers had to admit he was amazingly clever at keeping the initiative; indeed he *was* representing the centrist majority of voters, both Republican and Democratic. The majority of Americans wanted the US military to leave Vietnam, as did Nixon. The majority favoured détente with the Russians – as did Nixon, however irrationally he conducted negotiations and however specious the first SALT agreement. The majority wished for a rapprochement with Communist China – as did Nixon. The very man who had fanned the flames of fear and even hysteria against the Communists of the USSR and China for two long decades, trampling every liberal in his path, became the first president to obtain a signed agreement that codified nuclear parity and coexistence with the Soviets. And then, to the disbelief of diehard Republican anti-Communists but to the applause of the 'silent majority', Nixon reversed his attitude towards Communist China too, going all out to woo Chairman Mao. Observers could only scratch their heads in astonishment. Had the politician who had, at the start of his career, called himself a 'progressive liberal' actually become a liberal?

On Sunday August 15, 1971, after a secret economic summit at Camp David involving thirteen helicoptered assistants and advisers, including the chairman of the Federal Reserve Board, Arthur Burns, Nixon had gone on national television to make an important announcement. With inflation continually rising, along with unemployment, foreign speculators were demanding gold for their dollars. The United States, then, would simply abandon the gold standard and allow the dollar to float, effectively devaluing it at a stroke.

Foreign governments, oil producers and currency speculators were stunned by such a unilateral, surprise decision, which Nixon managed to keep from leaking until the moment he went on air. Moreover he announced a temporary freeze on prices and wages, as well as a raft of economic measures that scandalized right-wing Republican backers and reduced George McGovern, his probable opponent in the 1972 presidential election, to apoplexy. McGovern called the speech 'sheer bunk, irrelevancy and mystery' – especially the abandonment of the gold standard as 'a disgrace that amounts to a backdoor devaluation'.[47]

It did – but a highly effective one. As a result, the Dow Jones recorded the biggest one-day rise in its history. Nixon's address, moreover, was masterly. American troops were coming home faster than anyone had believed possible the year before; South Vietnam would soon be left on its own, leaving the United States to do what it did best: create wealth. 'America has its best opportunity today to achieve two of its greatest ideals,' Nixon began: 'to bring about a full generation of peace and to create a new era of prosperity.' The American dollar was never again to be 'a hostage in the hands of international speculators.' A 10 per cent tax on all imports would be levied, with price controls to ensure American speculators did not get in on the act. Federal spending would be cut, while investment credits would be given to businesses and a fifty-dollar bonus to every taxpayer. Foreign aid would be cut by 10 per cent. Lest this sound like Father Christmas in America and Scrooge abroad, Nixon ended with a call to economic arms. 'Every action I have taken tonight is designed to nurture and stimulate that competitive spirit to help us snap out of self-doubt, the self-disparagement that saps our energy and erodes our confidence in ourselves . . . Whether the nation stays number one depends on your competitive spirit, your sense of personal destiny, your pride in your country and yourself.'[48]

As a lawyer and as a campaign pugilist Nixon had always looked for weaknesses in an opponent's defences. Recognizing that the tensions between the USSR and China could be exploited to American advantage, Nixon the global strategist attempted to offer himself as an ally to the Soviets in their gathering dispute with Mao, while doing the same with the Chinese in their growing hostility towards the Soviet Union. He thus discussed (but did not agree to) a Soviet pre-emptive strike against Chinese nuclear weapon-producing sites; simultaneously he pressed for a personal meeting with Mao, and eventually got it. 'They're scared of the Russians. That's got to be it', Nixon remarked to Kissinger, on hearing Chou En-lai's invitation that he visit Peking.[49]

Nixon was right – and rightly seized the opportunity. His epithet 'Tricky Dick' was now earned in spades as he cast aside his long-held loyalty to Chinese Nationalist leader Chiang Kai-shek, buttered up Mao Zedong ('The Chairman's writings moved a nation and have changed the world' he said unctuously, when Mao deprecated his own books), expressed awe at the Great Wall of China, accepted two pandas for the Washington National Zoo, and agreed a communiqué which

not only obligated the United States to oppose with China any move
by the USSR to achieve 'hegemony in the Asia Pacific region', but also
recognized Communist China's claim that Taiwan was 'a part of
China'. Recommending that there be a 'peaceful settlement of the
Taiwan question by the Chinese themselves', the president committed
the US to an 'ultimate objective of the withdrawal of all US forces
and military installations from Taiwan'.[50] Such a statement, had it been
issued by a politician when Nixon was in Congress, would have had
him on the floor denouncing the speaker as a traitor. Now it was
wisdom – Nixon's wisdom.

Back home, where the president's extraordinary week-long trip in
February 1972 had been broadcast on evening network television
(thanks to the time difference), he immediately declared 'This was the
week that changed the world' – a play on John Reed's famous account
of the Russian Revolution. Inasmuch as he had spent half a lifetime
opposing the change, it was patently disingenuous. Nixon the maverick
had every reason to crow, however, since only a maverick could have
changed his spots so swiftly, utterly and shamelessly. The leader of
the free world, after decades of 'pinko-trashing', had entered the lion's
den, and stretched out a hand of potential friendship between the
world's foremost capitalist superpower and the world's most populous Communist nation (871 million people, having added 200 million,
the size of the US population, in a single decade). This was an extraordinary achievement, however much of a turncoat Nixon might be
as a Republican. 'Tricky Dick' had, in effect, tricked his own right-wing
anti-Communist funders and supporters, confounding them by his use
of the 'silent majority', which by an overwhelming margin supported
his initiative.

Later that year Nixon won re-nomination as the Republican presidential candidate, despite outrage among Republican hardliners,
diehards and extremists over his liberal actions. Then, with a peace
agreement being tortuously negotiated with North Vietnam, he won
one of the biggest electoral landslide victories in presidential history,
trouncing George McGovern on November 5, 1972, by forty-seven
million votes to twenty-nine million. For a politician who had
committed genocide in South East Asia and provoked virtual civil war
at home in his first two years in office, this was a truly extraordinary
resurrection.

In his second term, Richard Nixon seemed determined to continue to recast America's power abroad. Moreover he would exercise it no longer as the leader of the western allies, but in the pursuit of raw American self-interest, as the world's strongest economic and military power. 'Here's those little cocksuckers right in there' Nixon had sneered when pointing to Vietnam on a map of the world in May 1972 shortly before his re-election, thumping the table as he spoke. 'Here's the United States (thump). Here's western (thump) Europe, that *cocky* little place that's caused so much devastation – Here's the Soviet Union (thump), here's the (thump) mid-East . . . Here's the (thump) silly Africans . . . And (thump) the not-quite-so-silly Latin Americans. Here *we* are. They're taking on the United States. Now, goddamit we're gonna *do* it. We're going to *cream* them [bomb the North Vietnamese]. This is not in anger or anything. This old business, that I'm "petu-lant", that's bullshit. I should have done it long ago,' he'd rasped in an almost Hitlerian monologue, 'I just didn't follow my instincts.'[51]

This maverick, individual, cynical, dangerous but also game-changing approach to global issues was Nixon's contribution to what became known the next year as the 'Imperial Presidency'.[52] Instead of working in conjunction with Congress, Nixon directed his US bombing oper-ations and simultaneous negotiating efforts with Hanoi almost entirely without reference to Capitol Hill – just as he made each of his about-turns *ex cathedra*, from his visit to China to his abandonment of the gold standard. But such benevolent-dictator behaviour could only work successfully if there were no leaks; and leaks came to obsess him to the point of paranoia.

Nixon had always hated the press for criticizing him; now he hated it for daring to publish the truth – truths which people on his own team must be leaking, he suspected. In this respect, Nixon was not Richard the Lionheart but Richard III: an inveterate schemer, suspi-cious even of his colleagues, and constantly issuing vindictive, retalia-tory orders, which his loyal chief of staff, John Haldeman, for the most part took upon himself to execute – and often quietly ditched. Among the orders that Haldeman didn't ditch was one that would have disas-trous results for the president and his trusted servants: Watergate.

Had Nixon been psychologically better balanced, or had he had a sense of humour, the break-in that became known as Watergate might never have happened.

Watergate would be the iceberg that sank his presidency, but it was only the tip. Blaming 'fucking Jews' and using a Special Investigations Unit, familiarly known as 'the Plumbers', Nixon had already personally ordered the burglary of the office and files of a psychiatrist believed to be treating an opponent of the Vietnam War, Daniel Ellsberg. The president had also demanded IRS investigations of all who had contributed to his Democratic opponent Hubert Humphrey, and Senator Muskie: 'the Jews, you know, that are stealing—'. When his White House aide John Ehrlichman suggested the Plumbers break into the National Archives – the very repository of the US Constitution – Nixon concurred. 'You can do that,' the president said, his voice captured for posterity on his own self-taping system.

Even before his re-election, Nixon had prompted growing concern for the way he shut out members of his own administration, of Congress and even senior military leaders who threatened to steal his limelight. He had his own national security adviser, Dr Kissinger, wiretapped, and accused him of entertaining 'delusions of grandeur' when Kissinger offered to fly personally to Hanoi to negotiate with the North Vietnamese.[53] In a bizarre twist, Nixon insisted Kissinger see a psychiatrist, so paranoid did he feel Kissinger was becoming about leaks and 'internal weakness'.[54] (Kissinger even began taping his own telephone conversations to protect himself.)

It was small wonder, then, that in a White House morass of mutual suspicion, wiretapping, burglary, leak and planted denunciatory rumour, one of the Plumbers' illegal 'investigations' would eventually backfire. On May 28, 1972, a year after the Ellsberg affair began, with Nixon still in Leningrad after signing the SALT I treaty with Leonid Brezhnev, First Secretary of the Communist Party, the Plumbers managed to pick the locks of a new target: the headquarters of the National Democratic Committee, on the sixth floor of the Watergate office and apartment complex in Foggy Bottom, Washington DC.

The first break-in went without a hitch. Three weeks later, however, hubris overtook caution. On June 13, 1972, Nixon ordered his special counsel, Charles Colson, to carry out round-the-clock secret surveillance of his Democratic opponent, Senator McGovern, up to the November election. The next night, dissatisfied with the results from the bugs they'd earlier planted in the Democratic National Committee headquarters, Nixon's aides Gordon Liddy and Howard Hunt ordered the burglars back into the Watergate building. This time the President's men were caught *in flagrante*: three Cuban Americans and two former CIA agents, one of whom worked for the Committee to Re-elect the President (the CRP or, later, CREEP).

'Well, it sounds like a comic opera' Nixon chuckled as he listened to initial stories circulating about the burglary, mocking the accents of the Cubans and shaking his head over the $100 bills found in their pockets.[55] He felt secure: Gordon Liddy, his strong-arm lieutenant, was willing to be put 'in front of a firing squad' rather than betray his president, he was assured. The Democratic National Committee duly sued the CRP for $1 million for invasion of privacy, while Nixon – who had ordered the burglary, and had paid the Plumbers – attempted to remain above the fray, issuing a statement from the White House that 'this kind of activity has no place whatever in our electoral process, or in our governmental process'. This was followed by the categorical declaration that 'the White House has had no involvement whatever in this particular incident'.[56]

For a while it seemed as if the murky scandal would blow over, despite the detective work of two *Washington Post* reporters, Bob Woodward and Carl Bernstein. Nixon thus rejoiced in his massive victory at the November 1972 polls – validation, as he saw it, of all his efforts as president during his first term. Having withdrawn virtually all ground forces from Vietnam, he was relying on the might of the US Air Force, once again, to obtain a formal end to the war – or rather, America's part in it. This, he decided, would be achieved by massive new bombing of military targets in Hanoi and Haiphong, code-named Linebacker II. Over twelve days at Christmas 1972 (while Congress was in recess for the holiday break and could not object) vast aerial armadas of B-52 bombers were ordered to drop more tons of high explosive on North Vietnam than in World War II – 'the most savage and senseless act of war ever visited, over a scant ten days, by one sovereign people over another' as the *Washington Post* protested – a 'stone-age tactic' that might cause the president to be impeached, once congressmen returned to Washington.[57]

Since North Vietnam persisted in its refusal to sign a peace treaty guaranteeing South Vietnamese independence, Dr Kissinger's deputy, General Alexander Haig, favoured even more aggressive bombing to compel the North Vietnamese to withdraw their forces from the South.

Kissinger, in Paris, also wanted to end the fruitless negotiations, blaming the Vietnamese, whom he called 'Tawdry, filthy shits. They make the Russians look good.' But the South Vietnamese junta leader, President Thieu, was no better – an 'insane son-of-a-bitch', in Kissinger's parlance, since Thieu obstinately, but understandably, still refused the settlement Nixon had got him to reject four years before.

Times had changed, however. Almost 70 per cent of Americans now felt the war to have been a mistake, from the start. The ceaseless American bombing was becoming an international disgrace, with calls for Nuremberg war trials, given the untold civilian casualties; and all because, from Kissinger's viewpoint, President Thieu would not agree to South Vietnam's suicide. A 'bilateral arrangement' between the US and North Vietnam – one that would simply ignore the South Vietnamese – thus became the American position. The North Vietnamese, who had exhausted their last anti-aircraft missiles around Hanoi, had had enough too. A ceasefire was therefore announced in Paris on January 23, 1973, with President Thieu bowing to the inevitable.

All parties, including the Vietcong who signed up to the agreement, knew the Paris Peace Accords were a charade. Kissinger confided to a journalist that the North Vietnamese would 'probably start the war again on the first of February' 1973 – i.e. after Nixon's re-inauguration – and President Thieu's deputy denounced it as 'a sell-out'. Nevertheless American honour, if it could be called that, had been satisfied, and the US could finally and legally abandon South Vietnam to its fate. Kissinger predicted that, if lucky, South Vietnam could last a year before being overrun by the North Vietnamese, while he sought to get back some 600 American POWs.[58] It was a sad conclusion to a war that could have been terminated in the same way some four years before, had Nixon not sabotaged President Johnson's negotiations. A further 20,000 US servicemen had been killed, but at least it was now over for America.

Behind the general rejoicing, however, all was not well as the president's role in the Watergate burglary became the subject of a media manhunt.

Why Nixon's aides and subordinates should have been willing to go to the wall for him would never be clear, beyond promises of cash; but by continuing to operate his secret taping system, and keeping his incriminating tapes rather than destroying them, the president – who was pathologically anxious lest Kissinger upstage him and write memoirs that would steal the credit for Nixon's triumphs over China, SALT I and the ending of the war in Vietnam – sealed his own ultimate demise. On February 7, 1973, a Senate Watergate Committee was established. By April 30, the first resignations of White House staff began with those of Haldeman and Ehrlichman (both of whom would go to prison, as well as White House counsel John Dean). On May 18, Archibald Cox was then appointed Special Prosecutor by the Attorney General.

Cox's hearings were televised, just as the McCarthy hearings had been. Some 85 per cent of Americans watched at least some of the process. The first crack came in late June, when the 'master manipulator of the cover-up', John Dean, became a witness for the prosecution in return for a reduced jail sentence. Nixon asked Haig, who had become the White House chief of staff in May, if he thought he should resign as president, the first such resignation in US history.

Haig recommended against, as did Kissinger, who blamed 'bastard traitors', namely the press and members of Congress who 'are now trying to deprive you of any success'. By hanging tough, 'You can go down in history', he promised the president as his would-be Bismarck ('My idol', Kissinger boasted), 'as the man who brought about the greatest revolution in foreign policy ever'.[59]

Kissinger, born in Germany, had never truly understood the system of checks and balances that made the US Constitution such a unique document in world history, or the anti-monarchical sentiment that had fuelled the American Revolution. As the rats began to leave the sinking ship, however, Nixon's downfall became inevitable. On July 13, 1973, the deputy White House chief of staff, Alexander Butterfield, a decorated air force pilot, revealed under questioning the existence of White House audio surveillance tapes, a secret originally known only to three people. Immediately the tapes were subpoenaed both by Cox and by Congress. Nixon resisted, citing – like Eisenhower during the McCarthy hearings – 'executive privilege'.

Eisenhower had had, at least, the backing of his Attorney General in asserting such a privilege. Nixon did not; indeed he now fired his newly minted Attorney General, Elliot Richardson, and the Deputy Attorney General, for refusing to fire Cox. Fighting the Congress and his own Justice Department was, however, a poker-driven strategy that could only end badly. Although the Solicitor General, Robert Bork, agreed to do the president's bidding by firing Cox, a move to impeach Nixon in Congress began to gather momentum.

The president now knew what it was like to be Alger Hiss. Weighing his options, Nixon nevertheless decided he would hang on to the presidency, come what may. At a meeting of 400 Associated Press editors in Orlando, Florida, he admitted mistakes but said he had not obstructed justice, would not resign, and, while he acknowledged that 'people have got to know whether or not their president is a crook', he wanted them to know, via the editors, he wasn't.[60]

Adopting a stonewalling strategy, Nixon lurched between self-pity and bravado. His whole life, since childhood, had been a struggle to offset his disadvantages – his humble background, his morose character – by exercising his tough, relentless, competitive and wily intellect. At times he seemed actually to relish the cat-and-mouse struggle to deflect the long arm of the law, in a constitutional system he considered weighted towards dunces and second-raters. 'How much money do you need?' he asked John Dean, on March 21, 1973 – their conversation captured on tape. 'If you need the money, you could get the money . . . You could get it in cash. I know where it could be gotten . . . I mean it's not easy but it could be done,' he confided, assuring Haldeman he could raise a million dollars.[61] 'There is no problem in that.'[62] He could not, however, promise his Plumbers would avoid prison. 'We can't provide the clemency', he made clear; the money would have to compensate for that, he explained – and thereupon arranged for $75,000 to be taken from his secret safe and delivered to Hunt's home that night.[63]

More and more, the president's machinations resembled those of Caligula. Alternating daily between illegal and drastic options – the provision of illegal hush-money; efforts to get Mitchell, Dean and others to take sole blame for Watergate; instructions to the prosecutor not to offer immunity (which would encourage whistle-blowers); pretending meanwhile to his Plumbers that they could rely on him to grant them a presidential pardon so they would not go to jail – Nixon seemed to relish the adrenalin rush of playing, as always, such a high-stakes game. 'For a guy who you say is sometimes a little loose upstairs, he looks pretty clever to me', Dean's attorney was moved to remark.[64]

American affairs of state, meanwhile, went to pot as the president became more and more embattled, leaving Kissinger to conduct US foreign policy. Kissinger's indifference to civilian suffering in Cambodia and Laos – where another 350,000 civilians lost their lives – caused observers, historians and, later, genocide lawyers, to question his role as national security adviser in the Nixon administration, even to call for his indictment. Cambodia and Laos, moreover, were not the only areas where Kissinger indulged, it would be claimed, in mass murder and even individual murder – as when, on September 11, 1973, a second CIA-sponsored coup against the democratically elected president of Chile, Dr Salvador Allende, led to him being surrounded in his presidential palace and forced to commit suicide. 'I mean,' Kissinger congratulated the president five days later, 'we helped them – created the conditions as great as possible' for the coup to succeed. To which Nixon added, thinking of Watergate, he was grateful that 'our hand doesn't show on this one' – yet.[65] Nor did it the following month, when war broke out in the Middle East.

The first news of war in the Middle East came early on October 6, 1973. More than any other ill tidings, its reception in Washington DC bespoke the state of Nixon's crippled presidency, sixteen days before impeachment proceedings were opened by the House Judiciary Committee. 'For two and a half hours after he heard about war dangers from the Israelis at 6 a.m. on October 6,' one historian later wrote, the newly promoted Secretary of State, Kissinger, 'did not consult Nixon, who was in Key Biscayne, Florida, where he had taken shelter from mounting judicial and congressional pressures.'[66]

The president was, in fact, seldom in Washington. Records indicate that, in the seven months between April and the end of November 1973, Nixon only spent a total of thirty-two days in the capital, 'ten of them as a patient, with pneumonia, at Walter Reed Army Hospital'.[67]

Nixon's absenteeism, after sidelining the State Department throughout his presidency in order to concentrate power in his own and Kissinger's hands, now proved fatal to peace in the Middle East. The fact was, 'in October 1973, Nixon was in no condition to execute US policy in the Middle East' wrote another historian.[68] Depressed, he reverted to drinking; his new national security adviser, Brent Scowcroft, was told to refuse a call from the British prime minister Edward Heath, during the crisis, because the president of the United States was 'loaded'.[69]

Egypt's and Syria's attack, launched to retrieve the Sinai and the Golan Heights that Israel had refused to vacate after the 1967 war, made far more headway than Kissinger's analysts had forecast. Besieged by Israeli pleas for urgent military help, however, Kissinger presented the crisis to President Nixon not as a war between Jews and Arabs over the Occupied Territories, but as a war between America and the Soviet Union for domination of the Middle East and its oil for the next generation.

Sobering up, Nixon allowed himself to be persuaded, despite his concern over the consequences. He therefore approved Kissinger's rescue plan: a larger airlift of military supplies to Israel in a few days than the entire humanitarian Berlin airlift against Soviet pressure in 1948–9. The twenty-day Yom Kippur War thus ended on October 26 in a triumph not for the Egyptians and Syrians in liberating the Occupied Territories, but for the intransigent Israelis. Kissinger would claim it was his greatest achievement, a great coup against the Soviets – the very empire with which the president was seeking détente – but in terms of peace in the Middle East, it would prove to be a disaster.

To add to Nixon's misfortunes, a new scandal took place in Washington as the Yom Kippur War raged. On October 10, 1973, Nixon's vice president, Spiro T. Agnew, was forced to resign and face charges over earlier financial improprieties while governor of Maryland.

Characteristically, Nixon refused to grant Agnew a pardon, and looked for a replacement vice president who would help him fight Congress' ongoing Watergate investigation. Eventually he settled on a member of Congress itself: Minority House Leader Gerald R. Ford of Michigan.

If the president hoped thereby to mollify the Congress, however, he was to be bitterly disappointed. The Watergate hearings continued apace, taking a terrible toll on Nixon's mental health. As 1973 came to an end, his sanity seemed, to those who were allowed to meet him in person, to be deteriorating alarmingly. At Christmas, Senator Goldwater found him talking 'gibberish' and 'making no sense'.[70] 'I asked myself whether I was witnessing a slow-motion collapse of Nixon's mental balance', Goldwater noted, but declined to raise the issue of the president's competence in the Senate.[71] Fearful for the implications for the Republican lock on the presidency after the recent resignation of the vice president, Goldwater merely put his notes in his safe.

From landslide popular re-election in 1972, a bare year before, President Nixon's second term in office had turned into a travesty, his family, doctor and remaining intimates aware that he was no longer rational. The chief of naval operations, Admiral Zumwalt, considered that Nixon, Kissinger and General Haig were now clinically 'paranoid', raising grave concerns for the safety of the world. 'It was clear he saw the attacks on him', Zumwalt afterwards described, 'as part of a vast plot by intellectual snobs to destroy a president who was representative of the man in the street.'[72]

Had Nixon been a man in the street, he might well have been locked up, but with Kissinger feeding Nixon's paranoia ('They are out to get you . . . We will show them') the tragedy for America would drag on for many more months, with the danger that the very office of president of the United States would lose its dignity and authority unless the President, whose polls had dipped to the twenties, resigned.[73]

Behind Nixon's back, Kissinger promised Vice President Ford he would stay on as Secretary of State in a Ford administration, if the president was persuaded to step down; but Kissinger continued to toady and fawn to Nixon, as he had since Nixon's campaign of 1968. Emboldened, and despite rumours of resignation swirling throughout January 1974, Nixon warned Congress he would not resign 'under any circumstances'. The alternative was for Congress to impeach him, but if it did, he warned in what was in effect blackmail, it would bring upon the nation an even greater humiliation, for he would 'fight like hell, even if only one senator stands with him'.[74]

In truth there existed one other alternative: a Caine Mutiny. Under the Twenty-fifth Amendment, Section 3, passed by Congress in 1965 and ratified by the states in 1967, a president could stand down or be removed by virtue of his inability to 'discharge the powers and duties of his office'. But with no one yet willing to officially challenge the president's sanity, the future of America thus rested on judicial process: namely whether Congress dared proceed with the first impeachment of an incumbent president in the twentieth century, based on subpoenaing Nixon's tapes as material evidence.

Vainly, Nixon hoped he could rescue his fortunes, as he had so often managed before, by another Checkers-style speech. He therefore made plans to announce with great fanfare in his State of the Union address in January 1974 that he had personally persuaded Middle East oil producers to drop their oil embargo, currently crippling the American economy. The Arab oil-producing states, however, declined to oblige until they saw real progress in getting a withdrawal by Israel from the Occupied Territories. Israel simply refused to pull back from the captured Golan Heights; the Arabs would not lift their oil embargo; and nothing Nixon could say or threaten would move either side. The lines he'd planned for his State of the Union address were dropped, while the lines at American gas stations grew longer and longer throughout the spring of 1974.

For the president the punitive Arab oil embargo was a catastrophe. Inflation rose to 15 per cent, affecting everyone, while thanks to the Watergate revelations, distrust of the government rose to a near 70 per cent level. Once again Nixon attempted a Checkers-like broadcast on April 29, 1974, after issuing a sanitized version of transcripts of some of the tapes he was withholding.

Nixon's 1952 Checkers speech had saved his vice-presidential candidacy. Twenty-two years later, with the indictment of no less than seven White House officials by a federal grand jury announced in Washington in March 1974, and the Supreme Court rejecting Nixon's appeal to withhold subpoenaed tapes from the Public Prosecutor on the grounds of 'executive privilege', it didn't work. Despite acute phlebitis, the president then insisted on travelling to Europe and the Middle East in June, in an effort to show that, for the time being at least, he was too critical to world peace for Congress to start the impeachment process. That effort, too, led nowhere. Kissinger merely raised the question whether, by deliberately flying against his doctor's advice, Nixon had a death wish. (General Haig thought he had.) In Moscow, Nixon's attempt to get a SALT II agreement proved abortive and he was unfocused, purportedly 'listening to White House tapes' in his room rather than preparing for the next day's talks.

In public (or semi-public) Nixon claimed 'the Office of the presidency must never be weakened, because a strong America and a strong American president is something which is absolutely indispensable' – but this begged the question of whether by hanging on, Nixon was deliberately weakening the office.[75] In any event, his protracted manoeuvrings proved to no avail. On July 27, 1974, the House Judiciary Committee passed its historic vote to recommend impeachment of the president for only the second time in the nation's history. The specified articles of suggested impeachment extended in succeeding days to a total of three: first, obstruction of justice; second, the illegal use of executive agencies; and third, defying committee subpoenas.

All attention now narrowed to the tapes themselves, which were combed for incriminating material before being released. When the president's aides listened to the 'smoking gun' tape of June 23, 1972, however, with its record of Nixon's role in ordering the CIA to deliberately prevent the FBI from investigating the Watergate break-in, the die was cast. A brief segment, short enough to appear accidental, had been erased; nevertheless it was reported to the president that, in view of what remained, he now had no chance of fighting off a successful impeachment in the House, let alone winning the subsequent trial in the Senate. Nixon himself described the tape as resembling 'slow-fused dynamite waiting to explode,' and he rued the day when, suffering pneumonia in July 1973, he had resisted the temptation (and others' recommendations) to destroy it.[76]

The final farce now began. On August 1, 1974, Nixon told his chief of staff, General Haig, he would resign – but wanted Vice President Ford to promise he would pardon him, once Ford succeeded to the presidency. Ford baulked, unsure of the implications and consequences. At Camp David that weekend Nixon, now in limbo, was persuaded to fight on and face impeachment by his distraught family, who had no idea of the true contents of the tapes, or his involvement in the Watergate and other burglaries. (Later, Nixon's wife suffered a stroke when reading transcripts of the tapes.)

On August 7, the White House issued a statement saying the president 'had no intention of resigning'. But the truth was he had made the decision to resign, as he confided to Kissinger that evening, after hearing his support in the Senate was down to six or seven votes, meaning certain defeat. Nixon vividly foresaw not only the end of all his political dreams, but prosecution for his High Crimes and Misdemeanors – and burst into tears.

Kissinger sobbed as well, saying he too would resign, prompting Nixon to beg him not to. As Kissinger, relieved, made his way to the elevator, Nixon asked him to stop, and to kneel with him and pray. Afterwards the president called Kissinger and begged him never to reveal what had happened. Kissinger promised, but once Nixon was gone, reneged.

The next day, August 8, 1974, at 9.01 p.m., Nixon finally ended the excruciating saga of Watergate, broadcasting live from the Oval Office to some 160 million people. 'In all the decisions I have made in my public life, I have always tried to do what was best for the nation', he claimed – parsing the 'wrong' decisions he'd made not as criminal or vengeful, but as mere 'judgements' in what he believed 'at the time to be the best interests of the country'. It was vintage RN, as he liked to refer to himself, as 'duplicitous as the man himself', Senator Goldwater sneered, standing on the Stage of History, with one of the largest audiences in the annals of television and radio for a presidential broadcast.[77]

At moments the voice of another Richard could be discerned by viewers and listeners: Shakespeare's Richard II, which Nixon had devoured at school. Schlock and bathos were larded for maximum effect, echoing his Checkers speech two decades before. 'I have never been a quitter' he claimed in one final attempt to paint himself as victim rather than as responsible for his own misfortune. 'To leave office before my term is completed is abhorrent to every instinct in my body' he explained truthfully. 'But as president, I must put the interest of America first. America needs a full-time president and a full-time Congress, particularly at this time with problems we face at home and abroad.' After more than a year of covering up, of lies to Congress, of indictments of his closest aides – a whole year after the Watergate conspiracy began to consume his attention – he would now therefore set aside the selfish temptation to 'continue to fight through the months ahead for my personal vindication' and would ask Vice President Ford to take over the presidency at noon the following day.

On August 9, as Nixon boarded his helicopter to be whisked to Andrews Air Force Base and then by jet to exile in California, demonstrators waved placards reading 'Jail to the Chief'. It was a sorry end to a genocidal presidency.

Part Three: Private Life

Of all American Caesars, Richard Milhouse Nixon's personality was the most conflicted. Fear of his irascible, Irish-American father was balanced by adoration of his Quaker, saintly mother. Neither parent, however, believed in showing physical affection. 'No one projected warmth and affection more than my mother did', Nixon later explained. 'But she never indulged in the present-day custom, which I find nauseating, of hugging and kissing her children or others for whom she had great affection.'[78]

Nauseated or not, with two of his brothers dying of tuberculosis, Nixon seems to have felt guilty at surviving, tormented especially by the memory of his youngest brother, Arthur, who, when Nixon returned home from nearly a year away at a grammar school, asked if he could buck the Milhous-Nixon family rule, and kiss his older brother. 'He put his arms around me and kissed me on the cheek', Nixon later remembered – recalling, too, the weeks during which he wept in secret when little Arthur, whom the whole family loved, died at age six. The next year his older brother Harold also came down with tuberculosis, which took five heartbreaking years before it killed him.

Snubbed at school for his brains and for being teacher's pet, Nixon was nicknamed 'Gloomy Gus' by girls (for whom the shy, studious and intensely private student, lonely and lacking a sister, showed zero interest). Later, he would analyze his own competitive streak and relentless ambition, in the face of constant taunts and snubs as a child. 'If you are reasonably intelligent and if your anger is deep enough and strong enough,' he reflected, 'you learn that you can change those attitudes by excellence, personal gut performance, while those who have everything are sitting on their fat butts.'[79]

Nixon had many significant relationships with men in his life, from his father and brothers to men like Haldeman, Ehrlichman, Dean, Mitchell, Rebozo and Kissinger. He had only three significant relationships with women, however, in his whole life.

The first was Hannah Milhous, Nixon's mother. Hannah had trained as a schoolteacher before her wedding, and was proficient in Latin and Greek; she was considered to have 'married beneath her'. Nixon became her star pupil, able to translate Latin without difficulty, and well versed in Roman history. Her moral rectitude hung over him all his life; in fact part of Nixon's later objection to publication of transcripts of his tapes was his horror lest the 'damns and 'goddamns' be made public, which would make his mother 'turn in her grave'.

While his brothers faced down his cantankerous father (there were times when 'shouting could be heard all through the neighborhood', a contemporary recalled), Nixon was too afraid of his father's notorious Irish temper to risk his ire – or a belting.[80] 'Perhaps my own aversion to personal confrontations dates back to these', he later reflected, having watched his mother's quiet, tenacious way of defeating his father, who had left school with only a third-grade education.[81] Hannah's incisive tongue was, to the children, more stinging than their father's strap. 'Tell her to give me a spanking', Nixon's younger brother is said to have cried when caught smoking. 'I just can't stand it to have her talk to me.'[82]

His first girlfriend was initially out of his romantic league. Ola Welch was the stunningly beautiful daughter of the local police chief, a Democrat who revered Franklin Roosevelt and espoused opposing views to those of Nixon's father, a stalwart Republican. 'Oh, how I hate Richard Nixon' Ola wrote in her diary at Whittier High School.[83] But when they acted together in a (Latin) school play, in which the school 'nerd' had to kiss her, she softened her stance, and became intrigued by the talented but psychologically contorted valedictorian, a young man she thought amazingly gifted in his stage presence and 'rapport with an audience', and the speed with which he learned his lines and stage directions.[84] She thus allowed Nixon to date her, platonically, for the following five years, during which they became engaged and saved for a wedding ring. 'He was a real enigma' she said of him later.[85] 'Most of the time I just couldn't figure him out.'[86]

Moody, hard-working, riven between morality and ambition, Nixon worried people early on by his brilliant potential, which might be put to ill use. Ola's sister Dorothy read Nixon's palm at age nineteen, when he was in college. 'I got quite a shock' she remembered later. 'What I saw in his palm was a path of incredibly brilliant success and then the most terrible black cloud like a disaster or something.'[87]

Returning for the vacation from Duke Graduate Law School in the summer of 1935, Nixon asked to come over to Ola's home in Whittier. Pressed to give a reason why she said no, Ola explained that she had another boyfriend there, talking to her parents.

Nixon was beside himself. 'He was really furious. He shouted, "If I ever see you again it will be too soon."'[88] Though Ola returned the money he had contributed towards the purchase of a wedding ring, he kept writing to her, calling himself 'a bad penny' yet unable to relent.[89] Finally, in February 1936, after nine months he gave up, writing that he 'realized more than ever the perfection, the splendor, the grandeur of my mother's character. Incapable of selfishness she is to me a supreme ideal. And you', he explained to Ola, 'have taken her place in my heart – as an example for which all men should strive.'[90]

Nixon's stilted, idealizing prose masked a black hole in his psyche. Between his 'superdrive' on the one hand, and his 'inhibitions' on the other, even his psychiatrist later found him 'an enigma, not only to me but to himself'.[91] Though Ola Welch's termination of their engagement hurt him deeply, Nixon was fortunate enough, two years later, to meet – again through amateur dramatics – another beautiful woman. This time it was a twenty-six-year-old schoolteacher, blessed with golden-red hair and film-star looks, Thelma Ryan, who'd changed her name to Patricia. Nixon asked her for a date on January 16, 1938, the evening he first met her (acting in the ominously named play *The Dark Tower*). When she turned him down, he announced: 'You may not believe this but I am going to marry you some day.'[92]

Pat Ryan rebuffed Nixon's notions of courtship throughout the spring of 1938, but found it impossible to shake him off. They shared similar family stories, as well as common feelings of resentment towards those who came from more privileged backgrounds. Her father had also been a virtually uneducated, poverty-stricken Irish-American, a goldminer-trucker-farmer with a foul temper who died of silicosis when Pat was sixteen. Her mother had been a German immigrant, who bore her husband's violent outbursts with stoicism until she died in 1924, when Pat was twelve. Pat had worked her way all through college (in part as a movie extra in Hollywood), was a non-believer, and though, like Ola, she definitively terminated the relationship with Gloomy Gus, no better or more tenacious candidate came forward during the ensuing two years; Nixon even ferried her to and from her dates with other men to show the depth of his attachment. Pat finally agreed to marry him in the summer of 1940, when she was twenty-eight. She refused, however, to go through the hypocrisy of a church wedding, and the ceremony took place at an inn in Riverside, California, attended by only a handful of relatives. Pat and Dick would remain married for over fifty years until her death, in 1993, at eighty-one; but it was often a triumph of willpower more than affection.

Like many a young bride, Pat attempted to reinforce the better side of her husband's nature. She was, however, unable to thwart its darker, more satanic elements. As Stephen Ambrose, Nixon's biographer, later wrote, 'she hated politics' and there was no joy in the marriage beyond their two daughters.[93] Though they separated for a time in 1956, and he promised time and again thereafter to give up politics, he could not do so, addicted as he was to the excitement and dismissive of the 'boredom' that life as a lawyer would entail, indeed claiming it would 'kill him in four years'.

Nixon's mother had wanted him to become a preacher, but he had had insufficient faith; for politics, however, he possessed many of the most important credentials, beginning with deceit. 'You're never going to make it in politics', he told a fellow law student. 'You just don't know how to lie.'[94] In Nixon's mind, lies – especially political lies – were white, as long as they led to power, the greatest aphrodisiac. 'Nixon depended on Pat because he trusted her, and she stayed with him', Nixon's psychiatrist remarked after Nixon's death and his oath of confidentiality was at an end. 'But that was for politics. The truth is, his only passion was politics.'[95]

Between deceit and power there was the field of political battle, which energized and obsessed the grocer's son. Politics – especially taking on 'the Establishment' – challenged his theatrical, debating, analytical, predictive and conspiratorial abilities as nothing else. Weaving a personal myth of noble quest in pursuit of high ideals, moreover, permitted him to play upon public gullibility, excusing his less attractive traits. For this outwardly noble quest he needed Pat as a public symbol of his purity, even as he overruled her objections. 'His destiny', she recognized, 'was her fate.'[96]

Henry Kissinger later wondered how much more Nixon might have accomplished, had the president been 'loved' – failing to recognize that Nixon *had* been loved by his family, despite (perhaps because of) his awkward personality.[97] Amazingly, he drew copious examples of love, of admiration, and, above all, of extraordinary loyalty from his family, from certain companions, and from his intimate staff, even when they should have known better. The problem was not, then, in the lack of available love and devotion, but that it was never enough to satisfy Nixon's tormented psyche, which expressed itself in a constant mix of high rhetoric and black vindictiveness. Together they formed a relentless, insatiable ambition to vault the necessary steps leading to the highest political office in the empire, and then to retain it at any cost, however duplicitous, immoral, illegal, illicit or criminal his conduct became, as his tapes would ultimately reveal.

For his wife Pat, as for those innocents who had supported the rise of a hugely gifted American lawyer from a humble background, this was the deepest disappointment. For those who knew the demon in Richard Nixon, either in private or as evidenced early in his public career during the Hiss case and rampant McCarthyism, there was, by contrast, only a sense of déjà vu – as well as fear as to where a man of such profound narcissism, hate, depression and bouts of paranoia might, together with his many talents, lead (or mislead) America.

Behind Nixon's devotion to mythic political ideals such as anti-Communism and his low-life, vindictive pursuit of power at any cost, his psychiatrist saw a never-ending struggle between idealization of his saintly, puritanical mother and anger over the fear inspired in him as a child by his tyrannical, brutal and loud-mouthed father. It was not a struggle that Nixon succeeded in overcoming, the doctor lamented, especially when dishonesty and vindictiveness actually *rewarded* Nixon, emotionally, financially and politically.[98] As a candle draws moths to the flame, Nixon drew men of dubious, dishonest nature to him, attracting them not only to indulge their greed and eye for opportunity, but also appealing beyond them to a 'silent majority': the great white jury of American, mostly male, voters who did not know his underlying character, and who, once won over by his bathos-ridden theatrics, unwittingly licensed his secretive criminal behaviour and megalomaniacal conduct of America's vast military power.

In this latter-day role of Iago, Nixon demonstrated unmatched talents. Of all post-war US presidents, he was by far and away the most skilful in his use of courtroom techniques. His childhood love of Latin and his reading of Roman history gave him a powerful command of outward 'order and logic' in forming his appeal; to this he added telling infusions of sentimentality, schlock, entertaining invective and well-chosen lies, making him a compelling orator as well as formidable opponent whom even Ronald Reagan, in his prime, could not match.

Nixon always kept by him a lined yellow legal pad on which he would draft his thoughts, his speeches, his ambitions. He was forever *calculating*, and forever manipulating others for his own purposes. He worked at times as if demented, requiring at one point nine secretaries. His wife recalled that when he was a senator, he would often spend the whole night on the Hill. 'He'll work over there until the small hours of the morning . . . He'll curl up on the couch and get a few hours' sleep. Then he'll get a little breakfast and shave, and go right down to the Senate chambers to work.'[99] Posing as a man with a noble mission – beginning with anti-Communism, then switching to the accommodation of Communism – each time he was defeated he was able to solicit personal pity and compassion; so much so, in fact, that his own wife, and later his daughters, would refuse each time to believe the bad things said or documented about him. 'Richard Nixon is a man who has never lied, not even a white lie, to his family or to the American people', his daughter Tricia would say,[100] despite the testimony of Nixon's own Watergate attorney, Fred Buzhardt, who considered Nixon 'the most transparent liar he had ever met'.[101]

It was a masterly real-life performance in which the actor never actually paid for any of his sins, but was always rewarded or pardoned, forgiven and rehabilitated to the very end of his life, despite the swathe of destruction he left around and behind him. Thus the one-time pauper, who rented a hut without plumbing as a law student at Duke to save money, became, despite his defeats and criminal conduct, rich beyond his early dreams, able to dispose of huge amounts of cash from dubious sources to further his nefarious plots, like a medieval caliph.

Herein, sadly, lay the deeper tragedy for America, since not only was Richard Nixon irremediably corrupt, but in his manic determination to gain and to wield absolute power as president or Caesar of the United States, he succeeded in overturning a two-centuries-old American system of governance, claiming he was doing the best thing for his country of 'silent' Americans, but setting an example of quasi-dictatorship in which his contempt for the Senate and House of Representatives, two chambers in which he himself had briefly served, was absolute.

By a brilliant, Ciceronian ability to spin his own presidential story, Nixon had continually gilded a public self-portrait in which he, in search of greatness, was the noble victim of spite and snobbery, rather than an increasingly unstable, even mad quasi-dictator. 'The only place

where you and I disagree,' Nixon had told Kissinger in the spring of
1972, 'is with regard to the bombing' of North Vietnam, Cambodia
and Laos. 'You're so goddamned concerned about civilians,' Nixon
remarked, 'and I don't give a damn. I don't care.'[102] Contemptuous of
humanitarian-minded critics, Nixon insisted 'we ought to take the
North Vietnamese dikes out now. Will that drown people?' he asked
his national security adviser, who responded that it would kill 'About
200,000.' 'No, no, no' protested Nixon, not from compassion but from
the very insufficiency of such measures. 'I'd rather use the nuclear
bomb', he told the open-mouthed Kissinger. 'Have you got that,
Henry?'

Kissinger, though tantamount to a fellow mass-murderer by this
point, thought it 'would just be too much'. Nixon sneered. 'The nuclear
bomb, does that bother you?' he said. 'I just want you to think big,
Henry, for Christsakes.'[103]

'Hare-brained scheming, half-baked conclusions and hasty decisions
and actions divorced from reality, bragging and bluster, attraction to
rule by fiat' – these and other accusations had been made by *Pravda*
against another emperor, Premier Nikita Khrushchev, who had had
to be removed by his political colleagues before he endangered the
planet, in 1964.[104] Nixon and Khrushchev were thus both considered
by their peers to be dangerously loose cannons: clever but unstable,
relentless in the pursuit of power, and propelled by deep resentments
and feelings of personal insecurity. Both were responsible for the deaths
of tens of thousands of people. To Nixon it was immaterial whether
or not Thieu's South Vietnam, or its people, survived; what was important was 'the United States *cannot* lose. Which means, basically, I have
made the decision. Whatever happens to South Vietnam, we are going
to *cream* North Vietnam', irrespective of congressional approval. 'For
once, we've got to use the maximum power of this country . . . against
this *shit-ass* little country: to win the war.' Surgical strikes against
Haiphong were not what Nixon had in mind. 'I want that place bombed
to *smithereens*. If we draw the sword, we're gonna bomb those bastards
all over the place. Let it fly, *let it fly*.'[105]

It was small wonder Pat Nixon was stricken by thrombosis, reading
transcripts such as these. Nixon had, as his psychiatrist later confided,
always been on the margin of sanity; by the end, even Kissinger called
him 'a basket case'.[106] Whether he was truly mad is impossible to

know, but the 'Madman Theory' (or practice) certainly came in handy
– invoking compassion and, astonishingly, even forgiveness, once he
left office.

Spinning tales of innocence in the pursuit of greatness for his
country, he would decline ever to admit to deliberate wrongdoing;
obtained a controversial presidential pardon; fought tooth and nail to
keep his tapes from being made available to the general public; and
lived out his remaining twenty years in considerable wealth, dying in
New York on April 22, 1994. His funeral in Yorba Linda, California
was attended by five US presidents.

CHAPTER SEVEN

GERALD FORD

Respected

Republican
38th President
(August 9, 1974–January 20, 1977)

Part One: The Road to the White House

Baptized as Leslie Lynch King Jr, Ford was born in Omaha, Nebraska, on July 14, 1913. Two weeks later his mother took him to her family's home in Grand Rapids, Michigan, refusing to tolerate the violent, abusive behaviour of her husband, wool-merchant-heir Leslie Lynch King Sr.

Four years after her return to Grand Rapids, the divorcee remarried, this time choosing a humble local housepainter, Gerald Rudolf Ford, whose name was informally taken by her little son, once he went to school in Grand Rapids. Only in his twenties in 1934 did 'Jerry', as he was known to all, then legally change his name to Gerald Rudolph Ford Jr.

'I am a Ford, not a Lincoln' was the self-deprecating line Gerald Ford would later use. No great intellect but sensible, focused, tenacious and a fiercely loyal youth, Ford grew up to be six feet tall, broad-shouldered, fair-haired, blue-eyed, good-looking, and a fine football player – which counted for more in conservative Michigan than brains.[1] Gaining a football scholarship to Michigan State University, he played in the famous match against Georgia Tech, who refused to compete if Michigan's only coloured player, Willis Ward (who roomed with Ford on away-game trips), were allowed on to the field. Ward insisted Ford should play – and win. The Michigan Wolverines trounced the racists 9–2, to Ward's delight.

On graduation Ford, who had waited tables and washed dishes to survive, took a position as an athletics coach at Yale, where he was eventually accepted into the university's famed law school. Genial and respected, he was a young man 'who has an attractive personality, and is a gentleman of considerable bearing and poise', but was 'not conceited in the slightest, and is very handsome', as the athletics director reported.[2] Ford then returned to his home state to practise law.

As for many of Ford's contemporaries – men such as McCarthy, Kennedy, Lyndon Johnson and George H. W. Bush – World War II proved for him the stepping stone to political success. His application to serve in naval intelligence (as John F. Kennedy did) was not accepted, but despite bad knees he was accepted into the seagoing US Navy in April 1942, serving with courage and distinction as an anti-aircraft gun director and assistant navigator aboard the converted aircraft carrier, USS *Monterey*, in the South Pacific. He left the service, like Nixon, as a lieutenant commander, in 1946 – but, unlike Nixon, having earned some sixteen battle stars in 1943 and 1944.

From Midwest American isolationism (Ford had worked for Wendell Willkie's presidential campaign in 1940, and attended the Republican National Convention in Philadelphia), Ford became an ardent internationalist once the United States was attacked, and then defeated the Japanese and German empires. Thereafter he favoured America accepting the leadership of the free world in confronting Soviet postwar domination. Keen on carving out a political career in Grand Rapids, however, he found his path stymied by a Michigan political machine boss, Frank D. McKay.

Ignoring McKay, Ford filed at the last minute in the local Michigan Republican primary for Congress. To the surprise of all (including himself and his fiancée) he beat the incumbent congressman for the Fifth District, isolationist Bartel Jonkman, 23,632 votes to 14,341, on his first attempt – thereby assuring himself, in a safe Republican district, election to the House of Representatives in November 1948. It was a seat he never lost, in thirteen consecutive elections.

Given his popularity and principled, hard-working conduct, Ford would be repeatedly asked to stand for the Senate, but his seat on the Appropriations Committee in the House of Representatives guaranteed him growing importance and fulfilment. Unlike 'Tricky Dick' Nixon, who had immediately befriended him as a fellow congressman in 1949, Ford thus rested content with his political lot, becoming in due course Republican Minority Leader and nursing the hope that, if the Republicans ever won back their majority in the House after the 1950 debacle, he would one day become Speaker of the House.

In the event, the Republicans not only failed to gain a majority in Congress, but suffered a 'negative landslide' when Senator Goldwater contested the presidential election, resulting in the loss of some thirty-six Republican seats in the House in 1964. Ford declared his own agenda as pursuing 'the high middle road of moderation'. He was, he made clear, committed to 'firmly resist[ing] the takeover of our party by any elements that are not interested in building a party, but only in advancing their own narrow interests'.[3]

As a moderate Republican and stalwart, anti-Communist patriot Ford supported President Johnson's commitment of American troops to combat in Vietnam, as well as the president's subsequent escalation of the war, having rejected the Senate Republican Policy Committee's 1967 report that recommended peace and withdrawal. Ford was not a gifted speaker, but his position in Congress, his Eisenhowerian integrity and his moderate views on domestic issues made him a welcome mid-American middle-of-the-road speaker across the country with Republican audiences, so much so that he was tipped to be chosen as Nixon's running mate in the summer of 1968.

Former Vice President Richard Nixon had other ideas, however, preferring an unknown, inexperienced and therefore uncompeting understudy: the former governor of Maryland, Spiro T. Agnew. 'I shook my head in disbelief', Ford later recalled.[4]

Returning to the Capitol following Nixon's narrow victory in November 1968, Ford loyally backed Nixon's re-escalation of the Vietnam War, but was otherwise ignored by the president. To Ford's face, Nixon was unctuously grateful for the 'little errands' he did for him, such as denouncing Teddy Kennedy 'on the House floor', as Ford's chief of staff complained. But behind his back, Nixon did not even bother to disguise his contempt for Congress or its Republican Minority Leader, John Ehrlichman sneering that 'Jerry might have become a pretty good Grand Rapids insurance salesman' if he had not chosen politics; 'he played a good game of golf, but he wasn't excessively bright'.[5]

Ford had promised his wife he would step down from his congressional seat at the 1976 election, given the Republican Party's disappointing showing in the 1972 congressional elections and the unlikelihood that he would ever reach his cherished goal of Speaker of the House. But Nixon's trust in Ford's loyalty was well placed. When Agnew was compelled to resign for financial impropriety in October 1973, Nixon made his historic choice, which was approved by the House without serious objection. In accordance with the Twenty-fifth Amendment to the US Constitution, the former Leslie Lynch King Jr thus became, on December 6, 1973, the first appointed vice president of the United States of America – under a president increasingly besieged by Watergate investigators.

Had Nelson Rockefeller, Ronald Reagan or John Connally – the three alternatives recommended by senior members of the Republican Party – been appointed vice president, they would have had few qualms in condemning Nixon's abuse of presidential authority, and – as experienced governors of major states – in subsequently wielding their own new brooms once he was forced to resign. Jerry Ford, by contrast, was made of different stuff – a prisoner, in many ways, of his own high sense of loyalty. As vice president he now remained stubbornly and personally beholden to President Nixon for having chosen him, rather than to Congress for having favoured him in representations to the president, as mandated under the Twenty-fifth Amendment; moreover he continued to defer to Nixon as a leader who he thought, correctly, was significantly smarter than himself. In the following months he flew more than 100,000 miles across America as vice president to reassure Republicans and voters of Nixon's innocence – a noble, if obtuse, effort, given mounting suspicions, evidence and White House obstructionism. To the last moments, Ford refused to read or listen to evidence of Nixon's transgressions, enabling him to claim he was sincere in considering the president to be the victim of a vast left-wing conspiracy.

Ford, an Episcopalian, was a devout Christian, and prayed a lot for strength and guidance. He worked hard, meant well, and took people at their word. His radiant honesty and defence of the President, however, could not keep the chief executive afloat forever. Once the Supreme Court ruled that the 'smoking gun' tape be handed over to Judge Sirica, Nixon was cornered. On Thursday August 1, 1974, with Nixon confiding to Al Haig, his chief of staff, that he would resign if he could be spared prison, Haig embarked on a unique form of extortion. He asked to meet secretly, one on one, with the vice president, and made clear that Nixon would resign only if promised an a priori pardon.

Haig explained he had consulted a lawyer who claimed that the Founding Fathers had specifically mentioned the preservation of the 'tranquility of the Commonwealth', in the words of Alexander Hamilton, as the exceptional circumstance giving a president the right to grant such clemency.

Though trained at Yale Law School, Ford had never studied Hamilton's argument, which warned against taking any step that might, in the offering of a pardon, 'hold out the prospect of impunity' to rebels or miscreants in obstructing justice, and thereby set a poor example.[6] Instead the vice president fatefully took it for granted Haig and his lawyer were correct.

Ford's staff was aghast at the implications, which would destroy Ford's one great virtue, his integrity, if the claim was made he had exchanged a pardon in order to attain the presidency. Even his wife told him 'You can't do that, Jerry.'[7]

Reluctantly Ford, whose commendable and natural instinct was to spare the country the shame and humiliation of impeachment if the president hung on to power, called Haig the next day to tell him he had misspoken, and that there was 'No deal'. He even destroyed Haig's colleague's notes, lest they implicate him later.[8]

Nixon was stunned by Ford's reversal, and told his chief of staff that in that case he had changed his mind about resigning. 'Let them impeach me' Nixon told Haig. 'We'll fight it out to the end.'[9] The *opéra bouffe* of Nixon's last days in office now approached its climax.

Loyal as ever, Ford continued to claim in public that the president was innocent of any wrongdoing. 'I believe the president is innocent of any impeachable offense and I haven't changed my mind,' he stated on August 3, 1974.[10] But with the revelations of the 'smoking gun' tape on August 4, which proved Nixon had had full knowledge of the Watergate burglary from the very beginning, Ford could no longer pretend they would ride out the storm. Even Al Haig admitted to Republican leaders 'I don't see how we can survive this one.'[11]

With impeachment in the House now inevitable – and the prospect of losing his pension if convicted in a consequent Senate trial – Nixon was skewered. Publication of the transcript of the 'smoking gun' tape made even his own family recognize the game might be up. Yet *still* the president held on to his crown, issuing a crazed, thousand-word statement denying culpability, and asking his cabinet to meet on August 6, 1974.

For the first time Nixon was not applauded as he entered. Clearing his throat he began the meeting with the words 'I would like to discuss the most important issue confronting the nation, inflation.'[12]

'My God!' Ford later recalled thinking, it was surreal.[13] It became more so when the president, once they got round to the constitutional crisis, insisted that his decision to order the CIA to stop the FBI investigation of Watergate had been made solely for reasons of national security. He was, therefore, determined to go ahead and face impeachment and trial by Congress. With an air of injured nobility, Nixon added, 'I will accept whatever verdict the Senate hands down.'

Was Nixon acting? It seemed 'ludicrous' to Ford, especially when the president explained he had made the tapes available to prove his innocence, not because the Supreme Court had compelled him to. Yet so amazing was Nixon's performance in its pathos – like a wounded fox, before the kill – that he elicited personal compassion rather than concern for the interests of the nation. Finally, the vice president spoke.

Instead of explaining that the president must, in all conscience, stand down to save the nation, Ford looked ahead to impeachment proceedings in the House, following by a trial in the Senate, whose outcome 'I can't predict.' As vice president, Ford would of course have to recuse himself in public, during the trial, as he was 'a party of interest' – meaning he stood to gain if the president was forced to resign. Nevertheless he wanted Nixon to know he had 'given us the finest foreign policy this country has ever had', and that, if the president was convicted and Ford succeeded him, he would 'expect to support the administration's foreign policy and the fight against inflation'.[14]

There was stunned silence. The declaration, as Ford's aide afterwards recalled, fell far short of the 'Declaration of Independence' they had hoped for; indeed it seemed positively mealy-mouthed.[15] The other cabinet officers were as bad; in the worst domestic crisis of modern American government, no one dared ask the president to step down.

Could this really be the epicentre of the world's most powerful empire? Had Richard Nixon reduced his administration to a handful of gibbering idiots? Ford's chief of staff Robert Hartmann found himself in shock. After the meeting, when Republican members of Congress begged the vice president again to speak up, in order to end what was now a constitutional crisis of the first magnitude, Ford demurred, citing his conflict of interest – though he assured his aides it was only a matter of days before Nixon surrendered to the inevitable. It was important, Ford declared, to avoid rocking the sinking ship; rumours were circulating in the White House that the president might commit suicide if pressed further.[16] In the circumstances, Ford made clear, no one should push the president of the United States, with his finger on the nuclear trigger, into doing something crazy. Patiently allowing Nixon the time to accept his fate gracefully seemed the wisest policy.

Graceful would never be an appropriate epithet for Nixon, but finally, on August 7, 1974, three long days after the 'smoking gun' evidence pulled the rug from beneath him, he capitulated. He would, he decided, resign – after another two days. He did not even summon Ford to tell him the decision, but relied on his chief of staff to relay his decision – and to describe his state of mind. The next day the president agreed to see Ford. 'I have made my decision to resign', he told the vice president in the Oval Office, as if for the first time. 'It's in the best interests of the country.'[17] Watergate was never mentioned. Nixon then put his feet on the desk, and proceeded to give his successor an hour-long tutorial on American foreign and domestic policy – something he had failed to do for the past ten months.

Nixon's behaviour defied comprehension, at one moment in another world, the next, earnest and engaged with the real world. Ford, rendered almost speechless by Nixon's latest performance, told him he felt he was 'ready to do the job and I think I am fully qualified to do it'.[18] But was he?

When he read the draft of the speech the new president would give after taking the oath of office, written by his chief of staff Bob Hartmann, Ford said he wanted to remove the phrase 'Our long national nightmare is over.' 'Isn't that a little hard on Dick?' the vice president asked Hartmann. 'Could we soften that?'

'No, no, no!' Hartmann protested. 'Don't you see, that's your whole speech. That's what you have to proclaim to the whole country – to the whole world. That's what everybody needs to hear, wants to hear, has got to hear you say . . . You have to turn the country around.'[19]

'Okay, Bob' Ford responded. 'I guess you're right. I hadn't thought about it that way.'[20]

What, then, *had* the former Michigan football star been thinking? The phrase stayed in, to Hartmann's relief, but Ford's anxiety not to be seen by the outgoing President as hard-hearted raised serious concerns about the new President's backbone, as well as connection with his fellow Americans.

President Nixon left the White House on the morning of August 9, 1976. Gerald Ford's inauguration followed at 12.03 in the East Room.

Part Two: The Presidency

'I think he'll make a good president', Ford's new deputy press secretary, Bill Roberts – a former *Time* correspondent – noted on the eve of the handover. The nation's new chief executive 'had some dark circles under his eyes and it looked as though he hadn't slept very much. But he also was very calm and very serious and very intent on what he was doing. Whatever happens to me, I have great confidence in him. I think he'll make a good president simply because he does have confidence in himself, which is one of the things Richard Nixon lacked, and which I think a president needs.' Roberts also thought 'Harry Truman and Gerald R. Ford have a great deal in common in their approach to life and to the presidency.'[21]

Rarely can a former Washington bureau chief of *Time* magazine have been so mistaken. Ford was no Truman. His 'simplicity', however, certainly came as a relief after the tortured character of 'Tricky Dick'. Nixon had even insisted the press be locked inside the press room lest they see him emerge for a final time from his secret hideaway in the Eisenhower Executive Office Building. 'What a sad commentary on the Nixon administration', Roberts reflected, delighting in the fact that, by contrast, after dancing with Queen Alia of Jordan at a White House reception, the new president came back inside and had a long dance with his press secretary's wife, 'who is a very attractive Asiatic gal, dancing to the tune of "Big Bad LeRoy Brown" with a whole crowd attending and clapping hands. Mrs Nessen was doing a sort of modified rock and roll . . . The girls all say the president's a very good dancer. But the whole point was that people kept saying, "What a change. What a change. What a wonderful place this White House can be, people are having fun."'[22]

The days of fun, however, would be short-lived – something the president-to-be had been warned about the night before. 'Christ, Jerry, isn't this a wonderful country?' the Democratic House Majority Leader Tip O'Neill had remarked when Ford had called him. 'Here we can talk like this and you and I can be friends, and eighteen months from now I'll be going around the country kicking your ass in.' Ford had been taken aback. 'That's a hell of a way to speak to the next President of the United States' he'd responded, and they'd both erupted in laughter.

Ford's unique ascent to the office of president and his lack of personal preparation would hold many lessons for future rulers of the empire. He had read little or no history, had limited vision, and no foresight. What he did have was a very attractive, dependable, loyal yet obstinate personality – which now worked to his own impediment.

Instead of asserting his new authority, Ford made the inexplicable decision to keep General Haig on, for the time being, as his own White House chief of staff.

Ford's staff, accompanying him from the vice president's office, were disbelieving. Haig had made no secret of the fact that he would not leave Washington until he had got Nixon a pardon, and had deliberately shipped Nixon's subpoenaed tapes to Nixon's home in San Clemente, California, even as 'staff members were stuffing an inordinately high amount of papers in their "burn bags". These bags later were macerated chemically', Ford's legal adviser, Benton Becker, recalled with shock.[23]

Haig's hubris was, in fact, stunning. He considered he had been 'acting president' in Nixon's last months, and seemed intent on continuing that role for as long as possible thereafter. Thus on Ford's first day as president, August 9, 1974, Haig asked him if he would address Nixon's old staff, both to thank them and to ask them to stay on for the moment, to facilitate an orderly transition. He even asked Ford to especially emphasize in his address, as Haig put it in a briefing memo, 'Point 3': namely the 'special and heroic role of Al Haig'.

Haig's self-aggrandizing memorandum was just one indication of the 'arrogance of the people who worked for the Nixon administration', Roberts noted several days later. Another was the attitude of

Nixon's other henchman, Henry Kissinger, who had, in a supreme historical irony, been awarded the 1973 Nobel Peace Prize.

Instead of considering an alternative Secretary of State, Ford had immediately given in to Kissinger's pressure not only to be left in control of the State Department, but to be the sole conduit of foreign affairs information, cutting out Ford's own team of advisers. Ford's vice-presidential staff begged him not to listen so cravenly to Haig or to Kissinger, especially in their recommendations of a pardon for the disgraced Nixon. By a substantial margin public opinion polls showed voters were opposed to an immediate pardon, at least until the truth be divulged, now that Nixon could no longer stonewall the Justice Department, the Special Prosecutor or Congress.

Having watched the tragicomedy of Nixon's last year in office, Ford's staff were now treated to a fresh episode of Nixonian man-oeuvring as Ford listened to Haig's recommendations. The new president 'does like and respect Al Haig and thinks he's a great guy', Bill Roberts noted. 'I'm not so sure of that.'[24]

Nor were others, especially when Haig kept urging that Ford re-employ Nixon's White House staff. As Ford's speechwriter Milton Friedman confided to Bill Roberts on August 18, 'there is a very serious and intense battle going on between General Haig and Bob Hartmann . . . General Haig simply wants to take over the whole operation and is arguing with the president that he should not throw away this great structure of administration which has been built up over so many years, and Hartmann is going completely the other way, arguing that the structure is what brought about the Nixon downfall.'[25]

As Ford's chief aide, Hartmann had good cause to be worried. Haig, who had never commanded a unit higher than a battalion in combat but had got himself promoted to general, remained in intimate, secret communication with Nixon. Throughout the rest of August 1974, they were in daily, sometimes hourly contact while Haig was running the transition.

Finally, on August 28, Ford gave in to Haig's importunings on Nixon's behalf. In a secret meeting to prepare his staff for his decision, he explained he was going to trust not the polls, or congressional advice, but his 'conscience'. Rather than placing a terrible burden on the official Watergate prosecutor, Leon Jaworski, he would therefore, as president, take sole responsibility for the pardon-in-advance. 'My conscience tells me I must do this' he repeated. 'I have followed my conscience before – and look where it has brought me. I like where I am. I would like to stay. If what I am doing is judged wrong, I am willing to accept the consequences.'[26]

There was quiet consternation in the Oval Office at these words. The antique clock in the room shattered 'the silence like a burst of machine-gun fire', one adviser recalled.[27]

Why did Ford do it, and why had he moved towards his ultimate decision so privately, withholding his 'intention' from his own White House staff, save Haig and Hartmann? Was he really not aware of Haig's disloyalty? Or was it the performance of a lifetime by the disgraced former president himself?

Between them, General Haig and Richard Nixon certainly fooled Ford. Alarmed by Haig's reports that Nixon was sinking into suicidal despair in San Clemente, Ford sent a personal emissary, Benton Becker, to California, hoping Nixon would agree to an admission of guilt that would make a pardon palatable to the nation.

Nixon, however, was in no mood to admit guilt. Haig had secretly called him in advance to tell him the pardon would not be predicated on the admission of guilt. 'You don't have to give up anything, you don't have to apologize, you're gonna get the pardon', Haig assured him before Becker's plane even reached California.[28] Thus, to Becker's astonishment on arrival, no admission of guilt was forthcoming. As Nixon's lawyer announced to Becker, Nixon would 'make no statement of admission of complicity in return for a pardon from Jerry Ford'.[29]

Becker was furious. In that case, he made clear, he would return to the White House immediately. Persuaded to stay the night, however, the next day he was shown a draft statement. It 'reeked', Becker later recalled, with 'protestations of innocence'. When finally Becker got Nixon's lawyers to agree at least a vague statement acknowledging there had been an 'obstruction of justice', he was at last allowed to meet Nixon, who now played the part of mad King Richard II. 'He rose upon my entrance,' Becker noted several days afterwards in a memorandum, 'and appeared to demonstrate a sense of nervousness or almost fright at meeting me in person.'[30] Becker's 'first impression' of the former president in his new role was of 'freakish grotesqueness . . . [his] arms and body were so thin and frail as to project an image of a head size disproportionate to a body . . . a man whom I might more reasonably expect to meet at an octogenarian nursing home. He was old. Had I never known of the man before and met him for the first time, I would have estimated his age to be eighty-five.'[31] Tears mingled with ramblings, musings, self-pity, football allusions, small gifts and defiance, in no apparent order, as Nixon played his part to perfection. 'If it was an act, it was a convincing one', his admiring Conservative biographer, Jonathan Aitken, later acknowledged.[32] With his 'hair disheveled', Nixon appeared 'in the most pathetic, sad frame of mind that I believe I have ever seen anyone in my life', Becker noted, Whittier's star college drama student having put on a mesmerizing show.[33]

Returning to the White House the next day, Ford's emissary, full of compassion, thus gave a deeply sympathetic yet erroneous view of Nixon's state of mind and health, unaware that Nixon was playacting, and would live another twenty years. An incomparable poker player since college, Nixon had played for the very highest stakes, and was way above Ford's league in manipulation. Bound by his old-fashioned sense of honour, and urged on by Haig (who was delighted by his latest achievement and, deceitful to the very end of his life, claimed in his memoirs that 'where Nixon's pardon was concerned, I played no role at all'), Ford had allowed himself to be played for a sucker.[34]

In retirement, Ford would admit he'd been outfoxed by the wily Nixon. 'I had thought he would be very receptive to the idea of clearing the decks', he confided to a friend, but Nixon had 'not been as forthcoming as I had hoped. He didn't admit guilt . . . I was taking one hell of a risk [in granting a pre-indictment pardon], and he didn't seem to be responsive at all.'[35] Instead of calling Nixon's bluff, however, Ford had nobly allowed his sympathy to overcome his scepticism, and on the morning of Sunday September 8, he began to telephone the leaders of Congress to inform them of his decision, beginning with the House Majority Leader, Tip O'Neill.

'Tip,' he explained, 'I've made up my mind to pardon Nixon. I'm doing it because I think it's right for the country, and because it feels right in my heart. The man is so depressed, and I don't want to see a former president go to jail.'

O'Neill was amazed. 'You're crazy' he responded. 'I'm telling you right now, this will cost you the [next] election.' O'Neill added that he hoped it was 'not part of any deal'. Ford denied that it was. 'Then why the hell are you doing it?' O'Neill asked, pertinently.[36]

Ford could only sigh: 'Tip, Nixon is a sick man.' Nixon's daughter Julie had, he added, kept 'calling me because her father is so depressed'.[37]

Ford's compassion for Nixon's 'suffering' did him proud as a human being, but his openness to manipulation was ominous for the world's most powerful new head of state. Nixon had aroused deep concern abroad by his maverick 'imperial presidency', so that the prospect of a new president with long experience in the House of Representatives, and seven months of on-the-job training as vice president, had calmed diplomats and financial markets across the globe. At home, however, the public was sure to be outraged by the 'deal', his staff warned, a prospect that became daily more worrying as Nixon kept altering the wording of the pardon document, demanding that his White House tapes be maintained under his complete control (with the Archivist of the United States acting merely as a temporary trustee).

The pardon – a 'Get Out of Jail Free' pass, as Senator Goldwater aptly called it – was finally announced publicly on September 8, 1974.[38] Ford's new press secretary, Jerald terHorst, immediately resigned in protest, saying he had been kept in the dark. Bill Roberts, Ford's loyal deputy press secretary, noted that night in his diary that 'I feel there must be some compelling reason that caused him to make the decision to grant the Pardon now, either health or mental problems with Nixon or something else. The Nixon people deny this, but it just seems to me there must be something that changed the president's mind', for 'at his first news conference in August, he'd stated he'd let the legal action take its course before he made his decision. Now he's moving to subvert the whole legal action which of course irritates a lot of people.' The press were disbelieving; Thomas DeFrank, *Newsweek*'s White House correspondent and Ford's friend, told Roberts: 'Oh he's blown it. The election is down the drain in 1976.'[39]

Ford's poll ratings immediately slumped more than 20 per cent – the largest and most precipitous drop since presidential polling began. Even his former law partner, Phil Buchen, whom Ford had promoted to White House Counsel, threatened to resign (though was talked out of it). Buchen's wife would note, several weeks later, that Buchen 'is constantly discouraged by Jerry's decisions, boners in making statements, and wavering (changing) positions. He doesn't trust Jerry's "instincts".'[40]

Far from unifying the country by his pardon, Ford found to his chagrin that the majority of American citizens were appalled, making his task as a national caretaker/healer president harder, not easier. 'Overnight the healing stopped', Tom DeFrank would later write. 'Ford had sought to cauterize the wound of Watergate; instead he'd ripped off the scab.'[41]

Tip O'Neill had been right. Instead of putting the Nixon 'nightmare' to rest, Ford had permitted Nixon to evade justice and avoid admitting anything other than a few 'mistakes', even allowing him to keep legal (though not physical) possession of the taped proof of his own criminal behaviour. Meanwhile the innocent Ford found himself being accused across the nation of everything from egregious conspiracy to wilful ignorance. The pardon was 'nothing less than the continuation of a cover-up', the Washington Post declared.[42] 'In granting President Nixon an inappropriate and premature grant of clemency,' the New York Times commented, 'President Ford has affronted the Constitution and the American system of justice. This blundering intervention is a body blow to the president's own credibility and to the public's reviving sense of confidence in the integrity of its government.'[43]

Belatedly, Ford recognized he'd misunderstood the temper of American voters, just as he had done when rooting for Nixon against what he'd labelled 'a relatively small group of activists'. The small group had become the majority of Americans.

Ford vainly attempted to make good on his mistake. His honour impugned, he cast aside all precedent and agreed, for the first time in the history of the American presidency, to testify in person and on oath before the House Judiciary Subcommittee, which had convened to ask for an explanation of the premature pardon. This prompted Congresswoman Elizabeth Holzman to pose the $64,000 question 'whether or not in fact there was a deal'.[44] The president hotly denied it ('no deal, period, under no circumstances'), but the precipitate, blanket, pardon-in-advance left a sour, suspicious taste across the nation.

It was clear that Gerald Ford's honeymoon was over. Henceforth he would have to prove himself, in his own right, if he was to have any chance of being elected in 1976. The first issue would be pardons for Vietnam draft dodgers.

Objection to Vietnam as an unjust war had caused huge numbers of young Americans to burn their draft cards, refuse to register, flee abroad, go underground, or go AWOL when inducted. As a former World War II naval combatant Ford had little sympathy for such lack of patriotism, and had always objected to amnesty for Vietnam draft dodgers and deserters. Nevertheless he now hoped that by a demonstration of compassion ('I am throwing the weight of the presidency on the side of leniency'), he might show himself to be a conciliatory commander-in-chief.[45] He thus proposed, in August 1974, 'earned re-entry' into American society for the 115,000 or more offenders. Their cases, he proposed, would be reviewed by a specially created Presidential Clemency Board, with a requirement that offenders perform alternative service to the state.

As a compromise solution to an awkward issue for diehard patriotic Republicans, the proposal was perfectly sensible, but it immediately fell victim to Ford's controversial simultaneous announcement of the blanket pardon for the very man who had, for four years, prolonged the Vietnam War at the cost of more than 20,000 American soldiers' lives – the majority of them draftees. When the establishment of the new board was made public in mid-September 1974, its potential for healing the wounds of Vietnam was thus completely drowned out. Once convened, moreover, the board proved a bureaucratic nightmare. It only processed a handful of cases (less than twenty) before the November election meltdown, and over subsequent years processed but a tiny minority of eligible cases.

Congress' fury over the Nixon pardon would meanwhile be manifested in multiple ways. One of these was the treatment of Ford's nominee for appointment as vice president. Taking a secret straw poll, Ford was minded to recommend to Congress former congressman George Bush of Texas, currently chairman of the Republican National Party after serving as ambassador to the United Nations. However, *Newsweek* published a report that Bush had been given no less than $100,000 from Nixon's secret White House slush fund for his unsuccessful bid for a Senate seat in 1970. On August 17, 1974, Ford had therefore turned to Governor Nelson Rockefeller, the millionaire former governor of New York who had retired the previous December in order to prepare for his own renewed presidential run in 1976. (He had already run in three Republican primary campaigns in 1960, 1964 and 1968.)

Though by most people's standards a conservative who was tough on crime and favoured capital punishment, Rockefeller was considered a liberal by Republican diehards such as Senator Goldwater and Governor Reagan. A notable womanizer in the same mould as John F. Kennedy, Rockefeller rattled 'the cages of the [Republican] Right', as Nixon's speechwriter Pat Buchanan put it, while on the left, outraged Democrats, furious over the Nixon pardon, sharpened their sabres to punish Ford by delaying a confirmation vote. Governor Rockefeller was required to testify before Congress on seventeen separate days before he was finally confirmed by Congress on December 5, 1974, leaving Ford and the nation without a vice president for almost four months.

Meanwhile, matters were no easier in the White House itself. General Haig still attempted to run the Ford White House as his own fiefdom, but this time under a weak, instead of mad, president.

Ford's supine response in dealing with General Haig was galling to the president's staff, especially when Haig told him to fire his long-time chief assistant, Bob Hartmann. The problem, however, was not simply Haig's megalomania. Ford had clearly not prepared himself in any way for the presidency. He had no personnel plan lined up, either for a White House staff or a new cabinet, no clear idea how to manage a big organization, in fact no notion of how to choose or discipline subordinates. Haig – who aspired to be the next chairman of the Joint Chiefs of Staff, despite his nominal experience as a general – was for months allowed to run amok at the White House until Ford finally plucked up enough courage to get rid of him, by promoting him to supreme command of NATO in Europe (a move which, although deeply unpopular in Europe, did not require Senate confirmation).

Ford had said, both in fear of Haig and in ignorance of how a huge organization needs to be run, that he would dispense with a chief of staff altogether on Haig's eventual departure. Once again, this was a well-meant notion that sought to make him accessible to as many as possible, in contrast to his bunker-protected predecessor. In the modern, accelerated world of communications and decision-making, however, it was yet another major mistake.

Nature abhors a vacuum; so does empire. Ford's notion of six or seven co-equal assistants meeting him every day had worked well for him as a mere legislative congressman, but he was now president of

the United States. The entire world was watching how he commanded
his White House team, as well as how he directed American imperial
policy across the globe. As Ford himself acknowledged later, 'I started
out in effect not having a chief of staff and it didn't work . . . You
need a filter, a person that you have total confidence in, who works
so closely with you that in effect his is almost an alter ego. I just can't
imagine a president not having an effective chief of staff.'[46] This was
said, however, almost three decades later.

The challenge Ford faced in 1974 was to restore the American public's
trust in government. On paper, he was the very best possible appointee.
But, with the best of intentions, he blundered at every step.

Nixon, when president, had been almost invisible to the general
public, concealing himself in his various hideaways, yet managing
White House operations on the phone and through dedicated, ultra-
loyal, combative henchmen; Ford was now not only visible, but visibly
inept, along with an incompetent White House staff. In the months
after the transition the White House turned into a managerial and
public relations mess, with the right hand seeming not to know what
the left hand was doing, and top meetings with Ford either ill-attended
or him rambling without purpose or order: 'a White House staff
completely incapable of structuring a workable White House–Cabinet
relationship', as one political scientist put it, let alone a successful
White House–Congress one.[47]

Aware that his new administration was tanking and his own polls
sinking, Ford eventually recognized he must take restorative action.
Instead of bringing in an experienced bipartisan manager who would
reflect his own centrist approach, however, Ford chose yet another
Nixon holdover to head up White House operations: former
congressman Donald Rumsfeld.

Rumsfeld had loyally served in Nixon's White House, then been
sent as US ambassador to NATO in August 1974, only to be brought
back from his brief job to help Al Haig manage the initial transition,
and had thereafter departed. Now Rumsfeld was brought in yet again,
as chief of staff to the president. In this role he was eventually able
to carry out Haig's plan to destroy Hartmann, as well as other Ford
loyalists. In their place, Rumsfeld brought in yet another of Nixon's
'praetorian' guards, as his deputy: former congressman Dick Cheney.

Managerial order was thereby restored to the chaotic White House, but at a high ethical and political cost. Both Rumsfeld and Cheney were highly competent managers who proved effective administrators, but they were conservative Republicans harbouring a Nixonian view of imperial White House power wholly at odds with a charming, well-intentioned non-imperialist on the throne. Thus arose the basic problem of the Ford presidency: a Caesar with no clear vision of what he wished to achieve, other than continuing Nixon's policies abroad and at home, and so incompetent in command of his White House team that he had found himself forced to use Nixon's most detestable but effective civil servants, who were constantly at loggerheads with Ford's diminishing number of loyalists. The result was a White House split into feuding camps, lacking presidential direction; a poor prescription, when added to his disastrous Nixon pardon, for Ford's chances of election in 1976, if he chose to run.

The US inflation rate had reached 12.8 per cent that summer, in large part due to the Arab oil embargo. Economists across the western world were divided about how best to tackle rocketing prices, higher wages *and* rising unemployment – a vicious circle they termed stagflation. With signs of a major recession, Ford – who refused to re-impose a cap on wages and prices – felt compelled to act, but found himself none the wiser after convening a high-level economic summit in August 1974. His decision to declare a national voluntary campaign to reduce demand (and thus prices) by cutting consumption, waste and unnecessary travel, entitled 'Whip Inflation Now' (WIN), became an object of national ridicule. The Secretary of the Treasury called the campaign – complete with WIN lapel-buttons – 'ludicrous', while Ford's own Economic Policy Board hid their 'heads in embarrassment'.[48] One corporation president wrote to the White House: 'Your appeal to the American public with the juvenile "WIN" promotion was more fitting for a high school pep club than a leader of one of the world's great countries.'[49] WIN became, in short, lose.

Ford's more important proposal, namely to impose a surtax on high-income earners, corporations and especially oil companies, fared no better. Congress forced him to rescind the measure and propose instead a tax cut, in order to stimulate the economy and bring down unemployment, which had already reached 7.1 per cent.[50] This only resulted in claims of 'flip-flopping', yet few would have traded shoes with Ford as he attempted to curb inflation on the one hand, and

1. President-elect.
Franklin Delano Roosevelt, Democratic governor of New York, November 1932.

2. On the battlefield. President Roosevelt visits US troops in North Africa, 1943 – the first president to appear on the battlefield since Lincoln.

3. At the summit.
FDR confers with fellow Allied war leaders Churchill and Stalin, Yalta, January 1945.

4. Victory in Europe. President Harry Truman arrives in Berlin after the German surrender, 15 July 1945.

5. Potsdam. Truman studies his Soviet counterpart.

6. Dividing the spoils. Truman presides over the Potsdam conference.

7. Ike and Mamie.
Lieutenant Dwight D. Eisenhower and Miss Doud on their wedding day,
Denver, Colorado, 1 July 1916.

9. Korea.
President-elect Dwight Eisenhower
inspects UN troops, November 1952.

8. D–Day.
Supreme Commander
General Eisenhower
briefs US troops before
the invasion,
5 June 1944.

10. Sputnik.
President Eisenhower
and Vice President
Nixon humour
Premier Khrushchev
on his visit to the
Oval Office, 1958.

11. War in the Pacific.
Lieutenant John F. Kennedy skippers PT 109, Tulagi, Solomon Islands, 1943.

12. PT 109.
Skipper John F. Kennedy and his crew, shortly before their ship was sunk in the Blackett Strait.

13. The torch is passed. President Kennedy's inauguration on 20 January 1961 excited worldwide attention.

14. 'Ask not what your country …' Flanked by a former and two future incumbents, the 35th president holds forth.

15. Missile Crisis. President Kennedy works in the Oval Office, 1962.

16. Assassination.
The body of the murdered 35th president lies in state in the Capitol Rotunda, November 1963.

17. Vietnam.
As commander-in-chief,
President Johnson makes a
surprise visit to the battlefield, October 1966.

18. Debacle.
The 36th president listens to
a tape sent by his son-in-law,
marine serving in the quagmire
of Vietnam, 1968.

19. Treason.
The would-be 37th president promises to support President Johnson in peace negotiations over Vietnam, 1968.

20. Disgrace.
Flanked by the First Lady and his daughter Tricia, President Nixon announces his historic resignation, 9 August 1974.

21. Pardon.
Dooming his chances
election, President Ford
ardons his predecessor,
Oval Office,
8 September 1974.

22. Exit Vietnam.
A US Navy helicopter
evacuates the last personnel
from the American Embassy
in Saigon, 29 April 1975.

23. A winning smi[le]
Lieutenant Jimm[y]
Carter, US Navy[,]
on his wedding da[y]
7 July 1946.

24. Camp David Accord.
President Carter takes President Sadat and Prime Minister Begin to Gettysburg, 10 September 197[8.]

25. Hollywood actor.
Ronald Reagan's movie career earned
him the title 'the Errol Flynn of
the B's' – *Santa Fe Trail*, 1940.

26. Activist.
Reagan's anti-Communist career
began early. Here he testifies before
HUAC, Washington, 1947.

27. 'Mr Gorbachev, tear down this wall!'
President Reagan in Berlin, 12 June 1987.

28. Navy combat pilot. Nineteen-year-old Lieutenant George H.W. Bush, in his TBM Avenger South Pacific, 1944.

29. Desert Storm. President George H.W. Bush spends Thanksgiving with his troops in Iraq, 1990.

30. End of an empire. Congratulating President Gorbachev on the end of Soviet occupation of Europe, 1991.

31. The man from Hope.
The youngest-ever ex-governor of Arkansas,
Bill Clinton, with his wife Hillary, 1982.

32. Peace in Bosnia.
After a difficult start, President
Clinton proved an able peacemaker,
ending the war in Bosnia, 1995.

33. Democracy on trial.
In January 1999 William
Jefferson Clinton became
the first president to be
impeached since 1868.

34. Mission accomplished. President George W. Bush announces victory in Iraq, aboard USS *Abraham Lincoln*, 2003.

35. End of an era. The 44th president bids farewell to George W. Bush outside the US Capitol, 2009

avoid a looming recession on the other. Both William Simon, the Treasury Secretary, and Alan Greenspan, the chair of the Council of Economic Advisers, counselled ignoring unemployment – a policy of 'let 'em eat cake' as Ford's adviser Robert Hartmann – worried about a midterm meltdown for Republicans in congressional elections – sneered.[51]

America's dilemma was little different from that of most European economies, and Ford's response – taking considered advice from a plethora of economists and business leaders – well motivated. But, thanks to the Nixon pardon, his relations with Congress had soured, dooming his attempts to restore unity and common purpose in leading the nation. The result was a near-catastrophic midterm election defeat in November 1974, when Democrats took a further forty-nine seats from the Republicans in the House. In the Senate the Republican Party lost a further four members, giving Democrats a 61–38 majority. The Democrats thereby achieved a veto-proof majority – marking the end of the 'imperial presidency'.

The disastrous midterm election now gave the whip hand to a Democratic-controlled Congress, not the Oval Office. The very advantage Ford had held over rivals Rockefeller, Reagan and Connally the previous year as a vice-presidential appointee – namely his fine, bipartisan record in Congress – had evaporated. When Ford vetoed Congress' bill to embargo any aid to America's ally, Turkey, after its invasion of Cyprus in response to a Greek military coup there, the House simply overrode the veto, and although he was allowed to delay implementation, the embargo was duly instituted by Congress, causing Turkey, a crucial member of NATO, to close all US intelligence and military installations save a single NATO base. 'The enormous reservoir of goodwill Ford had enjoyed, especially with his Democratic cronies on Capitol Hill, swiftly dissipated. His popularity plummeted', DeFrank recalled, making it impossible for Ford to 'craft a bipartisan agenda' and even 'harder for Ford to rally support for dealing with runaway inflation or the Vietnam War'.[52]

If few political leaders would have traded places with Ford in dealing with stagflation, even fewer would have done so with respect to Vietnam, where on December 13, 1974, the North Vietnamese launched their long-awaited offensive to unify the two halves of the country by force. Their military campaign was planned to take two years, but in the event it took only a few months. By January 6, 1975, the Communists had captured the provincial capital Phuoc Binh. Ford begged Congress to authorize emergency funds to at least aid the South Vietnamese military, but as one group of congressmen explained to him, 'We face our own war here at home against crippling economic developments, the crisis in energy and other public resources and other serious problems . . . We cannot confront and resolve these crises while the United States continues involvement in South East Asia.'[53]

Ford seemed genuinely distraught. 'It cannot be in our interest to cause our friends all over the world to wonder whether we will support them' he countered, but the die was cast.[54] His pardon to Nixon had made him a pariah to many Democrats in Congress, and the policy of 'Vietnamization' Nixon had used to cover the American retreat from Vietnam was a sham that had convinced no one. Financial aid and military supplies would not affect the course of the campaign. Even the South Vietnamese dictator, Thieu, was under no illusions now. He had long labelled the Paris Peace Accords 'tantamount to surrender' by leaving 150,000 North Vietnamese troops in South Vietnam, and had known it was only a matter of time before his own right-wing junta fell. Nevertheless, as the North Vietnamese forces advanced, he begged Ford for a B-52 bombing campaign and the 'necessary means' to repel the offensive. He was supported not only by Kissinger but also by General Weyand, the chief of staff of the army, who had flown to Saigon. 'We must not abandon our goal of a free and independent South Vietnam', Weyand reported to Ford.[55]

The young White House photographer who had accompanied Weyand to Asia, however, was blunt when Ford asked his opinion. 'Mr President, Vietnam has no more than a month left,' David Kennerly warned, 'and anyone who tells you different is bullshitting.'[56]

Kennerly was right. Amid rumours he was about to be deposed in yet another coup, Thieu resigned, but the fantasy that South Vietnam could become a South Korea, protected by huge numbers of US troops, was over. Ford stopped showing the drafts of his speeches to Kissinger, his Secretary of State, and at Tulane University, New Orleans, the president unequivocally announced (to tumultuous applause) that America would not be 'refighting a war that is finished as far as America is concerned'.[57] A coded message was broadcast on Saigon radio announcing a temperature of '105 degrees and rising', as thirty-four helicopters from aircraft carriers in the South China Sea swooped down to the American embassy which was besieged by Vietnamese civilians seeking flight to safety.

As evening fell on April 29, 1975, the last helicopter lifted above the building, having evacuated 1,400 Americans and 5,600 South Vietnamese. The next day, and only fifty-five days since the North Vietnamese offensive began, Saigon fell. It was then renamed Ho Chi Minh City. Meanwhile, as North Vietnamese forces overwhelmed Saigon, a simultaneous assault took place on the capital of Cambodia, Phnom Penh. The American-funded dictator, Lon Nol, stepped down on April 1, 1975, and a week later, Ford authorized commencement of the US evacuation plan for Cambodia, code-named Eagle Pull, which 'saved' 276 people in helicopter rescues.

The Nixon Doctrine 'in its purest form' had come to final grief, having served only to ruin two small countries, far from Washington, in a misbegotten effort to demonstrate American imperial determination.

With unemployment and inflation rising, growing dependency on foreign oil and a new president who had inexplicably made Congress his enemy, as well as polls showing increasing isolationism on the part of voters, America's leadership role in the free world looked greatly diminished. 'America – A Helpless Giant', the German *Frankfurter Allgemeine Zeitung* headed an editorial that spring, while *The Economist* used the headline: 'The Fading of America'.

Ford later acknowledged the necessity to listen less to the rhetoric of Nixon's former apparatchiks and be more realistic. 'Maybe we weren't a giant power, throwing our [weight] around, trying to tell everybody to do what we wanted', he reflected on the change. The American Empire was no longer quite the giant that it had been; but it was not, as Ford added, 'without power'.[58]

In which direction would the president now steer the American ship of state, diplomats across the world wondered. With America's allies questioning US resolve in the aftermath of the fall of South Vietnam and Cambodia, as well as its economic problems at home, Ford was given an opportunity to show where he stood – and what advice, as Caesar, he would and wouldn't take.

Less than a month after the fall of Saigon and Phnom Penh an American merchant ship, carrying military spare parts, was seized by Khmer Rouge sailors in the Gulf of Siam on its way to Thailand. As

Ford was informed on May 12, 1975, the captors declared the unarmed vessel, the SS *Mayaguez*, to have deliberately entered newly expanded Cambodian territorial waters. Summoning his national security staff and alerting US naval and military staffs in South East Asia, Ford decided to make the incident a test of his presidential resolve. The Secretary of Defense, James R. Schlesinger, favoured downplaying the incident, but Kissinger (who had joked he was 'the only Secretary of State who has lost two countries in three weeks'[59]) was loath to see America lose further face, and recommended 'ferocious' air bombing countermeasures on the Cambodian mainland.[60]

Ford listened patiently to Kissinger, and realized belatedly that his Secretary of State was, in some respects, as reckless, even as feral as Nixon. Yet a response of some sort was required. Dismissing Kissinger's notion of a massive aerial attack on the mainland, the former naval lieutenant commander now ordered US forces to instantly retake the ship, which had been anchored fifty miles off the coast of Cambodia, by the island of Koh Tang, before its crew could be taken to a mainland port.

Luck favoured the president. In the first ship-to-ship boarding by an American naval vessel since 1826, the US destroyer *Holt* secured the *Mayaguez* on May 15, 1975, using air-dropped tear-gas bombs. The next morning, responding to pressure from the Communist Chinese government, the captive sailors were ordered to be released from a fishing vessel where they'd been secreted by the Khmer Rouge, and transferred to the USS *Holt* unharmed.

Ford's approval rating leaped eleven points at home. He had weathered the first international crisis not attributable to his predecessor, and had drawn a line in the proverbial sand, refusing to escalate the incident, as Kissinger wished, but avoiding accusations of pusillanimity that had attached to North Korea's seizure of the USS *Pueblo* six years before.[61] It was, despite its relatively trivial nature, 'the biggest political victory of the Ford presidency', as one Ford biographer called it.[62]

With his polls rising, Ford now decided to assert his own post-Nixonite Ford Doctrine on a much larger stage. He not only announced he would be a candidate for the 1976 presidential nomination, but also that he would personally attend the Helsinki Conference on Security and Cooperation.

For the American right, still vexed over Nixon's accommodation with Mao Zedong and then the 'loss' of South Vietnam and Cambodia to Communist regimes, Ford's willingness to go to Europe and sign off on what conservative Republicans continued to consider the 'Yalta betrayal' aroused a firestorm of protest. In thunderous indignation from his exile in Vermont, the Nobel-prizewinning novelist Aleksandr Solzhenitsyn denounced the president's July trip as appeasement, the aim of the conference being to settle the ongoing dispute over post-war borders of eastern European nations, including the legitimization of Soviet control of Poland and 'bloc' countries, in the interests of détente.

Once again, Ford demonstrated his growing stature. An inter-nationalist since his distinguished naval service in World War II, and a centrist in the manner of President Eisenhower, who had tried desper-ately hard to find common ground with the Soviets, Ford had never espoused Nixon's earlier rabid anti-Communism, and had welcomed Nixon's volte-face and efforts at détente. He thus had no trouble in now openly pursuing his own sincere détente agenda, without need of Nixon's magic tricks. Bravely ignoring the right wing of his own party, Ford proposed the opposite of the 'Madman Theory': an open, common-sense policy of global security through good relations between governments, shared agreements, and transparency.

'Jerry, Don't Go' the *Wall Street Journal* implored. The president did go, however, meeting the Soviet leader Leonid Brezhnev for a second time, and seating himself among the leaders of thirty-five non-Communist and Communist nations, including a representative from the Vatican. The four categories of agreements, from human rights to trade and travel and future monitoring, represented a willingness by western countries not to threaten the ever touchy Soviet Union, in return for liberalizing contact, commerce, information and human rights in Europe – part of a common will 'to broaden, deepen and make continuing and lasting the process of détente', as the signatories accepted.[63]

Travelling to the conference in Finland, Ford was the first US presi-dent to visit eastern Europe since World War II – a trip that, along with the Helsinki Accords, had profound consequences in the years that followed.

'The fact is,' General Wesley Clark, the supreme commander of NATO, later pointed out when running himself for presidential

nomination, 'that the Soviet Union did not fall the way the neoconservatives say it did. The 1975 Helsinki Accords proved to be the crucial
step in opening the way for the subsequent peaceful democratization
of the Soviet bloc. The accords, signed by the Communist governments of the East, guaranteed individual human and political rights
to all peoples and limited the authority of governments to act against
their own citizens. However flimsy the human rights provisions seemed
at the time, they provided a crucial platform for dissidents such as
Russian physicist Andrei Sakharov. These dissidents, though often jailed
and exiled, built organizations that publicized their governments' many
violations of the accords, garnering western attention and support
and inspiring their countrymen with the knowledge that it was possible
to stand up to the political powers that be.'[64]

John Lewis Gaddis, historian of the Cold War, seconded General
Clark's view the following year, writing that the Helsinki commitment
to 'human rights and fundamental freedoms' became a trap for the
Soviet Union, as it faced ever bolder condemnations by dissidents.
'Thousands of people who lacked the prominence of Solzhenitsyn
and Sakharov', Gaddis reflected, 'began to stand with them in holding
the USSR and its satellites accountable for human rights.' In other
words, the 1975 Helsinki Accords became, as he put it, 'the basis for
legitimizing opposition to Soviet rule'.[65]

If Ford hoped his successful statesmanship in Finland and eastern
Europe would improve his approval polls at home, however, he was
to be disappointed. In conforming to his new Ford Doctrine in
American foreign policy, based on patience, stability and goodwill,
he relied like Eisenhower on his own reputation for honesty and
integrity. But the America of the 1970s was not that of the 1950s. To
redirect American foreign policy towards détente and accommodation with both China and the USSR, Nixon had relied on his genius
for self-contradiction and counter-attack to confuse his opponents.
Ford, however, was honest to a fault, lacked courtroom skills, and
had no knack for manipulating public opinion. The result was that,
instead of being hailed at home as the Peace President, he was treated
to a chorus of right-wing Republican disapproval – with ominous
repercussions.

Long frustrated by Richard Nixon's ability to outwit, outtalk and
outmanoeuvre their star mouthpieces from Barry Goldwater to Ronald

Reagan, the right wing of the Republican Party now charged that their new president was 'selling out' their platform, and was guilty of a 'betrayal of eastern Europe', as Solzhenitsyn called it.[66] Still rabidly anti-Communist, vexed over American defeat in Vietnam, and virulently anti-government in domestic matters, Republican ideologues derided Ford for his participation in the Helsinki Accords, and began to promote an alternative, right-wing candidate as the Republican presidential nominee for the 1976 election. This was ominous.

Ford himself acknowledged he had not done enough to communicate the rationale and importance of the Helsinki Accords ('a failure in public relations' for which 'I will have to accept a large share of the blame', he admitted later), or to proselytize his moderate, longsighted gospel of détente after Helsinki, allowing right-wing Republicans and even his eventual Democratic opponent to scorn his statesmanlike efforts on behalf of America.[67] Over domestic issues, meanwhile, he was faced by the same problem: how to explain to an American public the difficulty of dealing with runaway inflation at the same time as rising unemployment – stagflation.

As over the Helsinki Accords, Ford found himself unable to garner due credit for what, in historical terms, would prove the second major achievement of his presidency: his efforts to goad Congress into passing an emergency tax-rebate bill in the spring of 1975 in order to stimulate the economy, while at the same time cutting government expenditure and closing tax loopholes in order to maintain government programmes without increasing the national deficit.

These efforts were, in retrospect, heroic. Ford's $23 billion tax rebate – largely confined to lower-income families, who would spend the money and thus hopefully cure the Great Recession – worked. Passed by Congress in May 1975, the consequences proved remarkable: unemployment fell, the stock market rose, and GNP increased by a staggering 11.2 per cent by the third quarter – the highest in two decades. But the public gave Ford little immediate credit; indeed in September, 1975, he would experience no less than two assassination attempts.

On September 5, 1975, Ford was in Sacramento, the state capital of California, to give a speech to its legislature and hold a private meeting with its Democratic governor, Jerry Brown, who had succeeded Ronald Reagan. Ironically, the subject of Ford's speech was crime.

'The weather that morning was clear; the sun was shining brightly'

Ford recalled, so he decided to walk from the Senator Hotel.[68] There were 'several rows of people standing behind a rope that lined the sidewalk to my left. They were applauding and saying nice things' Ford remembered; 'I was in a good mood, so I started shaking hands.'[69]

'That's when I spotted a woman, wearing a bright red dress. She was in the second or third row, moving right along with me as if she wanted to shake my hand. When I slowed down, I noticed immediately that she thrust her hand under the arms of the other spectators, I reached down to shake it – and looked into the barrel of a .45 caliber pistol pointed directly at me.'[70]

'I ducked' he said – but even so, he was extraordinarily lucky.[71] The twenty-six-year-old lover of mass-murderer Charles Manson was heard by a bystander to complain 'It didn't go off. Can you believe it?', astonished at her ill-luck as a secret service agent wrestled the gun from her hand.

Lynette 'Squeaky' Fromme was sentenced to jail for life, after warning the judge that 'If Nixon's reality-wearing-a-Ford-Face continues to run this country, your homes will be bloodier than the Tate-LaBianca houses and My Lai put together.' Her fellow concubine, Sandra Good, also warned that 'many people all over the world are due to be assassinated. This is just the beginning. Just the beginning of the many, many assassinations . . . People will be killed.'[72]

Good was right. Two weeks later, Ford was leaving the St Francis Hotel in San Francisco, following a television interview, when Sara Jane Moore, a bookkeeper for People in Need, drew a .38 calibre revolver and fired. This time the gun went off. The bullet missed the president, ricocheting off the hotel entrance fascia and hitting a taxi driver in the groin, at which point a fellow bystander grabbed Moore's arm and pulled her to the ground before she could fire a second time. 'I do regret I didn't succeed and allow the winds of change to start', the assassin – an admirer of Patty Hearst, the heiress who was abducted by terrorists and had joined the Symbionese Liberation Army – said afterwards. 'I wish I had killed him. I did it to create chaos.'[73]

In both assassination attempts President Ford showed the same physical courage he'd demonstrated aboard the USS *Monterey* as kamikaze pilots zeroed in on his vessel, and continued his schedule for the day without even mentioning the 'incident'. But if Ford joked to his scheduling staff that 'we're not going to schedule any more trips like that'[74] and refused to 'capitulate to those who want to undercut all that's good in America', the writing was on the wall.[75] 'You wouldn't be standing before me if we had an effective capital punishment law', the sentencing judge complained to Ms Moore, denouncing her as 'a product of our permissive society'.[76] Whether capital punishment could rectify the problems of the permissive society was debatable, but with the spectre of anarchy facing the country there would be a price to be paid for the excesses of the counter-culture 1960s radicals – a price that would now be paid in political currency, as right-wing Republicans began to gain greater traction within their own party. For Gerald Ford, as a centrist, progressive Republican, this would be bad news.

Détente with the USSR was hard enough, but 'No foreign policy challenges occupied more of my time in the early months of 1975', Ford later recalled, than Israel's refusal to withdraw from the territories it had occupied.[77] Thanks to American support, the Israelis 'were stronger militarily than all their Arab neighbors combined, yet peace was no closer than it had ever been. So I began to question the rationale for our policy. I wanted the Israelis to recognize that there had to be some quid pro quo. If we were going to build up their military capabilities, we in turn had to see some flexibility to achieve a fair, secure and permanent peace.'[78] Though the president attempted to bully the Israelis into withdrawal and negotiation by threatening, on NBC television, to turn resolution of the conflict and the future of Palestine over to a Geneva peace conference, and thus abandon Israel to its fate, it was to no avail. By providing Israel with the arms to win the October War, then arranging a ceasefire that left Israel in control of all its war spoils, Kissinger had turned Israel into an American puppet-state – but with the Israelis refusing to be a puppet. 'The Israelis kept stalling', Ford recalled his own exasperation. However, as one historian chronicled, Ford's threat to abandon Israel 'backfired. Instead of caving in to Ford's threat, the Israelis stiffened their resolve' – and with Kissinger cautioning against iron insistence, the president was stymied.[79] 'Their antics frustrated the Egyptians and made me mad as hell', Ford later said of the Israeli prime minister, Yitzhak Rabin (a former terrorist during the British Mandate in Palestine), and his colleagues.[80] 'Rabin fought over every kilometer', Ford lamented, but 'he didn't under-stand that only by giving do you get something in return'.[81]

In the end the United States, not the UN, became committed to providing a permanent monitoring force (the Sinai Field Mission) on a new border that was established between Egypt and Israel. In a series of secret side agreements or Memorandums of Understanding, later known as Sinai II, the US also committed to providing support 'on an ongoing and long-term basis' for 'Israel's military equipment and other defense requirements, and to its economic needs' at a cost of $4 billion annually, as well as making available F-16 fighter planes for its air force (already the third largest in the world) and Pershing missiles, guaranteeing Israel's oil requirements, and preparing plans for any future airlifts of military weapons during a crisis.[82] In addition, the US secretly promised (without informing the Egyptians) not to negotiate with the Palestine Liberation Organization (PLO) until it recognized Israel's right to exist, nor to negotiate with anyone in the Middle East before first consulting with Israel, or to follow any course of negotiation other than following existing UN resolutions. Rabin was justly delighted.

Pleased at least to have got back the Sinai and his surrounded Egyptian Army, as well as the Israeli-occupied Egyptian oilfields and the crucial Suez Canal (which Israelis would henceforth be permitted to use for non-military cargo vessels), in September 1975 Egypt's President Sadat reluctantly signed the Israel–Egypt Peace Treaty – and his own death warrant. He was assassinated six years later. (Rabin, too, would be assassinated twenty years later, after seeking too late in the day a compromise Israeli route to permanent peace, via the Oslo Accords.)

From the Middle East, President Ford then turned his attention back to a more peaceful approach to America's problems at home. In his State of the Union speech in January he had stated frankly that 'the state of the union is not good. Millions of Americans are out of work. Recession and inflation are eroding the money of millions more.' He accepted there were no simple solutions, and vowed now to continue to steer a centrist-Republican middle course. 'I believe that being in the middle of the road, as far as the Republicans are concerned, on a nationwide basis, is the right policy.'

Former governor of California Ronald Reagan disagreed, as did the Republican right. The right-wing *Manchester Union-Leader* began referring to the president as 'Jerry the Jerk', and deplored his vision of the

Republican Party as an 'umbrella of many colors' that could, and would, welcome independents and moderate Democrats. Reagan indicated he might well challenge for the party's presidential nomination, by coming forward as the standard-bearer of the right, which coerced Ford to move to the right himself, in order to deprive Reagan of a clear wind.

Ford now committed 'one of the few cowardly things I did in my life', as he later termed it.[83] At the urging of his chief of staff Donald Rumsfeld, who hoped he himself would then be picked, Ford decided to turn his back on his loyal, centrist vice president.[84] On October 28, 1975, after discussing 'the growing strength of the [Republican] right wing' with Vice President Nelson Rockefeller, the president asked him not to stand for election in 1976 as his prospective running mate.[85] Rockefeller agreed to stand down. It was, Ford acknowledged afterwards, not only the most egregious, but 'the biggest political mistake of my life'.[86]

The removal of Rockefeller from the prospective presidential ticket, while keeping Kissinger as Secretary of State, in no way appeased the right wing of the Republican Party, which was spoiling for a fight. On November 19, 1975, Ford took a phone call from Reagan, who had refused a cabinet post in the Ford administration. 'I am going to run for president' Reagan announced. 'I trust we can have a good contest, and I hope it won't be too divisive.'[87]

'How can you challenge an incumbent president of your own party and *not* be divisive?' Ford asked later.[88] Reagan's challenge hurt him deeply, yet in it he recognized much more than a personal duel. It would be, he saw, a struggle to define the very conception of Republicanism in modern America, as a centrist approach to government, governing, and imperial leadership across the globe.

The omens were not promising. By December 1975 a Gallup poll was already showing Ronald Reagan leading Ford by 40 per cent to 32 per cent among Republican voters.

For Ford's campaign team this was, belatedly, a wake-up call. Thereafter the campaign became the most memorable example of an incumbent having to fight off a fellow Republican rival since that of Robert Taft in 1912, a titanic struggle that had split the Republican Party, alienated voters by its venom, and had resulted in a Democrat (Woodrow Wilson) regaining the White House. Would that be the case in 1976, pundits wondered?

The president certainly had his work cut out. Not only did he not possess Reagan's silver-tongued, screen actor's performance skills on the campaign trail, but he lacked Nixon's flair for theatrics. Nixon, moreover, refused to help the man who had pardoned him; indeed, far from being grateful for his liberty, Nixon now astonished Ford by appearing in rude good health, and reneging on his promise not to visit China before the election. Disregarding Ford's pleas, Nixon flew to Beijing on February 21, 1976, a bare three days before the crucial, traditionally first-held presidential primary, in New Hampshire. 'Nixon's a shit!' Ford's national security adviser, Brent Scowcroft – a man who never cursed – was heard to exclaim on hearing the news.[89]

The president did manage, in the event, to beat Reagan in the New Hampshire primary, but it was only by a sliver: 1,000 votes out of 100,000 cast. This presaged an even more divisive battle in the subsequent primaries.

Buoyed by his near-win, Reagan stepped up his attacks on the president and his Republican administration, with so many false accusations that neither Ford nor observers could keep up with them. Reagan accused Ford – a stalwart maintainer of American military supremacy, who got Congress to authorize the largest budget for the Pentagon since World War II – of allowing the US to become number two militarily among world empires. The accusation was knowingly and completely false, but it allowed Reagan to campaign on a platform to 'Make America No. 1 Again'.

Ford had tackled the American inflation-recession crisis with considerable managerial skill, utilizing the best economic advisers in the nation and working hand in hand with the Democratic-controlled Congress. The result had been that unemployment rolls had begun to tumble, productivity rose and inflation fell. Yet day after day Reagan battered the president for poor economic growth, proposed shifting most taxation to the states rather than federal IRS authority, criticized government as a useless bureaucracy, and vilified Ford for his foreign policy, to the point where, after losing the Nebraska primary to Reagan, Ford had to postpone announcement of an agreement with the Russians on the peaceful use of nuclear explosions, lest it add fuel to Reagan's denunciatory rhetoric. The president was even forced to back off a new SALT arms reduction agreement, and found himself assailed by Reagan over his Panama Canal talks. ('When it comes to the canal,'

Reagan declared in one-liner speeches across the country, 'we built it, we paid for it, it's ours, and . . . we're going to keep it.'[90])

If President Ford, the most honest and moderate chief executive since World War II, was often outmanoeuvred by Reagan in media coverage, he was equally schemed against by his own White House staff. In the so-called 'Sunday Morning Massacre' of November 2, 1975, the 'Vulcans' – a cabal of former Nixon adherents, marshalled by Donald Rumsfeld – had shown their teeth. William Colby, the CIA chief who had testified honestly before the Church and Rockefeller committees, was fired, and Ambassador George Bush, Nixon's protégé, was brought back from China to take his place at CIA headquarters, lest he become Ford's choice as vice-presidential nominee. Simultaneously Rumsfeld engineered the removal of the Secretary of Defense, James Schlesinger, for not having carried out the bombing of the Cambodian mainland during the *Mayaguez* incident, and succeeded in making himself Defense Secretary. Dick Cheney – a man who had avoided the Vietnam draft – then took over Rumsfeld's job as chief of staff. Cheney was a Thomas Cromwell-type figure of ice-cold ambition, whose penchant for secrecy, illegality and Nixon-like targeting of individuals worried colleagues.[91]

Ford ultimately had no one to blame but himself. He was, in effect, 'too much Mr Nice Guy', as the White House press secretary put it, which meant his only hope of surviving as president was either to steal Reagan's right-wing thunder, or to govern more imperially from the White House, as Nixon had done.[92] By dropping his loyal, centrist vice president and massacring moderate members of his administration on the one hand, and promoting Nixon's least ethical henchmen on the other, Ford had made a last-ditch effort to do both; whether this would win the party nomination, let alone save his presidency in November 1976, was an open question.

Amazingly, Ford had been elected thirteen times to Congress, yet had never fought an election for anything larger than his own congressional district of Grand Rapids. 'All of a sudden I found myself in a different ballpark', he later conceded. 'I didn't comprehend the vast difference between running in my district and running for president.'[93] It was an extraordinary admission.

Faced with relentless attack from the right, he proved all too vulnerable, especially in combating Reagan's memorable but outrageous anecdotal claims. The president's first campaign manager resigned, and his replacement inspired little confidence when declaring that his job was to continue his predecessor's work rather than 'rearrange the furniture on the deck of the *Titanic*'.[94]

Reagan's relentless criticism of his presidency, Ford later confided, was 'a demagogic attack. And I resented it.'[95] With the contestants barely a hundred delegates apart at the Republican National Convention, it was clear that, win or lose, Reagan was leading a massive conservative revolt against Ford's centrist policies. As the convention chairman John J. Rhodes recalled, 'The Reagan people were intent on doing everything they could to embarrass President Ford', especially in pressing the president to alter his foreign policy by voting a new platform, 'Morality in Foreign Policy'. Instead of steady détente and gradualism in encouraging Communist regimes to liberalize, Reagan insisted upon a new, anti-Communist crusade, with himself as chief crusader.

In the end Ford, honourable and admired by all for his integrity, scraped by, winning the nomination on the convention floor by a bare 117 votes on August 19, 1976. 'Thus ended one of the most tense and unpleasant chapters of my political life', the convention chairman later wrote. The next chapter, however, proved if anything worse.

With Reagan and his disappointed supporters refusing thereafter to come out and campaign for Ford (or even, in many cases, to vote for the man they mocked as 'Bozo the president'), the president led a fatally divided party. He could – and did – boast that, like President Eisenhower, he had ended a foreign war and that the nation was now at peace; détente was producing remarkable stability in the once threatening Cold War; stagflation was being beaten (inflation cut by half, unemployment way down), and economic indicators were positive. Yet the president's near-defeat for the Republican nomination at the hands of a sixty-five-year-old right-wing ideologue betokened more than political schism in the Republican Party. In a celebrity-led society in which modern media and advertising played a burgeoning role, it spotlighted the ever increasing importance of public relations in modern politics. And in this respect, the president was at a grave disadvantage, blessed with neither acting ability nor televisual presence. Without them, however hard they tried, his team was unable to present the public with a winning presence. Ford's second campaign manager, Rogers Morton, was soon fired. A third then took on the role as Ford, severely wounded by Reagan's earlier attacks, now faced former governor Jimmy Carter of Georgia, the charismatic nominee of the Democratic Party.

With two months to go before the November election, Ford pinned his hopes on three prime-time television debates, the first such debates since those between Kennedy and Nixon sixteen years before. Although he won the first debate on domestic policy, he made a bad stumble in the second. In defending the Helsinki Accords, he took issue with Carter's criticism of détente as appeasement. 'There is no Soviet domination of eastern Europe,' the President defended his policy, adding 'and there never will be under a Ford administration.'

No Soviet domination of eastern Europe? Seventy-five million viewers rubbed their eyes in disbelief as Ford added insult to injury, claiming that not only Yugoslavs but Romanians and Poles did not 'consider themselves dominated by the Soviet Union'. Seeking to explain what he meant, Ford claimed that 'each of those countries is independent, autonomous; it has its own territorial integrity. And the United States does not concede that those countries are under the domination of the Soviet Union.'

Carter, handed such a gaffe, responded that he'd like to see 'Mr Ford convince the Polish-Americans and the Czech-Americans and the Hungarian-Americans in this country' that their countries were 'not under the domination and supervision of the Soviet Union behind the Iron Curtain'.

Though the president attempted to fudge the issue afterwards, he failed, unwilling to correct his mistake. His assertion, in such a tight election race, proved disastrous, especially when his running mate, Senator Robert Dole, committed an additional faux pas. In his one vice-presidential debate, he excoriated Democrats as collectively responsible for all American wars in the twentieth century, resulting in the death of 1.6 million Americans – 'enough to fill the city of Detroit' as Dole, who was known for his snarling tongue, sneered. The deliberate smear struck a very poor chord among patriotic citizens of both parties; it was an outrageous remark that Vice President Rockefeller, had Ford kept him on, would never have delivered. Not only did Dole thereby lose the debate to Walter Mondale, but centrist public confidence in the Republican ticket plummeted, following an already divisive nomination campaign.

'Mister President,' even Ford's own chief strategist said to him in the Oval Office, 'as a campaigner, you're no fucking good.'[96] Still, compared with polls taken in the summer at the time of the party conventions, Ford did remarkably well in improving his opinion poll numbers by late October, erasing the inexperienced Carter's twenty-point lead in eight weeks to a statistical tie, convincing Ford he might just breast the tape ahead of his rival.

The president's comeback, however, was a mirage. A low turnout – a mere 54 per cent of eligible voters, the lowest in twenty-eight years – cast their ballots on November 2, 1976. Counting went on into the early hours of the next morning. Even at 1 a.m. Ford's chief of staff, Dick Cheney, was calculating that with Hawaii, California, Illinois, Michigan and Ohio, the president might just reach the fabled 270 electoral votes. 'Hawaii?' reporters muttered, looking at each other.

At 9 a.m. on November 3, 1976, Cheney finally conveyed the bitter news. Carter had won 297 electoral votes against Ford's 240: a comfortable win for the former peanut farmer from Plains, Georgia.[97] The president was gutted.

President Ford remained in the Oval Office a further two and a half months until his term ended, but he seemed inconsolable, leading to newspaper reports of 'Jerry Ford's Blues'. On January 20, 1977, the only US president never to have been elected flew off aboard Air Force 2600[98] to Rancho Mirage, the retirement home he had bought in the California desert near Palm Springs.[99] He had served only 816 days in the White House, the shortest tenure of the US presidency in the twentieth century.[100]

Part Three: Private Life

Gerald Ford grew up in a strait-laced home, in the strait-laced community of Grand Rapids, his mother his sternest critic if he failed her expectations as a devout Episcopalian, his hard-working but financially strapped stepfather equally devout and principled. Watching over his three younger half-brothers, Ford knew he would have to work for everything he might covet.

For a time Ford struggled with a stutter. At age fifteen he was working in a local Grand Rapids restaurant, dishwashing and flipping hamburgers, when a man came in and, after twenty minutes staring at him, introduced himself: 'I'm Leslie King, your father. Can I take you to lunch?'[101]

King – who had never once paid the $50–75 per month he was supposed to contribute in child support – gave the boy $25 in cash, and lunch at another establishment. He also introduced his second wife. Then, in a brand new Lincoln – not a Ford – which he'd purchased in Detroit, he drove off home to Wyoming. That night, after telling his parents, Ford wept. He never saw his biological father again.

Ford had a fiery temper, which his mother taught him to control by dispatching him to his room, only allowing him to come down when ready to 'discuss rationally whatever I'd done wrong'.[102] Both parents drilled into him 'the importance of honesty'.[103] He was unusual in being left-handed when sitting down, but became right-handed when standing up. Ford thus wrote with his left hand, but threw a football with his right. His handsome features, his star athletic perform-ance at college, his willingness to work hard both on the field and in his studies, finally got him into Yale Law School in New Haven, along-side Cyrus Vance and Sargent Shriver. They also got him into the arms of eighteen-year-old Phyllis Brown who was slim, equally blonde, and stunningly beautiful, and who was attending nearby Connecticut College for Women.

Ford fell 'deeply in love for the first time in my life', as he later recorded, and the two quickly became an item.[104] Bewitchingly attrac-tive, Phyllis soon gave up her junior degree course and moved to New York as a Powers model, appearing frequently on the covers of Cosmopolitan and Look magazines. Her beau, the handsome law student and college football coach, even featured alongside her in a major five-page pictorial in Look in 1940, entitled: 'A New York girl and her Yale boy friend spend a hilarious holiday on skis' in Stowe, Vermont. One caption read: 'After a hot dinner at the Inn, they loaf, sing, drink beer, dance, talk skiing – and so to bed.'

Using his Yale coaching salary, Ford invested $1,000 in Phyllis' modelling agency. The 'torrid four-year love affair', as he termed it, transformed the retiring Midwesterner into a New York would-be playboy, as the couple wined and dined, played bridge and tennis, and embraced the theatre as well as skiing.[105] Ford was more in love than Phyllis, however; though they 'talked of getting married as soon as I earned my law degree and found a decent job', there was no marriage.[106] Ford was offered a job with a New York law firm, but felt out of his league and hankered to return to Grand Rapids. 'Phyllis' modeling career was blossoming in New York and she didn't think she could afford to leave', he recalled – as well as the 'anguish' their break-up caused.[107] She was 'very smart, very beautiful, very great', he reflected in the evening of life, 'really a great gal'. 'I talk to her on the phone about once every five years, or if I'm in Reno, I call up', he confided to a friend. 'But I don't have her come to my hotel room', he giggled, like 'the lovelorn young buck he once was'.[108]

It was not until after World War II, still living with his mother and stepfather – despite his three younger half-brothers having all married and moved out – that Ford was encouraged by his parents to date a pretty local divorcée, Betty Anne Bloomer Warren, a former dancer and model, who was working as a fashion coordinator for a department store in Grand Rapids. 'At first,' Ford candidly confessed, 'neither of us had thought the relationship was serious' but over time they recognized their compatibility. They became engaged, though Ford explained he had a secret he could not vouchsafe to her for another six months.

The Duke of Wellington, who became not only a great military field commander but a distinguished British prime minister, once said that the Battle of Waterloo was won on the playing fields of his old school, Eton. So, too, Gerald Ford believed competitive sport had prepared him not only for combat, but also, thanks to its fierce aficionados, for politics. 'As a football player,' he later reflected, 'you have critics in the stands and critics in the press', opinionated individuals who 'assume they know all the answers. Their comments helped me to develop a thick hide, and in later years whenever critics assailed me, I just let their jibes roll off my back.'[109]

Ford's secret was that he was going to run as a Republican for Congress and 'wasn't sure how voters might feel about his marrying a divorced ex-dancer'.[110] Betty did not take umbrage or demur (though the marriage was to cost her her health and, to some degree, her happiness). Ford still had campaigning mud on his shoes when he arrived at the altar for his wedding on October 15, 1948 – and the mud stuck. Handsome, honourable and dependable, he made it a rule to be home every Sunday, but was always 'on call' to his constituents, who came to revere him. (One local farmer was astonished when Ford, who had promised he'd milk the farmer's cows for two weeks if he won the election, arrived at 4.30 a.m. to do exactly that, following his victory.) But for Betty, the one-day-a-week marriage, while she raised their four children, was tough, and in part explained her addiction to painkillers, after a pinched nerve in the neck led to continuous suffering.

Ford, in his genial, dedicated way, found himself more fulfilled than he had ever dreamed possible, but Betty was not. By the mid-1960s Betty was mixing painkillers with alcohol and suffered a 'crack-up' as she put it, when she simply walked out on her home, unsure whether she would go back – one of a silent army of dissatisfied wives and mothers who 'have no selves, no sense of self'.[111] As she later wrote, 'Jerry, who has always been supportive, blamed himself for a good deal of my misery. He once admitted to a reporter that, because of his schedule, I'd had to be both mother and father to the children.'[112] She suffered pancreatitis, but once Ford became president, she 'flowered. Jerry was no longer away so much. And I was somebody, the First Lady.'[113]

Unfortunately, it was as First Lady that Betty was found, on routine examination, to have breast cancer – an upset that explained, in part, Ford's distracted mind at the time of his disastrous pardon of Nixon. Like the cancer, Ford wanted the Nixon problem to go away, as fast as possible. Betty recovered well from surgery, but alcohol certainly loosened her tongue when she gave what would become a famed interview with Morley Safer, for CBS' programme *Sixty Minutes*, broadcast on August 10, 1975. In this she described the Supreme Court's 1973 decision to legalize abortion, *Roe* vs *Wade*, as 'the best thing in the world . . . a great, great decision' and admitted that, as a girl, she 'probably' would have tried marijuana had it been widely used. She also said she assumed her children had 'all probably tried marijuana' since there was 'complete freedom among young people now'. The First Lady's most scandalous admission, however, was the one with which the next day's *New York Times* led its shocked report, under the headline 'Betty Ford Would Accept "An Affair" by Daughter'. Asked what her reaction would be if her eighteen-year-old daughter, Susan, confided that she was having an affair, the First Lady countered: 'Well, I wouldn't be surprised. She's a perfectly normal human being like all young girls.'

Stunned, the (male) interviewer had responded: 'She's pretty young to start affairs.' The First Lady had not batted an eyelid. 'Oh, yes,' Betty responded with pride, 'she's a big girl', and even 'suggested that in general, premarital relations with the right partner might lower the divorce rate'. Asked about the 'pressures on a woman living in Washington', the First Lady had then confessed there were many, 'And it depends on the family, the type of husband you have, whether he's a wanderer or whether he's a homebody.'[114]

No First Lady had ever spoken so candidly on national television, sending moralists of both parties into a tailspin. In Dallas, the pastor of the world's largest southern Baptist congregation declared at a news conference that he was 'aghast'. 'I cannot think', he fulminated, 'that the First Lady of this land would descend to such a gutter type of mentality. For her to offer her own daughter in this kind of illicit sexual relationship with a man is unthinkable. Her own daughter!'[115] CBS was inundated with the most mail it had ever received for a broadcast. Demonstrations took place outside the White House. After watching the programme, the President sighed as he puffed on his trademark pipe. 'Well, honey, there goes about twenty million votes,' he commented, 'but we'll make it.'[116]

'He didn't kick me out of the house,' the First Lady observed laughingly on holiday in Vail, Colorado, a week later, 'but he did throw a pillow at me.'[117]

William Loeb, publisher of the militant right-wing *Manchester Union-Leader*, called Betty 'stupid' and 'immoral'. As the days went by, however, pollsters found that although her pro-choice stance over abortion, premarital sex and mild drugs caused apoplexy among Christian fundamentalists and diehard Republican conservatives, the vast majority of respondents, some 75 per cent, supported the First Lady's right to speak her mind, and hold her own independent views. So did the chief executive of the country. 'The president', announced the White House press secretary in the aftermath, 'has long since ceased to be perturbed or surprised by his wife's remarks.'[118]

Voters were reminded of Eleanor Roosevelt. Though not a feminist, Betty became, overnight, a feminist icon – 'the very best kind of liberated woman', even Betty Friedan commented approvingly.[119]

Others, however, could not bring themselves to approve, nor were they amused. In his memoirs, Ford acknowledged that Reagan's challenge in the Republican primaries was, in part, triggered by the CBS interview, and certainly drew support from the outraged moralists it had provoked across middle and southern states.

In tolerating Betty's candour in such a public way, President Ford was, of course, demonstrating his love, loyalty and genuine respect for his wife. Unfortunately, he was also enabling her in other ways, too – such as her drinking. Ford's defeat in the 1976 presidential election, and their move to California, led to an alcoholic spiral that only ended when the whole family confronted Betty in 1978. To her great credit, she then faced up to the truth, admitting she now accepted she had become an alcoholic, even in the White House, 'because I was preoccupied whether alcohol was going to be served or not'. She went into rehab, and became the most eminent spokesperson for the treatment of alcoholism and medicinal drug addiction in the United States in the twentieth century, as president of the Betty Ford Center.

The two presidents – honest, courageous and devoted to each other – lived together in retirement in Rancho Mirage, in the Coachella Valley, ten miles from Palm Springs, California. One day Phyllis Brown appeared, asking if she could 'drop by for a quick hello with her old flame. Much to her chagrin,' Ford's friend recorded, 'the answer was no. They never spoke, but no doubt he was torn; his days with Phyllis Brown were among his happiest memories. But Betty Ford, understandably, had never been high on the brassy babe' who was married 'at least three times, maybe four', Ford recalled. There was simply 'no way the straightest of arrows would have seen her without telling Betty,' Thomas DeFrank considered, 'and after nearly sixty years of marital bliss, he wasn't about to risk hurting the uncontested love of his life, the woman he described a few weeks before his death as "the greatest of all my blessings".'[120]

Ford, the former isolationist, had become the humblest, least ambitious, most moderate and most tolerant of all American Caesars. He had stabilized the conduct of American power in the world, reassuring its allies and finding common ground with its adversaries – no small achievement in the history of empire. On December 26, 2006, the decorated World War II veteran suffered a fatal coronary thrombosis. He was ninety-three – the oldest man ever to have held the office of president of the United States – and was buried in the grounds of his museum in Grand Rapids.

CHAPTER EIGHT

JIMMY CARTER

Mocked, but later respected

Democrat
39th President
(January 20, 1977–January 20, 1981)

Part One: The Road to the White House

James Earl Carter Jr – named after his father, James Earl Carter Sr – was born on October 1, 1924, in the hamlet of Plains, 120 miles south of Savannah, Georgia. 'Jesus and even Moses would have felt at home on a farm in the deep South during the first third of the century' Carter later wrote, for without mechanization life in rural Georgia was primitive.[1] As Richard Nixon's parents had built a family house in Yorba Linda, California, from a Sears, Roebuck catalogue, so Carter's parents had traded their first home for a similar dwelling, made from a Sears, Roebuck catalogue in Archery, next door to Plains.

James Earl Carter Sr was not tall (5' 8") but was powerfully built, and had been a lieutenant in the Quartermaster Corps in World War I. He had what neighbours enviously called 'the Midas touch': everything he touched seemed to turn to gold, from businesses to agriculture and property. Mixing strictness – especially with regard to punctuality – with after-hours pleasure, he liked to play poker away from home on Friday nights, as Carter's mother recalled, and 'raise hell' at the Elks Club on Saturday, where 'he would dance with most of the pretty women in our crowd'.[2]

Jimmy Carter, the eldest of James Earl Carter Sr's four children, idealized his father. Though he loved his son, Jimmy's father did not idealize Jimmy, however – indeed he mockingly gave him the ambiguous nickname 'Hot'. This was short for 'Hotshot', which aptly captured the boy's diminutive size and precociously righteous ego. It was a nickname that would stick to Carter all the way to college and beyond.

'Hot' was still only 5' 3" tall when he left high school, and weighed only 121 lb. He was determined, nevertheless, to leave Georgia and enter the US Navy, despite never having seen the sea, much less spent time afloat. His father spent two years working on the local congressman to support Jimmy's application to go to the naval academy at Annapolis. Eventually, having cooled his heels for a year at junior college in Archery, then another year at the Georgia Institute of Technology studying engineering and other subjects he would need, Carter was admitted to Annapolis. By then, the summer of 1943, America had been at war for almost two years and 'Hot' had grown to his full height – 5' 9" – with unusually thick lips and wide mouth, a permanent toothy smile, thick cornfield-blond hair, and still weighing less than 130 lb.

'Hot' Carter's self-confidence, for an eighteen-year-old peanut farmer's son, none of whose male family had ever finished high school, let alone college, and who himself had never before been East, was astonishing. It certainly irritated his seniors, resulting in hazing that bordered on savagery as they attempted to put him 'in his place' and wipe the smile off his face.

The hazing did not succeed. Carter had encountered similar confrontations for several years already, some of them potentially lethal. As a sixteen-year-old, for example, he had been physically assaulted for insisting that a certain farmer not be awarded the federal soil-conservation payment he expected. 'I was meticulous in my work' (as a part-time crop-planting surveyor on behalf of the government's Agricultural Adjustment Administration) Carter later maintained, proud that the area supervisor had upheld his calculations. Given that his own grandfather had been murdered as a result of just such a local 'disagreement' (over ownership of an office desk), however, it had been foolhardy for Carter to insist. He was 'relieved', he later admitted, when the next planting season came and he departed to college, thus avoiding a second murder in the family.[3]

Carter's moral rectitude was impressive, the sign of a fierce and unyielding determination, despite his small size. Having been whipped many times by his father as a child he did not object to the tradition of hazing at Annapolis, which he did not take personally; yet his failure to recognize or seek to alter the effect of his priggish, righteous attitudes upon others would become an Achilles heel in someone so otherwise gifted.

The Annapolis Class of '47 graduated in 1946, with Carter having already served aboard the battleship USS *New York* on coastal escort duty in 1944, then aboard the battleship USS *Wyoming*, and finally being allotted, on graduation, a berth on the bruised battleship USS *Mississippi*, veteran of the war in the Pacific. With President Truman's decision to drop the atom bomb and the ending of the war in the Pacific, however, a large part of the rest of the American fleet was mothballed, and Carter became, as he put it, 'most disillusioned with the navy and the military in general'.[4]

According to one classmate who later became a doctor, Francis Hertzog, Carter was 'a loner' unable or unwilling to form 'close intimate friendships'. In retrospect Hertzog saw this as a sign of strength, not weakness. Though genial in his general outlook and behaviour, Carter 'didn't need' people to support 'his own ego and personality – he had a very strong character'; indeed Carter already demonstrated at Annapolis outstanding leadership ability and a rare, analytical mind that he remained bent on putting to practical use, like his father. But was the contracting post-war US Navy the appropriate place, or was there another, more challenging platform? 'Maybe once in a thousand years,' Dr Hertzog mused later, 'a person comes along who will have the control of their mind and utilize it to the extent he can his.'[5]

Carter seriously considered resigning from the navy. His application for a Rhodes scholarship to Oxford was, however, rejected by a committee of former Rhodes scholars at the final screening interview. It was, Carter later maintained, the first of only two great 'failures' he was willing to acknowledge in his life before he became president. Typically, Carter blamed the committee; after all, he complained, he had answered correctly and fully 'every question they could think of', from current events to nuclear physics. Never having been to Oxford, Carter could not understand how the successful student, who declared he had zero interest in anything after the death of Elizabeth I in 1603, would be more at home amidst Oxford's ancient spires than himself. On the rebound, though, he applied to join the US Navy's submarine service.

This time, Carter's application – in both senses – succeeded. Following a simple wedding to a local Georgia girl in Plains, Georgia, and then submarine training in New London, Connecticut, the young lieutenant served long tours of duty aboard the USS *Pomfret*, a three-year-old 1,500-ton Baloa-class diesel-electric submarine. In one storm he was swept thirty feet off the conning tower, but miraculously landed on the deck, adding to his sense that Providence was on his side. He claimed to enjoy the claustrophobic isolation of life below sea level, where his leadership skills – a powerful intelligence, absolute confidence in his ability, and ease in getting along with a small team of colleagues and subordinates while maintaining a consistent personal reserve – were honed. Like his father he looked after his men – 'Watch it, these are my engineers' was the tag line given to him – and like his father (who had several hundred tenant farmers working on his various lands) he asked that they trust in his professionalism, in return for his own trust in them. He was subsequently assigned as engineering officer to a brand-new diesel-electric submarine USS *K-1*, later named the *Barracuda*, launched and commissioned in 1951, becoming over time its executive officer and 'Qualified for Command of Submarine'. When no command ensued, the following year, however, he applied for service in the US Navy's futuristic nuclear-powered submarine project, requiring special interview by legendary Captain Hyman Rickover, generally considered the most abusive commander in the navy. Rickover accepted him in October 1952.

Again, Lieutenant Carter made no friends, but was respected for his professionalism in carrying out his duties in a perfectionist environment (Rickover's famous 'Why not the best?'), as the US Navy set about modernizing its submarine fleet in the frigid waters of a Cold War growing ever colder.

Rickover proved a stern taskmaster, but prized his elite team. Carter was posted to the US Atomic Energy Commission in New York, then Washington DC, to help develop the navy's first two nuclear-powered submarines, following the laying down of the USS *Nautilus* (whose keel had been laid by President Truman in June 1952) and the USS *Seawolf*, a 337-foot vessel with thirteen officers and ninety-two enlisted men, whose engineering officer Senior Lieutenant Carter was slated to become.

When commissioned, the *Seawolf* would break the world record for continuous submersion, as well as achieving speeds of more than twenty knots under water – but Lieutenant Carter would not be aboard. In July 1953, he was summoned to Plains, Georgia, where his father, who had been appointed to the seat of a retired Democratic

Georgia state legislator, was unexpectedly diagnosed with terminal pancreatic cancer. He was fifty-eight.

Jimmy Carter was present in the room in Plains when on July 23, 1953, his father exhaled his 'last terrible breath'.[6]

'I was at the pinnacle of success for a young officer of my rank', Carter later recalled, certain that he could 'attain the navy's highest rank'.[7] The brief compassionate leave he spent at his father's deathbed in rural Georgia raised, however, the uncomfortable question whether God had in store for him a different challenge: namely that he should resign his commission and save the family agribusiness, comprising over 5,000 acres of land, stores, houses, warehouses and other buildings, which in his will his father had instructed should be divided up, so that they could more easily be sold off.

Jimmy Carter's wife, Rosalynn, had been proud to become the wife of a deep-diving, ambitious submarine officer; indeed they had barely revisited Plains in the past seven and a half years. She was understandably 'shocked and furious a few days later' when Lieutenant Carter, returning to Washington, told her he was set upon resigning from the US Navy and returning 'home'.[8] 'She almost quit me' Carter confided forty years later.[9] As in a biblical saga, Jimmy Carter's brother, aged sixteen, was also distraught at his older brother's decision to return. 'I was mad as hell' Billy admitted later.[10] Captain Rickover – embroiled at that time in a bitter struggle to be made an admiral – was also angry at losing one of his chosen disciples, and damned Carter's resignation of his commission as 'a breach of loyalty'.[11] The move to Plains thus proved traumatic. 'I became more and more dejected', Rosalynn recalled. 'I didn't want to live in Plains. I had left there, moved on, and changed . . . I thought the best part of my life had ended.'[12]

In fact the best part was beginning. 'Miss' Lillian, Carter's mother, was delighted. 'He had to come back', she later made clear. 'Everything we had was on the line.'[13]

Back in Plains, aged only twenty-nine, Carter turned out to have inherited his father's Midas touch, collecting over time the sums owed to his father, rationalizing the family's land holdings and properties, and above all investing in mechanization of the peanut business. He encouraged his mother to leave Plains, and forced his wife to overcome her shyness. Finally, in 1962, while serving as chairman of the

Sumter County school board, Carter was asked to run for Congress for the district.

He said no, having calculated he had no chance of winning; moreover, if he did win, a seat in Congress would take him away from his business. Soon afterwards, however, having been halted in his attempts to modernize the local educational system, he decided to swallow his dislike of most politicians and to stand as prospective Georgia state senator, under new rules of direct election.

In rural Georgia, which lagged almost a century behind the rest of the country, electoral felony was still endemic. Ballot boxes were routinely stuffed, non-compliant white voters were intimidated, while black voters were simply excluded, on pain of death. Though popular in his county, and though he won in lawful votes cast, the former nuclear submarine engineer lost the special primary.

With his wife's backing, Carter – who had witnessed in person the fraud being openly and unapologetically perpetrated at several voting stations – contested the outcome. More than 10 per cent of registered voters in the worst-affected county signed his petition declaring the state Senate race, like its predecessors, to have been cooked. To everyone's astonishment, after initially being rebuffed, and despite ongoing threats against his life and property, Carter succeeded – the *Atlanta Journal*, and then local radio and television news, reporting that 'every election law in the book' had been violated.[14] Having won his lawsuit, Jimmy Carter thus claimed his rightful place in the Georgia state Senate at the eleventh hour. He later said 'If I have one political attribute as the cause of my success, it would be tenacity.'[15]

Tenacity was certainly needed. Not only was southern politics a 'dirty business', as Carter's wife – fearful of threats to burn down their peanut warehouse – described it, but the issue of desegregation in schools and colleges was reaching its climax. President Kennedy had been reviled for his civil rights speech when enforcing the admission of black students to the University of Alabama. Lyndon Johnson's successful 'Great Society' Civil Rights Bill had been followed by a backlash: the rise of the white Republican right under Senator Barry Goldwater (using 'states' rights' as a code word for anti-integration). Even Carter's own father opposed integration (though dying in the arms of his loyal black nurse). Democratic state senator Jimmy Carter nevertheless plunged into the vortex of the defining issue of his age, and announced he would run for governor on a platform of civil rights.

It proved a mistake. Though Carter campaigned tirelessly as a fiscal conservative and moderate, he lost to the openly racist Lester Maddox. Denied a bed in the governor's mansion, Carter gave way to despair ('acute reactive depression' in the words of his friend, aide and biographer, psychiatrist Dr Peter Bourne). He was rescued by his sister Ruth, a fervent Baptist. Though dismissed from her job as an English teacher for talking exclusively about God, her impact on her older brother, at a moment of profound personal crisis, was seminal. Carter 'reassessed' his relationship with God and became a born-again Christian. It was the turning point in his life.

Accepting defeat and proselytizing for the Baptist missionary movement in Pennsylvania and Massachusetts as a 'witness' for Christ, Carter not only discovered the joy of helping make other people's lives 'more enjoyable' through direct Christian teaching in 1968, but was gradually able to integrate his evangelical dedication into renewed political ambition – namely to stand again for the Democratic nomination for governor of Georgia in 1970.

This time the tide began to run with Carter. On television and on radio the fair-haired, blue-eyed candidate with big lips came across well. In person, his charisma was mesmerizing as he radiated integrity, high intelligence and complete conviction. Even his most hostile political critic in Georgia considered Carter 'as good a campaigner as anybody you've seen in the last twenty-five or thirty years in American politics. One-on-one, he's probably as convincing as anybody I've ever seen.'[16] With opinion polls showing him ahead of his rivals – including the former governor, Carl Sanders, who was standing again – money flowed in from the very 'special interests' that Carter condemned as a populist.

Carter duly won the Democratic Party's gubernatorial nomination. On a platform of government reorganization, tax reform, open government, racial harmony and protection of the environment, the peanut farmer went on to win handily against his Republican rival in November 1970.

Reorganizing Georgia's staggeringly diffuse government bureaucracy, increasing its revenues, reforming its crony-run judicial system, and leaving a healthy surplus at the end of his four years in office,

Jimmy Carter proved a model governor of his state. In his inaugural address he had unabashedly announced 'The time for racial discrimination is past', and since Georgia then practised what its governor preached, Jimmy Carter was widely applauded as the embodiment of the 'New South'.[17]

Carter's eyes, however, were on a higher prize. In 1972, halfway through his gubernatorial term, he made a quiet bid for the vice-presidential post, correctly seeing himself as a politician who could deliver a healing New South to the Democratic Party's presidential ticket. He was thus mortified when George McGovern, the victorious Democratic anti-Vietnam War nominee, failed to choose him as his vice-presidential running mate at the party's National Convention that summer. Instead, McGovern chose Senator Thomas Eagleton, without doing a careful background check. When Eagleton was found to have a medical history of depression, requiring hospitalization, and had to drop his candidacy, McGovern still did not take Carter but chose Ted Kennedy's brother-in-law Sargent Shriver, who had directed the Peace Corps but had never been elected to anything. McGovern and Shriver were then trounced by President Nixon, 521 to seventeen in the Electoral College, and 46.6 million to 28.4 million in votes cast.

Disappointed by McGovern's snub, Carter vowed never again to try for second spot. 'You have to sidle up to people,' he explained, 'and I don't like that.'[18] Emboldened by a loyal coterie of enthusiasts who saw him as a new JFK, he began preparations for a personal march on Washington and the White House. He could be unabashedly acerbic, alongside his positive personality. Richard Nixon, especially, aroused his scorn. 'In 200 years of history,' he remarked following revelations about the Watergate break-in but before the 'smoking gun' tapes were made public, 'he's the most dishonest president we've ever had. I think he's disgraced the presidency. I'm a long-time Nixon hater from way back', he confessed. 'I lived in California when he ran against Helen Gahagan Douglas. It's not in the nature of that man [to resign]' he judged – rightly. But hanging on to the Oval Office would do Nixon no good; Nixon would be 'impeached', he was certain. 'I think the evidence is there . . . the accumulated impact of a dozen culpable acts.'[19] When asked by the New York Times reporter Scotty Reston what he himself planned to do when his gubernatorial term ended

(Georgia governors could not run for office in consecutive elections), he stunned the *Times'* editorial board by declaring 'I plan to run for president.'[20]

No sooner had he left the Georgia governor's mansion in January 1975 than Carter did just that, hoping as he did so that Senator Ted Kennedy of Massachusetts, the best-known Democrat in the country, would continue to sit out the quadrennial contest.

Carter's prayers were answered and Ted Kennedy did not enter the 1976 race. In a field of mediocrities Carter was initially unknown; in fact, at the National Press Club in Washington in December 1975, one editor was quoted saying 'Carter? Running for president? Nobody's ever heard of him. It's a joke.'[21] Carter soon made up for this on the campaign trail, however. Short in physical stature he might have been, but he towered above his rivals, Birch Bayh, George Wallace, Fred Harris, Morris Udall, Lloyd Bentsen, Henry Jackson and other presidential wannabees. Sharp in intellect, politically focused, and driven by determination and strong religious faith, he proved a formidable opponent. Boasting a commendable earlier career in uniform, a highly successful career in business and stellar current performance in state lawmaking and governance in the New South, he possessed outstanding credentials as a presidential candidate.

Wisely, Carter chose not to run against the interim president, Gerald Ford, but against the image of Ford's disgraced predecessor, Richard Nixon. Carter's election mantra became: 'I will never lie to you.' Time and again he reinforced his oath. 'If I ever tell a lie, if I ever mislead you, if I ever betray a trust or a confidence,' he would state, 'I want you to come and take me out of the White House.'[22]

Ford's Republican image of honesty and healing took some of the wind from Carter's planned sails, since both men were at heart conservative moderates, but here the former governor of Georgia was rescued by none other than the former governor of California: Republican Ronald Reagan, who month after month, from one state primary election and caucus to the next, hammered his party colleague from the right – and right on to the floor of the Republican convention. Thus, although President Ford emerged the ultimate Republican nominee, he was left with only a few post-convention weeks to repair the damage and fend off the challenge posed by Carter and his running mate, Senator Walter Mondale of Minnesota.

Ford managed to cut Carter's lead in the polls from twenty points to a dead heat, but there was insufficient time to reverse it. When, in the second presidential debate, Ford made a serious error in discussing Soviet domination of eastern Europe, Carter was able to exploit the gaffe and keep Ford in his sights as they approached the winning post. This, despite Carter's own gaffe when giving an interview to *Playboy* magazine.

Carter's inner strength was his born-again Christian religion. In a secular country founded upon a constitutional division between church and state, however, Carter's Baptist zeal had become the source of considerable anxiety among Catholic voters and non-Baptists. At the end of an unwise *Playboy* interview designed to prove he was not a religious fanatic, Carter went too far. Just as he was leaving the journalist's office, he attempted to show his independence of mind by taking direct issue with the teachings of Jesus. 'Christ said, "I tell you that anyone who looks on a woman with lust has already committed adultery."' As the former Governor pointed out, this was ridiculous, in fact, since taken literally it set 'impossible standards for us'. Like the majority of heterosexual men Carter himself had 'looked on a lot of women with lust; I've committed adultery, in my heart many times'.[23]

Carter's point went grievously awry; indeed it caused a sensation in cold print. As an evangelical Christian he was already unpopular amongst Jews. They liked his references to the Old Testament well enough, but not to the New. After the *Playboy* interview – gleefully distorted by a post-Watergate national press, dizzy with its new power to ridicule, even bring down a politician – Carter found himself being denounced by others, too – even fellow Baptists. Although most voters, in the end, chose to overlook the gaffe, it did raise the question of whether the nuclear submarine officer, peanut farmer and Georgia legislator was really up to the searing business of national politics, in a 'take no prisoners' age of journalistic muckraking and political smearing.

Exhausted, but still wearing his red 'good luck' tie, he watched television in Atlanta, Georgia, on election night, November 2, 1976, as Massachusetts, which had eluded him in the Democratic primary, fell into the Carter column. At 3.30 a.m. the next morning the state of Mississippi was conceded by Republicans, giving Carter the necessary

Electoral College numbers he needed to take the White House. He had won – just.[24]

Part Two: The Presidency

True to his populist mantra, Carter insisted on becoming, after a brief inaugural speech and lunch in the Capitol, the first president in modern times to get out of his armoured limousine and walk on foot to the White House, accompanied by his wife. In addition he decided to send their youngest child – nine-year-old daughter Amy – to a local public school, Stevens Elementary.

These symbolic gestures were carried out with absolute sincerity on his part, determined as he was not to allow pride to turn his head. He banished the playing of 'Hail to the Chief' at official appearances, insisted on being driven in a sedan rather than an armoured limousine, and even invited his wife to become the first ever First Lady to sit in on the president's meetings, even cabinet meetings, as an adviser. At special 'town meetings' with ordinary citizens he tried to make every American feel he or she also had equal access to his decision-making.

An outsider from the South he might be, but Carter was equally courageous in the issues he proposed to tackle. Though he had long since left the US Navy, he was now commander-in-chief. 'I don't care if all one hundred of them are against me,' he snapped, when told that the majority of senators opposed a pardon for Vietnam War draft evaders. 'It's the right thing to do.'[25] And the day after the inauguration, January 21, 1977, he simply did it, signing an executive order to that effect. He also began the arduous process of preparing new legislation on a whole raft of issues, from health and welfare reform to energy conservation. The political missionary was up and running.

Initially the public responded well to Carter's new democratic approach. By March 1977, his public approval rating was the highest any president had enjoyed in the aftermath of inauguration since World War II. No empire, however, operates successfully without a measure of arrogance and pride; indeed these had been considered virtues at the height of the Roman Empire, replete as it was with monuments, arches, games, a Coliseum and Triumphs honouring victors of foreign wars (who were required to have killed at least 5,000 enemy soldiers in battle). Now, by contrast, the American Empire had as president a former navy lieutenant who immediately *pardoned* those who had refused to fight in such wars! Worse still, in the eyes of Washington insiders, he showed scant respect for senators, congressmen and even the number three in line to the presidency: the Speaker of the House of Representatives, and fellow member of the Democratic Party, Tip O'Neill.

O'Neill, in confidence, had warned the president-elect during the transition not to treat Congress as he had the Georgia legislature, namely going over the heads of elected representatives to the people. Carter said that was exactly what he was proposing to do. 'Hell, Mr President, you're making a big mistake' O'Neill had responded.[26] When Carter assigned O'Neill 'the worst seats in the room' for the pre-inaugural gala at the Kennedy Center, O'Neill was outraged – but the insults continued. 'Hell,' the corpulent Speaker complained when only coffee and a roll were served for the first congressional breakfast at the White House, instead of a full English meal, '*Nixon* treated us better than this!'[27]

The main course was the same. Crucial to the relationship between president and Congress was the liaison official whom the president selected to act as go-between. Carter's insistence, against all protes-tations, on appointing a Georgia friend, Frank Moore – a dud who was deeply unpopular on the Hill – was seen as a shot in the foot. 'I knew the Carter administration was finished the day I heard Moore was to be in charge' said the very man Carter had asked to head up his transition planning team, Jack Watson.[28] 'It immediately signaled the Congress that this was a bunch of amateurs,' commented another, an experienced Georgia congressman.[29] Tip O'Neill confided later that relations between the two supposedly allied strongholds were, as he put it, 'like a bad dream'.[30]

Had Carter been able to appoint and lead a tough and capable imper-ial team at the White House, he might just have got away with his treatment of Congress, especially by spinning the media to maintain the public support he was counting upon. But to the dismay of veteran politicians, he refused to appoint a chief of staff at all. 'I never wanted to have a major chief of staff between me and the people who worked for me', he later explained. 'I have always wanted to have a multiple, perhaps as many as ten people who had direct access to me all of the time without having to go through an interim boss . . . I don't even mind if those ten or twelve people are incompatible with each other.'[31]

This 'spokes of a wheel' approach to command (as Carter called it), with himself at the hub of a diffused (and often confused) White House administrative command structure, ensured that everyone competed for his attention and imprimatur. Ford at least later saw the error of having begun his presidency that way, but Jimmy Carter was constitutionally unable ever to admit error, then or later. After all, his reasoning went, had not President John F. Kennedy operated without a chief of staff, and made himself the most visible and accessible president since World War II, alongside his young wife? Had not President Lincoln encouraged a 'team of rivals' in his administration, with himself as the arbiter and visionary?

Unfortunately, Jimmy Carter was no Lincoln, nor Jack Kennedy, who had first spent fourteen years as a politician in Washington and had employed a de facto enforcer in his brother Bobby.

Carter's visionary agenda and accessibility did him proud, but his failure to recognize the limits of his own leadership ability in the White House was alarming to his staff. Flooding the Capitol with new proposals, they watched as almost all of them foundered. 'Look, we're trying to do too much' one of Carter's assistants from Georgia, Jody Powell, acknowledged in April 1977, only weeks after the inauguration.[32] The president, like Captain Queeg, refused to listen to his crew, however, and the chaos in the White House grew only worse.

The issue Carter most wanted to resolve was America's energy crisis. In 1910 the United States had produced almost 70 per cent of the world's oil. By the time of his inauguration, it was importing 50 per cent. The empire had become an oil addict, which would inevitably affect its global hegemony unless it moved to rectify the situation. 'There was no doubt in my mind that our national security was at stake' Carter would later write, calling the energy challenge 'the moral equivalent of war'.[33]

The solution to that war, he maintained, was to cut American dependency, thereby helping also to save the environment. By an open fire in the White House library, wearing a cardigan sweater to emphasize his point, Carter gave his first fireside chat, in the manner of Franklin D. Roosevelt, asking the American people on a freezing day in early February 1977 to turn down their thermostats (after the most severe winter in living memory) to sixty-five degrees Fahrenheit by day; at night, fifty-five degrees would be acceptable. In return he promised a new national energy plan within ninety days.

The president was buoyed by the immediate positive public response. Unfortunately it proved premature, and his plan too green – in the half-baked sense, not the environmental. Linking the main cities, commercial hubs and manufacturing centres of America, US highways were the modern equivalent of Roman roads. Though willing perhaps to wear an occasional cardigan or pullover, few American automobile or truck drivers were eager to trade down for more fuel-efficient vehicles. 'It was like pulling teeth' Carter later described the difficulty in getting Americans to accept that, as privileged citizens of the world's dominant empire, 'they should be ready to make some sacrifices or change their habits' without a Pearl Harbor or similar crisis to shock them into reality.[34] Despite heroic efforts by the House Speaker, Tip O'Neill, Congress failed to rise to Carter's challenge. All too soon the president's bill was stymied by seventeen different committees in the House of Representatives, and five in the Senate. It became clear that, as commander-in-chief, Carter could seek to protect the American Empire and its oil sources, but as president he was almost powerless to alter citizens' behaviour, especially in the buying and use of automobiles.

Carter's appreciation of both the short-term and long-term energy crisis for America was a credit to his intellect, but it spoke little of his realism. Thirty years later the situation would be little different, but in the meantime Carter lamented in his diary on June 9, 1977, how the 'influence of the special interest lobbies is almost unbelievable' as summer came and the Senate crushed the House's energy bill into a proliferation of committees working on the issue, while Republican intransigence was fuelled by the automobile and oil companies urging senators to threaten a filibuster. The acronym for the Moral Equivalent of War was 'MEOW', critics mocked. Carter's ninety-day wonder hadn't worked.

Observers noted Carter was not whim-driven so much as hyper-active, and in a strangely obstinate, wilful way, absorbing huge amounts of written and verbal information via his 'spokes of a wheel' staffing system, but a stranger to the business of commanding a unified political team. In a man who had trained to be a submarine commander this seemed difficult to understand, until analysts asked navy personnel and learned of the special conditions in which underwater vessels operate: comprising small, elite crews, whose few officers worked together without needing a strict hierarchical system to put orders into effect. Moreover, under the moniker 'the silent service', their job was to remain invisible, not only to the enemy but to the rest of the navy and shore.

The White House, however, was not a submarine. Far from working together in a collegial fashion, the president's staff fought like dogs, using deliberate leaks to an all too grateful press for extra leverage when internal methods failed. Moreover, to cap the litany of White House errors and disputes, there was another difficulty: unlike President Kennedy, who had captained a PT boat in combat against the Japanese, Lieutenant Carter had never actually commanded his submarine, and this lack of experience now showed as he gave orders then countermanded them. His promised support to American farmers was quickly dumped, once the fiscally conservative president weighed the costs, which would militate against his efforts to achieve a balanced budget. His promised $50 per person tax giveaway was withdrawn, he abandoned his welfare spending reform as too expensive, and his big, much-heralded tax reform bill, designed to be simpler and fairer to the less wealthy, also stalled in Congress, its provisions contested in every which way.

From 75 per cent initial approval, Carter's rating dipped to below 50 per cent by summer's end in 1977. The public deplored the dissension, bickering and mish-mash legislation coming out of Congress, which retaliated by blaming the White House and demanded if not the head of the emperor, then one of his henchmen. The director of the White House's Office of Management and Budget (OMB), Carter's close friend Bert Lance, was thus targeted by the Democrat-led Congress. On September 21, 1977, the president fed the innocent Lance to the lions – 'Probably one of the worst days I've ever spent', Carter noted in his diary.[35] But the sacrifice led to no amelioration, and by the end of the year, noting the rise in unfavourable impressions of the president from 6 per cent to more than 30 per cent of poll respondents, *Time* magazine described the two most common explanations: 'that Carter had not lived up to his promises and seems unable to get things done'.[36]

The political commentator Victor Lasky was far more trenchant: 'Rarely in the history of the Republic has there been an occupant of the Oval Office', he wrote unkindly, paraphrasing Winston Churchill, 'who demonstrated so quickly an inability to conduct even the simplest affairs of state.'[37]

What had gone wrong? James Schlesinger, the man Carter appointed to head up his new Energy Department, probably summed up the problem best. Jimmy Carter was, Schlesinger later noted, 'an instinctive reformer, not a calculating one'; he had 'blundered' into Washington on a magic carpet, feeling 'he had this relationship with the American public that would transcend the need to get along with the traditional power centers'. In addition, there seemed to be something about the president that the press did not *like* – though Schlesinger was unable to explain why, in a leader so patently sincere, and thus the opposite of the arch-villain Richard Nixon. Even more worrying, that hostility became mutual. Carter called the journalists who had helped bring down his friend Bert Lance 'vultures'. In the media, Schlesinger noted, the president became stereotyped as 'cold and mean' – which was just 'plain wrong' since, from his perspective, Jimmy Carter was a 'kind, considerate warm attractive man'. However, in his missionary zeal the president did take 'on too many things and scattered his efforts', with impossible deadlines. He had 'regarded himself as a man of destiny, in that he had been chosen by destiny – or the Almighty – to be president of the United States. But by the fall of 1977, he was in serious trouble, barely able to keep his nose above water.'[38]

Carter was working eighty hours a week instead of the fifty he had promised, was still without a chief of staff, and continued to rely on a 'spokes of a wheel' White House staff structure in which none of the nine or ten spokes ever met in the same room, let alone agreed on a combined strategy. 'The imperial presidency of Franklin Delano Roosevelt and his successors was no more' commented Victor Lasky, distraught at the sight of the White House deliberately transformed into a cacophonous town hall.[39]

Worse, Carter remained as anxious to avoid the accusation (or sin) of running an 'imperial presidency' abroad as well as at home. To Schlesinger the president had confided his hope that 'in my administration I will be able to put our relations with the Soviet Union on the same basis as they are with England'.[40]

The Soviet Union the same as the UK, America's main NATO ally? What could the president possibly mean by such a remark? That he would hold the USSR to the same standards as any western democracy? Or that, thanks to détente, the Cold War was over, in his mind? Bill Moyers, in a television interview with Carter long before the election, had observed that people 'have more doubts about your perception of reality than they do about your integrity'.[41] It was a profound insight.

The SALT I arms control agreement with the Russians was set to expire in October 1977; a SALT II was urgently needed, and was more or less ready to be signed when Carter took over the presidency. To assist him in dealing with foreign affairs, he appointed two highly competent but competing individuals, Cyrus Vance, a 'dove', as Secretary of State, and Zbigniew Brzezinski, a 'hawk,' as his national security adviser. But if Carter hoped he could thereby be both liberal and conservative on the world stage, he was to be cruelly educated. All too soon his plan unravelled, as Carter publicly lambasted Moscow for the trials of human rights activists such as Anatoly Sharansky, while at the same time encouraging Communist China's rivalry with the Soviet Union and refusing to compromise over SALT II treaty provisions enshrining America's nuclear advantage. By the summer of 1977 Leonid Brezhnev, the Soviet premier, was refusing Carter's offer of a summit meeting, raising the spectre of détente evaporating, and producing fury in Europe, where Chancellor Helmut Schmidt of West Germany was driven to exasperation by Carter's approach to imperial diplomacy.

Once again, Carter had allowed himself to speak from moral conviction, incensed at the Soviet arrest of Alexander Ginsburg, Yuri Orlov and Sharansky. By deliberately making himself the spokesman of the American in the street, however, he lost presidential authority, with the Kremlin confused as to the true intentions of the American Empire. It took a further two years to get SALT II signed, by which time it was too late to count upon Senate ratification. (It was never formally ratified.)

Chaired by Carter's vice president, Walter Mondale, the first meeting of the National Security Council had set Panama as one of the two top priorities for the incoming Carter administration, along with the Middle East. Disputed ownership of the Suez Canal had nearly led to world war in 1956 when Egypt's President Nasser seized it from its French and British owner-operators; Carter wished to avoid the same from happening over the Panama Canal, especially since Ronald Reagan had used the issue as his biggest stick in beating – but not defeating – President Ford for the Republican presidential nomination in 1976.

Reagan was intent on keeping America's vital waterway between the Pacific and Atlantic – a 553 square mile strip that had been signed over to the US in a dubious land deal in 1903 – in American hands. By contrast President Carter, as an anti-imperialist, felt that not only should the canal revert to Panamanian ownership in due course, but restitution should be effected in good time. Serious rioting in the 1960s had raised the spectre of armed conflict over ownership, with a Pentagon report indicating it would require 100,000 troops to re-secure the canal in the event of a Panamanian insurgency and seizure. If a renegotiated treaty safeguarded neutrality, security and the passage of vessels from all nations, the president argued, all sides would be satisfied. To his lasting credit, the Carter–Torrijos treaties were not only signed in September 1977, but ratified by the Senate the following year, after a titanic struggle on Capitol Hill and the final ratification vote a cliffhanger. 'I think', Carter admitted in a press conference, 'I would almost equate it with the difficulty of being elected president.'[42]

If securing agreement over a Panama Canal treaty was tough, securing peace in the Middle East was even more difficult.

The irony of US 'interference' (as Brezhnev called it) in the internal affairs of another nation was that while Carter was willing to pressure the USSR about its treatment of its own and its neighbours' citizens, he found himself unable to criticize Israel's actions without accusations of anti-Semitism within America. Carter had a special interest in Palestine from his long devotion to the Bible, and had visited Israel at Prime Minister Golda Meir's invitation in 1973, while governor of Georgia. His support for the security of Israel had rested on a distant concern to preserve the antiquities of the biblical land, considered as sacred to Christians as to Jews. 'I had no strong feelings about the Arab countries' he explained later. 'I had never visited one and knew no Arab leaders.'[43] All this changed once he became president.

Since Israel, having fought four wars of self-creation and survival, seemed adamant it would neither return the territories it had won nor accept a Palestinian state (which the 1947 UN Commission had mandated), the prospect for American mediation – especially in view of the power of the Jewish vote and lobby in US elections – was slight. Nevertheless Carter decided to tackle the issue, which even his staff and advisers considered a 'losing proposition'.[44] He wanted to help Israel achieve lasting security, but he could not see this happening as long as Israel remained wedded to the lands it had conquered in the Sinai, Gaza, the West Bank and Golan Heights – territories it not only occupied by military force, but where it was encouraging Zionists to create expanding Jewish settlements. These would require road corridors from Israel for access, and military protection for each settlement, thus making eventual Jewish withdrawal – as called for in UN Resolution 242 – difficult, if not impossible.

To absorb Palestinians in a Greater Israel, given the fact that Palestinian Arabs outnumbered Jews, would be hard for Israeli politicians to accept; but to withdraw Israeli troops from the occupied territories and agree to a Palestinian nation alongside Israel would be a leap of faith beyond the will of most Israelis, given the vehemence of most Arabs to 'wipe Israel off the map'. Better to keep the upper hand militarily over the neighbouring states of Lebanon, Syria, Jordan and Egypt, Israeli right-wingers like Ariel Sharon and Yitzhak Rabin argued, while expanding Jewish settlements and keeping the dispossessed Palestinians destitute, impotent and as divided as possible.

To President Carter's credit, he foresaw no good coming of Israeli intransigence. Given the US need for oil from the Middle East, it was neither in America's strategic interest nor that of Israel, ultimately, if Israel wished to continue to be supported politically, militarily and economically by the western powers. Palestinians, Carter therefore declared, *must* have a homeland.

Seen in retrospect, Palestinian leaders had made a huge mistake in not accepting the British Peel Commission Partition Plan of 1937, which would have given Jewish settlers 15 per cent of Palestine, with 85 per cent for the Palestinians; they had then made another mistake in rejecting (along with Arab neighbours) the UN Partition Plan of 1947, at the end of the British Mandate, when 56 per cent of the Mandate territory of Palestine was still slated for them.[45] But should those past errors of judgement – the second made at a time when Palestinian Arabs outnumbered Jews by two to one, thus making the division seem unfair – necessitate their permanent enslavement under

Jewish military occupation as the result of war, or as hand-to-mouth refugees in other countries? President Carter wanted for the Palestinians 'the right to vote, the right to assemble and to debate issues that affected their lives, the right to own property without fear of its being confiscated, and the right to be free of military rule', leading to Palestinian statehood – albeit with 77 per cent of the former Arab country permanently ceded to the Israelis, once the Israelis withdrew from the occupied Arab territories.

Prospects for a positive solution in the Middle East did not look good when Carter became president. Nor did they improve when Prime Minister Yitzhak Rabin overreacted to the killing of thirty-five Israelis aboard a bus by a rogue element of the PLO, which sought to represent Palestinian Arabs. Invading South Lebanon, Rabin's forces killed many thousands of innocent civilians – raising comparisons, critics claimed, with Nazi brutality, even concern whether Israel might be seeking more *Lebensraum*, this time in Lebanon. Yet beyond banning the sale of more cluster bombs to Israel, there was little Carter was able to do, given the power of the Israeli lobby in America.

Almost in desperation, once Rabin was succeeded as prime minister by Menachem Begin, another right-wing Israeli, Carter called a summit at Camp David to see if he could at least get a resolution of the ongoing state of war between Israel and Egypt, whose president was Anwar Sadat. Reading the biographies of the two leaders, Carter learned that Begin had been born in Brest Litovsk, Belarus, and had been wanted by the British for mass murder as an Irgun terrorist in Palestine in 1946–7 (responsible for killing 91 people). As leader of the Herut Party in Israel, and advised by his Irgun associate Shmuel Katz, Begin had then become committed to the expansion of the Jewish settlements, especially in Judea and Samaria, rather than a permanent peace treaty (considered illusory) that would secure peace guarantees for the fragile state of Israel.

For his part, President Sadat had *also* opposed British rule, indeed had been imprisoned by the British in Egypt in World War II for helping Hitler's and Mussolini's 'liberating' efforts in North Africa. He too had become a revolutionary, and had later taken part in the Egyptian officers' coup that ousted King Farouk, becoming thereafter vice president to Colonel Nasser. Sadat's decision to attack the Sinai

Peninsula in the 1973 'October War', though it ultimately failed, had made Sadat the 'hero of the Crossing' in the Arab world – a status which, Carter astutely realized, might actually make Sadat strong enough to be able to reverse engines and sign a peace treaty with Israel, if Carter could wring concessions from Begin.

The three days assigned for the Camp David meeting with Sadat and Begin, beginning on September 5, 1978, became thirteen. Only the United States, as Israel's chief supplier of arms and funding, could pressure Israel into concessions that might lead to peace; but given the perceived power of Jewish opinion makers, lobbyists and voters in the US, no American president had ever dared risk the furore (and electoral backlash) that such a Palestinian-oriented approach would entail. Failure of the 'summit' would, Carter's aides warned, feed a growing impression that the president was well meaning but inept.

At Camp David, Begin proved more intransigent than Sadat. In the West Bank – the almost exclusively Muslim and Christian area which Jordan had administered after 1948 but which Jewish Israeli forces had occupied since the 1967 Suez war – the Palestinian Arab population had grown from 600,000 to 700,000, with fewer than 1 per cent Jews. Begin remained fiercely determined to change this. His aim was to increase the Jewish West Bank population from its 1977 level by a hundred times – a demographic strategy that would inevitably inflame Palestinian inhabitants, but if successful would present the world with a fait accompli, thus making a complete Israeli withdrawal politically impossible in the face of Zionist demands that the settlements be made permanent.[46]

The Camp David Accords that President Carter successfully negotiated in September 1978 were to bring lasting peace between Egypt and Israel, and rightly won the Nobel Peace Prize for President Sadat and Prime Minister Begin. Americans were awed by Carter's seemingly magic peace wand, and his polls rose fifteen points in four weeks; even the *Wall Street Journal* complimented him on his 'inspired leadership'.[47]

Behind the scenes, however, Camp David proved an unmitigated disaster, for although Begin agreed to pull Israeli troops and would-be settlers out of the Sinai, and thus release the still-surrounded Egyptian Army, for the Palestinians there was no improvement. Begin simply reneged on his commitment to stop Jewish settlement and withdraw Israeli military forces from the West Bank and Gaza. As Carter wrote in sadness thirty years later, 'The Israelis have never granted any appreciable autonomy to the Palestinians and instead of withdrawing their military and political forces, Israeli leaders have tightened their hold on the occupied territories.'[48] Belatedly, the president realized he had been 'had'.

As Carter's White House aide and biographer Peter Bourne wrote, Begin had fooled Carter into believing the Israelis had agreed to end all construction of Jewish settlements in the Palestinian West Bank. 'Although the record is clear', Bourne chronicled, Begin had simply twisted the truth to suit his Zionist agenda. 'Begin would later claim, after violating the agreement, that he had meant the building of settlements would be suspended for only three months' – indeed Begin and succeeding prime ministers authorized the settling of more than a quarter of a million Israelis in the West Bank in the thirty years after the accords, despite the express provisions agreed at Camp David for complete withdrawal.[49]

Carter was understandably disappointed as the full import of his failure became clear in subsequent decades. 'With the bilateral treaty, Israel removed Egypt's considerable strength from the military equation of the Middle East', allowing Israel 'renewed freedom to pursue the goals of a fervent and dedicated minority of its citizens to confiscate, settle, and fortify the occupied territories'.[50] For fanatical Zionists this was divine delivery, but for the United States it would prove ruinous, leading to anti-American protests across the Arab world, attacks on American installations and personnel, and mounting threats to America's homeland security. It was, in hindsight, a disaster.

Leadership of a mighty empire rather than a nation, historians noted, requires more than peaceful sincerity. Carter had attempted to act merely as an honest broker between two warring adversaries, not as an American emperor who, by virtue of Israel's dependence on the US for military and economic support, could compel Israel not only to withdraw from the Sinai, but halt its illegal settlement activity in Gaza and the West Bank, and ensure at least a moderate Palestinian homeland in the region. The threat of Soviet expansion in the region had evaporated as Egypt sent home its Russian advisers; indeed there was no Arab state in the Middle East that showed any significant interest in Communism. In the absence of a Soviet presence in the

Middle East, the United States could have acted as the region's impartial guarantor of peace – and oil. Instead, thanks to Camp David, Israel was seen to have formed 'an alliance with America in all but name'.

The consequences were not slow in coming. Other Arab nations, including Jordan and Saudi Arabia, were appalled and refused to cooperate in efforts at a wider, regional peace agreement, which had been Carter's real aim. At the Tokyo G7 economic summit in 1979, Carter was condemned by Chancellor Schmidt and other NATO nations for his 'meddling' in the Middle East that had infuriated Arab oil producers, who lifted oil prices for a fourth time in five months. Oil prices in America rose higher and higher, presaging serious domestic problems for a president who had relied upon popular rather than congressional or party support. With 90 per cent of gas stations in the New York area being closed over the July 4 weekend, people began to wonder 'What in hell is Carter doing in Japan and Korea when all the problems are here at home?' as his senior aide, Hamilton Jordan, told him.[51]

Deemed too soft by conservatives, and too conservative (and confusing) by liberals, Carter's presidency seemed not so much centrist as lacking in cohesion, judgement and direction. Walter Mondale, the vice president, confided he would like to resign since the president did not seem to be representing the Democratic Party any more, sharing 'the view of much of Washington that Carter and his staff were politically inept, incapable of understanding the inner workings of Congress, and unable to project a clear and compelling vision to the public', as Peter Bourne put it.[52] Eventually Mondale told Carter to his face that his approach to the presidency was all wrong.

To his credit, Carter made history by inviting 150 people to Camp David, over eight days, while he listened carefully to their criticisms and complaints. On July 15, 1979, he gave a thoughtful, well-received televised address to the nation, cognizant of the frustration felt by ordinary Americans waiting in gas lines, and focusing on energy as the great test of the nation's will. He then asked his entire cabinet and White House staff to resign.

The White House Massacre, as it was quickly termed, created the opposite impression from the house cleaning which Carter had intended. An air of national crisis now pervaded Washington. The president made Hamilton Jordan his chief of staff, but Zbigniew Brzezinski, the national security adviser, simply refused to take orders from him, and was not alone. As the weeks went by, the president's admired address of July 15 was conflated with the 'massacre' and the sense of crisis; it thereafter became known as 'the malaise' speech.

Malaise, indeed, seemed to afflict the president himself – literally. On September 15, 1979, having overruled the warnings of his entire staff, he ran in a sponsored ten-kilometre race near Camp David, collapsed before the cameras and had to be carried off – inviting every cartoonist in the world to use the incident as a symbol of the president's demise. This despite inflation held down to 6 per cent, while the economy grew at a similar pace and unemployment also stabilized at 6 per cent, as well as a raft of legislation that was finally passing through Congress: bills that dealt with energy conservation, created a Department of Education, accepted a major welfare reform package, provided financial assistance to middle-income students, ensured better funding for schools, and deregulated trucking, railways, banking and communications.

It was too little, too late, and too diffuse. At a lunch at the White House on September 20, 1979, Senator Ted Kennedy delivered his own bad news. Carter's chances of re-election were slight (70 per cent of people polled disbelieved he could win re-election), and Kennedy had therefore decided to run against him for their party's nomination.

Early in November, Kennedy duly prepared the formal announcement of his candidacy. Before he could do so, however, disaster of another kind struck.

The Shah of Persia had chosen temporary exile in January 1979, for 'rest and recuperation'. From exile in Paris the seventy-eight-year-old Ayatollah Khomeini had then flown into Tehran in February. Millions had paraded on the streets. The military had held back, waiting to see what would happen. A group of Marxist guerrillas had besieged the American embassy, only to be chased away by Khomeini supporters. Soon armed revolutionaries loyal to Khomeini were arresting and executing people across the country. Over the ensuing months Mehdi Bazargan's civil government and Khomeini's de facto religious authority had worked in an uneasy tandem, the Iranian government declaring its commitment to the Palestinian cause, reversing the Shah's pro-Israel policy, and yet declaring an equal commitment to good relations with the US. In the streets, however, mobs still rampaged shouting anti-US slogans, in view of its military and economic support for Israel, and demanding the return of the Shah to face trial.

How, in these circumstances, Carter allowed the fabulously wealthy Shah – who had moved his place of exile to the Bahamas, then to Mexico – to visit America for medical treatment is difficult in retrospect to understand. Carter was certainly warned by the remaining staff of the US embassy in Tehran not to do so, but Henry Kissinger and Zbigniew Brzezinski lobbied on the Shah's behalf, and thus contributed to one of the most disastrous decisions of the era (though characteristically neither would ever accept responsibility for it). The Bazargan government gave an assurance there would be no reprisals, but given the state of turmoil in the country, it was an empty promise. The Shah was duly admitted to the Sloan-Kettering Memorial Hospital, New York, in October 1979. Once word of this reached Iran, an armed mob of revolutionaries attacked the US embassy on November 4, this time without interference or objection by government or Khomeini forces. The insurgents took all sixty-three members of the embassy staff hostage, as well as three US diplomats visiting the Iranian foreign ministry that day.[53] They did so, moreover, in the name of Khomeini, demanding that the Shah be returned to Iran to face 'revolutionary justice'.

'Does somebody have the answer to what we do if the diplomats in our embassy are taken hostage?' Carter had asked his staff, presciently, some months earlier. Silence, even on the part of the vice president, had greeted the question. 'I gather not', the president had commented, and delivered his own prophecy. 'On that day,' he'd mused, 'we will all sit here with long drawn, white faces and realize we've been had.'[54]

The day had now come, and Brzezinski had no contingency plan. Carter ordered the US Sixth Fleet, with two aircraft carriers, closer to the Persian coast; but with Ayatollah Khomeini threatening to put the American hostages on trial and destroy the embassy if the US attempted to rescue them, Carter had to admit that, beyond terminating oil purchases from Iran and the freezing of all Iranian assets in the US, he was powerless unless he wished to go to war over the matter. He broke off diplomatic relations with Iran on April 7, 1980, then, on April 11, he told his national security staff he wanted a rescue mission, which the Pentagon had now planned, to go ahead.

Launched as Operation Eagle Claw on April 24, the mission used helicopters from the aircraft carrier USS *Nimitz* to rendezvous in the Iranian desert with the rescue force, ferried there aboard six C130s. Transferring to the *Nimitz*'s helicopters, the rescue force was then intended to land secretly outside Tehran in darkness, and snatch the hostages from their captors the following day.

That the president, a trained naval officer, could have approved such a cockamamie plan said little for his youthful ambition to become chief of naval operations. 'I'll guarantee you something will go wrong' the Secretary of State, Cyrus Vance, warned the vice president and tendered his resignation, to be effective as soon as the operation had taken place. 'It never works out the way they say it's going to work', Vance sighed.[55]

Amid dust storms, the unexpected presence of Iranian military personnel and a catastrophic fatal accident, Carter ordered the mission to be aborted, leaving not only eight American servicemen dead but six abandoned helicopters in the desert, a burned-out C130, and secret documents with the names of all CIA agents in Tehran. As Peter Bourne chronicled, the botched rescue attempt 'compounded the impression of a president impotent in defending the nation's honor against a Third World power'.[56]

The seizure of the American embassy in Tehran was not the only nightmare that afflicted Carter's presidency at this time. Instead of following his cautious prescription for détente with the USSR, he made another disastrous mistake, this time in relation to Afghanistan. The Soviet Union had supplied military advisers and weaponry to the Afghan monarch since 1933, and its Marxist dictator since 1973. In the summer of 1979, Carter allowed Zbigniew Brzezinski to try a new version of the 'Great Game', the age-old imperial contest for supremacy in Central Asia.

Brzezinski's plan was stunning in its stupidity, especially in a period of détente: to secretly provoke the Soviet Union into invading Afghanistan, where their armies would get bogged down in a Vietnam-style quagmire. The US would then be doing 'something', Brzezinski later boasted, 'that had never been done in the entire history of the Cold War . . . actively and directly supporting the resistance movement in Afghanistan, the purpose of which was to fight the Soviet army'.[57] According to the official version, 'CIA aid didn't start until after the

Russian invasion of Afghanistan,' Brzezinski later explained with pride, 'But the reality, which has been kept secret to this day [1998], was different: that in fact President Carter signed the first directive six months earlier, on July 3, 1979, instructing the CIA to give assistance to the opponents of the pro-Soviet Afghan regime. And on that day I wrote a note to the president in which I explained my view that this aid would lure the Soviets into an invasion.'[58]

Operation Cyclone, which President Carter authorized that day, began a major effort to secretly arm and fund the mujahidin insurrection in order to destabilize the Afghan regime and force the Soviets to intervene with more than advisers – just as the US had done in Vietnam in 1964. The killing of a hundred Russian advisers provided the *casus belli*. Wearing Afghan uniforms, the Russians seized Kabul by *coup de main* on December 27, 1979, murdered the Communist president, Hafizullah Amin, and installed a new, more compliant Communist puppet dictator. Under command of Marshal Sokolov, Soviet ground forces simultaneously invaded Afghanistan from the north. Brzezinski was over the moon.

Given that the Russians, however brutally, were intent on modernizing a fractious, feudal Islamic society in Afghanistan through the Kabul government, the United States would have been well advised to stay clear of the imbroglio, having no apparent dog in the fight. Thanks to Brzezinski, however, they did not.

Keeping silent over the CIA's deliberate enticement to invade, President Carter pretended to be shocked and disgusted by the Russian incursion. To the American public and to the world, he announced on January 4, 1980, that he was imposing a punitive grain embargo on the USSR, thus hurting his own highly productive American farmers as well as the Russians. He also decided that the US would boycott the 1980 Olympic Games in Moscow.

'You don't regret it today?' Brzezinski was asked in 1998. 'Regret what?' he retorted. 'The CIA operation was a *wonderful* idea . . . It succeeded in luring the Soviets into the Afghan trap and you want me to regret *that*? The day the Russians officially crossed the Afghan border I wrote President Carter, saying, in effect, "We've now our chance of giving the Russians their own Vietnam."'

In this, at least, he was right. The ten-year Russian war, fought in Afghanistan's mountainous, often impassable terrain, required more than 620,000 Soviet troops, almost 15,000 of whom would be killed, 54,000 wounded, and more than 415,000 fall sick before the Kremlin withdrew. It was, Brzezinski boasted, a decade-long millstone which 'in the end put paid to the Soviet empire'. 'What is more important in terms of world history?' he asked. 'The fall of the Soviet empire – or the Taliban? A handful of hysterical Islamists, or the liberation of central Europe and the end of the Cold War?' When reminded that Islamic fundamentalism was, by 1998, posing a 'global threat', Brzezinski cut the interviewer short with the immortal words: 'Don't be daft! . . . There is no global Islamic threat from the Orient. The notion of global Islamism is utterly stupid!'[59]

Born in Poland and stranded in Canada as a youngster during World War II, when Poland was invaded by the Nazis and then turned into a Soviet Communist puppet state, Zbigniew Brzezinski was a Cold War fanatic. Détente made no sense to him. Instead of seeing a faltering Communist empire that would gradually disintegrate through its own inherent disabilities, he subscribed to the Republican fear that the Soviets were once again on the march and would soon be at the gates of Washington DC and other capitals of the free world. 'The Soviets at that time were proclaiming over and over again', he claimed, 'that the scales of history were tipping in the favor of the Soviet Union: that the Soviet Union would outstrip us in economic performance, the Soviet Union was getting a strategic edge, the Soviet Union was riding the crest of the so-called national liberation struggles. The Soviet Union was moving into Africa, it had a foothold in Latin America.' To him this fully warranted the ditching of détente in favour of a more aggressive American policy, such as support for the Taliban insurgency in Afghanistan and – in 1980 – warnings to the Russians not to send more troops into Poland to crush Lech Walesa's Solidarity movement. '[W]e'll not have détente: we'll have competition across the board', Brzezinski characterized the new Carter Doctrine – a revived Cold War strategy that missed completely the growth of Islamism, and how this, rather than supposed Soviet expansionism, would affect the problem of America's huge dependence on oil.[60]

With détente out the window, unrestrained Israeli settlement activity in the occupied territories, continuing oil shortages and soaring gas prices at home, inflation rising again, the SALT II treaty unratified and the Iran hostage crisis unresolved, President Carter's appeal for each individual American to 'look and say what can we do to make our country great' looked moribund. Carter was now asking Congress for 5 per cent annual increases in defence spending – raised from 3 per cent – while in April 1980 inflation ballooned to 20 per cent, and the Federal Reserve's prime interest rate rose to 18 per cent. Unemployment in some urban areas like Chicago reached 25 per cent.[61] Despite Carter's rightward turn in confronting the Soviet Union, the economic outlook for ordinary Americans looked far bleaker than when Carter took office – playing into the hands of his opponents.

Whether the Carter administration's lurch to the right reflected an inevitable trend in American culture and politics, Brzezinski's obsession with Russian Communism opened the floodgates to Republicans such as Barry Goldwater and Ronald Reagan, especially when the Iran hostage crisis was not quickly resolved.

Brzezinski acknowledged the Iran hostage crisis was 'politically devastating' for his boss, but not for America. For Brzezinski it was of no significance beside America's larger imperial strategy – which he did not see as concerning itself with the rise of militant Islam.[62] If the Soviets could send an army into Afghanistan, might they not also send troops into Iran, he argued. 'Iran would be even more vulnerable to the Soviet Union,' he claimed, 'and in any case, the Persian Gulf would be accessible even to Soviet tactical air force from bases in Afghanistan. Therefore, the Soviet intervention in Afghanistan was viewed by us as of serious strategic consequence, irrespective of whatever may have been the Soviet motives for it.'[63]

Brzezinski's obsession with the Soviet Communist threat thus not only hijacked Carter's peace agenda, but left the president squarely between a rock and a hard place, since Carter believed passionately in human rights, but, compared with diehard right-wingers, was unconvincing in his Cold War rhetoric. His record in foreign affairs had become as convoluted as his domestic efforts, and he could easily be dislodged from his eyrie by a sufficiently right-wing opponent, Republican strategists calculated. Equally, his conservative domestic policies, ditching of détente and increase in military spending made him vulnerable to a liberal Democratic challenger such as Senator Ted Kennedy, Democratic strategists argued in the spring of 1980.

The majority of Americans had rallied patriotically behind their president in the first weeks of the Iran hostage crisis, but the 'long wait' thereafter (including ever higher gas prices) had become a ball and chain Carter could not escape. Jewish voters abandoned him in droves when he instructed his administration to support the UN resolution to dismantle the illegal settlements in the West Bank. 'Either the vote is reversed or you can kiss New York goodbye', Carter's campaign manager warned – and he was right: the president lost the New York Democratic primary (and neighbouring Connecticut) to Senator Kennedy by 16 per cent.[64] With Carter running two White Houses – 'one working on the hostages, the other working on everything else' – and his polls dropping ever lower, it looked increasingly as if the ultimate presidential election contest would be a knockabout between Kennedy and Reagan.[65]

In primary after primary in the spring of 1980, Kennedy excoriated his fellow Democrat from the left, while Reagan hammered him from the right. Carter refused to give in, though, counting on his religious faith as well as his faith in ordinary voters to see him through. Eventually, on the floor of the National Democratic Convention on August 12, 1980, President Carter clinched his re-nomination, but it was a near-run thing. According to most opinion polls he was estimated to be running a staggering 30 per cent behind Reagan with barely two months to close the gap.[66] Carter could only hope that, in an October surprise, he could negotiate the release of the remaining American hostages in Iran, and be seen to have triumphed through Christian patience and dedication rather than loudmouth bravado.

Jimmy Carter's stoicism did him great credit, but his time was up. Reagan had campaigned across the South proclaiming 'states rights' – a code for anti-integration, or racism – and despite the fact that he never attended church himself, he had mobilized widespread support among Christian evangelicals, who now abandoned their devout Baptist president in surprising numbers. In a period of economic distress and international confusion, Reagan's no-nonsense anti-Communist rhetoric – ridiculed for years by East Coast liberals – sounded a clearer note than the president's speeches. Carter's pardon of Vietnam draft evaders still irked right-wing patriots, while Reagan's simplistic calls for tax cuts and further deregulation of trade and industry found receptive ears among lobbyists, funders and voters.

Though a Democrat, Carter had never truly had a Democratic Party base, whether among party organizers, trade unions, congressmen or senators. He had always relied on the nebulous public, who in 1976 had responded to his idealistic promise of honesty after the years of Nixonian deceit, as well as his declared willingness to tackle the problem of energy and oil. But he hadn't tackled them, at least, not effectively – unless gas lines at the pump were considered an effective way of reducing consumption. Even his efforts at governmental reform – streamlining departments, vetoing pork-barrel spending, urging welfare reform – had failed to stop Reagan from urging his supporters to see government as the problem, not the solution, to America's problems.

In previous campaigns, Carter had always been the challenger, not the incumbent. Instead of presenting himself as the confident occupant of the Oval Office in difficult times, calmly setting out a vision of what a second Carter term would bring, he scrapped with Reagan's image as if in a dogfight, attacking him as a semi-psychopath who would 'launch an all-out nuclear arms race' while dismantling Johnson's Great Society; he was a hollow man, a B-movie actor, with stock lines but no substance: a public danger in a hostile world.[67] Against the advice of his staff, but to show the public what he meant, Carter agreed to a televised debate with Reagan. This proved a terrible mistake.

'When it came to understanding the issues of the day, Jimmy Carter was the smartest public official I've ever known', Tip O'Neill reflected later. 'The range and extent of his knowledge were outstanding: he could speak with authority about energy, the nuclear issue, space travel, the Middle East, Latin America, human rights, American history, and just about any other topic that came up.'[68] Intelligence, however, was not the issue: effective leadership and character were. Reagan had spent a lifetime portraying himself on the screen; now, in a single prime-time television duel, he had the chance to disprove Carter's characterization of him – and even Carter's aides trembled at the prospect.

By dint of energetic campaigning the president had by October 19, 1980 effaced Reagan's lead in opinion polls. In fact he was supposedly two points ahead as the debate in Cleveland, Ohio, approached on October 28, 1980. As virtually the entire television audience of the country got to listen to Reagan's slightly gravelly voice and humour, and compare his tall, ageing Hollywood good looks with the diminutive, smiling, smart, self-righteous but tense and sometimes irritable president, the maverick right-wing screen actor was elevated in the public mind to Oval Office status.

Despite everything Carter threw at him, Reagan was composed and difficult to rattle – and for a good reason. Incredibly, the president's secret briefing book on foreign policy had come into Reagan's hands, allowing him to meet every Carter argument or thrust. Carter's attempts to paint his opponent as a loose cannon now failed miserably. 'There you go again' Reagan would sigh, unperturbed, humorous and supremely confident.

'We rushed downstairs and greeted the president and Rosalynn as they came offstage' recalled Hamilton Jordan, Carter's chief of staff. 'How did I do?' Carter asked in trepidation. 'Grasping his hand,' Jordan recounted, 'I exclaimed, "You won, Mr President! You did it!"'[69]

He hadn't, however, as polls soon showed. Even Jordan's own brother admitted in a telephone call that it had been a failure. 'My boy, the Gipper did well' he told Jordan. 'He did better than Carter.'[70] Reagan's summing up had proved especially devastating. 'Looking straight into the television camera with an almost pained look, he asked, "Are you better off than you were four years ago? Is it easier for you to go and buy things in the store than it was four years ago? Is there less unemployment than there was four years ago? Is America as respected throughout the world as it was? Do you feel that our security is as safe, that we're as strong as we were four years ago?"' Jordan afterwards related that he had got Carter to use the same tactic – the so-called 'Misery Index' – against President Ford in 1976. Now it had come back to haunt them, and Carter looked as wooden in the limelight as Ford had done.

As if Reagan's possession of Carter's briefing book and his victory in the single presidential debate were not enough, there was – as in the case of Richard Nixon's sabotage of President Johnson's peace negotiations in October, 1968 – another, even more egregious reason for his success. Frightened of the president producing an 'October Surprise' by obtaining the release of the American embassy hostages in Iran, Reagan had for months used his campaign manager, William Casey, to pursue a secret 'arms for hostages' deal with Iran (which desperately needed weapons, once the Iran–Iraq War had broken out in September 1980). Carter had ruled out a deal on moral grounds, but Reagan had not. Release of the hostages, therefore, would be deliberately held back, Ayatollah Khomeini assured Casey, until after the US election, thus dooming Carter's last hope of beating Reagan.

In the history of US electoral politics there were few examples of such treasonable, yet effective, misconduct in gaining supreme power. Unaware of Reagan's malfeasance, Carter kept pursuing the release of the hostages along conventional diplomatic lines. No deals were made, and the administration waited for the Iranian government to decide. Thus, with the contenders 'neck and neck', as Hamilton Jordan remembered, the result of the election 'was now in the hands of unpredictable fanatics halfway around the world, revolutionaries who hated the United States and its chief executive. If something dramatic happened Monday [November 2] – like the release of the hostages – it would probably allow us to nose Reagan out; a bad signal from the Iranian Parliament Sunday would probably mean Reagan's election.'[71]

The news from Tehran when the president flew back to the White House from Chicago, where he was campaigning, was bad: the Majlis were setting *new* conditions. Casey's secret machinations (he would be rewarded by being made director of the CIA) had worked. On board Air Force One, Jordan recalled, Carter confessed it was 'a hell of a note' on which to end a presidential election, knowing the outcome would not be decided 'in Michigan or Pennsylvania or New York – but in Iran'.[72]

In truth the outcome had already been decided in America – by William Casey. On November 4, 1980, Carter duly lost the low-turnout election, buried by a landslide in the winner-takes-all Electoral College, where Carter managed only forty-nine votes to Reagan's 489.

Carter was gutted. Still unaware of Reagan's treason, the White House continued its efforts to obtain the release of the hostages in Tehran, buoyed by Ayatollah Khomeini's promise they would soon be freed. Even that post-election achievement would be denied Carter, however; he planned, if all went well, to fly to Germany to greet the hostages and be able to get back for the inauguration ceremony, but Reagan's team had promised yet more illegal arms to the Iranians if only they delayed signing off on the deal. Only at 6 o'clock on in-auguration morning, January 20, 1981, was the deal finally signed by Iranian negotiators (in Algiers, as the US had broken off diplomatic relations with Iran). When Carter called Reagan to tell him the glad tidings, he was informed that Mr Reagan was still asleep and could not be disturbed. It was a humiliating end to a deeply disappointing, luckless presidency.

Part Three: Private Life

Only a psychologist could divine the glue that bonded James Earl Carter Jr to Rosalynn Smith, a woman who, as Carter said in 1976 when running for the presidency, became an 'equal extension of myself'.[73] At eighteen Rosalynn was profoundly shy, even antisocial, having no close friends except perhaps Ruth Carter, Jimmy's sister. After one movie date, however, Ensign Carter announced to his mother he'd found the person he would marry: a consort to his own loner personality who would not only keep house for him and bear his children, but be his 'other half' – the only person in the world to whom he would be willing to unburden himself wholeheartedly, completely.

This Rosalynn became. She had been her 'Daddy's girl' until the age of thirteen when her father died, and like Jimmy, she became the older responsible sibling to the three other children in the Smith family. Trim, pretty, smart and neat – and having studied decorating and secretarial duties at Georgia Southwestern – she became a model officer's wife and then a model agribusinessman's wife (she acted as bookkeeper for the growing Carter peanut company). They did everything together, as one. Jimmy's adored mother Lillian had caused him to surrender his naval career to save the family business, against Rosalynn's wishes, but once Rosalynn accepted the career change, the competition between the two women was quickly over. Lillian moved out of the family home, even travelling to India to serve in the Peace Corps, while Rosalynn helped Jimmy run the agribusiness – and run for elective office.

Rosalynn saw her husband's political destiny as others often, in her view, did not. After all, she reasoned, one only had to look at Jimmy's brother, 'Buckshot' Billy Carter, to see how differently 'Hotshot' Jimmy's life could have wandered off course. Raised in the same family, in identical circumstances, Billy became Jimmy's polar opposite: a Republican segregationist who, after leaving the Marines and selling his share of the Carter inheritance, drove a manure spreader

for the agribusiness, wasted much of his life as an a
twice jailed, scorned the Baptist church (calling it
hypocrites'), used his older brother's name to enrich h
rise to a Senate investigation (Billygate), failed to get ele
of Plains, sired six children, and died of cancer at age fifty
was nevertheless known in Georgia as a 'good ol' boy'.[74]

As a faithful Christian, Jimmy Carter never criticized or turned against his brother, however much trouble and embarrassment he caused. Billy Carter represented lack of willpower – and willpower was the defining element of Jimmy Carter's character, the factor that caused others, over time, to follow him in his quest for political stardom. 'All the Carters submerge their needs to his', Carter's psychiatrist friend Dr Peter Bourne noted before the presidential election, starting with Rosalynn, who became Jimmy's backbone when matters looked bleak or they spun out of control, his companion by day and by night, able to read his thoughts, finish his sentences, pray with him, even, at times, bend him to her will (as when insisting he put her in charge of a Mental Health Commission, and allow her to sit in on cabinet meetings).

Whether such a close modern marital bond, in the case of a politician who needed to communicate to *others* his strength of will and authority, was a blessing or proved an impediment is a moot point. In that Rosalynn became Jimmy's rock, she certainly contributed more than any other human being to his rise to power and to his many achievements. But this tightest of bonds also walled him off from the the most important requirement of the US presidency at a time of empire – the leadership of others. For all his ambition, intelligence (Katharine Graham, publisher of the *Washington Post*, considered Carter 'by far the most intelligent president of my lifetime') self-training and moral determination, and for all that he had spent ten years of his adult life in the US Navy, Carter failed to apply the two most fundamental elements of command, at least at a higher national and international level of politics: the need to impose a clear vision that others can subscribe to, and the ability to delegate to others if that vision is to be carried out successfully.[75]

Jimmy Carter was hobbled by the fact that, from childhood on, he was a 'control freak': a term that was launched in the general vocabulary shortly after his inauguration in 1977.[76] It was said that when his son received poor grades in school, he spent a week learning the lessons himself, in order to instruct the child privately and improve his grade – which to Jimmy, not his son, was all-important. (*Why Not the Best?* was the title of Carter's campaign book in 1976.) It was also said that at the White House he not only read mountains of paperwork that an assistant or chief of staff should have first winnowed, but even drew up the precise daily schedule for use of the White House tennis court.

While exemplary in his commitment to his son's education, and to an orderly use of the White House tennis court, these instances spotlight the unfortunate, micromanaging flaw at the heart of Jimmy Carter's gem-like character: a flaw which his devoted, loyal, committed, sincere and caring wife Rosalynn kept from him, as did his uncritical staff.

Flanked by his wife and surrounding himself with his 'Georgia Mafia' on whose loyalty he could depend, the Prince of Plains betrayed, at times, a surprising insecurity, which perhaps reflected his backwoods roots. For all his high intellect, he seemed stilted and uncomfortable with people of equal or greater talent, expertise or facility. In turn this reflected a further, perhaps more significant facet: his failure to mature in the office of president. Almost all his predecessors had, in the course of their tenure in the White House, grown more, not less presidential, from FDR to Gerald Ford. But as his problems mounted, Jimmy Carter seemed to turn more inward than outward, increasingly relying on prayer and Rosalynn's encouragement. He also retreated more regularly to Camp David in his own version of Nixon's bunker mentality – but without Nixon's ability to manipulate, deceive, and magically produce his own swamp rabbit in virtuoso television performances that would reconnect him to the 'silent majority'. Carter's 'malaise' speech became an unfortunate illustration of his misreading of the public's expectations of their president. Instead, many felt his most compelling compact was with Rosalynn, proving to her and to God, not the public, his nobility of heart, his sincerity, integrity and stoic determination. 'There was no way I could understand our defeat' Rosalynn said after it, tellingly using the word 'our'. 'It didn't seem fair that everything we had hoped for, all our plans and dreams for the country, could have gone when the votes were counted on election day.'[77]

Abjuring until it was too late a tough chief of staff and a hierarchical system of command, Jimmy Carter had posed as a democrat, a common man, while acting often as a control-freak – moreover a weak and sometimes misguided one. Seldom if ever did he transmit to his staff genuine confidence in *their* abilities, which could be passed on and down to others in the pyramid of imperial power. Too often he conveyed, in fact, the very opposite: the feeling that, had he but the time, he would do their jobs so much better than they. Incensed at the many mistakes made by the Carter administration and the president's know-all airs, his holier-than-thou hardworking piety and his self-righteousness, the press turned against him. Eventually, so did the voters, his only real constituency.

That a former B-movie actor, with right-wing, often wacky ideas and misconceptions, would be able not only to defeat Carter in 1980, but also to demonstrate thereafter how a president *should* act, in terms of White House leadership, would provide the ultimate demonstration of Jimmy Carter's failure as an emperor.

Spurned by the new president, by the press and even by those subordinates whom he had mistakenly thought of as friends, Carter bought a twenty-acre lot in the mountains of Ellijay, Georgia, building with his own hands a cabin (and its furniture) for himself and Rosalynn. Such humility on the part of an ex-president found few admirers. There were difficulties over his Presidential Library (the mandatory repository for ex-emperors' papers) in Atlanta, and accusations that behind the facade of humility and ordinariness, he was too full of 'self-importance', that the people of Georgia were tired of his 'acting like a stuffed shirt' and 'puffing up like a blowfish'. 'We've always felt a little guilty about palming Carter off on the other forty-nine states,' the political editor of the *Atlanta Journal* sneered in 1983, 'and we don't appreciate having him around as a constant reminder.'[78]

Deeply distressed by his sister's and his mother's deaths in September and October 1983, Jimmy Carter never understood the hostility he provoked in certain people, just as he never understood his own role in the failure of his presidency. Nor, crucially, did Rosalynn, who effaced her humble origins with an unfortunate air of entitlement. Nevertheless, after their two-year self-exile in Ellijay they eventually picked themselves up, dusted themselves off, and thereupon, with Rosalynn at his side, Carter began a new life: devoting himself over the next three decades to peace, reconciliation and volunteer projects that addressed poverty, diplomacy and self-sustaining agriculture.

Carter's work for Habitat for Humanity would show his idealism at its most practical, yet it was his faith and sheer personal courage – physical and intellectual – in the pursuit of peace that would take him to every corner of the globe, from Port au Prince to Pyongyang, Darfur to the West Bank, Eritrea to Cuba, and which would be finally recognized in the United Nations Human Rights Award in 1998, and the Nobel Peace Prize in 2002.

James Earl Carter Jr might have lacked the priceless asset of good luck, and been a failure as an American emperor, but he was far from a failure after he left the White House, transforming the lives of countless people in need across the globe. Rather than be buried at his Presidential Library in Atlanta, or the National Cemetery at Arlington, Virginia, he characteristically asked that when he die, he be laid to rest in Plains, the little hamlet in Georgia he came from. As the eminent Indian scientist Dr Swaminathan remarked reflecting on Carter's relentless post-presidential work for humanity in retirement, Carter is 'the American Gandhi'.[79]

CHAPTER NINE

RONALD REAGAN

Later deified – by conservatives

Republican
40th President
(January 20, 1981–January 20, 1989)

Part One: The Road to the White House

Ronald Wilson Reagan was born on February 6, 1911, in a rented apartment above a bank in the small town of Tampico, Illinois, where his father Jack was an itinerant shoe salesman. Wilson was his mother Nelle's maiden name, and Ronald was chosen as a last-minute substitute for Donald, which a sister of Nelle had used for her own child. Reagan hated it, and asked to be called 'Dutch' after the family anecdote in which his father, looking at the newborn, had said 'He looks like a fat little Dutchman. But who knows, he might grow up to be president one day.'[1]

Jack Reagan was of Irish-American stock, a lapsed Roman Catholic with dark good looks, and a born storyteller who, as Reagan later described him, was 'endowed with the gift of blarney and the charm of a leprechaun'.[2] Neither Jack nor Nelle – a devout, churchgoing Protestant, daughter of American Scots-English parents – had more than a few years' grade school education, and they assumed their children would follow their father (who hoped one day to own a shoe store) as shoe salesmen.

Deeply shy, small as a boy, the last of the Reagans' four children and for many years unaware he was short-sighted, Reagan grew to be tall (6' 1") and an athlete at the high school in nearby Dixon, where the family had moved when he was nine. Helped by his mother, who both acted in plays and recited dramatic passages at her church, he was also a thespian who relished acclaim. 'I don't remember what I said,' he later recalled – or couldn't recall – of his first performance, 'but I'll never forget the response: *People laughed and applauded*.'[3]

The shy Illinois shoe salesman's son who suffered from insecurity and claustrophobia (which later gave him a fear of flying) found himself liberated by applause. Almost everything he would undertake in life, from football to lifesaving to politics, stemmed from an unrelenting determination to earn the music of acclamation.

In 1928, Reagan won a Needy Student scholarship at the tiny Eureka College, Illinois. Washing dishes and waiting tables during term time, and working as a lifeguard in his vacations (he claimed to have rescued seventy-seven people from drowning), he graduated in economics with a C. He was hardly an intellectual, but, like Richard Nixon at Whittier, he was a talented amateur actor, bursting with ambition to play upon a larger stage. His father lost his job in the Depression – rescued only by President Roosevelt's Works Program – while Reagan coveted a career in radio as an announcer. He duly got it, at WOC in Davenport, Illinois. As 'Dutch' Reagan he performed so well he was made sports announcer at a 50,000-watt station, WHO in Des Moines, earning $75 a week. His father gave up work altogether, suffering the ravages of an alcoholism he couldn't beat.

Reagan's skill as a radio announcer, especially his ability to dramatize in listeners' minds a vivid ball-game from the ticker-tape he was handed, made him an Illinois legend. After paying a visit to a Gene Autry film being shot at Republic Pictures in Hollywood, however, he was smitten by the movie bug. Following a screen test, Reagan received a telegram in April 1937 informing him Warner Brothers were willing to offer a seven-year contract at $200 per week. 'SIGN,' Reagan wisely wired his agent from Des Moines, 'BEFORE THEY CHANGE THEIR MINDS.'

Reagan's mother Nelle, as a stalwart member of the Dixon Disciples of Christ congregation, worried about 'Dutch' going 'to such a wicked place as Hollywood'.[4] By 1941 Reagan was already earning $52,000 per film, and his fan mail was second only to that of Errol Flynn – in fact Reagan began to call himself 'the Errol Flynn of Bs'.[5] He was drafted in August 1941, some months before Pearl Harbor, but obtained deferments. Only after the Japanese attack, and finishing a new film with Errol Flynn (*Desperate Journey*), did Reagan report for duty in the Army Cavalry – where, to his chagrin, his poor eyesight caused him to be disqualified for combat duty.

Seconded to Lieutenant Colonel Jack Warner's new First Motion Picture Unit of the Army Air Corps, Reagan rose to the rank of captain, introducing training films and acting as personnel director for the FMP unit.

Joining the Hollywood Democratic Committee, Reagan – an admirer of President Roosevelt throughout the Depression – remained a loyal party member. Putting the skills he'd developed in introducing air force training films to good use, Reagan volunteered as a speech-maker on behalf of Democratic organizations such as the American Veterans Committee, and the 3,000-strong Hollywood Independent Citizens Committee of the Arts, Sciences and Professions, which espoused an anti-nuclear war agenda. Asked in 1946 to stand for Congress as a Democrat, though, Reagan demurred. Not only could he not bring himself to abandon his movie ambitions, but, as East Coast Democrats tore themselves apart in left-wing power struggles and fears of Communist infiltration, he witnessed first-hand mob violence – in Hollywood.

Reagan had never seen combat, but at the Warner Brothers main gate he now did, beginning on October 5, 1945, in what would be called the Battle of Burbank. Striking carpenters fought with competing union workers, with the fate of 30,000 workers and film production in Hollywood held to ransom. Tear gas, chains, pipes and hammers were used, as well as fire-brigade hoses to cool tempers and the violence. So disenchanted did Reagan's boss Jack Warner become by the inter-union saga, he vowed never to vote Democrat again. Once Regan received an anonymous death threat, requiring the studio to issue him with a .32 Smith & Wesson pistol and shoulder holster, he found himself in the same position. As Robert Mitchum remarked, when being threatened in a similar fashion by union thugs, 'as an American you can ask me what to do, but damn it, don't *tell* me what to do'.[6]

The threats to his own life by left-wing unionists soured Reagan against liberals for the rest of his life. The Warner Brothers bus, on which he usually commuted to the Warners lot, was firebombed in front of him. As a member of the board of the Screen Actors Union he had become their chief negotiator, and in the fall of 1946, suspecting a Communist conspiracy to destroy Hollywood, he began to inform on his left-wing colleagues, taking the codename T-10, as one of eighteen FBI 'informants' in Hollywood.[7]

Without Screen Actors Guild support, the carpenters' fight eventually collapsed, and in March 1947 Reagan was voted president of the

SAG, beating Gene Kelly. In 1948 Reagan voted Republican in a presidential election for the first time, casting his ballot for Thomas Dewey. Though Reagan would not formally change his registered Democratic Party membership for several years, he confided to a friend 'I've switched.'[8]

Reagan had sworn he would never 'sink' to television. When his Hollywood acting career tanked, however, General Electric offered Reagan a contract to introduce their weekly CBS television drama broadcast, at a princely salary of $125,000, which he accepted. At his own request, moreover, the handsome new TV host was permitted to tour America giving live speeches in GE's many factories, as part of their Employee and Community Relations Program. The television contract thus gave Reagan two new career boosts: national television name recognition, plus live audiences as a political preacher. Within four years he had spoken, it was claimed, to some 200,000 GE workers, with as many as fifteen speeches a day in company cafeterias, plants and auditoria. One GE executive told him he was 'more in demand as a public speaker than anyone in the country except President Eisenhower'.[9]

Anti-Communist to his bootstraps after the Battle of Burbank, Reagan relished the Cold War; indeed he stood considerably to the right of the Republican in the White House, refusing, for example, to attend the gala which President Eisenhower arranged for Nikita Khrushchev on his visit to Hollywood.

Though Reagan's views delighted his rich friends in California, men like millionaire Walter Annenberg, they drove his first wife to distraction and divorce, and disappointed his liberal acquaintances – especially when Reagan supported the John Birch Society and its political candidates, who were dedicated to getting rid of graduated income tax, social security, and opposed school buses. Reagan voted for Republican Richard Nixon in the 1960 presidential election, and again for Nixon in the California gubernatorial race in 1962. Finally, and irrevocably, Reagan then changed his political registration, later excusing his desertion with the claim that 'I didn't leave the Democrats, they left me.'[10] General Electric, however, also left him, after he refused to tone down the right-wing rhetoric in his speeches to employees. 'Ronnie was devastated', his second wife, Nancy, acknowledged.[11] 'What can I do, Charley,' Reagan begged the chairman of the agency handling the GE contract, 'I can't act anymore, I can't do anything else. How can I support my family?'[12]

The answer, as Senator Barry Goldwater – the most conservative ideologue in the Senate – and others told Reagan, was obvious: seek political office. In an age of increasing celebrity worship, the former movie actor – fondly known as 'the Gipper' for his role in *Knute Rockne: All American* – should set about translating his television name recognition into Republican electoral votes.

Reagan remained reluctant, not only embarrassed by his divorce, which might lead to nastiness in an election battle, but also sensing it was not the right moment, with Nixon trounced in his gubernatorial bid and President Kennedy's popularity growing, not declining. In 1963 Reagan thus made one last, desperate attempt to be a movie actor, in a made-for-TV film called *The Killers*. The film flopped, however, leaving him with only one avenue to money and acclamation: politics.

Communications, especially television, were everything in the modern world, Reagan recognized – as did his financial backers. Reagan's televised half-hour speech in support of Goldwater's 1964 campaign at the Republican National Convention became its highlight, with quotations from Lincoln (Republican) and FDR (Democrat). His ability to mask his right-wing views with folksy humour and deference to Democratic gods such as FDR made him far more acceptable to centrist voters than Goldwater himself. Money poured into the Republican Party coffers.

Finally, in February 1965, Reagan agreed to enter the 1966 California gubernatorial race as a Republican. California had now overtaken New York as the most populous state in the US, boasting nineteen million residents, and an economy estimated to be the sixth largest in the world. For Reagan it would mean overcoming his fear of flying, which he had refused to undertake since 1939 after a traumatic snowbound landing in Chicago, but with medication and therapeutic advice he was prepared to face the challenge. Nancy became his campaign personnel director, while his friends and movie colleagues became his financial backers and fund-raisers.

Reagan was already fifty-four, and had never previously stood for public office. He had no knowledge or understanding of how the California state government worked, or what its obligations were. Though he had backed Democratic and Republican candidates with speeches in the past, his rhetoric had been anti-Communist and anti-federal, with little indication of what he was *for*, beyond patriotism, individual liberty, lower taxes and opposition to government – especially government 'in a distant capital'. To his foes he was nothing but a divorced actor who had been born and raised in another state, and an anti-intellectual who had never been seen with a book (though he read voraciously the funny pages, the newspapers and *Reader's Digest*). Political observers noted, however, that the actor possessed credentials that opponents, in a televisual age, were unwise to ignore.

Like Richard Nixon, Ronald Reagan had an excellent memory for the things he wished to recall, and moreover was able to recall them when speaking extempore. Also like Nixon, Reagan came from a humble background, with an Irish-American father and a tough, devout mother whom he revered, thus upsetting any notion in the voter's mind that Republicans were de facto all snobs. Furthermore, as Richard Nixon parlayed his humble origins into a special relationship with the 'silent majority', so too did Ronald Reagan. Having erected such a broad tent and easily won the Republican nomination, on polling day in the autumn of 1966 Reagan attracted not only a record number of independents but almost half a million renegade Democrats, who liked what they saw as he travelled the state, as well as what he said. Above all they liked *how* he said it; speeches that he scripted himself were peppered with homey remarks that put people at ease, and which harped on basic American values that were for the most part not, per se, Republican or Democratic. Most of all, his old-time values were welcomed by voters appalled by the 1965 summer race riots in Watts, as well as the anarchy at UC Berkeley, the state's largest campus, where the university president seemed incapable of asserting authority.

Reagan beat the incumbent Democratic governor of California, Pat Brown, by almost a million votes in November 1966. Journalists tittered when he insisted on taking his inaugural oath at two minutes past midnight on January 2, 1967, because his wife's pet astrologer, Jeanne Dixon, deemed the timing more propitious. Their mockery gave way to reluctant admiration, however, as reporters watched the former movie actor in his new role. In a nation increasingly partisan – whether supporting sports teams or political parties – Governor Reagan was maddeningly, disarmingly polite. Moreover he was humorous and confident. He was obstinately attached to his core principles, which he drew from his reading of the Constitution (which he liked for its brevity), but was otherwise pragmatic. His ignorance of California politics or state administration did not embarrass him in any way; indeed he had a way of deflecting criticism that would one day merit the name 'the Teflon president'. 'I don't know – I've never played governor before', he would answer a difficult question. Asked aboard a plane how he had overcome his fear of flying, he retorted: 'Overcome it, hell. I'm holding this plane up in the air by sheer willpower.'[13]

Truman had had a sign on his desk: 'The buck stops here.' Reagan had a sign placed over his door that read 'Observe the rules or get out.'[14] He chose key or signature issues to tackle which would set the tone of his governorship and which would be remembered, come the next election. He got the president of UC Berkeley dismissed within days of his own inauguration. He authorized the execution of Aaron Mitchell, a black who had killed a policeman. (Outside Reagan's rented house in Sacramento a candlelight vigil was held, prompting Reagan to say only that he wondered why no bells rang 'every time there is a murder'.[15]) But, ever the lifeguard, he saved the life of a little black girl he saw drowning in his pool during a staff party (his seventy-eighth rescue), and signed into law an abortion bill he did not personally favour. As Martin Luther King was assassinated in Tennessee, then Senator Robert Kennedy in California, and the capital of France erupted in what looked like urban politico-civil war, Reagan remained calm, firm and amazingly upbeat. His ability to pick effective subordinates harked back to his time as personnel officer in the Army Air Corps' film unit, but most of all it was his cool demeanour that inspired his staff – responsible for directing 115,000 state employees – to serve him loyally and leak-free. As his official biographer would write, his governing style as chief executive was, for a man who said very little in meetings and worked short hours in the Capitol, stunningly effective: 'I can compare it only to the phenomenon of the conductor who beats time imperceptibly, often with eyes closed, before a band of players, few of whom even look up from their decks. Somehow, a concerted sound emerges.'[16]

Sending in the National Guard to Berkeley, which had descended into People's Park anarchy, Governor Reagan became a scourge of 1960s' hippies, and increasingly a hero to the right. Yet he was able to get the Speaker of the California Assembly, macho Democrat Bob

Moretti, to work with him on welfare reform. ('Governor, I don't like you. And I know you don't like me,' Moretti declared, 'but we don't have to be in love to work together.'[17])

Step by step, by charm and focus, Reagan appeared to be preparing himself for national, indeed international stewardship. It was noted, for example, how he seemed to fix on even the most elderly statesmen he met, studying them for their comportment, dignity, resolution and distinctive traits. After all, Churchill had made his bowler hat, cigar and romper suit trademark fixtures; why should Reagan not also stamp his personal image on his era? Tall, lanky, with broad shoulders and a short neck requiring specially tailored shirts, he decided he would avoid hats and make do with what his official biographer called his 'pompadour': his immaculate, signature, slicked-back hairstyle.

Democratic politicians, who had done little to keep Reagan in their ranks, excoriated the apostate. 'As a human being and an American,' former governor Pat Brown wrote in 1970, 'I am chilled to the bone at the thought of Ronald Reagan one day becoming president of the United States.'[18] But Brown's political days were over (he never won another electoral office), while Reagan's ascent seemed inexorable – stalled only by his fellow Republicans.

Reagan's contest with President Ford for the Republican Party nomination in 1976, two years after Reagan left Sacramento at the end of his second gubernatorial term (the state limit), came agonizingly close to victory. Reagan's 'Kitchen Cabinet' (as it was later called) told him not to worry, however: Ford's defeat in the November 1976 election, against Jimmy Carter, would leave Reagan as the heir presumptive four years on. And so it proved.

No other Republican candidate possessed Reagan's speaking skills, both live and on television, or his unique temperament as a leader. To the fury of his opponents he seemed unruffled by criticism, patient in adversity, dogged in stating his convictions, and supremely confident he could run America, Inc., if given the electoral support to win the White House as a 'responsible conservative'.

Martin Anderson, who advised Nixon and then Reagan on domestic policy, later characterized Reagan's leadership style as totally different from 'the model of the classic executive who exercised leadership by planning and scheming, and barking out orders to his subordinates'. He was like 'an ancient king or a Turkish pasha', Anderson described, 'passively letting his subjects serve him, selecting only those morsels of public policy that were especially tasty . . . He just sat back in a supremely calm, relaxed manner and waited until important things were brought to him. And then he would act, quickly, decisively.'[19]

Nowhere was Reagan's decisiveness better demonstrated than at the Republican National Convention in Detroit in the summer of 1980. As the Republican presidential candidate, Reagan offered the vice-presidential place on his ticket to the former president, Gerald Ford, never dreaming that Ford would accept. He was thus taken aback when Ford agreed to 'consider' it with his wife Betty.

Watching Ford being interviewed on television the next night, and hearing the interviewer use the term 'co-presidency', Reagan was appalled. He had heard rumours that Henry Kissinger, Alan Greenspan and Dick Cheney – all of them former Nixon men – had set up a triumvirate, as in ancient Rome, and were busy presenting a 'power-sharing' proposal to Reagan's aides whereby they, behind Ford as a vice-presidential figurehead, would become Reagan's chief-of-staff council and decide who would be appointed Secretary of State and Secretary of Defense. It was, as another of Reagan's biographers put it, 'one of the most bizarre episodes in modern political history'.[20] Infuriated, Reagan told his senior aide to get Kissinger on the phone immediately, and told him to back off. At 11 p.m. on July 15, 1980, Ford was pressed to withdraw his candidacy for the vice presidency. Then Reagan picked up the phone, explaining to his staff his purpose: 'I'm calling George Bush. I want this settled. Anyone have any objections?'[21]

No one did. George Herbert Walker Bush became the official Republican vice-presidential candidate, and twelve weeks later, at 8.15 p.m. on November 4, 1980, NBC News called the election for Ronald Wilson Reagan: 'a sports announcer, a film actor, a governor of California',[22] Reagan had beaten President Carter by forty-three million votes to thirty-five million. He would be the fortieth president of the United States.

Part Two: The Presidency

In his inaugural address on January 20, 1981, Reagan cleared his throat and declared that 'in this present crisis government is not the solution to our problem, government *is* the problem'.

The speech, given for the first time from the West Front of the Capitol, was considered to be the most inspiring since that of John F. Kennedy twenty years before; this time, however, it was not a call to do what one could for one's country, but for oneself. Taxes – at least for the wealthy – would be reduced, not increased, stimulating economic growth and generating more government revenue – an erroneous idea espoused by Arthur Laffer, and thereafter known as the Laffer Curve. 'If we look at the answer as to why, for so many years, we achieved so much, prospered as no other people on earth,' Reagan nonetheless declared, 'it was because here, in this land, we unleashed the energy and individual genius of man to a greater extent than has ever been done before.'

Reagan was determined to be the herald of a new era for the individual, beginning unashamedly with himself and the First Lady. Whereas the Carters had shown a cheese-paring presidential style, with reduced hospitality, smaller cars and carry-one's-own-luggage humility, Reagan deliberately espoused the opposite. Frank Sinatra – a Democrat – performed at the gala ball. The new First Lady wore a $10,000 gown. Hollywood glamour now replaced Plains-style in Washington DC. 'Hail to the Chief' was reintroduced. Limousines came back with a vengeance.

The son of the Irish-American shoe salesman from Dixon, Illinois understood the nature of symbolism and imperial leadership in a way that his predecessor, for all his intelligence and sincerity, had not. 'Can we solve the problems confronting us?' he asked in his inaugural address. 'Well, the answer is yes. To paraphrase Winston Churchill, I did not take the oath I have just taken with the intention of presiding over the dissolution of the world's strongest economy.'

Reagan's faith in himself was stunning. Whereas Carter had seemed to know very few people in Washington, and to trust even fewer, causing him to rely on an amateur 'Georgia Mafia' to help run the White House, Reagan brought in his own experienced people from California and augmented them with Washington and other insiders. He made Bush's campaign manager, James Baker, his chief of staff, working alongside Ed Meese and Mike Deaver – 'the troika', as they would be called, Baker overseeing politics and Congress, Deaver his deputy in charge of scheduling and packaging the president's image, while Meese watched over policy and the National Security Council.

The troika met at 7.30 every morning, and one of them was with Reagan every hour of the day, filtering out inessential items before they reached his desk. Reagan was thereby allowed to do what he did best: decide among options, then communicate his decisions. With 1,700 employees in the Executive Office of the President, 350 White House staffers and almost two million federal government workers, it was seen initially as a model White House command structure, one that put his predecessor's to shame.

A Hollywood film, ironically, lay the behind the assassination attempt on the life of the former Hollywood movie actor on March 30, 1981, only two months after his new and greatest role had begun: Martin Scorcese's *Taxi Driver*. Spurred by an obsession with its star, Jodie Foster, a paranoid twenty-three-year-old Texas college student, John Hinckley Jr, came to Washington by Greyhound bus, determined to prove the depth of his love for Ms Foster by killing the US president. He very nearly succeeded, catching Reagan leaving the Washington Hilton where he had been giving a speech.

Reagan had been arguing the case for his forthcoming federal government cost-cutting programme, in order to reduce the 'wild and irresponsible spending' that was ballooning the national deficit, conveniently ignoring his Defense Secretary's push to increase defence funding by a mammoth 10 per cent. Cleverly reminding the union audience that he had been a lifetime card-carrying member of the AFL-CIO, Reagan presented his one-sided appeal as if it were the gospel word, and shortly after 2 p.m. left by a side entrance to get into his armoured limousine.

Hinckley's .22 'Devastator' bullet was designed to explode on impact. Mercifully it missed the president, hitting the bodywork of the limousine, which then squashed the projectile into a careening disc that bounced through the narrow gap between the open door and the car, where it carved its way under Reagan's arm, hit a rib, was deflected into his lung and stopped only a few millimetres from his heart. Ordering the secret service agent who had been shielding him to get off, Reagan accused the agent of having broken one of his ribs. Then, as blood began to pour from his lips, he commented. 'I think I've cut my mouth.'[23] At that point the agent ordered the driver to race to the nearest hospital, not the White House.

Although Reagan insisted on walking from the limousine to the

George Washington University hospital entrance, which the limo reached in three and a half minutes, he collapsed inside. 'I think we've lost him' the secret service agent muttered when the emergency nurse in Trauma Bay 5 was unable to register a pulse.

At the White House, an even more surreal drama was played out as the Nixon henchman whom Reagan had appointed Secretary of State, Al Haig, declared himself to be the acting president – and put the military on high alert. To the disbelief of those present who knew the presidential succession procedures as set out in the Twenty-fifth Amendment, Haig announced: 'Constitutionally, gentlemen, you have the president, the vice president, and the Secretary of State in that order.' Since the vice president was away in Texas, 'I am in control here, in the White House', he claimed.

'He's wrong,' the Secretary of Defense, Caspar Weinberger, commented. 'He doesn't have any such authority.' Donald Regan, the Treasury Secretary – responsible for the secret service – was even more aghast, asking: 'Is he mad?'[24]

White House aides, watching the unholy struggle for power, worried lest Haig was, as one reporter put it to Reagan's communications director, plotting 'a *coup d'état*'.[25] Even if the seventy-year-old president survived the assassination attempt, would he be weakened, either physically or mentally – or both? Would the rump-administration of Haig and his warring colleagues then be able to direct government operations? Would a debilitated Reagan – who had always been thought of by many as a mere movie actor, an empty shell, even 'an amiable dunce' in the parlance of Clark Clifford, the former Secretary of Defense (and adviser to four presidents) – be able to guide, let alone rule, the American Empire?

It is impossible to overstate the effect of Reagan's recovery on America's recovery, as significant in its own way as Franklin Delano Roosevelt's courage in triumphing over his paralysis when stricken by polio. Reagan's five hours of surgery, with copious amounts of morphine still required after the operation (during which he lost over half his blood), certainly tested his resilience.[26] His courage, insisting on walking to the hospital entrance despite a bullet lodged next to his heart, then his jokes to the doctors, nurses and his wife, became legendary. Was the doctor a Republican, he asked jokingly, before undergoing surgery. ('We're all Republicans now', the surgeon, a

Democrat, responded.) 'Who's holding my hand? Who's holding my hand?' he enquired of the nurse who was checking his pulse, 'Does Nancy know about us?'[27] And when Nancy got there, only ten minutes later, he was quick to explain: 'Honey, I forgot to duck.'[28] Unable to speak after regaining consciousness, he scribbled: 'I'd like to do this scene again – starting at the hotel.'[29]

Treating the murder attempt as a joke, indeed as a Hollywood film comedy, Reagan transformed a terrible moment – certainly the worst moment since the assassinations of JFK, Bobby Kennedy and Martin Luther King – into a moment of national deliverance, not mourning. His approval polls shot up – by more than ten points, to 73 per cent – as did the stock exchange. Presidential weakness was buried, not Reagan. After his emergence from hospital, Reagan was never again traduced as a mere Hollywood movie actor. 'As long as people remember the hospitalized president joshing his doctors and nurses' wrote David Broder in the *Washington Post*, '– and they will remember – no critic will be able to portray Reagan as a cruel or callow or heartless man.'[30]

As he worked his phone to get congressional backing for his cost-cutting, tax-cutting, increased military-spending budget – a plan that might otherwise have been trashed by the Democrat-led House of Representatives – the president breathed new life into his ambitious agenda, launching the 'Reagan Revolution': a new era of unfettered, low-tax entrepreneurial capitalism in which the rich would be encouraged to get richer, while the middle class would be palliated with a diet of revived nationalism and a steadying drumbeat of conservative 'American values'.

The Democratic Majority Leader in the House, Jim Wright, noted in his diary that the president's 'philosophical approach is superficial, overly simplistic and one-dimensional. What he preaches is pure economic pap, glossed over with uplifting homilies and inspirational chatter. Yet so far the guy is making it work', Wright admitted. By unrelenting behind-the-scenes phone calls and meetings, the recuperating chief executive overcame Democratic resistance to his budget bill, which passed 232 to 192 in the House, and eighty to fifteen in the Senate. 'Appalled by what seems to me a lack of depth,' Wright wrote, 'I stand in awe nevertheless of his political skill. I am not sure that I have seen its equal.'[31]

From a seasoned political opponent, a liberal Democrat from Texas, this was praise indeed. Reagan had personally met or talked with some 479 members of Congress – 'about 400 more than Jimmy Carter had spoken to in four years', as one biographer chronicled.[32] A political scientist put the transformation into a nutshell: 'Reagan has demonstrated, in a way that Jimmy Carter never did, that he understands how to be president' – not least in 'developing a working relationship with Congress'.[33]

By appointing the first woman ever to sit on the Supreme Court, Sandra Day O'Connor, Reagan bit back at right-wing conservatives demanding not only an anti-Communist crusader but an anti-abortionist whom religious fundamentalists could applaud. The president had interviewed O'Connor at the White House, and liked the fact that she loved horses, having grown up on a ranch, the Lazy-B. Reagan phoned Jerry Falwell, the leader of the Moral Majority movement, who opposed the choice of O'Connor. 'Jerry, I'm going to put forth a lady on the Supreme Court. You don't know anything about her. Nobody does, but I want you to trust me on this one.' 'I'll do that, sir' Falwell responded.[34]

The day the president returned to his desk in the Oval Office in May 1981, he was confronted by an air traffic controllers' strike. By law, air controllers could not walk off their jobs, but 'the only illegal strike is an unsuccessful one', their union leader, Robert Poli, sneered, and declared the strike would go ahead, however illegally. 'They cannot fly this country's planes without us' he taunted, and 'they can't get us to do our jobs if we are in jail, or facing excessive fines'.[35]

Clearly Poli had not read the president's bio. Reagan labelled the illegal walkout 'Desertion in the face of duty', and at 11 a.m. on August 3, 1981, in the White House Rose Garden, he gave the strikers exactly forty-eight hours to return to their posts or their positions would be 'terminated' – forever.

Thirteen thousand strikers ignored him. This proved a gross miscalculation on their part. On orders of the president in his role as commander-in-chief, military air controllers now took over from those men who did not return to their posts. New controllers were then taken on, breaking the strike. The strikers were never re-employed. Even the Soviets took note – 'a man who, when aroused, will go to the limit to back up his principles', a Kremlin watcher noted.[36]

The Russians were right to be concerned. On July 1, 1981, America had gone officially into recession, with the worst unemployment since 1941, and was facing ballooning national deficits for the foreseeable future. Reagan refused to give up the 'no new taxes' mantra of his Republican crusade, and he would not countenance the only possible alternative to cuts in federal welfare, education and health costs: a cut in military spending, which would adversely affect his key goal, the destruction of the Soviet Empire.

Reagan had never been to the USSR, nor had he ever met a Communist outside Beverly Hills. Nevertheless he was certain that behind its Cold War curtain the Soviet Union was faring even less well than the United States economically, and that the way to cause it to collapse was to compete more aggressively in military spending.[37]

This was a risky strategy in that it would intensify, not reduce, the risk of misunderstanding or accidental nuclear war. Moreover it left the Soviet Union no room to reduce military spending and reform its economy (as Communist China would be encouraged to do in subsequent years). Simplistic, deliberately confrontational and draconian, it was Reagan's personal plan: a proposal to ignore America's current economic woes, accept the biggest deficit in American history and go all out for broke, breaking the will of the Soviet Empire as it struggled in Afghanistan and in Europe, where the Polish Solidarity movement was again protesting the USSR's iron occupation, prompting the Polish puppet leader, Jaruzelski, to declare martial law to crush opposition more effectively on the Kremlin's behalf.

All American presidents since Harry Truman – who established the doctrine of 'containment' – had believed the Soviet Union would topple on its own, eventually. Reagan, however, was the first to be convinced that it could be 'encouraged' to fall. He was increasingly driven by a growing conviction he could topple the USSR not only by fending off its expansionist efforts worldwide, but by deliberately inciting a new arms race that, if successful, would bankrupt a bloated military empire that was already overstretched, especially in eastern Europe.

Thus, where Brzezinski had persuaded President Carter to end détente and react defensively to presumed Soviet intentions in the Near East and Middle East, Reagan used his degree in economics to back his intuition, as well as 'raw intelligence on the Soviet economy' from his national security adviser and the CIA, not to worry about the Soviet Union's strengths, but rather, to identify its weaknesses.[38] The Russians 'are in very bad shape', he wrote in his diary, 'and if we can cut off their credit they'll have to yell "Uncle" or starve'.[39] In a secret Decision Directive, he laid down America's express strategy against the Soviet Empire as a policy 'to weaken the Soviet alliance system by forcing the USSR to bear the brunt of its economic shortcomings'.[40]

Trident submarine missiles, a B-1 stealth bomber, navy F-14 fighters, the M-1 tank and an MX programme of new ICBMs were amongst the programmes that indicated the seriousness of Reagan's gamble. He would, at the very least, 'force them to the bargaining table', but his goal was even more ambitious. American policy would now be not only to 'contain' the Soviet Union, but to 'reverse' its postwar expansion.[41]

Although three quarters of British members of Parliament boycotted President Reagan's address to the British legislature on his official visit to London and Europe – with millions of people across the western world demonstrating in favour of a 'nuclear freeze', not a new American nuclear arms race – he seemed undeterred. No one, he was determined, would now stop him from explaining in his own words his 'plan'. In the cradle of parliamentary democracy Reagan thus reversed Marx's claim that it was the capitalist world that was in crisis and could only be rescued by Communism. Instead, he described a Soviet Union 'in deep economic difficulty', unable to 'feed its own people' and in 'decay', while it was the democratic societies that were 'prosperous'. 'I don't want to sound overly optimistic,' he stated in his address, but Marxism-Leninism would soon be left 'on the ash heap of history'.[42]

At a time when the United States was officially in recession and heading for its largest ever deficit, Reagan's boast sounded impossibly blinkered. Marvin Kalb, the dean of Washington correspondents, nevertheless saw it as a milestone that 'after sixty years in power' the Soviet leadership was, in Reagan's eyes, not only illegitimate, protected by guns, gulags and secret police, but doomed to *economic* defeat – with the seventy-year-old president mounted on his steed and ready to 'take on the entire Communist world'.[43] Even Reagan's colleagues were stunned by his confidence in this respect. 'We must keep the heat on these people', Reagan had told Senator Howard Baker, the Republican Majority Leader, in March. 'What I want is to bring them to their knees so that they will disarm and let us disarm; but we have got to do it by keeping the heat on. We can do it. We have them on the ropes economically', he emphasized.[44] And to prove his thesis, he added his trademark coda: a little detail, often erroneous, but which brought his point right home, into the family parlour: 'They are selling rat meat in the markets in Russia today.'[45]

Could the Soviet system of police and military oppression that had enforced the slavery of the peoples of eastern Europe since World War II have been challenged in a less dangerous American manner, via continued containment and détente? Historians were tempted to think so. Certainly it was the view held by most European liberals at the time, and by many in the US. Yet the history of dictatorship in the twentieth century did not proffer many examples of happy endings. Karl Marx's supposed 'withering away of the state' once true Communism was achieved, never happened anywhere – in fact the reverse was the case. By challenging the Soviet Union to an arms race it could not win, the former Eureka C-student and B-movie actor was determined, as an alpha president, to end Marx's nonsense. Moreover he had another arrow in his quiver: Star Wars.

Following his insistence on the largest increase in American military spending in the country's entire peacetime history, in 1981, the ageing president began to rethink the whole concept of nuclear deterrence. He had made a visit to the North American Aerospace Defense Command in Colorado, on Cheyenne Mountain, in 1979, and had talked there with the inventor of the hydrogen bomb, Professor Edward Teller, who suggested that modern technology might eventually make it possible to create a defensive shield against missile attack, much as the British had set up radar stations before World War II to help counter German bomber fleets in the event of hostilities. The discussion was filed away in Reagan's highly selective memory, and when, early in March 1983, he attended a five-day, top-level computerized war game code-named Ivy League, the die was cast.

Reagan, who had made his reputation simulating baseball play from ticker tapes, was enthralled by the game – and alarmed, especially by its culmination, namely the death of the president. The entire notion of MAD – mutually assured destruction – appeared more pointless to him than ever, since American retaliation for the loss of the president and his command staff would be punitive, but pyrrhic: the world irradiated, and literally in flames.

With the Russians having installed more than 500 SS-20 missiles with multiple independent re-entry nuclear warheads, and given the vulnerability of American land-based missiles to Soviet targeting, there were only two 'good' options: either nuclear disarmament or the development of defensive weapons to disable Russian long-range missiles in flight. Knowing that the former had been proposed, but would never be accepted either by the American or Russian militaries, Reagan now chose the latter. Several weeks after Ivy League, with only a handful of people informed in advance, Reagan announced in a televised speech from the Oval Office at 8 p.m. on March 23, 1983, that he was launching a new military programme 'with the promise of changing the course of human history': a Strategic Defensive Initiative, SDI, or, as it was instantly dubbed, 'Star Wars'.

Almost the entire White House staff and Reagan administration, including the Joint Chiefs, were against the idea. Even the speechwriter helping prepare the television address did so under duress and in disbelief. Vice President Bush was aghast, his chief of staff bursting into his office, waving the speech and shouting: 'We've got to take this out! If we go off half-cocked on this idea, we're going to bring on the biggest arms race in history!' George Shultz, the new Secretary of State (following the much-welcomed resignation of Al Haig), declared 'This is lunacy.'[46] Within hours it was being denounced on Soviet radio and television, as well as the capitals of Europe. It appeared to defy the ABM Treaty which President Nixon had signed, as well as committing the US to vast expenditure on research and development that would make the Manhattan Project look like child's play.

It was a measure of Reagan's utter self-confidence that, in his diary that night and in subsequent days, he stuck to his belief that his initiative 'would render nuclear missiles obsolete', even though this might 'take 20 yrs. or more but we had to do it. I felt good.'[47]

Few others did; indeed the storm that Reagan's announcement triggered damaged his standing in Europe and elsewhere for decades after. The world's press had a field day, trashing the notion of such a deterrent and accusing Reagan of ratcheting up the Cold War, with NATO's European citadels targeted as the first victims of a nuclear holocaust, instead of becoming, as was hoped, a nuclear-free zone by patient accommodation with the Soviets.

Reagan ignored his critics, even those on his own staff. 'I didn't expect them to cheer' he remarked.[48] A week later he explained to sceptical reporters that, once developed, the SDI shield could be offered to the Soviets in a real disarmament negotiation, 'to prove that there was no longer any need for keeping those [nuclear] missiles'.[49]

Few journalists, if any, believed Reagan, or even the feasibility of a missile shield. But public reaction in America warmed to the president's rhetoric of a 'shield', even if it was mythological. Was not Reagan a favourite son of Hollywood, the dream factory that had just produced the third film of the Star Wars series, *Return of the Jedi*, replete with Red Guards, an implacable emperor aboard a Death Star, defensive shields, a renewed arms race, space stations, dark sides and fighter planes in the form of cannon-armoured space craft? Reagan's conduct, rhetoric and vision thus seemed unexceptional to most moviegoing Americans. Indeed his earlier assertion of American power in the Mediterranean, off the coast of Libya, had appeared scripted for a Lucas movie: American F-14 fighters were ordered to shoot down (and did) any Libyan jets that attempted to overfly US naval manoeuvres in the Gulf of Sidra, which Libyan dictator Muammar Qaddafi had declared Libyan territory.

Despite protests across the world, Reagan was implacable. The Soviets offered to dismantle half their SS-20s if the president would cancel the deployment of the Tomahawks and Pershings. Reagan rejected the offer. The two-year-long efforts at nuclear arms reduction agreements in Geneva were then abandoned. The crunch, officials on both sides agreed, was now coming – the 'countdown to nuclear war', as Soviet officers put it, when Able Archer 83, a secret ten-day NATO war game in November 1983, caused Russian and Warsaw Pact forces to go on high alert.[50]

Having waved his big stick, Reagan then stunned the Soviets by a new announcement on national television in January 1984. The United States was back in a position of global nuclear superiority. He therefore wanted to revert to 'peaceful competition' – i.e. economic war – and embrace 'constructive cooperation' with the Soviets.[51] Was he serious, the Russians wondered, and what did he mean?

Gromyko, the Russian foreign minister, had denounced Reagan in Stockholm as the author of 'maniacal plans', and of using 'criminal and dishonest methods' in pursuit of a 'pathological obsession' over SDI – a sign that Reagan's tough stance was unnerving the Kremlin.

However, the SDI research programme, his defiant deployment of new missiles in Europe and then appeal for cooperation or even a return to détente, not only caught the Russians off guard, but leaderless – for on February 9, 1984, the Russian premier, Yuri Andropov, a former KGB chief who was four years younger than Reagan, passed away. Asked if he would attend the Andropov funeral, Reagan snapped: 'I don't want to honor that prick.'[52]

Andropov's successor, Konstantin Chernenko, was a master of wiretapping and Politburo bureaucracy, but he too was a sick man, hardly seen in public. In an attempt to match Reagan's stepped-up Cold War symbolism, he ordered a Russian boycott of the 1984 summer Olympics in Los Angeles; refused to allow the East German ruler, Erich Honecker, to visit West Germany; and attempted to dampen talk of liberalization in eastern Europe. He also pointed to the economic difficulties being suffered by western capitalist economies.

It was too late, however, for such counter-rhetoric to sound plausible. The American economy had picked up dramatically, and Reagan was on a roll. He had stalwartly backed the tough anti-inflationary measures of the chairman of the Federal Reserve Bank, via high interest rates, and Americans were now seeing positive results. Inflation and unemployment were down, while the Soviet Union's prospects – weighed down by its own Vietnam-like struggle in Afghanistan – looked dimmer than for decades. To Reagan it seemed clear that the Russian straitjacket, which had kept eastern Europe colonized and enslaved for almost forty years, was nearing its demise, or 'assisted suicide'.

That summer, on the fortieth anniversary of D-Day, Reagan gave perhaps the most celebrated speech of his life, at the top of a near-vertical cliff in Normandy that US Rangers, despite great losses, had stormed on June 6, 1944, during the invasion of France: 'The boys of Pointe du Hoc'. 'These are the men', the president said, pointing to the sixty-two survivors present, 'who took the cliffs. These are the champions who helped free a continent.'

In the context of the Cold War, Reagan's words possessed an added piquancy. The sheer courage of young US servicemen in liberating an occupied continent was Reagan's deliberate theme. The days of iron-fisted Soviet military repression in the cause of a faded and failing ideology were numbered – the Soviet Empire, as successor to Hitler's

Third Reich, was on the defensive as Soviet occupation troops guarded a new form of the Atlantic Wall, stretching from the Baltic Sea almost to the Adriatic and into Asia. Reagan's certainty that the US would win was remarkable – worryingly so. 'My fellow Americans,' he announced on his return when testing a microphone at his ranch, which he thought was not recording, 'I am pleased to tell you I just signed legislation which outlaws Russia forever. The bombing will begin in five minutes.'[53]

The joke caused many to be concerned that Reagan was losing his marbles. He made further slips that year, his mental agility showing signs of deterioration at age seventy-three, having survived a near-fatal assassination attempt. But with the United States winning the majority of the Olympic medals in Los Angeles to patriotic glee, and the economy beginning to boom, it was a very different America from four years previously. The prospect of electoral victory for Democratic nominee Walter Mondale, Carter's former vice president, looked steeper than the Pointe du Hoc. Democrats who had predicted disaster for global stability and for the American economy found themselves embarrassingly wrong-footed.

Increasingly, voters gave Reagan credit for the eventual upturn in their personal lives since the Carter era – which seemed all the more dreary in retrospect. There were now no gasoline lines. Inflation was a thing of the past. Taxes had been reduced by a whopping 25 per cent. Real incomes were rising. A new era in America seemed afoot, encapsulated in Reagan's re-election advertising campaign mantra, 'It's morning in America.'

Many critics, though, felt the chill, pointing out that by encouraging people to see taxes as a form of government theft, Reagan was deliberately appealing to ordinary citizens' self-centredness – thereby destroying a collective moral responsibility that had existed since FDR's New Deal, and had been continued under presidents Truman, Kennedy and Johnson: the notion that, as Supreme Court Justice Oliver Wendell Holmes Jr had once put it, 'taxes are what we pay for civilized society'. Vilifying federal government as an obstacle to economic and social progress; seeking to shift the burden of welfare from the federal government to the (often poor) states; seeking to 'liberate' entrepreneurship by deregulating business, but at the risk of unfettered freedom, corruption and unchecked market manipulation – these and other aspects of the Reagan domestic agenda threatened not only to alter the social fabric of American society, but also its communal wealth, in rapidly deteriorating transportation infrastructure and environmental damage. Supply-side, Laffer-curved, 'trickle-down' (from tax cuts for the rich) 'Reaganomics' became, such critics argued, a recipe for simple American materialism, greed, consumerism and collective myopia. Reagan's own response to a CBS news reporter's question seemed to epitomize a new indifference at the very top. Under his new tax-cut programme, the president stood to save, the reporter noted, some $28,000 on his joint tax return, if his proposal to reduce taxes for the rich went through. 'I think that just points out for everyone how advantageous the new tax system is', Reagan had remarked – oblivious to the meaning of the word 'everyone'.[54]

Critics might blame Reagan for inspiring rampant greed, in contrast to FDR's vision of collective security or Carter's appeals for collective Christian charity. Reagan, however, had demographics on his side in the 1980s: a two-to-one majority of voters under twenty-five years of age, casting their ballots for a seventy-three-year-old presidential nominee when he stood for re-election.

Reagan's war on Communism, meanwhile, was obsessive, consuming the majority of his waking hours and diary entries. He could not, and would not, let up. Blaming Congress for not supporting him over what amounted to serial right-wing dictatorship across Central America, he resorted to whatever illegal measures he deemed 'necessary'. In a special address to Congress on April 27, 1983, he had even dared, as a Republican, quote the Truman Doctrine, in order to picture El Salvador, Honduras, Guatemala, Costa Rica and Nicaragua as a sort of collective Korea far closer to the American heartland than the Asian peninsula. El Salvador 'is nearer to Texas than Texas is to Massachusetts', he pointed out. 'The national security of all the Americas is at stake in Central America . . . If we cannot defend ourselves there we cannot be expected to prevail elsewhere' – despite the absence of any Americans to be defended there. 'Our credibility would collapse, our alliances would crumble, and the safety of our homeland would be put in jeopardy.'

For all the president's magical communication skills, this peroration, for once, was received in stony silence – save when he promised, at least, not to send American troops to the 'new Korea'. American intervention would thus have to remain, he reluctantly accepted, illegal – while keeping voters' attention focused on the Soviet Union. The fate of twenty-five million mostly poor inhabitants of Central America, with an average income of only $500 per year, was thus ignored by most Americans in the US, who thought their elderly president misguided, even a bit wacky, on the issue, and simply looked the other way. As the Secretary of State, George Shultz, put it when silencing a senior State Department official who was fulminating against Reagan for his continuing support for Ferdinand Marcos, the corrupt former president of the Philippines, in the face of incontrovertible evidence that Marcos had attempted to rig the election: 'The president is the president. He has strong views; that is how he got to be president.'[55]

Seen historically, however, it was in the Middle East that Reagan's obsession with Communism most clearly mortgaged the future for Americans. By refusing to negotiate with any Palestinian group that did not first acknowledge Israel's right to exist, Israel's prime minister Menachim Begin made certain there would be no obstacles to his settler policies, and proceeded to order accelerated expansion of illegal Jewish settlements in the West Bank, ignoring Palestinian objections, as well as UN and world protests. Nor did he stop at that, once he made General Ariel Sharon his defence minister. In June 1981 Begin had ordered an air attack on Saddam Hussein's French-built nuclear power station outside Baghdad, using American F-4 and F-16 fighters in violation of US agreements barring their use in offensive actions, rather than working with allies to stop shipment from France of enriched uranium. 'I swear I believe Armageddon is near' Reagan had noted anxiously in his diary on June 7, 1981, but beyond suspending delivery of more F-16 fighters to Israel in the aftermath, Reagan had done nothing to halt the approach of war.[56] 'That fellow Begin makes it very hard for us to support Israel' the president confided to staffers.[57] But in his diary he noted that even if Congress decided to punish Israel for violating its agreement, he would 'grant a presidential waiver', given his own belief that Saddam Hussein, as well as Israel, was building an atomic bomb.[58]

Licensing Israel to become America's uncontrolled proxy in the Middle East, however, was a policy fraught with consequences. Seeing so much American ambivalence, Begin unilaterally moved ahead with his West Bank settlement policy and his plans to destroy the PLO. By the following summer Reagan had 'known for at least a year' that Begin – 'the waspishly aggressive little prime minister of Israel', as Reagan's official biographer wrote – 'was spoiling for war in the Middle East', which had come appreciably closer once Begin's government officially annexed the Golan Heights.[59] Though the Israeli ambassador was 'called in' to the State Department in Washington in protest, little beyond an American vote in the UN condemning the action had been done; indeed in Tel Aviv the protesting American ambassador to Israel was handed Prime Minister Begin's response: 'What kind of talk is this "punishing Israel"? Are we a vassal state of yours? Are we a banana republic? You will not frighten us with punishments.'[60] On June 6, 1982, Begin ordered the launching of his ill-fated re-invasion of the Lebanon, backed by his defence minister Ariel Sharon, but in open defiance of the majority of Israelis.

Attempting not only to clear southern Lebanon of PLO insurgents, but also to cleanse it of Palestinian refugees and punish the city of Beirut, the Israeli assault resulted in massive civilian casualties. Such calculated bloodshed aroused condemnation across the world, not least for the deployment of American-supplied cluster bombs, which Israel was forbidden to employ except in self-defence. 'The world is waiting for us to use our muscle and order Israel out', Reagan acknowledged in his diary on June 16, 1982. He declined to do so, however, believing that, even if guilty of literal overkill, Israel's proxy-intervention might provide 'the best opportunity we've had to reconcile the warring factors in Lebanon and bring about peace after seven years'.[61]

Such a fantasy proved short-lived. A new frenzy descended as the Israeli Air Force – the third largest in the world and almost entirely dependent on US aircraft and spare parts – got busy. 'Watching the Israeli Air Force smashing Beirut to pieces was like having to stand and watch a man slowly beating a sick dog to death' *Newsweek* reported, as the eighth week of Israeli bombing ended, and a ninth began.[62] Secretary of State George Shultz pleaded with the president to do something to stop the killing, lest American influence and standing in the Arab world be permanently destroyed. Reagan's loyal deputy chief of staff Mike Deaver then offered his resignation, saying to Reagan 'I can't be part of this anymore, the bombings, the killing of children. It's wrong. And you're the one person on the face of the earth who can stop it.'[63]

For a man so unshakeable in his simplistic beliefs and attitudes, whether about Communism or taxes, Reagan was surprisingly unwilling to face unpleasantness among his own staff. 'All you have to do is tell Begin you want it stopped', Deaver pleaded. This time the president listened and phoned Begin, shaming him by calling the Israeli assault by its proper name. 'I used the word holocaust deliberately' Reagan noted that night in his diary, having angrily told Begin that 'our entire future relationship was endangered'.[64] Twenty minutes later Begin called back to say the aerial massacre had been halted, 'and pled for our continued friendship' as well as blaming Sharon for ordering it.[65] 'I didn't know I had that power' Reagan confessed, amazed.[66]

Why, Reagan's aide wondered, had it taken two *months* of Israeli blitzkrieg in Lebanon and the relentless bombing of the city of Beirut – with its overtones of Guernica in 1937 – before Reagan would lift the phone? Above all, why did Reagan not recognize that Begin's and Sharon's oppression of the Palestinian Arabs (a policy opposed by Shimon Peres, the leader of the opposition party in Israel) would inevitably cause the United States to carry the can in the Islamic world for Israel's misdeeds? As Reagan sought to defuse the Lebanese time-bomb by sending in American peacekeepers, after the fact, the following months gave him ample demonstration of the anti-US sentiment which his sponsorship of Israeli aggression and expansion had inspired.

From his California ranch, on holiday on August 8, 1982, Reagan ordered some 800 American Marines to land in Beirut and take part in an ad hoc peacekeeping mission with French and Italian troops – the Multinational Force, or MNF. From an NBC studio in Hollywood he then declared in a prime-time address to the nation and to the world that the Palestinian problem *had* to be addressed, not simply crushed, as Hitler had crushed the Warsaw uprising.

Although he appreciated Israeli fury at being shelled 'by hostile Arabs' from across its borders and explained that he was not 'about to ask Israel to live that way again', he declared he was not impressed by Israel's response. 'The war in Lebanon has demonstrated another reality in the region . . . The departure of the Palestinians from Beirut dramatizes more than ever the homelessness of the Palestinian people. Palestinians feel strongly that their cause is more than a question of refugees. I agree.'[67] On September 1, 1982, he proposed a Reagan Plan, granting full autonomy to Palestinians in the West Bank and Gaza, in a federation supervised by Jordan, and the freezing of Israeli settlements installed and defended by Israeli forces in the years since their victory in 1967.

Reagan's speech fell on deaf ears. 'ISRAEL REJECTS REAGAN PLAN FOR PALESTINIAN SELF-RULE' was the *New York Times* headline on September 3. Two days later Begin announced he was giving $18.5 million for another ten settlements in the West Bank, and indeed hoped to increase the number of Jewish settlers by more than 300 per cent.

Saddened, Reagan washed his hands of the problem and pulled out the 800 Marines on September 10. On humanitarian grounds, however, he felt compelled to send them back in again on September 29, for by then the situation had spiralled into a mad bloodbath. Far from reconciling 'the warring factors' and enforcing peace after seven years of quasi-tribal violence, the Israeli invasion had produced unadulterated turmoil, with the entire world sickened over what were seen as Israel's crimes against humanity and the aftermath, in which Christian Lebanese militias were abetted by a secret pact with Israeli forces.

The president's second humanitarian intervention was no better than the first, and merely demonstrated the weakness of the belated American hand. Instead of destroying the PLO, Israel's invasion had turned its members into martyrs, had helped spawn Hezbollah, had sucked Syria into deeper involvement, and had intensified lingering civil strife in the country. As Israel finally abandoned its failed blitzkrieg and left Beirut, American peacekeepers were forced to call for American battleship firepower to defend themselves. By so doing, however, the peacekeepers became combatants – surrogates for the departed Israelis. The result was inevitable.

On October 22, 1983, an Islamic suicide bomber drove a truck carrying six tons of high explosive into the US Marine peacekeeping barracks at Beirut airport, setting off an explosion that lifted the entire building into the air and slaughtered at one stroke some 241 Americans. It was a harbinger of a new kind of kamikaze-style suicidal guerrilla warfare, against which simple roadblocks and security checks were ineffective.

The slaughter of hundreds of young Americans sickened the

American public, who urged the president to pull out the Marines altogether. Reagan, having refused to rein in Begin until it was too late, now refused to pull out American peacekeepers lest in doing so it broadcast the same signal that had come out of Carter's administration: the US was weak and would back down if challenged.[68] However, he did nothing to pressure the Israelis into backing the Reagan Plan. Instead, he gave the go-ahead for an American invasion of an island ninety miles off Venezuela.

With a population of 11,000, Grenada was the smallest independent nation in the western hemisphere, a former British colony ruled by a Marxist dictator, Maurice Bishop. When a second Marxist coup took place there on October 20, 1983, supported by Cuban troops and Russian trainers, some 250 American medical students were placed in possible peril, it was alleged. Questioning the chairman of the Joint Chiefs, John Vessey, as to how many men he had committed to a possible US invasion, if it was supported by neighbouring Caribbean nations and went ahead, Reagan listened to the general's response – then stunned him by ordering that Vessey double the number. Asked why, the president responded 'Because if Jimmy Carter had used eighteen helicopters for Desert One instead of nine, you'd be briefing him now instead of me.'[69]

Mocked by cartoonists and columnists in Europe, where millions had been protesting against the placement of new American intermediate nuclear missiles, Reagan showed remarkable self-assurance for a man who had, all his early life, yearned for applause, not derision. 'You are informing us, not asking us?' Speaker Tip O'Neill reacted, stunned, when Reagan summoned congressional leaders to the White House. 'Yes', the president coolly replied.

Despite his fury at Reagan's high-handedness, Tip O'Neill cautioned his colleagues and the press not to fault the president while American lives were at risk in Grenada, where Cuban mercenaries put up stiff resistance. Finally, as American forces mopped up, Reagan went on television on October 27 to explain the tragic loss of American life in Beirut in a peacekeeping role, and the reasons for invading Grenada. 'Grenada, we were told, was a friendly island paradise for tourism. Well, it wasn't. It was a Soviet-Cuba colony readied as a major bastion to export Communism and undermine democracy. We got there just in time.'[70] As the Defense Department paraded evidence at Andrews

Air Force base outside Washington – from armoured personnel carriers to anti-aircraft guns, and almost six million rounds of ammunition for rifles and machine guns, as well as records of almost 700 Cuban soldiers (almost as many as there were Grenadian soldiers) – Reagan's approval polls rose twenty points to 84 per cent. Days later, triggering yet more protests, the first shipment to American air bases in Europe of nuclear-tipped Tomahawk and Pershing II missiles duly arrived at Greenham Common in England. The message for those who confronted the American Empire was: beware.

Reagan's magic, like Roosevelt's, was his sheer optimism: a quality considered deeply American, however naive, and which, together with a sense of humour, had been in short supply since JFK's presidency. In speechmaking Reagan had a brilliant eye for the telling detail, whether sentimental or inspiring, and a fantastically deflating sense of humour. 'I've come to the conclusion that there is a worldwide plot to make my job more difficult on almost any day that I go to the office' was one typical aphorism that delighted his admirers, and in turn made the job of any contender for the office of president a tougher sell. Tall, always immaculately groomed and attired, even in cowboy gear, with a studied air of confident distinction (standing before the mirror, shaving in the morning, he would recite his mantra: 'I am the president'), he was hard to humble – as President Carter had relentlessly been humbled – by the press, by opponents, or even angry voters. 'I want you all to know,' Reagan jested in the second of the presidential debates against the former vice president Walter Mondale, the Democratic nominee, in October 1984, 'that I also will not make age an issue in this campaign. I am not going to exploit, for political purposes,' he added with a smile, 'my opponent's youth and inexperience.'[71]

Despite Mondale's criticisms of Reagan's leadership and of his command of the military, Reagan remained polite, reasonable, principled – and above all, firm. 'I know it will come as a surprise to Mr Mondale, but I *am* in charge', he retorted in the debate, not only confident in his vision of America's future prosperity and security, but pleasantly surprised to know, according to a new poll, he was leading the much younger Mondale (aged fifty-six) two to one among voters aged between eighteen and twenty-four – voters who were the future of America.

On November 6, 1984, Reagan won re-election for four more years, carrying forty-eight states to two: a landslide vindication of a presidency that would now witness an even more dramatic term.

A routine medical examination in 1985 found Reagan to be suffering from cancer of the skin and of the colon, requiring a three-hour operation to remove two feet of his intestine around the malignant polyp.

With a new, arrogant chief of staff, Donald Regan, running the White House, some pundits wondered – and worried – who was really running the country. If anything, however, Reagan seemed even more presidential than before, narrowing the focus of his leadership skills still further to concentrate on those issues central to his imperial vision of America: defeating the 'spread' of Communism, achieving military superiority over the Soviet Union, cutting taxes for the rich, and reviving American confidence and pride.

Abroad, this gave rise to greater protest and unpopularity, especially his continued funding of right-wing rebels in Nicaragua and his Star Wars programme, but at home his Teflon coating became increasingly impermeable as the economy continued to flourish, despite a $2 trillion national debt, with a $125 billion annual trade deficit. Moreover the ageing president remained endlessly patient, consistent, and humorous. Informed he would have to have the three-hour abdominal operation to remove his cancerous lesions he quipped 'You mean, the bad news is that I don't get to eat supper tonight?'[72] Like Margaret Thatcher, the British prime minister who was his most constant ally and cheerleader, he kept to his simple script, ignoring and deflecting the views of others – and since he was infinitely more likeable and self-deprecating than Mrs Thatcher, he won most of his battles at home without arousing the sort of personal vilification that greeted him (and her) abroad.

For a president who had attempted to savage social security in order to increase national security – failing in the first, but succeeding in the second – Reagan's continuing domestic popularity was no mean achievement. Certainly no one would ever forget his national television address on the day the US space shuttle *Challenger* blew up, killing all on board, including Christa McAuliffe, a thirty-six-year-old social sciences teacher from Concord, New Hampshire. Many of the nation's children had been watching on television screens at school as *Challenger* lifted off from Cape Canaveral on January 28, 1986, and then exploded a bare ten miles above the launch pad. Stricken, the president cancelled his scheduled State of the Union address in Congress and instead addressed a nation in shock. The 'Challenger crew were pulling us into the future,' he declared, 'and we'll continue to follow them. We will never forget them, nor the last time we saw them, this morning as they prepared for their journey and waved goodbye – and "slipped the surly bonds of Earth" to "touch the face of God".'[73]

In the majority of American voters' eyes the president had reasserted American military and economic superpower. In terms of imperial politics, Reagan was certainly playing a brilliant hand – indeed a far more ruthless one than most observers knew at the time. Not only did he persuade the Saudis to increase oil output from two million barrels a year to nine million, thus flooding the world market, in return for military supplies, but via the CIA he also stepped up Brzezinski's surreptitious programme of support to the Taliban and mujahidin in Afghanistan. In a still-secret presidential directive, NSDD-166, Reagan ordered the CIA not simply to help the Muslim rebels in 'harassing' Russian forces in Afghanistan – as President Carter had done – but to start 'driving them out'. In 1985 the CIA proceeded to deliver 10,000 rocket-propelled grenades and 200,000 rockets – more than five times the total for the previous five years (and fifteen times more in dollar terms). The operation became the 'largest US covert action program in the history of the CIA', as Reagan-apologist Paul Kengor later crowed.[74] Reagan's CIA director, William Casey, was reputed to have ordered one of his subordinates to 'go out and kill me 10,000 Soviets until they give up'.[75] Sixteen thousand Soviet troops were, in fact, killed in Afghanistan, and an incredible 269 Russian helicopters downed by 340 American-furnished Stinger anti-aircraft missiles.

On March 10, 1985, however, an event of far greater global consequence than the Russian quagmire in Afghanistan took place: Konstantin Chernenko, the Soviet premier, died in Moscow. Reagan had assumed it would be another decade before the colossus of Soviet Communism could be brought down, but the advent of a new Soviet leader, fifty-four-year-old Mikhail Gorbachev, altered Reagan's time frame and his strategy.

Star Wars held out no prospect of being realized in the short term, but such was America's lead in technology that the Russians could not make this assumption; they were thus cornered, desperately hoping they could trade an American decision not to proceed with the programme in return for nuclear arms reduction. Gorbachev was quick to respond to Reagan's invitation to visit Washington or, if not there, an alternative venue. In due course it was in Geneva, where Calvin had launched his Reformation four centuries earlier, that the two men met in November 1985.

Month after month in his diary, during preparations for the summit meeting, the president had set down his absolute determination in relation to Star Wars. 'I stand firm we cannot retreat on that,' he had already noted in December 1984, 'no matter what they offer.'[76] Nine months later, on September 10, 1985, he remained just as determined. 'Gorbachev is adamant we must cave in our SDI – well this will be a case of an irresistible force meeting an unmovable object.'[77] On November 19 the two emperors met, 'the "No. 1 Communist" and the "No. 1 Imperialist"' as Gorbachev later wrote.[78]

'[W]e did about 2 hours on SDI,' Reagan noted that evening in his rented house in Geneva. 'He's adamant but so am I.'[79] The next day 'the stuff really hit the fan' as Gorbachev 'fired back about SDI creating an arms race in space . . . He was really belligerent,' the son of the Irish-American alcoholic shoe salesman described, '& d—n it I stood firm.'[80]

Reagan was sure Gorbachev – hugely intelligent and representing a generation that had participated neither in the Russian Revolution nor World War II – was blustering, and would fold his cards if Reagan remained cool but implacable. Like the British government after World War II, the Politburo was having to face up to the fact that the Soviet Union could no longer afford the huge costs of empire, with restive colonies or puppet states agitating behind the Iron Curtain, and in competition with a far more economically productive western world; moreover, it was becoming prohibitively expensive for the USSR to maintain direct military rivalry with the United States on one flank and the Communist Chinese, boasting almost limitless manpower and soldiers, on the other.

Knowing Gorbachev's travails, the question for historians would thus arise, in the aftermath: could another, less ideologically driven American president have helped Gorbachev and the Soviet Union to retreat from its own empire and to modernize – as the Chinese Communist empire was encouraged to do – without deliberately

seeking to bankrupt it? A second question became: would an alternative American Caesar – a President Mondale, for example, had he
won the 1984 election – have thought through the consequences of
destroying the Soviet Union? While the world would be – and eventually became – undoubtedly a safer place without a nuclear arms
race, was it necessarily likely to be a safer place with the United States
exercising sole global hegemony? Would such monolithic power not
permit, even encourage, the US, under a future Caesar, to wield its
superpower unilaterally and irresponsibly?

At Geneva in November 1985, Gorbachev decided to come clean.
He astonished Reagan by describing openly how US policy was hurting
the Soviet Union, with an arms race it could not afford.[81] Gorbachev's
frankness, however, did not alter Reagan's agenda. Reagan had been
informed by his diplomatic and intelligence sources that the Soviet
Union was near-moribund; he now had it from the mouth of its
emperor, who begged Reagan to ditch SDI and improve US–Soviet
relations by agreeing arms limitation.[82] Moreover he pleaded with
Reagan to discard the American obsession with Soviet 'expansionism',
which he felt 'either a delusion or deliberate distortion', since such
post-McCarthyites, he assured Reagan, 'overemphasize the power of
the Soviet Union. We have no secret plans for world domination . . .
We support a settlement in Afghanistan, a political settlement under
the United Nations, if you help us. You accuse us of deploying troops,
but you work against us. You want our troops there, the longer the
better.'[83]

American commanders struggling in Afghanistan, twenty years later,
would have cause to remember such plaintive truth-telling. Reagan,
though, simply smiled at his adversary on December 21, 1985, and
refused to back down. Reagan 'appeared to me not simply a conservative, but a political "dinosaur",' the young Russian leader reported
sadly to his colleagues when he returned to Moscow, recognizing he
would have to launch perestroika without American help or support.
As his memoirs attest, it was a thankless, excruciating exercise,
mounted against entrenched bureaucracies and personalities. A catastrophic accident at Chernobyl in April 1986 was the worst nuclear
accident in history, a symbol of all that was wrong in Marxist-Leninist
Utopia. At a meeting of the Politburo two months after the disaster,
Gorbachev openly called Chernobyl a 'fiasco' that reflected bleakly

on state-run Communism. 'Throughout the entire system there has reigned a spirit of servility, fawning, clannishness and persecution of independent thinkers, window dressing, and personal and clan ties between leaders.'[84]

Had he seen the transcript of Gorbachev's peroration, Reagan would have chuckled. But he did not need to. Following his experience of inter-union venom in Hollywood, Reagan had seen the light. Reagan had never thereafter been seduced or intimidated by Communist or Russian posturing, and though he felt he could work with Gorbachev ('You're right,' he told one of his negotiating team, 'I did like him'), he was not about to agree to a draw in a global Cold War chess game that had gone on for four decades.[85] He did agree, however, to a second summit at Reykjavik the next year.

On October 10, 1986, Gorbachev again went all out to persuade Reagan to scrap SDI. When Reagan baulked, but promised to 'share' the fruits of SDI as a defensive shield rather than to protect aggression, Gorbachev burst out laughing – and asked the president not to talk in such 'banalities'. 'Excuse me, Mr President, but I cannot take your idea of sharing SDI seriously. You are not willing to share with us well equipment, digitally guided machine tools, or even milking machines. Sharing SDI would provoke a second American revolution! Let's be realistic.'[86]

Reagan held firm, however, and though the two leaders agreed to massive mutual reductions in their deployed nuclear arsenals under a new treaty – thus effectively freezing the nuclear arms race – there would be no rest for the Soviet Empire in military research spending requirements. Nor would American help be offered in resolving Russia's quagmire in Afghanistan.

A year later, on December 7, 1987, Gorbachev came to Washington for a third summit, where he asked Reagan even more plaintively, 'Why can't we be allies? We were allies at one time, why can't we be allies now?'[87] Beyond the smiles, however, Reagan remained – as always – implacable; indeed some months earlier he had gone on the offensive, at least rhetorically.

On June 12, 1987, before a huge crowd in West Berlin celebrating the city's 750th anniversary at the Brandenburg Gate, Reagan had delivered his *coup de grâce*. Against the advice of his staff, he decided to make a Kennedyesque declaration that would go down in history. He had already forced the Soviets – who had finally prepared plans to pull out their vanquished army from Afghanistan in January – on the defensive. 'We hear much from Moscow about a new policy of reform and openness. Are these the beginnings of profound changes in the Soviet state? Or, are they token gestures?'

The former radio announcer from Dixon, Illinois paused, having come to the high point of his speech. 'There is one sign the Soviets can make that would be unmistakable, that would advance dramatically the cause of freedom and peace', he declared, then lifted his voice almost into a shout as he addressed himself directly to the emperor of the Soviet Union: 'General Secretary Gorbachev, if you seek peace, if you seek prosperity for the Soviet Union and eastern Europe, if you seek liberalization: come here to this gate! Mr Gorbachev, open this gate! Mr Gorbachev, tear down this wall!'[88]

Poor Gorbachev, already dicing with death in challenging the ossified Communist military-political power structure in the Soviet Union, felt stabbed in the back and embarrassed. He could only hope that in a fourth summit, he could convince President Reagan to back off, and give Russia real assistance.

Reagan happily accepted the invitation to Moscow on May 29, 1988, where he made it his business to talk openly to young people and raise the question of freedom of speech and religion in the Russian heartland.

If anything Reagan's 'ideological luggage' (as Gorbachev called it when talking to George Shultz)[89] was getting heavier as his second and final term of office neared its end. His agenda remained implacably the same: continuation of SDI research, arms reductions only according to an American agenda, zero trade improvements, zero financial help. Even the piece of paper Gorbachev proffered containing the draft of a joint statement declaring that neither country would infringe on the independence or sovereignty of the other, was rejected after Reagan promised to think about it. 'I don't want to do it,' the president announced his decision, as eastern European countries rattled their chains.[90]

It was their last session together, June 2, 1988. Disappointed that Reagan would not sign the 'peaceful coexistence' protocol he'd drafted, Gorbachev seemed momentarily at a loss. Recovering, however, he stood up and took the seventy-seven-year-old president's hand. 'Mr President,' he smiled as he put his arm around Reagan's shoulder, 'we had a great time.'[91] Reagan, by contrast, seemed unaffected by the get-together. 'I think it's clear that Gorbachev wants to restore the Soviet economy' he told congressional leaders on his return. 'It's a terrific job and it will take him a long time if he succeeds at all, because he's got opposition there, very obviously so.' In sum, he concluded, 'we have to consider them an adversary, because of their foreign policy and controlled society at home'.[92]

Reagan's role in crippling the Soviet Union and causing its imminent demise would be the signature achievement of his presidency in most Americans' eyes. Certainly he was later proud of his part in the ending of the 'evil empire' (though in Moscow he had claimed that he no longer believed it was evil). In other respects, however, his second term as president proved less fortunate than his first.

Reagan's wife had opposed his decision to stand for re-election in 1984, fearing his health would not stand the strain, especially in the wake of near-assassination. The First Lady had been right, for his health declined visibly and audibly as he went into his seventies. Prostate surgery followed his colon cancer operation. His hearing became progressively more impaired. His memory – once so strong – began to fail, and he often appeared muddled, dropping his cue cards when negotiating with Gorbachev, for example, and seemingly at a loss as the young Russian leader bent to help him pick them up.

Inevitably Reagan's cabinet colleagues and staff acted according to what they thought the president had in mind, or wanted, rather than what he actually instructed. For the most part his legendary Lady Luck held, and he was able to maintain his presidential dignity in a manner that had eluded his predecessor. The raging increase in the national deficit he managed to sweep under the rug, given the prolonged economic boom the country was experiencing, with GNP doubling since the recession of 1981–2. Other things were not so easy to bat away with silver words.

As a conservative Republican, Reagan necessarily drew to himself the biggest anti-Communist loudmouths in America, including his Defense Secretary Caspar Weinberger, his ambassador to the UN Jeanne Kirkpatrick and his CIA chief William Casey. Their misreading of a Soviet 'threat' in the Middle East – particularly their concern about a Soviet influence in Iran – would skew the history of the

western world, as they worked on their 'boss' to approve illegal sales
of American arms, and even more illegal use of the money they thereby
pocketed. In return for supposed Iranian 'influence' in getting the
release of Americans who had been taken hostage in Lebanon, the
plotters would not only sell clandestine arms to Tehran, but then use
proceeds from those sales to fund illegal weapons and support for
Nicaraguan right-wing insurgents fighting against the democratically
elected government of Daniel Ortega in Nicaragua.

Secretary of State George Shultz had, from the beginning, warned
the president that 'if we go out and try to get money' for the Contra
insurgents 'from third countries, it is an impeachable offense'.[93] But,
as Reagan's national security adviser 'Bud' McFarlane later explained
when hauled before Congress, he had failed to stop his colleagues.
'To tell you the truth, probably the reason I didn't is because if I had
done that, Bill Casey, Jeanne Kirkpatrick and Cap Weinberger would
have said I was some kind of commie.'[94] It was a telling admission.

Reagan's anti-Soviet stance could, at least, be understood and vindicated in terms of the forty years of totalitarian repression of the
nations of eastern Europe. But Iran and Nicaragua? It was a measure
of Reagan's limited interest in any subject outside the crushing of the
Soviet Empire, and his failure ever to think through the consequences
of his policies, that he not only tolerated an arms-for-hostages
imbroglio, organized illicitly by his national security adviser, but happily
acted as the undoubted godfather to the scheme, which had gone
underground in June 1984 when Speaker Tip O'Neill turned down a
supplemental appropriation bill to fund pro-Contra support. 'Thursday,
December 5, 1985: NSC briefing' Reagan had written in his diary, noting the 'complex undertaking with only a few of us in on it. I won't
even write in the diary what we're up to.'[95]

An inner sanctum of Reagan operatives, nicknamed 'The
Establishment', had been created in the White House, on much the
same lines as Richard Nixon's Plumbers: men who were united in
their contempt for Congress and love of clandestine operations.
Reagan's pet henchman in carrying out the secret deal was the
heavily decorated Vietnam veteran, Lieutenant Colonel Oliver North,
who claimed 'The old man loves my ass.'[96] North was exaggerating
– but not by much, since the president saw in the young colonel's
brash adventurism a sort of active alter ego, as well as a quasi-son,

whose patriotism and devotion to the military bespoke Reagan's sentimental nature. Though Reagan had signed Boland II in 1984 – a bill
expressly forbidding the CIA from giving non-military support to the
Contras, in conjunction with Boland I of 1982, which forbade the Reagan
administration from giving any funds to overthrow the Sandinista
government – the President had then authorized Robert MacFarlane,
the national security adviser, to do just that.

The deal stank from start to finish, especially since it could only
encourage Hezbollah to seize more hostages. First, an American pilot
who was shot down in October 1986 confessed that the CIA were clan-
destinely directing the Contra insurgency using their own ships, planes,
pilots, arms, airfields and radio equipment. Several weeks later on
November 3, 1986, the Iranian arms-for-hostages deal hit the headlines
when the *Washington Post* reported stories in Beirut that, in connection with the release of an American hostage there, 'the United States
had sent spare parts and ammunition for American-built fighter planes
and tanks' to Iran. 'We will never pay off terrorists,' President Reagan
said, 'because that only encourages more of it' – yet this was precisely,
it became clear, what he *had* done, with even more clandestine machinations still to be uncovered: namely, that the proceeds from the arms
sales to Iran would be used to illegally fund the Contras in Nicaragua,
in defiance of Congress.

By March 4, 1987, Reagan was having to apologize to the whole
nation. On prime-time television he took 'full responsibility for my
own actions and for those of my administration' and expressed disappointment 'in some who served me'.[97] He then admitted that, only
a 'few months ago [November 13, 1986] I told the American people I
did not trade arms for hostages. My heart and my best intentions still
tell me that's true, but the facts and evidence tell me it is not' – words
that did not make sense but, rather, implied that the ageing president
was losing his mind.

The inference, however, was clear: he was a patriotic American who
had desperately wanted to rescue the five American hostages held by
Hezbollah in Lebanon. It was a brilliant stratagem, and to the consternation of most critics he was forgiven on grounds of old age for one
of the shoddiest contraventions of congressional and constitutional
injunctions.

Reagan's elliptical confession masked a sad truth. His actions had merely encouraged Hezbollah – supported by the Iranians – to take more American hostages. By the time Congress put a stop to it, six further hostages had been seized in place of the five traded, while 1,508 TOW missiles, eight Hawk missiles and top secret intelligence information had been given to the Iranians. Reagan's national security adviser, Robert McFarlane, resigned and attempted suicide, the CIA director William Casey developed a brain tumour and also resigned, and Reagan's approval ratings plummeted from 67 per cent to a meagre 36. Meanwhile for six months, while awaiting the report of the Tower investigative panel that Reagan himself appointed to get to the heart of the matter, the White House came to a near standstill. Oliver North shredded as much evidence of the matter as possible, and the president's staff and senior members of the administration, from the White House to the Secretary of Defense, laboured to protect the president while trying to avoid prison themselves for malfeasance and perjury.

The revelations of deliberate deceit, lying, secret fund-solicitations both in the United States and abroad, use of foreign countries to facilitate illegal transactions, criminal acts and, above all, the mix of presidential whim and vacuity, were devastating, barely a decade since Watergate – and for what? Disgusted by a saga so reminiscent of Richard Nixon's imperial presidency and contempt for Congress, the House of Representatives rejected Reagan's appeal for another $36.25 million to aid the Contras in February 1988, and under the Sapoa Accord ceasefire, the Contras were completely disbanded. More than 40,000 Nicaraguan people had by then become casualties, with an estimated 29,000 dead on both sides, more than 3,000 of whom were civilians.[98] Reagan's efforts had been for nought, and his good name, some claimed, ruined forever.

'Reagan Now Viewed as an Irrelevant President' ran one newspaper headline in the aftermath of Iran-Contra.[99] Most of his right-wing staff were indicted by the federal prosecutor. His nomination of the conservative ideologue Judge Robert Bork to the Supreme Court was rejected by the Senate. In acknowledging the AIDS epidemic Reagan had been forced to acknowledge the need for the use of condoms – the bête noire of conservatives. Memory lapses and moments of confusion suggested an elderly man, almost eighty, facing the onslaught of dementia. Though he anointed his vice president, George Bush, as his preferred successor – 'win one for the Gipper' as he exhorted at the finale of the Republican National Convention in New Orleans on August 15, 1988 – he seemed either too tired or too indifferent to campaign heartily for Bush as the Republican nominee. Parallels with Eisenhower's last year in office were abundant, with many Republicans fearing the same outcome: a Democratic administration.

As pundits pondered his eight years as emperor, Reagan's legacy seemed strangely contradictory. He had doubled the national debt in six years. Behind a smokescreen of 'no new taxes' they had increased by more than $80 billion per year. Unemployment – though down in his last year – had averaged 7.7 per cent, compared with 6.4 under Carter. US output had averaged only 2.6 per cent growth under Reagan, compared with 3 under Carter (though the figure was 4.2 if reckoned from the time the Reagan recession ended). Meanwhile federal government spending, far from being slashed as Reagan had promised his conservative base, had risen to its highest level in relation to national output in American history. Reagan's efforts to deregulate the economy, moreover, resulted in a Savings and Loan scandal that exploded in his second term, resulting in taxpayers being asked to cover probable losses of $64 billion by the time of his final budget – a sum that would in due course require $200 billion in taxpayers' bailout funding, to compensate customers of failed and often fraudulent, unregulated American companies. The income of the poorest 20 per cent of the population fell by more than a tenth during his presidency, while the income of the top 20 per cent increased by a fifth, hugely enlarging the gap between them. He deliberately reversed Carter's efforts on environmental protection and energy conservation, while refusing to take seriously Gorbachev's warning about the threat of fundamentalist Islamic terror in Afghanistan and in the Middle East. Revelations of Reagan administration malfeasance in the Iran-Contra scandal continued to remind citizens of the excesses of Richard Nixon's White House – Oliver North's secretary (who had dated the son of a Nicaraguan Contra leader[100]) claimed that 'There are times when you have to go above the written law',[101] and North himself defended his decision to shred incriminating documents with the words 'That's why the government of the United States gave me a shredder.'[102] This was hardly a presidential scoreboard of which to be proud.

Was it smoke and mirrors, then, that explained the American public's continuing love affair with Reagan as his second term of office came to an end? Aware that the Soviet Union's Communist empire was fraying – its troops withdrawing from Afghanistan, its occupied countries in eastern Europe showing signs of revolt – American voters for the most part sensed an uncertain new era approaching, at once positive in signs of change in Russia, yet aware that traditional American manufacturing industry jobs were diminishing and being assigned overseas, in what came to be called 'globalization' and 'outsourcing'.

For this reason, perhaps, voters seemed reluctant to see the ageing but unwavering 'Gipper' go, indulging, as Richard Reeves later put it, in 'premature nostalgia'.[103] The president's sins of omission, his forgetfulness, even manipulation of the facts, were forgivable, it was felt, in a man who had restored the prestige of America across the world, after Jimmy Carter's brief but haunted occupation of the Oval Office. Whether or not Reagan had twisted the truth, indulged in false statistics, quoted phony economic indicators, misconstrued strategic threats, or engaged in occasional deliberate deceit, the Soviet Union was now on the defensive, while the president of the United States 'stood tall'. 'We meant to change a nation,' he declared in his farewell address from the Oval Office on January 11, 1989, in words crafted by his favourite speechwriter, Peggy Noonan, 'and, instead, we changed a world.'[104]

Leaving the White House and Washington on January 20, 1989 the fortieth president retired to Bel Air, California, keeping his 688-acre property in the hills north-west of Santa Barbara as his vacation home, where the seventy-seven-year-old, who had so wanted to be a cowboy actor, could ride to his heart's content.

Part Three: Private Life

Reagan's 'inner life remained a mystery,' admitted Lou Cannon, the California journalist who knew and reported on Reagan for a quarter-century, 'even to his friends'.[105]

It remained a mystery, too, to Reagan's wives, and his children. The wall that Reagan had begged Gorbachev to tear down seems never to have come down in his own private life. Most biographers, in explanation, pointed their psychological fingers at Reagan's childhood. The

Reagan family, it was noted, moved some ten times while Reagan was growing up. Even when settled, briefly, in one place, Reagan's father Jack would suffer 'week-long benders' unable to control 'the Irish disease' as his son called it. At one point, living away from the family, Jack took up with another woman and divorce was threatened, though eventually he returned to Nelle. She, meanwhile, did her best to keep the shame from the rest of the world, but it was impossible to conceal it at home. At age eleven, for example, Reagan found his father spread-eagled on the front porch and had to drag him by his overcoat into the house.

Though Nelle Reagan tried to help her boys see their father's downfall as a disease, not a choice, Ronald, as the youngest child, grew an outer shell that became impervious to insult or condescension, while his older brother Neil tackled such abuse with his fists, to the point of getting a police record.

The Reagan boys went their separate ways as adults, Ronald following his own star: half in the real world, half in his own. Like Richard Nixon he worshipped his devout Christian mother to the day she died. Like Nixon he worked menial jobs throughout his youth, uncomplainingly. Like Nixon he even paid for his parents to retire early to a house he bought for them, in California. But unlike Nixon, Reagan exuded goodwill and gratitude for the better things in life, especially the simple ones. Clean living and clean speaking, he got the reputation of a Mr Goody-two-shoes, was the idol of his Disciple of Christ mother, and the diametric opposite of his wastrel father, who died of drink and heart disease at age fifty-seven.

As with Richard Nixon, theatre allowed Reagan to express himself in a new dimension. Again like Nixon he fell in love with a fellow thespian, Margaret Cleaver, daughter of his local Christian Church pastor. Fiercely intelligent, Margaret at first rejected him because of his alcoholic father, but eventually consented to his courtship. She acted with him first in high school, then in college. It was she who encouraged him to study at tiny Eureka College – itself half the size of Nixon's college, Whittier. 'I loved three things: drama, politics, and sports' Reagan later said of his time in Eureka, omitting his love affair with Margaret, his constant companion, who even returned to Eureka from the University of Missouri to spend her senior year with him.[106] ('Oh, you found out about her, huh?' he

sighed when his official biographer, Edmund Morris, tracked her down
and told Reagan he had done so.[107])

Ms Cleaver was the smartest and sharpest-tongued student in her
class – so sharp Reagan's brother Neil said she 'spat tacks'.[108]) Reagan
and Margaret became engaged on graduation, Reagan forcing himself
to live up to Margaret's high moral expectations of him. Seven years
into their relationship, however, Margaret went with her sister to stay
in Paris and fell in love with a young American diplomat. She returned
Reagan's ring, married the diplomat, and shattered Reagan's romantic
dreams. He wasn't, it was clear, good enough for her.

Reagan's career in the less serious realm of entertainment fared
better, however, leading him from radio to the dream factory itself:
Hollywood. His swift ascent there, at the seeming brink of movie
fame, earned the 6' 1" hunk easy dates and unusual bedding rights in
a prudish era, yet his partners all later described him as impossible to
fathom behind his facade of good and gentle manners. He seemed
happiest on the beach or riding on the ranch he soon bought, when
not required on the film set; he remained devoted to his parents, whom
he took care to see every week; and allowed no one to get too close,
save for one individual: 'Little Button Nose', as he affectionately called
the twenty-year-old he acted alongside in the film *Brother Rat* in 1938:
Jane Wyman.

Née Sarah Jane Mayfield, Jane Wyman had first met Reagan at the
Warner Brothers studio in 1937, where they were both under contract.
She had also had a difficult domestic upbringing, fostered out when
her father died, and 'raised with such strict discipline', she later said,
'that it was years before I could reason myself out of the bitterness I
brought from my childhood'.[109] Blessed with a good singing voice, she
had pursued a part-time career in radio, then, having faked her birth
certificate, left high school in Missouri at age fifteen to get into movies
in Hollywood. With her petite figure, snub nose, her sunny smile and
her big dark brown eyes, the diminutive, twice-married (in fact still
married) blonde captivated Reagan.

After Jane obtained her second divorce she and Ronald became,
under the aegis of Hollywood gossip columnist Louella Parsons,
the model married couple of the movie industry, once they were
wedded in January 1940: Reagan turning twenty-nine, Jane turning
twenty-three. They soon had a daughter, they adopted a son, had

another baby (a daughter who died), but in 1948, after eight years of marriage, they divorced – an experience from which Reagan never quite recovered.

Tiny Ms Wyman was both girlish and all-woman – 'hard-boiled, intense and passionate' as a friend described. She loved gaiety, singing and nightclubs. Reagan, by contrast, was tall, handsome – 'a very sexy-looking man, of course – looked wonderful in swimming trunks' – but 'rather square'.[110] In a movie world of self-preening and insecure artists he exuded unusual steadiness, wholesomeness and a persistent, unshakeable optimism, as if he would allow nothing bad ever to get to him, and would always think the best of people. He was loyal to Wyman, even to the point of accompanying her to her sessions with her psychiatrist and encouraging her to have 'a fling' with her co-star Lew Ayres during the filming of *Johnny Belinda*.[111] 'I know Jane and I know she loves me' he insisted to Hedda Hopper when there were rumours of impending separation. 'I don't know what this is all about, and I don't know why Jane has done it. For my part, I hope to live with her for the rest of my life.'[112]

Wyman's defection – she was the cause of the divorce, he insisted – crippled him. She ejected him from their house, then gave him a turquoise Cadillac convertible for his thirty-seventh birthday on February 6, 1948. She took him back into their house, then threw him out again and filed for divorce for his unceasing, boorish talk of politics. 'The plain truth was that such a thing was so far from ever being imagined by me that I had no resources to call on' Reagan acknowledged later. He had been 'a prince' of Hollywood, the perfect gentleman of the Sunset Strip.

For months Reagan went into denial, certain his wife would take him back. Hope faded as the lawyers sharpened their quills and in June 1948 a divorce decree was granted, which became absolute in July 1949. By then Reagan was a wreck. 'He was heartbroken. He really was' recalled Patricia Neal, who'd replaced Wyman in Reagan's next movie, *John Loves Mary* (which flopped). At midnight on New Year's Eve 1948, Reagan had 'wept and wept on an older woman's arm'.[113]

Though he met Nancy Robbins Davis, a young aspiring actress, in the autumn of 1949, Reagan was simply unable to get over his divorce, simultaneously dating a seemingly unending series of 'Hollywood starlets, singers, models, and beauticians' as one biographer of Nancy Davis put it, from Doris Day and Rhonda Fleming to Adele Jergens, Kay Stewart, Ruth Roman, Monica Lewis, Penny Edwards, Ann Sothern . . . 'I hate to say he was weak,' recalled Doris Lilly, one of his many 'conquests', 'maybe a nicer word would be passive.' This was understandable because, as another of his companions recalled, Jane Wyman haunted him to the point of impotence. 'He was so in love with that woman that she had become an obsession with him. When she walked out on him, he couldn't function – couldn't go out of the house, couldn't work, couldn't cook, couldn't perform sexually', Jacqueline Park recalled – as well as the time he dropped his glass and, pointing to the shards, told her: 'That is what is going to happen to your heart if you stay in this town. One way or the other – if you make it or if you don't make it – this town will break your heart. That's how your heart will look if you decide to stay here.'[114] He got Jacqueline pregnant, but then refused to have anything to do with her, or the abortion she ended up having.[115] 'I woke up one morning,' he confessed later, 'and I couldn't remember the name of the girl I was in bed with. I said, "Hey, I gotta get a grip here."'[116] When Nancy Robbins Davis became pregnant by him at the end of 1949, he finally agreed to marry her, and reform his broken life.

Reagan's private reformation was not easy. It would be claimed he was seeing at least six other women at the time he agreed to marry Nancy; embarrassed and ashamed, he would only agree to a small wedding. Two witnesses were invited, and only afterwards did Reagan dare tell his mother what he had done. He even went on seeing one of his mistresses, red-headed actress Christine Larson, in the months afterwards – and was with her in bed, she claimed, when Nancy gave birth to their first child, Patti. He told Christine his life was ruined, and that he had been 'tricked' into marriage.[117] But it was too late. He had made his marital bed and must lie in it, he recognized, though he would, in consequence, grow a secret layer around his heart that no one would ever be able to pierce. 'You can get just so far with Ronnie, and then something happens' Nancy later confessed.[118] And she added, thoughtfully: 'Although he loves people, he often seems remote, and he doesn't let anybody get too close. There's a wall around him. He lets me come closer than anyone else, but there are times when even I feel that barrier.'[119] This view was seconded by

Reagan's son Ron who, like his mother, later puzzled over the fact that there was 'something that he holds back. You get just so far, and then the curtain drops.'[120] Ron described his relationship with his father as 'friendly and loving', but 'he gets a little bit antsy if you try and get too close and personal and too father-and-sonny'.[121] Reagan's daughter Patti was more forthright, however. 'I never knew who he was,' she described her disappointment, 'I could never get through to him.'[122]

Without Nancy Davis – stepdaughter of a Republican doctor – Reagan would probably not have managed to overcome his hurt at all. Nancy's tough, no-nonsense, businesslike approach to marriage and to the world transformed Reagan's life in Hollywood. Petite, prim, pointy-nosed and with a pronounced chin, at thirty years old she became, in effect, his business manager. She had pressed him to get her a seat on the Screen Actors Guild, she applauded rather than deplored his political views, pushed him in new directions – and erected a fence around his daily life as his moral guardian, effacing any mention of his former wife. Within the safety zone created around him by 'Mrs Nancy Reagan' – as she recast herself in Tinseltown, having given up acting – Reagan gradually blossomed: his faltering career was rescued by television work and increasing political engagements that eventually led him towards elected office. By learning to operate his memory selectively, he was able not only to erase Jane Wyman from his conscious life (he only gave Jane and his first marriage twenty-nine words in his 748-page autobiography, *An American Life*), but also to blot out what he did not wish to see, or recall, in politics. Instead he focused relentlessly on the reality show he was scripting for California and then America, in which he would take the leading role, and which in time he would direct.

What Jane Wyman had considered boring, Nancy Davis recognized as American genius as she set about creating a home environment that would glue Reagan's broken doll together and make him whole, the better to fulfil his unique talent as a political communicator: at once folksy and inspiring, passionately sincere and disarmingly humorous. Since he was gentle, almost passive, she would play bad cop to his good cop. In doing so she offended people who either didn't share her reverence for his leadership or who resented her KGB style of policing behind the scenes. ('There was no ambiguity ever with regard to her power' a long-time colleague noted. 'If she thought someone was disloyal to her Ronnie, that was a nuclear holocaust!' Any 'dealings with her were difficult at best'.)[123] Others mocked her abject reliance on soothsayers and astrologers, as in ancient Rome, considering her a witch. But by her absolute devotion to his welfare, contentment and success, she earned his admiration and loyalty, not least when he recognized that his once photographic memory was fading into dementia, and finally Alzheimer's, which was diagnosed in 1994.

Ronald Reagan died at his home in Bel Air on June 5, 2004, not having opened his eyes for four years.[124] He was buried on the hill below his Presidential Library in Simi Valley, California, six days later.

CHAPTER TEN

GEORGE H. W. BUSH

Republican
41st President
(January 20, 1989–January 20, 1993)

Part One: The Road to the White House

Born in a suburb of Boston, Massachusetts on June 12, 1924, George Herbert Walker Bush was considered a quintessential American WASP, following a long line of American worthies: his great-grandfather was an Episcopalian minister on Staten Island, New York, his grandfather a fabulously wealthy industrialist in Ohio. His father, Prescott Bush, became a senator, having served in combat in France in World War I as a field artillery captain, like Harry Truman.

Prescott Bush had married a wealthy woman, Dorothy Walker, and worked in her father's big investment firm in New York. There, he became both rich and a pillar of the establishment. Commuting each day to Manhattan, but living in Greenwich, Connecticut, Prescott Bush employed a cook, a maid and a chauffeur; he also served as moderator of the 148-strong Greenwich Representative Town Meeting as 'an active practising Republican', and was founder of the Greenwich Taxpayers Association.

Gloomy and uncommunicative, the giant (6' 4") Prescott Bush left the upbringing of his five children largely to his wife Dorothy, a no-nonsense martinet who shared his conservative views. When the master of Saybrook College told an off-colour joke, Prescott turned to his wife and said: 'Dorothy, we're leaving.' And they left.[1] When his brother abandoned his wife and children to marry a Philadelphia socialite, Prescott severed all connection with his sibling.[2] There was right and there was wrong – and Dorothy, schooled at Miss Porter's, was equally firm in her judgement.

On his eighteenth birthday in June 1942, straight out of Phillips Andover school, George – who was expected to attend Yale, like his elder brother – registered instead at the navy recruiting station in New York. By the following summer he was the youngest trained pilot in the US Navy, and by January 1944, at age nineteen, he was flying off the aircraft carrier USS *San Jacito* in the Pacific, first in bombing runs against Wake Island, then on Chichi Jima, where on September 2 his plane – a TBF Avenger – was hit but managed to drop four 500 lb bombs on its target. Baling out at 2,000 feet with another of his three-man crew, whose parachute did not open, he was the only one to survive, rescued by a US submarine, the *Finback*, while fellow pilots strafed approaching Japanese vessels.[3] Like Lieutenant John F. Kennedy, he refused to be repatriated to the United States, but flew a further eight combat missions over the Japanese-occupied Philippines before going home aged twenty-one, with the Distinguished Flying Cross, fifty-eight missions and 126 carrier landings to his credit.

After marrying the daughter of the company director of a big women's magazine, Bush duly attended Yale, where he was accepted into the exclusive Skull and Bones society, captained the university baseball team, concentrated on business and finance, and graduated in 1948 after only two and a half years. Anxious to escape his mother and mother-in-law's critical gaze, he declined to join his father's investment company in New York, and instead obeyed the American injunction 'Go West, young man, and grow up with the country.' Working for a Yale classmate, Neil Mallon, and his company the International Derrick & Equipment Company, he moved to West Texas as an oilman. Settling down with his growing family among cattle ranchers and 'black gold' riggers and prospectors, the 'Ivy League' salesman learned to mask his preppy background and barbecue with people of all stripes.

From supplying equipment to the Texas oil industry, George Bush moved into lease prospecting for mineral rights, starting his own company, Bush-Overby, with $350,000 loaned from his father, his uncle and his family's friends, including one of his father's clients, the owner of the *Washington Post*, Eugene Meyer. Switching then from leases to oil drilling, Bush formed a new company, Zapata Oil, in 1953. Striking rich in Coke County, he became a prospective millionaire in Midland, Texas, moving to a house with a swimming pool, while his father Prescott went to Washington as senator for Connecticut.

Though two inches shorter than his father, George Bush was still tall at 6' 2", a certified World War II hero, handsome and personable, a born conciliator-adventurer with few fixed views on anything. Wherever he was, he blended in: popular, well connected, modest, and open to suggestion. Soon he was building special rigs and drilling offshore, on contract to major distributors in the Gulf of Mexico, and going international in the Persian Gulf, in the South China Sea off Brunei, and in the Caribbean off Trinidad. As the first self-made millionaire among his transplanted Yale cohort, he was the envy of his colleagues. What they could not understand was why Bush – who seemed apolitical except where offshore drilling legislation was concerned – then decided to go into politics.

In part Bush was floating on the tide of oil, which made Houston, Texas – where Bush moved in 1960 – the 'oil and chemical capital' of America. In part, though, he was borne by the same political tide on which his father, as an Eisenhower Republican, had risen to prominence. Prescott Bush suffered ill health and had decided not to run again for the Senate, after two terms, in 1962. Though George gave no thought to succeeding him in Connecticut, which would have meant carpet-bagging, he decided to make a run for political office in his new home state of Texas which, in the wake of the Civil Rights tsunami, was turning increasingly Republican.

In the long run, Bush's political prescience was as marked as his oil prospecting instinct. However, it involved moral compromises that caused his 'leviathan of a father' deep concern.[4] In February 1963 Bush was elected chairman of the Republican Party of Harris County, embracing two congressional districts. He'd affected a slight Texas drawl, but still found it hard to evade his 'preppy Yale' persona among ten-gallon hats, Bible-thumpers, diehard anti-Communist nationalists and John Birch Society stalwarts. 'It was his nature to try to get along with everybody', a campaign colleague recalled, appalled that, in his naivety, Bush would even think of bringing Birchers into the Republican hierarchy.[5] 'He didn't understand', the campaigner remarked, not recognizing Bush's instinctive appreciation that, in order to offset his educated East Coast carpetbagger image, he needed to get the backing of good, Goldwater, values-obsessed, Texas extremists. In 1964, approaching his fortieth birthday, George Bush made his first run for the Senate, easily winning the Republican Party primary as a 'Goldwater Republican'.

Like Goldwater, Bush opposed Johnson's civil rights bill, declaring it a 'new civil rights bill to protect fourteen per cent of the people', and excoriated his anti-poverty measures. He also opposed admission of Red China to the United Nations, and even the Nuclear Test Ban Treaty, which he called 'foolishness'. 'The sun's going to shine in the Senate some day / George Bush is going to chase them liberals away' his Bush Bonnett Belles chanted in 200 Texas town squares, while Bush recklessly defamed his opponent and other Democrats, using guilt by association.[6] Anyone who had given money to Martin Luther King's movement, for example, he tarred as a near-terrorist, while the right-wing fanatical Birchers who were supporting him were lauded as sanctified patriots. On election day, however, he failed to dislodge Senator Ralph Yarborough, the popular sitting Democratic senator, for whom President Johnson campaigned, losing by a massive 300,000 votes. 'I just don't know how it happened', Bush confessed in shock to reporters. 'I guess I have a lot to learn about.'[7]

He had a lot to be ashamed of, also, his opponents felt.

Afterwards, Bush was contrite. So concerned were his parents by the extreme positions he'd taken that neither of them had come out to Texas to help campaign for him. To his Episcopalian minister, Bush confessed: 'You know, John, I took some of the far right positions to get elected. I hope I never do it again. I regret it.'[8] He even admitted in a speech the next year he was 'ashamed' not to have spoken out against the 'pandemonium' of right-wing hate groups and racists.[9] Shame could not obscure the fact, however, that oceans of oil money had 'talked' in the election, more than a million formerly Democratic votes in Texas helping to produce the biggest Republican turnout in Texan history.

If Senator Yarborough, once elected, expected the young war hero to go back to his oil wells, he was much mistaken. Political ambition now became an addiction for Bush, and with President Johnson starting the Vietnam War, then escalating it, Bush (who supported it) felt confident in standing for election as a congressman for the predominantly (90 per cent) white Seventh District of Texas in 1966, comprising Houston's north-west city and suburban wards.

To show his absolute determination, moreover, Bush resigned his CEO and chairman's position with Zapata, sold his stock and this time ran to the *left* of his Dixiecrat opponent, an old-fashioned district attorney, racist Frank Briscoe. Completely reversing his anti-civil rights platform of only two years before, Bush sponsored a black girls' softball team, the George Bush All-Stars, who went on to challenge and beat all five white teams in the Houston league. He deliberately had himself photographed presenting the trophies to winners and losers, yet the volte-face did him no harm, especially in the context of young students representing a new generation. From a six-to-one majority for the Democratic candidate in the previous election, voters not only turned out in record numbers, but gave Bush, as a Republican, a 57.6 per cent majority.

One of forty-seven freshman Republican representatives in January 1967, Congressman Bush was, a colleague recalled, 'pretty innocent of political ideas generally': a politician still in the making, and bereft of political vision other than to serve in the nation's Capitol. In some ways, this helped him stand out against the more partisan members of the House. He was strangely inarticulate on the stump or in front of large gatherings, yet movie-star handsome, alert, ambitious, but modest in person. With his father's help, he got a seat on the Ways and Means Committee and soon set his sights on higher things, namely the vice presidency, if the Democratic administration was brought down thanks to the very Vietnam War that Republicans, ironically, had pressed Johnson to declare.

Aware how strong LBJ's influence still was in Texas, Bush went out to Vietnam, where he was encouraged by what he saw of American soldiers fighting on the ground, as well as navy fliers setting off to bomb Hanoi. With General Westmoreland demanding another 200,000 troops, and the Tet Offensive demonstrating the weakness of the South Vietnamese junta, however, he had to acknowledge it was the 'wrong war' to have started. He felt certain the 'next struggle will be in the Middle East', not South East Asia. Yet how withdraw, without dishonouring the flag? He did not oppose Johnson or the war – but he did oppose an aspect of it that surprised his Texas constituents.

Seeing the disproportionate number of African Americans fighting in Vietnam, Bush found himself ashamed over housing discrimination at home. Bush therefore voted in the House for President Johnson's bill to outlaw discrimination in housing, knowing it could end his political career in Texas. 'I voted for the bill,' he wrote a Yale friend, 'and the roof is falling in – boy does the hatred surface. I have had more mail on this subject than on Vietnam and taxes and sex all put together.'[10] He even received death threats but persevered, announcing to voters of the Seventh District that he would be betraying his sacred duty to follow his own moral judgement as their elected representative if he did not stand up for basic American decency. As someone who had himself served his country in combat, he declared that no one 'should have the door slammed in his face because he is a Negro or speaks with a Latin-American accent. Open housing offers a ray of hope for blacks and other minorities locked out by habit and discrimination.'[11] With those words Congressman Bush demonstrated, finally, a moral backbone missing in action since he went into politics – and to his astonishment no one dared oppose his 1968 re-election candidacy from either party.

Bush's moral courage, however, had been spurred by the fact that he was not overly concerned about re-election. The truth was, he had hoped the Republican nominee for president, Nixon, might select him as his running mate that year, since no lesser person than President Eisenhower – who had admired Senator Prescott Bush – had recommended young Bush as a candidate for the post, just as young Nixon had been recommended to Eisenhower in 1952. Nixon, however, chose an unknown former Democrat and former governor of Maryland, Spiro T. Agnew.

Spurned by the president, Bush now set his sights for a second time on a seat in the Senate, not only toadying up to Johnson in the hope of getting his imprimatur (he attended Johnson's farewell to Washington at Andrews Air Force Base instead of Nixon's post-inaugural ceremonies), but also visiting the former president at his Texas ranch later, asking Johnson if he should run. 'Son, the difference between being a member of the Senate and a member of the House is the difference between chicken salad and chicken shit', Johnson memorably advised. 'Do I make my point?'[12]

Bush took the advice, even where it meant transgressing campaign ethics – approaching President Nixon for financial backing in 1970, and happily taking $106,000 from Nixon's illegal 'Townhouse Fund', in violation of campaign finance law.[13]

Bush's behaviour reflected the two sides of his political personality: the fawning young man, willing to compromise his integrity and self-respect in order to get ahead, and the *noblesse oblige*, an honourable and courageous individual whom his high-minded aides – particularly his Texas lawyer friend and campaign manager, James Baker III – admired and respected.

Neither Bush's toadying nor his financial impropriety worked, however. Democratic Congressman Lloyd Bentsen, a self-made Texas millionaire in insurance and an even greater war hero than Bush (having been awarded the Distinguished Flying Cross, the Air Medal and three Oak Leaf Clusters as a bomber pilot in World War II in Europe) won.

'Like Custer, who said there were just too many Indians,' Bush said in an attempt to make light of his second defeat running for the Senate, 'I guess there were too many Democrats.' In truth, he was 'shattered by the loss', a close friend recalled, 'he said it was just the end of everything'.[14]

In his campaign Bush had, to his credit, refused to use the odious 'attack ads' that Nixon's 'evil genius', Charles Colson, had suggested to him as Special White House Counsel; in fact Bush had called the White House in a fury to say: 'Don't ever send anything of that nature up here again. Tell Mr Colson I called and be sure he understands.'[15] Such moral revulsion bespoke Bush's better nature: Colson would be indicted as one of the Watergate Seven, and later went to jail for organizing the burglary of whistle-blower Daniel Ellsberg's psychiatrist's office. The lesson of Bush's defeat was that, without using such 'derogatory' attack ads, as a Republican politician with poor speaking ability he simply could not get elected. As another friend noted, Bush was too inarticulate: 'his sentences were ragged, ran into each other, and tended to leave thoughts hanging and ideas incomplete' – much like 'General Eisenhower whom I had observed in 1952'.[16]

It was an apt comparison, save that Bush was not a world-famous American general. Distraught and determined not to be left out in the cold two years into a Republican administration, Bush appealed directly to President Nixon for the job of Treasury Secretary, which was becoming vacant. Nixon said no. Disappointed, Bush begged Nixon to appoint him, instead, to the post of US ambassador to the UN. Nixon expressed surprise. Even Bush's associates were nonplussed. 'George,' Bush's old Skull and Bones friend, Lud Ashley, exclaimed when he heard of the plan, 'what the fuck do you know about foreign affairs?'[17]

The answer was very little – but a willingness to learn, and a place in the Nixon cabinet. Duly appointed to the post at age forty-seven, Ambassador Bush underwent a crash course in world politics in New York. As important as it was as an introduction to world affairs, the position also offered a ringside cabinet seat in the secretive, manipulative world of Nixon's imperial White House, since Nixon and Kissinger, he soon found, were double-crossing him, especially over Taiwan and Communist China. Bush belatedly favoured American recognition of Red China, which he saw as a 'brilliant move', but resented being used as a fall guy at the United Nations, where on October 24, 1971, Taiwan was duly expelled by a 59–55 vote in the General Assembly.

'A total Nixon man. Doubt if you can do better than Bush', Nixon commented with smug gratitude at Camp David when Bush's name came up for the post of Deputy Treasury Secretary, following Nixon's re-election in 1972.[18] Bush was not impressed. He had brought rich gifts to the president's secret campaign table, including $100,000 from Bush's old partner in Texas, William Liedke; he therefore felt he was 'owed', and baulked at the notion of being appointed a mere 'super-secretary' troubleshooter at the Treasury. There was an alternative sinecure Nixon could bestow, Bush knew – and desired. However, it was one that would mean firing the current chairman of the Republican National Committee, Senator Bob Dole, whom Nixon in any case considered insufficiently obsequious. Stirred by the financial and electoral implications, Nixon warmed to the idea. Dole duly stood down, remarking later that he had been 'Bushwhacked'.

Bush's wife Barbara, who'd enjoyed living in New York, hated the idea of the RNC post in Washington – 'the last thing in the world' she thought her husband should do.[19] Her instinct was right. But from his illegal cash transactions, Bush knew exactly what he was getting into by entering the lion's den; indeed his eye for the main chance within government and politics was unerring. Dissembling, he told his wife he couldn't 'turn a president down', whereas in truth the idea had been his own.[20] The Republican chairmanship would allow him access to the Nixon administration at all levels, and to meet all the top people in Republican politics, sitting with the cabinet and networking with the richest funders across the country. At the very least this would guarantee a soft landing if his political career came to an early end.

No soft landing, however, was to be had. No sooner had Bush moved to Washington and taken over the Republican Party's national office than Nixon's house of cards began to shake, thanks to Watergate. Bush admitted privately he was 'sickened' by the growing revelations, yet he continued to tour the country as chairman of the RNC, defending the president and denying anything illegal had been done: a *tour d'excuse* in which he gave some 101 speeches, held seventy-eight news conferences, made eleven appearances on television and travelled almost 100,000 miles visiting thirty-three states.[21]

Bush's desperate cover-up of malfeasance did no good. In October 1973, Vice President Agnew was forced to resign on corruption charges. Once again Bush's name was touted as a possible appointee for the post, which would put him in the White House if Nixon was successfully impeached. Despite his stalwart, transnational defence of the president, however, Bush was turned down yet again by Nixon. Instead, the president selected the Minority Leader in the House, Congressman Gerald R. Ford.

Disappointed, Bush continued to support the president, though even his wife noted in her diary she was 'worried about George as he does not love his work. How could he? All this scandal.'[22] Nor was Nixon even grateful, calling Bush a 'worrywart' for his anxieties over Watergate. Nixon's daughter Julie was more direct: she telephoned Bush directly, 'and asked him why', as Barbara Bush later recalled, 'he wasn't defending her dad more'.[23]

Such loyal stonewalling by Bush merely helped buy Nixon time to explore further ways of evading justice. The president was able to erase the most criminal eight minutes from his White House tapes, but the many hundreds of undeleted hours were subpoenaed. Still George Bush defended his chief, however, for whom he felt genuine compassion. 'He has a different sense than the rest of people', Bush noted in his diary on August 5, 1974 as Nixon vowed to fight impeachment in Congress to the bitter end. 'He came up the hard way. He hung tough. He hunkered down. He stonewalled. He became president of the United States and a damn good one in many ways, but now it had all caught up with him. All the people he hated – Ivy League, press, Establishment, Democrats, privileged – all of this ended up biting him and bringing him down.'[24]

Bush's sensitivity to the president's inferiority complex did credit to the Ivy Leaguer's social antennae, but not to his moral compass. 'My temptation was to blast the president,' he noted in his diary, 'blast the lie, and then I thought, why add to the personal tragedy and the personal grief? Events were moving so fast that it just didn't seem right to kind of "pile it on".'[25]

At a cabinet meeting on August 6, 1974, Bush was, like Vice President Ford, less than courageous in declining to raise the issue of resignation, and contenting himself with remarks about the effect of Watergate on Republican chances at the forthcoming midterm election. 'Am I failing to lead?' Bush asked in his diary. On August 7, he plucked up courage to at least send a letter to the president, advising him to resign. With Senator Goldwater and others telling Nixon in person that he would not survive impeachment, the president caved in and agreed to stand down. Ford's succession then raised the question of who would fill the vice-presidential vacancy.

Once again, Bush's name was shortlisted for the post. His supporters, led by James Baker III, hounded the White House and engineered calls from across the nation on his behalf. It did no good. 'I let my hopes zoom unrealistically' Bush confided to a friend, gutted to learn he had been turned down in favour of the four-times governor of New York, moderate Republican Nelson Rockefeller.[26] Deeply disappointed, Bush went to China as head of the US Mission in Beijing, wondering as he flew there with his wife, 'Am I running away from something?'[27]

Unknown to him, he was – from a White House disaster. His year and a half in Beijing, meanwhile, allowed him to grow up politically, convincing him that the United States had nothing 'to fear' from China. 'The talk about how we lost China infuriates the Chinese and *now* it infuriates me. I can see where it is very clearly wrong. China was not ours to lose,' Bush candidly acknowledged in his diary, 'and that has been part of the problem.'[28] He determined, if he could get back on to the political ladder, that he would do his best to make Republican foreign policy more realistic and less ideological.

President Ford felt the same, but was a poor picker of men to serve him. Instead of distancing himself from the disgraced president, Ford pardoned Nixon and kept on Henry Kissinger as combined national security adviser and Secretary of State despite his involvement in Watergate. ('Bullshit', Nixon told his lawyer. '[Kissinger] knew what was going on in the Plumbers' activities . . . Don't let him give you that crap. He was – he was clear up to his ankles himself'.[29]) Ford then found himself so out of his depth he had to summon Donald Rumsfeld, Nixon's *éminence grise*, to restore order as his chief of staff. And to George Bush's chagrin, Rumsfeld hated George Bush.

After Saigon was overrun by the North Vietnamese, Rumsfeld got himself promoted to Secretary of Defense. Dick Cheney, Rumsfeld's right-hand man, then became chief of staff and together the two urged Ford to axe the centrist, progressive Republican, Vice President Rockefeller, from the forthcoming 1976 presidential ticket. Lest George Bush again became contender for the vice-presidential post, which Rumsfeld coveted for himself, they also arranged for Ford to recall Bush from Beijing and park him at the CIA, with a promise to Congress not to run for electoral office in 1976.

Bush's old partner, Hugh Liedke, warned Bush the appointment was political homicide. Even Bush himself saw it as a move to 'Bury Bush at the CIA', which he called 'a graveyard for politics', prompting his wife to invite more guests to Beijing to drive away her husband's blues.[30] For his part Rumsfeld was heard to say the appointment would 'sink the sonofabitch for good'.[31] His and Cheney's Machiavellian manipulations had succeeded, it appeared, in ending Bush's political career.

Directing 15,000 spooks and their handlers on a 'black budget' traditionally kept secret from the public and Congress, Bush now received a new crash course in imperial strategy and tactics – this time not in diplomacy, but below the radar. Given the corrupt way in which Nixon had sought to use the CIA, the spy agency was up against the ropes. Not only was Bush summoned fifty-one times to go before Congress – where the Church Committee held its celebrated hearings into government-sanctioned assassination and illegal wiretapping – but he also inherited the problem that his predecessor William Colby had postponed, but which was rearing its ugly head once more: pressure from right-wing extremists to bust détente.

Later known as the Rise of the Vulcans, this was Goldwater II: a clique of American diehards, indifferent to Chinese Communism but virulently anti-Soviet, and driven to despair over military defeat in Vietnam, as symbolized in the last American helicopters lifting people away from the abandoned US embassy in Saigon.[32] Their venom was now directed at the empire that had got away scot-free from the imbroglios in South East Asia: the Russians, whom they now accused of an accelerated military build-up, and of planning a pre-emptive nuclear strike against the US, concealed behind détente.

Should George Bush, as CIA director, have permitted what became known as the 'Team B Panel Report on Strategic Objectives', an infamous minority report which damned current CIA estimates of Russian capabilities and argued for a tough termination of détente? Disciples of right-wing professors Leo Strauss (who had died in 1973) and Albert Wohlstetter of the University of Chicago, the self-styled 'neocons' included Norman Podhoretz, Irving Kristol, Richard Pipes, Harry Jaffa, Paul Wolfowitz and Abram Shulsky. Under Professor Pipes' Team B – which boasted Paul Nitze and Paul Wolfowitz – the team objected to the CIA's view of Russia as a crumbling economic edifice, best cauterized by containment. Instead, Pipes' radical right-wing team not only invented fantasy Russian military programmes, from nuclear-powered beam weapons to non-acoustic submarines, but refused to accept the role of the CIA as an objective intelligence-gathering body. Pipes thus damned existing CIA estimates, to which he became privy, as a gross underestimation of the Soviet Union's 'intensity, scope and implicit threat', arguing that, even if correct, the CIA had hitherto only assessed 'the adversary's *capabilities*', not 'his ideas, motives and aspirations'.[33]

Almost every claim in the Team B Report – in particular the assertion that the Soviet Union had a 'large and expanding Gross National Product' and was working towards a 'first strike' capability – was right-wing moonshine. 'I would say that all of it was fantasy' commented Dr Anne Cahn of the Arms Control and Disarmament Agency later. 'If you go through most of Team B's specific allegations about weapons systems, and you just examine them one by one, they were all wrong. *All* of them.'[34] Even Bush's CIA deputy director, Admiral Daniel Murphy, derided Team B's 'reality check' as a brash challenge that 'did not amount to a hill of beans'.[35] Giving them access to 'data' that was denied to any other group outside the CIA, Bush had, however, taken a tremendous risk, the more so once Team B leaked 'a tough estimate of the USSR's military build-up in order to stop [president-elect] Carter from cutting the defense budget' – a charge that 'couldn't be further from the truth', Bush protested on television.[36]

Was it, though? Right-wing extremism was certainly mounting in America. Carter won the 1976 presidential election, but his victory, though sufficient in Electoral College votes, was garnered by a mere percentage point in the popular vote. The entire western half of America, from the Pacific Ocean eastwards to a line running from Minnesota to Texas, had swung to the Republicans. Despite his failure to beat President Ford for the Republican nomination, Reagan vowed to continue his crusade for the presidency. Caught between two stools – a defeated but resurgent Republican right and an incoming Democratic president with a liberal agenda – Bush was playing safe: not siding with the neocons, but not opposing them either. Moreover, in a telling illustration of his essentially apolitical character he actually offered to serve a further year as CIA director under Carter.

Fortunately for Bush's political career, the president – a deeply religious man and genuine southerner, who had a visceral antipathy to the East Coast Establishment – took an instant dislike to Bush as a dissembler without convictions, and fired him. On January 20, 1977, Bush thus found himself without a job, an oil company, or – when leaving Washington – a home.

In Texas no Republican electoral office looked winnable to Bush, and he was proven right when his lawyer-aide James Baker III failed to win the Texas governorship in 1978, and Bush's eldest son George Jr, who ran for Congress in the Nineteenth District, was defeated. For a while, as Rumsfeld had intended, George H. W. Bush, the chameleon of the Republican Party, with ties to all but no fixed convictions, was all washed up.

Many men might have given up further political ambitions at this point. The Republican Party which his father had served as a senator, with its old-fashioned fiscal conservatism, libertarian creed and paternalistic sense of social responsibility, was dying. In its place a new confluence of evangelical Christians, moneybags and virulent ideological anti-Communists were moulding a potent greed-machine, peculiarly suited to a nation of immigrants imbued with the American dream of becoming individually rich, or at least richer. Led by Ronald Reagan, the 'father' of the American revolt against taxes (he had supported a ballot referendum that capped property taxes, Proposition 1, as governor of California in 1973), the simplistic prosperity gospel movement cast off old-fashioned European values of compassion and social responsibility. In their place the movement espoused a muscular, born-again Christianity based on personal faith, a community of fellow Born-Agains, and vilification of government, whether good or bad, for daring to redistribute personal wealth. Since George Bush had not been born again as a Christian, but remained the same Christian he had always been, this posed a challenge.

In the event Bush refused to advocate the teaching of creationism in science classes. He also refused to oppose abortion even in cases of rape or incest, or to demand the overthrow of the Equal Rights Amendment – the campaign planks of Ronald Reagan. Instead, drawing comfort from polls showing that Gerald Ford, a moderate, was still the most popular Republican in the nation, and on the assumption that Ford would not run a second time, George Bush announced his candidacy for his party's nomination for president of the United States on May 1, 1979.

Why, Bush's friends asked, did he do so when he had little or no chance of defeating Reagan? Bush was unfazed. If Reagan, aged sixty-eight, were to falter, Bush countered, he would be left in pole position. Against a weak field of competitors (the former vice-presidential candidate Senator Dole, Senator Howard Baker and Congressman John Anderson), he felt himself to be the strongest contender behind Reagan. Besides, Reagan might overreach himself in demonizing the Russians, leading the majority of registered Republicans to plump for Bush as a moderate. And finally, there was, once again, the matter of the second spot, the vice presidency. Although it had never happened in practice, in theory the successful candidate might select the runner-up at the Republican National Convention in a bid for swift party unity following the gruelling campaign for the nomination.

Given that George Bush was still virtually unknown to the general population, he performed remarkably well, beating Reagan in the first caucus of the campaign in Ohio in January 1980. With James Baker III as his campaign manager, Bush went on to win a number of import-ant states thereafter. But in calling Reagan's economics 'voodoo' it was he, not Reagan, who overreached. If he attacked or ridiculed Reagan, his chief strategist warned, 'they'll hate you. You can't do that', Reagan being simply too popular among his Republican fans. What he had to do, Bush was advised, was to attack the *other* candi-dates, 'and you're there. And if [Reagan] fails, then you can get it.'[37]

Though Bush eventually dropped his strategist, he did as advised, prudently withdrawing from the contest well before the National Convention lest he become a spoiler in Reagan's quest to unseat President Carter. Reagan duly won the Republican nomination, and telephoned Bush personally to offer him the second slot – if Bush was willing to subscribe to Reagan's right-wing platform. He was.

Cresting a patriotic, evangelical tide of greed and indifference to the poor, the Reagan-Bush ticket duly won both the 1980 and 1984 elections, the latter by the largest landslide in electoral history, when Reagan took forty-nine states to Mondale's one. Before the embers had died down, however, the race to become Reagan's successor began. As Barbara Bush noted, on January 21, 1985, 'the 1988 campaign started'.[38]

By the spring of that year Vice President Bush was already holding his first formal campaign strategy meeting for the 1988 election, with a ruthless young advertising genius named Lee Atwater as his political director, and Bush's eldest son George Jr working as his enforcer. At their urging, Bush also began to court the nation's top televangelists – Jerry Falwell, Jim and Tammy Faye Baker, Jimmy Swaggart and Pat Robertson – while positioning himself to meet or roll with any challenge from the right of his own party. He got rid of all his old staff 'because he knew the mission he needed was different', explained a new Bush operative, Ron Kaufman. 'George Bush is much smarter, much tougher than people give him credit for, much more Machiavellian.'[39]

Ruthless ambition allied to opportunism was now propelling Bush closer and closer to the extremist fire, at whatever cost. 'I've got to fulfill this mission' he wrote in his diary as the election grew closer, aware that he had broken the law over Iran-Contra to keep both Reagan and himself from possible impeachment.[40] He thus continued to serve the faltering president in the waning months of the Reagan presidency loyally and uncritically. Then on October 13, 1987, he finally declared his official candidacy for the Republican Party's presidential nomination.

With President Reagan's tepid yet crucial imprimatur, and the backing of Falwell's Moral Majority, Bush was able to win the Republican primary campaign in the spring of 1988. However, Iran-Contra hearings in Congress and an economic recession made his aim

to win the election seem dubious; indeed the Democrats were reported
to be some seventeen points ahead, a lead they kept into the summer
of 1988 when the party conventions were held.

Governor Mike Dukakis, the Democratic nominee and son of Greek
immigrants, had a two-term reputation for sober governance of a
large, modern state, Massachusetts, but had no idea what he would
be up against. The chameleon vice president proclaimed his new, right-
wing credentials – anti-abortion, anti-regulatory agencies, denial of
the spiralling deficit, anti-taxes ('The Congress will push me to raise
taxes, and I'll say no . . . And I'll say to them, Read my lips: no new
taxes') as well as a mandatory Pledge of Allegiance in schools.
Meanwhile Bush's hit squad, under Lee Atwater, went for Dukakis as
a wild, out of control 'Liberal,' sneering at his environmental record
in failing to clean up Boston Harbor, and putting out their infamous
'Willie Horton' racist ads: using the photo of a black Massachusetts
murderer who had committed armed robbery and rape while on
furlough, fourteen years after he was imprisoned.[41]

This was a new Bush, licensing Atwater and his accomplices to aim
directly at Dukakis' supposed strength, namely his record as an effective modernizing governor of Massachusetts. Having 'test-marketed'
the Willie Horton ads, Atwater later boasted to reporters: 'I realized
right then that the sky was the limit on Dukakis' negatives.'[42] It was
a tactic to 'strip the bark off the little bastard' and 'make Willie Horton
his running mate'.[43]

American politics had always had a Wild West frontier quality,
expressed in elections that were rife with real or supposed skullduggery. But Atwater's evil genius was to see, like the Nazis in the 1920s
and 1930s, how modern media could be cynically manipulated to vilify
opponents. As Bush's media consultant Roger Ailes confided to a journalist, Bush 'hates it, but he knows we'd be getting killed if we didn't
go negative'.[44] Saturating television with the Willie Horton ads some
600 times, it was estimated eighty million Americans saw them at least
once.

This was Bush's personal pact with the devil, which his honourable,
loyal campaign manager and friend James Baker III abhorred.[45] In a
moment of unusual misjudgement Bush had overruled Baker and chosen
as his running mate a young, unknown, semi-literate but photogenic
conservative senator from Indiana, Dan Quayle, who would appeal to

evangelicals and the party's anti-abortionist, supply-sider base, yet was entirely unqualified to be 'a heartbeat away from the presidency', as the vice presidency was termed.

With the press revealing Quayle's draft-dodging and lack of credentials, Bush confessed in his diary that 'it was my decision, and I blew it, but I'm not about to say that I blew it'.[46] Instead, he licensed Atwater and Republican national campaign operatives and their funders to work even harder to destroy Dukakis. The *New York Times* observed that Ronald Reagan had at least run his campaigns on the basis of gaining the confidence of the American people, whereas Bush was aiming to destroy it, at least in relation to his presidential opponent.[47] Reeling, Dukakis found himself unable to beat off Atwater's personal attacks on his character, his liberalism, his environmental record, his patriotism, and, above all, his 'guilt' over Willie Horton, even though Dukakis had not been responsible for the Massachusetts rehabilitation-furlough programme, which his predecessor had introduced, and which Dukakis had terminated in the spring of 1988 as a failure. 'The only question is whether we depict Willie Horton with a knife in his hand or without it', Atwater admitted.[48] As Dukakis belatedly did his best to fight back, Atwater worried lest he might have overdone his tactic: 'If this sucker lasted forty-eight hours longer, I'm not sure we would make it.'[49] In the event, however, the 'sucker' failed to beat off Atwater's evisceration. Vice President George H. W. Bush won the White House on November 8, 1988, by a comfortable margin: 426 electoral votes to 112, and thereby became the forty-first President, at age sixty-four.

Part Two: The Presidency

Aware that his father Senator Prescott Bush would turn in his grave had he known of his son's (and grandson's) use of Lee Atwater, the new president began his inaugural speech on January 20, 1989, with a plea to God. 'For we are given power not to advance our own purposes' his prayer for atonement ran, but to 'serve people. Help us to remember it, Lord. Amen.' Bush then declared he would do his best to celebrate the 'quieter successes that are made not of gold and silk, but of better hearts and finer souls'. His purpose was 'to make kinder the face of the nation and gentler the face of the world. My friends, we have work to do', from helping the homeless to assisting pregnant teenagers and the recovering junkies, in a 'thousand points of light'. 'And so,' he ended, 'today a chapter begins, a small and stately story of unity, diversity, and generosity – shared, and written, together.'

Clearly, the speech had not been written by Atwater, who was made chairman of the Republican National Committee. There, with the help of the young right-wing firebrand, Congressman Newt Gingrich, Atwater began another campaign of character assassination, targeting the new Democratic Speaker of Congress, Tom Foley, whom they insinuated was gay. Bush found Atwater's latest attack so 'disgusting' that although he allowed Atwater to keep his job, in deference to his role in his presidential victory, the president made Atwater fire his odious RNC communications director, Mark Goodin. When Gingrich then became Republican Minority Whip in the House of Representatives, however, there was nothing President Bush could do; the political stage was now set for bloodletting on a deeply divisive, partisan scale. It was as if Atwater's newly diagnosed brain cancer was metastasizing in the polity of America, dooming Bush's inaugural vision of America as a 'proud, free nation, decent and civil'.[50]

Bush had pleaded for more civility in politics, but to get elected he had adopted platforms he did not believe in, and made promises he could not keep. Anti-abortionists were outraged he would not appoint a diehard conservative to the Supreme Court to overthrow *Roe* vs *Wade*, while rabid conservatives became apoplectic when, to balance the budget and begin paying down the spiralling national deficit, he agreed to Congress' demand that he abandon his 'no new taxes' pledge. To the chagrin of New Right conservatives, Bush was proving no different from the very man he had destroyed, Governor Dukakis: a centrist. Unlike Dukakis, however, Bush had no vision of what he wanted to achieve in the White House.

Not having won electoral office on his own account in more than twenty years, Bush found himself at sea – a 'free-form presidency' as one political scientist called it, that had little sway over the Democratic-controlled chambers of Congress and even less over the Republican right. The only terrain where the president could make his mark was foreign affairs, and in 1989 and early 1990 the charismatically challenged

American emperor duly applied himself alongside the wildly popular young leader of the Soviet Union, Mikhail Gorbachev.

Gorbachev had wowed the young not only of Europe but also of the Far East. As China emerged from the long nightmare of Mao's Cultural Revolution, Gorbachev travelled to Beijing in May 1989 to celebrate the 'normalization' of relations between the two tottering empires, some ten days after students occupied Tiananmen Square. As he was driven to meet the eighty-four-year-old Chinese leader Deng Xiaoping, past students screaming his name and the word 'perestroika', Gorbachev wondered 'Who the hell is in charge here?'[51] Only when he returned to Moscow did he get his answer. In a ruthless massacre to re-establish Communist 'order' in the capital, 3,000 students were slaughtered and 10,000 wounded.

Observing the massacre from afar, Bush said nothing, wondering whether Tiananmen Square would preface similar crackdowns in the Communist countries of eastern Europe, where Gorbachev's rhetoric had aroused identical student expectations and unrest. It was becoming clear that, although the Cold War was thawing with glasnost, the *Götterdämmerung* would inevitably be contested by reactionaries – and could be bloody.

Lacking Gorbachev's rhetorical ability, President Bush, as leader of the most powerful empire in the world, nevertheless seemed born to the role of elder statesman. His often apolitical past proved now an asset, insulating him from Republican fealty and allowing him, as former US representative to the UN and Communist China, to see America's best interests in global, rather than local, terms. Given his CIA directorship, successive political appointments and lack of elective credentials, he was, ironically, more akin to a typical Russian leader than Mikhail Gorbachev himself. Guardedly, the two men – who had met at the United Nations General Assembly in New York in November 1988 – thus cosied up to one another in the aftermath of Tiananmen Square, with the fate of the world in their hands.

Anxious not to provoke a military coup in Russia that might lead to a new freeze or Cold War, Bush overruled his new Secretary of Defense, Dick Cheney, who counselled a policy of taking advantage of Soviet weakness to assert US global hegemony, and letting Gorbachev fail.[52] Equally, he ignored the 'hotheads', impatient human rights activists calling for more robust American support for pro-democracy movements not only in China but in the East European bloc – which could only give ammunition to Russia's hardliners. In defiance of Margaret Thatcher's howls of protest, he therefore talked openly of armed force reductions in western Europe, and of acceptance of eventual German reunification. In this quest Bush travelled to Amsterdam, Bonn, Paris, London, and then, in July 1989, to Warsaw and Budapest behind the once seemingly impenetrable Iron Curtain. There, he saw for himself the pent-up public aspiration for freedom from the shackles of Communism in everyday life, as half a million people turned out in Kossuth Square to greet him – much like Americans had been fêted at the end of World War II. Joyfully, Bush threw away his speech and basked in the glow of being an American who simply stood for good things, not guided missiles.

The times, Bush now recognized, were changing faster than American militarists, in their bunkers, had anticipated or thought possible. General Colin Powell, Bush's new chairman of the Joint Chiefs of Staff, had been told by Kremlinologists at the CIA in 1988 that Gorbachev could not last and would be rubbed out; instead, Gorbachev had 'fired a dozen or so generals and hardliners' and had defied the odds. As Powell noted later, 'With all their expertise' the Kremlinologists 'could no longer anticipate events much better than a layman watching television.'[53]

Whatever hawks or 'Vulcans' in America warned, President Bush decided to do his best to keep Gorbachev in power by offering serious reductions and compromises in American military strength, both in men and weapons. Second, he would not tempt fate by threatening American intervention in eastern Europe, as the countdown to Russian relaxation of its control over the bloc countries began. And third, by a personal, one-on-one relationship with Gorbachev, he would attempt to talk down the ailing but heavily armed Soviet nuclear airship, pilot to pilot. Grabbing a sheet of White House notepaper on Air Force One while travelling back to the United States, Bush secretly proposed a meeting with Gorbachev, to take place on battleships anchored by the island of Malta, much like Roosevelt and Churchill when drawing up the Atlantic Charter in August 1941, off Newfoundland – 'without thousands of assistants hovering over our shoulders'.

Gorbachev immediately agreed to the summit, which was duly scheduled to take place at the beginning of December 1989. Even that early date was outpaced by events, however. On October 16, 100,000 anti-government protesters marched through Leipzig, but Gorbachev issued an order that not a single one of the 380,000 Russian troops occupying East Germany would be allowed out of their barracks to support a government crackdown. Two days later, with a nod from Gorbachev, the East German dictator Erich Honecker was deposed. On October 23, Hungary – which had got Gorbachev to promise Soviet troops would not invade or intervene in the country's democratization, and had begun permitting East German holidaymakers to cross freely into Austria – declared itself an independent republic with free elections set for the spring of 1990. Two days later, as the *New York Times* reported on October 26, President Mikhail S. Gorbachev 'declared today that the Soviet Union has no moral or political right to interfere in the affairs of its East European neighbors'.[54]

This was, for a Soviet emperor, a most extraordinary public statement. Though he would exclude his remark from his memoirs, Gorbachev had, in truth, given protesters across the Soviet-occupied nations of eastern Europe the green light. In the most sensational month in post-war European history, the unimaginable happened: on November 9, 1989 the Berlin Wall, erected in 1962 to stem the flood of East German refugees to West Berlin and thence to West Germany, was stormed by a crowd of Germans who, hearing from the post-Honecker government that East Germans were free to visit the West, dared the guards to shoot them as they took sledgehammers to the iconic concrete Mauer.[55]

At the White House President Bush found himself agog at the televised coverage – the fruit of his 'hands-off' policy, trusting that Gorbachev would succeed. The Brezhnev Doctrine (namely the Soviet Right to Intervene) was unmistakably over. The next day the Bulgarian leader, Todor Zhivkov, was dismissed by his own Politburo, and on November 24 the entire Politburo of Czechoslovakia resigned. It was clear that no one save elderly, privileged or self-serving functionaries believed in the old Communist system any more, at least in central and eastern Europe.

Like a snowball, Gorbachev's words and, most of all, his refusal to take or support punitive action by the Communist authorities, now accelerated across Europe. Those who mocked Bush for not showing more emotion at the fall of the Berlin Wall were mistaken. In truth he could hardly believe his eyes, and was minded to jump for joy. He was determined, however, not to do, say, or give anything away, even by gesture, that might make Gorbachev's position in the Kremlin less secure – encapsulated in his quiet dictum 'I'm not going to dance on the wall.'[56] He wrote to Gorbachev to assure him the US, under his leadership, wanted a 'calm and peaceful' transition to full democracy in Europe.[57]

Meeting aboard their battleships anchored in Valetta Harbour on December 2, 1989, the two emperors were lashed by sixteen-foot waves in a freak Mediterranean storm. Both men emerged from the Malta summit satisfied, however. Not only did they establish the basis for a real strategic arms reduction agreement the next year (START), but President Bush obtained a Russian promise not to intervene in the Baltic States as the tiny, defenceless countries declared their independence; meanwhile Gorbachev got verbal assurances Russia would obtain a free trade agreement with America and observer status at the next GATT tariff talks, as well as promises of American help in creating a stock market and establishing private investment and property laws.

Most important of all, perhaps, given Russia's history of being invaded first by Napoleon's imperial armies, then by Kaiser Wilhelm's Second Reich, then by Hitler's Third Reich forces, Malta ended forever the understandable Russian fear that it would be attacked again from the west – either by the forces of the United States or by European nations, including Germany. After forty years of Cold War, Gorbachev recognized that as the Soviet Union adjusted to a different ideological model for economic and political life, the presence of US forces as peacekeepers would actually be essential to the Soviet Union for stability in Europe – especially if Russian troops were withdrawn from the bloc countries. In other words, the American Empire, not the Russian Empire, would henceforth be the responsible guarantor of peace in liberated Europe, ensuring that a reunified Germany, in particular, would never threaten Russia again.

'The summit suggested to Gorbachev', wrote Kremlin watchers, 'that Bush was at last emerging from his fear of the American Right.'[58] Whether Gorbachev was entirely correct was, however, debatable. Even as they met in Valetta Harbour, Bush ordered jets to streak over the Philippines and indicate American willingness to intervene if the coup against President Cori Aquino's elected government succeeded, prompting one of Gorbachev's staff to quip that while the Soviets had abandoned the Brezhnev Doctrine, the US had adopted it. More dramatically, three weeks later, US troops invaded Panama in response to an unwise declaration of war by the Panamanian legislature.

Operation Just Cause was the biggest US military assault conducted since World War II. Moreover, it made US history since there was no rationale of anti-Communism or even anti-socialism, the invasion this time being classically imperial: to remove from power a leader in a foreign country deemed inimical to American interests. Gambling on his decades of paid service to the CIA and US Defense Department, Noriega – the self-styled 'chief executive officer' of the Panamanian Republic – had considered himself immune to American intervention as he ordered the murder of any who confronted or competed with him, assassinated one of the main opposition leaders, voided the spring 1989 elections, foiled two coup attempts and controlled the drug trade as an agent of the Medellin cartel. When the Panamanian legislature, under pressure from Noriega, objected to US military exercises staged in the Canal area on December 15, 1989 and declared 'a state of war' with America, war was exactly what they got.

Almost 57,000 American troops were sent into combat immediately after midnight on December 20, 1989, backed by 300 aircraft. Though the Panamanian defence forces could supposedly field 46,000 troops, the result was (in retrospect) inevitable. At a cost of twenty-four fatalities, the US government was able to put Guillermo Endara – the presumed victor in the voided spring election – on the presidential throne. Noriega himself took refuge in the Vatican embassy in Panama City but was eventually hounded out – ironically, by loud American music – and arrested on January 3, 1990 to stand trial in America on drug-trafficking charges.

In a free vote, the United Nations condemned the invasion as an act of rank imperialism, as did most of the civilized world, especially in view of the several thousand innocent civilian casualties incurred. However, it was difficult to claim sympathy for General Noriega himself, or to argue that the country was not better off without him (as proved to be the case). Above all, American troops were withdrawn into the Canal Zone or to the American mainland within weeks. The invasion thus passed into history as a model modern

American military intervention – if creating, as it did so, a worrying precedent. Noriega himself was unmourned. But what if a similar US invasion was to be inspired by more rabid, ideologically driven American militarists in the vein of Barry Goldwater? What if such an invasion proved less surgically swift and efficient, involving higher casualties among innocent civilians? And what if it got bogged down, either in a long conventional war, or, despite initial success, what if it met a consequential insurgency – thus saddling the United States with a classic imperial conquest that required huge expenditures in men and materiel to maintain? At what point, in such a case, should American troops be withdrawn?

Only six months later, these questions would be raised for real, when another military dictator, Saddam Hussein, marshalled his forces by the border between Iraq and tiny Kuwait.[59]

Hussein had invaded Iran in 1980, compelling the Iraqi Army to fight a futile, eight-year war which ended in the loss of an estimated half a million Iranian and Iraqi lives. Now Hussein appeared to be on the warpath once more. Or was he merely grandstanding, in order to wring territorial and oil concessions from defenceless neighbouring Kuwaitis? No one, apart from Hussein himself, seemed quite sure.

Complaining vociferously of Israel's continuing military occupation of the West Bank (seventeen years since the October War and the UN resolution demanding Israeli withdrawal), Hussein was able to garner considerable Arab support for his Middle East sabre-rattling, even though Kuwait had no connection with Israel. Moreover, American intelligence services were deceived, as were the Russians, who had more than 8,000 oil, arms and other personnel in the country. When Hussein's army crossed the Kuwait border on August 2, 1990 – conducting its own version of the invasion of Panama – there was consternation in Washington and Moscow. The head of US Central Command, General Norman Schwarzkopf, had predicted Hussein might possibly seize a Kuwaiti island, but would go no further. When Hussein's forces swept on into Kuwait City, the West was faced with a fait accompli. Or seemingly so.

Panama might have emboldened Saddam Hussein, as an example of *coup de main* warfare, but the lightning success of American forces in Panama had also served to restore the confidence of the Pentagon – and voters. 'In breaking the mindset of the American people about the use of force in the post-Vietnam era,' Bush's Secretary of State, James Baker, later noted, 'Panama established an emotional predicate that permitted us to build the public support so essential for the success of Operation Desert Storm.'[60]

Brilliantly executed six months after Hussein's own territorial strike, Operation Desert Storm would demonstrate the new ability of the American Empire to act effectively not only at its own back door, but also far away in the Middle East, and as the leader, moreover, of a huge Allied force assembled under the aegis of the UN. The reason for its effectiveness as a counterstrike was not just the modernization of American military command, performance and weaponry, but the diminishing ability, even willingness, of the Soviet Union to contest American diplomatic or military decisions. With economic conditions deteriorating within the Soviet Union – the Central Committee was unable even to raise the artificially low price of bread lest there be a popular revolt – Gorbachev's latitude for manoeuvre was becoming daily more restricted as he sought to be seen as an equal partner rather than opponent of American hegemony in the looming post-Cold War world. The result, in the Middle East, was farce, as Gorbachev's Foreign Secretary, Eduard Shevardnadze, attempted to act as the West's negotiator-in-chief with Saddam Hussein and avert a world war. Since Hussein was mad and Russia not only near to bankruptcy but power-less to protect its thousands of advisers and engineers in Iraq – who could be held hostage by Hussein – the Soviets merely resembled amateurs on the new global democratic stage.

Astute participants and observers were aware that not only the fate of oil ownership and production in the Middle East but also the future of the world order now hung in the balance. A prime participant was General Colin Powell, who had been Reagan's national security adviser and was now Bush's chairman of the Joint Chiefs of Staff.

As a Vietnam veteran, General Powell would become famous for the Powell Doctrine, based on Field Marshal Montgomery's campaign doctrine in World War II: soldiers should never be committed to combat unless their objectives were established in clear terms, and sufficient forces were assembled and applied not only to start, but also to finish the job. There was, however, a less well-known part of the Powell Doctrine: asking whether military intervention was, in all honesty, the best policy to achieve political and economic ends. When

Powell asked President Bush and the cabinet whether it was worth going to war to liberate Kuwait, rather than moving troops to protect Saudi Arabia and applying sanctions and the threat of war to Hussein, 'I detected a chill in the room' he recalled.[61]

It was clear that Bush, after initially maintaining his composure with reporters asking whether the US would respond militarily ('I am not discussing intervention . . . I'm not contemplating such action'), was angling for another war. After the meeting, the Secretary of Defense, Dick Cheney, took Powell aside. 'Colin, he said, you're chairman of the Joint Chiefs. You're not Secretary of State. You're not the national security adviser anymore. And you're not Secretary of Defense. *So stick to military matters.*'[62]

Chastened, Powell was even more stunned when he learned that Cheney had taken directly to President Bush a wacky, secret plan to seize Baghdad from the desert rear, without consulting with Powell as head of the combined US military. Clearly, as an alleged Vietnam draft dodger (five deferments, without completing his further degree), Cheney had no conception of military command or logistics and was worryingly myopic.

Though gagged by Cheney over the expediency of military action, Powell afterwards recalled asking himself how far – even if he did go ahead and order military action – Bush would want to take the American counterstrike, given Cheney's secret machinations. 'Do we want to go beyond Kuwait to Baghdad? Do we try to force Saddam out of power? How weakened do we want to leave Iraq?' And if Hussein was removed, 'Do we necessarily benefit from a Gulf oil region dominated by an unfriendly Syria and a hostile Iran?'[63]

These were crucial questions in relation to the impending post-Cold War world order. The direct use of American military power in a combat role for the first time in the history of the Middle East – rather than the threat of force – raised huge questions for the future stability of the world's most volatile region. Would the United States then be seen by Muslim countries as the bullying protector not only of its puppet oil state, Saudi Arabia, but of Israel, which had still not complied with UN resolutions for it to withdraw from the territories it had seized in the October War? Was such an outcome beneficial for long-term American interests? Would war simply beget further war down the road?

Mikhail Gorbachev vainly attempted to act in concert with George

Bush, warning Saddam Hussein to negotiate a withdrawal of Iraqi forces and appealing for an Israeli–Palestinian peace conference to tackle the primary problem in the Middle East. The Soviet leader was ignored by the mad dictator in Baghdad, however, while his attempt to turn the Iraqi malfeasance into a Soviet–US triumph of concerted diplomacy fell foul of lobbyists for Israel in Washington. Bush later said that 'There will be, and is, no linkage to the West Bank question',[64] and rejected Gorbachev's plea at the Helsinki talks in September 1990 for an 'international conference' on a solution to the Israeli–Palestinian problem.[65]

With 200,000 US troops dispatched to Saudi Arabia, as well as warships and a huge air force capability, plus UN pressure building on him to withdraw from Kuwait, Saddam Hussein had nowhere to go save to reverse engines. Had Hussein been rational, the Israelis less intransigent, and had the Soviet Union not been in freefall, the Kuwait debacle might well have led to an improvement in the Middle East situation rather than war. But Saddam Hussein was not rational, and with the Baltic States increasingly restless, the two Germanies uniting as the Federal Republic of Germany on October 3, 1990, as well as rising unemployment and inflation across the Soviet Union and fifty million Soviet Muslims who would 'rise up in fury against the Kremlin' if Gorbachev assigned Russian troops to the impending Desert Storm Coalition counterstrike, there was no ideal outcome.

In conversation with Brent Scowcroft, his national security adviser, Bush had reflected on the way the crisis in the Gulf had encouraged him to see both the UN and the Soviet Union in a new way – a chance for 'real cooperation' between the US and the USSR in enforcing peace and stability in the world, with the backing of the UN. But with Hussein first refusing Gorbachev's effort in February 1991 to negotiate an Iraqi withdrawal except on a six-week timetable, with numerous caveats and linkage to an international conference to address the Israeli–Palestinian problem, then spinning out the endgame to the point where no one believed Hussein's word any longer, Bush felt that for good or ill, egged on by Cheney, he had no option but to issue the order to begin military action.

In his memoirs, Gorbachev metaphorically shook his head at Hussein's tactics. In Moscow, Hussein's foreign minister Tariq Aziz declared he was 'not afraid of confrontation with the Americans', despite knowing full well 'that confrontation could lead to a wide-scale conflict, the consequences of which would affect not only the Arab region but the entire world. That prospect does not frighten us, though.' Gorbachev was appalled. 'The Iraqi leaders were "not frightened" by the possibility of global catastrophe! Such were the kind of people with whom the world community had to deal' he commented sadly.[66]

Following the Hussein–Aziz version of Russian roulette, and the US decision to launch Operation Desert Storm on February 24, 1991, Gorbachev saw his reputation as a world statesman shattered. His political survival was as threatened, in fact, as Hussein's. Hussein surrendered only four days later, as Coalition Forces numbering 540,000 made mincemeat of his men in Kuwait. Hussein now agreed not only to the immediate unconditional withdrawal of all his troops but to all UN conditions, prompting President Bush to halt the Allied counteroffensive, and agree a ceasefire.

With its Coalition allies, the US had won the swiftest major war in modern history (one hundred hours of ground combat). America had demonstrated not only its renewed military prowess, moreover, but also the sagacity of its emperor, who wisely refused to countenance the recommendations of those members of his administration who wanted him to ignore the UN resolutions and send his troops on to Baghdad. If Saddam Hussein was to fall, Bush reasoned, the dictator should fall as the result of Iraqi discontent, not American interference – which could only inflame anti-American feelings in the Arab world.

Instead, of course, it was Gorbachev who fell, later that year.

Was it illness, in the meantime, that assailed President Bush at the seeming height of his presidency, and affected his mind? No other Caesar save President Johnson had suffered a crisis of nerve at the very point of acclamation, as when he baulked at running for nomination in the summer of 1964, just as his great civil rights bill passed Congress. Now, in the spring of 1991, with his Gallup polls running at an extraordinary 87 per cent public approval and a ticker-tape parade slated for June in New York, similar to that of General Eisenhower after World War II, Bush felt the very ground beneath him slipping away.

Bush's father had suffered a similar affliction in 1962, when in exhaustion and depression at age sixty-seven he had decided not to run for re-election as senator for Connecticut – a decision he had afterwards regretted.[67] George Bush was now the same age, and in his diary he confessed he not only felt depressed after his historic victory in Kuwait, but also little if any interest in running for re-election as president the following year.

Bush vainly attempted to quieten his anxiety in patriotic gore, revelling in the victory tributes, American 'flags, patriotism . . . music' and 'praying' – but he was continually haunted by something else: the imminent death of his Mephistopheles, Lee Atwater, and the price he himself would have to pay for his Faustian bargain in 1988: vengeance by Democrats for his egregious vaporization of Governor Dukakis. 'I feel the build-up now on the domestic side' the president noted in his diary. 'When will Bush stumble; what about the domestic agenda; can he handle it? . . . I don't know whether it's the anticlimax or that I'm too tired to enjoy anything, but I just seem to be losing my perspective.'[68] Maybe, he pondered, he should step down. 'I don't seem to have the drive,' he confided to his journal, sickened at the thought of 'the political stuff' he'd have to face if he ran: not only fund-raising, but also campaigning on behalf of a Republican Party that had no respect for statesmanship, and seemed hell-bent on neoconservative Goldwaterland.[69]

Bush's vice president, Dan Quayle, was busy spreading mischief, complaining that American forces should have invaded Iraq – 'a new right-wing theme', Bush noted – while deploring the National Rifle Association's lobbying against the Senate bill in Congress to restrict automatic weapons in America. Even in international affairs the right wing was rampant, saying that the president and his Secretary of State, James Baker, were being too soft on Gorbachev and should unilaterally recognize Lithuania's independence. ('Fuck you!' Baker had snarled at the Secretary of Housing, Jack Kemp, who was attempting to interfere in Baker's patient diplomacy.[70]) Meanwhile Israel's government, under Yitzhak Shamir, had proven as myopic and intransigent as ever.

'Israel rolled us', Bush lamented in his diary in March 1991, as disappointed as presidents Carter and Reagan had been. 'They are very, very difficult.' Despite the fact that the US had 'kicked Saddam Hussein and solved their problem in the area', they were demanding more weaponry but refusing to offer 'land for peace' and delaying the international peace conference that Gorbachev had vainly pleaded to tie to Desert Storm, insisting instead on expanding their illegal West Bank settlements which could only make eventual reconciliation with the Palestinians impossible.[71] 'They are never going to get peace in the Middle East without solving the Palestinian question' Bush wrote. 'I know it; they know it; the Arabs know it; the French and Europeans know it; and we're standing alone against reason a lot of times' in supporting Israel. He even swore he would do what 'no president has done since Ike': forgo Jewish support for his election campaign, preferring to 'stand up for what is fair and right'.[72] But would he even stand?

'Sometimes I really like the spotlight,' Bush confided, 'but I'm tired of it. I've been at the head table for many years, and now I wonder what else is out there.' He felt dead tired, and acknowledged he didn't 'really care' any more for politics. He'd lost fifteen pounds, and even his handwriting, his doctor noted, had altered. Could the Republicans not get someone else to lead them, he wondered – someone better equipped for the 'rough and tumble', moreover someone 'who likes it better'.[73]

The chief of staff, John Sununu, was instructed to keep the majority of problems away from the president's desk, while Bush made the fateful decision not to begin his campaign for re-election until the following year, relying on his credentials as a victorious war president. With unemployment exceeding 8.5 per cent, and interest rates so high that house mortgages were unobtainable save for the rich, this was potentially fatal to his chances for re-election – if, indeed, he decided to run. 'I haven't made up my mind' he told his eldest son George Jr, who in turn told the deputy chief of staff 'there is a good chance that he won't' – a concern they must keep quiet about, since 'if we told anybody else that, we were dead meat'.[74]

Graves' disease was diagnosed after an attack of arrhythmia, but even after treatment the president did not appear to recover his former elan. As the ticker tape drifted away in the summer of 1991, Bush seemed uncharacteristically distant, listless and unwilling to make decisions. He was going to bed in August at the family dacha at Kennebunkport, Maine, bracing for Hurricane Bob to hit the New England coast, when he was told there was another storm coming: CNN was reporting a putsch at Gorbachev's dacha on the Black Sea, claiming he had been overthrown and replaced by his deputy, Gennadi Yanayev, in what became known as 'the putsch of fools'. Bush, who had been warned in June this might happen, had personally warned Gorbachev of the danger during his own trip to London, Moscow and Ukraine.

Upset and anxious, the president hastened back to Washington. He had wisely, if cold-heartedly, left Saddam Hussein in power in Iraq, lest the United States be encumbered with the burden of imperial responsibility for the country, with its myriad internal ethnic and religious problems dividing Shiites, Sunnis and Kurds. A complete collapse of the Soviet Union, however, posed far greater problems, given the vast nuclear arsenals and the economic black hole facing a moribund Communist system, as well as the pent-up aspirations for independence among the Soviet republics.

In March 1990, Mikhail Gorbachev had got himself retitled 'president' by the new Congress of People's Deputies, for a term of five years – but president of what? For his part, Bush hoped the USSR could cast off its Communist past and yet be preserved as a political, governing structure, in the interests of stability in eastern Europe – but such divestiture was never going to be easy. This was not, after all, a case like Europe after the fall of Napoleon's empire, or after World War I, or even the Allies winding up World War II and establishing the United Nations in the hope once again of arbitrated peace in the world: masking the desperate arms race between the two ideologically driven superpowers that emerged from the ruins of a global anti-fascist struggle. Now was different. The only other competing major world empire to that of the US was spinning increasingly out of control and towards its possible doom, leaving the American Empire the world's sole superpower, but without a clear doctrine espoused by its president, beyond pragmatism.

The news of the Russian putsch, if it was true, raised an uncomfortable new challenge for the American leader. A review of US policy towards the USSR which he had commissioned immediately after his inauguration had been disappointing – 'mush', as Secretary of State Baker had called it. Trusting his instincts Bush had decided to back Gorbachev with rhetoric, summits and diplomatic respect, but no money or real partnership over Iraq and the future of the Middle East. Now that Gorbachev was seemingly gone, what would happen in Russia, and what should be the agenda and role of the United States? The right-wing Secretary of Defense, Dick Cheney, had long proposed

American rearmament in anticipation of Soviet right-wingers seizing control from Gorbachev. Bush had overruled Cheney, in the hope that Gorbachev would succeed in reforming the Soviet economy and downsizing its military. But if the military was now in the ascendant, should Bush therefore recognize the Soviet coup, and face up to Cheney's vision of a resurgent Soviet 'iron first', with all its nuclear implications for America and the world?

Bush's dilatory state of mind, whether the result of his illness or his fear of having to campaign again, now ironically came to his rescue. At his dacha, Gorbachev had refused to sign the transfer of power to his vice president, which the cabal of plotters presented to him. They thus flew off empty-handed, and into the dustbin of history. In Moscow the new populist president of the Russian Republic, Boris Yeltsin, was more than a match for them – but his victory, though welcomed with relief by President Bush several days later, raised new worries for the stability of the world. Yeltsin was only interested in Russia, not the Union.

More than 70 per cent of Soviet citizens had voted in a referendum in the spring for keeping the USSR as an overarching federal system of government, similar to the federal system of the United States; indeed Boris Yeltsin had put his signature to the continuation of the Soviet Union as a supranational body. But the putsch exposed Gorbachev's helplessness and lack of electoral support. By the time Gorbachev was freed at his dacha and returned to Moscow, his star had fallen. He had already resigned from the Communist Party (which was soon banned as a party of putschist traitors). This left Gorbachev as an emperor without clothes: an appointed but unelected president of the Soviet Union, his standing fatally diminished by the putsch, and Yeltsin's heroism. Though Gorbachev subsequently attempted to act as President Bush's equal in Madrid at the belated Middle East peace conference in October 1991, it was a charade. The USSR, born like the United States out of revolution and civil war, was, unlike the USA, dissolving.

The Soviet military had stayed out of the struggle between Yeltsin and the plotters in August. With Yeltsin's emergence as the big man on the Russian campus, the military threw in their lot with him when he proposed a Commonwealth of Independent States, not a Soviet Union. It would mean the end of Mikhail Gorbachev's history-making.

On Christmas Day 1991, as the Bush family opened their presents at Camp David, protected by the secret service, a call came through to President Bush from the Kremlin. Gorbachev had already announced that the USSR would cease to exist the next day. Meanwhile, Gorbachev told Bush on the telephone, he was resigning his meaningless presidency to become a private citizen.

For George Bush it was an extraordinary moment, at the end of more than four decades of Cold War. A couple of hours later Gorbachev went on television in Moscow to tell the people of a now moribund empire the truth. He refused to be blamed for the collapse of the Soviet Union, or the economic and political chaos of the past several years. 'All the half-hearted reforms – and there were a lot of them – fell through, one after another. This country was going nowhere, and we couldn't possibly live the way we had been living. We had to change everything' – but 'dismembering this country and breaking up the state' was not what he'd had in mind.[75] He was distraught.

On the telephone at Camp David, President Bush had been compassionate and dignified. Speaking later the same night on television from the Oval Office, he again decided not to rub salt in Gorbachev's wound, announcing merely that the historic 'confrontation' with Communism 'is over'. Several weeks later, however, as the New Year began, he dropped diplomatic niceties. He would be facing re-election in November, if he won the Republican nomination. America, he therefore announced to Congress and many millions of voters watching on television, had 'won the Cold War'. Gorbachev shuddered but could say nothing, for it was true.

In three years, Bush had thus won three wars – two by the application of surgical force, the third by patience and cautious diplomacy, overriding the hawks in his administration. He had every reason to feel proud, despite his sense of psychic exhaustion.

Had the president now announced he would stand down at the end of his successful first term and join Gorbachev in retirement, he might have gone down in history as one of the most effective transitional presidents of modern times, inaugurating a new era.

The gene that makes people want to win the presidency, however, does not make it easy for them to relinquish the office, once attained. Haunted by the memory of Atwater's evil but effective tactics in his last campaign and its consequences, Bush had held off making a final decision, but in the end, he felt, it had to be done – and on February 12, 1992, he formally announced his candidacy for re-election.

Twelve months previously, Bush's approval rating had hit an astonishing 84 per cent in opinion polls, prompting George Jr to boastfully predict victory at the next election: 'Do you think the American people are going to turn to a Democrat now?'[76] The ancient Greeks had always mistrusted hubris, however – and with reason. Bush's stratospheric numbers had tumbled, cascading into a worrying slide, and by February 1992 he was down to an ominous 42 per cent in polls – a number that did not guarantee re-election. The very man who, with Atwater's help, had stopped America from electing an effective modern, managerial governor in 1988 was now seen, ironically, to be a disappointingly incompetent manager of the economy, prompting millions of people, especially the unemployed, to look for a possible national saviour, either in the young, five-times elected Democratic governor of Arkansas, Bill Clinton, or a paranoid but successful independent, billionaire businessman Ross Perot.[77]

'Our whole political problem is the recession,' warned one of Bush's aides only a month after the president's announcement of his candidacy. 'We face a twenty-month recession, a 78 per cent [on the] "wrong track" [poll] number, and likely a southern conservative Democrat [Clinton]. The situation is about as bad as it could be.'[78]

Like Mikhail Gorbachev, then, President Bush was faced by menacing failure not as a statesman, since he had proved himself a master steward of America's interests on a global stage, but by his inability to master the domestic challenges that faced him. Lacking a clear vision of what he wanted to achieve at home, as well as the rhetoric to back such a vision, he was seen more and more as a 'flip-flopper' – too much like a Democrat by right-wing conservative Republicans, too conservative by Democrats – and by all as too willing to respond to lobbying pressure rather than his own convictions, whatever they might be.

A 1988-style personal-attack campaign might just have saved the president. However, Lee Atwater had died of a brain tumour and Roger Ailes, Atwater's chief accomplice, had resigned long ago. With all too little fund-raising done, the president now found himself bereft, with no political weaponry, or strategy, or even driving desire. The result was visible when Pat Buchanan, a right-wing Republican journalist and former speechwriter for Richard Nixon, almost toppled him in the New Hampshire primary.

Winning the Republican nomination but lagging in the polls that summer, Bush's fortunes seemed briefly to rise when Ross Perot, having left the race once, re-entered it, and threatened as an independent to split the vote of the Democratic nominee, Governor Bill Clinton. But in the all-important presidential debates, Perot was dismissed as a weirdo, President Bush appeared out of touch with ordinary Americans' lives, and it was Governor Clinton of Arkansas who came across as a centrist, southern politician with an IQ off the charts, yet full of optimism, compassion, energy, goodwill and good domestic ideas – especially in dealing with the recession.

A last-minute attempt to use Atwaterian tactics – raiding Clinton's passport files at the State Department, labelling him and his running mate, Senator Al Gore, as covert Marxists and 'Those Bozos' – failed to destroy the Democratic challenge. Bush lost the election in November, 38 per cent to Clinton's 43 per cent, with Ross Perot winning 19 per cent as an independent.[79] Bill Clinton, not George Bush, would be the forty-second US president.

Bush was as devastated as President Carter had been to lose after a single term. Though he went on to sign the North American Free Trade Agreement which he and James Baker had negotiated in December 1992 with Canada and Mexico – his final example of statesmanship – and though he sent troops to Somalia to ensure humanitarian aid to the starving population, he seemed a broken man. His mother had died shortly after his defeat.

At Camp David he confided to Colin Powell, who had come up with his wife to commiserate: 'Colin, it hurts. It really hurts.'[80] Referring to the president-elect, he wailed: 'I just never thought they'd elect him.'[81]

Part Three: Private Life

JFK once said his mother, Rose Fitzgerald Kennedy, was the 'glue that held the family together'. In the Bush family, Dorothy Walker Bush performed the same role: another tiny American matriarch, whose longevity and moral expectations profoundly influenced her son, as in so many cases of the American Caesars. It was not that their sons necessarily met their exacting standards of honesty, courage or behaviour. For good or ill, however, their sons were moulded in that crucible, answering – and at times denying or subverting – the powerful maternal aspirations held up for them.

At age sixteen Barbara Pierce, a beautiful girl with brownish-red hair, met the seventeen-year-old George H. W. Bush at a Christmas dance while he was still a schoolboy at Andover Academy. They became secretly engaged, and in 1943 publicly so, when the USS *San Jacinto* was commissioned at Philadelphia and an expensive diamond ring was held up in evidence before the family. Barbara played tennis and 'could talk to absolutely anybody', Dorothy Walker Bush pronounced, giving her blessing. 'The Bush family liked my mom from the start' their daughter Doro later wrote in her family memoir.[82] She fitted right in to a family of do-ers, with little time or inclination for books, history or music. As Doro Bush related, her father couldn't 'play the piano or carry a tune', indeed suffered what he himself called a 'genetic power outage' in relation to music – an outage that extended to the public-speaking gene, too, which made electoral politics ever tougher, especially in the age of the twenty-four-hour media news cycle.[83]

Failing twice to win election to the Senate, and warned he had no chance of winning office as Texas governor, Bush's path to the White House thus followed a different course from his nine predecessors in its non-electoral course – a path based upon networking, fund-raising and the series of political appointments and job offers he secured. His ascent was not, however, without arduous personal demands, in patience, loyalty and in fortitude. The death of his daughter Robin from leukaemia almost destroyed his marriage; Barbara's beautiful brown-red hair, at age twenty-eight, turned white overnight, and she refused to colour it, lest it signify she was forgetting little Robin's tragic fate. In grief she 'kind of smothered' her eldest boy, George Jr.[84]

More children (Neil, Marvin, Doro) helped, as did a growing sense of family destiny: that of Senator Prescott Bush's four sons it would be the second son, not George's elder brother Bucky or younger brothers Johnny or Pres, who had been singled out by God to be the anointed Bush family standard-bearer: the war hero and self-made oil millionaire who would continue the family's prominence, and hopefully raise it still further.

That high expectation had its downside, however; friends became anxious when George took on a new secretary at the Republican National Committee, and then asked her to come to China as his personal assistant in 1974.

For years, even after he was forced by James Baker to sideline her, Bush would be tormented by rumours that he and Jennifer Fitzgerald, the English-born divorcée and martinet who ruled his office schedule as executive assistant with a rod of iron, had a romantic relationship – much as speculation never ceased over Eisenhower's relationship with his English driver and office assistant, Kay Summersby. Bush travelled everywhere with Jennifer, but as with Eisenhower there was no real danger he would end his marriage to wed her, if only because such a decision, made in a moment of madness or passion, would have ended his presidential ambitions, and his family's hopes for him. Besides, he had no wish to divorce Barbara.

Bush, who had been genuinely infatuated with Barbara when a young man – even painting her name on his warplane – continued to love 'Bar' loyally as the mother of his five surviving children. Barbara, however, left Beijing to spend Thanksgiving and then Christmas with her children back home, thus leaving George to his own devices: and to Jennifer Fitzgerald. George's mother Dorothy came out on a special mission to China, there to guard the chicken coop. 'Mother arrives tomorrow' Bush wrote in his diary. 'I have that kind of high school excitement – first vacation feeling.'[85] Alarmed by what she found, Dorothy warned Barbara to start dying her hair, the better to compete with Jennifer.

Whether this would have helped is doubtful. As one congressman's wife noted, 'George and Barbara married young and had those kids when the hormones were working well.' Gradually Barbara had turned into a devoted-mother figure, indeed many people initially thought she *was* George's mother, so debonair did he seem, so dowdy did she. 'He came into the Green Room', noted a CBS television staffer, 'with a gray-haired woman who I thought was his mother. Someone told me she was his wife, and I became fascinated by their dynamic because they were not a matched pair . . . He engaged women immediately. He's not a lecher, but he makes eye contact with sexual energy. He's polite and does not behave improperly – he's no Bill Clinton – but the sexual message is there. She [Barbara] is oblivious to it all. She's supremely confident and in charge of him like a mother who totally wears the pants . . . and it's also clear that he relies on her.'[86] Another congressman's wife, who visited Bush in China, noted that Barbara 'adored George. Pure love . . . I think she saw that her biggest strength was to imitate his mother, almost become his mother.' And in terms of her hair and her clothes, 'Barbara let herself look the way she did on purpose. If George had wanted her to look any other way, she would have' – and whatever disappointment there might have been, romantically, 'with Barbara her kids made up for everything'.[87]

Short, blonde, loyal, available when he needed her and in love with George, the forty-two-year-old Jennifer Fitzgerald, by contrast, suited the chameleon in Bush in a different way. He took her with him on travels, and to the CIA when he became head spy. Even after he quit the CIA, he got her a job as special assistant to the US ambassador to Britain, Kingman Brewster, and continued to see her. Though Brewster was irritated by her 'frequent absences' flying back to the US 'to see George', there was little the ambassador could do. 'Their relationship was no secret to the embassy staff', Ambassador Brewster's biographer claimed, though without offering proof. 'Everyone knew that she was George's mistress.'[88]

True or not, Barbara had only herself to blame. She had, after all, made her own marital bed: not only imbibing, but herself enforcing the Bush family imperative that, if accepted into the family, wives of the Bushes must stay at home, raise children and not compete with their husbands. 'I went through sort of a difficult time' Barbara later admitted, when her children became adults and she suffered midlife depression; 'suddenly women's lib had made me feel that my life had been wasted . . . But I got over it, thank heavens.'[89] She watched over her children's lives and marriage choices, attempting vainly to stop her son Jeb from marrying a Mexican teenager, and watching stonily as her husband thrived on Jennifer Fitzgerald's undistracted feminine adulation at his office.[90] Anxious lest the relationship cause a scandal, James Baker insisted Fitzgerald be removed from the abortive 1980 campaign for the presidency. Bush consented, but paid out of his own pocket for her to work for him privately in New York.

When Bush became vice president to Ronald Reagan, Barbara Bush got the vice president's imposing huge white official mansion on Massachusetts Avenue, and a distinguished interior designer (Mark Hampton) to upgrade its decor. But at his office Bush got Jennifer back – in a mink coat. When Bush's top aide, Rich Bond, objected, Bush fired Bond, not Fitzgerald. 'Jim Baker made me make that choice once before,' he told Bond, 'and I made the wrong choice.'[91]

The press ignored the relationship, as did the Bush family. Bush's sister Nancy remarked: 'Dumpy little Jennifer! She's like the most reliable, good person you know. We've all known her forever. She just absolutely adores George.'[92] 'She became in essence his other wife,' another intimate reflected, 'his office wife.'[93] There was 'no denying the connection between them' one staffer commented. 'Jennifer was a doter. She made George feel that he was God's gift to mankind. She'd bat her eyes and gush all over him. She'd poof her hair, put on lipstick, and spray perfume every time she walked into his office in her high stiletto heels. She was a courtesan, but not that gifted', the assistant sniffed, deriding Fitzgerald's middle age and lack of fashionable style. 'Still, she was a treat from Bar[bara], who is no gusher. Bar would just as soon say, "George, cut the crap," as "Open the door." Jennifer was an ego trip for him.'[94]

Fitzgerald's quasi-courtship flattered the 'femme' in Bush, a perceptive female friend also reflected. The person who seemed to object the most, ironically, was the First Lady, Nancy Davis Reagan, who hated both Bushes for their Yankee rather than Californian manners, but derided Barbara Bush especially for her size sixteen, overweight figure, and her complete lack of dress sense. By contrast, Nancy – a fashion devotee, reminiscent of Mrs Simpson, the Duchess of Windsor – wore a size four dress, spent a fortune on designer clothes, and was suspicious to the point of paranoia of other women, as well as men who might compete with her 'Ronnie' for the limelight. To Nancy, George was a 'wimp' and a 'Whiner'. She positively revelled in the incident of 'George and his girlfriend' – the widow of a former congressman – when the car Bush was driving in was involved in an accident, and the secret service had to be called in to airbrush the episode.[95] 'I always knew Nancy didn't like me very much,' Bush later noted in his diary, when president, 'but there is nothing much we can do about all that.'[96]

Not even Nancy Reagan, however, had dared leak the supposed secrets of George Bush's love life, which could damage the public image of the White House. Moreover, the serious press still abided by an unwritten rule over scandal-mongering, until in 1987, handsome senator and Democratic contender Gary Hart dared the press to report his dalliance with Donna Rice – and paid the price.

The consequences for Vice President George Bush and all who wished to run for public office in the republic, after Hart, were dire. Republican candidates especially were now expected to pass muster not only on political issues, such as their anti-abortion stance or anti-tax and anti-government posture, but in terms of squeaky-clean family conduct, a demand that also drew enthusiastic support from feminists sick of patriarchal behaviour. Donna Brazile, a senior aide to Governor Dukakis, thus challenged Bush in the 1988 campaign with the words 'The American people have every right to know,' in view of the rumours about Jennifer Fitzgerald, 'if Barbara Bush will share that bed with him in the White House.'

To his lasting credit, Governor Dukakis promptly fired Ms Brazile, never wavering in the correctness of his decision in later years. 'To hell with all that' he told Bush's daughter Doro. 'When you decide you're going to go into this business, you've got to decide who you are, what standards you're going to set for yourself and the people around you. If folks get out of line, you can't accept that.'[97]

To his lasting discredit Bush did not return the favour. By pioneering the use of personal and racial smear strategy by Lee Atwater to destroy Dukakis over Willie Horton, Bush reversed his losing campaign and won the post he had craved during the preceding eight years, failing thereby to live up to the moral precepts his father had lived and died by. His daughter later blamed the press: 'one more example of how people who run for office become public property, and how some people in the media will stop at nothing to bring them down', she excoriated the Fitzgerald stories. But in truth it was her own, beloved father – like Julie Nixon's father – who had made his pact with the Devil, in the form of Lee Atwater and his squad of character-assassins.

Four years later George Herbert Walker Bush lost the office he had spent a lifetime pursuing, and the Bush family, saddened by the death of Dorothy Walker Bush ('Ganny'), went into double mourning. Retiring to Texas on January 20, 1993, the forty-first President had only himself to blame for his failure to be re-elected, yet blamed the media instead. He was determined neither to write his memoirs nor to say anything in public, lest he give vent to his bitterness. He was resolved, as he put it, to 'stay out of Dodge'. 'He stayed out of Dodge', the journalist Bob Woodward subsequently noted, but in retirement 'he never seemed to reach a state of peace, relaxation or happiness' as Reagan did.[98]

More significantly, however, was the effect that Bush's unhappy retirement had on his sons. He had brought them up to tell the truth, yet he allowed his resentment to overshadow the positive aspects of his legacy – the peaceful collapse of the Soviet Union, and the liberation of Kuwait – as well as failing to express remorse for the campaign tactics he'd employed to destroy Governor Dukakis in 1988. His legacy to his sons became not pride and honesty, but a haunting sense of unfair failure: a failure for which his sons could and should, if they were truly loyal – like the Kennedys when making up for their father Joe Kennedy's fiasco as ambassador to Britain – make amends. Thus would arise one of the greatest ironies in the history of the American Caesars: that the man who had guided his empire's fortunes with great responsibility and flexibility in a transitional world, would, with his wife Barbara, live to see his own son do the opposite.

CHAPTER ELEVEN

BILL CLINTON

Democrat
42nd President
(January 20, 1993–January 20, 2001)

Part One: The Road to the White House

Bill Clinton was born a Baptist, in Hope, Arkansas, on August 19, 1946, not as a Clinton, but as William Jefferson Blythe IV. His supposed father, Bill Blythe III, was a bigamous salesman who died in an automobile accident before his son's birth.

Bill Clinton's mother, Virginia, was the only daughter of a Hope ice deliverer and storekeeper with no education, and his wife, an auxiliary nurse. While his widowed mother went away for two years to New Orleans to train as a nurse-anaesthetist, little Billy Blythe IV was looked after by his grandparents in Hope.

Who Billy Blythe IV's real father was would never be known, but the boy's astonishing intelligence revealed itself once his widowed mother remarried and moved along with her flamboyant, reckless second husband, Roger Clinton – a divorced car dealer – and her little son to Hot Springs: the 'dunghill' of Arkansas, as one local ideologue called it.

In 1959, when Billy was twelve, Virginia filed for divorce, but withdrew the application. A witness to continuing domestic, male-dominated family violence, Billy finally grew tall enough to challenge his drunken stepfather to stop beating his mother – and won, temporarily, when Roger Clinton was again hauled off to spend the night in a police cell. The drunkenness, threats and beatings did not, however, cease, and Virginia finally re-filed for divorce in 1962, this time definitively.

Delighted, Billy changed his family name from Blythe to Bill Clinton, at age fifteen. Throwing himself into his schoolwork, he grew to be exceptionally tall (6' 3"). He excelled at the saxophone, maths, English and general studies – and was mortified when his mother, in a fit of compassion, remarried Roger Clinton.

Virginia's remarriage proved a mistake, Roger Clinton remaining an abusive drunk, and their son Roger Clinton Jr becoming a wastrel like his father, eventually landing in jail for drug dealing and addiction.

Bill Clinton was of a different calibre, however, blessed with a phenomenal intelligence, photographic memory, deep compassion – and a determination, after meeting President Kennedy as a high-school senior on a visit to Washington in the summer of 1963, to see the world and make a difference. He applied for a place at Georgetown University's School of Foreign Service, a predominantly Catholic academy in the capital, set up in the 1930s to educate would-be diplomats and political scientists, and was accepted.

Working as a university student intern in the DC office of Democratic Senator William Fulbright, chairman of the Senate Foreign Relations Committee during the first years of the Vietnam War, Clinton became, like his mentor, an increasingly bitter opponent of the conflict and was personally reluctant to fight there, if drafted. Awarded a Rhodes Scholarship to Oxford, he continued his postgraduate studies and took part in peace protests in London. Finally, however, after what amounted to a mental breakdown, he changed his mind. All presidents since Harry Truman had served in the military. Abandoning further possible deferments or the National Guard service he had been offered, Clinton formally re-registered for the draft, come what might.

Clinton proved – as he'd secretly hoped – lucky, his number, in 1969, too low to be called-up (311th out of 365). Freed of that obligation he was thus eligible to apply to Yale, attending in the autumn of 1970.

Returning to Arkansas as a law professor in 1973, after being awarded a top-grade law degree at Yale, Clinton exhibited both brilliance as a teacher and a precocious ambition to represent the district in Congress as a Democrat.

After indefatigable personal campaigning, during which the twenty-eight-year-old attempted to shake the hand of every living constituent, Clinton failed to unseat the incumbent Republican congressman – shy of only 3,000 votes he was certain had been purloined. Disappointed but unbowed by his defeat, he then married his loyal girlfriend from Yale Law School, Hillary Rodham, and in 1976 ran for state Attorney General, a post he won without difficulty, aged only thirty. Two years later, when the popular governor ran for the Senate, Clinton took aim at the vacant governor's mansion and won, becoming the youngest governor in America.

Two further years later, however, after a rocky first term characterized by indiscipline, competing objectives and no chief of staff, Clinton became the youngest ex-governor. He was, in the words of his best friend, 'really very upset, in tears', unable to admit to himself what he'd done wrong.[1]

This failure to admit to personal error would prove a serious defect in an otherwise extraordinarily talented young politician. His friend begged him to enlarge his resumé by earning a living in another field, for a time. 'You need to go out and make some money!' he advised. 'You know, do something out in the real economic world.'[2] Clinton, however, was obsessed with politics, and had no interest in learning a new trade or earning money, leaving that to his wife, who had joined the prestigious Rose Law Firm in Little Rock. 'He looked me straight in the eyes,' his friend recalled, 'and he said, "There's nothing else I want to do." I thought, man! You're a sick butt!'[3]

Sick butt or not, Clinton was serious. He unashamedly invited a Republican strategist from New York, Dick Morris, to work for his campaign, and appointed a new chief of staff, Betsey Wright, to run his team, winning back the governor's mansion in 1982 and again in 1984.

In 1987, the now four-times governor of Arkansas, still aged only forty-one, gave serious thought to running for the presidency. President Reagan remained immensely popular, but the core Republican Party was moving further and further to the right, leaving the centre unmanned. Clinton's wife urged him to try, if only to achieve national name recognition, but Betsey Wright, who knew the skeletons in the governor's cupboard, confronted him with their names. 'What Bill thought he was getting away with for a number of years', she later recalled of his philandering, now 'caught up with him.'[4] Senator Gary Hart had already been compelled to abandon his intended campaign for the presidency when exposed as a Kennedy-style philanderer in a post-Kennedy political age. There was no way, Wright made clear, the governor could avoid his private life being investigated by the national press, and his being eviscerated like Hart if he ran. Reluctantly, with his wife weeping at the decision, Clinton announced he would not be a candidate.

Given Governor Mike Dukakis' treatment at the hands of Lee Atwater in 1988, it was just as well. In 1990, Clinton contented himself with a fifth term as governor of Arkansas, population 2.3 million, as opposed to the 248 million of the US.

Left to his own devices, however, Clinton was in danger of becoming self-destructive. Convinced he was the smartest Democratic politician of his generation, the most charismatic and the most energetic, Clinton finally decided to fire Betsey Wright. It was at this point, in July 1991, that he received a telephone call from one of President George H.W. Bush's White House advisers, Roger Porter, asking the governor if he was going to run.

When Clinton said he was unsure but lectured Porter – a Harvard business professor – on the crucial issues facing the nation, Porter cut him off. 'Cut the crap, Governor,' Porter snarled, warning that, if he did run, 'they would have to destroy [him] personally'. 'Here's how Washington works', Porter explained, likening America's system to that of the Coliseum in amusing the mob in ancient Rome. 'The press has to have somebody in every election, and we're going to give them *you.*' The media 'would believe any tales they were told about back-water Arkansas. "We'll spend whatever we have to spend, to get whoever we have to get to say whatever they have to say to take you out. And we'll do it early." I tried to stay calm,' Clinton recalled later, 'but I was mad.'[5]

Porter's challenge now swept away Betsey Wright's earlier warnings regarding collateral damage. By fighting on a national stage for the things he believed in, he would banish his demons, please Hillary, and engage in the fight of his life against an Atwater-trained enemy out to destroy him.

Even Clinton's own staff would be minded to throw in the towel during the ensuing campaign for the Democratic nomination, as revelation after revelation was – just as Porter had predicted – fed to a voracious press to gratify a greedy-for-scandal public. Porter's parallel with Rome was, in fact, extraordinary.

A supermarket tabloid began the assault, in the all-important first primary in New Hampshire, by claiming Clinton had enjoyed a twelve-year dalliance with a pretty nightclub singer, Gennifer Flowers. The story instantly migrated into the serious press. As if this was not enough, allegations over financial malfeasance relating to a long-buried, loss-making real estate deal, Whitewater, were bruited, while the back-story of Clinton's slippery evasion of military service during the Vietnam War also emerged. When George Stephanopoulos, Clinton's young communications director and a former Greek Orthodox Church altar boy, read the letter Clinton had sent to the Arkansas National Guard ROTC chief, thanking him 'for saving me from the draft', he initially said to himself: 'That's it. We're done.'[6]

Stephanopoulos, however, had no idea how tough was the governor's hide, or how prepared Clinton was to dissemble in order to confound the Republican trashing machine. 'Ted,' Clinton snapped at the television presenter of *Nightline*, on which Clinton had agreed to appear, 'the only times you've invited me on the show are to discuss a woman I never slept with and a draft I never dodged.'[7]

Given that seemingly authentic audiotapes of Clinton's phone conversations with Ms Flowers were played at a specially convened press conference in New York, and Clinton's draft-avoidance letter was made public, the majority of viewers found it hard to believe the governor's denial. To Stephanopoulos' delight, however, voters seemed willing to excuse Clinton because, in the end, such allegations were irrelevant to his potential stewardship of the White House in a time of economic adversity. Governor Jimmy Carter had, after all, prom-ised he would 'never lie' to the American public; it had not made him a better president, indeed in some respects – as in his 'malaise' speech – it had made him a worse one. In a poor field of candidates, Bill Clinton stood out as a larger-than-life personality, possessing rhetorical skills that could help inspire the country to embrace the new, global era of trade, finance and technological innovation, while seeking peace abroad. Thus, Stephanopoulos later conceded, he also became, like Hillary and his campaign colleagues, an 'enabler'.[8]

Stephanopoulos was later ashamed. But could the young Arkansas governor have won the Democratic presidential nomination and the subsequent election if he *had* admitted the truth? In truth there was probably only one Democratic presidential candidate in America with the necessary intellect, charisma, cunning, shamelessness and sheer willpower to overcome the cynical red tide of Republican hawks in elections: 'Slick Willie', as he was affectionately known in Arkansas.

Clinton's tough childhood, and especially his two electoral defeats in Arkansas, were crucial elements in his political maturation. Few, if any, bested Governor Bill Clinton on the campaign trail. He talked articulately, had total recall, was a born teacher, exuded energy and idealism, hugged and glad-handed, felt people's pain, never tired – and raised prodigious amounts of campaign finance by showing no inhibition in asking for funding support. Thus when, in the wake of the damaging allegations in the New Hampshire primary in February 1992, he placed second, the governor was over the moon. He had weathered a veritable hurricane of revelations meant to destroy his candidacy, and had survived. His positive, articulate, centrist message, looking ahead to an exciting future for the American Empire, made President Bush's campaign, based as it was on negativism, seem all too deficient in ideas, especially after the long Reagan years preceding it. In the weeks thereafter Clinton won primary after primary. By the late spring he had sewn up the Democratic nomination to become the official party candidate. He also made a much-admired choice of vice-presidential candidate in selecting Senator Al Gore, two years younger than himself. The two baby boomers then stormed the country pounding out an upbeat message of responsibility and renewal, making the billionaire independent candidate, Ross Perot, look odd, and the president passé. By the time Bush recognized the danger and sought new revelations by raiding Clinton's passport files at the State Department, it was too late: the Clinton-Gore team was unstoppable.

In the Electoral College, in the November 1992 presidential election, Governor Bill Clinton trounced President Bush 370 to 168; in the popular vote he bested Bush by almost six million votes, and Ross Perot by more than twenty-five million. To the delight of Democrats, Bill Clinton was the undisputed victor.

Part Two: The Presidency

What became lamentably clear as the Clintons moved into their new home at 1600 Pennsylvania Avenue following the inauguration on January 20, 1993, was that Bill Clinton was the cleverest man ever to win the presidency, but had done no thinking about the Oval Office.

Bill Clinton loved ideas and discussion. Proud of the three-day conference on economics he'd held in Little Rock during his transition the new president pulsed with initiatives, but proceeded to make every conceivable mistake in terms of presidential leadership. White House appointments had been left to the last moment, in favour of cosmetic obsession with selecting a multiracial 'rainbow' cabinet. His appointment of a kindergarten friend as chief of staff sent shivers of apprehension through Washington; then, instead of using his vice president, Al Gore, he stunned the capital by announcing that his own wife, Hillary, would head up a Health Care Reform Task Force, charged with delivering a solution to America's health care woes in a hundred days.

Since Hillary confessed she knew next to nothing of health care, and since reforming health care was the most intractable problem in American politics which no previous president had been able to tackle since FDR, it was the assignment from hell. Not only would Hillary's Task Force take almost 1,000 days, but its eventual proposal would be rejected by both houses of Congress, and delay health care reform in America by more than a decade.

Without an experienced chief of staff to guide him and without any idea as to the command, operations and culture of the military, young President Clinton meanwhile turned half the nation against him by announcing, on his first full day in office, that he would press for 'gays in the military' as his first presidential priority.

Without preparation or prior public debate (since the issue was at the bottom of gay people's agenda), the announcement – by a draft dodger who had been 'saved from service in Vietnam' – provoked immediate opposition from an already sceptical Joint Chiefs of Staff Committee, and a menacing backlash in Congress. Clinton found himself facing a barrage of fury across the nation, at the very moment he was seeking to deal with a spiralling national deficit and an ailing economy, with unemployment the highest in ten years – and the world abroad in post-Communist transition.

Almost everything he touched or tackled in his first year in office turned into a similar disaster or near-disaster. The bombing of the World Trade Center in New York by disaffected Muslim terrorists, in February 1993, pointed to a new threat to western civilization. Clinton's deliberately cautious, lawyerly response certainly kept public outrage at the death toll (five people) to a minimum, but the lack of experience and clear lines of authority at the White House worried those charged with national, indeed international, security.

After George H. W. Bush's steady hand at the American tiller, the new White House's missteps alarmed even Clinton's most ardent supporters. The handling of the Waco stand-off in Texas was watched with especial alarm. In a heavily armed compound a mad, self-appointed messiah calling himself David Koresh had barricaded himself and more than a hundred adherents to await Armageddon. Government officers who attempted to enter the compound were slaughtered by Koresh, who welcomed death. It came in due course, on April 19, 1993, when Koresh and almost a hundred men, women and their innocent children were torched to death by federal agents. The president, having authorized the government assault, passed the buck, however, leaving his Attorney General, Janet Reno, to take responsibility. It was clear he was no John F. Kennedy.

In the White House Rose Garden, the President had hosted the signing of the historic, Norwegian-brokered Oslo Peace Accord between Israel and Palestine by Yasser Arafat and Menachim Begin, on September 13, 1993 – but any hopes that the tall, photogenic president was maturing as a leader were dashed in Somalia three weeks later. On October 3, an attempt was made to take out two top lieutenants of the chief warlord, Mohamed Aideed, who had been disrupting UN humanitarian operations. Like President Carter's abortive attempt to rescue the American embassy hostages in Iran in 1975, however, Operation Gothic Serpent went disastrously wrong. The raid failed and nineteen American Rangers died. Worldwide horror was expressed as their naked bodies were dragged through the streets of Mogadishu, in ridicule at the efforts of the world's last remaining superpower.

For Clinton, the Battle of Mogadishu was bad enough for his freshman standing as president and commander-in-chief, but it was soon followed by yet another disaster for American prestige. Transporting the elected president of Haiti, Jean-Bertrand Aristide, back to his Caribbean island following a UN agreement with the military junta there on October 8, 1993, the USS *Harlan County* tank-landing warship was forced to retreat when faced by mere stick-waving thugs at Port au Prince, shouting 'Somalia! Somalia!'

Clinton's national security adviser, Tony Lake, was appalled, anxious lest such humiliations 'put a bull's eye on the backs of American soldiers around the world'.[9] Lake was not alone, the chief of staff of the US Army, General Sullivan, saying to NATO's naval chief, Admiral Miller, 'we can't live with this'.[10] After the long years of muscular American responsibility in maintaining peace and security across the globe, and with the Soviet Union having recently collapsed, the vacuum in the Oval Office was viewed with alarm as much by diplomats as servicemen, nervous lest the lack of world leadership at the White House encourage further factionalism abroad at the very moment when Reagan's vision of the triumph of democratic capitalism, however simplistic, had proven itself so stunningly successful.

Clinton's travails were made worse, moreover, by a series of past scandals that – as Betsey Wright had foretold – came back to bite him: Whitewater, Troopergate and Paula Jones. Each new revelation – whether true or false – diminished the young president's frail standing. The First Lady's massive health care reform bill was trashed and finally voted down in Congress on August 26, 1994, as right-wing millionaires like Richard Mellon Scaife lined up eagerly to force Clinton's resignation as a failed emperor.[11] In television advertising, Clinton's face was morphed on to the faces of Democratic candidates standing for midterm re-election. As a result, in what Clinton's media director (who resigned) called 'a negative referendum on the Clinton presidency', the Democratic Party suffered one of the biggest electoral defeats in its history, not only losing eight Senate and forty-four House seats, but their majorities in both chambers.[12] The whole country was stunned. The big Arkansan with the silvery tongue looked as if he was finished.

For several weeks the wounded president went into a 'funk', his press secretary later described. The election result was a 'full-blown disaster', even the First Lady admitted, bursting into tears in front of her all-female staff in the White House, the so-called 'Chix'. Her much-vaunted attempt at health care reform having foundered, she was left openly wondering 'whether I had gambled on the country's acceptance of my active role and lost'.[13] Out on the road, campaigning for her health care plan, she'd been shocked by the personal animosity she evoked, becoming, as she put it later, 'a lightning rod for people's anger'.[14] 'Everything I do seems not to work' she cried in a phone call to Clinton's old Republican pollster and strategist, Dick Morris. 'Nothing goes right, I just don't know what to do.'[15]

The first thing, Morris recommended to the president, was to get rid of Hillary as 'co-president'. Then, Morris strategized, Clinton should co-opt the new Republican Speaker's capitalist manifesto in Congress, drawn up by Representative Newt Gingrich and called the 'Contract With America' – a call to Republican arms in which the rich had nothing to lose but their taxable chains. In short, Clinton should become like Morris, a Republican.

Hillary, beaten down, agreed to vacate her West Wing office and abandon her effort at co-presidency, but Clinton obstinately refused to accept personal responsibility for the electoral catastrophe, as was his wont. He did, however, admit to collective Democratic guilt. As he put it, 'we got the living daylights beat out of us'.[16] However, he suddenly saw what no one else, including Morris, seemed to realize: the Republican tsunami had removed from office all internal competition within the Democratic Party, from Governor Mario Cuomo of New York to the Speaker of the US House of Representatives, Jim Wright. The president was almost literally the last Democrat standing, offering him the chance not to become a Republican, as Morris recommended, but by virtue of his phenomenal intelligence and public speaking ability, to become the Moses of his generation: leading his beaten tribe of Democrats, trashed and trampled by Newt Gingrich and his fellow travellers of the right, out of the land of misery and back towards the Promised Land.

Mercifully, to make this epic journey easier, the president had finally been persuaded to dismiss his ineffective kindergarten friend Mack McLarty as his chief of staff, and to take instead, upon Al Gore's advice, Leon Panetta, a former nine-times congressman and currently the director of the White House Office of Management and Budget. Knowing Gingrich and his mercenaries at first hand, Panetta – the son of Italian immigrants and a politician who had served in the military – was certain the Republicans would overreach. Without the First Lady interfering, Clinton empowered Panetta to run the government while he, as the Democrats' Last Hope, travelled the country with a new vision of the presidency. No longer would he be the easily traduced mad, bad, dangerous-to-know liberal, pushing progressive agendas from gays in the military to ambitious health care and environmental reform. Instead, he would be like Winston Churchill in June 1940 after the evacuation of Dunkirk: the last defender of civilized, centrist values, and armed, moreover, with the most potent weapon in the US Constitution: the power of presidential veto.

For his part the new Speaker of the House, Newt Gingrich – fat, short, mop-haired and self-important – strutted the halls of the Capitol, imagining himself to be Napoleon. He was in for a rude awakening. The retiring Secretary of the Treasury, Lloyd Bentsen, had warned that Bill Clinton was not called 'The Comeback Kid' for nothing – he was 'a Comeback fellow'.[17] And so it proved. Dick Morris was used as a sort of double agent, reporting to the Republican Deputy Senate Majority Leader in secret on the White House's plans, but also secretly reporting back on Republican plans to the president.[18] Clinton fashioned a strategy of 'triangulated' defence, allowing Gingrich to win trophy victories to appease the lunatic right, such as the firing of the black Surgeon General, Joycelyn Elders.[19] Meanwhile he ring-fenced those issues over which Democrats would never surrender: Medicare, Medicaid, education and social security.[20]

Thus unfolded one of the most extraordinary reversals of presidential political fortune in American political annals, as Clinton's 1994 *annus horribilis* gave way to his *annus mirabilis*: a year in which he not only confronted, on behalf of the nation, the mass murder of innocents by an American terrorist, but brought the nightmare of genocidal civil war in Bosnia to an end.

At first, news of a massive explosion bringing down the main federal government building in Oklahoma City like a pack of cards suggested another Islamic terrorist outrage, like the attempted destruction of the World Trade Center. More thoughtful analysts, however, noted the date: April 19, 1995 – two years to the day since the storming of Koresh's 'Branch Davidian' complex at Waco. Could the mass murder be the work of right-wing *Americans*, responding to the drumbeat of Newt Gingrich's endlessly anti-government rhetoric and antics in Washington?

'Go for a head shot; they're gonna be wearing bulletproof vests' recommended Gordon Liddy, Nixon's jailed 'Plumber' who had been released and now offered his expertise in how to 'resist' the Bureau of Alcohol, Tobacco and Firearms if its officers came to confiscate listeners' weapons, as at Waco. First and foremost, Liddy urged, they should to shoot to kill: 'Head shots, head shots.'[21] Rush Limbaugh, another right-wing syndicated radio talk-show host, was similarly irresponsible, with the result that anti-government militias were springing up and increasing across the nation. One such member of the Michigan

Militia was Timothy McVeigh, a gun enthusiast who was arrested by a traffic cop less than ninety minutes after the Oklahoma City explosion for driving a vehicle without registration plates. With another white supremacist militiaman, Terry Nicholls, the unrepentant McVeigh was soon charged with committing the deadliest hate crime on American soil in US history, in which almost 1,000 people were wounded and 168 innocent victims died, including nineteen small children in the building's Day Care Center.

Against the backdrop of nationwide grief and outrage, the president finally became presidential. 'The bombing in Oklahoma City was an attack on innocent children and defenseless citizens' he immediately declared on national television, flanked by the Attorney General, Janet Reno, promising that he would not 'allow the people of this country to be intimidated by evil cowards'. Flags flew at half mast across the country, and in the White House, the president gathered together and addressed the children of his staff.

No longer was Bill Clinton the widely ridiculed former governor with a woman problem, but a parent himself: incredulous at such cold-blooded mass murder, yet anxious to calm the fears of millions of fellow parents. 'I know it is always – or, at least, it's often difficult', he began, 'to talk to children about things that are this painful' (the photograph of a city firefighter carrying the dead body of a small child emblazoned across newspaper pages and television screens). 'But at times like this, nothing is more important for parents to do than to simply explain what has happened to the children and then to reassure your own children about their future . . . This is a frightening and troubling time. But we cannot let the actions of a few terrible people frighten us any more than they already have. So reach out to one another and come together. We will triumph over those who would divide us. And we will overcome them by doing it together, putting our children first.'[22]

In Oklahoma City the next day Clinton seemed to channel the grief of the nation as he vowed to bring to justice 'those who did this terrible evil. This terrible sin took the lives of our American family: innocent children, in that building only because their parents were trying to be good parents as well as good workers; citizens in the building going about their business; and many who served the rest of us, who worked to help the elderly and the disabled, who worked to support our farmers and our veterans, who worked to enforce our laws and to protect us . . . To all my fellow Americans beyond this hall, I say: one thing we owe those who have sacrificed is the duty to purge ourselves of the dark forces which gave rise to this evil. They are the forces that threaten our common peace, our freedom, our way of life. Let us teach our children that the God of comfort is also the God of righteousness. Those who trouble their own house will inherit the wind. Justice will prevail. Let us let our children know that we will stand against the forces of fear. When there is talk of hatred, let us stand up and talk against it. When there is talk of violence, let us stand up and talk against it. In the face of death, let us honor life. As St Paul admonished us, let us not be overcome by evil but overcome evil with good.'[23]

The president's handling of the mass murder in Oklahoma proved healing and inspiring – 'a moment he was born to be president for', Stephanopoulos afterwards commented.[24] Leon Panetta saw it as 'a real turning point' in Clinton's presidency, not only in putting a damper on the vitriolic Gingrich rhetoric of the right, but in establishing Clinton's 'traction with the American people about who he was'.[25]

Ronald Reagan had maintained that government was not the solution to America's problem, government *was* the problem – a mantra Gingrich had mercilessly repeated. The Oklahoma City bombing, however, showed that Speaker Gingrich, not the government, was the problem, and people like him: anti-government, anti-gun control, anti-birth control, anti-tax, anti-everything that might regulate society rather than promoting free enterprise and personal profit.

For all his personal faults, President Clinton emerged as the real voice of centrist America. Qualities that had seemed so bumbling and ineffectual the year before now looked, as he found his embattled feet, remarkably caring and wise. While Speaker Gingrich's polls plunged, Clinton's rose, giving him, along with his power of veto, a second string to his presidential bow. Whatever Speaker Gingrich might railroad through the House of Representatives, even if rubber-stamped by Republicans in the Senate, the president could simply strike down – and did. Assault weapons would not be permitted back on the streets, whatever pressure the NRA exerted on congressmen. One by one, the ten vaunted items of Gingrich's proposed 'Contract With America' crumbled.

As Clinton's authority increased in relation to domestic issues, so too did his willingness to act abroad. He had successfully evicted the military junta from Haiti in the late summer of 1994 by launching, after due warning, an invasion of the island by sea and air, causing the junta to surrender without a shot being fired. He had celebrated the anniversary of the ending of World War II in Red Square, Moscow – having got the Russian president, Boris Yeltsin, to join the Partnership For Peace programme, ensuring its cooperation with NATO. Using the threat of NATO intercession, moreover, he had caused the Serbs to suspend their attack on Sarajevo in Bosnia; but when the Serbs renewed their ethnic-cleansing in the summer of 1995, Clinton finally decided to act, not only in his role as commander-in-chief of the US, but as the effective captain of NATO.

The Serb massacre at Srebrenitsa of more than 7,000 Bosnian males in the second week of July, and mass rape of Muslim women, proved the point of departure, like Oklahoma City, for a transformed emperor. With Vice President Gore at his side, and his national security adviser Tony Lake pursuing an endgame strategy that would force the Serbs to the negotiating table to hammer out a peace treaty, the president ignored Gingrich's calls to stay out of Europe and fused his NATO allies in the biggest and most concentrated application of military force as deterrent in its post-war history. Tens of thousands of NATO troops assembled in south-east Europe while NATO aircraft, on August 30, 1995, pummelled Serb artillery positions. 'Shouts of joy could be heard from balconies all over Sarajevo' the Washington Post reported, following yet another Serb mortar attack that had killed thirty-seven innocent civilians in a marketplace. 'My God, the Serbs are bombing us' a resident had exclaimed as she heard the planes come overhead. 'When I realized it was NATO, I was literally jumping through my flat with joy.'[26]

Flying the leaders of Bosnia, Croatia and Serbia to Dayton Air Force Base in Ohio on November 1, 1995, President Clinton then used the threat of further NATO force to get the parties to agree a peace accord in a matter of weeks. It would hold for more than a decade.

Poor Gingrich, who had earlier that year basked in the widely touted moniker 'Prime Minister of America', was distraught, and in his frustration now committed the biggest error of his life. He wanted automatic weapons back on the streets, to curry favour with the NRA;

moreover, with power having gone to his head, earlier that summer he had threatened Clinton with what he called a 'train wreck' if the president did not agree to his legislative proposals to abolish the federal departments of education, commerce and housing, and to curtail Medicare and Medicaid. Clinton had said no, however, warning he would use his veto. Gingrich had then made history by carrying out his threat.

Gingrich's shutdown of the US government, halfway through the Dayton negotiations, began on November 14, 1995, causing almost a million federal workers to be sent home, forcing the government to default on its loans, US embassies and consulates worldwide to close, and tens of millions to go without cheques. All federal museums closed, as well as national parks and institutions. Gingrich's right-hand man and House Majority Leader, Congressman Dick Armey of Texas, warned the president in a midnight meeting that it was going to be the end of his presidency.

Instead it would mark the end of Gingrich's posturing. When the Speaker then complained that he had not been allowed to exit Air Force One by the front ramp, beside the president, on his way back from the funeral of the terrorist-assassinated Yitzhak Rabin in Tel Aviv ('You just wonder, where is their sense of manners? Where is their sense of courtesy?') and gave this as his reason for continuing the government shutdown, his infantile whining struck a risible note. A cartoon was published in the *New York Daily News* showing Gingrich dressed in nappies, captioned: 'CRY BABY'.

Gingrich's stock plummeted while Clinton's, in the wake of the historic Dayton Peace Accords, rocketed. Even the Majority Leader of the Senate, Bob Dole, was ashamed. When Gingrich, having temporarily ended the shutdown for a few weeks, reimposed it over the Christmas holiday, Republican defectors finally forced him to back down on January 5, 1996. The 'train wreck' had been an unmitigated disaster, not only for the country, but also for any hopes of 'Prime Minister' Gingrich – or Senator Dole – becoming president.

President Clinton, so belittled in his first year in office and knocked to the canvas in his second, now began to emerge as the master politician of the age. Even journalists began to look at him differently. In London, journalist Hamish McRae had warned those of his colleagues who had written Clinton off after the midterm tsunami not to underestimate the American president. Two years before the election of Tony Blair as prime minister of Great Britain, McRae pointed out that the old politics of union solidarity and entitlements were out of date in a global economy, and that a new, practical liberalism could only arise from the ashes if leaders sought a fresh compact between politicians and the people. Clinton's makeover 'should be studied carefully by all politicians in Europe. For it signposts a way down the path they are likely to have to travel themselves' – a 'roadmap that will be useful to us all'.[27]

Young, indefatigable, smart, well read, willing to listen and determined to do good in the world, Bill Clinton was coming into his own, his nation's best ambassador both in pursuing peace, and where necessary applying force to obtain it. From Turkey to Japan, political leaders were wowed by his sheer energy and positive outlook; indeed he achieved rock-star status wherever he travelled abroad, pressing for improvement in trade, greater environmental protection, and reduction in ethnic and nationalist violence. His ability to articulate the different sides and aspects of any problem, and review solutions, was unique among world leaders. Moreover, with an American economy undergoing an information technology revolution as profound as the Industrial Revolution more than a century before, he wore something of FDR's mantle in foreign eyes: a president with benevolent, compassionate feelings, as well as an extraordinary curiosity about other cultures. It was small wonder his popularity abroad exceeded even that of John F. Kennedy.

At home, the president's increasing self-confidence was best demonstrated in his State of the Union address on January 23, 1996. In the course of a spellbinding, eighty-minute *tour d'horizon*, he pointed to a Vietnam veteran in the gallery who had entered the bombed wreckage of the Murrah Federal Building in Oklahoma City to save the lives of three women. As the audience rose to applaud Richard Dean's courage, Clinton thundered 'I challenge all of you in this chamber. Never – ever – shut the federal government again.'[28]

Viewers and commentators expressed amazement at Bill Clinton's extraordinary journey, from fumbling naivety to mastery of the presidential office. Why had it taken him so long, people wondered? Certainly there was no one on the Republican benches who had a hope of beating him if he stood for re-election in 1996, as polls made

savagely clear to the ragbag of Republican wannabes, from Lamar
Alexander and Steve Forbes to Newt Gingrich and Bob Dole.

Only one man could have given Clinton a fight: the former chairman
of the Joint Chiefs of Staff, General Colin Powell, and he removed
himself from contention, citing domestic reasons. The way for Clinton
was clear.

Had Bill Clinton decided at this, his proudest and most successful
moment as president, to stand down in favour of his stalwart, rock-
steady vice president, Al Gore, he would – like Lyndon Johnson in 1964,
after passing his civil rights bill – undoubtedly have gone down in history
as one of the most effective of American Caesars, after a rocky start. At
home the national deficit had already been halved since he took office,
thanks to his 1993 economic bill; ten million new jobs had been added;
new businesses were starting up at a record rate; unemployment was at
its lowest level for twenty-eight years; the minimum wage had increased
to $4.75 per hour, and portability of medical insurance was ensured from
job to job. Moreover, these achievements had been won in direct refutation of the Reagan-Republican mantra against tax hikes. Disproving
Reagan's dictum, the president had increased the highest tax bracket to
36 per cent, with a 10 per cent surcharge on the highest earnings – making
a tax bracket of 39.6 per cent. Moreover he had raised the corporate
income tax rate to 36 per cent, as well as increasing the federal tax on
gas – and the American economy had flourished, not dwindled as
Republicans had predicted. Abroad he had not only brought Serbian
genocide in Bosnia to an end, but he had, using the US as an independent
arbitrator, helped the move towards peace in Northern Ireland and an
Israeli–Jordan Peace Accord. Like Lyndon Baines Johnson in 1964,
however, Bill Clinton could not say no to the lure of another term in
the White House, whatever attacks might be unleashed by his enemies.

Second Acts had rarely proven successful in the history of the
American Caesars, after FDR; indeed in many ways they contradicted
the feature that best characterized America: its constant self-reinvention
and renewal. But Bill Clinton, having finally found his feet as American
president, had no wish to hand over his hard-won spurs to his deputy
marshal, Al Gore. Not only did he see himself as the most intelligent
person he knew, but – as when he was defeated as governor of Arkansas
after a single term – he had no idea what he would do with himself
outside of politics. Jimmy Carter had taken up carpentry and Habitat

for Humanity, as well as service to peacemaking, from North Korea to Haiti. But Carter had perhaps the deepest well of humility of any Caesar, whereas Bill Clinton's hubris had since his student years made it impossible for him to play second fiddle to another human being, let alone multiple beings. He *had to* shine, to wow, to win over, to seduce, lest the demons in his psyche take him over and bring him down – as they had his drug-addicted, imprisoned brother Roger. For the president, this was a powerful argument for staying put in the White House.

His decision to run for re-election thus looked, on the surface, a no-brainer; indeed he told his aides that, if he campaigned well enough, he might even reverse the Republican landslide in the House of Representatives, thus felling the egregious Speaker, Newt Gingrich. Against that, however, as would emerge in due course, he had a very personal, and highly secret, reason *not* to run.

Despite the efforts of the Republican nominee, Senator Dole, to sink his opponent with a missile aimed at the president's 'character' and financial probity, the presidential debates resulted in three resounding victories for the patient, endlessly positive, articulate Clinton. The independent candidate, Ross Perot – who had not been permitted to participate in the debates – garnered ten million votes fewer than in 1992, while Dole, who had resigned his seat in the Senate to devote himself to the campaign, came nowhere close, winning only 159 to Clinton's 379 Electoral College votes on November 3, 1996. William Jefferson Clinton would get to stay in the White House, becoming the first Democrat since Franklin Roosevelt to win and serve a second elected term.

Instead of welcoming the president's belated learning curve in the Oval Office, Republican opponents continued to see him as the prime target of their resentment; indeed the more he succeeded in rallying the nation after the Oklahoma City bombing and the Dayton Peace Accords, the more determined their diehards became to find some way to take the Democratic polymath down. The fact that his Omnibus economic bill, on the wheel of which they had almost broken him in the spring and early summer of 1993, had proven an historic turning point in steering the American economy back into sustained growth and reduction in national debt only maddened such opponents more. They had blocked health care reform in 1994, and had forced the president to sign a welfare reform bill in the summer of 1996 (preferring lower welfare rolls to a healthier country), but otherwise they were unable to point to anything constructive that they had proposed – in part because Clinton seemed to co-opt in advance every issue they addressed, from urban crime (where the president got federal funding to provide 100,000 more police on the streets of American cities) to V-chips on televisions to safeguard children from violence and pornography.

In the view of diehard anti-Clintonistas, then, the president had to be brought down not for the good of America, but for the good of the Republican Party. That such a conspiracy might amount to near-treason, at a moment when the nation required the legislature and security officials to unite and concentrate on dealing with the growing threat of Islamic terrorism, was not something, lamentably, that worried them – as shown by the behaviour of the director of the FBI, Louis Freeh.

Freeh would later boast that, from the spring of 1993, when he was made FBI director, he met with the president 'one time, maybe two, maybe three times in the entire seven-plus years I worked under Bill Clinton'.[29]

Historians rubbed their eyes in disbelief. How, when plot after plot was being hatched against America at home and abroad, by terrorists concerted by al-Qaeda – an organization formed and financed by a Yemeni-Saudi millionaire, Osama Bin Laden – was it conceivable that the director of the FBI, a Republican, refused to meet with his own president – and would later *boast* of this?

Freeh's hatred for the president reflected the blinkered venom that Clinton seemed to stir in a minority of Americans, even as his popularity with the majority reached record levels of approval. Certainly, thanks to his upbringing and political career in one of the most bigoted states in the nation, President Clinton was no stranger to the hatred he inspired as a 'liberal' in the minds of bigots and right-wing fanatics. Nonetheless he tried, again and again, to hold out an olive branch to his opponents. His last act before his second inauguration had been to award the Presidential Medal of Freedom to his defeated opponent, Bob Dole, a hero of World War II, in which he had served as an infantry officer. 'I liked Dole' Clinton later wrote. 'He could be mean and tough in a fight, but he lacked the fanaticism and hunger for personal destruction that characterized so many of the hard-right Republicans who now dominated his party in Washington.'[30]

The president also decided not to press for criminal charges against the Speaker, Newt Gingrich, who was found guilty by the House Ethics Committee of violating tax and ethics laws, for which he was fined $300,000 by Congress. Instead, in his second inaugural address on January 20, 1997, Clinton called for 'a new spirit of community for a new century'. He pointed to the 'divide of race' which had been 'America's constant curse', as well as other evils. Each 'new wave of immigrants gives new targets to old prejudices' he stated. 'Prejudice and contempt, cloaked in the pretense of religious or political conviction, are no different. These forces have nearly destroyed our nation in the past. They plague us still. They fuel the fanaticism of terror. And they torment the lives of millions in fractured nations all around the world. Those obsessions cripple both those who hate and, of course, those who are hated, robbing both of what they might become. We cannot, will not, succumb to the dark impulses that lurk in the far regions of the soul everywhere. We shall overcome them', he promised – leading, in the next century, to renewed opportunity, thanks to 'our rich texture of racial, religious and political diversity'. After all, he pointed out, 'Ten years ago the Internet was the mystical province of physicists; today it is a commonplace encyclopedia of schoolchildren.' And in that increased level of communication, he foresaw a situation in which 'the voice of the people' would 'speak louder than the din of narrow interests', redeeming the promise of America to its citizens. It was time, he declared, to end 'acrimony and division' at home, the better to be able to spread 'America's bright flame of freedom' throughout the world.

These were famous last words. Whatever Clinton might do to disarm his opponents, and whatever he now did to prove himself a worthy, bipartisan president, he could neither change his own dark urges nor the minds of those who had hated him for his early incompetence, but who now seemed to hate him all the more for his success. Shortly before the election he had signed the Comprehensive Test Ban Treaty, together with Russia, China, France and the UK. In the twelve months following his second inauguration he signed off on a balanced budget passed by Congress, a primary supposed objective of Republicans, and an important step in achieving federal fiscal responsibility. Abroad he

ensured, in a personal meeting with Boris Yeltsin, Russia's acquiescence to the expansion of NATO to include the Czech Republic,
Hungary and Poland. These were signal achievements, but his signature was, literally, on hundreds of other initiatives, from Internet
funding to cancer research and clean water initiatives. Like Lyndon
Johnson he was a force of nature, as he met with foreign leaders from
Britain's new prime minister, Tony Blair, to China's leader, Jiang Zemin,
visited American troops in Bosnia, travelled across South America, got
the Chemical Weapons Convention Treaty ratified by Congress over
the sworn opposition of Caspar Weinberger and Donald Rumsfeld, yet
seemed as knowledgeable and involved in domestic initiatives as their
progenitors, from children's health care to middle-class tax cuts – which
he persuaded the Republican-controlled House of Representatives to
pass, in return for a reduction in capital gains tax. Asked by the *Wall
Street Journal* 'at what point', given the depth of animosity he inspired
in his detractors, 'do you consider that it's just not worth it, and do
you consider resigning the office?' he responded sharply: 'Never. I
would never walk away from the people of this country and the trust
they have placed in me.'[31]

Begged by right-wing fanatics not to give up on the Whitewater
investigation regarding possible culpability by the Clintons, Kenneth
Starr, the Independent Investigator appointed by the Republican House
of Representatives to examine allegations of malfeasance in the
imbroglio, decided *not* to terminate his investigation of the Clintons'
role, as he had promised. Instead, with the help of Louis Freeh, on
February 21, 1987 Starr renewed his detective inquiry, this time focusing
on the keyhole to the president's boudoir.

Never in American presidential history had such a sex-investigation
taken place while a president was in office. The notion of executive
privilege was now cast to the four winds by Republican right-wingers
– often the very people who had objected to Nixon being investigated
while in office – as the Supreme Court awarded Paula Jones, who was
attempting to sue Clinton for previous sexual harassment in Arkansas
in 1991, the right to have her civil case heard in court while Clinton
was still president.

Alarmed, Clinton eventually offered what he should have offered four
years before: a financial settlement, more than $700,000. Even Jones'
own lawyers acknowledged that, according to the then-operative

Arkansas law under which she had brought her case, she could point to no monetary or professional suffering incurred by the alleged harassment. Her lawyers thus urged her to accept the money and to run. When she refused, her lawyers resigned, leaving the right-wing 'Rutherford Institute' to fund new lawyers for her case.

Ms Jones demanded from Clinton an admission of guilt and an apology. 'I couldn't do that because it wasn't true,' Clinton would later maintain. Few, however, believed him then, or later. Assuming Ms Jones' allegations of sexual harassment were true, there were, chroniclers could see in retrospect, only two possible reasons why the president was unable to bring himself to issue an apology. The first was entirely rational.

No other president in modern times possessed Clinton's ability to calculate political expediency in advance. Since childhood, he had used his brains to stay ahead of others, however aggressive. He was, in effect, a modern Houdini, able not only to contort himself to accommodate every political belief, from capital punishment to compulsory recitation of the pledge of allegiance, but to escape from every net thrown over him by his political enemies. Believing that such an open apology to Ms Jones would only encourage other women from his exotic past to come forward with similar, perhaps even worse, examples of his sexual self-indulgence, he calculated it would be political suicide – in the media and possibly the courts – to agree to her demand.

Besides this, though, there was the matter of pathology.

Despite his extraordinary ability to empathize, indeed a legendary ability to 'feel your pain', Bill Clinton had always suffered from the opposite, too: namely sexual sociopathy, or bipolar behaviour. In Clinton's case this took the form of an initial inability to say no to high-risk sexual misconduct, however much it might threaten to ruin him, followed afterwards by an inability to acknowledge his guilt. Only his wife Hillary, possibly, could have got him to confess to his addiction, but even she, who was an intensely private person, could not now get him to issue a public apology, since her own distrust of the media and right-wing fanatics went deeper even than his: a distrust so pronounced that, whatever her private feelings (fury, disappointment, lamentations at yet another example of her husband's bad behaviour), she simply could not countenance such a public *mea culpa*.

Thus, inexorably, the tragedy unfolded as Paula Jones' new legal team began, in the absence of an apology from the president, and in the hope of establishing a pattern of sexual misbehaviour, to seek to unearth other examples from the past – never dreaming they would find examples from the present. It was this 'fishing expedition' that Kenneth Starr and the director of the FBI, Louis Freeh, decided to join.

Pointing to Clinton's stellar polls for a second-term president, the White House staff did not take the news of Starr's sex-trawling seriously; but they did not know what the president was hiding from them, indeed from his own wife. Only Clinton himself knew that at the very moment his enemies were seeking to corral evidence of past sexual impropriety against him in the spring of 1997, he had yet again indulged in an 'inappropriate' extramarital liaison: to wit, a 'friendship with benefits' in the hallowed confines of the Oval Office, conducted with a young former intern.[32]

His conduct – or misconduct, given that it involved a government employee in the president's official, government-funded work quarters – defied subsequent belief. It was true that previous presidents had indulged in far more egregious extramarital practices while in the White House, especially John F. Kennedy and Lyndon Johnson, but those practices had been unknown by the general public in their day, thanks to patriarchal attitudes and self-censorship by (male) editors in the serious American press. Times had changed since then, as Clinton well knew. Public expectations of presidential morality had, if anything, become all the more idealistic, the further that public mores – whether in the entertainment industry or in ordinary people's lives – declined, relative to supposed earlier standards. The president, however briefly in that imperial role, was in an almost sacred position of trust. Why would anyone in that role in the late twentieth century put not only his career but the very office of the presidency at risk, to gratify a fleeting sexual impulse?

The word hubris, then, could not begin to describe Clinton's departure from his senses as a man *already* facing a major lawsuit over earlier sexual misbehaviour when Arkansas governor. It suggested more than the power to misbehave, as emperor; indeed it seemed so deliberately self-destructive that many subsequent chroniclers ascribed it to a sort of metaphorical death wish, when details of the alleged liaison finally emerged.

The 'victim' chosen by Starr and Freeh to illustrate Clinton's pattern of misconduct was unfortunate: a plump, twenty-two-year-old Jewish intern who had previously been the willing mistress of a married teacher at her college in California, before coming to Washington for an internship at the White House arranged through her divorced mother. She then boasted to her companions that she was setting her beret, as well as 'presidential knee-pads', for the president. Once successful in that quest – her innocent seduction of Clinton taking place during the Gingrich government shutdown, when only a skeleton White House staff was operating – Monica Lewinsky would not thereafter let go. Nor, however, would Ms Jones' team or Ken Starr's, once they got wind of the affair. The more the investigation delved, the more it took on the form of a cat-and-mouse contest: Jones, Starr and Freeh determined to entrap the president, and, Clinton, like Richard Nixon before him, determined to prove himself cleverer than his accusers.

Blessed with an ability to multitask that no president in American history had evinced, Clinton was amazingly successful. He was observed to complete in minutes the *New York Times* crossword puzzle, sign letters, read documents and take telephone calls, all simultaneously. As a narcissistic genius and former law professor trained at Yale, he knew he could not admit to his closest friends or family the truth of what he had done, in case they were subpoenaed.[33] He therefore stopped all but phone sex and chaste meetings with the former intern, to keep her from turning against him; meanwhile, knowing her gossipy, loose-tongued, childlike personality, he braced himself, throughout the second half of 1997, for the impending legal challenge, without ever asking himself whether it was right and proper for the American people to be put through another wrenching drama, once Starr got evidence of the 'affair'.

Finally, on January 18, 1998, news broke on the very medium the president had extolled in his State of the Union address, the Internet: a '23-year-old, former White House intern' had had a 'sex relationship with president. World Exclusive.'[34]

The news reverberated across the world like an earthquake, fulfilling the worst nightmares of Democrats as they continued their efforts to rebuild the party following the 1994 meltdown. The last thing they needed was *another* Clinton sex scandal.

Telling the truth, however, seems never to have entered the president's calculating brain. Clinton had already used his friendship with a successful outside lawyer, Vernon Jordan, to get the former intern a job in New York, thereby whisking her away from the prying eyes of Washington journalists and mischief-makers. He had also colluded with Ms Lewinsky in drawing up an affidavit to sign, lest she be formally deposed and cross-examined by the Jones team. (In this she denied, on oath, that there had been a sexual or improper relationship.) Meanwhile Clinton had responded to a subpoena from the Jones team by giving them a six-hour deposition at the offices of his lawyers in downtown Washington on January 16, 1998, in which he denied virtually all allegations about sexual misbehaviour in his past, and denied any recollection of having met, let alone lewdly exposed himself to an Arkansas employee, Paula Jones. With reference to Ms Lewinsky, he had, by shrewd use of the past and present tenses, been able to deceive the team about the nature of his White House relationship, and the extent of his connection with the former intern.

Any relief, or Yalie pride, in having evaded the Jones legal team's most searching questions evaporated, however, when less than thirty hours later the Internet news story broke in the *Drudge Report*, indicating that Ms Lewinsky – and thus the president – had been entrapped by Starr's men using illegally recorded telephone tape recordings and concealed body-wires, supplied by the FBI, as in a Hollywood movie. It was thus no rumour, but a story backed by FBI evidence. All hell broke loose.

The Clinton administration would in effect be shut down again, by yet another arm of the Republican-controlled Congress: its so-called Independent – though unashamedly Republican – Counsel. Having already wasted $28 million of American taxpayers' money in pursuit of Whitewater, Starr's fruitless efforts would now make presidential history.

In a televised press conference in the White House on January 26, 1998, the president attempted to tamp down media speculation, given that he had not in fact had sex with Ms Lewinsky, if sex meant sexual intercourse, as defined by the law. After lengthy remarks on children's reading and after-school programmes, he declared 'I want to say one thing to the American people. I want you to listen to me. I'm going to say this again. I did not have sexual relations with that woman. I never told anybody to lie, not a single time – never. These allegations are false. And I need to go back to work for the American people.'[35]

Starr could only smile. Day by day, week by week, month by month, leaking evidence and rumours as they went along, the members of his team now took up the baton of the Jones team, threatening the former White House intern with twenty-eight years in penitentiary if she did not cooperate in bringing down the president with whom she had become besotted. Like the Dreyfus case in France in the final decade of the nineteenth century the matter became a cause célèbre, pitting liberals against conservatives, puritans against tolerants and seniors against the younger generation, in a strangely symbolic *fin de siècle* struggle.

That the world's most powerful empire, attempting to maintain Pax Americana across a fractious globe, should become so embroiled in the minutiae of its president's most private parts and the legal definition of 'sexual relations' was not only demeaning but dangerously distracting, given the rise of 1990s Islamic terrorism. Yet as long as Clinton refused to resign and instead made it his mission to slay the 'vast right-wing conspiracy' seeking to bring him down, the United States – and the world – was doomed to watch while the two sides slugged it out. All hope of constructive, bipartisan legislation in 1998 was abandoned, and in foreign affairs America's leading role became fatally tarnished.

As Clinton's counter-terrorism czar Richard Clarke would later write, he found himself seething with fury that the serving president could have put himself, and thus the nation, into such a ridiculous situation, owing to his lack of 'discretion or self-control'. But Clarke was even 'angrier, almost incredulous, that the bitterness of Clinton's enemies knew no bounds, that they intended to hurt not just Clinton but the country by turning the president's problem into a global, public circus for their own political ends'.[36]

Several days after the scandal erupted, the group calling itself al-Qaeda – named after the foundation stone or base of a building, and having merged with its counterpart in Egypt, Egyptian Islamic Jihad – declared official 'war' on the American Empire. In March, the president summoned his cabinet and senior officials from the State Department, Department of Defense, CIA, FBI, Health, the Federal

Emergency Management Agency (FEMA), Energy, OMB and other agencies, under Clarke, to plan for a possible nuclear, chemical or biological terrorist attack in the US.[37] In June, Osama Bin Laden was indicted *in absentia* by a federal grand jury in New York, and the president issued his third Counter-terrorism Directive (PDD-62, 63 and 67). Soon after that – just as had been feared – the next massive terrorist attack on America took place, aimed this time at American sovereign territory and personnel in Africa.

On August 7, 1998, the American embassies in Kenya and Tanzania were simultaneously blown up by al-Qaeda mass murderers. In Nairobi, 257 people were killed and 5,000 wounded. This was deliberate Islamist slaughter and maiming of innocents, forbidden in the Koran, but excused by a disputed interpretation of jihad on a new, global scale. Though the bombings aroused shock and condemnation in the US, the American press and news channels on radio, television and the Internet simply ignored the tragedy and concentrated on the president's sex life, as Clinton was compelled by Starr to go before a grand jury and fight for what was left of his reputation. On August 17, 1998, the FBI, working for Starr's Republican Whitewater team, arranged to record, then deliberately leak to the media, yet another deposition by the serving president. This time the interrogation was given in the Map Room of the White House and on videotape, owing to an absent juror. In almost surreal comic opera, Clinton was grilled not on the subject of national security and the measures being taken to combat Islamist terrorism, but the exact nature of his consensual trysts with Ms Monica Lewinsky in the White House during and after Gingrich's government shutdown in 1995, when she succeeded in entering the otherwise off-limits area of the West Wing. Starr's prosecutor and the president battled not over sarin and other threats to the homeland, but over the definition of the word 'sex' and even 'what the meaning of the word "is" is'.[38]

The Lewinsky business had now become tragic farce. That night Clinton again went on television to address the nation. Not even his wife knew whether he would resign or what he would say in his speech, let alone his lawyers and staff.

In the event, Clinton's announcement to the nation was not, as many assumed, to resign honourably and spare the country further shame and embarrassment. Instead, the former Rhodes Scholar and

Yale Law School graduate decided to see whether he could extricate himself by turning the tables on Starr. The president still denied having committed perjury or an obstruction of justice, claiming he had put no pressure on his former intern to lie to the Jones and Starr teams. He still insisted that he and Ms Lewinsky had not, in any biblical sense, had full 'sexual relations' since sexual intercourse had not taken place, and only heavy petting had been involved. However, Clinton did admit he had obfuscated the truth of his relationship, in understandable embarrassment. 'I misled people, including even my wife' he now admitted. 'I deeply regret that.' Nevertheless, he asserted, the matter was strictly a private matter 'between me, the two people I love most – my wife and our daughter – and our God', not with Ken Starr or the people of the United States who had elected him. 'It's nobody's business but ours' Clinton insisted. 'Even presidents have private lives.'[39] And with that he promised to dedicate the rest of his presidency to his job – 'the challenges and all the promise of the next American century'.

By turning the tables on Starr, Clinton demonstrated yet again why he was called 'The Comeback Kid', daring the prosecutor to escalate yet further a sordid but relatively benign sex scandal that had consumed the attention of the country's media for the past seven months. As 60 per cent of respondents believed he was doing a good job as president, Clinton felt convinced of his own essential goodness, compassion, competence, and his elected right to remain in the job until officially removed by Congress. Thus, he made clear, he would *not* stand down just to appease Republican assassins. He had figured out the way to deal with diehards such as Newt Gingrich and Dick Armey, Gingrich's odious henchman in Congress, and now saw himself in the same embattled light as Nixon, determined to focus on idealistic causes and foreign affairs in order to distract the media from its obsession with his own private affairs.

Tirelessly he sought to get Yasser Arafat to negotiate peace with Benjamin Netanyahu, the Israeli prime minister; worked with the new British prime minister, Tony Blair, on the historic 'Good Friday' settlement in Northern Ireland; sent military forces to the Gulf to threaten Saddam Hussein, when the dictator got out of line; visited China, where he pressed for more open trade and mutual investment; and on August 20, 1998, authorized a cruise-missile strike on a training camp in Afghanistan where Osama Bin Laden was reported to be, just as President Reagan had sought to take out Muammar Qaddafi after the bombing of Pan Am Flight 103 over Lockerbie.

To Clinton's disappointment, Bin Laden was not hit – Clinton was. Where Reagan had not been faulted for seeking the demise of an evil, mass-murdering enemy of the US, the fallout from Clinton's failure demonstrated how wounded he was. He looked not only incompetent to Americans at home, but also, thanks to the continuing Lewinsky scandal and his refusal to resign, deceitful, accused by the media not of seriously attempting to keep America safe by killing Bin Laden, but of wanting to distract attention from his continuing woes over the Lewinsky sex saga – and impending impeachment.

The crippling effect of the Lewinsky farce on Bill Clinton's ability to carry out his duties as president is almost impossible to overstate. Faced with impeachment Richard Nixon had maintained he was 'not a quitter'; in the same manner, Clinton swore to friend and foe alike he would fight Starr and his men 'till the last dog dies' – regardless of the consequences for his beloved country. Moreover, standing behind him, the First Lady hardened his resolve. She had told a succession of reporters in January that her husband's 'relationship' with Ms Lewinsky 'was not sexual', had denied it was an 'improper relationship', had insisted the scandal would disappear ('I have seen how these charges evaporate and disappear as they're given the light of day'), and on January 27, 1998, she had famously spoken of a 'vast right-wing conspiracy'.[40] Emboldened by her loyalty – even after she had heard from his own tainted lips, in August, the truth of his relationship with Ms Lewinsky – the president stood firm as Starr delivered his 452-page report and its official recommendation to Congress on September 9, 1998: namely that the president should be impeached.

Two days later, the House voted to release the Starr Report in its entirety to the public, including a long, sexually explicit autobiographical memoir of transgression by Ms Lewinsky, forced from her under threat of imprisonment by one of Starr's female prosecutors.

The world now gulped, as in fastidious, fully footnoted pornographic prose, Starr's dissertation on the serving president's private life and his deplorable sexual mores, even the use of his cigars, was made public. As one of the best chroniclers of the impeachment noted, in the 'first weekend after the release of the Starr Report, the Clinton presidency teetered' – and not because of a right-wing conspiracy.[41] Even honourable, God-fearing and ethical Democrats were, along with Republicans, appalled by the revelations. Just as the Nixon tapes had scandalized a nation used to thinking of the president as an almost sacred personage, and were then shocked by transcripts of his mafia-like gutter-language, so now both Democrats and Republicans alike were outraged at the implicit scorn for presidential dignity displayed by the nation's chief executive in the Oval Office. One liberal Democrat, Congressman David Obey, declared to the Democratic Minority Leader as the House voted: 'We have to get rid of this guy. He will destroy the Democratic Party for a generation', and recommended that the Democratic Minority Leader and his colleague in the Senate, Tom Daschle, would 'have to go tell [the President] to get out'.[42]

For a third time, however, the president refused to budge. Millions downloaded the text of the Starr Report from the Internet, even before it was bound and widely published in paper form. The 'facts', as cajoled from Ms Lewinsky, seemed incontrovertible, as well as disgusting in their intimate details, but as Clinton had calculated, they hardly comprised grounds for impeachment, given Alexander Hamilton's original view, in helping to draw up the Constitution, that impeachment was to guard against a genuine threat to America. Was Speaker Gingrich once again overreaching, as he had been in shutting down the US government in 1995? Asked why he was pushing for impeachment of the President over the Lewinsky scandal Gingrich replied, simply, 'because we can'.[43]

Given that the effective administration of America and its empire had been seriously hobbled by the Lewinsky business for almost a year, if an impeachment of the serving President was authorized by Speaker Gingrich things could only get worse. They did. Instead of getting support for the president's executive order 13099 to halt funding to al-Qaeda, the Taliban and other terrorist organizations, obstructionism now ruled in Washington.[44] The personal had truly become the political – with a vengeance. In Congress and elsewhere, especially the media, the impeachment saga became a sort of metaphorical Gettysburg, with charges and counter-charges, artillery barrages and counter-battery fire. By refusing to resign, and instead framing the issue as *Clinton* vs *A Right-Wing Conspiracy*, the president had deftly managed to reorientate the national debate from 'doing the right thing' to 'doing in' the right wing.[45]

The longer he could stretch out the process, Clinton reckoned, the more likely the public would eventually tire of it and turn against the Republicans, who seemed to fatally underestimate his Darwinian ability to survive when cornered. How long could it go on, people wondered?

Rather than gaining seats in the midterm elections in November 1998, as Gingrich had hoped, the Republicans lost yet more, ratifying the president's decision to mount his version of Custer's Last Stand. Republican hypocrisy now came under the spotlight, as investigations were made regarding legislators' own private lives. As Gingrich's marital infidelity came to light, the Speaker wisely decided not to seek re-election but to resign at the end of the session. The wisdom of this was soon demonstrated when, amid a flurry of new revelations, his elected successor, Bob Livingstone, the Republican Speaker-designate of the House of Representatives, was also compelled to resign. To the fury of Republicans, however, Clinton refused to follow suit.

Relentlessly, implacably, the impeachment process was therefore pressed by the Republican-controlled House of Representatives. On December 19, 1998, in Resolution 611, the House unwisely rejected the simpler alternative of censure. Instead it voted by 228 to 206 to have the president put on trial by the Senate for 'perjury committed before a grand jury', and by 221 to 212 for his 'obstruction of justice' – both claims relating to Clinton's attempt to mislead investigators over his relationship with Ms Lewinsky, a private matter that was of no concern to Congress or to the law, which Clinton had not broken.

For only the second time in American history (and the first time ever for an elected president) a full impeachment trial in the Senate was now prepared against the president. Presided over by the Chief Justice of the Supreme Court, the comic opera opened on January 7, 1999, and stretched across five weeks during which the business of the state, as well as the Supreme Court, was yet further disrupted. America became the laughing stock of the world.

Finally, on February 12, 1999, the trial ended with acquittal (just) on all counts. William Jefferson Clinton had won, but had America? After owning up to Hillary in August 1998, Clinton had begun 'a serious counseling program, one day a week', while being exiled for months to sleep on the couch 'in the small living room that adjoined our bedroom' in the White House, in a renewed effort to 'unify my parallel lives', the first of which he saw as noble, the other as deeply self-destructive – a trait he attributed to unaddressed anger and grief, stemming from his abused childhood. His acquittal he saw as the consequence of majority public support among ordinary Americans, as evidenced by his approval ratings in opinion polls. 'It would have been much harder' to maintain his sanity, he afterwards claimed, 'if the American people hadn't made an early judgement that I should remain president and stuck with it.'[46]

Once again, however, Bill Clinton was parsing history, since the majority of voters had no quarrel with the president's performance in running the country, especially the economy – but they had less and less faith in his honesty, his ethics, his integrity, his dignity or his moral character. In a nation where the president is the embodiment not only of American power but also of self-respect, this was a grave shortcoming that could only have been addressed by his resignation – which he refused to concede.

Ever the narcissist, Clinton wanted the public's love and forgiveness rather than banishment, and to his credit was prepared to work harder than ever to merit it, in a spirit of 'reconciliation and renewal for America'. The final two years of the Clinton presidency thus took place in a strange political twilight: the public was relieved the Lewinsky saga was finally over and pleased at the continuing strength of the economy as it continued its longest sustained boom ever, yet also ashamed of its president whom few now respected.

Clinton might – and did – proudly point to statistics showing how the country was moving towards a historic surplus and the paying-down of the once spiralling national debt; might – and did – pride himself on showing strong leadership in NATO's intervention in the former Yugoslavia, when Serbs were compelled to halt their ethnic cleansing in Kosovo and, on June 3, 1999, to accept NATO administration of the enclave; and might – and did – take credit for seeing the country safely into the new millennium without another Islamic terrorist outrage, or millennium-induced computer meltdown. These were, however, hardly matters which President Gore, had he been appointed, would have been unable or unwilling to manage; indeed by the autumn of 2000 it became ever more evident that a new American president was needed, one who would have the trust and authority to meld together the FBI, CIA, defence and security agencies, given the ongoing refusal of the director of the FBI, Louis Freeh, to meet with

President Clinton for a single meeting in his second term, or to resign in favour of a new FBI director. ('I spent most of the eight years as director investigating the man who appointed me' Freeh later said.[47] Then he admitted he stayed on 'longer' at the FBI because he 'didn't want to give Clinton a chance to name his successor', 'I was going to stay there and make sure he couldn't replace me' he confessed.[48])

The fact was, America needed a tough, respected president, for the threat to America was not going away – indeed it was magnified, to Richard Clarke's chagrin, by the president's reduced stature and authority. Despite titanic efforts between Israeli and Palestinian negotiators at Camp David in July 2000, Yassar Arafat rejected Clinton's compromise peace agreement: a two-state solution in which the Palestinians would eventually get back 91 per cent of the West Bank, all of Gaza, and control of East Jerusalem, including custodianship, though not sovereignty, of the Temple Mount. Once Ariel Sharon blithely insisted on walking across the Temple Mount, on September 28, to rub in Israeli sovereignty in his bid to oust Ehud Barak as prime minister, the Middle East exploded. Protest begat violence. A second intifada or Palestinian uprising commenced – leading to thousands of deaths, suicide bombings, reprisals and targeted assassinations, and arousing yet more Muslim hostility towards the 'Great Satan', America, which was perceived as Israel's military protector and primary funder, yet lacked the power or will to rein its expansionist policies in, or compel Israel to compromise.

Clinton refused to give up on his peace proposals, knowing how America's security depended on the outcome. He took pride in the fact that every attack planned against Americans on American soil since the World Trade Center bombing shortly after his first inauguration had been successfully disrupted. But with the Palestinian intifada fanning the flames of Islamist terror groups, he knew time was running out. On October 12, 2000, three weeks before the presidential election, two suicide bombers approached the anchored USS *Cole* in Aden, Yemen, and blew themselves up, killing seventeen American sailors as they did so. It was clear the clash of civilizations was growing ever more earnest, and with Osama Bin Laden still at large in southern Afghanistan, and unless there was a peace agreement between the Israelis and the Palestinians under Yasser Arafat, the future of the American Empire under its next president would be severely tested.

Who that president would be was a moot point. At the beginning of August, Republicans had nominated as their candidate for the White House – after a bruising fight with competitors – the eldest son of former president George H. W. Bush, Governor George W. Bush. Two weeks later, on August 17, 2000, Democrats nominated as their candidate Vice President Al Gore. Secret polls indicated a disturbing groundswell of residual public anger, 'still mad as hell over the Year of Monica' and at President Clinton's moral failings, however much they abhorred the tactics which Ken Starr had adopted.[49] In view of this alarming information, Gore decided it would be unwise to ask the president to campaign for him – indeed that he must take as his running mate a 'squeaky clean' but little-known vice-presidential running mate, Senator Joe Lieberman, an observant Jew from Connecticut.

The result, for Gore, was not encouraging. The country was deemed by the public to be on the right track politically and economically, but on the wrong track in terms of ethics and ethical leadership. By a five-to-one margin, voters felt that the born-again Christian, Governor Bush, was more 'honest' than the vice president who was tainted by his loyal service to Clinton. In the closest election in American history, on November 7, 2000, Vice President Gore won the majority of votes cast, but after a Supreme Court ruling of five votes to four on December 12, lost in the Electoral College (266 to 271) thanks to a number of disputed paper chads in Florida. Clinton's refusal to resign had ensured his own survival in the Oval Office, but had ruined Gore's chances of succeeding him.

Just as President Carter had worked to the last hours of his presidency to secure the release of the American embassy hostages in Tehran, so President Clinton worked to get an Israeli–Palestinian settlement while the centrist Israeli prime minister, Ehud Barak, was still in power. Clinton even passed up the possibility of flying to North Korea to get an agreement banning long-range missiles, in a last-ditch attempt to get Arafat to accept an American-brokered Middle East peace deal. To his chagrin Arafat declined the deal, thereby surrendering the best opportunity for an Israeli–Palestinian settlement since 1948. In one of their last conversations, as Clinton recalled, Arafat 'thanked me for all my efforts and told me what a great man I was. "Mr Chairman," I replied, "I am not a great man. I am a failure, and you have made me one." I warned Arafat that he was single-handedly electing Sharon and that he would reap the whirlwind.'[50] Arafat did – but so too did America.

That Clinton, for all his brilliance as a politician, was simply too shameless and self-centred to put the dignity of the office and the good of the nation first seemed to be symbolized as he left the White House. In the final hour of his presidency he chose to grant a controversial pardon to Mark Rich, the ex-husband of a major donor promising to give more than $150,000 to Clinton's Presidential Library and museum project in Little Rock – but a man still wanted for massive IRS tax fraud and evasion.[51]

Many of Clinton's staffers and subordinates had already left his administration in disgust at the Lewinsky scandal. Even the most loyal remaining Friends of Bill, however, wondered if the departing president had taken leave of his senses. Despite his weekly counselling, months spent on the marital couch and two post-impeachment years trying to demonstrate his still-remarkable skills as president, Clinton had shown yet again that personal interest had triumphed.

The Rich pardon thus marred the by now traditional departure of the former president from Washington. In an emotional speech at Andrews Air Force Base on January 20, 2001, the charismatic, indefatigable but narcissistic arch-egoist of the United States lauded his time and achievements in the White House as 'the ride of my life' and flew into retirement – not to Arkansas, but to Chappaqua, New York, where his wife had won a thrilling election that had put her in the Senate, and on track for her own eventual bid for the imperial crown.[52]

Part Three: Private Life

From earliest infancy Bill Clinton wanted to please. His absolute determination to be liked and admired masked, however, deep inner turmoil, something he later described as 'the difficulty I've had in letting anyone into the deepest recesses of my internal life. It was dark down there.'[53] His lack of a real father, his abusive, alcoholic stepfather, his mother's divorce and remarriage all contributed to this black hole; indeed it was remarkable the boy from Hope was in most respects so normal.

At elementary school in Hot Springs one of his Catholic teachers jokingly told his mother he was so smart he would land either in jail or in the White House.

Over time this need to please, and his propensity to over-promise, became a serious moral hazard. He was, in his way, too gifted to be true, especially given his underlying demons. As the 6' 3" All State saxophone-player prodigy from Hot Springs High School went out into the wider world, he was like an accident waiting to happen, at once brilliant and yet, in his overweening ambition, lacking a reliable core moral fibre. Somehow, he continued to hope, his positives – a genuine compassion for the underprivileged, a determination to improve the conditions of life in which most people struggled, an ability to synthesize smart thinking, and a promise of betterment to those in need of hope – would outweigh his inability to say no to temptation. As his neighbour Carolyn Staley, the daughter of a Baptist minister, put it, he wore 'good on one shoulder, and bad on the other'.[54] For many – indeed ultimately for tens of millions, who came to see him as a political rock star – the good would outweigh the bad. But for many others, the bad aroused contempt and even hatred, sometimes of a distinctly malevolent kind, suggesting that Clinton's transgressions – his occasionally callous behaviour, his over-promising, and his lying – were experienced as a betrayal of their high expectations, like scorned lovers.

In some cases, this was no more than the truth. Bill Clinton's private life abounded with such cases. In Hot Springs his best female friend, Carolyn Yeldell, loved him and expected him to propose to her, so close did she feel to him. One night, on her way to meet him, she saw him on his doorstep, on vacation from Georgetown University, kissing another woman. She assumed it was a fellow Georgetown undergraduate whom Bill had been seeing – only to find it was Miss Arkansas.[55]

Wherever he went, Bill Clinton seemed to arouse – and disappoint – such dreams; indeed when he became president, a whole book, *Dreams of Bill*, was published, recording actual nocturnal dreams people had experienced and recorded in which they found themselves – men as well as women – seduced by the Man From Hope: romantically, companionably, erotically, sexually.[56] He was, some claimed, a sort of throwback to the great studio stars of Hollywood,

BILL CLINTON   471

about whom millions had also dreamed: big, bushy-haired, hugely
intelligent, fun-loving like his mother, rippling with energy and in
his positivism promising more than he could possibly deliver – especially once he met Hillary Rodham at Yale Law School and became
engaged to her.

The fact was, among women in a 1970s American culture of women's
lib, Bill Clinton's unusually open nature, at once inquisitive and compassionate, invited friendship and easy intimacy. For men who hewed to
a more moral line in their behaviour, or were less successful in
attracting women, Bill Clinton's ability to 'have it all' aroused fear-
some envy, even in his twenties. It didn't seem fair that a man from
such a humble background should have such mega-intelligence, such
an abundant love of life, such a confident ability to network and
promote himself, and such success with the fairer sex. 'Did I feel he
was exploiting her?' one friend asked rhetorically, learning that Bill
was having sex with one of his congressional campaign aides, despite
his engagement to Hillary Rodham. 'I did, I did! I mean this was just
one example that happened to involve a female, an example that
happened to involve sex. But he does it with men, too! He seduces
men – and when I say seduce, I mean the minds, the commitments,
the emotions – yes, the affections. He demands a kind of loyalty,
complete, consummate loyalty, while giving nothing in return!'[57]

This objection, amounting to moral outrage, had little to do with
politics, and everything to do with envy, though envy of an interesting
kind. Clinton's friend, over time, would become his nemesis – and
lawyer for the Arkansas Troopers whose scandalous story of unending
sexual conquests, which they were expected to facilitate, led to the
Paula Jones harassment case, setting in motion a process that would
lead to impeachment.

Politics, as such, did not figure in this equation. What it boiled
down to, in essence, was the spectacle of a hugely charismatic, idealistic individual whose amoral conduct defied and thus threatened
the moral code that others were trying to live up to in their own
lives. That Bill Clinton not only indulged himself, but *got away with
it* – his Gingerbread Man, catch-me-if-you-can casualness – infuriated such observers, some of whom became determined to try and
take him down, not as Republicans but as moral human beings struggling in their own lives to be good. It was not for nothing that Clinton

sneeringly referred to the director of the FBI, Louis Freeh, as the 'Boy Scout'.

As if to make the syndrome more galling still, Hillary Rodham's refusal to take Bill's surname upon their marriage in 1975 aroused yet more ire, in Arkansas, since this too took the matter of enviable success and amorality to a fourth dimension: not only was the super-gifted Attorney General, then governor, committing adultery with nightclub singers such as Gennifer Flowers with marital impunity, but his wife was meanwhile benefiting as a corporate lawyer from his political eminence, without even having to pay the traditional dues by surrendering her name. Indeed those who did not know the Clintons assumed it must be nothing short of a marriage of convenience.

They were wrong, however convenient the bond between such ambitious, self-seeking individuals, besotted by the nobility of their mutual enterprise. Bill Clinton *did* genuinely love Hillary, his friends agreed – but then, Bill Clinton genuinely loved everybody, from his grandma to his neighbour. What was different, they noted, was that he also *needed* Hillary. In the intimate company of the Gennifer Flowers-type women he bedded (or who bedded him), he might complain that Hillary – the eldest daughter of a tough, self-made Republican millionaire from Chicago – was too hard, too anti-erotic, too workaholic, too humourless. But from the moment he had stared at her in the Yale Law School library in 1971 and the fateful conversation they'd had on the steps outside after she deliberately accosted him, the Arkansas prodigy from the wrong side of the tracks had known Hillary was the only woman who could possibly share his political goals, keep him focused, and rein him in for his own good. This was not convenience, it was necessity. As one aide later reflected, without Hillary, Bill Clinton could easily have ended up a convicted drug addict like his younger half-brother Roger, pumping gas on prison furlough in Arkansas.

The marriage to Hillary Rodham in 1975 was, in short, a lifesaver for Bill Clinton, however much he thereafter strayed and thereby strained Hillary's patience, loyalty and perseverance. Without Chelsea, the daughter Hillary gave birth to in 1980, the union might well have collapsed, but as in many marriages, parental responsibility trumped dreams of flight. It was never easy, however: Bill's self-indulgence, his narcissism and his love of sexual adventure led him to acts of lunacy for a politician aspiring to a larger stage than that of landlocked little Arkansas, with its two million souls. As chairperson for Northwest Arkansas Democrats, Ann Henry later recalled how her daughter had telephoned her, sobbing. 'She was so angry, so upset!' Ann explained. 'She'd been to dinner at a friend's house – one of my friend's houses, who was then Bill's big supporter – and there was a woman there talking about *her affair with Bill Clinton!*' Going to Diane Blair, a political science professor and close friend of the Clintons, Mrs Henry said: 'I can't support him . . . Chelsea is eight years old, and this is going to devastate her – I mean he *cares* about his daughter.'[58]

Bill did, but the urge to play off-reservation was simply too enticing, and Hillary's leash too elastic for a state governor with a whole security detail willing to pimp and lie for him, as long as he controlled their jobs.

Thus, though Bill Clinton withdrew from a possible presidential run in the 1988 election, the leopard in him could not, and did not, change its spots. Clinton reasoned that his country needed him, despite his failings. For Hillary it was often a form of purgatory knowing that every so often a new scandal would arise, which they would have to deal with as best they could, unable to protect their daughter from the shame. That a man of such unique talents – the most gifted politician of his generation – should be so much a prey to his sexual, self-gratificatory urges, was a cross Hillary continued to bear, hoping others would bear it too, since they were, after all, not even *married* to him. What they both declined ever to address, though, was the effect that an adult lifetime of deceit and inevitable lying, however white the lies, and however well intentioned, would have on the trust that electors place upon those they empower – especially presidents.

The net result, then, of Hillary turning a blind eye to her husband's private failings, and her unquestioned conviction that others should ignore them too – the First Lady loudly contesting every allegation until her husband was eventually forced, each time, to confess his guilt – was to prolong the agony of a nation crippled by a sex scandal. Only Hillary, perhaps, could have persuaded Bill to resign. Concerned that she should have his fund-raising and politicking skills behind her when she began to eye a seat in the Senate for herself, she did not do so.

Thus did the tragedy of Bill Clinton's presidency unravel, a reign at once so positive and yet so negative for America. As the national exchequer filled, public trust in the silver-tongued Democratic president diminished, creating a deep public yearning in America for a more disciplined, authoritative leadership, such as that being offered by an unseasoned, seemingly simple-minded Republican: the born-again Christian son of the forty-first president.

CHAPTER TWELVE

GEORGE W. BUSH

Later Reviled

Republican
43rd President
(20 January, 2001–20 January, 2009)

Part One: The Road to the White House

George Walker Bush was born on July 6, 1946, in New Haven, Connecticut, the first child of Lieutenant George Herbert Walker Bush, a distinguished navy flier who was taking his undergraduate degree at Yale, postponed by his service in World War II.

George W. – nicknamed 'Dubya' or 'Junior' once the Bush family moved to Odessa and then Midland, Texas – proved a tormented child. He suffered learning disabilities and attention deficit disorder at school which left him with a lifelong inadequacy, a deficit he masked in a variety of ways, from hellraising to sneering contempt for those more intellectually gifted. His father's long absences as an oil prospector and entrepreneur, his mother Barbara's rocky, peremptory attempts to bring up the growing family largely on her own, and the early death of his young sister Robin from leukaemia when he was seven, left him flailing as eldest son, wanting to do what was responsible, yet by nature a rebel: insecure, provocative, a jester, but often angry with himself, sullen, and driven to flight.

Doing what was responsible involved emulating his father's record – a high bar for any child of George H. W. Bush to vault. At Andover boarding school George W.'s teachers despaired of him, and assumed he would not be accepted at Yale on his grades. The records of his grandfather – senator for Connecticut – and his father at the university, however, along with his father's run for the Senate that year (1964), ensured his acceptance.

Leaving Yale, W. told his family he hadn't 'learned a damn thing'.[1] Ineligible for graduate school deferment due to his poor grades, he was only able to avoid service in Vietnam by his acceptance, thanks to his father, in the Texas Air National Guard as a part-time fighter-interceptor pilot trainee, but without a regular job.[2] His father then bailed him out when he was arrested and charged for possession of cocaine in 1972. Instead of going to prison, the Houston judge arranged for him to do community service, and the legal record to be expunged.[3] Thus ended George W. Bush's National Guard author-ization to fly nuclear-capable F-102 Interceptors.[4] Leaving Texas, he did not complete the final two years of his ANG air force service in any capacity, or indeed any of the work projects to which he was assigned by his father.

Though many partied with 'Junior' (a name he hated), few liked the bullying George W. Bush – including himself. His permanent sneer or smirk, his insecurity vis-à-vis his father, his love of alcohol, his awkward, antagonistic relationship with his siblings, his use of nick-names for people – as if he could only cope with others in his own cartoon-like world – conspired to produce an often obnoxious and resentful figure, at odds with the world around him and the expect-ations placed upon him. He was turned down by the University of Texas Law School and seemed locked in a downward, binge-drinking spiral. However, his father's reputation as a loyal public servant and rising figure in the Republican Party once again came to his rescue, and to widespread astonishment W. was accepted into Harvard University's MBA programme in the autumn of 1973 ('I got lots of help', as he put it).[5]

W. was 'dumber than dumb', one of his classmates recalled, 'so inarticulate it was frightening'.[6] In a class discussion of the Great Depression, George W. announced: 'People are poor because they are lazy' – words he would rue twenty-four years later, when Wall Street imploded.[7] His macroeconomics professor was sickened by his arro-gance and deliberately closed mind – a young man 'totally lacking in compassion, with no sense of history, completely devoid of social responsibility, and unconcerned with the welfare of others . . . I gave him a low pass.'[8]

George W. was arrested and charged with drink-driving in Maine in September 1976; even his Harvard MBA did not lead to success in the oil prospecting business in Texas.[9] In 1977 he therefore tried an alternative route to success, by entering politics as a Republican. Despite his father's best efforts – including the help of one of George

Sr's political action committee aides, of Karl Rove, and of Bush's brother Neil – he lost his bid for the seat of a retiring Texas Democratic congressman in the 1978 elections by over 6,000 votes. Bush's sneer lengthened. Repeated attempts at business in the 1980s fared as badly as in the 1970s, his energy companies soaking up investment from rich family friends and others, but teetering always on the edge of bankruptcy. It was then that the sudden advent of evangelical Christianity changed W.'s life.

W.'s 'conversion', or submission to the saving grace of Jesus Christ, intrigued those watching the Bush dynasty. Though for campaign purposes it was later ascribed to the intercession of the Revd Billy Graham, who visited the Bush family at their summer home in Kennebunkport, Maine, in 1986, George W.'s epiphany took place in Texas, and was the triumph of an evangelical preacher, Arthur Blessitt, who brought W. to 'know Jesus' in 1984. Famous for ministering to dropouts and drug addicts in San Francisco, and for carrying a twelve-foot-high, forty-five-pound cross around the world, Blessitt was proselytizing on Midland local radio when George W. asked for a private meeting at the Midland Holiday Inn. 'A good and powerful day', Blessitt noted triumphantly in his diary that night, April 3: 'Led vice president's son to Jesus today. George Bush Jr! This is great! Glory to God!'[10] Holding hands with Blessitt and an oilman friend, Jim Sale, Bush prayed and received Blessitt's benediction: 'You are saved!'[11]

Jesus alone was not enough to get the vice president's son to quit drinking, however. Rather, it was finding himself under threat of divorce by his long-suffering, pretty, librarian wife for his binge drinking and neglect of their twin daughters that, on W.'s fortieth birthday on July 6, 1986, finally caused him to give up alcohol completely, and start his life on a new basis of paternal responsibility and temperance.[12]

Evangelical Christianity did not make George Bush Jr into a good person, but it incontrovertibly made him into a less bad one, as he himself was the first to admit. 'I wasn't pleasant to be around', he said, describing his drinking bouts. 'All you have to do is ask my wife.'[13] His wife joked that 'it was when he got the bar bill' that the penny dropped.[14] The truth, however, was more prosaic. 'His marriage was falling apart,' a friend confided, 'and he cared about his girls. That's what turned him around.'[15] 'George is pretty impulsive,' Laura Bush observed, 'and does pretty much everything to excess. Drinking is not one of the good things to do to excess.'[16] As W.'s doctor explained, he just couldn't stop drinking, once he started.[17]

The vice president was delighted by his son swearing off alcohol, though he denied in public that George W. was ever 'an alcoholic. It's just he knows he can't hold his liquor.'

Alcohol, W. confided, had begun to 'compete with my energies', causing him to 'lose focus'.[18] He had never bothered to learn the oil business from the ground up, as his father had done, or to nurture relationships based on goodwill, trust and earned respect. What he offered investors and partners, however, was access to his father, the vice president, and to his father's Rolodex.

With commercial success in the oil industry still eluding him, W. moved in 1987 to Washington DC to work for George Sr as he prepared his run for the presidency, acting as the campaign's family 'enforcer', side by side with the egregious Lee Atwater and Roger Ailes.

The success of Lee Atwater's tactics in destroying Governor Dukakis in the 1988 presidential campaign exhilarated the younger members of the Bush team, even if it rewarded the destructive aspect of his character that W. had, in embracing born-again Christianity, sought to overcome. 'If we lose this one, we're dead' George W. warned Atwater before the all-important New Hampshire primary in February 1988. 'Get out a dirty tricks book, Lee, and start reading.'[19]

Atwater did – and George H. W. Bush was elected president. At the climax of the campaign, however, George W. organized a quite different, personal coup from the campaign office: the purchase of the Texas Rangers baseball team.

W.'s financial gamble of a mere $600,000 towards the $86 million purchase price for the team turned out a windfall, since the investors – culled from his father's Rolodex – gave W. a full 10 per cent stake as the 'rainmaker'. When taxpayers then financed the building of a new $135 million stadium in Arlington for the Rangers, he became a multimillionaire overnight. More significantly, it gave W., at last, his *own* claim to fame, irrespective of his father – despite the disappointing subsequent performance of the baseball team. 'This is as good as it gets' he later recalled thinking. 'Life cannot be better than this.'[20]

But it could be, he was assured by his cronies – by entering politics again, on his own behalf. He was asked by his mother not to run for the governorship of Texas in 1990, however, or for a seat in the

Senate in 1992, given the huge funds his father would need for his 1992 re-election. Instead, W. once again offered his paid services as war-room 'enabler' to the president in the 1992 campaign.

W.'s father, to the chagrin of his staff, was not re-elected that year. For W. himself, it was a bitter blow, since he attributed his father's demise to his refusal to use dirty tricks in the campaign against Governor Bill Clinton until it was too late. The failure of his father thus became a turning point in W.'s life trajectory, since he saw himself as tougher and more streetwise and yearned to demonstrate his own skills. He thus announced he would stand for the governorship of Texas against the incumbent, Ann Richards, in the 1994 election.

W.'s younger brother Jeb did likewise, in Florida, challenging the incumbent Democratic governor Lawton Chiles. Where Jeb did so, however, on a clearly articulated right-wing Republican platform, W. decided to employ a strategy recommended by the political aide who'd worked closely with Lee Atwater in the 1970s: Karl Rove.

Karl Rove was short, ugly, prematurely balding and ambitious. He had been instantly drawn to the ruggedly good-looking political wannabe with the big family pedigree and money, George W. Bush. 'He was the kind of guy political hacks like me wait a lifetime to be associated with' explained Rove, who considered himself hitherto a 'diehard Nixonite'.[21] Rove, a non-believer, told his new idol that the support of evangelists would trump all other political advantages and issues, if properly marshalled. 'This is just great!' Bush responded. 'I can become governor of Texas just with the evangelical vote.'[22]

Having formally hired Rove as his 'brain', W. now went into electoral battle with Governor Richards, having carefully lined up the support of evangelical Christian leaders in the state. Guns, too, provided a platform. Reclining by his swimming pool and smoking a cigar, W. threw in a tennis ball for his dog to fetch. 'Sip, my man,' he said to Don Sipple, his media consultant, 'don't underestimate what you can learn from a failed presidency.'[23] His father, W. maintained, had permitted 'Bill Clinton [to] decide what issues the two of them were going to talk about' – a 'major mistake' that he, George W. Bush, wasn't going to make, at least not when he could bang the twin drums, God and guns.

Bush's Texas gubernatorial campaign in 1994 represented the culmination of disciplined modern partisan political campaigning in America:

cynical, relentlessly focused, manipulative, largely dishonest, negative
– and hugely funded. Claiming he had never once been unfaithful to
his porcelain-pretty wife (who had asked him not to run), but was a
born-again Christian and successful Texas businessman now that he
owned the Texas Rangers baseball team, Bush was able not only to
separate himself from his East Coast father, but to contrast himself
against his baby-boomer contemporary in the White House: the
scandal-dogged, incompetent-looking President Bill Clinton, who in
the summer of 1994 was the proverbial elephant in the room.[24] Thus,
to Governor Richards' chagrin, in a triumphant year for Republicans
as they captured control of both the Senate and House of
Representatives for the first time in forty years, Bush won the Texas
gubernatorial battle that autumn by an astonishing 352,000 votes. The
'black sheep of the family', as his mother had ribbed him in conversation with the Queen of England, had redeemed himself as the
Prodigal Son. He would now be governor of the second largest and
second most populous state of the union.

To the amazement of those like Ann Richards who had predicted
disaster for the state if 'the jerk' (as she called him) was elected, George
W. Bush proved, thanks to the checks and balances of the Texas polity
in the 1990s, a popular and remarkably effective governor in the public's
perception. He had promised he would permit Texans the right to carry
concealed weapons, and he did – persuading a sceptical legislature, in
defiance of the recent passing of the Brady Background Check and
Assault Weapons Ban bills in Congress, to pass his pro-gun bill, which
he then signed into law. In a period of otherwise diminishing violent
crime, over time it would prove a Texas nightmare. Yet for the moment
he basked in his achievement, gaining the same bipartisan success in
pushing through three other primary platform promises he'd made:
ending automatic parole for prisoners, instituting civil court tort reform,
and reforming welfare. Though each measure was considerably altered
by the Democratic legislature, the governor was lauded for his clear
agenda, tight focus, and the way he worked with the state's Democratic
lawmakers. Best of all, from Texans' perspective, was the fact he did
not seem to be, as former Governor Richards had claimed, an out-
of-depth greenhorn in politics, or a poor copy of his privileged,
sugar-daddy East Coast father. Eating peanut-butter sandwiches and
Mexican food, visiting with every legislator in their own offices rather

than the governor's mansion, drinking beer with ordinary folk, befriending journalists and insisting on a ceaseless schedule of public events as governor, Bush soon earned the moniker 'the Energizer Bunny' – casually dressed in jeans and cowboy boots, sincere, simplistic and willing to listen to opponents, even to compromise.[25] In 1998, after four years in office, he was re-elected governor by a landslide. Given his pedigree, people began to talk of a presidential run in 2000, when Clinton's scandal-ridden second term would come to an end.

With his wavy, wiry hair, the blue-eyed ease with which he joshed people, and his ability to memorize their names and faces, the Texas governor seemed a paragon of simple, homey virtues. He rose at dawn and cycled three to six miles before breakfast. He neither chased women nor allowed them to chase him. And he went to bed with his pretty wife ritually at 9 p.m., even before his daughters retired.

Texas was booming thanks to the NAFTA free trade agreement with Mexico that had led to surging growth, especially in high-tech and maquiladora cross-border manufacturing assembly areas. Hand in hand with W.'s confidence in his growing political leadership skills went another, darker piece of knowledge: he had cracked the secret code of success in modern American campaigning – character assassination.

It was W.'s ability to sleep soundly every night, knowing this and not being ashamed of it, that finally convinced him he had the necessary toughness to be president. Though capable of surprising empathy with less privileged, ordinary individuals in Texas, he had displayed no qualms or compassion when approving some 152 executions as governor, even where doubts lingered as to the culpability or mental health of the criminal.[26] With the help of his strategist Karl Rove and his communications director Karen Hughes, he felt he was ready to face his rivals if he ran.

The Bush Tragedy, as it came to be called, was that however popular he was in his home state, he had no business seeking to be leader of the free world. His wife begged him not to do it. He had virtually never travelled abroad. As his national security adviser Dr Condoleezza Rice, a Stanford University professor, put it, he was conversant only with Mexico across the border. 'He has on-the-ground experience there,' she explained, 'which I would say is much more valuable than if he had been attending seminars at the Council on Foreign Relations for the last five years.' Guffaws of laughter contested her view.[27]

When Senator McCain won the first Republican primary in New

Hampshire by a huge margin of nineteen percentage points, Bush was distraught. McCain had campaigned in a bus he called 'The Straight Talk Express' while Bush had travelled in a private jet and, nervous lest his ignorance show, had not given a single in-depth interview to the hundred reporters following his campaign.

Bush's response, as it had been when helping his father defeat Governor Dukakis, was to get out the dirty tricks book. In the case of McCain, this required trashing the senator's war record and his character, spreading rumours that he had fathered an illegitimate child who was black.[28]

The accusations defied belief in their viciousness, pillorying Senator McCain 'with lies that he was a liberal reprobate who abandoned a crippled wife to father black children with black prostitutes. Preposterous charges of extramarital affairs, abortion, wife beating, mob ties, venereal diseases, and illegitimate children were flung at him, while his wife Cindy was tarred as a wayward woman and drug addict who had stolen to support her habit, his children were vilified as bastards' – the 'poison drip' saturating South Carolina 'for eighteen days and nights of slaughterhouse politics'.[29]

Had Atwater lived, he would have been proud of Karl Rove, but McCain – who lost the second primary – was so disgusted he never forgave Bush. 'Don't give me that shit,' the senator snarled when, after their one televised debate, Bush apologized and claimed 'We've got to start running a better campaign.'[30]

'The deeply personal, usually anonymous allegations that make up a smear campaign are aimed at a candidate's most precious asset: his reputation', McCain's campaign director said when watching Bush and Rove repeat their tactics in 2004. 'The reason this blackest of the dark arts is likely to continue is simple: It often works.'[31] It did. Though McCain countered by resorting to bare-knuckle tactics in the Michigan primary, and won it by seven percentage points, his heart wasn't in such methods. Nor, more significantly, could he raise the tens of millions of dollars W. was assembling. On March 9, 2000, Senator McCain dropped out of the race, and Bush's path to nomination as the Republican candidate was cleared.

There remained just one major decision to make, in the summer of 2000, as the Republican National Convention approached: who Governor Bush should invite to be his Republican vice-presidential nominee.

With a Harvard MBA but no administrative experience outside Texas,

Bush looked for an older man to be his vice-presidential partner. All polls showed the revered four-star general, Colin Powell, to be the most popular choice he could make. When asked if he would serve, however, Power declined, though he left his door open to a possible cabinet post.

George H. W. Bush, Powell's former boss, begged him to reconsider, but Powell struck to his decision – which doomed both Governor Bush and America. The only other nominee for the vice presidency with major public approval was Senator McCain, who would not even speak to Bush after the primary campaign, let alone serve under him. Bush therefore entrusted the selection process to his father's former Secretary of Defense, Richard B. Cheney.

Cheney gave a thumbs down to all contenders – save himself. To Governor Bush the idea of Dick Cheney as vice president seemed a welcome, unthreatening idea, one that would appeal not only to those Republicans who revered W.'s father but also to those pundits who claimed the governor of Texas was an inexperienced lightweight. On July 25, 2000, the announcement was made and the Bush–Cheney ticket was born. On November 7, the dead heat that polls predicted actually transpired. It was the tightest presidential election since 1876.

Early results in Florida caused the Democratic candidate, Vice President Gore, to concede the presidential election to Bush, but then to retract his concession when a recount looked necessary. Thirty-five excruciating days of tallying, recounting, legal objection, appeals to state Supreme Court jurisdiction, and finally Republican appeals to the US Supreme Court, ensued.

Despite Gore having won the popular vote by an estimated 200,000 (later certified to be more than half a million) out of a total 105 million votes cast, the Supreme Court overthrew the Florida Court's decision to continue the recount process.[32] By virtue of Florida's twenty-five Electoral College votes, Governor Bush was thus declared the president-elect on December 12, 2000, in a split vote of the nine Justices, five to four.

Part Two: The Presidency

Given the controversial nature of the election result, most pundits expected the forty-third president to be humble, and to seek to unify the country through compromise and goodwill. After all, he gave a 'solemn pledge' in his inaugural address to 'build a single nation of justice and opportunity', especially in tackling reform of American public education, the social security system and Medicare sectors of the economy. Abroad he promised to 'show purpose without arrogance'. Seldom were a president's inaugural vows so neglected.

In the White House, the new president was determined to make his mark, both in dress and in speech, and thereby provide a contrast to his predecessor. He insisted on new standards of behaviour and clothing, ordering that everyone wear shirts, ties and jackets at all times, and be punctual to the minute. (Unpunctuality had been Clinton's second name.) Within that professional formality for others, however, Bush sought to etch his own image not only as commander-in-chief, but also a 'regular guy'. He thus continued his practice of calling people by nicknames he bestowed on them, such as 'Pablo' for the astonished new Treasury Secretary, Paul O'Neill, or 'Fredo' for his new Attorney General, Alberto Gonzales. In this way he asserted his distinctive new Bush leadership style: friendly, personal, yet strictly focused and expeditious.

It did not, however, fool those who were significantly cleverer, especially the former president. 'He doesn't know anything', commented Clinton in frustration, after meeting Bush during the transition and attempting to warn him of the grave dangers posed by Islamic terrorism. 'He doesn't *want* to know anything.'[33]

Sensing the intellectual void at the heart of the imperial presidency, Bush's new chief of staff Andrew Card (who had served under George Sr as a deputy chief of staff) redoubled his efforts to protect the prince from scrutiny while he found his feet. Presidential press conferences and interviews were therefore not permitted, lest Bush stumble or reveal his lacunae. Visits to the inner sanctum were carefully screened and kept to a minimum.

If the press was thereby held at bay, however, Bush's shallowness of intellect and limited understanding were not easy to conceal from his close colleagues. In meetings with the cabinet it was almost impossible to hide the President's lack of knowledge, or even interest, in most subjects discussed, beyond the wish to get decisions made, whatever the consequences.

There were some issues the president seemed genuinely to care about, Card was relieved to know. For example, Bush wanted to promote education reform through new national testing – a subject the First Lady, as a trained librarian, felt strongly about. He also wished to push through a major tax cut for the wealthy, who would – he hoped – use the money to invest in the economy, which was faltering at the end of a sustained boom. But beyond that he seemed remarkably . . . vacant. When a Texas friend had asked during the campaign what would happen if he lost the election, W. had shrugged. 'Oh, I don't know, Jimmy. That wouldn't be the worst thing that could happen. I guess I'd just go back to Dallas, watch a lot of baseball games, spend time with my friends and Laura and the girls, make a living, enjoy life. Do what other people do.' 'Simple as that?' the friend had pressed. 'Yep, that simple.'[34]

In Austin, Texas, where the legislature only met once every two years for 140 days, and where the lieutenant governor was arguably more powerful than the governor, Bush's empty-headedness hadn't really mattered. But in Washington, at the citadel of the world's mightiest empire, power was the meat and drink of daily life. People fought for it, used it, abused it, manipulated it, and had done so long before the nation became an empire. If the president saw his role merely as a mediator-manager, a chairman of the board of America Inc., would there not then be a struggle for power among the directors of the board?

Meeting for a full hour with the president in the Oval Office shortly after the coronation, Treasury Secretary Paul O'Neill – who had served under presidents Ford and George H. W. Bush – was stunned by Bush's inability to ask a single question. 'Strange', O'Neill reflected.[35] Over subsequent weeks, he recognized Bush had already ceded control of economic policy and tax cuts to his new presidential adviser, Karl Rove. Moreover, in the very first National Security Council meeting he attended, on January 30, 2001, O'Neill was astonished to hear the Secretary of Defense, Donald Rumsfeld, and the vice president, Dick Cheney, talking about invading Iraq.[36]

To O'Neill's near-disbelief the president then announced, in confidence, that America was pulling out of further attempts to obtain peace in the Middle East through an Israeli–Palestinian accord. 'Clinton overreached', Bush declared simply. 'If the two sides don't want peace, there's no way to force them.' And W. went on to extol the new prime minister of Israel, Ariel Sharon – who had a black

name for intransigence, provoking the Palestinian intifada, and expanding Jewish settlements in the West Bank. 'I'm not going to go on
past reputations when it comes to Sharon' the president said. Sharon
had taken Bush on a helicopter flight over Palestinian camps in 1998,
on one of his handful of trips outside the United States. That seemed
to be enough. 'Just saw him that one time', Bush explained. 'Looked
real bad down there. I think it's time to pull out of that situation.'[37]

Astonished, the new Secretary of State, General Colin Powell,
warned that an American withdrawal from Clinton's Middle East peace
process would offer a green light for Sharon and the Israeli Army to
use force, undeterred. 'The consequences of that could be dire,' Powell
cautioned, 'especially for the Palestinians.' To which the president
responded with a shrug, followed by the fateful words that 'a show
of strength by one side can really clarify things'.[38] And with that, the
meeting was invited by the national security adviser, Dr Condoleezza
Rice, to discuss an alternative way of imposing democracy on the
Middle East – via the ousting of Saddam Hussein, and the colonization of Iraq! To this end, the president instructed Rumsfeld and the
chairman of the Joint Chiefs, General Shelton, to 'examine our military options'.[39]

O'Neill and Powell were dumbfounded. Neither Gerald Ford nor
George H.W. Bush had been men of the highest intellect, but both
had learned to listen, and to process competing interpretations of the
facts, consider carefully the consequences of a proposed action, and
make an informed ultimate decision as president and commander-in-
chief. Now, behind the mask of tight-lipped, leak-proof, disciplined,
crisp new management style, O'Neill began to realize a palace coup
seemed already to have taken place under Karl Rove, who proceeded
to set up no less than four new Republican Political Offices on the
second floor of the White House, and insisted he have a point-man
on every White House committee. Moreover, Rove had a twin: the
vice president.

Cheney had also immediately set up his political store in the White
House. He insisted that his chief of staff, Scooter Libby, not only hold
the job of national security adviser to the vice president but also the
position of presidential assistant to Bush – entitled, like Rove's capos,
to see all documents before they reached the president. Cheney, Libby
or the vice president's legal adviser, David Addington ('the most

powerful man you've never heard of'), thus not only sat in on every committee and panel in the White House, but ensured that every presidential letter, email or document be copied to them – yet that no vice-presidential document be copied to the president.[40]

Treasury Secretary Paul O'Neill was not the only official worried by the Rove–Cheney palace takeover. Counter-terrorism czar Richard Clarke, for example, had already felt concern during the election campaign at the Bush team's apparent indifference to the growing threat of terrorism. Very soon Clarke was reprimanded by the national security adviser. 'You know,' Dr Rice said to him, 'don't give the president a lot of long memos, he's not a big reader.' Clarke was amazed. 'Well shit. I mean,' Clarke said later, *the president of the United States is not a big reader?*'[41]

The vice president was, though.

John Nance Garner had described the office of vice president as 'not worth a pitcher of warm piss', since it carried no constitutional responsibilities beyond certifying the election result, and then presiding over the Senate with a deciding vote in the event of a tie. The position *did* offer a literal and metaphorical side door to the presidency, though – however much Cheney assured Governor Bush he had no intention of ever running for the office himself.

At the core of Cheney's agenda, from the very start, was a determination to make himself as indispensible to the new monarch as Thomas Cromwell had been to King Henry VIII – only in Cheney's case, the throne would be his should the president be assassinated or incapacitated.

From the start of the Bush presidency, Cheney, sensing the ignorance and naivety of the new president in the Oval Office, was deferential to Bush in person, but a law unto himself outside. 'Bush's staff is terrified of Cheney's people', one White House staffer confided.[42] Another commented: 'They are too smart, too powerful for Bush and his team.' A third, a colonel who had admired Cheney earlier as Secretary of Defense, found himself appalled by the calculating way Cheney went about his task as vice president. Under George H.W. Bush, Dick Cheney had been brought back to earth whenever he moved out of line, such as the occasion when he openly criticized Mikhail Gorbachev in 1989 without presidential approval. 'Dump on Dick with all possible alacrity', had been Secretary of State James Baker's classic order at the time.

But now, with a callow, inexperienced, outmanoeuvred, outstaffed, and fatally incurious president in the Oval Office, there was a void – and it did not take Cheney long to fill it, Colonel Wilkerson reflected later. 'What in effect happened was that a very astute, probably the most astute, bureaucratic entrepreneur I've ever run into in my life became the vice president of the United States.' Seeing his opportunity, Cheney then waded 'into the vacuums that existed around George Bush – personality vacuum, details vacuum, experience vacuum'.[43]

To those around him, Bush insisted that his agenda was still 'compassionate conservatism', as his speechwriter, David Frum, recalled, especially with regard to public education. Cheney, however, did not care a fig for public schooling; indeed as a congressman he had voted to close down the nation's Department of Education completely. What he wanted was less federal interference in people's daily lives, and more imperial power in the White House to advance America's interests abroad: securing its energy supplies and requisite raw materials, disarming those who threatened it in any way, and maintaining military superiority. To achieve these aims would require beating back the inroads he felt Congress had made on presidential power since Watergate. So strongly did he feel about this, and so contemptuous of the Senate as an institution, he was willing to drive the White House off a cliff – as he did when persuading Bush not to compromise with the Republican senator Jim Jeffords over funding of the Disabilities Education Act. Even Karl Rove felt the president should make a concession to Jeffords, who wanted more budget money for special education programmes rather than giving it away in tax reduction. Rove memorably remarked that Senator Jeffords could be 'fucked over' later.[44] Cheney, however, got his way. Appalled, Senator Jeffords then carried out his threat to vote with the Democrats, causing the Senate to change hands in what was called a 'political earthquake'.[45]

This was not how Governor Bush had operated in Texas, insiders complained. But much worse was to follow.

Although Cheney had, as he himself put it, 'flunked' his further degree at Yale, whereas Dr Rice was a tenured professor at Stanford, she was no match for him. Cheney saw the same national intelligence information as Rice, and all her communications, but did not allow her to see *his* communications. Cheney would rise at 4.30 a.m. and hold his own intelligence briefing before Rice convened her morning security panel, prior to briefing the president. He dogged her every meeting, and oversaw her every recommendation. He even attended every meeting of the National Security Council Principals, and relentlessly demanded, from day one, that despite the deadly suicide attack on the USS *Cole* the previous autumn, they focus not on terrorism or al-Qaeda, but on Iraq.

Richard Clarke had no doubt that Osama Bin Laden had been behind the *Cole* bombing in Aden. Day after day, week after week, month after month, Clarke attempted to convince his new colleagues there was going to be another attack, either on American installations abroad or at home. Clarke, however, could make no headway with Cheney, Rice or Donald Rumsfeld, nor with Rumsfeld's number two, Paul Wolfowitz; indeed in the entire first eight months of the Bush presidency, Clarke was not permitted to brief President Bush a single time, despite mounting evidence of plans for a new al-Qaeda outrage.

To her subsequent shame, Rice first refused to agree to a meeting of Principals on the subject, then insisted the matter be handled only by a more junior Deputy Principals meeting, in April 2000, at which Wolfowitz announced he could not understand 'why we are beginning by talking about this one man Bin Laden'. Even after Clarke explained the al-Qaeda network, Wolfowitz protested: 'You give Bin Laden too much credit', and claimed Bin Laden could not achieve his ends without the aid of a state sponsor – namely Iraq, which Wolfowitz blamed for the 1993 World Trade Center bombing.

Clarke was dismayed. 'I could hardly believe it' he later wrote, given the utter discrediting of any Iraqi connection to the attack in New York. Attempting to keep his temper, Clarke prophesied: 'Al-Qaeda plans major acts of terrorism against the US' – indeed Osama Bin Laden and his terrorist group had actually published their plans. Sometimes, he said, 'as with Hitler in *Mein Kampf*, you have to believe that these people will actually do what they say they will do'.[46]

Clarke regretted the words as soon as they were out of his mouth, for Wolfowitz immediately declared he resented 'any comparison between the Holocaust and this little terrorist in Afghanistan'.[47]

For Clarke, the sheer obtuseness and sneering contempt of Bush's senior advisers and colleagues towards officials who had served in the Clinton administration was galling. It was as if a sort of wilful blindness seemed to afflict the new president, the vice president, the national security adviser and her deputy, and the Secretary of Defense and his deputy – leaving only Secretary of State Colin Powell and his deputy, Richard Clarke and a sceptical Treasury Secretary in a lonely battle to waken a seemingly deranged new administration, obsessed with Iraq, and with ending the ABM missile treaty with Russia, which was about to expire.

In vain Clarke sent out word that 'al-Qaeda is planning a major attack on us'; ordered all agencies on to high-alert status; asked the FBI and CIA to report to the downgraded Counterterrorism Group everything they could find out about suspicious individuals or activity inside and outside the United States.[48] Then, in a final challenge to Rice at the Principals meeting which she belatedly convened on September 4, 2001, Clarke asked her to picture herself at a moment 'when in the very near future al-Qaeda has killed hundreds of Americans', and to imagine asking herself what 'you wish then that you had already done'.[49]

Neither the president, Rice, nor other senior members of the Bush administration would ever admit afterwards to their somnambulance. Nor would any of them be brought to account. It made Clarke's blood boil.

On the morning of September 11, 2001, four small teams of al Qaeda suicide bombers, armed with simple boxcutters, boarded without hindrance four commercial US airliners: American Airlines flights 11 and 175 at Boston's Logan airport; American Airlines flight 77 at Dulles International, outside Washington DC; and United Airlines flight 93 at Newark Airport, outside New York. Using the very simplest of weapons to kill the pilots and fly the aircraft as guided missiles on to carefully chosen targets, they sought to create the maximum symbolic effect, killing thousands of innocent American citizens.

Though one team's effort was aborted in mid-flight, when passengers attacked the hijackers, the outrage achieved its object: the United States suffered more deaths that sunlit morning, in New York and Washington, than at Pearl Harbor in 1941.

As film and video of the collapsing Twin Towers at New York's World Trade Center were broadcast across the world, America went into shock. The president himself, sitting in on a class of second-graders in a school in Sarasota, Florida, seemed as stunned as ordinary people. He appeared unable to comprehend the footage of an aircraft flying into a high-rise building in Manhattan playing on a television screen as he went into the classroom, or the news whispered to him some minutes later that another plane had crashed into the second tower. Vice President Cheney was equally stunned.

The news came as no surprise, however, to the demoted counter-terrorism czar Richard Clarke, who knew immediately the organization behind the attack.

The president's message to the nation and the world, written by Karen Hughes and videotaped on board Air Force One, was forceful in asserting that the United States would not be intimidated by terrorists. Yet when Bush finally spoke, for the very first time in his presidency, to Richard Clarke the next evening in the Situation Room, it was to make what seemed an amazing presidential request: 'Look, I know you have a lot to do and all, but I want you, as soon as you can, to go back over everything, everything. See if Saddam did this. See if he's linked in any way.'[50]

Clarke, who had scarcely slept or eaten in two days as he grounded the nation's air traffic and attempted to thwart possible follow-up terrorist attacks, was 'taken aback, incredulous', he recalled. 'But Mr President, al-Qaeda did this' he protested. 'I know, I know,' Bush said, 'but . . . see if Saddam was involved. Just look. I want to know.'[51]

Dutifully, Clarke did so, suspecting that in the space of a few hours, Bush must already have been 'gotten at' by the madmen controlling National Security: Cheney, Rumsfeld and Wolfowitz, men who had, on the very night of the attack, held meetings not to avert further terrorism, or pursue al-Qaeda, but to have 'discussions about Iraq'.

Vice President Cheney had advised the president to stay out of Washington in a 'secure location' – a euphemism for cowardice. To his credit, Bush insisted on returning to the White House, joined by the First Lady. Cheney, who hid away for the next weeks, would not allow his obsession with Iraq to be defused or sidelined. As in surreal-ist science fiction, Cheney continued to participate in all discussions via 'secure video' communications, encouraging Bush to see the 9/11 attack not as the premeditated plot of demented Islamic terrorists answering to Osama Bin Laden, but as a global *casus belli*. George W. Bush could then become the war leader of the American Empire.

The president needed little persuasion. Without consulting his Secretary of State,[52] Bush announced to assembled reporters in the

Roosevelt Room at the White House on September 12, 2001, that the 'deliberate and deadly attacks' on New York were 'more than acts of terror. They were acts of war.' America would respond with full-scale war, a 'monumental struggle between good and evil' in which, if other countries did not join the US, 'we'll go it alone'.[53]

Had the last half-century of American experience as the leader of the free, democratic nations of the world, with decades of diplomacy and careful nurturing of allies, been discarded overnight? Half an hour later, when Bush again used the word 'war', the Senate Majority Leader, Democratic senator Tom Daschle, cautioned that 'War is a powerful word.' The president ignored him – and it was left to eighty-three-year-old Senator Robert Byrd, president *pro tempore* of the Senate, to warn that Congress would not give the blank cheque it had given Lyndon Johnson over the Tonkin incident, pulling from his pocket a copy of the Constitution to prove his point. To obtain congressional approval under the Constitution, any riposte would have to be targeted on al-Qaeda, not take America to war on a massive, open-ended scale like Vietnam.

Undeterred, Bush attended a fateful National Security Council meeting at 4 p.m. that day. 'Why shouldn't we go against Iraq, not just al-Qaeda?' Rumsfeld asked the president.

Cheney emphatically agreed, concerned that it might take time to 'get' the 'little terrorist' Bin Laden in Afghanistan, whereas a massive US invasion of a Muslim country like Iraq would make a powerful 'statement' of American imperial power and resolve. It was left to Secretary Powell to bring the meeting, which was advocating something very close to treason in its indifference to the need for Congress to approve such a war, back to its senses. Not only was there no evidence Iraq had anything to do with 9/11 or al-Qaeda, but 'Any action needs public support', Powell reminded his colleagues, in addition to congressional approval. 'It's not just what the international coalition' – should he be able to put together such a coalition – 'supports, it's what the American people want to support.' And lest there be any misunderstanding, he spelled it out again: 'The American people want us to do something about al-Qaeda.'[54]

The president seemed not hear his Secretary of State. Indeed, if ever there was a wrong man for the job of Caesar of the world's most powerful nation, it was the 'toxic Texan', as Bush proudly called himself after his withdrawal from the Kyoto Protocol. Hitherto he had seen his role as being that of a crisp, decisive chairman of the board of America, Inc, 9/11, however, changed him into a buffoon – to the delight of Cheney, who urged him to talk in public not just of locating and removing Bin Laden, but of launching a hopefully long and profitable war. Stepping down from his Marine One helicopter on September 16, 2001, Bush announced that 'this crusade, this war on terrorism is going to take a while'.

Rather than marginalizing al-Qaeda terrorists as freakish Islamic hotheads, was it not more likely that talk of a 'crusade' would raise the spectre of a new Judaeo-Christian military campaign against the Muslim world – and thus inflame such radicals, driving fringe groups to join with al-Qaeda as their inspiration, their strategic and ideological brain? Congress remained cautious. On September 18, 2001, a joint assembly of Congress authorized the president to 'use all necessary and appropriate force', but only 'against those nations, organizations, or persons he determines planned, authorized, or aided the terrorist attacks that occurred on September 11, 2001'.[55] Beyond that, Congress insisted on retaining its constitutional War Powers authority.

Rather than dampening Bush's zeal, Congress' cautionary language only seemed to galvanize him and Cheney. Addressing Congress in person on September 20, 2001, for the second time in his presidency, the president initially backtracked, assuring Muslims in America and across the world that they were not to blame, and would not be blamed, for their faith. Nevertheless, he made clear, the attack on the World Trade Center and the Pentagon constituted, like Pearl Harbor, a declaration of 'war' and the United States was thus a nation *at* war, one unlike any previous war America had waged. 'Americans are asking, "How will we fight and win this war?" We will direct every resource at our command – every means of diplomacy, every tool of intelligence, every instrument of law enforcement, every financial influence, and every necessary weapon of war – to the destruction and to the defeat of the global terror network.'

Diplomats across the world found this worrying. Bush's demeanour and language suggested that of a hastily deputized town marshal in a Wild West movie, rather than the heir of George Washington. 'It will not look like the air war above Kosovo two years ago, where no ground troops were used and not a single American was lost in combat', the president asserted. This time there would be blood – for America's new 'war on terrorism' would be war with a capital W – and without foreseeable end. 'Americans should not expect one battle, but a lengthy campaign unlike any other we have ever seen. It may include dramatic strikes visible on TV and covert operations, secret even in success. We will starve terrorists of funding, turn them one against another, drive them from place to place until there is no refuge or no rest. And we will pursue nations that provide aid or safe haven to terrorism. Every nation in every region now has a decision to make: either you are with us or you are with the terrorists.'

What did these words really mean, viewers and diplomats across the world wondered? Was not Congress, constitutionally, the only body entitled to declare war – especially such a vague 'war on terror' rather than on al-Qaeda, as the plotters specifically responsible for 9/11? What exactly would it mean to 'pursue' whole nations that aided terrorism? 'Our war on terror begins with al-Qaeda,' the president had declared, 'but it does not end there. It will not end until every terrorist group of global reach has been found, stopped and defeated.'

Every terrorist group found, stopped, defeated – not simply al-Qaeda? In the context of a president who had only *once* referred to the problem of terrorism in the eight and a half months since being inaugurated, and had now been given only specific, limited authorization by Congress, it seemed vague, messianic, emotional and ill-considered. Also – something that could not be said of Osama Bin Laden – not a little stupid, since it would be the very response Bin Laden wanted, energizing jihadists across the Muslim world.

As Colin Powell, would later remark, 'Bush had a lot of .45-caliber instincts, cowboy instincts.'[56] The president certainly seemed overex-cited, or on mood-enhancing medication. In his address to the joint session of Congress he had added, ominously and almost sotto voce, 'tonight a few miles from the damaged Pentagon I have a message for our military: be ready. I have called the armed forces to alert, and there is a reason. The hour is coming when America will act, and you will make us proud.'

The president's first 'act' of war took place four weeks later – in Afghanistan, not Iraq, to Rumsfeld's and Wolfowitz's chagrin. Blitzed by US and British air power, the Taliban forces that had harboured Bin Laden's jihadists ran away. Kabul fell on November 13, 2001, and Kandahar on December 7 as more than 1,000 Marines joined CIA, paramilitaries and US Commandos supporting the anti-Taliban forces of the Northern Alliance on the ground.

Casualties among innocent Afghan civilians (referred to as 'collateral damage') mounted, however; indeed by Christmas 2001 they exceeded those killed in the 9/11 attacks in America. Neither the president nor Rumsfeld, nor Cheney, nor Rice, took heed. The US was magnificently 'winning' – so far. Bin Laden and the Taliban leader, Mullah Omar, fell back towards the Pakistani border, resolving to fight a guerilla, mujahidin-style campaign, just as they had done against the Russians. Retreating to the well-known caves of Bora Bora, Bin Laden seemed cornered in December, 2001. As Gary Berntsen, the CIA intelligence commander at Bora Bora later recounted, the Eastern Alliance blocked any escape route back into Afghanistan – but not into Pakistan. A 15,000 lb 'daisy cutter' was dropped, but though it wounded Bin Laden, it did not kill him. Hundreds of innocent villagers were hit by stray bombs. Berntsen requested American boots on the ground – 800 Rangers – to make sure Bin Laden did not escape, but Secretary Rumsfeld, anxious to avoid American casualties and insisting that Afghan anti-Taliban forces take them instead, denied the request – and President Bush, the commander-in-chief, declined to overrule him.

'Unfortunately,' Berntsen recalled, 'the decision was made at the White House to use the Pakistani Frontier Force' for the job of capturing or killing the arch-terrorist. 'What the White House didn't understand', he explained, 'was that the frontier force had cooperated with the Taliban' and had no desire to see it exterminated.[57]

The result was that both Bin Laden and Omar evaded the American dragnet.

Neither Bush nor his courtiers Cheney, Rumsfeld, Wolfowitz and Rice, recognized the enormity of their mistake at the time. 'The great Don' Rumsfeld, self-preening and arrogant, was proud he had toppled the Taliban, the harbourers of Bin Laden, in a matter of weeks without a single American soldier's death, and only a tiny number of American 'boots on the ground'. But beyond shock and awe, what had really been achieved, if Bin Laden, architect of the 9/11 attack, escaped?

'We proceeded systematically, village by village, and we destroyed the houses, filled up the wells, blew down the towers, cut down the great shady trees, burned the crops and broke the reservoirs in punitive devastation', Second Lieutenant Winston Churchill had described the Malakand Field Force's campaign against the 'Mad Mullah of Swat' and his 12,000 Pathan tribesmen a century before, in 1897. 'Whether it was all worth it I cannot tell.'[58] Beyond the weaponry, little seemed to have changed.

The entire Islamic world watched, mesmerized and often with admiration, as their Jesse James, Osama Bin Laden, escaped – leaving egg on Marshal Bush's face, and unending combat in the forbidding mountains of Afghanistan ahead. As one Russian officer warned the head of the US Counter-terrorism Center when told in advance of American plans to go to war in Afghanistan, the mountainous region they would encounter was guerilla heaven: 'With regret, I have to say you're really going to get the hell kicked out of you.'[59]

Bush's next war would prove an even greater calamity. Fevered madness once again infected him and his war cabinet as Kabul fell. On November 21, 2001, only ten weeks after 9/11, Bush 'took Rumsfeld aside', having, in Bob Woodward's triumphal account at the time, 'decided it was time to turn to Iraq'.[60]

Previous leaders of empires had come unstuck for just such thoughtless, obsessional hubris. 'I'm not a textbook player, I'm a gut player', the president described himself to the admiring *Washington Post* journalist. In Condoleezza Rice's even more admiring eyes, Bush was less a player than 'the coach', urging his all-star team to 'victory'.[61] Offence, not defence, was the president's creed, which sounded fine in football, but masked the saddest truth: with regard to war he was a gambler, with a 'devil take the consequences' attitude, when other men's lives were at stake.

The head of US Central Command, General Tommy Franks, was certainly appalled once Cheney passed on the president's instruction that he investigate 'what it would take' to 'remove Saddam Hussein if we have to'. In the midst of a difficult logistical challenge in sending more forces to bring order to Afghanistan, Franks let loose 'a string of obscenities'.[62] Then he obediently did as instructed, with a possible D-Day of June 2002, cognizant of the president's orders that not only did the invasion have 'the highest priority', but also that planning was to be kept entirely secret.[63] As Bush later explained to Woodward, he did not 'want others in on the secret because a leak would trigger "enormous international angst and domestic speculation. I knew what would happen if people thought we were developing a potential or a war plan for Iraq.'"[64]

The president was right; instead of angst, however, the country would get seven years of affliction. At the end of December 2001, with Cheney, Rumsfeld, Rice, George Tenet of the CIA and Powell participating via secure video link, General Franks duly briefed Bush in person at the president's ranch in Crawford, Texas. Under pressure, the general had reduced the anticipated requirement of 500,000 troops to just 230,000 in an effort not to alarm the American public – still a huge army for the US to field, however, while simultaneously attempting to stabilize the situation in Afghanistan, where complex security and logistics problems remained and Bin Laden was still at large.

At first, Colin Powell did not believe the president was serious. Saddam Hussein had few supporters in the world, given his ruthless Ba'ath Party regime. But taking America, without allies, into full-scale war in Iraq, when al-Qaeda had still not been dealt with, and Afghanistan posing huge problems in reconstruction and the restoration of civil order? Congress' 9/11 War Resolution did not currently authorize such an undertaking. Nor did the United Nations Security Council, which had backed Desert Storm a decade before, but which could not be counted upon to license regime change in a sovereign country, just for the sake of regime change.

Powell, who as chairman of the Joint Chiefs of Staff had masterminded the Gulf War in 1991, thus opposed the president's hare-brained imperial venture, knowing it was viewed with the utmost suspicion in the capitals of what Rumsfeld would call 'old Europe'. There was no evidence or serious suspicion that Saddam Hussein had any ties to al-Qaeda. Nor was there was any evidence that he was currently developing either biological or nuclear materials. What, then, was the justification for a proposed massive US invasion, involving a quarter of a million troops? What would be the exit strategy? Who would run a post-Hussein Iraq? A handful of unreliable Iraqi exiles? And why was the proposed attack so secret, on orders of the president? Was Bush afraid that, if discussed nationwide, the public would stay his warrior hand?

Those who heard, or overheard, members of the administration and the president himself on the subject, were not only alarmed that a second Bush war was being planned while the first was incomplete, but that the *raison d'être* was so puerile. 'Fuck Saddam!' the president told a group of senators at the White House in March 2002. 'We're going to take him out' – but with no serious examination of who would take Saddam's place.[65]

Powell vainly attempted to dissuade his colleagues, but Cheney, in particular, seemed gripped by a 'fever', as Powell later commented. Powell's reluctance to rush to war restrained, but did not stop, the president. Addressing Congress in a State of the Union speech on January 29, 2002, Bush now used a new term, 'axis of evil', to describe America's enemies – by which he meant, he explained, Iraq, Iran and North Korea.[66] (His speechwriter, David Frum, had suggested the phrase 'axis of hatred', but was overruled by Bush.)

Moral courage seemed to go out the window as the 'Vulcans' in the administration – named after the statue of the god of fire in Rice's home town of Birmingham, Alabama – now clamoured for another war.

A *casus belli* was, however, still required – and could best be manufactured if Saddam Hussein could be found to be developing weapons of mass destruction (WMD). The President thus insisted Saddam Hussein re-admit UN inspectors into Iraq, which Hussein reluctantly agreed to. When no evidence of WMD was found, Bush refused to back down. With the president's approval, Cheney's office ordered the false authentication of suspect secret intelligence, suggesting that an agent of Saddam Hussein had tried to buy uranium concentrate powder, or 'yellowcake', in Nigeria for Saddam's secret nuclear arms programme, and that the dictator was also sponsoring al-Qaeda plots against America.

The Bush administration's rush to a second war became unstoppable. At a meeting called by the prime minister in London on July 23, 2002, the head of British intelligence reported on his recent visit to Washington: 'Military action was now seen as inevitable' he confided, as noted in the minutes. 'Bush wanted to remove Saddam, through military action' to which end 'the intelligence and facts were being fixed around the policy'. Even more sobering was that 'there was little discussion in Washington of the aftermath after military action'.[67]

Even Blair's backing (he was soon dubbed 'Bush's poodle') was not enough, however, to convince Britain's European partners and enough members of UN Security Council, in the absence of any evidence of WMD, that the US should invade. Fatefully, therefore, President Bush decided to go to war without UN backing.

War hysteria now began to sweep America. Analogies with 1914 and myriad other wars that had begun with popular excitement were drawn, especially the example of Hitler's blitzkrieg in the spring of 1940, and then his doomed occupation of western Europe and invasion of the Soviet Union in 1941. Powell, in particular, had warned Bush in August 2002 that if he followed through with such a madcap plan, he would then 'own' Iraq and its '25 million people' – a people who had never known democracy, and were traditionally divided between Sunni and Shia clans, with a hostile Kurdish region in the north. A messy occupation could destabilize Saudi Arabia, Egypt and Jordan, and potentially ignite a firestorm of loathing for the United States throughout the Islamic world. And this at the very time when most Muslims still disapproved of al-Qaeda's dedication to violence, and deplored the 9/11 attacks on innocents, which went against the divinely inspired teachings of Mohammed as set down in the Koran.

Once again the president thanked Powell for the warning, but went ahead with his war plans. On March 19, 2003, he publicly announced that war with Iraq had 'reluctantly' begun. He had, he said, given the green light to the invasion out of sheer necessity, since 'the people of the United States will not live at the mercy of an outlaw regime that threatens the peace with weapons of mass destruction'.

Like Roman military campaigns in the time of the original Caesars, the initial Battle of Iraq proved another demonstration of American mastery of modern aerial, ground and logistical blitzkrieg warfare – its legions disciplined, well armed, well commanded, and focused. On April 9, 2003, only three weeks after the invasion began, Iraqis in the main square of Baghdad saw the great statue of Saddam Hussein being toppled from its column. Soon after, President Bush co-piloted a Navy S-3B Viking attack fighter on to the flight deck of the aircraft carrier USS *Abraham Lincoln* off the California coast. Wearing a green combat suit, the president stood under a vast banner prepared by the White House: 'Mission Accomplished'.

Relief among ordinary Americans soon turned to anxiety, however, as they heard worrying stories from their loved ones in the armed forces. No public acclamation had greeted the 'liberators' in Iraq; indeed they were almost instantly seen as infidel 'occupiers'. In Baghdad itself Donald Rumsfeld, reading an advance copy of the president's speech, was distraught: 'I just died, and I said my God, it's too conclusive.'[68] Though Rumsfeld recommended removing any mention of 'mission accomplished', Karl Rove's political team at the White House, who had produced the banner, had been too exultant to order it to be taken down – thus piling hubris upon hubris.

In subsequent weeks, everything in Iraq that could go wrong did go wrong. A quarter of a million American soldiers, backed by 40,000 British, Australian, Polish and Danish troops, found no weapons of mass destruction. Nor did they find evidence of an al-Qaeda connection. Mesopotamia had been one of the great centres of early civilization; in the absence of instructions from Washington, its historic treasures were openly pilfered from the National Museum by looters undeterred by the overstretched American troops who, under orders from the White House that would haunt them afterwards, disbanded the one organization capable of keeping order: the Iraqi Army.

Far from being a mission accomplished, the invasion of Iraq turned into a monumental debacle. The orgy of bloodletting and sectarian violence in Iraq soon escalated into civil war, exceeding the wildest warnings issued before the invasion, not only in numbers murdered and maimed, but in the utter inhumanity exhibited by human beings towards each other. US soldiers and 'contractors', however well-meaning, were seen neither as peacekeepers nor as philanthropists, simply as occupation forces. As the numbers of American body bags rose and the extent of the fiasco deepened, even 'embedded' journalists who had extolled the brilliance of the blitzkrieg invasion began to speak up and to report reality: a quagmire of internecine civil strife, suicide bombings, roadside bombings, assassinations, beheadings and sectarian-cleansing that reduced the world's oldest surviving civilization to mayhem.

As casualties mounted not only reporters but former generals spoke up. By 2004, a year after the invasion began, casualties exceeded 20,000 US soldiers wounded, with more than 1,000 American servicemen dead. 'We are now being viewed', lamented General Zinni, the former chief of US Central Command, 'as the modern crusaders, as the modern colonial power in this part of the world', and he called for

Rumsfeld, and Rumsfeld's fanatical deputy Wolfowitz (who had set up a rogue political unit, the Office of Special Plans at the Pentagon, to bypass normal chains of command), to tender their resignations, along with the other neocons: 'Undersecretary of Defense Douglas Feith; former Defense Policy Board member Richard Perle; National Security Council member Elliot Abrams; and Vice President Cheney's chief of staff, Lewis "Scooter" Libby.'[69]

Zinni's passionate call for heads to roll, and for the president to revert to his original, Congress-approved mission after 9/11 – to pursue al-Qaeda – went nowhere. Instead, Rove's political team went into action, trashing the four-star general – a distinguished Vietnam veteran – as an anti-Semite.

The treatment of Zinni symbolized not only the moral depravity of Rove's huge team, operating at the heart of the White House, but the double bind in which George Walker Bush found himself. By virtue of his chosen advisers and his own ignorant and 'gut player' personality, Bush was hoist with his own petard. It was he who had made a deliberate, emotion-driven choice to rush to war, using the most powerful military in the world, egged on by a gung-ho war cabinet of neoconservatives who had almost all avoided military service themselves. Even sceptics in his administration had been forced to choose between loyalty to their president and their own wisdom. 'Are you with me?' Bush had asked General Powell on the eve of the invasion of Iraq. To his distress later, Powell had loyally said yes to his commander-in-chief.[70]

In the midterm election of November 2002, the Senate had been won back by the Republican Party, along with the Republican-dominated House. Once the invasions of Afghanistan and Iraq proved pyrrhic victories, however, Rove's job became much more difficult. Scott McClellan, the president's press secretary, would later describe Rove's role in the US government under Bush as 'political manipulation, plain and simple'.[71] As the Iraq War spiralled into ever worsening violence, the president's re-election in 2004 could only be secured by further spin, obfuscation, deceit and cover-up.

Without 'transparency', noted McClellan – who had to fend off and manipulate the press each day – the White House was doomed to become a House of Lies. Had the president admitted his error and cleaned his stables by firing the 'Vulcans', exiling the vice president from the White House, and denying Cheney and his henchmen access to his presidential communications, he might just have rescued his presidency – and America's prestige in the world – before it was too late, even if it ended up costing him a second term.

George W. Bush, however, was no Jack Kennedy. Retaining his loyal team, he dug himself yet deeper into a morass of deception, secrecy and cover-up, all excused on the grounds of national security, but in reality done to conceal and protect the guilty from being exposed. 'That secrecy', McClellan wrote afterwards, 'ended up delaying but not preventing the consequences.'[72]

Refusing to set up an independent investigation into the 9/11 disaster, then making sure the commission, once set up, would not deliver its report until *after* the 2004 election, was only one of an increasing number of manipulations, misdemeanours and even crimes that would have merited impeachment of the president and vice president, had not the country remained, conveniently, 'at war'.[73] The head of the Office of Legal Counsel, Jack Goldsmith, recorded the effect of such high-level lack of accountability – indeed refusal to be held account-able – as it gradually permeated almost every area of government in the Bush administration, fusing lack of transparency and outright polit-ical skullduggery, as the embattled president – using Dick Cheney as his malevolent Lord Protector – attempted to ward off congressional oversight.[74]

For his part, the vice president relished his role. As President Nixon had once targeted whistle-blowers such as Daniel Ellsberg and Seymour Hersh, so now Cheney's staff swung into action against anyone of consequence who criticized the president or dared expose White House falsifications. When former US ambassador Joe Wilson debunked, from personal knowledge, claims that Iraq had been buying 'yellow-cake' from Nigeria, Cheney's office deliberately leaked the name of the ambassador's wife as a serving, covert CIA officer: a criminal, even treasonable act. Once Valerie Wilson's career had been ruined – endan-gering her life but sending a stern 'message' to would-be whistle-blowers – Cheney and his staff covered up their actions for as long as possible, ensuring that the ostensible culprit (Scooter Libby) was not indicted until after the 2004 presidential election.[75]

With each further deception Bush authorized or deliberately ignored, he not only empowered his subordinates' move towards the cynical abuse of power, but surrendered his own authority as chief executive. Osama Bin Laden's mad jihad and Saddam Hussein's notorious cold-blooded, vindictive savagery as dictator were condemned by all, but an America out of control – with revelations of American torture at Abu Ghraib, Guantanamo Bay and in secret foreign locations – could only lessen the righteousness of America's cause.[76]

The issue came to a head on March 11, 2004, when the president's authority to conduct surveillance of foreign communications came up for renewal by the Justice Department. Without informing Congress, Cheney had already, in 2001, set up a secret operation to monitor all domestic American communications – by telephone, cellphone, email and others[77] – and to torture suspects as he directed.[78] 'It is unlikely that the history of US intelligence includes another operation conceived and supervised by the office of the vice president'[79] Cheney's biographer would later write, in awe – for Cheney refused to inform the president's own counter-terrorism adviser of the programme. Not even the head of Homeland Security or Congress Intelligence Committee members were allowed to know what Cheney was doing, let alone be permitted to arrange congressional oversight or an extension of the law to cover it. Known only to a handful of people, the illegal programme smacked of the KGB at its worst. Shortly before March 11, 2004, it resulted in a stand-off when the acting Attorney General, refusing to sign off on further illegal acts, offered his resignation, along with seventeen senior members of the Justice Department.

To Cheney's fury, Bush backed down; the US would abide by the Geneva Convention in Iraq, and the programme itself was altered until the Justice Department could sign off on it. Meanwhile the drama was kept from the press and public until after the election.

As the dust settled in the White House, however, insiders wondered why the president so often gave in to Cheney's shadow presidency, when it brought him so much grief. At times the overweight Cheney appeared to be not only ill from heart disease (he had required implantation of a cardioverter-defibrillator in 2001), but also seemed mentally unbalanced. When a targeted anthrax mailing was discovered that killed five people in 2002, for example, Cheney had suspected (wrongly, and with no evidence) foreign terrorists rather than a domestic culprit. He had thereupon insisted that the *entire population of America* be

immediately vaccinated against an anthrax attack by foreign terrorists;[80] only the president's refusal to issue such an order (which would
have resulted in many allergic-reaction deaths) had stopped him.
Meanwhile Cheney's legal counsel, David Addington, terrorized the
Washington legal bureaucracy as Cheney's 'eyes, ear and voice', –
ensuring no decision was made without his permission, and treating
even the president's legal counsel, Alberto Gonzales, as a puppet.[81]
'Of probably a hundred meetings in Gonzales' office to discuss national
security,' Jack Goldsmith later wrote, 'I recall only one when Addington
was not there.'[82]

Instead of dropping the all-too-powerful Cheney from the 2004
re-election ticket, however, Bush kept him as his co-president. The
greatness of America as an open society, honest with itself and reliant
upon Congress to provide the necessary checks and balances to
monarchical-style presidency, had been abandoned, citing the
constraints of war – a war the president himself had manufactured; a
war being waged on three fronts without a clear vision; a war without
exit strategies; and a war which, in many people's eyes, had turned the
United States, in terms of torture and the rule of law, into a failed state.

Impetuous, impulsive, shallow and insecure, Bush had no one to
blame but himself. However, the tragedy did not end there, for on
November 2, 2004, he was re-elected.

Benefiting from a group masquerading as 'Swift Boats For Truth',
Karl Rove and the Bush campaigners had removed their gloves and –
as they had with Senator McCain four years before, and again with
the triple-amputee Senator Max Cleland in 2002 – had destroyed the
character and reputation of the Democratic nominee, Senator John
Kerry, whose courage in Vietnam should have put the president and
vice president to shame.

Triumphantly re-elected, Bush thanked Karl Rove as the 'brilliant
architect' of his victory.[83] It was a victory not even his father had been
able to win without a Rove or Atwater to 'push the envelope to the
limit of what is permissible ethically or legally', as McClellan later
commented, thinking of the way Rove – a 'savvy, shrewd and devious
strategist'[84] – had manipulated even national terror alerts during the
campaign to heighten domestic insecurity.[85]

It was now, in November 2004, that Bush had one final opportunity to secure his legacy as a 'compassionate conservative', however,

and reinsert the United States into the international fold alongside its allies and in step with the UN. Had he asked Dick Cheney to step back into an advisory rather than co-presidential role, and had he made Colin Powell the 'new face' of the administration in what promised to be difficult years of bridge-building or -rebuilding – thereby embarking on a four-year term in which he could be seen to be pursuing a course of moderation and peace, not unilateralism and contempt for international law – he might still have avoided the bottom tier of the pantheon of US presidents.

The next day, November 3, 2004, all eyes turned to the vice president at the midmorning cabinet meeting. There, Cheney told his colleagues how, in a conversation 'about whether to trim the sails' following the contested victory and long drawn-out election result in November 2000, the president had said compromise 'was not an option' – and it had 'paid off' in 2001. 'This time', the vice president claimed, the mandate was 'clear': to continue with their right-wing domestic and foreign agenda.[86]

McClellan later described them as living in a fool's paradise. The war in Iraq was still a sickening quagmire of violence, terrorism, corruption, ethnic cleansing and bloodshed, yet *still* the neocons contemptuously dismissed the United Nations, and the need for allies and congressional support. Several days later Bush fired Colin Powell for not having been a neocon 'team player'. In the months that followed, moreover, he nominated for promotion his most incompetent loyalists: Condoleezza Rice to replace Powell as Secretary of State, Alberto Gonzales to be Attorney General, and his legal counsel Harriet Miers to be a Supreme Court judge.[87] He also promoted Karl Rove to be Deputy Chief of Staff for Policy.

Not only Powell but American journalists and observers went into shock. Democrats went into depression. America's standing abroad plummeted to an all-time low.

The overriding – and cynical – influence of Karl Rove on the president was demonstrated in March 2005 when Bush rushed back to Washington from his ranch in Texas to sign 'critical' Republican legislation: a special bill pushed through Congress to keep a patient, Terri Schiavo, alive in Florida by federal fiat, against the wishes of her husband, after seven years in a brain-dead, vegetative state. At a time when thousands of American soldiers had died in Iraq, tens of thousands had been wounded and troops were complaining of poor body armour and insufficiently armoured vehicles to protect them in what had become a civil war and protracted new battleground for al-Qaeda insurgents, the Schiavo affair seemed to typify what had gone wrong with the Bush administration in its desperation to appease its 'base'.

Sickened by reports and imagery of the orgy of violence in towns such as Falluja and Mosul, the majority of respondents in opinion polls declared the war in Iraq to have been, as Senator Kerry had declared, 'a mistake'. As the tide turned against the president that year, so too did Congress, despite its Republican majorities. One by one the Bush team's sins of commission and omission were now revealed. On June 7, 2005, documents were published showing the source of the decision to abandon the Kyoto Protocol on climate change had been an Exxon-sponsored group; the chief of staff of the president's Council on Environmental Policy then resigned, only to be reported taking a job at Exxon.[88] On June 22, Karl Rove was widely condemned for traducing those who opposed the war in Iraq as liberals who 'saw the savagery of the 9/11 attacks and wanted to prepare indictments and offer therapy and understanding for our attackers'.[89] Days later, in July, not only Rove but Vice President Cheney and their staffs were investigated on behalf of a grand jury, with a view to indictment. Although Rove and Cheney managed to avoid indictment, Cheney's chief of staff Scooter Libby was arrested, charged, found guilty, and eventually sentenced to prison for his part in deliberately revealing the role of Ambassador Wilson's wife as a CIA operative to America's enemies.

More damning still, however, was the final release, on July 22, 2005, of the bipartisan 9/11 Commission Report, confirming its announcement the previous summer that, despite Cheney's insistent claims to the contrary, there was 'no credible evidence' there had been a link between al-Qaeda and Saddam Hussein's Iraq before 9/11.[90] Indeed the report quoted a secret investigation given to the then national security adviser, Condoleezza Rice, only a week after the 9/11 attack, that had found '"no compelling evidence" that Iraq either planned or perpetrated the attacks'.[91]

As if to mirror the turning of the tide against the 'Vulcans', a terrifying 175 mph hurricane hit New Orleans and the Louisiana Gulf coast on August 30, 2005. The Corps of Engineers' levees were breached, inundating the city and marooning scores of thousands of New Orleans residents, almost 2,000 of whom were then allowed to die.

When the president, returning to the Oval Office from his Texas ranch three days later, asked Cheney 'if he'd be interested in spearheading' a cabinet-level task force to deal with the crisis, he was told no. 'Let's just say I didn't get the most positive response', Bush mocked the vice president in front of his crisis team: Andy Card, Condoleezza Rice, Karl Rove, and the deputy press secretary, Dan Bartlett. Yet still the president did not order Cheney to take charge. Meekly he asked him: 'Will you at least go do a fact-finding trip for us?' The vice president again demurred.

Rove suggested the president himself fly over the flooded city in Air Force One, and a widely published photo was taken of the nation's commander-in-chief peering out of a porthole window thousands of feet above the devastation, having failed to federalize the emergency response. Any hope of saving the president's second term was extinguished. As Bush's own pollster and chief campaign strategist reflected afterwards, 'Katrina was the tipping point. The president broke his bond with the public. Once that bond was broken, he no longer had the capacity to talk to the American public. State of the Union addresses? Legislative initiatives? PR? Travel? It didn't matter.' Nothing could now help. 'I knew when Katrina – it was like, man, you know this is it man. We're done.'[92]

Pictures of Condoleezza Rice shopping for expensive shoes in New York only added to public outrage at the administration. Bush had promoted Michael D. Brown, a feckless Republican lawyer and long-time director of the Arabian Horse Association, of all people, to run the Federal Emergency Management Agency (FEMA) in 2002. Brown's utter mishandling of the Katrina disaster resulted in further outrage on all sides, compounded by the president's deplorable remark during the crisis, as he turned to the hapless FEMA director – the most incompetent in American annals – and said 'Brownie, you're doing a heck of a job!'[93]

Brown was forced to resign in ignominy several weeks later. Bush's failure to prepare for the disaster, despite warnings by the National Hurricane Center, his tardiness in responding to it, and his cronyism in promoting a horse breeder to such a crucial post, shocked the nation. For the president's press secretary, Katrina represented 'the defining turning point for Bush and his administration. It left an indelible stain on his presidency'.[94] In fact it came to 'define Bush's second term. And the perception of this catastrophe', McClellan added, 'was made worse by previous decisions President Bush had made, including, first and foremost, the failure to be open and forthright on Iraq and rushing to war with inadequate planning and preparation for its aftermath.'[95]

That aftermath, meanwhile, had grown worse and worse. Why, even jingoistic veterans wondered, had the president fired General Zinni for saying that at least 300,000 to 400,000 troops would be required to keep order after the invasion of Iraq? Why had the president not ordered a draft, if the military was overstretched and the need to avoid immediate chaos was so crucial? Why was the vice president allowed to secretly eavesdrop on conversations by US diplomats abroad, using the National Security Agency, in order to make sure no American officials strayed from his unilateralist line?[96] Orwell's nightmare of Nineteen Eighty-Four had come true, in America, with Big Brother watching and even the most senior American officials warned by well-meaning intelligence officers to be careful.[97]

The violence in Iraq, which Cheney claimed had already peaked, only grew worse. The famed Golden Mosque in Samarra was destroyed by Sunnis in February 2006; a Lancet medical journal report in June 2006 claimed that more than 600,000 Iraqis had died in the post-invasion violence, with millions more 'ethnically cleansed', displaced and living as refugees in camps or abroad. It seemed a heavy price for invading and ridding the country of a dictator, however much the president boasted of having 'done the absolute right thing in removing him from power', despite the lack of WMD.[98] In the New York Times, even Thomas Friedman, the war's biggest champion as a Middle East gamechanger, now admitted the US was 'not midwifing democracy in Iraq' but 'babysitting a civil war' – a civil war for which America, by virtue of its blitzkrieg invasion and failure to restore order in the aftermath, was wholly responsible.[99] With Israel, armed and unchecked by the United States, invading Lebanon for a second time, on July 12, 2006, to do battle with Hezbollah adherents – killing over 1,000 civilians and displacing over a million Lebanese – hopes for peaceful democracy in the Middle East looked bleaker than ever.[100]

On September 3, 2006, it was announced officially that 2,974 US servicemen had died since the start of the president's 'war on terror'.

More than 40,000 American soldiers had been either wounded or evacuated sick.[101] Osama Bin Laden still remained uncaptured, while al-Qaeda openly boasted of fielding 12,000 fighters now in combat in Iraq, with perhaps another 20,000 armed Iraqi insurgents attacking the 'infidel' US occupying forces for religious or nationalist reasons.

In what was called a 'referendum on Iraq', voters in the United States finally registered their assessment of the presidency on November 7, 2006: Democrats were elected back into control of the House of Representatives (233–202) and the Senate (fifty-one to forty-nine) in the midterm elections for the first time since 1992.

Six years into his presidency, Bush now had to reassess his own performance – and to his credit, he did. Bowing to pressure from Congress and members of his administration, he ignored the furious opposition of Dick Cheney and finally fired Donald Rumsfeld as Secretary of Defense the day after the elections. Then on December 6, 2006, he was faced with the sequel to the 9/11 Commission Report.

The new document, entitled *The Way Forward – A New Approach*, it was the work of an independent, bipartisan commission headed by his father's former Secretary of State, James Baker, to analyze what had gone wrong in Afghanistan and Iraq – and how to fix it. Far from 'winning' the 'war', the commission's authors concluded, the mire America had produced in Iraq was now 'grave and deteriorating' with no exit strategy beyond undefined 'victory'. 'The gist of what we had to say was a responsible exit. He [Bush] didn't like that', related the report's co-author, former congressman Lee Hamilton, afterwards. 'I don't recall, seriously, that he asked any questions', confided another of the authors, former Secretary of State Lawrence Eagleburger. Instead, the president 'ignored it so far as I can see', Hamilton sighed.[102]

In truth the president *did* read the report, however reluctantly, noting the authors' recommendation that he 'significantly increase the number of US personnel, including combat troops, imbedded and supporting Iraqi units' – which would thus allow US forces gradually to leave Iraq to the Iraqis. In this respect the Iraq Survey Group supported a short-term 'surge of American combat forces to stabilize Baghdad'.

It was close to midnight in terms of American failure, with the outgoing American commander in Iraq so pessimistic, in the face of an ever worsening orgy of bloodshed that he was recommending

American troops simply withdraw to safe havens and hand over responsibility to the provisional Iraqi government to deal with the chaos. Was he right, or were the authors of *The Way Forward*?

In the days and weeks that followed, Bush finally recognized he must listen to those commanders, statesmen and critics who had alternative ideas of how the US could get out of Iraq without too much shame, loss of face, and humiliation.

Six *years* to read, listen and ask searching questions? The president's father broke down in tears when launching the USS *Bush* and when interviewed on *Larry King Live*. Secrecy, contempt for democratic public debate and Congress ('Fuck yourself', Cheney had been heard to snort at Senator Patrick Leahy of Vermont, the ranking Democrat on the Judiciary Committee), and a bureaucracy of fear and intimidation had been the vice president's chief contribution to the twenty-first century American presidency – or co-presidency.[103] With Cheney's chief of staff formally indicted for deliberate felony, however, and his replacement denied the post of adviser or assistant to the president, Cheney's star had fallen. Rumsfeld, Wolfowitz, Perle, Feith, John Bolton and other outspoken proponents of unilateral American power, had gone – and both McLellan and the president's ineffective chief of staff, Andy Card, had resigned. The way was clear to reconstitute the chief executive.

In an interview with the press, Andy Card's successor, Josh Bolten, thus made clear that Cheney's co-presidency was over. 'The president took him as a *counselor*, not as a deputy', he explained. To be sure, the president might be seen as more 'courteous' to the vice president, but he was not, and would not be, 'more deferential' to Cheney than to others. Moreover, with regard to any presidential decision, 'the president will make it' – no one else. 'If it is not presidential,' Bolten added, 'it is going to be one of the cabinet officers [who] would make it – or me' – i.e. not the vice president.[104]

Bush was finally growing up, and in his careful weighing of the arguments for withdrawal, prolongation or change of direction in the military occupation of Iraq he finally donned the true mantle of the presidency. 'I am listening to a lot of advice to develop a strategy', he told reporters in December – who appeared stunned by the change in his vocabulary. Gone was the cowboy braggadocio. 'I will be delivering my plans after a long deliberation . . . I'm not going to be rushed into making a decision.'[105]

'Is he lucky?' Napoleon had famously asked when reviewing the recommendation of a new commander. Belatedly the president recognized the one man who could, perhaps, turn defeat into victory – or if not victory, then a successful exit from Iraq: Lieutenant General David Petraeus, author of the army's *Field Manual on Counterinsurgency*, whom Bush nominated to be the new American commander-in-chief in Iraq. Congress, impressed by Petraeus' testimony before the Senate Armed Services Committee on January 27, 2007, approved. Against a background of scepticism and conflicting views – especially from the new Democratic Majority Leaders of both House and Senate, Speaker Nancy Pelosi and Senator Harry Reid – the president authorized the temporary 'surge' the ISG had recommended, involving 30,000 more troops being sent to Iraq – as well as major funding to back Petraeus' strategy: to *pay* Iraqi militias to stop attacking American occupiers, and instead to turn their weapons on al-Qaeda insurgents.

Petraeus certainly proved lucky, and an inspired choice by Bush. With the Shiite warrior cleric Muqtada al-Sadr ordering his Mahdi Army militias to stand down, and the American-paid Sunnis, the Sons of Iraq, taking on al-Qaeda, the American surge – concentrated on combat operations in Baghdad – slowly but surely worked. By the autumn of 2007, sectarian violence began to diminish, and the road to gradual withdrawal of occupying forces from Iraq looked open.

Meanwhile Dick Cheney, who had suffered four heart attacks by the time he was fifty-nine, was treated for deep vein thrombosis in March 2007 and diagnosed with atrial fibrillation in November 2007, requiring electric shock treatment. Everywhere they went Vice President Cheney and Karl Rove – who resigned as deputy chief of staff on August 31, 2007 – were booed. On a visit to Afghanistan, Cheney even became the target of an assassination attempt which killed twenty-three innocent people outside a US air base. His approval rating dropped below 30 per cent, while his disapproval rating rose to 60 per cent. With rumours that he was urging a missile attack on Iran before it became a nuclear power, public anxiety grew even more pronounced. When asked on ABC News in the spring of 2008 whether he 'cared what the American people think', he answered bluntly: 'No.'[106]

President Bush, by contrast, cared – but found that, despite the improving situation in Iraq, it was too late to rehabilitate himself at home. The long housing bubble he had deliberately nurtured to distract from the war's negatives burst, and, as Republican and Democratic candidates for the 2008 presidential election argued over how best to end Bush's misguided wars, Wall Street began to totter – and collapse.

For this, the blinkered president had only himself to blame. As with the Hurricane Katrina fiasco, he seemed to be a man out of his depth, with no idea how to avoid what was soon predicted to become the worst recession since the Great Crash and Depression of the 1930s – the crisis that had brought the first American Caesar, Franklin D. Roosevelt, to power.

On the day of the presidential election in November 2008, Bush's approval rating, in a CBS tracking poll, dipped to 20 per cent – 'the lowest ever recorded by a president', as newspapers reported – while his disapproval rating soared to 72 per cent.[107] It was a sorry finale to a disastrous presidency, the crowds jeering at his departure, and hoping against hope that a new American Caesar could get their proud empire back on track.[108]

Part Three: Private Life

Of the American Caesars, George W. Bush resembled John F. Kennedy the most, at least in childhood – both men born into large, wealthy, competitive families, irreverent and content to cultivate their 'bad boy' images, especially with women.

Bush became engaged to a stunning blonde student at Rice University, Cathryn Wolfman, at age twenty. Plans were made for a wedding in 1967. 'Everybody agreed that she and George made a great couple', a friend recalled – the studious, mature but outgoing step-daughter of a wealthy clothier, and the wayward son of a Texas congressman. 'George, of course, prided himself in being a bad boy. But Cathy always seemed to be having an awful lot of fun whenever they were together. He made her laugh the way he made everybody laugh. Maybe she lived vicariously through him a little.'[109]

Wedding plans, however, were delayed, and then, over time, dropped. After college, Bush went into his 'nomadic years', as he later called them: restless, partying, smoking, binge drinking, drug-using, lost. When his father famously called him to account for driving drunk into a garbage can outside their house, W. challenged him to a fight, '*mano a mano*'.[110] Unable to stay in any job or assignment, he seemed bewildered by adult life: spoiled, purposeless, self-destructive, a James Dean in the making. As such, he was dangerously attractive to women who wished to rescue him, but who found his family, congregating at Kennebunkport every summer, too formidable to handle. 'I don't want to go to Maine' his fiancée Cathryn Wolfson had said when ending their relationship. 'And I don't think this is going to work out.'[111] Crushed, W. had burst into tears, but Cathryn was not taken in. 'He can have any woman he wants – and he knows it', she said later.[112]

Though in fun-loving, reckless behaviour the similarities between the two playboy sons of rich, high-profile fathers were striking, there were also fundamental differences between Kennedy and Bush. Kennedy was smart, with an IQ that stunned even his teachers, and a voracious reader – a habit which repeated illness and hospitalization in childhood and youth only deepened. His fourth-year undergraduate thesis at Harvard, *Why England Slept*, was published as a book in 1940, when Kennedy was twenty-three – and two years later the FBI, tapping his phone and listening to secretly installed tape-recorders, heard him talking world politics with his mistress, Inga Arvad, telling her he was determined one day to be president of the United States.

Political ambition, then, was in John F. Kennedy's blood from the start, as was courage. With the onset of World War II, Kennedy finagled his way from clear unacceptability on medical grounds into heroic combat service in the US Navy as a PT boat captain. By contrast, George W. Bush's problem, from the start, was his limited IQ, lack of military courage and refusal to study in order to succeed.

The fateful odyssey that was Bush's rise to the presidency we have outlined, together with its tragic denouement, as the once popular, bipartisan Texas governor turned into his opposite – with terrible consequences for the country. Within that sorry tale, affecting so many millions of people's lives across the globe, there was, however – as in the story of Tsar Nicholas and Empress Alexandra – an affecting inner saga which, though it could never make amends for the damage done to the United States and other nations, did touch people's hearts at a human level.

In 1977 Laura Lane Welch, thirty-one-year-old librarian and registered Democrat, was introduced to the wastrel thirty-one-year-old son of the then US ambassador to the United Nations. Finding him both

China

funny and tantalizingly unfulfilled, she consented to his dating her. Three months later, in a small ceremony after a lightning courtship, they were married. Where he was impetuous, Laura was cautious; where he was gregarious, she was private; where he was ill-read to the point of near-illiteracy, 'I read and I smoke' Laura had told her astonished future mother-in-law.

Calm, quiet, principled, an only daughter and the survivor of a terrible car crash at age seventeen (when inadvertently she ran a stop sign and killed her former high-school boyfriend), Laura Welch became George Walker Bush's lodestar. She turned his life around, threatened to leave him unless he stopped drinking, gave birth to twin daughters, and provided what he craved: trust in his essential worth, beneath the wastrel exterior. Though she didn't encourage him to run for the governorship of Texas and declined to give stump speeches or interviews, she stood by him, and became proud of his accomplishments in the governor's mansion. She brought out, people said, the best in W. and by her constancy banished the worst. He never strayed, and indeed hated to spend a night apart. If marriage is co-dependency, they were deeply, and movingly, co-dependent.

Why, then, did Laura Lane Bush not stop her beloved husband, the twice-elected and most popular governor of Texas since records began, from reaching for a yet higher political post, one he was not qualified to take? Bush saw himself at times as Reagan's disciple – folksy, humorous, and opposed to big government – but had no idea of Reagan's serious side, and the decades-long, arduous political path Reagan had taken, honing his skills as a speaker and spokesman for Republican causes. All W. had was a cheeky, friendly glamour, without political or intellectual depth. He had been at sea academically at both Yale and Harvard Business School, and would be overwhelmed by the complexity of economic, legal, congressional and diplomatic issues he would have to face if elected president. Laura had not enjoyed living in Washington when W. had worked for his father's 1988 presidential election campaign. She had no desire to live there again. She loved Texas; she loved the life that they had made there, and she worried what effect the White House – if Bush won the race – would have on their teenage daughters.

Sadly, fatefully, Laura did not stop her husband. Worse still, she innocently recommended that her husband take Dick Cheney, the man who was vetting vice-presidential candidates, as his number two, thinking the unvetted Cheney would lend 'gravitas' to the ticket. It was a decision she would come to deeply regret, once George W. Bush won the election, and the co-presidency turned into a haunting refutation of all that had characterized her husband's governorship in Texas.

Thanks to Cheney and Rove, George W. Bush quickly changed back to the bullying, snide, wilful and obstinate person he had been at school and at college. 'That's the interesting thing about being president,' W. said later in an unguarded moment, 'I don't feel like I owe anybody an explanation.'[113] Nothing Laura was able to do, as his wife and First Lady, seemed able to rescue him from the nefarious vice president or the manipulative Rove, the two men wheedling, urging, pressing, protecting and manoeuvring her naive, insecure and fatally ignorant spouse into imagining himself as a modern Cincinnatus, called to be dictator in troubling times.

Given the dynamic of the Bush dynasty and the quadrennial torrent of Republican Party money thrown at likely candidates for supreme power, was it inevitable that George W. Bush, a man of prankster charm but weak intellect, would be hauled to the apex of the political pyramid as a faux pharaoh of his nation, and then cast to the wolves when he failed to lead the American Empire wisely? Could it have been different, observers wondered, at the end of Bush's eight years in office, as they watched their beleaguered president fly into domestic exile, pursued by rumblings of possible international lawsuits calling him to account for torture and crimes against humanity? Looking at the slim, still delectably pretty woman in her pale grey coat holding the former president's hand as the couple strode to the helicopter that would take them away, those who knew them best could not help but ponder the role of the First Lady in the history of the American Empire. Eleanor, Bess, Mamie, Jackie, Lady Bird, Pat, Betty, Rosalind, Nancy, Barbara, Hillary, Laura . . . all had played their part, with varying success, in keeping their husbands sane as they carried ultimate executive responsibility for the world's most powerful hegemony; none had stopped them from accepting the challenge.

Within the Oval Office, the tragedy had then unfolded. The Cheney–Rove stranglehold had proved simply too powerful, and by the time Republican control of Congress was lost and bipartisanship became critical, it was too late. For all his African AIDS initiative, Prescription Drug, No Child Left Behind and other well-meaning programmes, the president's legacy would, like that of Lyndon B. Johnson, forever be his ill-considered, unilateral rush to war in Afghanistan and Iraq, and the quagmires they produced.

True to his image as Dr Strangelove, Dick Cheney attended the inauguration of the forty-fourth President in a wheelchair (he had hurt his back, packing more boxes of documents stolen from the government and the prying eyes of posterity, wags explained), and did everything possible in subsequent months to scorn the new Caesar's efforts to deal with the massive problems he was inheriting. By contrast a chastened George W. Bush not only refused to pardon Cheney's chief of staff, but said how delighted he was to have 'a front-row seat' at the impending 'historic event' on January 20, 2009, as the first black president mounted the inauguration podium.[114] When, after the swearing-in ceremony by the Capitol, the two men then embraced, arms around each other and cheek to cheek, it was as if a torch was truly passing from one generation, one race, and one approach to the responsibility of empire in the modern world, to another. Bending to say goodbye to Obama's little daughters, George W. Bush reminded watchers in Texas of what he had once been: a caring father, devoid of racial prejudice, blessed with a simple human touch.

As the two Caesars strode with their wives from the bottom of the Capitol steps towards the waiting helicopter, the compassionate hand of Obama laid across the shoulder of the departing former president seemed to symbolize the start of a new era for America: one in which humility and goodwill would mix with articulate idealism not seen for almost half a century, when President John F. Kennedy electrified the world.

Acknowledgements

American Caesars originated in 2007, when I was approached by Dan Hind of The Bodley Head, part of the Random House publishing group in London.

For several years I had taken time out from presidential biography to write two short books on biography – *Biography: A Brief History*, and *How To Do Biography: A Primer*. However, having spent more than ten years writing multi-volume, large-scale presidential biographies (*JFK: Reckless Youth*; *Bill Clinton: An American Journey*; *Bill Clinton: Mastering the Presidency*), I was actively exploring the idea of a group biography of US presidents I admire – in part because I so deprecated the performance of George W. Bush as 43rd President, as I explained in the Prologue to *Bill Clinton: Mastering the Presidency*.

Dan's idea of a book about modern American presidents in the manner of Suetonius' *The Twelve Caesars* – a book I have cherished (and quoted) for four decades – thus struck me as serendipitous. And intriguing. No author since Suetonius has, after all, emulated his portraits of the first Roman emperors by seeking to look at a succession of such world-historical rulers.

What I particularly liked about the Suetonian approach, when I examined it structurally, was the separation of his lives into first the public career, and only then the personal life, or love-life, of his subjects. I had never used this biographical paradigm, since every modern biographer is *de rigeur* a disciple of Freud, and must lace a modern understanding of the subject's psychology into the gradual unravelling of the subject's lifestory, from the start, to satisfy public expectation. A trial chapter addressing President Truman, however, demonstrated to me, and to Dan, that by focusing first on the public career of the President, and only then on the life of his heart, so to speak, it was possible to see the politician initially in the context of his historic imperial role, and then, by contrast, as a man with a private life story.

Would that *American Caesars* had followed such a straightforward trajectory! The number of excellent individual biographies of the presidents, over recent decades, made it unnecessary to seek out unpublished material for the new work – but it did pose a substantial challenge of printed digestion. Beyond that, my task became one of 'selection and design', as Lytton Strachey put it in the preface to his masterpiece *Eminent Victorians*: using the framework of modern American empire, or hegemony, as the backcloth to the Caesars' lives. In this respect, at least, it promised to be less forbidding for me to tackle, perhaps, than for a number of my fellow American historians. Not only because of my detailed previous work on Presidents John F. Kennedy and Bill Clinton (and, earlier, on Dwight D. Eisenhower as a general, when writing my official biography of Field Marshal Montgomery), but because of the years I had spent in Great Britain – which made the concept of empire perfectly normal for me. Britain had, after all, established the world's largest territorial empire in the nineteenth century. In my own lifetime it had then ceded that role as guardian of international order and prosperity to the United States. Nevertheless, the sheer epos – political and personal – of the presidents' lives within the imperial context soon ran away with me. By the time the manuscript was ready, after two years' research and writing, it was twice too long.

Dan's successor at the Bodley Head, Jörg Hensgen, rightly refused to publish the book *en gros* – indeed felt it to be unpublishable at such length (and digressiveness). There thus began the heartbreaking task of self-editing, or self-mutilation. Only by picturing myself back in the cutting room studios of the BBC's Film and Documentaries Department in the 1980s was I able to overcome my aversion to the sight of so much lexical blood (First Cut, Second Cut, Final Cut). In the end the necessary surgery was completed, however, and I was able to see how wise Jörg had been. The lives of the twelve American Caesars had become shorter, omitting many a crucial event or aspect, but were now significantly more focused in my narrative. And, perhaps most important to me – and hopefully the reader – the portraits were still *moving*. To my editor Jörg Hensgen, then, I owe a huge debt of gratitude.

All my writing life I have sought to examine the nature, vagaries and conduct of leadership: literary, military, and political. In large part, I suppose this is due to my late father, who from humble circumstances rose to become a decorated infantry battalion commander in World War II, and later Editor-in-Chief of the London *Times* and *Sunday Times*. He had arranged for me to intern at age nineteen on the *Washington Post* in the summer of 1963 – an experience which, though it did not make me a journalist, did make me into a lifelong student of American history and politics, spurred by that great American patriot and editor, Russ Wiggins. Over the years, in researching my military biographies, I gradually learned my way around myriad American archives – and in 1988, after my father's death, I moved to Boston, Massachusetts, to start work on a fresh life of President John F. Kennedy. Save for a stint teaching biography and history in England in the late 1990s, I have been at work in the US ever since, with my intellectual home located in the state's diverse and beautifully situated University of Massachusetts Boston, next to the Massachusetts State Archives and Kennedy Library. I want to thank therefore my many colleagues at UMass Boston, especially Professors Paul Bookbinder, Padraig O'Malley, William Percy, Robert Weiner, Carter Jefferson and Ed Beard, as well as the Director, Steve Crosby, the staff and all my colleagues in the John W. McCormack Graduate School of Policy Studies. I am particularly grateful to Steve Crosby for help in providing a student research trainee, Lisa Cathcart, who worked diligently and tirelessly to assemble relevant documentation for each chapter, following initial research assistance by Danielle Thompson. Bill Baer and the staff of UMass' Healey Library, likewise, were, once again, of invaluable assistance. The directors and archivists of the National Archives' John F. Kennedy, Richard M. Nixon, Gerald R. Ford, Jimmy Carter and Ronald Reagan Presidential Libraries were invariably hospitable and helpful on my visits; also my sojourn as a Visiting Scholar at George Washington University and at Georgetown University in 2005 proved immensely helpful – especially since, at the latter, my office was located in the Classics Department, where Greek and Roman parallels with modern America were constantly discussed! I am particularly grateful to those members of the Clinton Administration I was able to interview for my Clinton biography, from Rahm Emanuel to Leon Panetta and Larry Summers, but also to the historians of the US Senate, Richard A. Baker and Donald A. Ritchie, as well as distinguished authors belonging to the Washington Writers Group, led by Dan Moldea, for their constant kindnesses and encouragement.

The fact is, no serious historian can write a biography without the help of his or her literary peers. I was fortunate to be alerted by James McGrath Morris, the editor of thebiographerscraft.com, to the existence of the Boston Biographers Group – and to them I would like to extend my heartfelt gratitude for moral, emotional and intellectual support during the genesis of this work. To my fellow biographers, authors and professional colleagues Herbert Parmet, Carlo D'Este, David Kaiser, Clive Foss, Larry Leamer, David Chanoff, Mark Schneider, Timothy Naftali, Craig Howes, Andrew Phillips, David Sparks, John Gartner, Mel Yoken, and others who read or listened to parts of the manuscript, my deep gratitude. My lifelong friend and classmate from Cambridge University days, Robin Whitby, read each chapter of the original manuscript for readability and general interest, as did my brother Michael Hamilton, following his retirement from Briggs & Stratton, Milwaukee. Audience responses at Suffolk University in Boston, UMass Boston, UMass Dartmouth, Roxbury Latin School and the Cambridge Boat Club to preliminary readings from the evolving manuscript proved greatly encouraging. My wife, Dr Raynel Shepard, ESL Curriculum Developer of the Boston Public Schools, kept me focused and happier than perhaps I have ever been while undertaking a major book project. Bruce Hunter, of David Higham Associates, acted as not only my literary agent but, as always, my stalwart adviser, friend and reassurer-in-chief. I have much to be grateful for – and I am, especially for the faith of the Publishing Director of The Bodley Head, Will Sulkin, and his colleagues, in the merit of the project. I can only hope the book, for all its faults, is worthy of so much help and support across two continents.

Nigel Hamilton
Somerville
Massachusetts
October 2009

Select Bibliography

American Empire

Ambrose, Stephen, *Rise to Globalism: American Foreign Policy since 1938* (1971) (New York: Penguin Books, 1993)

Bacevich, Andrew, *American Empire: The Realities and Consequences of US Diplomacy* (Cambridge, MA: Harvard University Press, 2004)

— *The Limits of Power: The End of American Exceptionalism* (New York: Macmillan, 2008)

Bender, Peter, *Weltmacht Amerika: Das Neue Rom* (Munich: Deutscher Taschenbuch Verlag, 2005)

Beschloss, Michael R., and Strobe Talbott, *At the Highest Levels: The Inside Story of the Cold War* (Boston: Little Brown, 1993)

Brands, H. W., *The Devil We Knew: Americans and the Cold War* (New York: Oxford University Press, 1993)

— *Into the Labyrinth: The United States and the Middle East, 1945–1993* (New York: McGraw-Hill, 1994)

de Grazia, Victoria, *Irresistible Empire: America's Advance through 20th Century Europe* (Cambridge, MA: Harvard University Press, 2005)

Ferguson, Niall, *Colossus: The Price of America's Empire* (New York: Penguin Press, 2004)

— *The War of the World: Twentieth-Century Conflict and the Descent of the West* (New York: Penguin Press, 2006)

Gelb, Leslie H., *Power Rules: How Common Sense Can Rescue American Foreign Policy* (New York: HarperCollins, 2009)

Hardt, Michael, and Antonio Negri, *Empire* (Cambridge: Harvard University Press, 2001)

Hedges, Chris, *Empire of Illusion: The End of Literacy and the Triumph of Spectacle* (New York: Nation Books, 2009)

Herring, George C., *From Colony to Superpower: US Foreign Relations since 1776* (New York: Oxford University Press, 2008)

Hobson, J. A., *Imperialism: A Study* (1938) (Ann Arbor: University of Michigan Press, 1965)

Hoff, Joan, *A Faustian Foreign Policy: From Woodrow Wilson to George W. Bush – Dreams of Perfectibility* (New York: Cambridge University Press, 2008)

Johnson, Chalmers, *The Sorrows of Empire: Militarism, Secrecy, and the End of the Republic* (New York: Metropolitan Books, 2004)

Kagan, Robert, *Of Paradise and Power: America and Europe in the New World Order* (New York: Knopf, 2003)

Kennedy, Paul, *The Rise and Fall of the Great Powers* (New York: Random House, 1987)

Lapham, Lewis H., *Pretensions to Empire: Notes on the Criminal Folly of the Bush Administration* (New York: The New Press, 2006)

Lundestad, Geir, *Empire by Integration: The United States and European Integration, 1945–1997* (New York: Oxford University Press, 1998)

McMahon, Robert J., *The Cold War: A Very Short Introduction* (Oxford: Oxford University Press, 2003)

Maier, Charles S., *Among Empires: American Ascendancy and Its Predecessors* (Cambridge, MA: Harvard University Press, 2006)

Murphy, Cullen, *Are We Rome? The Fall of an Empire and the Fate of America* (Boston: Houghton Mifflin, 2007)

Robinson, Jeffrey, *The End of the American Century: Hidden Agendas of the Cold War* (London: Hutchinson, 1992)

Ross, Dennis, *Statecraft: And How to Restore America's Standing in the World* (New York: Farrar Straus and Giroux, 2008)

Turchin, Peter, *War and Peace and War: The Rise and Fall of Empires* (New York: Plume, 2006)

Tyler, Patrick, *A World of Trouble: The White House and the Middle East – From the Cold War to the War on Terror* (New York: Farrar Straus and Giroux, 2009)

Vidal, Gore, *The Decline and Fall of the American Empire* (1992) (Tucson, AZ: Odonian Press, 2004)

— *Imperial America: Reflections on the United States of Amnesia* (New York: Nation Books, 2004)

— *The Last Empire: Essays 1992–2000* (New York: Doubleday, 2001)

US Presidency

Andrew, Christopher, *For the President's Eyes Only: Secret Intelligence and the American Presidency from Washington to Bush* (New York: HarperCollins, 1995)

Anthony, Carl Sferrazza, *First Ladies: The Saga of the Presidents' Wives and Their Power, 1789–1961* (New York: William Morrow, 1990)

Bohn, Michael K., *Nerve Center: Inside the White House Situation Room* (Washington: Brassey's, 2003)

Caroli, Betty Boyd, *First Ladies: An Intimate Look at How 38 Women Handled What May Be the Most Demanding, Unpaid, Unelected Job in America* (New York: Oxford University Press, 1995)

Dallek, Robert, *Hail to the Chief: The Making and Unmaking of American Presidents* (New York: Hyperion, 1996)

Degregorio, William A., *The Complete Book of US Presidents* (New York: Avenel, 1993)

Doyle, William, *Inside the Oval Office: The White House Tapes – From FDR to Clinton* (New York: Kodansha America, 1999)

Edwards, George C., and Stephen J. Wayne (eds), *Studying the Presidency* (Knoxville: University of Tennessee Press, 1983)

Hess, Stephen, *Organizing the Presidency* (Washington, DC: Brookings Institution, 2002)

Jones, Charles O., *Passages to the Presidency: From Campaigning to Governing* (Washington, DC: Brookings Institution, 1998)

Milkis, Sidney M., and Michael Nelson, *The American Presidency: Origins and Development, 1776–1998* (Washington, DC: CQ Press, 1999)

Moore, Kathryn, *The American Presidency: A Complete History* (New York: Barnes & Noble, 2007)

Patterson, Bradley H., *The White House Staff: Inside the West Wing and Beyond* (Washington, DC: Brookings Institution, 2000)

Schlesinger, Arthur M., Jr, *The Imperial Presidency* (New York: Popular Library, 1974)

Smith, Carter, *Presidents: Every Question Answered* (Irvington, New York: Hylas Publishing, 2004)

Wilson, Robert A. (ed.), *Power and the Presidency* (New York: PublicAffairs, 1999)

Franklin D. Roosevelt

Black, Conrad, *Franklin Delano Roosevelt: Champion of Freedom* (New York: PublicAffairs, 2003)

Brands, H. W., *Traitor to His Class: The Privileged Life and Radical Presidency of Franklin Delano Roosevelt* (New York: Doubleday, 2008)

Dallek, Robert, *Franklin D. Roosevelt and American Foreign Policy, 1932–1945* (New York: Oxford University Press, 1979)

Davis, Kenneth S., *FDR: The War President, 1940-1943 – A History* (New York: Random House, 2000)

Freidel, Frank, *Franklin Roosevelt: A Rendezvous with Destiny* (Boston: Little Brown, 1990)

Jenkins, Roy, with Richard E. Neustadt, *Franklin Delano Roosevelt* (New York: Times Books, 2003)

Lash, Joseph P., *Eleanor and Franklin* (New York: Norton, 1971)

— *Roosevelt and Churchill 1939-1941: The Partnership That Saved the West* (New York: Norton, 1976)

Meacham, Jon, *Franklin and Winston: An Intimate Portrait of an Epic Friendship* (New York: Random House, 2003)

Perkins, Frances, *The Roosevelt I Knew* (New York: Viking Press, 1946)

Persico, Joseph E., *Franklin & Lucy: President Roosevelt, Mrs Rutherfurd, and the Other Remarkable Women in His Life* (New York: Random House, 2008)

Roosevelt, Eleanor, *The Autobiography of Eleanor Roosevelt* (1961) (New York: Da Capo Press, 1992)

Smith, Jean Edward, *FDR* (New York: Random House, 2007)

Ward, Geoffrey C., *Before the Trumpet: Young Franklin Roosevelt, 1882–1905* (New York: Harper & Row, 1985)

— *A First Class Temperament: The Emergence of Franklin Roosevelt* (New York: Harper & Row, 1989)

— (ed.), *Closest Companion: The Unknown Story of the Intimate Friendship between Franklin Roosevelt and Margaret Suckley* (Boston: Houghton Mifflin, 1995)

Harry S. Truman

Acheson, Dean, *Present at the Creation: My Years in the State Department* (New York: Norton, 1969)

Clifford, Clark, *Counsel to the President* (New York: Random House, 1991)

Donovan, Robert, *Conflict and Crisis: The Presidency of Harry S. Truman, 1945–1948* (New York: Norton, 1977)

— *Tumultuous Years: The Presidency of Harry S. Truman, 1949–1953* (New York: Norton, 1982)

Ferrell, Robert H., *Harry S. Truman, and the Modern American Presidency* (Boston: Little Brown, 1983)

— (ed.), *The Autobiography of Harry S. Truman* (Boulder, CO: Colorado Associated University Press, 1980)

— (ed.), *Dear Bess: The Letters from Harry to Bess Truman, 1910–1959* (New York: W. W. Norton, 1983)

— (ed.), *Off the Record: The Private Papers of Harry S. Truman* (New York: Harper & Row, 1980)

Hamby, Alonzo M., *Man of the People: A Life of Harry S. Truman* (New York: Oxford University Press, 1995)

Isaacson, Walter, and Evan Thomas, *The Wise Men: Six Friends and the World They Made – Acheson, Bohlen, Harriman, Kennan, Lovett, McCloy* (New York: Simon & Schuster, 1986)

Jenkins, Roy, *Truman* (New York: Harper & Row, 1986)

McCullough, David, *Truman* (New York: Simon & Schuster, 1992)

Miller, Merle, *Plain Speaking: An Oral Biography of Harry S. Truman* (New York: Berkley/G.B. Putnam's Sons, 1973)

Offner, Arnold A., *Another Such Victory: President Truman and the Cold War, 1945–1953* (Stanford: Stanford University Press, 2002)

Pemberton, William E., *Harry S. Truman: Fair Dealer and Cold Warrior* (Boston: Twayne Publishers, 1989)

Perret, Geoffrey, *Commander in Chief: How Truman, Johnson, and Bush Turned a Presidential Power into a Threat to America's Future* (New York: Farrar, Strauss and Giroux, 2007)

Poen, Monte M. (ed.), *Strictly Personal and Confidential: The Letters Harry Truman Never Mailed* (Boston: Little Brown, 1982)

Pogue, Forrest C., *George C. Marshall: Statesman 1945–1959* (New York: Viking, 1987)

Truman, Harry S., *Memoirs, Volume One: Year of Decisions* (New York: Doubleday, 1955)

— *Memoirs, Volume Two: Years of Trial and Hope* (New York: Doubleday, 1956)

Truman, Margaret, *Harry S. Truman* (New York: William Morrow, 1972)
— (ed.), *Where the Buck Stops: The Personal and Private Writings of Harry S. Truman* (New York: Warner Books, 1989)

Dwight D. Eisenhower

Adams, Sherman, *First Hand Report: The Inside Story of the Eisenhower Administration* (New York: Harper, 1961)

Ambrose, Stephen, *Eisenhower: Soldier, General of the Army, President-elect, 1890-1952* (New York: Simon & Schuster, 1983)

— *Eisenhower: The President* (New York: Simon & Schuster, 1984)

— *Ike's Spies: Eisenhower and the Espionage Establishment* (1981) (Jackson: University of Mississippi, 1999)

Beschloss, Michael R., *May-Day: Eisenhower, Khrushchev and the U2 Affair* (New York: Harper & Row, 1986)

Brendon, Piers, *Ike: His Life and Times* (New York: Harper, 1986)

Carlson, Peter, *K Blows Top: A Cold War Interlude, Starring Nikita Khrushchev, America's Most Unlikely Tourist* (New York: PublicAffairs, 2009)

David, Lester, and Irene David, *Ike and Mamie: The Story of the General and His Lady* (New York: G.B. Putnam's Sons, 1981)

D'Este, Carlo, *Eisenhower: A Soldier's Life* (New York: Holt, 2002)

Eisenhower, Dwight D., *The White House Years: Mandate for Change, 1953–1956* (New York: Doubleday, 1963)

— *The White House Years: Waging Peace, 1956-1961* (New York: Doubleday, 1965)

Ferrell, Robert H. (ed.), *The Eisenhower Diaries* (New York: Norton, 1981)

Fursenko, Aleksandr, and Timothy Naftali, *Khrushchev's Cold War: The Inside Story of an American Adversary* (New York, Norton, 2006)

Khrushchev, Nikita, *Khrushchev Remembers: The Last Testament* (Boston: Little Brown, 1974)

Pach, Chester J., and Elmo Richardson, *The Presidency of Dwight D. Eisenhower* (Lawrence: University Press of Kansas, 1991)

Perret, Geoffrey, *Eisenhower* (New York: Random House, 1999)

Powers, Thomas, *The Man Who Kept the Secrets: Richard Helms and the CIA* (New York: Knopf, 1979)

Taubman, William, *Khrushchev: The Man and His Era* (New York: Norton, 2003)

Taubman, William, et al. (eds), *Nikita Khrushchev* (New Haven: Yale University Press, 2000)

John F. Kennedy

Beschloss, Michael, *The Crisis Years: Kennedy and Khrushchev, 1960–1963* (New York: HarperCollins, 1991)

Blair, Joan, and Clay Blair, *The Search for JFK* (New York: Putnam, 1974)

Bradlee, Ben, *Conversations with Kennedy* (New York: Norton, 1997)

Dallek, Robert, *An Unfinished Life: John F. Kennedy 1917–1963* (Boston: Little Brown, 2003)

Giglio, James N., *The Presidency of John F. Kennedy* (Lawrence: University Press of Kansas, 1991)

Hamilton, Nigel, *JFK: Reckless Youth* (New York: Random House, 1992)

Hersh, Seymour, *The Dark Side of Camelot* (Boston: Little Brown, 1997)

Kaiser, David, *American Tragedy: Kennedy, Johnson, and the Origins of the Vietnam War* (Cambridge, MA: Harvard University Press, 2000)

Leamer, Laurence, *The Kennedy Men, 1901–1963* (New York: William Morrow, 2001)

May, Ernest R., and Philip D. Zelikow, *The Kennedy Tapes: Inside the White House during the Cuban Missile Crisis* (Cambridge, MA: Harvard University Press, 1997)

Parmet, Herbert, *JFK: The Presidency of John F. Kennedy* (New York: Dial Press, 1983)

Perret, Geoffrey, *Jack: A Life Like No Other* (New York: Random House, 2001)

Reeves, Richard, *President Kennedy: Profile of Power* (New York: Simon & Schuster, 1993)

Reeves, Thomas C., *A Question of Character: A Life of John F. Kennedy* (New York: Macmillan, 1991)

Rubin, Gretchen, *Forty Ways to Look at JFK* (New York: Ballantine, 2005)

Smith, Sally B., *Grace and Power: The Private World of the Kennedy White House* (New York: Random House, 2004)

Sorensen, Theodore C., *Kennedy* (New York: Bantam, 1966)

Lyndon B. Johnson

Beschloss, Michael R. (ed.), *Taking Charge: The Johnson White House Tapes, 1963–1964* (New York: Simon & Schuster, 1997)

— (ed.), *Reaching For Glory: Lyndon Johnson's Secret White House Tapes, 1964–1965* (New York: Simon & Schuster, 2001)

Bornet, Vaughn Davis, *The Presidency of Lyndon B. Johnson* (Lawrence: University Press of Kansas, 1983)

Caro, Robert, *The Years of Lyndon Johnson: Master of the Senate* (New York: Knopf, 2002)

— *The Years of Lyndon Johnson: Means of Ascent* (New York: Knopf, 1990)

— *The Years of Lyndon Johnson: The Path to Power* (New York: Knopf, 1982)

Christian, George, *The President Steps Down: A Personal Memoir of the Transfer of Power* (New York: Macmillan, 1970)

Dallek, Robert, *Flawed Giant: Lyndon Johnson and His Times, 1961–1973* (New York: Oxford University Press, 1998)

— *Lone Star Rising: Lyndon Johnson and His Times, 1908–1960* (New York: Oxford University Press, 1991)

— *Lyndon B. Johnson: Portrait of a President* (New York: Oxford University Press, 2004)

Gardner, Lloyd C., *Pay Any Price: Lyndon Johnson and the Wars for Vietnam* (Chicago: Ivan R. Dee, 1995)

Goldman, Eric F., *The Tragedy of Lyndon Johnson* (New York: Knopf, 1969)

Herring, George C., *LBJ and Vietnam: A Different Kind of War* (Austin: University of Texas, 1994)

Johnson, Lyndon Baines, *The Vantage Point: Perspectives on the Presidency, 1963–1969* (New York: Holt, Rinehart and Winston, 1971)

Johnson, Sam Houston, *My Brother Lyndon* (New York: Cowles, 1970)

Kearns, Doris, *Lyndon Johnson and the American Dream* (New York: Harper, 1976)

Kotz, Nick, *Judgment Days: Lyndon Baines Johnson, Martin Luther King Jr., and the Laws That Changed America* (Boston: Houghton Mifflin, 2005)

Miller, Merle, *Lyndon: An Oral Biography* (New York: G.B. Putnam's Sons, 1980)

Perlstein, Rick, *Before the Storm: Barry Goldwater and the Unmaking of the American Consensus* (New York: Hill and Wang, 2001)

Phipps, Joe, *Summer Stock: Behind the Scenes with LBJ in '48* (Fort Worth: Texas Christian Press, 1992)

Reedy, George, *Lyndon B. Johnson: A Memoir* (New York: Andrews and McMeel, 1982)

Schwartz, Thomas Alan, *Lyndon Johnson and Europe* (Cambridge, MA: Harvard University Press, 2003)

VanDeMark, Brian, *Into the Quagmire: Lyndon Johnson and the Escalation of the Vietnam War* (New York: Oxford University Press, 1991)

Vandiver, Frank E., *Shadows of Vietnam: Lyndon Johnson's Wars* (College Station: Texas A&M University Press, 1997)

Woods, Randall B., *LBJ: Architect of American Ambition* (New York: Free Press, 2006)

Richard M. Nixon

Aitken, Jonathan, *Nixon: A Life* (Washington DC: Regnery, 1993)

Ambrose, Stephen, *Nixon: The Education of a Politician, 1913–1962* (New York: Simon & Schuster, 1987)

— *Nixon: The Triumph of a Politician, 1962–1972* (New York: Simon & Schuster, 1988)

— *Nixon: Ruin and Recovery, 1973–1990* (New York: Simon & Schuster, 1991)

Black, Conrad, *Richard Milhous Nixon: The Invincible Quest* (New York: PublicAffairs, 2007)

Dallek, Robert, *Nixon and Kissinger: Partners in Power* (New York: HarperCollins, 2007)

Dean, John, *Blind Ambition: The White House Years* (New York: Simon & Schuster, 1976)

Ellsberg, Daniel, *Secrets: A Memoir of Vietnam and the Pentagon Papers* (New York: Viking Penguin, 2002)

Hahnimaki, Jussi, *The Flawed Architect: Henry Kissinger and American Foreign Policy* (New York: Oxford University Press, 2004)

Hersh, Seymour M., *The Price of Power: Kissinger in the White House* (New York: Summit Books, 1983)

Kutler, Stanley I., *Abuse of Power: The New Nixon Tapes* (New York: Free Press, 1997)

Macmillan, Margaret, *Nixon and Mao: The Week that Changed the World* (New York: Random House, 2007)

Morris, Roger, *Richard Milhous Nixon: The Rise of an American Politician* (New York: Holt, 1989)

Nixon, Richard, *RN: The Memoirs of Richard Nixon* (New York: Grosset & Dunlap, 1978)

— *Six Crises* (New York: Doubleday, 1962)

Parmet, Herbert, *Richard Nixon and His America* (Boston: Little Brown, 1990)

Reeves, Richard, *President Nixon: Alone in the White House* (New York: Simon & Schuster, 2001)

Small, Melvin, *The Presidency of Richard Nixon* (Lawrence: University Press of Kansas, 1999)

Summers, Anthony, *The Arrogance of Power: The Secret World of Richard Nixon* (New York: Viking, 2000)

Woodward, Bob, and Carl Bernstein, *The Final Days* (New York: Simon & Schuster, 1976)

Gerald R. Ford

Brinkley, Douglas, *Gerald R. Ford* (New York: Times Books, 2007)

Cannon, James, *Time and Chance: Gerald Ford's Appointment with History* (New York: HarperCollins, 1994)

DeFrank, Thomas M., *Write It When I'm Gone: Remarkable Off-the-Record Conversations with Gerald R. Ford* (New York: G.B. Putnam's Sons, 2007)

Ford, Gerald R., *A Time to Heal* (New York: Harper & Row, 1979)

Greene, John Robert, *The Presidency of Gerald R. Ford* (Lawrence: University Press of Kansas, 1995)

Mieczkowski, Yanek, *Gerald Ford, and the Challenges of the 1970s* (Lexington: University of Kentucky Press, 2005)

Mollenhoff, Clark, *The Man Who Pardoned Nixon* (New York: St. Martin's Press, 1976)

Werth, Barry, *31 Days: The Crisis That Gave Us the Government We Have Today* (New York: Doubleday, 2006)

Jimmy Carter

Bourne, Peter G., *Jimmy Carter: A Comprehensive Biography from Plains to Postpresidency* (New York: Scribner, 1997)

Carter, Jimmy, *An Hour Before Daylight* (New York: Simon & Schuster, 2001)

— *Keeping Faith: Memoirs of a President* (New York: Bantam, 1982)

— *Palestine Peace Not Apartheid* (New York: Simon & Schuster, 2007)

Carter, Rosalynn, *First Lady from Plains* (Boston: Houghton Mifflin, 1984)

Jones, Charles O., *The Trusteeship Presidency: Jimmy Carter and the United States Congress* (Baton Rouge: Louisiana State University Press, 1988)

Jordan, Hamilton, *Crisis: The Last Year of the Carter Presidency* (New York: Berkley Publishing, 1982)

Kaufman, Burton I., *James Earl Carter, Jr.* (Lawrence: University Press of Kansas, 1993)

Lasky, Victor, *Jimmy Carter: The Man and the Myth* (New York: Richard Marek, 1979)

Mazlish, Bruce, and Erwin Diamond, *Jimmy Carter: A Character Portrait* (New York: Simon and Schuster, 1979)

Meyer, Peter, *James Earl Carter: The Man and the Myth* (Kansas City: Sheed Andrews and McMeel, 1978)

Morris, Kenneth E., *Jimmy Carter: American Moralist* (Athens: University of Georgia Press, 1996)

Schramm, Martin, *Running for President: A Journal of the Carter Campaign* (New York: Pocket Books, 1978)

Strong, Robert A., *Working in the World: Jimmy Carter and the Making of American Foreign Policy* (Baton Rouge: Louisiana State University Press, 2000)

Stroud, Kandy, *How Jimmy Won: The Victory Campaign from Plains to the White House* (New York: Morrow, 1977)

Thompson, Kenneth W. (ed.), *The Carter Presidency: Fourteen Intimate Perspectives of Jimmy Carter* (Lanham, MD: University Press of America, 1990)

Witcover, Jules, *Marathon: The Pursuit of the Presidency, 1972–1976* (New York: Viking, 1977)

Ronald Reagan

Brown, Edmund G., *Reagan and Reality: The Two Californias* (New York: Praeger, 1970)

Cannon, Lou, *President Reagan: The Role of a Lifetime* (New York: PublicAffairs, 2000)

Colacello, Bob, *Ronnie and Nancy: Their Path to the White House – 1911–1980* (New York: Warner Books, 2004)

Dallek, Robert, *Ronald Reagan: The Politics of Symbolism* (Cambridge, MA: Harvard University Press, 1999)

Deaver, Michael, with Mickey Herkovitz, *Behind the Scenes* (New York: Morrow, 1987)

Diggins, John Patrick, *Ronald Reagan: Fate, Freedom, and the Making of History* (New York: Norton, 2007)

Donaldson, Sam, *Hold on, Mr President!* (New York: Random House, 1987)

D'Souza, Dinesh, *Ronald Reagan: How an Ordinary Man Became an Extraordinary Leader* (New York: Free Press, 1997)

Edwards, Anne, *Early Reagan* (New York: William Morrow, 1987)

Gorbachev, Mikhail, *Memoirs* (New York: Doubleday, 1995)

Kelley, Kitty, *Nancy Reagan: The Unauthorized Biography* (New York: Simon & Schuster, 1991)

Kengor, Paul, *The Crusader: Ronald Reagan and the Fall of Communism* (New York: HarperCollins, 2006)

Morris, Edmund, *Dutch: A Memoir of Ronald Reagan* (New York: Random House, 1999)

Noonan, Peggy, *When Character Was King: A Story of Ronald Reagan* (New York: Viking, 2001)

Pemberton, William E., *Exit with Honor: The Life and Presidency of Ronald Reagan* (Armonk, NY: M. E. Sharpe, 1997)

Reagan, Nancy, with William Novak, *My Turn: The Memoirs of Nancy Reagan* (New York: Random House, 1989)

Reagan, Ronald, *An American Life* (New York: Simon and Schuster, 1990)

— *The Reagan Diaries*, ed. Douglas Brinkley (New York: HarperCollins, 2007)

Reeves, Richard, *President Reagan* (New York: Simon & Schuster, 2005)

Troy, Gill, *Morning in America: How Ronald Reagan Invented the 1980s* (Princeton: Princeton University Press, 2005)

Wilentz, Sean, *The Age of Reagan: A History 1974–2008* (New York: Harper, 2008)

George H. W. Bush

Baker, James, with Thomas DeFrank, *The Politics of Diplomacy: Revolution, War and Peace, 1989–1992* (New York: G. B. Putnam's Sons, 1995)

Bush, Barbara, *A Memoir* (New York: Scribner, 1994)

Bush, George, *All the Best, George Bush: My Life in Letters and Other Writings* (New York: Scribner, 2000)

Bush, George, and Brent Scowcroft, *A World Transformed* (New York: Knopf, 1998)

Engel, Jeffrey A., *The China Diary of George H. W. Bush: The Making of a Global President* (Princeton: Princeton University Press, 2008)

Green, FitzHugh, *George Bush: An Intimate Portrait* (New York: Hippocrene Press, 1991)

Greene, John Robert, *The Presidency of George Bush* (Lawrence: University Press of Kansas, 2000)

Halberstam, David, *War in a Time of Peace: Bush, Clinton, and the Generals* (New York: Scribner, 2001)

Koch, Doro Bush, *My Father, My President: A Personal Account of the Life of George H. W. Bush* (New York: Grand Central Publishing, 2006)

McGrath, Jim, *Heartbeat: George Bush in His Own Words* (New York: Scribner, 2001)

Mervin, David, *George Bush and the Guardianship Presidency* (New York: St Martin's Press, 1996)

Naftali, Timothy, *George H. W. Bush* (New York: Times Books, 2007)

Parmet, Herbert, *George Bush: The Life of a Lone Star Yankee* (New York: Scribner, 1997)

Phillips, Kevin, *American Dynasty: Aristocracy, Fortune, and the Politics of Deceit in the House of Bush* (New York: Viking, 2004)

Powell, Colin, with Joseph E. Persico, *An American Journey* (New York: Random House, 1995)

Tarpley Webster G., and Anton Chaitkin, *George Bush: The Unauthorized Biography* (Washington, DC: Executive Intelligence Review, 1992)

Woodward, Bob, *The Commanders* (New York: Simon & Schuster, 1991)

— *Shadow: Five Presidents and the Legacy of Watergate* (New York: Simon & Schuster, 1999)

Bill Clinton

Blumenthal, Sidney, *The Clinton Wars* (New York: Farrar, Straus and Giroux, 2003)

Conason, Joe, and Gene Lyons, *The Hunting of the President: The Ten-Year Campaign to Destroy Bill and Hillary Clinton* (New York: St Martin's Press, 2000)

Clinton, Bill, *My Life* (New York: Knopf, 2004)

Clinton, Hillary Rodham, *Living History* (New York: Simon & Schuster, 2003)

Fick, Paul, *The Dysfunctional President: Understanding the Compulsions of Bill Clinton* (Secaucus, NJ: Carol Publishing, 1995, 1998)

Freeh, Louis B., *My FBI: Bringing down the Mafia, Investigating Bill Clinton, and Fighting the War on Terror* (New York: St Martin's Press, 2005)

Gartner, John D., *In Search of Bill Clinton: A Psychological Biography* (New York: St Martin's Press, 2008)

Gergen, David, *Eyewitness to Power: The Essence of Leadership – Nixon to Clinton* (New York: Simon & Schuster, 2000)

Hamilton, Nigel, *Bill Clinton: American Journey – Great Expectations* (New York: Random House 2003)

— *Bill Clinton: Mastering the Presidency* (New York: PublicAffairs, 2007)

Harris, John, *The Survivor: Bill Clinton in the White House* (New York: Random House, 2005)

Johnson, Haynes, *The Best of Times: America in the Clinton Years* (New York: Harcourt, 2001)

Johnson, Haynes, and David S. Broder: *The System: The American Way of Politics at the Breaking Point* (Boston: Little Brown, 1996)

Maraniss, David, *The Clinton Enigma: A Four-and-a-half Minute Speech Reveals the President's Entire Life* (New York: Simon & Schuster, 1998)

Morris, Dick, *Behind the Oval Office* (New York: Random House, 1997)

Renshon, Stanley A., *High Hopes: The Clinton Presidency and the Politics of Ambition* (New York: New York University Press, 1996, 1998)

Schmidt, Susan, and Michael Weisskopf, *Truth at Any Cost: Ken Starr and the Unmaking of Bill Clinton* (New York: HarperCollins, 2000)

Stephanopoulos, George, *All Too Human* (Boston: Little Brown, 1999)

Stewart, James B., *Blood Sport: The President and His Adversaries* (New York: Simon & Schuster, 1996)

Starr, Kenneth, *The Starr Evidence*, ed. *Washington Post* (New York: PublicAffairs, 1998)

Toobin, Jeffrey, *A Vast Conspiracy: The Real Story of the Sex Scandal That Nearly Brought down a President* (New York: Random House, 1999)

Woodward, Bob, *The Agenda: Inside the Clinton White House* (New York: Simon & Schuster, 1994)

— *The Choice* (Simon & Schuster, 1996)

George W. Bush

Anderson, Christopher, *George and Laura: Portrait of an American Marriage* (New York: William Morrow, 2002)

Bovard, James, *The Bush Betrayal* (New York: Palgrave Macmillan, 2004)

Bruni, Frank, *Ambling into History: The Unlikely Odyssey of George W. Bush* (New York: HarperCollins, 2002)

Cannon, Lou, and Carl M. Cannon, *Reagan's Disciple: George W. Bush's Troubled Quest for a Presidential Legacy* (New York: PublicAffairs, 2008)

Clarke, Richard A., *Against All Enemies: Inside America's War on Terror* (New York: Free Press, 2004)

Dean, John, *Worse than Watergate: The Secret Presidency of George W. Bush* (Boston: Little Brown, 2004)

Dubose, Lou, and Jake Bernstein, *Vice: Dick Cheney and the Hijacking of the American Presidency* (New York: Random House, 2006)

Feith, Douglas J., *War and Decision: Inside the Pentagon at the Dawn of the War on Terrorism* (New York: Harper, 2008)

Freiling, Thomas M., *George W. Bush: On God and Country* (Fairfax, VA: Allegiance Press, 2004)

Frum, David, *The Right Man: The Surprise Presidency of George W. Bush* (New York: Random House, 2003)

Gellman, Barton, *Angler: The Cheney Vice Presidency* (New York: Penguin Press, 2008)

Goldsmith, Jack, *The Terror Presidency: Law and Judgment inside the Bush Administration* (New York: Norton, 2007)

Hatfield, J. H., *Fortunate Son: George W. Bush and the Making of an American President* (New York: Soft Skull Press, 2001)

Kean, Jack, Lee H. Hamilton et al., *The 9/11 Commission Report: Final Report of the National Commission on Terrorist Attacks upon the United States* (New York: Norton, 2004)

Kelley, Kitty, *The Family: The Real Story of the Bush Dynasty* (New York: Doubleday, 2004)

Kessler, Ron, *A Matter of Character: Inside the White House of George W. Bush* (New York: Sentinel, 2004)

Mann, James, *Rise of the Vulcans: The History of Bush's War Cabinet* (New York: Viking, 2004)

McClellan, Scott, *What Happened: Inside the Bush White House and Washington's Culture of Deception* (New York: PublicAffairs, 2008)

Mayer, Jane, *The Dark Side: The Inside Story of How the War on Terror Turned into a War on American Ideals* (New York: Doubleday, 2008)

Miller, Mark Crispin, *Cruel and Unusual: Bush / Cheney's New World Order* (New York: Norton, 2004)

Moore, James, and Wayne Slater, *Bush's Brain: How Karl Rove Made George W. Bush Presidential* (Hoboken, NJ: John Wiley, 2003)

Suskind, Ron, *The Price of Loyalty: George W. Bush, the White House and the Education of Paul O'Neill* (New York: Simon & Schuster, 2004)

Unger, Craig, *American Armageddon: How the Delusions of the Neoconservatives and the Christian Right Triggered the Descent of America – and Still Imperil Our Future* (New York: Scribner, 2007)

Weisberg, Jacob, *The Bush Tragedy* (New York: Random House, 2008)

Woodward, Bob, *Bush at War* (New York: Simon & Schuster, 2002)

— *Plan of Attack: The Definitive Account of the Decision to Invade Iraq* (New York: Simon & Schuster, 2004)

— *State of Denial: Bush at War, Part III* (New York: Simon & Schuster, 2006)

Notes

Preface

1. Ron Suskind, 'Faith, Certainty and the Presidency of George W. Bush', *New York Times Magazine*, October 17, 2004. • **2.** At the end of President George W. Bush's final term in office, in January 2009, the US Government officially administered only six colonies or US Territories across the world: American Samoa, the Federated States of Micronesia, Guam, Midway Islands, Puerto Rico, and the US Virgin Islands. However, the US was still fighting two major wars, in Iraq and Afghanistan, and operating more than 900 officially acknowledged military bases overseas, in 130 countries (other than its official US Territories), as well as more than a hundred secret or disguised installations – up from only 14 overseas bases in 1938. Catherine Lutz, 'Obama's Empire,' *New Statesman*, July 30, 2009.

Chapter One: Franklin Roosevelt

1. Jean Edward Smith, *FDR*, p. 23. • **2.** Ibid., p. 50. • **3.** Ibid., p. 63. • **4.** Ibid., p. 61. • **5.** Ibid., p. 59. • **6.** Ibid., p. 102. • **7.** Ibid., p. 140. • **8.** H. W. Brands, *Traitor to His Class: The Privileged Life and Radical Presidency of Franklin Delano Roosevelt*, pp. 129–30. • **9.** Ibid., p. 137. • **10.** Ibid. • **11.** *New York Times*, September 16, 2001, in Smith, *FDR*, p. 192. • **12.** Smith, *FDR*, p. 211. • **13.** Ibid. • **14.** Brands, *Traitor to His Class*, p. 206. • **15.** Smith, *FDR*, p. 225. • **16.** Ibid., p. 251. • **17.** Ibid., p. 258. • **18.** Ibid., p. 263. • **19.** Ibid., p. 316. • **20.** Ibid., p. 299. • **21.** Ibid., pp. 350–1. • **22.** Initially, only 60 per cent of workers were covered, as firms employing less than ten people were exempt from contributions. • **23.** Smith, *FDR*, p. 359. • **24.** Ibid., p. 371. • **25.** Ibid., p. 419. • **26.** Ibid., p. 426. • **27.** Ibid.,

p. 445. • **28**. Conrad Black, *Franklin Delano Roosevelt: Champion of Freedom*, p. 290. • **29**. Smith, *FDR*, p. 441. • **30**. Ibid., p. 458. • **31**. Ibid., p. 466. • **32**. Ibid., p. 476. • **33**. Conrad Black, *Franklin Delano Roosevelt*, p. 595. • **34**. Smith, *FDR*, p. 477. • **35**. Ibid., p. 448. • **36**. Hamilton, *JFK*, p. 396. • **37**. Smith, *FDR*, pp. 485–6. • **38**. Ibid., p. 487. • **39**. Ibid., p. 490. • **40**. Joseph P. Lash, *Roosevelt and Churchill 1939–1941*, p. 391. • **41**. Ibid., p. 403. • **42**. Jon Meacham, *Franklin and Winston*, p. 122. • **43**. Lash, *Roosevelt and Churchill*, p. 401. • **44**. Meacham, *Franklin and Winston*, pp. 122–3. • **45**. Max Domarus, *Hitler: Speeches and Proclamations 1932–1945, and Commentary by a Contemporary*, Vol. 4 (Wauconda, IL: Bolchazy-Carducci Publishers, 2004), p. 2542. • **46**. Ibid., p. 2551. • **47**. FDR to Knox, in Smith, *FDR*, p. 537. • **48**. Ibid., p. 541. • **49**. Domarus, *Hitler: Speeches and Proclamations*, p. 2593. • **50**. Nigel Hamilton, *The Full Monty* (London: Allen Lane, 2001), p. 584. • **51**. Meacham, *Franklin and Winston*, p. 185. • **52**. Smith, *FDR*, p. 568. • **53**. Ibid., p. 567, quoting de Gaulle memoirs. • **54**. Morgan, *FDR*, pp. 656 and 723. • **55**. Mark A. Stoler, *The Politics of the Second Front* (Westport, CT: Greenwood Press, 1977) p. 158. • **56**. Ibid., p. 150. • **57**. Ibid. • **58**. Brands, *Traitor to His Class*, p. 701. • **59**. Bohlen, *Witness to History*, p. 140. • **60**. Frank Freidel, *Franklin Roosevelt: A Rendezvous with Destiny*, p. 481. • **61**. Keith Sainsbury, *The Turning Point*, p. 227. • **62**. Smith, *FDR*, p. 622. • **63**. Ibid., p. 623. • **64**. Ibid., p. 625. • **65**. Ibid., p. 627. • **66**. Frances Perkins, *The Roosevelt I Knew*, p. 393. • **67**. For an excellent historiographical survey of the 'supposed blunders and *naïveté* of President Franklin D. Roosevelt' theses and their rebuttal, see Mark Stoler, 'World War II', in Robert D. Schulzberger (ed.), *A Companion to American Foreign Relations* (Oxford: Blackwell, 2003), pp. 188-214. • **68**. Smith, *FDR*, p. 629. • **69**. Freidel, *Franklin Roosevelt*, p. 595. • **70**. Smith, *FDR*, p. 632. • **71**. Edward M. Bennett, *Franklin D. Roosevelt and the Search for Victory*, pp. 166. • **72**. Freidel, *Franklin Roosevelt*, p. 597. • **73**. The other two were Frances Dana, granddaughter of H. W. Longfellow, and Dorothy Quincy: Smith, *FDR*, p. 35. • **74**. Ibid., p. 36. • **75**. Joseph E. Persico, *Franklin & Lucy*, p. 60. • **76**. Ibid., p. 93. • **77**. Ibid., p. 124. • **78**. Ibid., p. 130. • **79**. Ibid., p. 131. • **80**. Ibid. • **81**. Ibid., p. 184. • **82**. Smith, *FDR*, p. 150. • **83**. Ibid., p. 207. • **84**. Persico, *Franklin & Lucy*, p. 227. • **85**. Ibid., p. 249. • **86**. Ibid., p. 250. • **87**. Ibid., p. 263. • **88**. Ibid. • **89**. Ibid., p. 264. • **90**. Ibid., p. 315. • **91**. Ibid., p. 316. • **92**. Ibid. • **93**. Ibid., p. 326. • **94**. Ibid., p. 335. • **95**. Ibid., p. 339.

Chapter Two: Harry Truman

1. David McCullough, *Truman*, p. 41. • **2**. Alonzo M. Hamby, *Man of the People*, p. 19. • **3**. Ibid., p. 27. • **4**. Robert H. Ferrell (ed.), *The Autobiography of Harry S. Truman*, p. 29. • **5**. Hamby, *Man of the People*, p. 30. • **6**. Robert H. Ferrell (ed.), *Dear Bess: The Letters from Harry to Bess Truman, 1910–1959*, p. 167. • **7**. Letter of October 11, 1918, in ibid., p. 275. • **8**. Hamby, *Man of the People*, p. 160. • **9**. Ibid., p. 191. • **10**. Ibid., p. 233. • **11**. Ibid., p. 235. • **12**. McCullough, *Truman*, p. 251. • **13**. Hamby, *Man of the People*, p. 262. • **14**. Ibid., p. 254. • **15**. Ibid., p. 258. • **16**. Letter of October 27, 1939, in Robert H. Ferrell (ed.), *Dear Bess*, p. 426. • **17**. Hamby, *Man of the People*, p. 283. • **18**. Frank Freidel, *Franklin Roosevelt: Rendezvous with Destiny*, p. 537. • **19**. McCullough, *Truman*, p. 327. • **20**. Hamby, *Man of the People*, p. 293. • **21**. Robert Donovan, *Conflict and Crisis*, p. 15. • **22**. Letter of June 6, 1945, in Robert H. Ferrell (ed.), *Dear Bess*, p. 514. • **23**. Martin Gilbert, *Winston Churchill* (New York: Holt, 1991), p. 6. • **24**. July 7, 1945, in Robert H. Ferrell (ed.), *Off the Record: The Private Papers of Harry S. Truman*, p. 49. • **25**. July 16, 1945, in ibid., p. 52. • **26**. Ibid., pp. 52–3. • **27**. July 17, 1945, in ibid., p. 53. • **28**. July 25, 1945, in ibid., p. 56. • **29**. July 26, 1945, in ibid., p. 57. • **30**. July 30, 1945, in ibid., p. 58. • **31**. March 15, 1957, in ibid., p. 348. • **32**. March 15, 1957, in ibid., p. 349. • **33**. March 15, 1957, in ibid., p. 348. • **34**. July 25, 1945, in ibid., p. 56. • **35**. McCullough, *Truman*, pp. 440 and 437. • **36**. July 25, 1945, in Ferrell (ed.), *Off the Record*, pp. 55–6. • **37**. William Rees-Mogg, 'The American empire, a fine old British tradition' (review of Niall Ferguson's UK Channel 4 television series, *Empire*), *The Times*, January 12, 2003. • **38**. Harry S. Truman, *Memoirs*, Vol. 2, p. 105. • **39**. Ibid., p. 101. • **40**. Ibid., p. 106. • **41**. Ibid. • **42**. John T. Woolley and Gerhard Peters (eds), *The American Presidency Project*, http://www.presidency.ucsb/edu/?pid=12859. • **43**. Truman, *Memoirs* Vol. 2, p. 111. • **44**. Merle Miller, *Plain Speaking*, p. 245. • **45**. Truman, *Memoirs*, Vol. 2, p. 111. • **46**. Ferrell (ed.), *Off the Record*, p. 145. • **47**. Truman, *Memoirs*, Vol. 2, p. 131. • **48**. Robert Fisk, *The Great War for Civilisation* (New York: Knopf, 2005), p. 365. • **49**. Robert Donovan, *Conflict and Crisis*, p. 319. • **50**. Hamby, *Man of the People*, p. 408. • **51**. Donovan, *Conflict and Crisis*, p. 319. • **52**. Hamby, *Man of the People*, p. 405. • **53**. Dean Acheson, *Present at the Creation: My Years in the State Department*, p. 175. • **54**. Donovan, *Conflict and Crisis*, p. 382. • **55**. Miller, *Plain Speaking*,

p. 216. • **56**. Donovan, *Conflict and Crisis*, p. 413. • **57**. Ibid., p. 423. • **58**. Ibid., p. 413. • **59**. Miller, *Plain Speaking*, p. 291. • **60**. Ibid., p. 292. • **61**. Forrest C. Pogue, *George C. Marshall: Statesman 1945–1959*, p. 47. • **62**. Donovan, *Conflict and Crisis*, pp. 286–7. • **63**. Geoffrey Perret, *Commander in Chief*, p. 169. • **64**. Arnold A. Offner, *Another Such Victory*, p. 398. • **65**. Robert Donovan, *Tumultuous Years*, p. 314. • **66**. Miller, *Plain Speaking*, p. 305. • **67**. Donovan, *Conflict and Crisis*, p. 294. • **68**. Miller, *Plain Speaking*, p. 366. • **69**. McCullough, *Truman*, p. 813. • **70**. Hamby, *Man of the People*, p. 429. • **71**. Rovere, *Senator Joe McCarthy*, pp. 123–4. • **72**. John Hersey, 'Truman Would Answer With Truth', *St Petersburg Times*, August 6, 1973. • **73**. John Hersey, *Aspects of the Presidency* (New Haven: Ticknor and Fields, 1980), p. 138. • **74**. Clark Clifford, *Counsel to the President*, p. 290. • **75**. Ibid., pp. 290–1. • **76**. Joseph Goulden, *The Best years: 1945–1950*, p. 427. • **77**. Acheson, *Present at the Creation*, p. 366. • **78**. Ibid., p. 369. • **79**. Clifford, *Counsel to the President*, p. 290. • **80**. Ferrell (ed.), *Off the record*, p. 178. • **81**. Margaret Truman, *Harry S. Truman*, pp. 551–2. • **82**. Letter of December 28, 1945, in Monte M. Poen (ed.), *Strictly Personal and Confidential*, p. 173. • **83**. Letter of December 7, 1950, in McCullough, *Truman*, p. 829. • **84**. Roy Jenkins, *Truman*, p. 15. • **85**. Letter of November 10, 1913, in Robert H. Ferrrell (ed.), *Dear Bess*, pp. 140–1. • **86**. Ibid., p. vii. • **87**. McCullough, *Truman*, p. 435. • **88**. Lord Moran, *The Struggle for Survival*, p. 298. • **89**. McCullough, *Truman*, p. 886. • **90**. Hamby, *Man of the People*, p. 473. • **91**. McCullough, *Truman*, p. 435. • **92**. Donovan, *Conflict and Crisis*, p. 148. • **93**. Ibid. p. 147. • **94**. Acheson, *Present at the Creation*, p. v.

Chapter Three: Dwight Eisenhower

1. Carlo D'Este, *Eisenhower: A Soldier's Life*, p. 39. • **2**. Ibid., p. 34. • **3**. James C. Humes, *Confessions of a White House Ghostwriter* (Washington DC: Regnery, 1997) p. 39. • **4**. D'Este, *Eisenhower*, p. 222. • **5**. Ibid., p. 224. • **6**. Ibid., p. 229. • **7**. Ibid., p. 235. • **8**. Ibid., p. 315. • **9**. Ibid., p. 375. • **10**. Stephen Ambrose, *Eisenhower: Soldier, General of the Army, President-elect, 1880–1952*, p. 273. • **11**. D'Este, *Eisenhower*, p. 467. • **12**. Piers Brendon, *Ike: His Life and Times*, p. 194. • **13**. Stephen Ambrose, *Eisenhower: Soldier, General of the Army, President-elect*, p. 409. • **14**. Geoffrey Perret, *Eisenhower*, p. 368. • **15**. Ambrose, *Eisenhower: Soldier, General of the Army, President-elect*, p. 441. • **16**. Ibid., p. 523. • **17**. Perret,

Eisenhower, p. 391. • **18**. Ambrose, *Eisenhower: Soldier, General of the Army, President-elect*, p. 523. • **19**. Robert Donovan, *Tumultuous Years: The Presidency of Harry S. Truman, 1949–1953*, p. 394. • **20**. Ambrose, *Eisenhower: Soldier, General of the Army, President-elect*, p. 53. • **21**. Ibid., p. 96. • **22**. Conrad Black, *Richard Milhous Nixon*, p. 185. • **23**. Ibid., p. 206–7. • **24**. Perret, *Eisenhower*, p. 426. • **25**. Stephen Ambrose, *Eisenhower: The President*, p. 42. • **26**. Perret, *Eisenhower*, p. 436. • **27**. Andrew Goodpaster, introduction to Robert R. Bowie and Richard H. Immerman, *Waging Peace: How Eisenhower Shaped an Enduring Cold War Strategy* (New York: Oxford University Press, 1997), p. vi. • **28**. Perret, *Eisenhower*, p. 456. • **29**. Brendon, *Ike*, p. 245. • **30**. Robert H. Ferrell (ed.), *The Eisenhower Diaries*, p. 234. • **31**. Ambrose, *Eisenhower: The President*, p. 55. • **32**. Ibid., p. 167. • **33**. Ibid., p. 60. • **34**. Ibid., p. 162. • **35**. David M. Oshinsky, *A Conspiracy So Immense: The World of Joe McCarthy* (New York: Free Press, 1983), pp. 462–5. • **36**. Perret, *Eisenhower*, p. 504. • **37**. Ambrose, *Eisenhower: The President*, p. 220. • **38**. Ibid., p. 200. • **39**. Ibid., pp. 220–1. • **40**. Ibid., p. 202. • **41**. Ibid. • **42**. Ibid., p. 184. • **43**. Conrad Black, *Nixon: The Invincible Quest*, pp. 323–4. • **44**. See Chester J. Pach, Jr., and Elmo Richardson, *The Presidency of Dwight D. Eisenhower*, pp. 123–4. • **45**. Dwight D. Eisenhower, *Waging Peace*, p. 34. • **46**. Ambrose, *Eisenhower: The President*, p. 332. • **47**. Ibid. • **48**. Ibid., p. 333. • **49**. Ibid., p. 339. • **50**. Ibid., p. 352. • **51**. Ibid. • **52**. Ibid., p. 353. • **53**. Ibid., p. 356. • **54**. Ibid., p. 358. • **55**. Ibid., p. 360. • **56**. Ibid., p. 361. • **57**. Ibid., p. 364. • **58**. Ibid., p. 367. • **59**. Ibid., p. 368. • **60**. Brendon, *Ike*, p. 319. • **61**. Ambrose, *Eisenhower: The President*, p. 406. • **62**. Senator Paul Douglas, in Robert Dallek, *Lone Star Rising: Lyndon Johnson and His Times, 1908–1960*, p. 526. • **63**. Dwight D. Eisenhower, *Waging Peace*, p. 166. • **64**. Ambrose, *Eisenhower: The President*, p. 421. • **65**. Ibid., p. 420. • **66**. Ibid., p. 422. • **67**. Ibid. • **68**. Ibid., p. 440. • **69**. Khrushchev, *Khrushchev Remembers: The Last Testament*, p. 374. • **70**. Ibid., p. 375. • **71**. Ibid., pp. 374–5. • **72**. Dwight D. Eisenhower, *Waging Peace*, p. 440. • **73**. Ambrose, *Eisenhower: The President*, p. 456. • **74**. Dwight D. Eisenhower, *Waging Peace*, p. 440. • **75**. Khrushchev, *Khrushchev Remembers: The Last Testament*, p. 411. • **76**. Ibid., p. 536. • **77**. Ibid., pp. 412–13. • **78**. Oleg Troyanovsky, 'The Making of Soviet Foreign Policy', in William Taubman et al. (eds), *Nikita Khrushchev*, p. 226. • **79**. Ambrose, *Eisenhower: The President*, p. 578. • **80**. Troyanovsky, 'The Making of Soviet Foreign Policy', p. 227. • **81**. Ambrose, *Eisenhower: The President*, p. 579. The Sputnik, which sent back extended telemetry, subsequently malfunctioned and eventually disintegrated on re-entry into the earth's atmosphere two years later; a chunk was supposedly found in a street in Wisconsin. • **82**. In his memoirs Khrushchev claimed he had demanded at the summit an apology from Eisenhower, and a promise that there would be no more U-2 flights, which Eisenhower repudiated, on the advice of Dulles's successor, Christian Herter. This was untrue – in fact Eisenhower assured him 'these flights were suspended after the recent incident and are not to be resumed.' Khrushchev, *Khrushchev Remembers: The Last Testament*, editor's note on p. 455. • **83**. Khrushchev, *Khrushchev Remembers: The Last Testament*, p. 455. • **84**. Ibid., p. 449. • **85**. Ambrose, *Eisenhower: The President*, p. 612. • **86**. Michael R. Beschloss, *May-Day: Eisenhower, Khrushchev and the U2 Affair*, p. 388. • **87**. D'Este, *Eisenhower*, p. 86. • **88**. Ibid., p. 88. • **89**. Ibid., p. 109. • **90**. Ibid., p. 101. • **91**. Ibid. • **92**. Ibid., p. 99. • **93**. Ibid., p. 110. • **94**. Ibid., p. 111. • **95**. Merle Miller, *Plain Speaking*, pp. 339–40. • **96**. Robert H. Ferrell and Francis H. Miller, 'Plain Faking', *American Heritage*, June 1995. • **97**. Ambrose, *Eisenhower: Soldier, General of the Army, President-elect*, p. 417. • **98**. Ambrose, *Eisenhower: The President*, p. 29. • **99**. Brendon, *Ike*, p. 288. • **100**. Samuel Lubell, *Revolt of the Moderates* (New York: Harper and Brothers, 1956), pp. 4–5. • **101**. Poll of seventy-five historians conducted by Arthur M. Schlesinger Sr in 1962, published in William A. DeGregorio, *The Complete Book of US Presidents*. By 1999, however, a C-Span viewer survey had raised Eisenhower to 8th place in American presidential history.

Chapter Four: John F. Kennedy

1. Nigel Hamilton, *JFK: Reckless Youth*, p. 130. • **2**. Ibid., p. 127. • **3**. Ibid., p. 391. • **4**. Ben Bradlee, *Conversations with Kennedy*, p. 33. • **5**. Geoffrey Perret, *Jack: A Life Like No Other*, p. 269. • **6**. Ambrose, *Eisenhower: The President*, p. 604. • **7**. Ibid., p. 606. • **8**. Ibid., p. 583. • **9**. Ibid., p. 608. • **10**. Barry Goldwater, *Goldwater* (New York: Doubleday, 1988), pp. 135–6. • **11**. Perret, *Jack*, p. 309. • **12**. E. B. Potter, *Admiral Arleigh Burke* (New York: Random House, 1990), pp. 437–8. The only formal air attack that President Kennedy finally authorized, to cover Cuban rebel B-26 bombers supporting the invasion force, proved a fiasco – the US naval pilots getting the time-zone in Cuba wrong. • **13**. Richard Reeves,

President Kennedy: Profile of Power, p. 101. • **14**. Ibid., p. 106. • **15**. James Reston, *Deadline: A Memoir* (New York: Random House, 1991), p. 290. • **16**. Michael Beschloss, *The Crisis Years: Kennedy and Khrushchev, 1960–1963*, p. 224. • **17**. William Taubman, *Khrushchev: The Man and His Era*, p. 496. • **18**. Ibid., p. 766. • **19**. Beschloss, *The Crisis Years*, p. 234. • **20**. *FRUS, 1961–1963*, Vol. 5 (Washington, DC: US Government Printing Office, 1991), pp. 229–30. • **21**. Taubman, *Khrushchev*, p. 495. • **22**. Ibid., p. 500. • **23**. Beschloss, *The Crisis Years*, p. 234. • **24**. Sergei Khrushchev, *Nikita Khrushchev and the Creation of a Superpower*, trans. Shirley Benson (University Park: The Pennsylvania State University Press, 2000), p. 436, and Taubman, *Khrushchev*, p. 493. • **25**. Taubman, *Khrushchev*, p. 766. • **26**. Richard Reeves, *President Kennedy: Profile of Power*, pp. 361–2. • **27**. 'Radio and Television Report to the Nation on the Situation at the University of Mississippi', September 30, 1962, www.jfklibrary.org/Historical+Resources/Archives. • **28**. Herbert Parmet, *JFK: The Presidency of John F. Kennedy*, p. 262. • **29**. Reeves, *President Kennedy*, p. 362. • **30**. Taubman, *Khrushchev*, p. 541. • **31**. Aleksandr Fursenko and Timothy Naftali, *Khrushchev's Cold War* (New York: Norton, 2006), p. 459. • **32**. Reeves, *President Kennedy: Profile of Power*, p. 370. • **33**. Robert, Dallek, *An Unfinished Life: John F. Kennedy 1917–1963*, p. 544. • **34**. Taubman, *Khrushchev*, p. 551. • **35**. Reeves, *President Kennedy*, p. 370. • **36**. Oleg Troyanovsky, 'The Making of Soviet Foreign Policy', in William Taubman et al. (eds), *Nikita Khrushchev*, p. 234. • **37**. Taubman, *Khrushchev*, p. 559. • **38**. Ibid., p. 551. • **39**. Beschloss, *The Crisis Years*, p. 456. • **40**. Taubman, *Khrushchev*, p. 561. • **41**. Ibid. • **42**. Ibid. • **43**. Beschloss, *The Crisis Years*, p. 498. • **44**. Taubman, *Khrushchev*, p. 581. • **45**. Ibid., p. 578. • **46**. Reeves, *President Kennedy*, p. 437. • **47**. Ibid., p. 438. • **48**. Ibid., p. 462. • **49**. Ibid., p. 522. • **50**. Ibid., p. 584. • **51**. Ibid., p. 585. • **52**. Ibid., p. 547. • **53**. Ibid., p. 149. • **54**. Dallek, *An Unfinished Life*, p. 666. • **55**. Reeves, *President Kennedy*, p. 309. • **56**. Geoffrey Perret, *Commander in Chief*, p. 188. • **57**. Dallek, *An Unfinished Life*, p. 672. • **58**. Ibid., p. 668. • **59**. Ibid., p. 682. • **60**. Ibid., p. 683. • **61**. Charles Spalding, NH Papers, Massachusetts Historical Society; Perret, *Jack*, p. 393. • **62**. Dallek, *An Unfinished Life*, p. 684. • **63**. Oswald was murdered by a Dallas nightclub operator, Jacob Rubenstein, who had legally changed his name to Jack Ruby. Whether or not Oswald was prompted, or funded, by others to assassinate President Kennedy has never been definitively established. Ruby died of aggressive lung, liver and brain cancer on January 3, 1967, at Parkland Hospital, Dallas, where Oswald had died and President Kennedy had been pronounced dead. In a last statement Ruby declared, 'There is nothing to hide. There was no one else'. ('A Last Wish,' *Time*, December 30, 1966). • **64**. Hamilton, *JFK*, p. 155. • **65**. Ibid., p. 440. • **66**. Ibid., p. 443. Inga, who married Hollywood actor Tim McCoy, lived to see JFK win the presidency, but also his assassination; she herself died of cancer ten years later, in 1973.• **67**. Ibid., p. 547. • **68**. Ibid., p. 617. • **69**. Ibid., p. 637. • **70**. Ibid., pp. 658–61. • **71**. Charles Spalding, interview with the author. • **72**. Laurence Leamer, *The Kennedy Men, 1901–1963*, p. 250. • **73**. Alistair Forbes, interview with the author. • **74**. James Reed, interview with the author. • **75**. James Reed, interview with the author. • **76**. Seymour Hersh, *The Dark Side of Camelot*, p. 22. • **77**. Beschloss, *The Crisis Years*, p. 473. • **78**. Richard N. Goodwin to author. • **79**. *New York Times*, June 3, 1961. • **80**. Gretchen Rubin, *Forty Ways to Look at JFK*, p. 185. • **81**. Ben Bradlee, interview with the author. • **82**. Anna 'Chiquita' Cárcanos, interview with the author. • **83**. Charles Spalding, interview with the author. • **84**. Rubin, *Forty Ways to Look at JFK*, p. 239. • **85**. Ibid. • **86**. Sally B. Smith, *Grace and Power: The Private World of the Kennedy White House*, p. 143. • **87**. Reeves, *President Kennedy*, p. 291. • **88**. Smith, *Grace and Power*, p. 143. • **89**. Hersh, *The Dark Side of Camelot*, p. 19. • **90**. Ibid., p. 18. • **91**. Ibid., p. 442–6; also Paul Corbin to author. • **92**. Rubin, *Forty Ways to Look at JFK*, p. 241. • **93**. Hersh, *The Dark Side of Camelot*, p. 238. • **94**. Perret, *Jack*, p. 397. • **95**. Ibid.

Chapter Five: Lyndon Johnson

1. Robert Caro, *The Years of Lyndon Johnson: The Path to Power* (New York: Knopf), 1982, p. 52. • **2**. Dallek, *Lone Star Rising: Lyndon Johnson and His Times, 1908–1960*, p. 143. • **3**. Robert Caro, *The Years of Lyndon Johnson: The Path to Power*, p. 448. • **4**. Ibid., p. 449. • **5**. Ibid., p. 742. • **6**. Robert Caro, *The Years of Lyndon Johnson: Means of Ascent*, p. 29. • **7**. Robert Dallek, *Lyndon B. Johnson: Portrait of a President*, p. 65. • **8**. Robert Caro, *The Years of Lyndon Johnson: Means of Ascent*, p. 214. Having worn out the Sikorski engine, Johnson then used a smaller, five-foot-long Bell 47-D helicopter, barely powerful enough to lift the candidate and his loudspeaker equipment, for the final weeks: Caro, pp. 247–8. • **9**. Ibid., p. 219. • **10**. Robert Dallek, *An Unfinished Life: John F. Kennedy,*

1917–1963, p. 189. • **11**. Ibid. • **12**. Michael Beschloss, *The Crisis Years: Kennedy and Khrushchev, 1960–1963*, p. 513. • **13**. Michael R. Beschloss (ed.), *Taking Charge: The Johnson White House Tapes, 1963–1964*, p. 30. • **14**. Ibid., p. 67. • **15**. *Public Papers of the Presidents: Lyndon B. Johnson, 1963–64*, Book I (Washington, DC: US Government Printing Office, 1965), p. 114. • **16**. Robert Dallek, *Flawed Giant: Lyndon Johnson and His Times, 1961–1973*, p. 63. • **17**. Doris Kearns, *Lyndon Johnson and the American Dream*, p. 178. • **18**. Dallek, *Flawed Giant*, p. 112. • **19**. Ibid., p. 120. • **20**. Ibid., p. 123. • **21**. Beschloss (ed.), *Taking Charge*, p. 388n. • **22**. Ibid. • **23**. Nineteenth-century populist. • **24**. Lyndon Baines Johnson, Tuesday, January 28, 1964, in Beschloss (ed.), *Taking Charge*, p. 190. • **25**. Lyndon Baines Johnson, Saturday, February 8, 1964, in ibid., 231. • **26**. Lyndon Baines Johnson, Saturday, March 7, 1964, in ibid., p. 271. • **27**. Lyndon Baines Johnson, Thursday, June 4, 1964, ibid., p. 382. • **28**. Barry Goldwater, Acceptance Speech, July 16, 1964, http://www.americanrhetoric.com/speeches/barrygoldwater1964rnc.html. • **29**. Lyndon Baines Johnson, Saturday February 8, 1964, in Beschloss (ed.), *Taking Charge*, passim. • **30**. Lyndon Baines Johnson, Thursday June 11, 1964, in ibid., p. 401. • **31**. Lyndon Baines Johnson, Wednesday, May 27, 1964, in ibid., p. 367. • **32**. Lyndon Baines Johnson, Wednesday, May 27, 1964, in ibid., p. 364. • **33**. Lyndon Baines Johnson, Wednesday, May 27, 1964, in ibid., p. 368. • **34**. Lyndon Baines Johnson, Wednesday, May 27, 1964, in ibid., p. 369. • **35**. Lyndon Baines Johnson, Tuesday, August 4, 1964, in ibid., p. 496. • **36**. Lyndon Baines Johnson, Saturday, December 7, 1963, in ibid., p. 95. • **37**. Dallek, *Flawed* Giant, p. 123. • **38**. Ibid. • **39**. Ibid. • **40**. Jack Valenti interview, *American Experience*, Vietnam Online, Transcript, PBS: www.pbs.org/wgbh/amex/vietnam/series/pt_03.html. • **41**. Lyndon Baines Johnson, *Vantage Point: Perspectives on the Presidency, 1963–1969*, p. 125. • **42**. David Kaiser, *American Tragedy: Kennedy, Johnson, and the Origins of the Vietnam War*, p. 398. • **43**. Frank E. Vandiver, *Shadows of Vietnam: Lyndon Johnson's Wars*, p. 30. • **44**. http://www.hawaii.edu/powerkills/SOD.TAB6.1A. • **45**. http://www.pbs.org/battlefieldvietnam/timeline/index2.html. • **46**. Dallek, *Flawed Giant*, p. 255. • **47**. Ibid., p. 249. • **48**. Brian VanDeMark, *Into the Quagmire: Lyndon Johnson and the Escalation of the Vietnam War*, p. 123. • **49**. Dallek, *Flawed Giant*, p. 361. • **50**. George C. Herring, *LBJ and Vietnam: A Different Kind of War*, p. 19. • **51**. Dallek, *Flawed Giant*, p. 427. • **52**. Ibid. • **53**. Ibid., p. 429. • **54**. Ibid., p. 430. • **55**.

'Chinese Checkers', *Time*, January 31, 1964. • **56**. Dallek, *Flawed Giant*, p. 494. • **57**. Clark Clifford, *Counsel to the President*, p. 485. • **58**. Dallek, *Flawed Giant*, p. 500. • **59**. Clark Clifford, *Counsel to the President*, p. 495. • **60**. Ibid., p. 518. • **61**. Sam Houston Johnson, *My Brother Lyndon*, p. 4. • **62**. George Reedy, *Lyndon B. Johnson: A Memoir*, 1982, p. 150. • **63**. Randall B. Woods, *LBJ: Architect of American Ambition*, p. 834. • **64**. Lloyd C. Gardner, *Pay Any Price: Lyndon Johnson and the Wars for Vietnam*, p. 463. • **65**. George Christian, in Dallek, *Flawed Giant*, p. 573. • **66**. Dallek, *Flawed Giant*, p. 573. • **67**. Ibid., p. 580. • **68**. Ibid. • **69**. Ibid., p. 583. • **70**. Ibid. • **71**. Ibid. • **72**. Ibid., p. 584. • **73**. Ibid., p. 591. • **74**. Ibid., p. 588. • **75**. Ibid., p. 590. • **76**. Ibid., p. 586. • **77**. Woods, *LBJ*, p. 290. • **78**. Caro, *The Years of Lyndon Johnson: The Path to Power*, p. 173. • **79**. Ibid., p. 162. • **80**. Sam Houston Johnson, *My Brother Lyndon*, p. 29 and Doris Kearns, *Lyndon Johnson and the American Dream*, p. 57. • **81**. Woods, *LBJ*, p. 80. • **82**. Caro, *The Years of Lyndon Johnson: The Path to Power*, p. 299. • **83**. Ibid. • **84**. Ibid. • **85**. Ibid., p. 300. • **86**. Ibid., p. 301. • **87**. Ibid., p. 302. • **88**. Ibid., p. 303. • **89**. Woods, *LBJ*, p. 105. • **90**. Ibid., p. 640. • **91**. Ibid., p. 132. • **92**. Ibid., p. 205. • **93**. Ibid., p. 290. • **94**. Dallek, *Lone Star Rising*, p. 189. • **95**. Ibid., p. 191. • **96**. Ibid. • **97**. Woods, *LBJ*, p. 247. • **98**. Ibid., p. 288. • **99**. Ibid., p. 481. • **100**. Ibid., p. 288. • **101**. Dallek, *Lone Star Rising*, p. 537. • **102**. Ibid., p. 189. • **103**. Ibid. • **104**. Eric F. Goldman, *The Tragedy of Lyndon Johnson*, p. 531. • **105**. Thomas Alan Schwartz, *Lyndon Johnson and Europe*, p. 237.

Chapter Six: Richard Nixon

1. Herbert Parmet, *Richard Nixon and His America*, p. 58. • **2**. Ibid., p. 113. • **3**. Ibid., p. 90. • **4**. Ibid., p.104. • **5**. Ibid., p. 94. • **6**. Ibid., p. 133. • **7**. Ibid., p. 141. • **8**. Ibid., p. 107. • **9**. Conrad Black, *Richard Milhous Nixon: The Invincible Quest*, p. 159. • **10**. Ibid., p. 149. • **11**. Parmet, *Richard Nixon and His America*, p. 182. • **12**. Black, *Richard Milhous Nixon*, p. 162. • **13**. Ibid., p. 149. • **14**. Ibid., p. 157. • **15**. Stephen Ambrose, *Nixon: The Education of a Politician, 1913–1962*, p. 282. • **16**. Black, *Richard Milhous Nixon*, p. 229. • **17**. Richard Nixon, *Six Crises*, p. 110. • **18**. Black, *Richard Milhous Nixon*, p. 248. • **19**. Quoted in ibid., p. 249. • **20**. Anthony Summers, *Arrogance of Power: The Secret World of Richard Nixon*, p. 225. • **21**. Ibid., p. 226. • **22**. Jonathan Aitken, *Nixon: A Life*, p. 305. • **23**. Ibid., p. 306. • **24**. Ibid., p. 323. • **25**. Ibid., p. 357. • **26**. Robert Dallek, *Nixon and*

Kissinger: Partners in Power, p. 91. • **27**. Ibid., p. 92. • **28**. Stephen Ambrose, *Nixon: The Triumph of a Politician*, p. 66. • **29**. Dallek, *Nixon and Kissinger*, p. 104. • **30**. Ibid., p. 107. • **31**. Richard Reeves, *President Nixon: Alone in the White House*, p. 33. • **32**. Ambrose, *Nixon: The Triumph of a Politician*, p. 309. • **33**. Dallek, *Nixon and Kissinger*, p. 107. • **34**. Ibid., p. 154–5. • **35**. Ambrose, *Nixon: The Triumph of a Politician*, p. 309. • **36**. Taylor Owen and Ben Kiernan, 'Bombs over Cambodia: New Light on US Air War', *The Walrus* (Canada), October 2006. • **37**. 'The problem is, Mr. President, the Air Force is designed to fight an air battle against the Soviet Union. They are not designed for this war . . . in fact, they are not designed for any war we are likely to have to fight.' Owen and Kiernan, 'Bombs over Cambodia'. • **38**. December 9, 1970. The Kissinger Telcons, National Security Archive, Washington, DC, accessed May 29, 2004 www.gwu.edu/~nsarchiv/NSAEBB/NSAEBB123/. Owen and Kiernan, 'Bombs over Cambodia'. • **39**. Ambrose, *Nixon: The Triumph of a Politician*, p. 285. • **40**. November 1971, in David Reynolds, *One World Divisible: A Global History Since 1945* (New York: Norton, 2001), p. 350. • **41**. Dallek, *Nixon and Kissinger*, p. 144. • **42**. Ibid., p. 91. • **43**. Ibid. • **44**. Reeves, *President Nixon*, p. 64. • **45**. Dallek, *Nixon and Kissinger*, p. 280. • **46**. Ibid. • **47**. Ibid., p. 288. • **48**. Ambrose, *Nixon: The Triumph of a Politician*, p. 516. • **49**. Ibid., p. 459. • **50**. Reeves, *President Nixon*, p. 363. • **51**. Nixon tapes, May 4, 1972, quoted in Daniel Ellsberg, *Secrets: A Memoir of Vietnam and the Pentagon Papers*, p. 419. • **52**. Arthur M. Schlesinger Jr, *The Imperial Presidency*. • **53**. Reeves, *President Nixon*, p. 368. • **54**. Ibid., p. 411. • **55**. Ibid., p. 506. • **56**. Ibid., p. 507. • **57**. Dallek, *Nixon and Kissinger*, p. 446. • **58**. Ibid., p. 455. • **59**. Ibid., p. 487. • **60**. Ibid., p. 539. • **61**. Reeves, *President Nixon*, p. 578. • **62**. Ibid. • **63**. Ibid. • **64**. Ibid., p. 590. • **65**. Dallek, *Nixon and Kissinger*, p. 512. • **66**. Ibid., p. 521. • **67**. Reeves, *President Nixon*, p. 604. • **68**. Jussi Hahnimaki, *The Flawed Architect: Henry Kissinger and American Foreign Policy*, p. 303. • **69**. Ibid. • **70**. Dallek, *Nixon and Kissinger*, p. 545. • **71**. Ibid. • **72**. Ibid., p. 546. • **73**. Ibid., p. 547. • **74**. Ibid., p. 556. • **75**. Ibid., p. 600. • **76**. Ibid., p. 601. • **77**. Ibid., p. 604. • **78**. Aitken, *Nixon*, p. 14. • **79**. Ibid., p. 29. • **80**. Ibid., p. 13. • **81**. Ibid. • **82**. Ibid., p. 14. • **83**. Ibid., p. 29. • **84**. Roger Morris, *Richard Milhous Nixon: The Rise of an American Politician*, p. 126. • **85**. Aitken, *Nixon*, p. 61. • **86**. Black, *Richard Milhous Nixon*, p. 31. • **87**. Aitken, *Nixon*, p. 61. • **88**. Ibid., p. 63. • **89**. Ibid. • **90**. Ibid., p. 64. • **91**. Summers, *Arrogance of Power*, p. 92. • **92**. Aitken, *Nixon*, p. 86.

• **93**. Ambrose, *Nixon: The Education of a Politician*, p. 350. • **94**. Summers, *Arrogance of Power*, p. 4. • **95**. Ibid., p. 40. • **96**. Stephen Ambrose, *Nixon: The Triumph of a Politician*, p. 111. • **97**. Summers, *Arrogance of Power*, p. 40. • **98**. Ibid., p. 88–99. • **99**. Ambrose, *Nixon: The Education of a Politician*, p. 244. • **100**. Summers, *Arrogance of Power*, p. 3. • **101**. Ibid., p. 2. • **102**. Ellsberg, *Secrets*, p. 419. • **103**. Ibid., p. 418. • **104**. William Taubman, *Khrushchev: The Man and His Era*, p. 620. • **105**. Ellsberg, *Secrets*, p. 418. • **106**. Dallek, *Nixon and Kissinger*, p. 609.

Chapter Seven: Gerald Ford

1. Ford's University of Michigan transcript showed he earned 74 hours of Bs, 28 hours of Cs, 14 hours of As, and 4 hours of Ds. Domestic Intelligence Report on Gerald Ford, né Lynch, Office of Naval Intelligence file, January 10, 1942, Ford Library, Michigan. • **2**. Gerald R. Ford, Personal Files, Ford Library, Michigan. • **3**. Douglas Brinkley, *Gerald R. Ford*, p. 26. • **4**. Thomas DeFrank, *Write It When I'm Gone: Remarkable Off-the-Record Conversations with Gerald R. Ford*, p. 103. • **5**. Brinkley, *Gerald R. Ford*, p. 36. • **6**. Alexander Hamilton's Federalist Papers No 74, published under the pseudonym Publius, in 1788. The essay argued, 'But the principal argument for reposing the power of pardoning in this case to the Chief Magistrate is this: in seasons of insurrection or rebellion, there are often critical moments, when a well-timed offer of pardon to the insurgents or rebels may restore the tranquillity of the commonwealth; and which, if suffered to pass un-improved, it may never be possible afterwards to recall. The dilatory process of convening the legislature, or one of its branches, for the purpose of obtaining its sanction to the measure, would frequently be the occasion of letting slip the golden opportunity. The loss of a week, a day, an hour, may sometimes be fatal.' As president, Nixon could not conceivably be seen as an insurgent, however. • **7**. Cannon, *Time and Chance*, p. 299. • **8**. Ibid., p. 308. • **9**. Ibid. • **10**. Ibid., p. 310. • **11**. Brinkley, *Gerald R. Ford*, p. 59. • **12**. Cannon, *Time and Chance: Gerald Ford's Appointment with History*, p. 316. • **13**. Ibid. • **14**. Ibid. • **15**. Ibid. • **16**. Ibid., p. 330. • **17**. Ibid., p. 333. • **18**. Ibid. • **19**. Ibid., p. 338. • **20**. Ibid. • **21**. Audiotaped diary entry, August 8, 1976, John W. (Bill) Roberts Papers, Ford Library, Michigan. • **22**. Audiotaped diary entry, August 11, 1976, ibid. • **23**. Memorandum, September 9, 1974, Benton

L. Becker Papers, Ford Library, Michigan. • **24**. Audiotaped diary entry, August 18, 1976, John W. (Bill) Roberts Papers, Ford Library, Michigan. • **25**. Ibid. • **26**. Bunny Buchan (wife of Philip Buchan, Counsel to the President), 'Diary' Notes, August 28, 1976, Ford Library, Michigan. • **27**. Cannon, *Time and Chance*, p. 373. • **28**. Barry Werth, 31 *Days: The Crisis That Gave Us the Government We Have Today*, p. 294. • **29**. Benton L. Becker Memorandum, September 9, 1974, Benton L. Becker Papers, Ford Library, Michigan. • **30**. Ibid. • **31**. Ibid. • **32**. Jonathan Aitken, *Nixon: A Life*, p. 531. • **33**. Benton L. Becker Memorandum, September 9, 1974, Benton L. Becker Papers, Ford Library, Michigan. • **34**. John Robert Greene, *The Presidency of Gerald R. Ford*, p. 42; Alexander M. Haig Jr, *Inner Circles: How America Changed the World*, (New York: Grand Central Publishing, 1992), p. 513. • **35**. Cannon, *Time and Chance*, p. 381. • **36**. Ibid., p. 383. • **37**. Ibid. • **38**. Brinkley, *Gerald R. Ford*, p. 81. • **39**. Audiotaped diary entry, September 8, 1976, John W. (Bill) Roberts Papers, Ford Library, Michigan. • **40**. Bunny Buchan, 'Diary' Notes, October 12, 1976, Ford Library, Michigan. • **41**. DeFrank, *Write It When I'm Gone*, p. 46. • **42**. Cannon, *Time and Chance*, p. 385. • **43**. *Washington Post* and *New York Times*, September 9, 1974. • **44**. Cannon, *Time and Chance*, p. 391. • **45**. Brinkley, *Gerald R. Ford*, p. 67. • **46**. Karen M. Hult and Charles E. Walcott, *Empowering the White House: Governance under Nixon, Ford, and Carter* (Lawrence: University Press of Kansas, 2004), p. 37. • **47**. Shirley Ann Warshaw, *Powersharing: White House-Cabinet Relations in the Modern Presidency* (Albany, NY: State University of New York Press, 1996), p. 67. • **48**. Yanek Mieczkowski, *Gerald Ford, and the Challenges of the 1970s*, p. 140. • **49**. Ibid. • **50**. Ibid., p. 148. • **51**. Ibid., p. 146. • **52**. DeFrank, *Write It When I'm Gone*, p. 46. • **53**. Mieczkowski, *Gerald Ford*, p. 290. • **54**. Ibid. • **55**. Greene, *The Presidency of Gerald R. Ford*, p. 137. • **56**. Ibid. • **57**. Brinkley, *Gerald R. Ford*, p. 91. • **58**. Mieczkowski, *Gerald Ford*, p. 289. • **59**. Greene, *The Presidency of Gerald R. Ford*, p. 141. • **60**. Ibid., p. 150. • **61**. The USS *Pueblo*, an American spy ship, had been boarded in international waters and taken into custody by North Korea in 1968; it had taken ten long months and a torture-induced confession of guilt by its captain to get back its 82-man naval crew – by which time the 1968 election was lost by Hubert Humphrey, the Democratic presidential nominee. • **62**. Greene, *The Presidency of Gerald R. Ford*, p. 151. Although a major conflagration was avoided, the incident was not without tragedy. Just as the *Mayanguez* crew were released, an abortive US helicopter-lifted attack on the island of Koh Tang was launched. Heavily defended against the North Vietnamese, who disputed its ownership, the Cambodians beat off the misguided assault, which resulted in the loss of 41 American lives. • **63**. Yves Berthelot, *Unity and Diversity in Development Ideas: Perspectives from the UN* (Bloomington: Indiana University Press, 2004). • **64**. Wesley Clark, 'Broken Engagement: The strategy that won the Cold War could help bring democracy to the Middle East – if only the Bush hawks understood it', *Washington Monthly*, May 2004 issue. • **65**. John Lewis Gaddis, *The Cold War: A New History* (New York: Penguin Press, 2005), p. 205. • **66**. Mieczkowski, *Gerald Ford,* p. 298. • **67**. Gerald R. Ford, *A Time to Heal,* p. 297. • **68**. Ibid., p. 300. • **69**. Ibid. • **70**. Ibid. • **71**. Ibid. • **72**. Barbara Frum, interview with Sandra Good, CBC Radio, September 10, 1975. • **73**. Eileen Keerdoja, 'Squeaky and Sara Jane', *Newsweek,* November 8, 1976. • **74**. Tom Matthews et al., 'Ford's Brush with Death', *Newsweek,* September 15, 1975. • **75**. 'Those gunslinging ladies of California', *The Economist,* September 27, 1975. • **76**. 'Trials: Life for Sara Jane', *Newsweek,* December 29, 1975. Moore was finally released in 2007, at age 77, having renounced her earlier views. • **77**. Ford, *A Time to Heal,* p. 238. • **78**. Ibid. • **79**. Greene, *The Presidency of Gerald R. Ford,* p. 128. • **80**. Ford, *A Time to Heal,* p. 240. • **81**. Ibid. • **82**. Avi Shlaim, *The Iron Wall: Israel and the Arab World* (New York: Norton, 2001), p. 339–40. See also Kenneth W. Stein, *Heroic Diplomacy: Sadat, Kissinger, Carter, Begin and the Quest for Arab-Israeli Peace* (New York: Routledge, 1999), pp. 178–81. • **83**. Mieczkowski, *Gerald Ford,* p. 311. • **84**. DeFrank, *Write It When I'm Gone,* p. 93. • **85**. Cannon, *Time and Chance,* p. 407. • **86**. Ibid. • **87**. Ford, *A Time to Heal,* p. 322. • **88**. Ibid. • **89**. Mieczkowski, *Gerald Ford,* p. 312. • **90**. Ibid., p. 315. • **91**. From the spring of 1975 Cheney explored ways to increase presidential power, avoid Congressional oversight, and hobble the investigatory role of the Fourth Estate in democracy, especially the *New York Times* itself, whose star reporter, Seymour Hersh, had aroused his ire. Cheney's notes, revealed thirty years later, posited an 'FBI investigation of the *Times*', a 'Grand Jury indictment of Hersh and the *Times*', and 'a search warrant to "go after Hersh papers in his ap[artmen]t"'. Lowell Bergman and Marlena Telvick, 'Dick Cheney's Memos from 30 Years Ago' (5/28/75, in Gerald R. Ford Library. http://www.pbs.org/wgbh/pages/frontline/newswar/preview/

documents.html, accessed April 1, 2008). • **92**. Mieczkowski, *Gerald Ford*, p. 161. • **93**. Ibid., p. 318. • **94**. Ibid., p. 316. • **95**. Ibid., p. 323. • **96**. Greene, *The Presidency of Gerald R. Ford*, p. 177. • **97**. In ballots cast, Carter won by 40.83 million to Ford's 39.14 million votes. • **98**. Air Force One and Angel are used when the President is aboard the aircraft. Air Force 2600 is used at all other times. • **99**. DeFrank, *Write It When I'm Gone*, p. 62. • **100**. In total, Ford served 896 days, until Carter's inauguration. Nineteenth-century presidents William Harrison, Zachary Taylor and James Garfield all died (or were assassinated) in office, having served shorter terms. • **101**. Ford, *A Time to Heal*, p. 46. • **102**. Ibid., p. 43. • **103**. Ibid., p. 44. • **104**. Ibid., p. 55. • **105**. Ibid., p. 63. • **106**. Ibid., p. 55. • **107**. Ibid. • **108**. DeFrank, *Write It When I'm Gone*, p. 181. • **109**. Ford, *A Time to Heal*, p. 52. • **110**. Jane Howard, 'The 38th First Lady: Not a Robot at All', *New York Times*, December 8, 1974. • **111**. Betty Ford, *Betty: A Glad Awakening* (New York: Doubleday, 1987), p. 30. • **112**. Ibid. • **113**. Ibid., p. 32. • **114**. Howard, 'The 38th First Lady'. • **115**. Sandra Salmans and Thomas DeFrank, 'A Family Affair', *Newsweek*, August 25, 1975. • **116**. CBS, January 7, 2007. • **117**. Salmans and DeFrank, 'A Family Affair'. • **118**. Howard, 'The 38th First Lady': • **119**. Salmans and DeFrank, 'A Family Affair'. • **120**. DeFrank, *Write It When I'm Gone*, pp. 181–2.

Chapter Eight: Jimmy Carter

1. Jimmy Carter, *An Hour Before Daylight*, p. 26. • **2**. Ibid., p. 121. • **3**. Ibid., p. 71. • **4**. Bruce Mazlish and Erwin Diamond, *Jimmy Carter: A Character Portrait*, p. 101. • **5**. Mazlish and Diamond, *Jimmy Carter*, p. 100. • **6**. Carter, *An Hour Before Daylight*, p. 75. • **7**. Ibid., p. 259. • **8**. Ibid. • **9**. Peter G. Bourne, *Jimmy Carter: A Comprehensive Biography from Plains to Postpresidency*, p. 81. • **10**. Bourne, *Jimmy Carter*, p. 86. • **11**. Mazlish and Diamond, *Jimmy Carter*, p. 100; Carter, *An Hour Before Daylight*, p. 118. • **12**. Bourne, *Jimmy Carter*, p. 82. • **13**. Ibid., p. 81. • **14**. Ibid., p. 123. • **15**. Ibid., p. 131. • **16**. Mazlish and Diamond, *Jimmy Carter*, p. 181. • **17**. Ibid., p. 193. • **18**. Kandy Stroud, *How Jimmy Won: The Victory Campaign from Plains to the White House*, p. 16. • **19**. Ibid. • **20**. Bourne, *Jimmy Carter*, p. 250. • **21**. Stroud, *How Jimmy Won*, p. 21. • **22**. Peter Meyer, *James Earl Carter: The Man and the Myth*, p. 3. • **23**. Bourne, *Jimmy Carter*, p. 347. • **24**. The final tally was 297 electoral votes to President Ford's 241. In the popular vote, Carter won 40.2 to 38.5 million. • **25.** Bourne, *Jimmy Carter*, p. 366. • **26.** Kenneth E. Morris, *Jimmy Carter: American Moralist*, p. 243. • **27.** Ibid. • **28.** Bourne, *Jimmy Carter*, p. 361. • **29.** Ibid. • **30.** Morris, *Jimmy Carter*, p. 244. • **31.** Bourne, *Jimmy Carter*, p. 360. • **32.** Burton I. Kaufman, *James Earl Carter, Jr.*, p. 22. • **33.** Jimmy Carter, *Keeping Faith: Memoirs of a President*, p. 91. • **34.** Ibid., p. 97. • **35.** Ibid., p. 135. • **36.** Meyer, *James Earl Carter*, p. 196. • **37.** Victor Lasky, *Jimmy Carter: The Man and the Myth*, p. 11. • **38.** James Schlesinger, Miller Center Oral History, July 1984, courtesy of Carter Library, Atlanta, Georgia. • **39.** Lasky, *Jimmy Carter*, p. 14. • **40.** James Schlesinger, Miller Center Oral History, July 1984. • **41.** Meyer, *James Earl Carter*, p. 4. • **42.** Robert A. Strong, *Working in the World: Jimmy Carter and the Making of American Foreign Policy*, p. 178. • **43.** Carter, *Keeping Faith*, p. 275. • **44.** Ibid., p. 315. • **45.** http://en.wikipedia.org/wiki/1947_UN_Partition_Plan#cite_note-5. • **46.** http://www.donteverstop.com/files/apn/upl/assets/pressconf 191005.ppt#256,3,Slide 3. • **47.** Bourne, *Jimmy Carter*, p. 411. • **48.** Carter, *Palestine Peace Not Apartheid*, p. 52. • **49.** Bourne, *Jimmy Carter*, p. 411. • **50.** Carter, *Palestine Peace Not Apartheid*, p. 52. • **51.** Bourne, *Jimmy Carter*, p. 441. • **52.** Ibid., p. 443. • **53.** Thirteen were released in November 1979, and one more in July 1980, leaving fifty-two. • **54.** Bourne, *Jimmy Carter*, p. 455. • **55.** Ibid., p. 460. • **56.** Ibid. • **57.** National Security Archives interview with Zbigniew Brzezinski, http://www.gwu.edu/~nsarchiv/coldwar/interviews/episode-17/brzezinski1.html. • **58.** Vincent Jauvert, 'Oui, la CIA est entrée en Afghanistan avant les Russes . . .' (interview with Zbigniew Brzezinski), *Le Nouvel Observateur*, January 15, 1998. • **59.** Ibid. • **60.** National Security Archives interview with Zbigniew Brzezinski. • **61.** Bourne, *Jimmy Carter*, p. 458. • **62.** National Security Archives interview with Zbigniew Brzezinski. • **63.** Ibid. • **64.** Bourne, *Jimmy Carter*, p. 459. • **65.** Ibid. • **66.** Ibid., p. 461. • **67.** Ibid., p. 462. • **68.** Ibid., p. 428. • **69.** Hamilton Jordan, *Crisis: The Last Year of the Carter Presidency*, p. 357. • **70.** Ibid., p. 358. • **71.** Ibid., p. 361. • **72.** Ibid., p. 362. • **73.** Mazlish and Diamond, *Jimmy Carter*, p. 104. • **74.** Kandy Stroud, *How Jimmy Won*, p. 47. • **75.** Bourne, *Jimmy Carter*, p. 428. • **76.** William Safire, 'On Language', *New York Times*, May 7, 2000. • **77.** Jimmy Carter and Rosalynn Carter, *Everything to Gain: Making the Most of the Rest of Your Life* (New York: Random House, 1987), p. 9. • **78.** Morris, *Jimmy Carter*, p. 293. • **79.** Dr. M. S. Swaminathan, agriculture scientist known as 'Father of the Green Revolution in India', Peter G. Bourne, *Jimmy Carter*, p. 490.

Chapter Nine: Ronald Reagan

1. Ronald Reagan, *An American Life*, p. 21. • 2. Ibid. • 3. Ibid., p. 35. • 4. Bob Colacello, *Ronnie and Nancy: Their Path to the White House – 1911–1980*, p. 70. • 5. Ibid., p. 118. • 6. Ibid., p. 176. • 7. Ibid., p. 171. • 8. Ibid., p. 252. • 9. Ibid., p. 279. • 10. Ibid., p. 316. • 11. Ibid. • 12. Edmund Morris, *Dutch: A Memoir of Ronald Reagan*, p. 321. • 13. 'Flying Scared', *Time*, November 8, 1968. • 14. Morris, *Dutch*, p. 348. • 15. Ibid., p. 351. • 16. Ibid., p. 349. • 17. Ibid., p. 375. • 18. Edmund G. Brown, *Reagan and Reality: The Two Californias*, p. 32. • 19. Martin Anderson, *Revolution*, pp. 289–90. • 20. Colacello, *Ronnie and Nancy*, p. 492. • 21. Michael Deaver, with Mickey Herkovitz, *Behind the Scenes*, p. 96. • 22. Colacello, *Ronnie and Nancy*, p. 505. • 23. Richard Reeves, *President Reagan*, p. 34. • 24. Ibid., p. 40. • 25. Ibid., p. 42. • 26. Ibid., p. 38. • 27. Ibid., p. 35. • 28. Ibid., p. 36. • 29. Morris, *Dutch*, p. 451. • 30. Reeves, *President Reagan*, p. 45; *Washington Post*, April 1, 1981. • 31. Reeves, *President Reagan*, p. 71. • 32. Ibid., p.60. • 33. Ibid., p. 62. • 34. Ibid., p. 75. • 35. Ibid., p. 78. • 36. Ibid., p. 104. • 37. Since the early 1960s Reagan had declared in speeches that the way to force the Russians to 'recognize' the superiority of the western 'way of life' over Soviet communism was to 'let their economy come unhinged so that the contrast is apparent'. Paul Kengor, *The Crusader: Ronald Reagan and the fall of Communism*, p. 118. • 38. Ibid., p. 120. • 39. Friday, March 26, 1982, in Ronald Reagan, *The Reagan Diaries*, ed. Douglas Brinkley, p. 75. • 40. Reeves, *President Reagan*, p. 105. • 41. Ibid., p. 102 and 105. • 42. Ibid., p. 109. • 43. Ibid., pp. 108–9. • 44. Ibid., p. 110. • 45. Ibid. • 46. Ibid., p. 143. • 47. Wednesday, March 23, 1983, in Reagan, *The Reagan Diaries*, p. 140. • 48. Reeves, *President Reagan*, p. 146. • 49. Ibid. • 50. John Patrick Diggins, *Ronald Reagan: Fate, Freedom, and the Making of History*, p. 348. • 51. Reeves, *President Reagan*, p. 205. • 52. Ibid. • 53. Ibid., p. 228. • 54. Ibid., p. 258. • 55. Ibid., p. 310. • 56. Reagan, *The Reagan Diaries*. • 57. Reeves, *President Reagan*, p. 69. • 58. Ibid.; Reagan, *The Reagan Diaries*, p. 25. • 59. Morris, *Dutch*, p. 462. • 60. Reeves, *President Reagan*, p. 114. • 61. Monday, June 21, in Reagan, *The Reagan Diaries*, p. 90. • 62. Reeves, *President Reagan*, p. 123. • 63. Ibid. • 64. Reagan, *The Reagan Diaries*, p. 98. • 65. Ibid. • 66. Reeves, *President*

Reagan, p. 124. • **67**. Ibid., p. 127. • **68**. The Marines were evacuated in February 1984, five months after the Beirut truck bombing. • **69**. Reeves, *President Reagan*, p. 183. • **70**. Ibid., p. 191. • **71**. Ibid., p. 234. • **72**. Ibid., p. 266. • **73**. From 'High Flight', a poem by Pilot Officer John Gillespie Magee Jr, who died on December 11, 1941, over Lincolnshire, England. Reagan's planned State of the Union address to Congress was delivered a week later. • **74**. Paul Kengor, *The Crusader*, p. 236. • **75**. Ibid., p. 234. • **76**. December 17, 1984, in Reagan, *The Reagan Diaries*, p. 287. • **77**. November 5, 1985, ibid. • **78**. Mikhail Gorbachev, *Memoirs*, pp. 405–6. • **79**. November 19, 1985, in Reagan, *The Reagan Diaries*. • **80**. November 20, 1985, ibid. • **81**. Reeves, *President Reagan*, p. 285. • **82**. CIA Study, State Department Intelligence and Research Report, and National Intelligence Estimate, in Reeves, *President Reagan*, p. 283. • **83**. Reeves, *President Reagan*, p. 286. • **84**. Gorbachev, *Memoirs*, p. 191. • **85**. Reeves, *President Reagan*, p. 285. • **86**. Ibid., p. 345. • **87**. Ibid., p. 433. • **88**. Ibid., p. 401. • **89**. Gorbachev, *Memoirs*, p. 452. • **90**. Reeves, *President Reagan*, p. 467. • **91**. Ibid., p. 475. • **92**. Ibid. • **93**. National Security Planning Group Minutes, 'Subject: Central America', SECRET, June 25, 1984, National Security Archive, George Washington University. • **94**. Robert McFarlane, Iran-Contra Hearings, May 14, 1987, in Holly Sklar, *Washington's War on Nicaragua* (Cambridge, MA: South End Press, 1988), p. 251. • **95**. Reagan, *The Reagan Diaries*, p. 374. • **96**. William E. Pemberton, *Exit with Honor: The Life and Presidency of Ronald Reagan*, p. 175. • **97**. Diggins, *Ronald Reagan*, p. 295. • **98**. Sklar, *Washington's War on Nicaragua*, p. 393; Lou Cannon, *President Reagan: Role of a Lifetime*, p. 309. • **99**. Reeves, *President Reagan*, p. 431. • **100**. The son was Arturo Cruz Jr: see Keith Schneider, 'Fawn Hall Steps into the Limelight', *New York Times*, February 26, 1987. • **101**. Reeves, *President Reagan*, p. 400. • **102**. Ibid., p. 408. • **103**. Ibid., p. 461. • **104**. Ibid., p. 486. • **105**. Cannon, *President Reagan*, p. 17. • **106**. Diggins, *Ronald Reagan*, p. 63. • **107**. Morris, *Dutch*, p. xi. • **108**. Ibid., p. 696. • **109**. Tom Vallance, 'Jane Wyman' (obituary), *The Independent* (London), September 11, 2007. • **110**. Colacello, *Ronnie and Nancy*, p. 106. • **111**. Lawrence J. Quirk, *Jane Wyman* (New York: Norton, 1987), p. 113. • **112**. Colacello, *Ronnie and Nancy*, p. 222. • **113**. Ibid., p. 223. • **114**. Kitty Kelley, *Nancy Reagan: The Unauthorized Biography*, p. 87. • **115**. Ibid., p. 88. • **116**. Ibid.; Morris, *Dutch*, pp. 282, 750; Anne Edwards, *Early Reagan*. • **117**. Kelley, *Nancy Reagan*, p. 91. • **118**. Cannon, *President Reagan*, p. 192. • **119**. Nancy Reagan,

My Turn: The Memoirs of Nancy Reagan, p. 106. • **120**. Cannon, *President Reagan*, p. 193. • **121**. Ibid., p. 82. • **122**. Ibid., p. 193. • **123**. Colacello, *Ronnie and Nancy*, p. 471. • **124**. Nancy Reagan to Richard Reeves, in Reeves, *President Reagan*, p. 492.

Chapter Ten: George H. W. Bush

1. Herbert Parmet, *George Bush: The Life of a Lone Star Yankee*, p. 30; Doro Bush Koch, *My Father, My President: A Personal Account of the Life of George H. W. Bush*, pp. 5–6. • **2**. Parmet, *George Bush*, p. 32. • **3**. Koch, *My Father, My President*, p. 19. • **4**. Parmet, *George Bush*, pp. 30–1. • **5**. Ibid., p. 96. • **6**. Ibid., p. 109. • **7**. Ibid., p. 113. • **8**. Ibid., p. 114. • **9**. Ibid., p. 115. • **10**. Ibid., p. 132. • **11**. Ibid. • **12**. Timothy Naftali, *George H. W. Bush*, p. 21. • **13**. Ibid., pp. 21–2; Parmet, *George Bush*, pp. 170–1. • **14**. Jack Steel, quoted in Parmet, *George Bush*, p. 145. • **15**. Parmet, *George Bush*, p. 144. • **16**. Fitzhugh Green, *George Bush: An Intimate Portrait*, p. 113. • **17**. Parmet, *George Bush*, p. 150. • **18**. Ibid., p. 157. • **19**. Ibid., p. 159. • **20**. Ibid. • **21**. Barbara Bush, *A Memoir*, p. 109. • **22**. Ibid., p. 111. • **23**. Ibid. • **24**. Parmet, *George Bush*, p. 165. • **25**. Ibid. • **26**. Ibid., p. 172. • **27**. Ibid. • **28**. Bush, *Peking Diary*, p. 294; Parmet, *George Bush*, p. 176. • **29**. Stanley I. Kutler, *Abuse of Power*, p. 553. • **30**. Parmet, *George Bush*, p. 191. • **31**. Victor Gold, *Invasion of the Party Snatchers: How the Holy-Rollers and the Neo-Cons Destroyed the GOP* (Chicago: Sourcebooks Trade, 2007), p. 92. • **32**. James Mann, *Rise of the Vulcans: The History of Bush's War Cabinet*, (New York: Viking, 2004). • **33**. 'Intelligence Community Experiment in Competitive Analysis: Soviet Strategic Objectives: An Alternative View, Report of Team 'B', December 1976,' 1 and 9, released by the CIA to the National Archives. See Anne H. Cahn, *Killing Detente: The Right Attacks the CIA* (University Park: Pennsylvania State University Press, 1998), p. 163. • **34**. Adam Curtis, *The Power of Nightmares*, Documentary series, BBC television, October 20–November 3, 2004, quoted in Thom Hartmann, 'Hyping Terror for Fun, Profit – and Power', December 7, 2004. www.common dreams.org. Retrieved November 26, 2008. • **35**. Parmet, *George Bush*, p. 200. • **36**. Webster G. Tarpley and Anton Chaitkin, *George Bush: The Unauthorized Biography*, Chapter XV. • **37**. David Keene to George Bush, in Parmet, *George Bush*, p. 220. • **38**. Barbara Bush, *A Memoir*,

p. 197. • **39**. Parmet, *George Bush*, p. 301. • **40**. Diary entry, May 28–30, 1988, in Parmet, *George Bush*, p. 333. • **41**. Starting in September 1988 with a month-long airing of an attack ad by 'Americans for Bush', the ads related the story of a black Massachusetts murderer, Willie Horton, who had been furloughed as part of a state programme, only to commit battery and rape in Maryland. This was then followed by official Bush campaign ads, known as 'The Revolving Door'. In this, prisoners in uniform went in and out of a revolving door – with an announcer declaring Governor Dukakis had vetoed the death penalty in Massachusetts and approved furloughs for prisoners, including those who had committed 'first-degree murder' – i.e. Willie Horton. Taken apart, Bush could not be accused of directly stirring racism, but taken together, they proved devastating to the Dukakis campaign. • **42**. Parmet, *George Bush*, p. 336. • **43**. Ibid. • **44**. Ibid., p. 341. • **45**. Ibid., p. 352. • **46**. Ibid., p. 349. • **47**. Ibid., p. 351. • **48**. Richard Stengel, 'The Republicans', *Time*, August 22, 1988. • **49**. Parmet, *George Bush*, p. 355. • **50**. Atwater's 'negative politics' were contagious, and rooted in the era. 'We both cut our teeth at the same time' recalled Karl Rove of the 1970s and 80s, on becoming chief strategist to Bush's eldest son in 1999 – proud to be compared with the chief smearer in America. 'He rose much faster, much farther than I did' Rove said of Atwater, while Texas Republican Party Chairman Tom Pauken remarked of Rove: 'Karl's very capable and wants to be the next Lee Atwater.' Rove had already been investigated in 1973 by the Republican National Committee for dirty tricks, and never gave up. Dan Balz, 'Team Bush: The Iron Triangle', *Washington Post*, July 23, 1991. • **51**. John Robert Greene, *The Presidency of George Bush*, p. 93. • **52**. Naftali, *George H. W. Bush*, p. 77. • **53**. Colin Powell, *An American Journey*, p. 376. • **54**. Bill Keller, 'Gorbachev, in Finland, Disavows Any Right of Regional Intervention', *New York Times*, October 26, 1989. • **55**. Michael Beschloss and Strobe Talbott, *At The Highest Levels: The Inside Story of the End of the Cold War*, p. 134. • **56**. Ibid., p. 135. • **57**. Ibid., p. 137. • **58**. Ibid., p. 165. • **59**. Kuwait had a population in 1990 of 2 million. • **60**. James Baker, *The Politics of Diplomacy: Revolution, War and Peace, 1989–1992*, p. 194. • **61**. Powell, *An American Journey*, p. 464. • **62**. Ibid., pp. 465–6. • **63**. Ibid., p. 470. • **64**. Beschloss and Talbott, *At the Highest Levels*, p. 262. • **65**. Ibid. • **66**. Gorbachev, *Memoirs*, p. 553. • **67**. Parmet, *George Bush*, p. 89. • **68**. Ibid., p. 488. • **69**. Ibid. • **70**. Ibid., p. 487. • **71**. Ibid.,

p. 499. • **72**. Ibid., p. 500. • **73**. Ibid., p. 488. • **74**. Ibid., p. 490. • **75**. Beschloss and Talbott, *At the Highest Levels*, p. 463. • **76**. Ibid., p. 434. • **77**. Nigel Hamilton, *Bill Clinton: An American Journey*, p. 681. • **78**. Greene, *The Presidency of George Bush*, p. 164. • **79**. In the Electoral College Clinton took 370 votes to Bush's 168. • **80**. Doro Bush Koch, *My Father, My President*, p. 417. • **81**. Colin Powell, *An American Journey*, p. 561. • **82**. Doro Bush Koch, *My Father, My President*, p. 17. • **83**. Ibid., p. 5. • **84**. Naftali, *George H. W. Bush*, p. 11. • **85**. Quoted in Kitty Kelley, *The Family: The Real Story of the Bush Dynasty*, p. 330. • **86**. Nadine Eckerts, in Kelley, *The Family*, p. 331. • **87**. Marian Javits, ibid. • **88**. Geoffrey Kabaservice, author of *The Guardian: Kingman Brewster, His Circle and the Rise of the Liberal Establishment* (New York: Henry Holt, 2004), interview in Kelley, *The Family*, pp. 353 and 653. Other interviewees claiming an affair included Roy Elson and Anne Woolston: ibid., pp. 329 and 435. The *New York Post* scandalously headlined a report 'The Bush Affair' on August 11, 1992, quoting Susan Trento's new book, *The Power House*. Again, no factual evidence was adduced beyond the account of a deceased US Ambassador, Louis Fields, who had arranged for Vice President Bush and Mrs Fitzgerald to share on romantic grounds a guest house in Switzerland. • **89**. Quoted in Kelley, *The Family*, p. 351. • **90**. Ibid., pp. 354–5. • **91**. Ibid., p. 375. • **92**. Parmet, *George Bush*, p. 241. • **93**. Kelley, *The Family*, p. 326. • **94**. Ibid., p. 435. • **95**. Parmet, *George Bush*, p. 273. • **96**. Ibid. • **97**. Koch, *My Father, My President*, p. 224. • **98**. Bob Woodward, *Shadow: Five Presidents and the Legacy of Watergate*, p. 223.

Chapter Eleven: Bill Clinton

1. Nigel Hamilton, *Bill Clinton: American Journey*, p. 362. • **2**. Ibid., p. 364. • **3**. Ibid., p. 370. • **4**. Ibid., p. 475. • **5**. Bill Clinton, *My Life*, p. 368. • **6**. George Stephanopoulos, *All Too Human*, p. 74. • **7**. Ibid., p. 77. Clinton finally admitted, in a legal deposition in 1998, that he had in fact slept with Gennifer Flowers. • **8**. Stephanopoulos, *All Too Human*, p. 61. • **9**. Hamilton, *Bill Clinton: American Journey*, p. 192. • **10**. Ibid., p. 195. • **11**. Joe Conason and Gene Lyons, *The Hunting of the President*, p. 173 et seq. • **12**. David Gergen, *Eyewitness to Power*, p. 314. • **13**. Hillary Rodham Clinton, *Living History*, p. 257. • **14**. Ibid. • **15**. Gail Sheehy, *Hillary's Choice* (New York: Random House, 1999), p. 253. • **16**. Clinton, *My Life*, p. 629. • **17**. Nigel Hamilton, *Bill Clinton: Mastering the Presidency*,

p. 421. • **18**. Ibid., p. 413. • **19**. Ibid., pp. 386–7. • **20**. Ibid., p. 415. • **21**. Hamilton, *Bill Clinton: Mastering the Presidency*, pp. 451–5 • **22**. Ibid., pp. 443–4. • **23**. Ibid., p. 445. • **24**. Stephanopoulos, interview with Chris Bury, 'The Clinton Years', PBS Television. • **25**. Leon Panetta interview, in Hamilton, *Bill Clinton: Mastering the Presidency*, p. 448. • **26**. Hamilton, *Bill Clinton: Mastering the Presidency*, p. 515. • **27**. Ibid., p. 424. • **28**. Ibid., p. 575. • **29**. Louis B. Freeh, *My FBI: Bringing down the Mafia, Investigating Bill Clinton, and Fighting the War on Terror*, p. 246. • **30**. Clinton, *My Life*, p. 741. • **31**. Ibid., p. 778. • **32**. Conason and Lyons, *The Hunting of the President*, p. 275. • **33**. Ibid., p. 343. • **34**. Matt Drudge, *The Drudge Report*. • **35**. 'Remarks to the After-School Child Care Initiative', January 26, 1998, in William J. Clinton, *Public Papers of the Presidents of the United States*, 1998, Book I (Washington, DC: US Government Printing Office, 1999), p. III. • **36**. Richard Clarke, *Against All Enemies*, p. 186. • **37**. Ibid., p. 163. • **38**. Sidney Blumenthal, *The Clinton Wars*, p. 463. • **39**. Ibid., p. 465. • **40**. Jeffrey Toobin, *A Vast Conspiracy: The Real Story of the Sex Scandal That Nearly Brought down a President*, pp. 254–6. • **41**. Ibid., p. 336. • **42**. Ibid., p. 332. • **43**. Clinton, *My Life*, p. 835. • **44**. Clarke, *Against All Enemies*, pp. 190–5. • **45**. Clinton, *My Life*, p. 834. • **46**. Ibid., p. 845. • **47**. Freeh, *My FBI*, p. viii. • **48**. Daniel Schorn, 'Louis Freeh talks about Terrible Relationship with Clinton', CBS *60 Minutes*, October 6, 2005. • **49**. 'Clinton and Gore Have It Out', Associated Press, February 8, 2001. • **50**. Clinton, *My Life*, p. 944. • **51**. John Harris, *The Survivor: Bill Clinton in the White House*, p. 429; Blumenthal, *The Clinton Wars*, p. 783. • **52**. 'Former President Clinton's Farewell Remarks', Saturday, January 20, 2001, http://www.australianpolitics.com/usa/Clinton/speeches/01-0120 farewell.shtml. • **53**. Clinton, *My Life*, p. 149. • **54**. Hamilton, *Bill Clinton: An American Journey*, p. 44. • **55**. Ibid., pp. 168–70. • **56**. Hamilton, *Bill Clinton: Mastering the Presidency*, pp. 217–18. • **57**. Hamilton, *Bill Clinton: An American Journey*, p. 293. • **58**. Ann Henry interview, ibid., p. 474.

Chapter Twelve: George W. Bush

I. Jacob Weisberg, *The Bush Tragedy*, p. 42. • **2**. 'My dad fixed it so I got into the Guard', Bush told Harvard professor Yoshi Tsurumi. Kitty Kelley, *The Family: The Real Story of the Bush Dynasty*, p. 310. • **3**. J. H. Hatfield, *Fortunate Son: George W. Bush and the Making of an American*

President, p. 313. • **4**. Ibid., pp. 316–17. • **5**. Kelley, *The Family*, p. 310. • **6**. Steve Arbeit, in Kelley, *The Family*, p. 309. • **7**. Professor Yoshi Tsurumi, in ibid., p. 309. • **8**. Ibid., p. 310. • **9**. Christopher Anderson, *George and Laura: Portrait of an American Marriage*, p. 109. • **10**. Weisberg, *The Bush Tragedy*, p. 76. • **11**. Ibid., p. 77. • **12**. Andersen, *George and Laura*, p. 146. • **13**. Hatfield, *Fortunate Son*, p. 73. • **14**. Ibid., p. 72. • **15**. Andersen, *George and Laura*, p. 150. • **16**. Hatfield, *Fortunate Son*, p. 73. • **17**. Ibid. • **18**. Ibid. • **19**. Ibid., p. 80. • **20**. Kelley, *The Family*, p. 489. • **21**. Ibid., p. 543. • **22**. Weisberg, *The Bush Tragedy*, p. 87. • **23**. Ibid., p. 63. • **24**. Hatfield, *Fortunate Son*, p. 122. • **25**. Ibid., p. 173. • **26**. Kelley, *The Family*, pp. 585–6; Hatfield, *Fortunate Son*, pp. 190–212 . • **27**. James Traub, 'The Bush Years: W.'s World', *New York Times Magazine*, January 14, 2001. • **28**. Richard H. Davis, 'The Anatomy of a Smear Campaign', *Boston Globe*, March 21, 2004. • **29**. Kelley, *The Family*, p. 595. • **30**. Ibid., p. 598. • **31**. Davis, 'The Anatomy of a Smear Campaign'. • **32**. Gore's final majority over Bush was 543,895 votes, out of a total 105,405,100 applicable votes cast. The electoral college, however, voted 271 to 266 for Governor Bush, with one abstention. • **33**. Weisberg, *The Bush Tragedy*, p. 67. • **34**. James Moore and Wayne Slater, *Bush's Brain: How Karl Rove Made George W. Bush Presidential*, p. 5. • **35**. Ron Suskind, *The Price of Loyalty: George W. Bush, the White House and the Education of Paul O'Neill*, p. 58. • **36**. Ibid., pp. 70–5. • **37**. Ibid., p. 71. • **38**. Ibid., p. 72. • **39**. Ibid., p. 75. • **40**. Chitra Ragavan, 'Cheney's Guy', *U.S. News & World Report*, May 29, 2006; Barton Gellman, *Angler: The Cheney Vice Presidency*, p. 376. • **41**. Cullen Murphy and Todd S. Purdum, 'Farewell to All That: An Oral History of the White House', *Vanity Fair*, February 2009, p. 93. • **42**. Lou Dubose and Jake Bernstein, *Vice: Dick Cheney and the Hijacking of the American Presidency*, p. 179. • **43**. Murphy and Purdum, 'Farewell to All That', p. 90. • **44**. Gellman, *Angler*, p. 78. • **45**. Ibid., p. 79. • **46**. Richard A. Clarke, *Against All Enemies: Inside America's War on Terror*, p. 232. • **47**. Ibid. • **48**. Ibid., p. 236. • **49**. Ibid., p. 237. • **50**. Ibid., p. 32. • **51**. Ibid. • **52**. Bob Woodward, *Bush at War*, p. 47. • **53**. Ibid., p. 45. • **54**. Ibid., p.49. • **55**. 'Authorization for Use of Military Force', Public Law 107-40, September 18, 2001. • **56**. Murphy and Purdum, 'Farewell to All That', p. 160. • **57**. Ibid., p. 99. • **58**. Winston S. Churchill, *My Early Life* (1930) (New York: Scribner, 1996), p. 147. • **59**. Woodward, *Bush at War*, p. 103. • **60**. Bob Woodward, *Plan of Attack: The Definitive Account of the Decision to Invade Iraq*, p. 30. • **61**. Woodward, *Bush at War*, p. 246.

• **62**. Associated Press, April 16, 2004. • **63**. Bob Woodward, *State of Denial: Bush at War, Part III*, p. 35. • **64**. Woodward, *Plan of Attack*, p. 3. • **65**. Daniel Eisenberg, 'We're Taking Him Out', *Time* magazine, May 5, 2002. • **66**. Technically, Bush's February 2001 Address was a 'Budget Message' to the Joint Session of Congress. • **67**. 'Iraq: Prime Minister's Meeting, 23 July', David Manning Memo, S 195/02, published in the *Sunday Times* (London), May 1, 2005. • **68**. DefenseLink News Transcript, Secretary of State Donald Rumsfeld interviews with Bob Woodward, July 6 and 7, 2006. • **69**. Rebecca Leung, 'Gen. Zinni: "They've Screwed Up", Former Top Commander Condemns Pentagon Officials Over Iraq', *60 Minutes*, CBS Television, May 21, 2004. • **70**. Woodward, *State of Denial*, p. 106. • **71**. Scott McClellan, *What Happened: Inside the Bush White House and Washington's Culture of Deception*, p. 117. • **72**. Ibid., p. 118. • **73**. Jane Meyer, *The Dark Side: The Inside Story of How the War on Terror Turned into a War on American Ideals*, p. 328. • **74**. Jack Goldsmith, *The Terror Presidency: Law and Judgment inside the Bush Administration*. • **75**. McClellan, *What Happened*, pp. 3–4. • **76**. Gellman, *Angler*, pp. 132–3, 174–5. • **77**. Ibid., pp. 144–9. • **78**. Ibid., pp. 177–9. • **79**. Ibid., p. 282. • **80**. Meyer, *The Dark Side*, p. 4. • **81**. Ibid., p. 77, quoting Ted Olson, Solicitor General. • **82**. Ibid., p. 76. • **83**. McClellan, *What Happened*, p. 237. • **84**. Ibid., p. 76. • **85**. Ibid., p. 77. • **86**. Ibid., p. 237. • **87**. Miers' nomination ultimately failed. • **88**. Philip Cooney: see Murphy and Purdum, 'Farewell to All That', p. 155. The Bush administration also directed that any references to the National Assessment of Climate Change Impacts effort of 1997–2000 should be excised from government agency documents: ibid. • **89**. 'White House defends Rove over 9/11 remarks', Associated Press, June 24, 2005. • **90**. Hope Yen, '9/11 Commission: No Link between al-Quaida and Saddam', Associated Press, June 16, 2004. • **91**. Jack Kean, Lee H. Hamilton et al., *The 9/11 Commission Report: Final Report of the National Commission on Terrorist Attacks upon the United States* (New York: Norton, 2004), p. 334. • **92**. Dan Bartlett, in Murphy and Purdum, 'Farewell to All That'. • **93**. McClellan, *What Happened*, p. 288. • **94**. Ibid., p. 290. • **95**. Ibid., p. 291. • **96**. Gellman, *Angler*, p. 243. • **97**. Ibid. • **98**. Hope Yen, '9/11 Commission'. • **99**. Thomas Friedman, Op-ed page column, *New York Times*, August 4, 2006. • **100**. Craig Unger, *American Armageddon: How the Delusions of the Neoconservatives and the Christian Right Triggered the Descent of America – and Still Imperil Our Future*, p.

341. • **101**. James Ridgeway, 'American Casualties in Iraq More than 44,000', *Mother Jones*, November 2, 2006. • **102**. Murphy and Purdum, 'Farewell to All That', p. 157. • **103**. Helen Dewar and Dana Milbank, 'Cheney Dismisses Critic with Obscenity', *Washington Post*, June 25, 2004. • **104**. Gellman, *Angler*, p. 365. • **105**. 'Bush says he won't be rushed on Iraqi changes', CNN, December 14, 2006. • **106**. Gellman, *Angler*, p. 391. • **107** 'Countdown to Crawford: As voters go to polls to pick his successor, George W. Bush hits new low in approval rating', *Los Angeles Times*, November 4, 2008. • **108**. Maria Recio, 'Bush, his approval in tatters, flies home to Texas', McClatchy Newspapers, January 20, 2009. • **109**. Christopher Andersen, *George and Laura*, p. 65. • **110**. Ibid., p. 109. • **111**. Ibid., p. 73. • **112**. Ibid., p. 74. • **113**. Woodward, *Bush at War*, p. 146. • **114**. Andrew Malcolm, 'The Long Farewell of George W. Bush', *Los Angeles Times*, January 12, 2009.

Picture Credits

Index